P9-CMF-619

HK
BW378w

THE

WORKS

OF

DANIEL WEBSTER.

VOLUME II.

FOURTH EDITION.

———

BOSTON:
LITTLE, BROWN AND COMPANY,
1853.

Entered according to Act of Congress, in the year 1851, by
GEORGE W. GORDON AND JAMES W. PAIGE,
in the Clerk's Office of the District Court of the District of Massachusetts.

CAMBRIDGE:
STEREOTYPED BY METCALF AND COMPANY,
PRINTERS TO THE UNIVERSITY.
PRINTED BY HOUGHTON AND HAYWOOD.

DEDICATION

OF THE SECOND VOLUME.

TO

ISAAC P. DAVIS, Esq.

My dear Sir:

A warm private friendship has subsisted between us for half our lives, interrupted by no untoward occurrence, and never for a moment cooling into indifference. Of this friendship, the source of so much happiness to me, I wish to leave, if not an enduring memorial, at least an affectionate and grateful acknowledgment.

I inscribe this volume of my Speeches to you.

DANIEL WEBSTER.

CONTENTS

OF THE SECOND VOLUME.

SPEECHES DELIVERED ON VARIOUS PUBLIC OCCASIONS.

MASS MEETING AT SARATOGA.

INTRODUCTORY NOTE.

THE political excitement which pervaded the Union during the year 1840 was greater than has existed on any other occasion, for many years. Immense meetings of the most animated kind were held throughout the country, and were addressed by the ablest men. In the month of August of that year, Mr. Webster was called to Saratoga by a professional engagement as counsel in an important lawsuit for the State of Illinois. A large number of persons from all parts of the Union are generally assembled at Saratoga at this season of the year, and a strong wish was felt that Mr. Webster would make a public address on the absorbing political topics of the day. Although the little time he was to pass at Saratoga was too much engrossed by his professional duties to leave leisure for the slightest preparation, he found it impossible to resist the general wish ; and the afternoon of the 19th — the day before his argument in court — was appointed for a grand political meeting.

From an early hour in the morning of that day, and along every avenue, crowded vehicles were arriving in Saratoga from the surrounding country. The railway trains from Troy and Schenectady (and they were all behind their time, by reason of the vast crowds in and upon them) poured their living multitudes into the village. About two o'clock, P. M., a dark, lowering cloud, which had been gathering in the west, burst in a deluge of rain, accompanied with vivid lightning and thunder. But the storm soon passed, and the earth smiled again under returning sunshine. The face of nature was refreshed ; and the grateful coolness of the air gave new spirits and animation to the assembling throng.

Just before the storm broke, a very long procession on horseback and in wagons, with banners and music, arrived from the neighboring towns, and passed down the main street. Every house and piazza was crowded. The desire to hear Mr. Webster had drawn together the entire movable population of the neighborhood. In addition to this attraction, the Court of Errors for the State of New York and the Court of Chancery were in session at Saratoga, and the Governor of the State was also in the village.

At half past three o'clock, the public meeting was called to order, and the Hon. John W. Taylor, of Ballston, formerly Speaker of the House of Representatives of the United States, was called to the chair. Other persons of eminence were near him. At this moment, in casting the eye from the platform (which had been hastily, and, as the event proved, not very securely, put together), the spectacle which presented itself was of a novel and most striking character. In front, in a fine grove of pines, without any undergrowth, covering a circular eminence, about eight or ten thousand persons were collected. Near the platform were seats of rough boards capable of containing as many more. These seats were partly filled by ladies. The upturned faces of this great assemblage, as Mr. Webster, personally a stranger to most of them, stepped to the front of the stage, evinced the most intense and eager expectation. Beyond and wholly round to the rear of the platform stood thousands closely pressed together. The appearance of the speaker was the signal for the most enthusiastic cheering on the part of this vast multitude.

As soon as silence was restored, he commenced the following speech, which for more than three hours held the immense crowd in attention the most fixed and profound, except as it was interrupted by constantly repeated cheers. Before he had spoken many moments, an incident occurred, which at the time threatened disaster, but happily had no serious result. As it furnishes a happy instance of self-possession, it is worth recording.

The platform, which was of rough boards elevated some seven or eight feet from the ground, on which the speaker, the chairman, and the official and distinguished persons present were seated, suddenly gave way and fell with a great crash. Mr. Webster, who was happily uninjured, was the first person on his feet; and, supporting himself on some fragments of the staging, announced to the anxious assembly that no one was hurt, adding the expression of his confidence and satisfaction, that "the great Whig platform was more solid than the frail structure on which he was standing." This annunciation relieved the apprehensions of the audience. The place of the shattered platform was supplied by a large wagon covered with planks, and from this extemporized rostrum Mr. Webster continued his address, without having been in the slightest degree disturbed in his tone of remark by the annoying incident.

MASS MEETING AT SARATOGA.*

We are, my friends, in the midst of a great movement of the people. That a revolution in public sentiment on some important questions of public policy has begun, and is in progress, it is vain to attempt to conceal, and folly to deny. What will be the extent of this revolution, what its immediate effects upon political men and political measures, what ultimate influence it may have on the integrity of the Constitution, and the permanent prosperity of the country, remains to be seen. Meantime, no one can deny that an extraordinary excitement exists in the country, such as has not been witnessed for more than half a century; not local, nor confined to any two, or three, or ten States, but pervading the whole, from north to south, and from east to west, with equal force and intensity. For an effect so general, a cause of equal extent must exist. No cause, local or partial, can produce consequences so general and universal. In some parts of the country, indeed, local causes may in some degree add to the flame; but no local cause, nor any number of local causes, can account for the generally excited state of the public mind.

In portions of the country devoted to agriculture and manufactures, we hear complaints of want of market and low prices. Yet there are other portions of the country, which are consumers, and not producers, of food and manufactures; and, as purchasers, they should, it would seem, be satisfied with the low prices of which the sellers complain; but in these portions, too, of the country, there are dissatisfaction and discontent. Everywhere we find complaining and a desire for change.

* Speech delivered at the Great Mass Meeting at Saratoga, New York, on the 19th of August, 1840.

1*

There are those who think that this excitement among the people will prove transitory and evanescent. I am not of that opinion. So far as I can judge, attention to public affairs among the people of the United States has increased, is increasing, and is not likely to be diminished; and this not in one part of the country, but all over it. This certainly is the fact, if we may judge from recent information. The breeze of popular excitement is blowing everywhere. It fans the air in Alabama and the Carolinas; and I am of opinion, that, when it shall cross the Potomac, and range along the Northern Alleghanies, it will grow stronger and stronger, until, mingling with the gales of the Empire State, and the mountain blasts of New England, it will blow a perfect hurricane.

There are those, again, who think these vast popular meetings are got up by effort; but I say that no effort could get them up, and no effort can keep them down. There must, then, be some general cause that animates the whole country. What is that cause? It is upon this point I propose to give my opinion to-day. I have no design to offend the feelings of any, but I mean in perfect plainness to express my views to the vast multitude assembled around. I know there are among them many who from first to last supported General Jackson. I know there are many who, if conscience and patriotism permitted, would support his successor;* and I should ill repay the attention with which they may honor me by any reviling or denunciation. Again, I come to play no part of oratory before you. If there have been times and occasions in my life when I might be supposed anxious to exhibit myself in such a light, that period has passed, and this is not one of the occasions. I come to dictate and prescribe to no man. If my experience, not now short, in the affairs of government, entitle my opinions to any respect, those opinions are at the service of my fellow-citizens. What I shall state as facts, I hold myself and my character responsible for; what I shall state as opinions, all are alike at liberty to reject or to receive. I ask such consideration for them only as the fairness and sincerity with which they are uttered may claim.

What, then, has excited the whole land, from Maine to Georgia, and gives us assurance, that, while we are meeting here

---

* Mr. Van Buren.

in New York in such vast numbers, other like meetings are holding throughout all the States? That this cause must be general is certain, for it agitates the whole country, and not parts only.

When that fluid in the human system indispensable to life becomes disordered, corrupted, or obstructed in its circulation, not the head or the heart alone suffers; but the whole body — head, heart, and hand, all the members, and all the extremities — is affected with debility, paralysis, numbness, and death. The analogy between the human system and the social and political system is complete; and what the lifeblood is to the former, circulation, money, currency, is to the latter; and if that be disordered or corrupted, paralysis must fall on the system.

The original, leading, main cause, then, of all our difficulties and disasters, is the disordered state of the circulation. This is, perhaps, not a perfectly obvious truth; and yet it is one susceptible of easy demonstration. In order to explain this the more readily, I wish to bring your minds to the consideration of the internal condition, and the vast domestic trade, of the United States. Our country is not a small province or canton, but an empire, extending over a large and diversified surface, with a population of various conditions and pursuits. It is in this variety that consists its prosperity; for the different parts become useful one to the other, not by identity, but by difference, of production, and thus each by interchange contributes to the interest of the other. Hence, our internal trade, that which carries on this exchange of the products and industry of the different portions of the United States, is one of our most important interests, I had almost said, the most important. Its operations are easy and silent, not always perceptible, but diffusing health and life throughout the system by the intercourse thus promoted, from neighborhood to neighborhood, and from State to State.

Let me explain this a little in detail. You are here in a grain-growing State. Your interest, then, is to have consumers, not growers, of grain. The hands that, in the broad belt which stretches across the country in which grain best succeeds, grow wheat, are interested to find mouths elsewhere to consume what they raise. The manufacturers of the North and East need the grain of the Middle States, and the cotton of the South, and

these in turn buy the manufactures of the East. Nor is this sole-
ly matter of interest, but it is in some degree brought about by
the regulations of foreign governments. Our manufactures find
no sale in Europe; and much of our grain is, under ordinary
circumstances, excluded from its markets. In France it is never
admitted, and in England in a manner so contingent and uncertain as to tantalize rather than gratify the American husband-
man.

The internal trade, moreover, moves as it were in a circle,
and not directly. The great imports of the country are at New
York, whence they pass to the South and to the West, while
our exports are not mainly from New York, but from the South.
Thus the main imports are at one quarter of the Union,
and the exports from another. The same thing is true of other
branches of trade. The produce of Ohio, much of it, descends
the river to New Orleans; but Ohio is supplied with foreign
commodities and domestic fabrics chiefly through the New York
canals, the Lakes, and the Ohio Canal. The live stock of Kentucky goes to the Carolinas; where, however, Kentucky buys
nothing, but transmits the money to Baltimore, Philadelphia,
and New York, and in those cities procures what she wants,
to be sent to her across the Alleghanies.

This circuit of trade, in a country of such great extent as ours,
demands, more than in any country under heaven, a uniform
currency for the whole people; that what is money in Carolina
shall be so elsewhere; that what the Kentucky drover receives,
what the planter of Alabama sells for, what the laborer in New
York gets in pay for his work, and carries home to support his
family, shall be of ascertained and uniform value.

This is not the time nor the occasion for an essay or dissertation on money; but I mean distinctly to express the opinion,
that until the general government shall take in hand the currency
of the country, until that government shall devise some means,
I say not what, of raising the whole currency to the level of gold
and silver, there can be no prosperity.

Let us retrace briefly the history of the currency question in
this country, a most important branch of the commercial question. I appeal to all who have studied the history of the times,
and of the Constitution, whether our fathers, in framing the
Constitution which should unite us in common rights and a

common glory, had not also among their chief objects to pro-vide a uniform system of commerce, including a uniform system of currency for the whole country. I especially invite the ingen-uous youth of the country to go back to the history of those times, and particularly to the Virginia resolutions of 1786, and to the proceedings of the convention at Annapolis, and they will there find that the prevailing motive for forming a general gov-ernment was, to secure a uniform system of commerce, of cus-tom-house duties, and a general regulation of the trade, external and internal, of the whole country. It was no longer to be the commerce of New York, or of Massachusetts, but of the United States, to be carried on under that star-spangled banner, which was to bear to every shore, and over every sea, the glorious motto, *E Pluribus Unum.*

This being a chief and cherished object, when the first Con-gress under the Constitution assembled in New York, General Washington, in his speech, naturally drew its attention to the necessity of a uniform currency, looking, probably, at that time, to the mint first established in Philadelphia, to produce that cur-rency.

What I wish to say is, that the difference in the currencies of the several States, and the want of a uniform system, both of commerce and currency, being among the chief inconveniences to be remedied by the establishment of the Constitution, the subject very naturally and properly attracted the early attention of the President, at the first session of the first Congress.

At the second session, the United States Bank was estab-lished. Without detaining you by quoting papers or speeches of that day, I will simply refer any one, curious to inquire, to the official documents of the time, and to the contemporaneous expressions of public opinion on the leading measures of that day, for proof that, while one object of incorporating a national bank was, that it might occasionally make loans to government, and take charge of the disbursement of its revenues, another object quite as prominent and important was to furnish a cir-culation, a paper circulation, founded on national resources, that should be current all over the country. General Washington had the sagacity to see, what, indeed, minds less sagacious than his could not fail to perceive, that the confidence reposed in the United States under the Constitution would impart to whatever came from Congress greater authority and value than could attach to any thing emanating from any single State.

The assumption by Congress of the State debts illustrates this remark; for the moment the United States became bound for those debts, and proceeded to fund them, they rose enormously and rapidly in value.

General Washington and his advisers saw that a mixed currency, if the paper had the mark of the Union, and bore on it the spread eagle, would command universal confidence throughout the country; and the result proved the wisdom of their foresight. From the incorporation of the bank to the expiration of its charter, embracing a period of great commercial and political vicissitudes, the currency furnished by that bank was never objected to: it, indeed, surpassed the hopes and equalled the desires of every body. The charter expired in 1811; how, or why, or from what state of parties, it is not my purpose to discuss, but the charter was not renewed. War with England was declared in June, 1812. Immediately upon the declaration of war, all the banks south of New England stopped payment, and those of New England ceased to issue notes; and thus, in fact, the payment of specie in those States amounted to little or nothing. At the close of the war, the condition of the currency, which had become very much deranged, not improving, Mr. Madison brought the subject before Congress. In his messages, both in 1814 and 1815, he dwelt earnestly on the subject; and in 1816 the second Bank of the United States was incorporated, and went at once into operation. At its outset, owing possibly to mismanagement, perhaps unavoidably, the bank met with heavy losses; but it fulfilled its functions in providing a currency for the whole country; and neither during the eight years of President Monroe's administration, nor the four years of President Adams's, were any complaints on that score heard. And now I desire to call attention to a particular fact. There were several candidates for the Presidency to succeed Mr. Monroe, — General Jackson, Mr. Adams, Mr. Crawford, and Mr. Clay. None of them received a sufficient number of votes from the electors to be chosen President. General Jackson received the largest number of any; but the House of Representatives chose John Quincy Adams President. From that moment a fierce opposition was commenced against his administration. I do not propose to discuss the character or conduct of this opposition. The fact of its existence is all that I have to do with now, together with the fact, that, from the inauguration, in March, 1825, to March, 1829, an opposition, distinguished for its remarkable ability, perseverance, and ultimate success, was carried on under the name and flag of General Jackson.

All other candidates had disappeared. General Jackson was the sole opponent; and four years of active, angry, political controversy ensued, during which every topic of complaint that could be drawn into the vortex was drawn in; and yet — I beg special attention to this fact — not once during this four years' controversy did General Jackson himself, or any press in his interest, or any of his friends in Congress or elsewhere, raise a single voice against the condition of the currency, or propose any change therein. Of the hundreds here, possibly, who supported General Jackson, not one dreamed that he was elected to put down established institutions and overthrow the currency of the country. Who, among all those that, in the honest convictions of their hearts, cried, Hurrah for Jackson! believed or expected or desired that he would interfere with the Bank of the United States, or destroy the circulating medium of the country? [Here there arose a cry from the crowd, "None! None!"] I stand here upon the fact, and defy contradiction from any quarter, that there was no complaint then, anywhere, of the bank. There never before was a country, of equal extent, where exchanges and circulation were carried on so cheaply, so conveniently, and so securely. General Jackson was inaugurated in March, 1829, and pronounced an address upon that occasion, which I heard, as I did the oath which he took to support the Constitution. In that address were enumerated various objects, requiring, as he said, reform; but among them was not the Bank of the United States, nor the currency. This was in March, 1829. In December, 1829, General Jackson came out with the declaration (than which none I have ever heard surprised me more), that "the constitutionality of the Bank of the United States might be well questioned," and that it had failed to furnish a sound and uniform currency to the country.

What produced this change of views? Down to March of the same year, nothing of this sort was indicated or threatened. What, then, induced the change? [A voice from the crowd said, " Martin Van Buren."]   If that be so, it was the production of mighty consequences by a cause not at all proportioned. I will state, in connection with, and in elucidation of, this subject, certain transactions, which constitute one of those contingencies in human affairs, in which casual circumstances, acting upon the peculiar temper and character of a man of very decided temper and character, affect the fate of nations.   A movement was made in the summer of 1829, for the purpose of effecting a change of certain officers of the branch of the Bank of the United States in Portsmouth, New Hampshire. Mr. Woodbury, then a Senator from New Hampshire, transmitted to the president of the bank at Philadelphia a request, purporting to proceed from merchants and men of business of all parties, asking the removal of the president of that branch, *not on political grounds*, but as acceptable and advantageous to the business community.   At the same time, Mr. Woodbury addressed a letter to the then Secretary of the Treasury, Mr. Ingham, suggesting that his department should, on *political* grounds, obtain from the mother bank the removal of the branch president. This letter was transmitted to the president of the mother bank, and reached him about the same time with the other; so that, looking upon this picture and upon that, upon one letter, which urged the removal on political grounds, and upon the other, which denied that political considerations entered into the matter at all, he concluded to let things remain as they were. Appeals were then artfully made to the President of the United States. His feelings were enlisted, and it is well known that, when he had an object in view, his character was to go ahead. I mean to speak no evil nor disrespect of General Jackson. He has passed off the stage to his retirement at the Hermitage, which it would be as well, perhaps, that friends should not disturb, and where I sincerely wish he may, in tranquillity, pass the residue of his days.   But General Jackson's character was imperious; he took the back track never; and however his friends might differ, or whether they concurred or dissented, they were fain always to submit. General Jackson put forth the pretension, that appointments by the bank should have regard to the wishes of the treasury; the matter was formally submitted to the directors of the bank, and they as formally determined that the treasury could not rightly or properly have any thing to say in the matter. A long and somewhat angry correspondence ensued; for General Jackson found in the president of the bank a man who had something of his own quality. The result was that the bank resisted, and refused the required acquiescence in the dictation of the treasury.

This happened in the summer and autumn of 1829, and in December we had the message in which, for the first time, the bank was arraigned and denounced. Then came the application of the bank for re-incorporation, the passage of a bill for that purpose through both houses, and the Presidential veto. The Bank of the United States being thus put down, a multitude of new State banks sprang up; and next came a law, adopting some of these as deposit banks. Now, what I have to say in regard to General Jackson in this matter is this: he said he could establish a better currency; and, whether successful or not in this, it is at least to be said in his favor and praise, that he never did renounce the obligation of the federal government to take care of the currency, paper as well as metallic, of the people. It was in furtherance of this duty, which he felt called on to discharge, of "providing a better currency," that he recommended the prohibition of small bills. Why? Because, as it was argued, it would improve the general mixed currency of the country; and although he did not as distinctly as Mr. Madison admit and urge the duty of the federal government to provide a currency for the people, *he never renounced it*, but, on the contrary, in his message of December, 1835, held this explicit language: —

"By the use of the State banks, which do not derive their charters from the general government, and are not controlled by its authority, it is ascertained that the moneys of the United States can be collected and distributed without loss or inconvenience, and that all the wants of the community, in relation to exchange and currency, are supplied as well as they have ever been before." *

It is not here a question whether these banks did, or did not, effect the purpose which General Jackson takes so much praise to himself for accomplishing through their agency, that of supplying the country with as good a currency as it ever enjoyed.

* Message, December 2, 1835.

But why, if this was not a duty of the federal government, is it mentioned at all? In his last message, in December, 1836, reviewing the benefits (!) of his experiments on the currency, he thus speaks: —

" At the time of the removal of the deposits, it was alleged by the advocates of the Bank of the United States, that the State banks, whatever might be the regulations of the treasury department, could not make the transfers required by the government, or negotiate the domestic exchanges of the country. It is now well ascertained, that the real domestic exchanges performed through discounts by the United States Bank and its twenty-five branches were one third less than those of the deposit banks for an equal period of time ; and if a comparison be instituted between the amounts of services rendered by these institutions on the broader basis which has been used by the advocates of the United States Bank, in estimating what they consider the domestic exchanges, the result will be still more favorable to the deposit banks."

Here we have the distinct assertion, that, through the State banks, he had accomplished more in establishing a good currency and easy exchanges than had been done by the Bank of the United States. However this fact may be, all this, I say, amounts to an acknowledgment of the duty of the general government, as a natural consequence of the power to coin money and regulate commerce, to take a supervision over that paper currency which is to supply the place of coin.

I contend for this truth, — that, down to the end of General Jackson's administration, no administration of this country had turned their back upon this power; and I now proceed to show, by extracts from Mr. Van Buren's letter to Sherrod Williams, to which, since he has largely referred to it of late, there can be no unfitness in my referring, that he, too, admitted the obligation of supplying a uniform currency and a convenient medium of exchange, which he thought could be effected by the State deposit banks.

" Sincerely believing, for the reasons which have just been stated, that the public funds may be as safely and conveniently transmitted from one portion of the Union to another, that domestic exchange can be as successfully and as cheaply effected, and the currency be rendered at least as sound, under the existing system, as those objects could be accomplished by means of a national bank, I would not seek a remedy for the evils to which you allude, should they unfortunately occur, through such a medium, even if the constitutional objections were not in the way." *

He denies not the duty of superintending the currency, but thinks the deposit banks of the States, under the control of Congress, can effect the purpose. This letter was written when Mr. Van Buren was a candidate for the Presidency.

Two months only after General Jackson had retired, and when his vigorous hand was no longer there to uphold it, the league of State banks fell, and crumbled into atoms; and when Mr. Van Buren had been only three months President, he convoked a special session of Congress for the ensuing September. The country was in wide-spread confusion, paralyzed in its commerce, its currency utterly deranged. What was to be done? What would Mr. Van Buren recommend? He could not go back to the Bank of the United States, for he had committed himself against its constitutionality; nor could he, with any great prospect of success, undertake to reconstruct the league of deposit banks; for it had recently failed, and the country had lost confidence in it. What, then, was to be done? He could go neither backward nor forward. What did he do? I mean not to speak disrespectfully, but I say he — *escaped!* Afraid to touch the fragments of the broken banks, unable to touch the United States Bank, he folded up his arms, and said, The government has nothing to do with providing a currency for the people. That I may do him no wrong, I will read his own language. His predecessors had all said, We *will not* turn our backs upon this duty of government to provide a uniform currency; his language is, We *will* turn our backs on this duty. He proposes nothing for the country, nothing for the relief of commerce, or the regulation of exchanges, but simply the means of getting money into the treasury without loss. In his first message to Congress, he thus expresses himself: —

" It is not the province of government to aid individuals in the transfer of their funds, otherwise than through the facilities of the Post-Office Department. As justly might it be called on to provide for the transportation of their merchandise.

* Mr. Van Buren's letter to Sherrod Williams of the 8th of August, 1836.

" If, therefore, I refrain from suggesting to Congress any specific plan for regulating the exchanges or the currency, relieving mercantile embarrassments, or interfering with the ordinary operations of foreign or domestic commerce, it is from a conviction that such are not within the constitutional province of the general government, and that their adoption would not promote the real and permanent welfare of those they might be designed to aid."

I put it to you, my friends, if this is a statesman's argument. You can transport your merchandise yourselves; you can build ships, and make your own wagons; but can you make a currency? Can you say what shall be money, and what shall not be money, and determine its value here and elsewhere? Why, it would be as reasonable to say, that the people may make war for themselves, and peace for themselves, as to say that they may exercise this other not less exclusive attribute of sovereignty, of making a currency for themselves. He insists that Congress has no power to regulate currency or exchanges, none to mitigate the embarrassments of the country, none to relieve its prostrate industry, and even if the power did exist, it would be unwise, in his opinion, to exercise it!

These are the doctrines of the President's first message; and I have no opinion of it now that I did not then entertain, and then express. I desire not to appear wise after the event, I am not a prophet nor the son of a prophet, and yet I declare that when I heard the declarations of this message, and reflected on its consequences, I saw, or thought I saw, all of suffering, loss, and evil that is now before us.

Let us compare this declaration with that of one now numbered with the mighty dead; of one who has left behind a reputation excelled by that of no other man, as understanding thoroughly the Constitution; of one taking a leading part in its inception, and closing his public career by administering its highest office; I need not name JAMES MADISON.

In his message to Congress, in December, 1815, when the war had closed, and the country was laboring under the disordered currency of that period, the President thus spoke: —

" It is essential to every modification of the finances, that the benefits of a uniform national currency should be restored to the community. The absence of the precious metals will, it is believed, be a temporary evil; but until they can again be rendered the general medium of exchange, it devolves on the wisdom of Congress to provide a substitute, which shall equally engage the confidence and accommodate the wants of the citizens throughout the Union. If the operation of the State banks cannot produce this result, the probable operation of a national bank will merit consideration," &c.

At that session, Congress incorporated the Bank of the United States; and at the next session, the President held this language respecting the currency and that bank: —

" For the interests of the community at large, as well as for the purposes of the treasury, it is essential that the nation should possess a currency of equal value, credit, and use, wherever it may circulate. The Constitution has intrusted Congress, exclusively, with the power of creating and regulating a currency of that description ; and the measures taken, during the last session, in execution of the power, give every promise of success. The Bank of the United States has been organized under auspices the most favorable, and cannot fail to be an important auxiliary to those measures."

How that sounds now as an argument for the sub-treasury! The new doctrine which the administration has set up is one vitally affecting the business and pursuits of the people at large, extending its efforts to the interests of every family, and of every individual ; and you must determine for yourselves if it shall be the doctrine of the country. But, before determining, look well at the Constitution, weigh all the precedents, and if names and authority are to be appealed to, contrast those of President Van Buren with those of the dead patriarch whose words I have just read to you, and decide accordingly.

We have heard much from the administration and its friends against banks and banking systems. I do not mean to discuss that topic; but I will say, that their tampering with the currency, and their course in relation to it, has, more than all other causes, increased the number of these banks.

But Mr. Van Buren's message contains a principle, — one altogether erroneous as a doctrine, and fatal in its operations, — the principle that the government has nothing to do with providing a currency for the country; in other words, proposing a separation between the money of the government and the money of the people. This is the great error, which cannot be compro-

mised with, which is susceptible of no amelioration or modification, like a disease which admits no remedy and no palliative
but the caustic which shall totally eradicate it.

Do we not know that there must always be bank paper? Is
there a man here who expects that he, or his children, or his
children's children, shall see the day when only gold coin, glittering through silk purses, will be the currency of the country, to
the entire exclusion of bank-notes? Not one. But we are told
that the value of these notes is questionable. It is the neglect
of government to perform its duties that makes them so. You
here, in New York, have sound bank paper, redeemable in coin;
and if you were surrounded by a Chinese wall, it might be indifferent to you whether government looked after the currency
elsewhere or not. But you have daily business relations with
Pennsylvania, and with the West, and East, and South, and
you have a direct interest that their currency too shall be sound;
for otherwise the very superiority of yours is, to a certain degree,
an injury and loss to you, since you pay in the equivalent of
specie for what you buy, and you sell for such money as may
circulate in the States with which you deal. But New York
cannot effect the general restoration of the currency, nor any
one State, nor any number of States short of the whole, and
hence the duty of the general government to superintend this
interest.

But what does the sub-treasury propose? Its basis is a separation of the concerns of the treasury from those of the people.
The law creating it directs, —

That there shall be provided, in the new treasury building at
Washington, rooms for the use of the treasurer, and fireproof
vaults and safes for the keeping of the public moneys; and these
vaults and safes are declared to be the treasury of the United
States:

That the vaults and safes of the mint in Philadelphia and the
branch mint at New Orleans shall also be places for the deposit and safe-keeping of the public moneys; and that there
shall be fireproof vaults and safes also in the custom-houses of
New York and Boston, and in Charleston, South Carolina,
and St. Louis, Missouri, and that these also shall be places of
deposit:

That there shall be a receiver-general at New York, Boston

Charleston, and St. Louis: that the treasurers of these mints, and the receivers-general, shall keep the public money, without loaning or using it, until ordered to be paid out; and into the hands of these treasurers and receivers-general all collectors of public money are to pay what they receive:

That the resolutions of Congress of April, 1816, be so far altered, as that hereafter, of all duties, taxes, and debts due and becoming due to the United States after June of this year, one fourth shall be paid in specie; after June of next year, one half; after June of 1842, three fourths; and after June, 1843, the whole; so that after June, 1843, all debts due the United States, whether for duties, taxes, sales of public lands, patents, postages of letters, or otherwise, "shall be paid in gold and silver only":

That from and after June, 1843, every officer or agent in the government, in making disbursements or payments on account of the United States, shall make such payments in gold and silver coin only:

The receiver-general in New York to be paid $ 4,000 salary, the others, each, $ 2,500.

I propose to say a few words on these provisions. In the first place, it seems very awkward to declare by law certain rooms in Washington, and certain safes and vaults therein, *the* treasury of the United States. We have been accustomed heretofore to look upon the treasury as a department of the government, recognized by the Constitution, which declares that no money shall be drawn from the treasury, but in consequence of appropriations made by law. It may, however, be made a question whether any thing but these rooms and safes at Washington are now within this protection of the Constitution. It is senseless. It is absurd. It is as if the Legislature of New York should declare that a certain large room in the United States Hotel, and certain desks and tables therein, should constitute the Court for the Correction of Errors of the State of New York.*

What else does this bill do? It directs that there shall be certain vaults, and safes, and rooms. But it has not been for want of adequate vaults and rooms that we have lost our money, but owing to the hands to which we have intrusted the keys. It is in

* The Court of Errors was at the time holding a session at the United States Hotel at Saratoga.

the character of the officers, and not in the strength of bars and vaults, that we must look for the security of the public treasure. What would be thought in private life, if some rich merchant, John Jacob Astor, for instance, should determine no longer to trust his money with banks and bank directors, who, nevertheless, have a common interest with him in upholding the credit and stability of the currency, and in the safe-keeping, too, of their own money, and should build for himself certain safes and vaults, and, having placed his treasures therein, should, of some forty or fifty hungry individuals who might apply for the office of treasurer, give the keys to him who would work the cheapest? You might not, perhaps, pronounce him insane, but you would certainly say he acted very unlike John Jacob Astor. Now, what is true of private affairs is equally true of public affairs; and what would be absurd in an individual is not less so in a government. What is doing in Boston, where I belong? There are banks, respectable, specie-paying, trustworthy banks, managed by prudent and discreet men; and yet the treasure of the country is withdrawn from the keeping of one of those institutions, with a capital paid in of two millions of dollars, and locked up in safes and vaults, and one of the President's political friends from another State is sent for to come and keep the key. There is, in this case, no president to watch the cashier, no cashier to watch the teller, and no directors to overlook and control all; but the whole responsibility is vested in one man. Do you believe that, if, under such circumstances, the United States, following the example of individuals, were to offer to receive private funds in deposit in such a safe, and allow interest on them, they would be intrusted with any? There are no securities under this new system of keeping the public moneys that we had not before; while many that did exist, in the personal character, high trusts, and diversified duties of the officers and directors of banks, are removed. Moreover, the number of receiving and disbursing officers is increased; and the danger to the public treasure is increased in proportion.

The next provision is, that money once received into the treasury is not to be lent out; and if this law is to be the law of the land, this provision is not to be complained of, for dangerous indeed would be the temptation, and pernicious the consequences, if these treasurers were to be left at liberty to lend to

favorites and party associates the moneys drawn from the people.
Yet the practice of this government hitherto has always been
opposed to this policy of locking up the money of the people,
when and while it is not required for the public service. Until
this time the public deposits, like private deposits, were used by
the banks in which they were placed, as some compensation for
the trouble of safe-keeping, and in furtherance of the general
convenience. When, in 1833, General Jackson formed the
league of the deposit State banks, they were specially directed
by Mr. Taney, then Secretary of the Treasury, to use the public
funds in discounts for the accommodation of the business of the
country. And why should this not be so? The President now
says, If the money is kept in banks, it will be used by them in
discounts, and they will derive benefit therefrom. What then?
Is it a sufficient reason for depriving the community of a beneficial measure, that the banks that carry it out will also derive
some benefit from it? The question is, Will the public be benefited? and if this be answered affirmatively, it is no objection
that the banks will be too. The government is not to play the
part of the dog in the manger. The doctrine is altogether pernicious, opposed to our experience, and to the habits and business
of the nation.

The next provision is that requiring, after 1843, all dues to the
government to be paid in gold and silver; and however onerous
or injurious this provision, it is to be conceded that the government can, if they choose, enforce it. They have the power; and,
as good citizens, we must submit. But such a practice will be
inconvenient, I will say, oppressive. How are those who occupy
three fourths of the surface of the United States to comply with
this provision? Here, in commercial neighborhoods, and in
large cities, and where the banks pay specie, the difficulty will
be less; but where is the man who is to take up lands in the
Western States to get specie? How transport it? The banks
around him pay none, he gets none for his labor. And yet, oppressive as all this is, I admit that the government have a right to
pass such a law, and that, while it is a law, it must be obeyed.

But what are we promised as the equivalent for all this inconvenience and oppression? Why, that the government in its
turn will pay its debts in specie, and that thus what it receives
with one hand it will pay out with the other, and a metallic cir-

culation will be established.   I undertake to say, that no greater fallacy than this was ever uttered; the thing is impossible, and for this plain reason.   The dues which the government collects come from individuals; each pays for himself.   But it is far otherwise with the disbursements of government.   They do not go down to individuals, and, seeking out the workmen and the laborers, pay to each his dues.   Government pays in large sums, to large contractors, and to these it may pay gold and silver But do the gold and silver reach those whom the contractor employs?   On the contrary, the contractors deal as they see fit with those whom they employ, or of whom they purchase.   The Army and the Navy are fed and clothed by contract; the materials for expensive custom-houses, fortifications, for the Cumberland Road, and for other public works, are all supplied by contract.   Large contractors flock to Washington, and receive their tons of gold and silver; but do they carry it with them to Maine, Mississippi, Michigan, or wherever their residence and vocation may be?   No, not a dollar; but, selling it for depreciated paper, the contractor swells his previous profits by this added premium, and pays off those he owes in depreciated bank-notes.   This is not an imaginary case.   I speak of what is in proof.   A contractor came to Washington last winter, and received a draft of $180,000 on a specie-paying bank in New York.   This he sold at ten per cent. premium, and with the avails purchased funds in the West, with which he paid the producer, the farmer, the laborer.   This is the operation of specie payments. It gives to the government hard money, to the rich contractor hard money; but to the producer and the laborer it gives paper, and bad paper only.   And yet this system is recommended as specially favoring the poor man, rather than the rich, and credit is claimed for this administration as the poor man's friend.

Let us look a little more nearly at this matter, and see whom, in truth, it does favor.   Who are the rich in this country? There is very little hereditary wealth among us; and large capitalists are not numerous.   But some there are, nevertheless, who live upon the interest of their money; and these, certainly, do not suffer by this new doctrine; for their revenues are increased in amount, while the means of living are reduced in value. There is the money-lender, too, who suffers not by the reduction of prices all around him.   Who else are the rich in this country? Why, the holders of office. He who has a fixed salary of from $2,500 to $5,000 finds prices falling; but does his salary fall? On the contrary, three fourths of that salary will now purchase more than the whole of it would purchase before; and he, therefore, is not dissatisfied with this new state of things.

There is, too, another class of our fellow-citizens, wealthy men, who have prospered during the last year; and they have prospered when nobody else has. I mean the owners of shipping. What is the reason? Give me a reason. Well, I will give you one. The shipping of the country carries on the trade, the larger vessels being chiefly in the foreign trade. Now, why have these been successful? I will answer by an example. I live on the sea-coast of New England, and one of my nearest neighbors is the largest ship-owner, probably, in the United States. During the past year, he has made what might suffice for two or three fortunes of moderate size; and how has he made it? He sends his ships to Alabama, Louisiana, Mississippi, to take freights of cotton. This staple, whatever may be the price abroad, cannot be suffered to rot at home; and therefore it is shipped. My friend tells his captain to provision his ship at Natchez, for instance, where he buys flour and stores in the currency of that region, which is so depreciated that he is able to sell his bills on Boston at forty-eight per cent. premium! Here, at once, it will be seen, he gets his provision for half price, because prices do not always rise suddenly, as money depreciates. He delivers his freight in Europe, and gets paid for it in good money. The disordered currency of the country to which he belongs does not follow and afflict him abroad. He gets his freight in good money, places it in the hands of his owner's banker, who again draws at a premium for it. The ship-owner, then, makes money, when all others are suffering, *because he can escape from the influence of the bad laws and bad currency of his own country.*

Now, I will contrast the story of this neighbor with that of another of my neighbors, not rich. He is a New England mechanic, hard-working, sober, and intelligent, a tool-maker by trade, who wields his own sledge-hammer. His particular business is the making of augers for the South and Southwest. He has for years employed many hands, and been the support thereby of many families around him, himself, meanwhile, moderately prosperous until these evil times came on. Annually, however, for some years, he has been going backwards. Not less industrious, not less frugal, he has yet found, that, however good nominally the prices he might receive at the South and South-west for his tools, the cost of converting his Southern or Western funds into money current in New England was ruinous. He has persevered, however, always hoping for some change for the better, and contracting gradually the circle of his work and the number of his workmen, until at length, the little earnings of the past wasted, and the condition of the currency becoming worse and worse, he is reduced to bankruptcy; and he, and the twenty families that he supported, are beggared by no fault of their own. What was his difficulty? He *could not escape* from the evils of bad laws and bad currency at home; and while his rich neighbor, who could and did, is made richer by these very causes, he, the honest and industrious mechanic, is crushed to the earth; and yet we are told that this is a system for pro-moting the interests of the poor!

This leads me naturally to the great subject of *American labor,* which has hardly been considered or discussed as carefully as it deserves. What is *American labor?* It is best described by saying, *it is not* European labor. Nine tenths of the whole labor of this country is performed by those who cultivate the land they or their fathers own, or who, in their workshops, em-ploy some little capital of their own own, and mix it up with their manual toil. No such thing exists in other countries. Look at the different departments of industry, whether agricul-tural, manufacturing, or mechanical, and you will find that, in almost all, the laborers mix up some little capital with the work of their hands. The laborer of the United States is the United States. Strike out the laborers of the United States, including therein all who in some way or other belong to the industrious and working classes, and you reduce the population of the United States from sixteen millions to one million. The Amer-ican laborer is expected to have a comfortable home, decent though frugal living, and to be able to clothe and educate his children, to qualify them to take part, as all are called to do, in the political affairs and government of their country. Can this be said of any European laborer? Does he take any share in the government of his country, or feel it an obligation to educate his children? In most parts of Europe, nine tenths of the laborers have no interest in the soil they cultivate, nor in the fabrics they produce; no hope, under any circumstances, of rising themselves, or of raising their children, above the condition of a day-laborer at wages; and only know the government under which they live by the sense of its burdens, which they have no voice in mitigating.

To compare such a state of labor with the labor of this country, or to reason from that to ours, is preposterous. And yet the doctrine now is, not of individuals only, but of the administration, that the wages of American labor must be brought down to the level of those of Europe.

I have said this is not the doctrine of a few individuals; and on that head I think injustice has been done to a Senator from Pennsylvania,* who has been made to bear a large share of the responsibility of suggesting such a policy. If I mistake not, the same idea is thrown out in the President's message at the commencement of the last session, and in the treasury report. Hear what Mr. Woodbury says: —

"Should the States not speedily suspend more of their undertakings which are unproductive, but, by new loans or otherwise, find means to employ armies of laborers in consuming rather than raising crops, and should prices thus continue in many cases to be unnaturally inflated, as they have been of late years, in the face of a contracting currency, the effect of it on our finances would be still more to lessen exports, and, consequently, the prosperity and revenue of our foreign trade."

He is for turning off from the public works these "armies of laborers," who consume without producing crops, and thus bring down prices, both of crops and labor. Diminish the mouths that consume, and multiply the arms that produce, and you have the treasury prescription for mitigating distress and raising prices! How would that operate in this great State? You have, perhaps, some fifteen thousand men employed on your public works, works of the kind that the Secretary calls "unproductive"; and, even with such a demand as they must produce for provisions, prices are very low. The Secretary's remedy is to set them to raise provisions themselves, and thus augment

* Mr. Buchanan.

the supply, while they diminish the demand. In this way, the wages of labor are to be reduced, as well as the prices of agricultural productions. But this is not all. I have in my hand an extract from a speech in the House of Representatives of a zealous supporter, as it appears, of the administration, who maintains that, other things being reduced in proportion, you may reduce the wages of labor, without evil consequences. And where does he seek this example? On the shores of the Mediterranean. He fixes upon Corsica and Sardinia. But what is the Corsican laborer, that he should be the model upon which American labor is to be formed? Does he know any thing himself? Has he any education, or does he give any to his children? Has he a home, a freehold, and the comforts of life around him? No: with a crust of bread and a handful of olives, his daily wants are satisfied. And yet, from such a state of society, the laborer of New England, the laborer of the United States, is to be taught submission to low wages. The extract before me states that the wages of Corsica are,

"For the male laborer, 24 cents a day;
And the female do. 11 cents do.";—

both, I presume, finding their own food. And the honorable gentleman argues, that, owing to the greater cheapness of other articles, this is relatively as much as the American laborer gets; and he illustrates the fact by this bill of clothing for a Corsican laborer:—

"Jacket,   lasting 24 months, 8 francs;
Cap,   do. 24   do.   2 do.
Waistcoat,   do. 36   do.   4 do.
Pantaloons,   do. 18   do.   5 do.
Shirt,   do. 12   do.   3 do.
Pair of shoes, do. 6   do.   6 do.
                                 ——
                              28 francs."

Eight francs are equal to one dollar and sixty cents, and five francs to one dollar. Now, what say you, my friends? What will the farmer of New York, of Pennsylvania, or of New England say to the idea of walking on Sunday to church, at the head of his family, in his jacket *two years old?* What will the young man say, when, his work ended, he desires to visit the families of his neighbors, to the one pair of pantaloons, not quite two years old, indeed, but, as the farmers say of a colt, "coming two next grass," and which, for eighteen months, have every day done yeoman's service? Away with it all! Away with this plan for humbling and degrading the free, intelligent, well-educated, and well-paid laborer of the United States to the level of the almost brute laborer of Europe!

There is not much danger that schemes and doctrines such as these shall find favor with the people. They understand their own interest too well for that. Gentlemen, I am a farmer, on the sea-shore, and have, of course, occasion to employ some degree of agricultural labor. I am sometimes also rowed out to sea, being, like other New England men, fond of occasionally catching a fish, and finding health and recreation, in warm weather, from the air of the ocean. For the few months during which I am able to enjoy this retreat from labor, public or professional, I do not often trouble my neighbors, or they me, with conversation on politics. It happened, however, about three weeks ago, that, on such an excursion as I have mentioned, with one man only with me, I mentioned this doctrine of the reduction of prices, and asked him his opinion of it. He said he did not like it. I replied, " The wages of labor, it is true, are reduced; but then flour and beef, and perhaps clothing, all of which you buy, are reduced also. What, then, can be your objections?" "Why," said he, "it is true that flour is now low; but then it is an article that may rise suddenly, by means of a scanty crop in England, or at home; and if it should rise from five dollars to ten, I do not know for certain that it would fetch the price of my labor up with it. But while wages are high, then I am safe; and if produce chances to fall, so much the better for me. But there is another thing. I have but one thing to sell, that is, my labor; but I must buy many things, not only flour, and meat, and clothing, but also some articles that come from other countries, — a little sugar, a little coffee, a little tea, a little of the common spices, and such like. Now, I do not see how these foreign articles will be brought down by reducing wages at home; and before the price is brought down of the only thing I have to sell, I want to be sure that the prices will fall also, not of a part, but of all the things which I must buy."

Now, Gentlemen, though he will be astonished, or amused,

that I should tell the story before such a vast and respectable assemblage as this, I will place this argument of *Seth Peterson*, sometimes farmer and sometimes fisherman on the coast of Massachusetts, stated to me while pulling an oar with each hand, and with the sleeves of his red shirt rolled up above his elbows, against the reasonings, the theories, and the speeches of the administration and all its friends, in or out of Congress, and take the verdict of the country, and of the civilized world, whether he has not the best of the argument.

Since I have adverted to this conversation, Gentlemen, allow me to say that this neighbor of mine is a man fifty years of age, one of several sons of a poor man; that by his labor he has obtained some few acres, his own unencumbered freehold, has a comfortable dwelling, and plenty of the poor man's blessings. Of these, I have known six, decently and cleanly clad, each with the book, the slate, and the map proper to its age, all going at the same time daily to enjoy the blessing of that which is the great glory of New England, the common free school. Who can contemplate this, and thousands of other cases like it, not as pictures, but as common facts, without feeling how much our free institutions, and the policy hitherto pursued, have done for the comfort and happiness of the great mass of our citizens? Where in Europe, where in any part of the world out of our own country, shall we find labor thus rewarded, and the general condition of the people so good? Nowhere; nowhere! Away, then, with the injustice and the folly of reducing the cost of productions with us to what is called the common standard of the world! Away, then, away at once and for ever, with the miserable policy which would bring the condition of a laborer in the United States to that of a laborer in Russia or Sweden, in France or Germany, in Italy or Corsica! Instead of following these examples, let us hold up our own, which all nations may well envy, and which, unhappily, in most parts of the earth, it is easier to envy than to imitate.

But it is the cry and effort of the times to stimulate those who are called poor against those who are called rich; and yet, among those who urge this cry, and seek to profit by it, there is betrayed sometimes an occasional sneer at whatever savors of humble life. Witness the reproach against a candidate now before the people for their highest honors, that a log cabin, with plenty of hard cider, is good enough for him!

It appears to some persons, that a great deal too much use is made of the symbol of the log cabin. No man of sense supposes, certainly, that the having lived in a log cabin is any further proof of qualification for the Presidency, than as it creates a presumption that any one who, rising from humble condition, or under unfavorable circumstances, has been able to attract a considerable degree of public attention, is possessed of reputable qualities, moral and intellectual.

But it is to be remembered, that this matter of the log cabin originated, not with the friends of the Whig candidate, but with his enemies. Soon after his nomination at Harrisburg, a writer for one of the leading administration papers spoke of his "log cabin," and his use of "hard cider," by way of sneer and reproach. As might have been expected, (for pretenders are apt to be thrown off their guard,) this taunt at humble life proceeded from the party which claims a monopoly of the purest democracy. The whole party appeared to enjoy it, or, at least, they countenanced it by silent acquiescence; for I do not know that, to this day, any eminent individual or any leading newspaper attached to the administration has rebuked this scornful jeering at the supposed humble condition or circumstances in life, past or present, of a worthy man and a war-worn soldier. But it touched a tender point in the public feeling. It naturally roused indignation. What was intended as reproach was immediately seized on as merit. "Be it so! Be it so!" was the instant burst of the public voice. "Let him be the log cabin candidate. What you say in scorn, we will shout with all our lungs. From this day forward, we have our cry of rally; and we shall see whether he who has dwelt in one of the rude abodes of the West may not become the best house in the country!"

All this is natural, and springs from sources of just feeling. Other things, Gentlemen, have had a similar origin. We all know that the term "Whig" was bestowed in derision, two hundred years ago, on those who were thought too fond of liberty; and our national air of "Yankee Doodle" was composed by British officers, in ridicule of the American troops. Yet, ere long, the last of the British armies laid down its arms at Yorktown, while this same air was playing in the ears of officers and men. Gentlemen, it is only shallow-minded pretenders who either make distinguished origin matter of personal merit, or obscure

3*

origin matter of personal reproach.   Taunt and scoffing at the humble condition of early life affect nobody, in this country, but those who are foolish enough to indulge in them, and they are generally sufficiently punished by public rebuke.   A man who is not ashamed of himself need not be ashamed of his early condition.

Gentlemen, it did not happen to me to be born in a log cabin; but my elder brothers and sisters were born in a log cabin, raised amid the snow-drifts of New Hampshire, at a period so early that, when the smoke first rose from its rude chimney, and curled over the frozen hills, there was no similar evidence of a white man's habitation between it and the settlements on the rivers of Canada.   Its remains still exist.   I make to it an annual visit.   I carry my children to it, to teach them the hardships endured by the generations which have gone before them.   I love to dwell on the tender recollections, the kindred ties, the early affections, and the touching narratives and incidents, which mingle with all I know of this primitive family abode.   I weep to think that none of those who inhabited it are now among the living; and if ever I am ashamed of it, or if I ever fail in affectionate veneration for him who reared it, and defended it against savage violence and destruction, cherished all the domestic virtues beneath its roof, and, through the fire and blood of a seven years' revolutionary war, shrunk from no danger, no toil, no sacrifice, to serve his country, and to raise his children to a condition better than his own, may my name and the name of my posterity be blotted for ever from the memory of mankind!

[Mr. Webster then reviewed the expenditures of the government; but the reporter finds, with regret, that the sheet containing this portion of the speech has been mislaid or lost.   We supply, therefore, from memory, a very brief, and, we are aware, a very inadequate, outline of the argument.]

The expenditures of this administration have been eminently wasteful and extravagant.   Over and above the ordinary revenue of the country, Mr. Van Buren has spent more than *twenty millions* that reached the treasury from other sources.   I specify,

Reserved under the Deposit Act, ...	$ 6,000,000
Fourth instalment of surplus, kept back, . .	9,000,000
Payment by the Bank of United States on its bonds,	5,000,000
	$ 20,000,000

But even this has been found insufficient for the prodigality of the administration; and we had not been long assembled in Congress before a demand was made upon it, notwithstanding the flattering representations of the message and the treasury report, for authority to issue *five millions* more of treasury notes. This, we were assured, if Congress would only keep within the estimates submitted by the departments, would be ample. Congress did keep within the estimates; and yet, before we broke up, intimations came from the treasury that they must have authority to borrow or issue treasury notes for four and a half millions more!

This time even the friends of the administration demurred, and, finally, refused to grant this new aid; and what then was the alternative? Why, after having voted appropriations for the various branches of the public service, all within the estimates, and all of which, they were told, were indispensable, Congress conferred on the President, by a special provision, authority to withhold these appropriations from such objects as he pleased, and, out of certain classes, to select, at his discretion, those upon which money should be expended. Entire authority was thus given to the President over all these expenditures, in evasion, as it seems to me, of that provision of the Constitution forbidding all expenditure except by virtue of appropriations, which, if it mean any thing, must mean the specification of distinct sums for distinct purposes.

In this way, then, it is proposed to keep back from indispensable works, or works declared by the administration to be indispensable, four and a half millions, which are, nevertheless, appropriated, and which, with five millions of treasury notes already issued, will constitute a debt of from nine to ten millions.

So, then, when General Harrison shall succeed, in March next, to the Presidential chair, all that he will inherit from his predecessors, besides their brilliant example, will be these treasury vaults and safes, without a dollar in them, and a debt of *ten millions of dollars.*

The whole revenue policy of this administration has been founded in error. While the treasury is becoming poorer and poorer, articles of luxury are admitted free of duty. Look at the custom-house returns, — twenty millions of dollars worth of silks imported in one year, free of duty, and other articles of luxury in proportion, that should be made to contribute to the revenue.

We have, in my judgment, imported *excessively;* and yet the President urges it as an objection to works of public improvement, to railroads and canals, that they diminish our importations, and thereby interfere with the comforts of the people. His message says, —

" Our people will not long be insensible to the extent of the burdens entailed upon them by the false system that has been operating on their sanguine, energetic, and industrious character; nor to the means necessary to extricate themselves from these embarrassments. The weight which presses upon a large portion of the people and the States is an enormous debt, foreign and domestic. The foreign debt of our States, corporations, and men of business can scarcely be less than two hundred millions of dollars, requiring more than ten millions of dollars a year to pay the interest. This sum has to be paid out of the exports of the country, and must of necessity cut off imports to that extent, or plunge the country more deeply in debt from year to year. It is easy to see that the increase of this foreign debt must augment the annual demand on the exports to pay the interest, and to the same extent diminish the imports; and in proportion to the enlargement of the foreign debt, and the consequent increase of interest, must be the decrease of the import trade. In lieu of the comforts which it now brings us, we might have one gigantic banking institution, and splendid, but in many instances profitless, railroads and canals, absorbing, to a great extent, in interest upon the capital borrowed to construct them, the surplus fruits of national industry for years to come, and securing to posterity no adequate return for the comforts which the labor of their hands might otherwise have secured."

What are these comforts that we are to get so much more of, if we will only stop our railroads and canals? Foreign goods, loss of employment at home, European wages, and, lastly, direct taxation.

One of the gentlemen of the South, of that nullifying State Rights party which has absorbed the administration, or been absorbed by it, comes boldly out with the declaration, that the period is arrived for a *direct tax on land;* and, holding up this idea, others have said *that it will bring the North to the grindstone.* We shall see, before this contest is over, who will be the parties ground, and who the grinders. It is, however, but just to add, that, thus far, this is only an expression of individual opinion, and I do not allege it to be otherwise.

I had proposed to say something of the militia bill; but it is already so late that I must forego this topic. [" No, no! Go on, go on!" — from the crowd.]

[Mr. Webster resumed, and briefly analyzed the bill. Owing, however, to the lateness of the hour, he did not go largely into the discussion. He did not, he said, mean to charge Mr. Van Buren with any purpose to play the part of a Cæsar or a Cromwell; but he did say that, in his judgment, the plan, as recommended by the President in his message, and of which the annual report of the Secretary of War, accompanying the message, developed the leading features, would, if carried into operation, be expensive, burdensome, in derogation of the Constitution, and dangerous to our liberties. Mr. Webster referred to the President's recent letter to some gentleman in Virginia, endeavoring to exculpate himself for the recommendation in the message, by attempting to show a difference between the plan then so strongly commended, and that submitted in detail, some months afterwards, by the Secretary of War, to Congress. Mr. Webster pronounced this attempt wholly unsatisfactory, and then went on to say,]

I have now frankly stated my opinions as to the nature of the present excitement, and have answered the question I propounded as to the causes of the revolution in public sentiment now in progress. Will this revolution succeed? Does it move the masses, or is it an ebullition merely on the surface? And who is it that opposes the change which seems to be going forward? [Here some one in the crowd cried out, " None, hardly, but the office-holders, oppose it."] I hear one say that the office-holders oppose it; and that is true. If they were quiet, in my opinion, a change would take place almost by common consent. I have heard of an anecdote, perhaps hardly suited to the sobriety and dignity of this occasion, but which confirms the answer which my friend in the crowd has given to my question. It happened to a farmer's son, that his load of hay was blown over by a sudden gust, on an exposed plain. Those near him, seeing him manifest a degree of distress, which such an accident would not usually occasion, asked him the reason; he said he should not *take on* so much about it, only father was under the load. I think it very probable, Gentlemen, that there are many now very active and zealous friends, who would not care much whether the wagon of the administration were blown over or not, if it were not for the fear that father, or son, or uncle, or brother, might be found under the load. Indeed, it is remarkable how frequently the fire of patriotism glows in the breasts of the holders of office. A thousand favored contractors shake with horrid fear, lest the proposed change should put the interests of the public in great danger. Ten thousand post-offices, moved by the same apprehension, join in the cry of alarm, while a perfect earthquake of disinterested remonstrance proceeds from the custom-houses. Patronage and favoritism tremble and quake, through every limb and every nerve, lest the people should be found in favor of a change, which might endanger the liberties of the country, or at least break down its present eminent and distinguished prosperity, by abandoning the measures, so wise, so beneficent, so successful, and so popular, which the present administration has pursued!

Fellow-citizens, we have all sober and important duties to perform. I have not addressed you to-day for the purpose of joining in a premature note of triumph, or raising a shout for anticipated victories. We are in the controversy, not through it. It is our duty to spare no pains to circulate information, and to spread the truth far and wide. Let us persuade those who differ from us, if we can, to hear both sides. Let us remind them that we are all embarked together, with a common interest and a common fate. And let us, without rebuke or unkindness, beseech them to consider what the good of the whole requires, what is best for them and for us.

There are two causes which keep back thousands of honest men from joining those who wish for a change. The first of these is the fear of reproach from former associates, and the pain which party denunciation is capable of inflicting. But, surely, the manliness of the American character is superior to this! Surely, no American citizen will feel himself chained to the wheels of any party, nor bound to follow it, against his conscience and his sense of the interest of the country. Resolution and decision ought to dissipate such restraints, and to leave men free at once to act upon their own convictions. Unless this can be done, party has entailed upon us a miserable slavery, by compelling us to act against our consciences on questions of the greatest importance.

The other cause is the constant cry that the party of the administration is the true democratic party, or the more popular party in the government and in the country. The falsity of this claim has not been sufficiently exposed. It should have been met, and should be now met, not only by denial, but by proof. If they mean the new democracy, — the cry against credit, against industry, against labor, against a man's right to leave his own earnings to his own children, — why, then, doubtless, they are right; all this sort of democracy is theirs. But if by democracy they mean a conscientious and stern adherence to the true popular principles of the Constitution and the government, then I think they have very little claim to it. Is the augmentation of executive power a democratic principle? Is the separation of the currency of the government from the currency of the people a democratic principle? Is the imbodying a large military force, in time of peace, a democratic principle?

Let us entreat honest men not to take names for things, nor pretences for proofs. If democracy, in any constitutional sense, belongs to our adversaries, let them show their title and produce their evidence. Let the question be examined; and let not intelligent and well-meaning citizens be kept to the support of measures which in their hearts and consciences they disapprove, because their authors put forth such loud claims to the sole possession of regard for the people.

Fellow-citizens of the County of Saratoga, in taking leave of you, I cannot but remind you how distinguished a place your county occupies in the history of the country. I cannot be ignorant, that in the midst of you are many, at this moment, who saw in this neighborhood the triumph of republican arms in the surrender of General Burgoyne. I cannot doubt that a fervent spirit of patriotism burns in their breasts and in the breasts of their children. They helped to save their country amidst the storms of war; they will help to save it, I am fully persuaded, in the present severe civil crisis. I verily believe it is true, that, of all that are left to us from the Revolution, nine tenths are with us in the existing contest. If there be living a Revolutionary officer, or soldier, who has joined in the attacks upon General Harrison's military character, I have not met with him. It is not, therefore, in the county of Saratoga, that a cause sustained by such means is likely to prevail.

Fellow-citizens, the great question is now before the country. If, with the experience of the past, the American people think proper to confirm power in the hands which now hold it, and thereby sanction the leading policy of the administration, it will be your duty and mine to bow, with submission, to the public will; but, for myself, I shall not believe it possible for me to be of service to the country, in any department of public life. I shall look on, with no less love of country than ever, but with fearful forebodings of what may be near at hand.

But I do not at all expect that result. I fully believe the change is coming. If we all do our duty, we shall restore the government to its former policy, and the country to its former prosperity. And let us here, to-day, fellow-citizens, with full resolution and patriotic purpose of heart, give and take pledges, that, until this great controversy be ended, our time, our talents, our efforts, are all due, and shall all be faithfully given, to OUR COUNTRY.

WHIG PRINCIPLES AND PURPOSES.

INTRODUCTORY NOTE.

AMONG the demonstrations of public opinion which preceded the election of General Harrison, in November, 1840, the convention held upon Bunker Hill, on the 10th of September, was perhaps the most imposing. The suggestion of a grand meeting upon this spot, to be attended by numerous delegates, not merely from Massachusetts and New England, but the other States of the Union, even those most remote, was received with great favor throughout the country, and was carried into full effect. Many persons from the distant States, travelling to the North, made their arrangements to be in Boston on this occasion. Respectable delegations from every section of the Union were specially appointed for this purpose, and every part of New England was fully represented. The number of strangers drawn to Boston to attend or witness the meeting was estimated by some persons as high as fifty thousand.

On the morning of the 10th, a vast procession was formed on the Common in Boston, and in the neighboring streets, and by eleven o'clock was ready to move. It was headed by one hundred and fifty truckmen, in white frocks, followed by more than a thousand well-mounted citizens. Fifty barouches and carriages succeeded, containing Revolutionary soldiers, gentlemen of distinction from other States, and persons specially invited. The different sections of the cavalcade were indicated by a variety of characteristic banners.

After the cavalcade came the pedestrian portion of the procession, the delegates from the New England States arranged in the rear, the others occupying places in the order in which the Constitution was adopted by their respective States. Appropriate banners, with significant devices, many of which were executed with great spirit, were borne by the several delegations. The appearance of these respectable bodies from the extremest South and West was the peculiar feature of the day, and added much to its interest. It was the first occasion on which any similar display had taken place, to any thing like the same extent, in this part of the Union.

The delegations from the States were followed by those from the various counties and towns in Massachusetts, that of Suffolk bringing up the rear. These, also, all carried appropriate banners, many with devices and inscriptions highly significant, original, and spirited, and wrought with great beauty. A large body of seamen appeared in the Suffolk delegation. In another section of the same delegation was a printing-press, in full operation, drawn by six horses.

The length of the procession was four miles, and two hours were required for its passage by any given point. It is impossible adequately to describe the enthusiasm which prevailed, or the extreme beauty and singularity of the spectacle. Numerous bands of music were placed in different parts of the procession. The entire line of streets through which it passed was filled with spectators. The windows and balconies were thronged with women and children, waving their handkerchiefs in token of sympathy with the delegates, while the latter acknowledged the attention with continual cheers. The streets were decorated with ensigns and pennons, and occasionally with triumphal arches adorned with evergreens and flowers. The whole city was alive with the festival.

In this manner the procession moved, in perfect order, through the principal streets, over Warren Bridge, and thence to the battle-ground on Bunker Hill. A general expectation of a speech from Mr. Webster had gone abroad. But the vast multitude anticipated had seemed to render it expedient to dispense with the usual mode of proceeding at political meetings, and, instead of a popular discussion, to put forth a carefully prepared and formal manifesto of the principles which governed the Whig party in the existing contest. A slight organization accordingly took place. Mr. Webster was invited to act as the presiding officer of the convention, and the following declaration of principles, previously drawn up by him, and signed by him on behalf of the assembly, was publicly read.

This closed the proceedings on the Hill, where the dispersion of the multitude was hastened by a heavy rain. In the evening, political meetings were held in Faneuil Hall, and other public halls in Boston, at which patriotic addresses of great ability were made by Messrs. Watkins Leigh of Virginia, Ellsworth of Connecticut, Pennington of New Jersey, O'Fallon of Missouri, Ogden Hoffman, Philip Hone, and Charles King, of New York, Upham of Vermont, Neal of Maine, Dawson of Michigan, and many other gentlemen of distinction from various parts of the Union.

The importance of this demonstration, as a display of sympathy between the people of the remotest members of the Union, and its tendency, in this way, to fortify and animate the true spirit of the Constitution, have seemed to warrant a notice in greater detail than would be due, in this place, to the ordinary manifestations of contemporary political feeling.

WHIG PRINCIPLES AND PURPOSES.*

WHEN men pause from their ordinary occupations, and assemble in great numbers, a proper respect for the judgment of the country and of the age requires that they should clearly set forth the grave causes which have brought them together, and the purposes which they seek to promote.

Feeling the force of this obligation, fifty thousand of the free electors of the New England States, honored also by the presence of like free electors from nearly every other State in the Union, having assembled on Bunker Hill, on this 10th day of September, 1840, proceed to set forth a declaration of their principles, and of the occasion and objects of their meeting.

In the first place, we declare our unalterable attachment to that public liberty, the purchase of so much blood and treasure, in the acquisition of which the field whereon we stand obtained early and imperishable renown. Bunker Hill is not a spot on which we shall forget the principles of our fathers, or suffer any thing to quench within our own bosoms the love of freedom which we have inherited from them.

In the next place, we declare our warm and hearty devotion to the Constitution of the country, and to that Union of the States which it has so happily cemented, and so long and so prosperously preserved. We call ourselves by no local names, we recognize no geographical divisions, while we give utterance to our sentiments on high constitutional and political subjects. We are Americans, citizens of the United States, knowing no other country, and desiring to be distinguished by no other ap-

* A Declaration of Principles and Purposes, adopted by a General Convention of the Whigs of New England, at Bunker Hill, on the 10th of September, 1840, prepared by Mr. Webster, and signed by him as President of the Convention.

pellation. We believe the Constitution, while administered wisely and in its proper spirit, to be capable of protecting all parts of the country, securing all interests, and perpetuating a national brotherhood among all the States. We believe that to foment local jealousies, to attempt to prove the existence of opposite interests between one part of the country and another, and thus to disseminate feelings of distrust and alienation, while it is in contemptuous disregard of the counsels of the great father of his country, is but one form in which irregular ambition, destitute of all true patriotism, and a love of power, reckless of the means of its gratification, exhibit their unsubdued and burning desire.

We believe, too, that party spirit, however natural or unavoidable it may be in free republics, yet, when it gains such an ascendency in men's minds as leads them to substitute party for country, to seek no ends but party ends, no approbation but party approbation, and to fear no reproach or contumely so that there be no party dissatisfaction, not only alloys the true enjoyment of such institutions, but weakens, every day, the foundations on which they stand.

We are in favor of the liberty of speech and of the press; we are friends of free discussion; we espouse the cause of popular education; we believe in man's capacity for self-government; we desire to see the freest and widest dissemination of knowledge and of truth; and we believe, especially, in the benign influence of religious feeling and moral instruction on the social, as well as on the individual, happiness of man.

Holding these general sentiments and opinions, we have come together to declare that, under the present administration of the general government, a course of measures has been adopted and pursued, in our judgments, disastrous to the best interests of the country, threatening the accumulation of still greater evils, utterly hostile to the true spirit of the Constitution and to the principles of civil liberty, and calling upon all men of honest purpose, disinterested patriotism, and unbiased intelligence, to put forth their utmost constitutional efforts in order to effect a change.

General Andrew Jackson was elected President of the United States, and took the oaths of office on the 4th of March, 1829; and we readily admit that, under his administration, certain portions of the public affairs were conducted with ability. But we have to lament that he was not proof against the insinuations and influences of evil counsellors, or perhaps against his own passions, when moved and excited. Hence, in one most important branch of the public interest, in that essential part of commercial regulation which respects the money, the currency, the circulation, and the internal exchanges of the country, accidental occurrences, acting on his characteristic love of rule, and uneasiness under opposition, led him to depart from all that was expected from him, and to enter upon measures which plunged both him and the country in greater and greater difficulties at every step, so that, in this respect, his whole course of administration was but a series of ill-fated experiments, and of projects framed in disregard of prudence and precedent, and bursting in rapid succession; the final explosion taking place a few months after his retirement from office.

General Jackson was not elected with any desire or expectation, on the part of any of his supporters, that he would interfere with the currency of the country. We affirm this as the truth of history. It is incapable of refutation or denial. It is as certain as that the American Revolution was not undertaken to destroy the rights of property, or overthrow the obligation of morals.

But, unhappily, he became involved in a controversy with the then existing Bank of the United States. He manifested a desire, how originating or by whom inspired is immaterial, to exercise a political influence over that institution, and to cause that institution to exercise, in turn, a political influence over the community. Published documents prove this, as plainly as they prove any other act of his administration. In this desire he was resisted, thwarted, and finally defeated. But what he could not govern, he supposed he could destroy; and the event showed that he did not overrate his popularity and his power. He pursued the bank to the death, and achieved his triumph by the veto of 1832. The accustomed means of maintaining a sound and a uniform currency, for the use of the whole country, having been thus trampled down and destroyed, recourse was had to those new modes of experimental administration, to which we have already adverted, and which terminated so disastrously, both for the reputation of his administration and for the welfare of the country.

But General Jackson did not deny his constitutional obligations, nor seek to escape from their force. He never professedly
abandoned all care over the general currency. His whole conduct shows that he admitted, throughout, the duty of the general government to maintain a supervision over the currency of
the country, both metallic and paper, for the general good and
use of the people ; and he congratulated both himself and the
nation, that, by the measures adopted by him, the currency and
the exchanges of the country were placed on a better footing
than they ever had been under the operation of a Bank of the
United States. This confidence in his own experiments, we
know, proved most illusory. But the frequency with which he
repeated this and similar declarations establishes incontestably
his own sense of the duty of government.

In all the measures of General Jackson upon the currency,
the present chief magistrate is known to have concurred. Like
him, he was opposed to the Bank of the United States ; like
him, he was in favor of the State deposit banks ; and, like him,
he insisted that, by the aid of such banks, the administration
had accomplished all that could be desired on the great subjects
of the currency and the exchange.

But the catastrophe of May, 1837, produced a new crisis, by
overthrowing the last in the series of experiments, and creating
an absolute necessity, either of returning to that policy of the
government which General Jackson had repudiated, or of re-
nouncing altogether the constitutional duty which it had been
the object of that policy to perform. The latter branch of the
alternative was adopted. Refuge was sought in escape. A
duty, up to that moment admitted by all, was suddenly denied,
and the fearful resolution announced, that government would
hereafter provide for its own revenues, and that, for the rest, the
people must take care of themselves.

Assembled here to-day, and feeling, in common with the whole
country, the evil consequences of these principles and these
measures, we pronounce against them all, from first to last,
our deep and solemn sentence of condemnation. We condemn the early departure of General Jackson from that line of
policy which he was expected to pursue. We deplore the temper which led him to his original quarrel with the bank. We
deplore the headstrong spirit which instigated him to pursue

that institution to its destruction. We deplore the timidity of some, the acquiescence of others, and the subserviency of all of his party, which enabled him to carry its whole, unbroken phalanx to the support of measures, and the accomplishment of purposes, which we know to have been against the wishes, the remonstrances, and the consciences of many of the most respectable and intelligent. We deplore his abandonment of those means for assuring a good currency, which had been successfully tried for forty years; his rash experiments with great interests; and the perseverance with which he persisted in them, when men of different temperament must have been satisfied of their uselessness and impotence.

But General Jackson's administration, authority, and influence are now historical. They belong to the past, while we have to do, to-day, with the serious evils, and the still more alarming portents, of the present. We remonstrate, therefore, most earnestly and emphatically, against the policy of the present administration upon this subject. We protest against the truth of its principles. We deny the propriety and justice of its measures. We are constrained to have too little respect for its objects, and we desire to rouse the country, so far as we can, to the evils which oppress and the dangers that surround us.

We insist that the present administration has consulted its own party ends, and the preservation of its own power, to the manifest neglect of great objects of public interest. We think there is no liberality, no political comprehension, no just or enlarged policy, in its leading measures. We look upon its abandonment of the currency as fatal; and we regard its system of sub-treasuries as but a poor device to avoid a high obligation, or as the first in a new series of ruthless experiments. We believe its professions in favor of a hard-money currency to be insincere; because we do not believe that any person of common information and ordinary understanding can suppose that the use of paper, as a circulating medium, will be discontinued, even if such discontinuance were desirable, unless the government shall break down the acknowledged authority of the State governments to establish banks. We believe the clamor against State banks, State bonds, and State credits, to have been raised by the friends of the administration to divert public attention from its own mismanagement, and to throw on others the consequence of its own conduct. We heard nothing of all this in the early part of General Jackson's administration, nor until his measures had brought the currency of the country into the utmost disorder. We know that, in times past, the present chief magistrate has, of all men, had most to do with the systems of State banks, the most faith in their usefulness, and no very severely chastened desire to profit by their influence. We believe that the purpose of exercising a money influence over the community has never departed from the administration. What it could not accomplish by an attempt to bend the Bank of the United States to its purposes, we believe it has sought, and now seeks, to effect by its project of the sub-treasury. We believe that, in order to maintain the principles upon which the system of the sub-treasury is founded, the friends of the administration have been led to espouse opinions destructive of the internal commerce of the country, paralyzing to its whole industry, tending to sink its labor, both in price and in character, to the degraded standard of the uninformed, the ignorant, the suffering labor of the worst parts of Europe. Led by the same necessity, or pushing the same principles still farther, and with a kind of revolutionary rapidity, we have seen the rights of property not only assailed, but denied; the boldest agrarian notions put forth; the power of transmission from father to son openly denounced; the right of one to participate in the earnings of another, to the rejection of the natural claims of his own children, asserted as a fundamental principle of the new democracy; — and all this by those who are in the pay of government, receiving large salaries, and whose offices would be nearly sinecures, but for the labor performed in the attempt to give currency to these principles and these opinions. We believe that the general tone of the measures of the administration, the manner in which it confers favors, its apparent preference for partisans of extreme opinions, and the readiness with which it bestows its confidence on the boldest and most violent, are producing serious injuries upon the political morals and general sentiments of the country. We believe that to this cause is fairly to be attributed the most lamentable change which has taken place in the temper, the sobriety, and the wisdom with which the high public counsels have been hitherto conducted. We look with alarm to the existing state of things, in this respect; and we would most earnestly, and with all our hearts, as well for the honor of the country as for its interests, beseech all good men to unite with us in an attempt to bring back the deliberative age of the government, to restore to the collected bodies of the people's representatives that self-respect, decorum, and dignity, without which the business of legislation can make no regular progress, and is always in danger either of accomplishing nothing, or of reaching its ends by unjustifiable and violent means.

We believe the conduct of the administration respecting the public revenue to be highly reprehensible. It has expended twenty millions, previously accumulated, besides all the accruing income since it came into power; and there seems at this moment to be no doubt, that it will leave to its successors a public debt of from five to ten millions of dollars. It has shrunk from its proper responsibilities. With the immediate prospect of an empty treasury, it has yet not had the manliness to recommend to Congress any adequate provision. It has constantly spoken of the excess of receipts over expenditures, until this excess has finally manifested itself in an absolute necessity for loans, and in a power conferred on the President, altogether new, and in our judgment hostile to the whole spirit of the Constitution, to meet the event of want of resources by withholding, out of certain classes of appropriations made by Congress, such as he chooses to think may be best spared. It lives by shifts and contrivances, by shallow artifices and delusive names, by what it calls "facilities," and the "exchange of treasury notes for specie"; while, in truth, it has been fast contracting a public debt, in the midst of all its boasting, without daring to lay the plain and naked truth of the case before the people.

We protest against the conduct of the House of Representatives in the case of the New Jersey election. This is not a local, but a general question. In the union of the States, on whatever link the blow of injustice or usurpation falls, it is felt, and ought to be felt, through the whole chain. The cause of New Jersey is the cause of every State, and every State is therefore bound to vindicate it.

That the regular commission, or certificate of return, signed by the chief magistrate of the State, according to the provisions of law, entitles those who produce it to be sworn in as members of Congress, to vote in the organization of the House, and to hold their seats until their right be disturbed by regular petition and proof, is a proposition of constitutional law, of such universal extent and universal acknowledgment, that it cannot be strengthened by argument or by analogy. There is nothing clearer, and nothing better settled. No legislative body could ever be organized without the adoption of this principle. Yet, in the case of the New Jersey members of Congress, it was entirely disregarded. And it is of awful portent, that on such a question, — a question in its nature strictly judicial, — the domination of party should lead men thus flagrantly to violate first principles. It is the first step that costs. After this open disregard of the elementary rules of law and justice, it should create no surprise, that, pending the labors of a committee especially appointed to ascertain who were duly elected, a set of men calling themselves representatives of the people of New Jersey, who had no certificates from the chief magistrate of the State or according to the laws of the State, were voted into their seats, under silence imposed by the previous question, and afterwards gave their votes for the passage of the sub-treasury law. We call most solemnly upon all who, with us, believe that these proceedings alike invade the rights of the States, and dishonor the cause of popular government and free institutions, to supply an efficient and decisive remedy, by the unsparing application of the elective franchise.

We protest against the plan of the administration respecting the training and disciplining of the militia. The President now admits it to be unconstitutional; and it is plainly so, on the face of it, for the training of the militia is by the Constitution expressly reserved to the States. If it were not unconstitutional, it would yet be unnecessary, burdensome, entailing enormous expenses, and placing dangerous powers in executive hands. It belongs to the prolific family of executive projects, and it is a consolation to find that at least one of its projects has been so scorched by public rebuke and reprobation, that no man raise his hand or opens his mouth in its favor.

It was during the progress of the late administration, and under the well-known auspices of the present chief magistrate, that the declaration was made in the Senate, that, in regard to public office, the spoils of victory belong to the conquerors; thus boldly proclaiming, as the creed of the party, that political contests are rightfully struggles for office and emolument. We protest against doctrines which thus regard offices as created for the sake of incumbents, and stimulate the basest passions to the pursuit of high public trusts.

We protest against the repeated instances of disregarding judicial decisions by officers of government, and others enjoying its countenance; thus setting up executive interpretation over the solemn adjudications of courts and juries, and showing marked disrespect for the usual and constitutional interpretation and execution of the laws.

This misgovernment and maladministration would have been the more tolerable, if they had not been committed, in most instances, in direct contradiction to the warmest professions and the most solemn assurances. Promises of a better currency, for example, have ended in the destruction of all national and uniform currency; assurances of the strictest economy have been but preludes to the most wasteful excess; even the Florida war has been conducted under loud pretences of severe frugality; and the most open, unblushing, and notorious interference with State elections has been systematically practised by the paid agents of an administration, which, in the full freshness of its oath of office, declared that one of its leading objects should be, *to accomplish that task of reform which particularly required the correction of those abuses by which the patronage of the federal government was brought into conflict with the freedom of elections.*

In the teeth of this solemn assurance, it has been proved that United States officers have been assessed, in sums bearing proportion to the whole amount they receive from the treasury, for the purpose of supporting their partisans even in State and municipal elections.

Whatever, in short, has been most professed, has been least practised; and it seems to have been taken for granted, that the American people would be satisfied with pretence, and a full-toned assurance of patriotic purpose. The history of the last twelve years has been but the history of broken promises and disappointed hopes. At every successive period of this history, an enchanting, rose-colored futurity has been spread out before the people, especially in regard to the great concerns of revenue, finance, and currency. But these colors have faded, as the object has been approached. Prospects of abundant revenue have resulted in the necessity of borrowing; the brilliant hopes of a better currency end in general derangement, stagnation, and distress; and while the whole country is roused to an unprecedented excitement by the pressure of the times, every state paper from the Cabinet at Washington comes forth fraught with congratulations on that happy state of things which the judicious policy of the administration is alleged to have brought about! Judged by the tone of these papers, every present movement of the people is quite unreasonable, and all attempts at change are only so many ungrateful returns for the wise and successful administration of public affairs!

There is yet another subject of complaint to which we feel bound to advert, by our veneration for the illustrious dead, by our respect for truth, by our love for the honor of our country, and by our own wounded pride as American citizens. We feel that the country has been dishonored, and we desire to free ourselves from all imputation of acquiescence in the parricidal act. The late President, in a communication to Congress, more than intimates that some of the earliest and most important measures of Washington's administration were the offspring of personal motives and private interests. His successor has repeated and extended this accusation, and given to it, we are compelled to say, a greater degree of offensiveness and grossness. No man, with an American heart in his bosom, can endure this without feeling the deepest humiliation, as well as the most burning scorn. The fame of Washington and his immediate associates is one of the richest treasures of the country. His is that name which an American may utter with pride in every part of the world, and which, wherever uttered, is shouted to the skies by the voices of all true lovers of human liberty. Imputations which assail his measures so rudely, while they are abominable violations of the truth of history, are an insult to the country, and an offence against the moral sentiments of civilized mankind. Miserable, miserable indeed, must be that cause which cannot support its party predominance, its ruinous schemes and senseless experiments, without thus attempting to poison the fountains of truth, and prove the government of our country disgracefully corrupt, even in its very cradle. Our hearts would sink within us, if we believed that such efforts could succeed; but they must be impotent. Neither the recent nor the present

President was born to cast a shade on the character of Washington or his associates. The destiny of both has been, rather, to illustrate, by contrast, that wisdom and those virtues which they have not imitated, and to hurl blows, which the affectionate veneration of American citizens, and the general justice of the civilized world, will render harmless to others, and powerful only in their recoil upon themselves. If this language be strong, so also is that feeling of indignation which has suggested it; and, on an occasion like this, we could not leave this consecrated spot without the consciousness of having omitted an indispensable duty, had we not thus given utterance to the fulness of our hearts, and marked with our severest rebuke, and most thorough reprobation and scorn, a labored effort to fix a deep and enduring stain on the early history of the government.

Finally, on this spot, the fame of which began with our liberty, and can only end with it, in the presence of these multitudes, of the whole country, and of the world, we declare our conscientious convictions, that the present administration has proved itself incapable of conducting the public affairs of the nation in such a manner as shall preserve the Constitution, maintain the public liberty, and secure general prosperity. We declare, with the utmost sincerity, that we believe its main purpose to have been, to continue its own power, influence, and popularity; that to this end it has abandoned indispensable, but highly responsible, constitutional duties; that it has trifled with the great concerns of finance and currency; that it has used the most reprehensible means for influencing public opinion; that it has countenanced the application of public money to party purposes; that it endeavors to consolidate and strengthen party by every form of public patronage; that it laboriously seeks to conceal the truth from the people on subjects of great interest; that it has shown itself to be selfish in its ends, and corrupt in its means; and that, if it should be able to maintain itself in power through another term, there is the most imminent danger that it will plunge the country in still further difficulty, bring on still greater disorder and distress, and undermine at once the foundations of the public prosperity and the institutions of the country.

Men thus false to their own professions, false to the principles of the Constitution, false to the interests of the people, and false to the highest honor of their country, are unfit to be the rulers of this republic.

The people of the United States have a right to good government. They have a right to an honest and faithful exercise of all the powers of the Constitution, as understood and practised in the best days of the republic for the general good. They have an inalienable right to all the blessings of that *Liberty* which their fathers achieved, and all the benefits of that *Union* which their fathers established.

And standing here, this day, with the memory of those fathers fresh on our hearts, and with the fields of their glory and the monuments of their fame full in our view, with Bunker Hill beneath us, and Concord, and Lexington, and Dorchester Heights, and Faneuil Hall all around us, we here, as a part of the people, pledge ourselves to each other, and to our country, to spare no lawful and honorable efforts to vindicate and maintain these rights, and to remove from the high places of the nation men who have thus contemned and violated them.

And we earnestly and solemnly invoke all good men and true patriots throughout the Union, foregoing all consideration of party, and forgetting all distinction of State or section, to rally once more, as our fathers did in 1775, against the common oppressors of our country, and to unite with us in restoring our glorious Constitution to its true interpretation, its practical administration, and its just supremacy.

In such a cause, principles are every thing; individuals nothing. Yet we cannot forget that we have worthy, honest, capable candidates for the offices from which we hope to remove the present incumbents.

Those who desire a change, throughout the whole country, have agreed, with extraordinary unanimity, to support General William Henry Harrison for the office of President. We believe him to be an honest and faithful citizen, who has served his country successfully, in divers civil trusts; and we believe him a veteran soldier, whose honor and bravery cannot be questioned. We give him our unhesitating confidence; and in that confidence we shall support him, and the distinguished citizen of Virginia who has been nominated for the Vice-Presidency, with all our efforts and all our hearts, through the present contest; convinced that by their election the true spirit of the Constitution will be restored, the prosperity of the people revived, the stability of our free institutions reassured, and the blessings of union and liberty secured to ourselves and our posterity.

SPEECH IN WALL STREET.

5*

SPEECH IN WALL STREET.*

I AM duly sensible, fellow-citizens, both of the honor and of the responsibility of the present occasion. An honor it certainly is to be requested to address a body of merchants such as I behold before me, as intelligent, as enterprising, and as respectable as any in the world. A responsible undertaking it is to address such an assembly, and on a subject which many of you understand scientifically and in its elements at least as well as I do, and with which most of you have more or less of practical acquaintance. The currency of a country is a subject always important, and in some measure complex; but it has become the great leading question of our time. I have not shrunk from the expression of my opinions, since I have been in public life, nor shall I now, especially since on this question another great political question seems likely to turn; namely, the question whether one administration is about to go out of power, and another administration to come into power. Under these circumstances, it becomes me to premise what I have now to say by remarking, in the first place, that I propose to speak for nobody but myself. My general opinions on the subject of the currency have been well known; and as it has now become highly probable that those who have opposed all that has recently been done by the government on that subject will be called on to propose some remedies of their own for the existing state of things, it is the more incumbent on me to notify all who hear me, that what I now say I say for myself alone; for in regard to the sentiments of the distinguished individual whom it is your purpose to support for the Presidency, I have no more authority

* A Speech delivered at the Merchants' Meeting in Wall Street, New York, on the 28th of September, 1840.

to speak than any of yourselves, nor any means of knowing his opinions more than is possessed by you, and by all the country.

I will, in the first place, state a few general propositions, which I believe to be founded on true principles of good, practical political economy, as understood in their application to the condition of a country like ours.

And first, I hold the opinion that a mixed currency, composed partly of gold and silver and partly of good paper, redeemable and steadily redeemed in specie on demand, is the most useful and convenient for such a country as we inhabit, and is sure to continue to be used, to a greater or less extent, in these United States; the idea of an exclusive metallic currency being either the mere fancy of theorists, or, what is probably nearer the truth, being employed as a means of popular delusion.

I believe, in the next place, that the management of a mixed currency, such as I have mentioned, has its difficulties, and requires considerable skill and care; and this position is as true in respect to England, the greatest commercial country of Europe, as it is of the United States. I believe, further, that there is danger of expansion and of contraction, both sudden in their recurrence, in the use of such a currency; yet I believe that where a currency altogether metallic exists, as it does in Cuba, and in countries where metallic coin is most in use, as in France, there are fluctuations in prices, there are disasters and commercial failures, occurring perhaps nearly as often, and being perhaps as bad in their character, as in countries where a well-regulated paper currency exists.

In the next place, I hold that the regulation of the currency, whether metallic or paper,—that a just and safe supervision over that which virtually performs the office of money, and constitutes the medium of exchange, whatever it may be,—necessarily pertains to government; that it is one of the necessary and indispensable prerogatives of government.

Every bank, as banks are now constituted in this country, performs two distinct offices or functions. First, it discounts bills or notes. This is merely the lending of money, and may be performed by corporations, by individuals, or by banks without circulation, acting as banks of discount merely. In this country, our banks are all banks of circulation, issuing

paper with an express view to circulation.   When such a bank
discounts notes, it pays the amount of discount in its own bills,
and thereby adds so much to the actual amount of circulation,
every such operation being, by so much, an increase of the circulating medium of the country.   Hence it is true, that, in the
absence of all government control and supervision, the wisdom
and discretion regulating the amount of money afloat at any
time in the community are but the aggregate of the wisdom and
discretion of all the banks collectively considered; each individual bank acting from the promptings of its own interest, without concert with others, and not from any sense of public duty.
In my judgment, such a regulator, or such a mode of regulating
the currency, and of deciding what shall be the amount of
money at any time existing in the community, is unsafe and
untrustworthy, and is one to which we never can look to guard
us against those excessive expansions and contractions which
have produced such injurious consequences.   Hence arises my
view of the duty of government to take the care and control
of the issues of these local institutions, and thereby to guard
the community against the evils of an excessive circulation.
I am of opinion, that the government may establish such a
control and supervision as shall accomplish these purposes in
two ways; and first, by restraining the issues of the local banks.
You all know, and from experience, perfectly well, that a general
institution for the circulation of a currency, which shall be as
good in one part of the country as in another, if it shall possess a competent capital and shall be empowered to act as the
fiscal agent of the government, is capable of controlling excessive issues, and keeping the bank paper in circulation in a community within reasonable limits.   Such an institution acts also
beneficially by supplying a currency which is of general credit,
and uniform in value throughout the country.

This brings us to the point.   What we need, and what we
must have, is some currency which shall be equally acceptable
in the Gulf of Mexico, in the valley of the Mississippi, on the
Canada frontier, on the Atlantic Ocean, and in every town, village, and hamlet of our extended land.   The question is, how
to get this.   Now, it seems to me that this question is to be answered by a plain reference to the condition of the country, to
the form of its government, and to the objects for which the

general government was constituted. Why is it that no State bank paper, however secure, under institutions however respectable, in cities however wealthy, and with a capital however ample, has ever succeeded, but has uniformly failed, to give a national character to the currency? The cause of this is obvious. We live under a government which makes us, in many important respects, one people, and which does this, and was intended to do it, especially in whatever relates to the commerce of the country. Yet the nation exists in twenty-six distinct and sovereign States, extending over a space as wide almost as the greatest empires of Europe. In this state of things, every man knows, and is bound to know, two governments; first, the government of his own State. If that State has established banks, he knows, and is bound to know, on what principles these banks have been established, whether they are safe as objects of credit, and whether the laws of their administration are wise. Generally speaking, these State institutions — I refer now more particularly to those in the central and the northern and eastern sections of the Union, because with these I am best acquainted — enjoy the confidence of the people of the several States where they exist. Their issues are in general well received, not only in the States where the banks are established, but frequently also in the neighboring States. Every citizen is also bound, in like manner, to know the laws of the general government, the security of the institutions it has founded, and their general character; and since this is a national subject, over which the general government acts as such, he regards its acts and provisions as of a national character. Every man looks to institutions founded by Congress as emanating from the national government, a government which he knows, and which, to a certain extent, he himself influences by the exercise of the elective franchise, and in which it is his duty, as a good citizen, to correct, so far as in his power, whatever may be amiss. He has confidence, therefore, in the national government, and in the institutions it sanctions, as in something of his own; but the case is very different when he is called to take the paper of banks chartered by a distant State, over which he has no control, with which he has little personal acquaintance, and of whose institutions he knows not whether they are well or ill founded, or well or ill administered.

In exemplification of this, if you take a note of one of the best banks in the city of New York, rich as this city is, and place upon it forty indorsements of the most substantial mercantile houses, and then carry that note to the frontier, and read it to the people there, such is the nature of man, and such is his habit of looking to the nation for that medium which is to circulate through the nation, that you cannot get that New York note, with all its indorsements, to circulate there as national money. Can I give a stronger proof of the truth of this assertion than is found in a fact which you all know? Your city banks pay specie; the banks of Philadelphia and the Bank of the United States do not pay specie, and their paper is consequently at a discount here of three, and I believe of five, per cent. But how is it on the frontier? I undertake to say that you may go to Arkansas, or Missouri, with a note of the specie-paying banks of New York, and with another of the non-specie-paying Bank of the United States, and the latter shall be preferred. And why? Because it is in the name of its national predecessor. There is an *odor of nationality* which hangs around it, and clings to it, and is long in being separated from it.

In the next place, my opinion is, that a currency emanating partly from a national authority as broad in its origin as the whole country, and partly from local banks organized as our banks now are, and issuing paper for local circulation, is a better currency for the whole people than ever before existed in the world. Each of these classes of institutions, and each of these kinds of currency, has its own proper use and value. I affirm that the banking institutions of New York and of New England are organized on better principles than the joint stock companies of Great Britain; and I hold that we are competent, with a tolerable intellect, and with an honest purpose, to establish a national institution which shall act with less fluctuation than is experienced in England under the Bank of England.

Now, Gentlemen, I do not at all mean to say that there is only one mode, or two modes, of accomplishing this great national object. I do not say that a national bank is the only means to effect it; but, in my judgment, it is indisputably true that the currency should, in some degree, or in some portion of it, be *nationalized* in its character. This is indispensable to the great ends of circulation and of business in these United States.

But I shall be asked (and it is a pertinent question), if there is to be a national institution, or if we are in any form to have national issues of bank paper, what security is there, or is there any security, that these national institutions shall not run to an excess in their issues of paper? Who is to guard the guardian? Who is to watch the sentinel? The last twenty years have been fruitful in experience on this subject, both in the United States and in England. In that time, the world has learnt much. I may say that we have learnt much; for our own experience has been our instructor; and I think that there are modes by which banking institutions may be so far restricted as to give us reasonable security against excessive issues.

From whatever source these institutions may emanate, the first security is to be found in entire publicity as to the amount of paper afloat. There is more in this than is sometimes supposed. It should be known to the whole community, from day to day, what is the actual amount of paper in circulation. When prices rise or fall, a merchant has a right to know whether the change of price springs from change in demand, or merely from change in the amount of money in circulation; and therefore the first duty of a banking institution is, to make it universally known, by a daily or a weekly publication, what amount of paper it has out. See what benefits would arise from such an arrangement, and that in a thousand ways. If the bank should thus make its issues public, those who control its affairs would be bound to respect public opinion, and the bank, while it controlled what is under it, would itself be controlled by something above it; and thus public opinion would be brought to regulate the regulator, and to watch the sentinel.

Then, again, if the government should act in this matter, what it does should rather be done in reference to the function of issue, in such an institution, than with a view to make it a money-getting concern; and that no temptation should lead the bank to excess, there ought to be a limit to the extent of its dividends; all receipts for discount beyond that point going, not into the private crib, but into the public treasury. Then there is another error, which has been common with the Bank of England. If you look at the monthly accounts which it has published of its affairs, it will at once appear that its directors seem to have judged of the condition of the institution by the amount of its circulation compared with its assets, including securities as well as bullion. They look chiefly to the amount payable and the amount receivable. As a mere lender of money, this is all very well; but if the bank is to act in regulating the circulation, it is an incorrect mode of stating the account. Admitting the object to be to keep its paper redeemable, and to exercise a general regulation, the true point of examination would be to see what proportion exists between the outstanding paper and the inlying bullion. The bank may be very rich, but she may expect her resources from the payment of the securities she holds. This may be all very well, as a means to show that she is solvent; but it is not the inquiry that belongs to her, as the source and preserver of a sound circulating medium.

I know very well that there are objections to the fixing of a positive limit for circulation. But until such limit can safely be dispensed with, it may be best to make it positive. When an institution has acquired general confidence, and there is no danger of a sudden and extensive panic in relation to it, it is in the power of such an institution, in case local panics should occur, to relieve the community, by that adaptation of the amount of outstanding circulation which discreet men may be trusted to regulate. Still I am of opinion that there ought to be a fixed limit, from which the bank should never depart.

I have not said, nor do I mean to say, that one or the other mode of accomplishing this great and desirable object is indispensable; but I affirm that, in his communication to Congress vetoing the bill to renew the charter of the United States Bank, President Jackson did say that, if he were applied to, he could furnish a plan for a United States Bank which would be adequate to all the purposes of such an institution, and should yet be constitutional. Therefore the thing is practicable, provided we of this generation can accomplish that which President Jackson said he could accomplish.

Now, Gentlemen, I have only stated what I receive as general principles, which the experience of the world has established, on the subject of currency and a paper currency. But all we can say is, that it seems the existing administration will do nothing of all this which I have stated as necessary to be done. They have done nothing to nationalize the currency in any degree; and so long as the government holds to that determination, there never will be in this country a currency of uniform value. This brings me to this inquiry: — Is the administration settled on the ground it has repeatedly avowed, and has for three years adhered to in practice, never to give us this uniform currency? That is the question. The administration will not go back to the policy sanctioned by forty years of prosperity. It will not trust the State banks. It will do nothing; and it will do nothing on principle; for Mr. Van Buren holds that the Constitution gives Congress no power to do any thing in the matter. I said at the time this assertion was uttered, and I still say, that I am hardly able to express the astonishment I feel at what would seem the presumptuousness of such a position; because, from the very cradle of the government, from the very commencement of its existence, those men who made the Constitution, who recommended it to the people, who procured its adoption, and who then undertook its administration, all approved that policy which is thus pronounced unconstitutional. It was followed for forty years by every Congress, and by every President, and its constitutionality was affirmed and sanctioned by the highest judicial tribunals. And yet here a gentleman stands up, at half a century's distance, and, disregarding all this legislative, executive, and judicial authority, says, " I am wiser than all of them, and I aver there is no such power in the Constitution."

The President says, " The people have decided this." But where did they so decide, and when? Why, he says that General Jackson declared the bank to be unconstitutional, and then the people reëlected him; but I have told you what General Jackson did declare. He said that a national bank might be established which would not be unconstitutional, although he held the particular bank then in existence to be against the Constitution. Now, if the people reëlected him after this declaration, why is it not just as fair to infer that they did so because he uttered this opinion, — because he said that there might be a national bank, and the Constitution still be preserved inviolate? No, Gentlemen; the truth is, that General Jackson was reëlected, not *because* he vetoed the Bank of the United States, but *notwithstanding* he vetoed it. It was the general popularity of General Jackson, and that paramount ascendency by which he ruled the party that placed him in power, and made it bend and bow to his own pleasure, that carried him again into office. To say that the constitutional power of creating a national bank and regulating the national currency was repudiated by the people, is a glaring instance of false reasoning and false philosophy. Nay, the President goes farther, and says he was himself against the bank, and the people elected *him* too for that reason. I do not say what actuated the people in his election; but this I will say, that if any man ever came into office by virtue and under power of will and testament, it is that same gentleman. I insist that no evidence can be produced that the American people have ever repudiated the doctrines of Washington, and condemned and rejected the decisions of their own highest judicial tribunals.

We must decide on these questions as men having a deep personal interest in them. Do you go to authority? Do you appeal to Madison? You may quote Mr. Madison's opinion from morning till noon, and from noon to night, on the longest day in summer, and you cannot get from the friends of the administration one particle of answer. I have again and again read, in my place in the Senate, Mr. Madison's doctrine, that it is the duty of government to establish a national currency. I have shown that Mr. Madison urges this with the utmost earnestness and solemnity. They say nothing against it, save that Mr. Van Buren, having expressed a different opinion, *got in* at the last election.

When the national bank was destroyed, or rather when its charter expired, and was not renewed, in consequence of the executive veto, what followed? I say that the government then put the entire business of this country, its commercial, its manufacturing, its shipping interest, its fisheries, — in a word, all that the people possessed, — on the tenterhooks of experiment; it put to the stretch every interest of the nation; it held them up, and tried curious devices upon them, just as if the institutions of our country were things not to be cherished and fostered with the most solicitous anxiety and care, but matters for political philosophers to try experiments upon. I need not remind you that General Jackson said he could give the country a better currency; that he took the national treasure from where it had been deposited by Congress, to place it in the State banks; and that Congress, by subsequent legislation, legalized the transfer,

under the assurance that it would work well for the country.
Yet I may be permitted to remind you that there were some
of us who from the first declared that these State banks never
could perform the duties of a national institution; that the
functions of such an institution were beyond their scope, without the range of their powers; that they were, after all, but
small arms, and not artillery, and could not reach an object so
distant. The State bank system exploded; but the administration did not expect it to explode. At that day, they no more
looked to the sub-treasury scheme than they looked for an
eclipse, and they did not expect an eclipse half as much as they
do just now. When the United States Bank was overthrown,
they turned, as the next expedient, to the State institutions; and
they had full confidence in them, for confidence is a quality in
which experimenters are seldom found wanting; but the expedient failed, — the banks exploded. And what then?

Why, in the speech delivered in this place, by one of the
ablest advocates of the measures of the administration, Mr.
Wright said, What could you expect? What could Mr. Van
Buren do? He could not adopt a national bank, because he
had declared himself opposed to it. He could not rely on the
State banks, for they had crumbled to pieces. What, then,
could he do, but recommend the sub-treasury? What does this
show, but that the government, as I have said, had departed
from the principles of the approved policy of forty years of national prosperity, and had put itself in such a situation that it
could not aid the country in any way? Mr. Van Buren would
not retract his opinion against the bank, although he could retract his opinion against the State bank deposit system fast
enough; but he would not retract the position he had taken
against the national bank. The State banks had failed him;
and he was driven, as his only refuge, to the suggestion of withdrawing all care over the national currency from the national
government, and confining the solicitude of government to itself
alone. But how far did he carry this doctrine? Look at the
draft of the sub-treasury bill. Does it contain a specie clause?
No such thing! It is a mere regulator of the revenue on the
principles of the resolution of 1816. But what happened next?
This bill was like to fail in the Senate for want of votes. There
was a certain division in that body, at the head of which stood

Mr. Calhoun, whose aid was indispensable to carry the measure, but who would not vote for it unless the *hard-money clause* should be inserted. It was inserted accordingly; and then the friends of the administration, for the first time, shouted in all quarters, "Hard money!" "Hard money!" "Hard money!"

By this cruel necessity, the government was driven to a measure which it had no more expected than you expect to see your houses on fire to-night. But such are the expedients, the miserable expedients, of a baffled and despairing administration, on which they have thrown themselves as a last resort, always hoping, and always deceived, and plunging deeper and deeper at every new effort.

I have said, and it may be proper enough, and involve no great self-complacency to say it, that there were some of us who never ceased to warn the government and the nation, that the deposit system must explode, as it has exploded. But what was our reward? What was the boon conferred upon us for thus apprising the administration of its danger? We were denounced as enemies to State banks, as opposed to State institutions, as anti-State-rights men, whom nothing would satisfy but the spectacle of a great national institution, riding over and treading down the institutions of the States.

But what happened? The whole State bank experiment, as I have said, utterly failed; and what did gentlemen of the administration do then? They instantly turned about, and, with the utmost bitterness of remark, reviled the banks which their experiment had crushed. They were vile, corrupt, faithless, treacherous institutions, leagued from the very beginning with the opposition, and not much better than British Whigs! And when we, who had opposed the placing of the national treasure in these banks, declared that they had failed only because they were applied to a purpose for which they never were calculated, and had perished in consequence of a rash and unwise experiment, we were instantly told, "You are bank aristocrats; you are leagued with a thousand corrupt banks, and are seeking, by the power of British gold, to destroy the purest administration that ever breathed the air of heaven!" Thus, when we said that State banks, though good for some purposes, were not good as a substitute for a national bank, we were denounced as the enemies of banks; but when we wished to shield these same banks from misapplied censure, and protect them from being totally destroyed by acts of bankruptcy, then we were reviled as "bank aristocrats."

I ask you, Gentlemen, as merchants, what confidence can you place in such an administration? Do you see any thing that they are disposed to do to restore the times you once enjoyed? (Loud cries of "No!" "No!") I perceive that your opinion corresponds with my own, and that you cannot lend your support to men who turn their backs on the experience, the interests, and the institutions of their country, and who openly declare that they will not exercise the powers which have been conferred on them for the public good.

Now, Gentlemen, I will observe to you further, that it appears to me that this administration has treated the States, in reference to their own affairs, just as it has treated the State banks. It has first involved them in the evils of extravagance (if any extravagance exists), and has then abused them for the very thing to which its own course has strongly invited them. Commencing with the messages of Mr. Van Buren himself, and then looking at the reports of his Secretaries, and the resolutions and speeches of Mr. Benton and Mr. Grundy in the Senate, and at the outcry of the whole administration press, there appears to be a systematic attempt to depress the character and credit of the States. It is everywhere said, that "the States have been rash and extravagant"; "the States will yet have to repent of their railroads and canals, and projects of internal improvements." This is the burden of the President's message, of the reports of his Secretaries, and of the resolutions of his friends. Now, I seriously ask, Is not the tendency of such a course of measures virtually to affect the credit of the States that have outstanding bonds and obligations in the market?

Let us look into this matter a little. Let us see under what circumstances it was that the States were induced to contract these large debts which now embarrass them. And here let me call your attention to a few facts, dates, and figures. And first, Gentlemen, in your presence, I charge upon the administration of the general government those great expansions and those sudden contractions of paper money, which have so deranged our affairs. I propose to prove the charge; and with that view now proceed to lay before you facts, and dates, and transactions, which must carry conviction to every honest and candid mind.

Let us go back to the year 1832, when it was perfectly settled by the veto of President Jackson, that the Bank of the United States would not be rechartered. Suppose we take a series of years by tens, and trace the history of the creation of State banks in this country. From 1820 to 1830, a period of ten years, there were created in the United States twenty-two new banks; and their creation added to the banking capital of the country but eight millions of dollars. During this period, the Bank of the United States was in full operation, and nobody entertained a doubt that it would be continued. How was it in the next ten years? From 1830 to 1840, the increase of banks, instead of twenty-two, as in the preceding ten years, was three hundred and forty-eight; and the increase of banking capital, instead of eight millions, amounted to two hundred and sixty-eight millions. Such has been the progress of bank expansion during the charming, the successful years of the experiment. But further, not only was there this great augmentation in the number and in the capital of the State banks, but when the extraordinary proceeding of the removal of the deposits in 1833 took place, it was declared by the government to be the duty of all its deposit banks to lend the public money freely to the commercial community. The Secretary of the Treasury, in his circular, issued, I think, in September, 1833, told these institutions expressly, that it was their duty to discount freely, and laid it down as a maxim, that the money of the government, between the periods of its collection and disbursement, ought to be at the service of the public. I remember, indeed, to have heard it said by the cashier of one of the banks in this street, that "he hardly knew what to do, for he was ordered to lend more of the public money than he could get security for." It is from this increase of banks, and this increase of issues, and from this alone, that the expansion so injurious to the country really sprang.

I know it may be said that there were expansions and contractions during the existence of the Bank of the United States. This I do not deny. The administration of that institution, I admit, was not always perfect; but I say, taking the whole period, of nearly half a century, during which such a bank existed, the country was freer from violent and sudden extremes of contraction and expansion than it has ever been since that time.   Why will not a fair reasoner draw his conclusions from the entire history of his country as a whole?   In his late speech from this place, Mr. Wright said he would not look back to the history of the first Bank of the United States; he said that under the second national bank there were great evils; but did he deny that, taking the whole forty years together, the country was less liable to fluctuations than it has since been? Not at all.   Well, in the midst of this great expansion of banks and banking capital came the Specie Circular, whose tendency was to produce, and which did in fact produce, great and sudden contractions.   This violent action and reaction, superinduced on a previous state of pecuniary expansion, is fairly chargeable to the administration itself, and is to be traced to the action of the government more than to all other causes.

But to return.   How does it stand with respect to the States? Under what patronage, and at whose recommendation, did they contract the large and onerous debt of two hundred millions of dollars?   Who induced this?   Under what circumstances at home was it done?   From 1820 to 1825, the aggregate of State debts amounted to twelve or thirteen millions.   From 1825 to 1830, it stood at thirteen millions; but during the period from 1830 to 1835, it rose to forty millions.   The effect of the increase of circulation did not begin fairly to develop itself in the country till 1834 and 1835.   Then the State debts were augmented to forty millions; and between 1835 and 1840, they rose to one hundred millions.

It appears, from tables supposed to be accurately compiled, that the amount of stock issued by the several States, for each period of five years since 1820, is as follows, viz.: —

From 1820 – 1825, somewhat over $ 12,000,000;
  " 1825 – 1830, " " 13,000,000;
  " 1830 – 1835, " " 40,000,000;
  " 1835 – 1840, " " 109,000,000.

Of this amount of one hundred and nine millions, nearly the whole was issued during 1835 and 1836, and part of 1837; that is to say, in the most palmy time of the experiment.

So it appears that these "extravagant" State debts were contracted when the currency was most redundant; when the States, in common with all the country, were urged, and goaded, and lashed on to borrow; and when all sorts of extravagant hopes and schemes were indulged among the people. To this very redundancy, thus caused by the government itself, in the vast multiplication of banks, and the free extension of loans, are to be traced these rash engagements of the States, for which they have been reviled in all quarters, from the head of the government down to its lowest agency. There were one hundred millions of debts created in 1835 and 1836, in the very midst of the glow and flow of the deposit system. It was in these very years, distinguished, as the administration say, for prudence and public prosperity, that the creation of the State debts kept pace with the bank creation and accommodation. The bank creation and accommodation kept pace with the government experiment, and the government experiment kept pace with the most rapid delusion which ever characterized any administration upon earth, or ever carried away an intelligent people.

And now I am on this subject, I must say a word or two on another topic, which it naturally suggests. One of the charges of the day is, that the opposition to the administration has come out with a project for the assumption of all these State debts by the general government. This charge was broached, as a subject of attack on the Whigs in the Senate, early in the last session. Let us look a little into facts. I have said that the general government encouraged the States to contract debts by making the currency plentiful; but they have also done this in another manner. It has been one of the favorite projects of the administration, since the removal of the deposits, to vest the surplus revenue, and the increased funds of the United States, in State bonds. I do not say this is an assumption of the State debts, but I do say that the general government did encourage the States to issue bonds, and did endeavor to give them all the credit it could.

In 1836, the project was taken up of distributing the surplus revenue among the States. This was not, indeed, a favorite measure of the leading men of the administration, but was carried rather against their wishes. In May of that year, it was moved by Mr. Wright of New York, then and now a prominent leader of the administration party in the Senate, that this surplus should be vested in State stocks, and that whenever any further surplus might occur, it should be vested in the same manner. When the bill to regulate the State banks was under consideration, and a new section was proposed, distributing the forty millions of surplus among the States, Mr. Wright moved to strike out that provision, and to insert instead another clause, vesting the whole of the money in State bonds. Again, when the first sub-treasury bill was brought forward, the same gentleman tacked to it a provision, that the surplus amounts in the treasury should be vested in State bonds. Finally, there were other sums, which we held in trust, from the sale of Indian lands, for the payment of Indian annuities, as well as the Smithsonian legacy, which were also authorized to be invested in State bonds. I say, therefore, that so long as the contraction of those State debts was favorable to the administration, they were the foremost of all men in fostering State credits, and in encouraging the States to enlarge their liabilities. For my associate, Mr. Wright, declared "that he would undertake to say, that he was not afraid to recommend such an investment of the national funds, as the States would issue *as many bonds as the government might choose to buy!*"

But now, after all this, these same gentlemen, overreaching the whole intervening period, and going back to the beginning, reproach and criminate the States, from the very outset, for contracting the engagements to which the government itself incited them. I do not say that this was an assumption of the State debts, but it certainly was holding them up to Europe and the world as worthy of confidence, so long as it suited the purposes of the administration so to do. And very pretty purposes it would have answered, in view of the coming election, had they succeeded in their object, and the Secretary of the Treasury been vested with unlimited discretion to purchase State bonds at his pleasure. Suppose such a power now existed, and Mr. Woodbury, conscientious and scrupulous as he is known to be, were asked by us of Massachusetts, for instance, or had lately been asked by our good sister of Maine, to invest money in State bonds; how do you think the money would have been applied? No doubt it would have been given freely to the *patriotic* States, but as carefully withheld from those not deemed worthy of that title.

For this declaration, that the Whigs in Congress are in favor of the assumption of the State debts by the general government, there exists not one particle of proof, nor the least possible foundation. I do not myself know a single man in Congress, who holds the opinion that the general government has any more right to pay the debts of a State, than it has to pay the debts of a private individual. Congress might as well undertake to pay the debts of John Jacob Astor, as of the State of New York. I exempt, however, from these remarks, the distribution among the States of the proceeds of the public lands, and their application to pay the debts of the States, should the States choose so to apply the money. But I say there is no foundation whatever for such a plan of assumption as Mr. Benton and Mr. Grundy have so zealously declaimed against in the United States Senate.

You have all heard in the public papers, (and it is one of the most despicable of all the inventions of the enemy,) that transactions took place, in which I had a part, the object of which was to persuade Congress to assume the State obligations, and that I went to England for the worthy purpose of furthering such a design. Now, as I am among you this day as among my friends, I will tell you all about it. I left this country in May, 1839. At that time I had neither read nor heard from living man of any such design. I went to England, and I must be permitted to say that it was a most gloomy time, so far as American securities in general, and the State debts in particular, were concerned. But I declare to you on my honor, that no European banker or foreign holder of State securities ever suggested to me, in the remotest manner, the least notion of the assumption of the State debts by the general government. Once, indeed, I did hear the idea started by an American citizen; but I immediately told him that such a thing was wholly unconstitutional, and never could be effected, unless the people should adopt a new constitution. It was quite natural that I should be applied to in reference to the State debts. The State to which I belong had sent out some stock to England to be sold, and so, I believe, had the State of New York. We heard, continually, the most gloomy accounts from the United States; and, in fact, this very thing was, to use a common expression, a great damper to my enjoyment while abroad. People frequently applied to me to know what security there was, that the American debts would be finally paid, and the interest, in the mean time, regularly discharged. I told them they might rely on the plighted faith of the States, and their ability to redeem their obligations. Nobody asked me whether there could be a United States guaranty to that effect, nor did I suggest such an idea to any one. Gentlemen came to me to ask about the Massachusetts bonds. They liked the offer of five per cent. interest very much, as this was high for an English capitalist; but they wanted to know what assurance I could give that the investment would be a safe one. I went to my trunk, and took out an abstract of the official return of the amount of the productive labor of Massachusetts. I put this into the hand of one of those inquirers, and told him to take it home and study it. He did so, and in two days returned, and invested forty thousand pounds sterling in Massachusetts stock. Others came, and made similar inquiries as to New York securities. I gave them a copy of the very able and admirable report made by your townsman, Mr. Ruggles, in 1838, and they came back satisfied. But to none did I suggest, or in the remotest manner hint, that they could look to the United States to secure the debt. I endeavored to uphold the credit of all the States. I remembered that they were all my countrymen, and I stated facts in relation to each as favorably as truth would allow. And what happened then? Gentlemen, it is fit that you should know that there exists a certain *clique* in London, who are animated by an inextinguishable hate of American credit. You may set it down as a fact, that it is their daily, their incessant vocation, to endeavor to impair the credit of every one of the States, and to represent the purchase of their bonds as an unwise and dangerous investment of money. On this subject their ferocity knows no mitigation; it is deaf to all justice, and proof against all reason. The more you show them it is wrong, the more tenacity of purpose do they exhibit. That part of the public press over which they have control is furnished, I am ashamed to say, with matter drawn from publications which originate in this city, and the object of which is to prove that State bonds are so much waste paper, the State having no right to issue any such obligations, and their holders being, therefore, utterly destitute of any security. And these miserable and contemptible speculations are put into the papers of the largest circulation in Europe, and enforced by all the aid they can derive from editorial sanction. It was under circumstances like these that a large banking-house in London put to me, as a lawyer, the professional question, whether the States were empowered to issue evidences of debt payable by the State. I answered that, for this purpose, they were as completely sovereign as any State in Europe; that they had a public faith to pledge, and did pledge it. This entire correspondence was published (though you might as well get any administration editor in this country to take hold of a pair of hot tongs as to insert it in his columns), in the face of those who have been shouting in all quarters, that I had a personal agency in attempting to bring about an assumption of State debts by the general government.

It so happened, that, in the latter part of October, the house of Barings issued a circular to foreign houses on this subject, which circular I never saw till I returned to America. In this paper they speak of such an assumption or guaranty; but as it went to foreign houses, I never saw nor heard of it till last December, when I also heard of the proceedings of Mr. Benton. But I here wish again to repeat, that, during the whole time I was in Europe, no English banker or foreign bondholder ever suggested an idea of such an assumption. The first I heard of it was from an American citizen there, and not again till my return to this country. I have said that, owing to the bad news which was constantly received from this country, the pleasure of my visit was much diminished. I will now say, that, during the whole time of my absence, I had the lowest hopes, as to the political state of the country, which I ever indulged. I saw the fatal workings of the experiment, and I saw that nothing wiser or better was in the mind of the administration. I knew that a vast majority of my countrymen were opposed to the existing policy, but I did not see them sufficiently roused, nor had I confidence that they would ever come to that cordial union in relation to any one candidate for the Presidency, which would enable them, as a party, to take the field with any rational hope of success.

Such were the gloomy feelings which possessed my mind when I first learned the result of the Harrisburg Convention. But when I saw a nomination which, though unwelcome at first to many, I thought the best that could possibly have been made, and learned that it was fast gaining the approbation of all who thought with me; and above all, when I beheld the warm enthusiasm and the heartfelt union which soon animated their ranks and concentrated their movements, I then began to entertain a confidence that the hour of deliverance was at hand, and that my long-suffering country would yet relieve herself from the disastrous condition to which she had been reduced.

I hope, Gentlemen, you will not be alarmed, if I take from my notes one more paper. I will detain you but a few moments in briefly expressing the opinions I entertain in regard to the sub-treasury. It appears to me to be a scheme entirely new to our history, and foreign to our habits, and to be the last of a series of baffled experiments, into which the representatives of the people have been lashed and driven by the continued exercise of executive power, through four mortal sessions of Congress.

I will say a word or two in relation to the system, under the various aspects in which its friends have supported it. What are the arguments in its favor? The leading argument was that of safety to the government. This was a plan to keep the public money where rogues could not run away with it. Now I think there is a way to prevent that, which would be much more effectual; and that is, not to trust rogues with the keeping of the public money. But as to the notion of vaults better and more secure than those of the banks, is it not the most ridiculous of all humbugs? I do not know in which of the bank vaults around me the receiver-general keeps his funds. If they are in a vault different from that which belongs to the bank, I will venture to say it is no better and no safer. It is said, however, that by this means government is to keep its own money. What does this mean? Who is that government? Who is that individual " I," who is to keep our money in his own pocket? Is not government a mere collection of agencies? Is not every dollar it possesses placed in trust with somebody? It may be put in vaults under a key, but the key is given to somebody to keep. Government is not a person with pockets.

The only question is, whether the government agents under the sub-treasury are any safer than the government agents before it was adopted? Mr. Wright, indeed, has assured us, that the agents under the sub-treasury are made responsible to the people. But how? In what respect? The receiver-general gives bonds; but how is he more responsible on that account than the collector in another street, who, like him, receives the public money, and like him gives bonds for its safe-keeping? It is just the same thing. One of these officers is just as far from the people, and just as near to the people, as the other. How, then, is the receiver-general more directly responsible? There is not a particle of truth or reason in the whole matter. If the vaults are not better, is the security better? I have no manner of doubt that the receiver-general in this city is a highly respect able man; but where is the proof that the government money is any safer in his vault than in the bank where he has his office? Suppose Mr. Allen had a private office of his own, at a distance from the bank, and should give the same bonds he now does for the safe-keeping of all moneys intrusted to him; how many of you would deposit your private funds in his office, rather than in a bank having half a million or a million of dollars capital, under the government of directors whose own fortunes were deposited in its vaults? Try the experiment, and see how many would resort to Mr. Allen, and how many to the banks.

So far from being safer, I maintain, on the contrary, that this sub-treasury scheme jeopards the public money, because it multiplies the hands through which it is to pass, and thereby multiplies the chances of corruption or of loss. Your collector, Mr. Hoyt, receives the money on duty bonds. He holds it subject to the draft or order of the Secretary of the Treasury, or else is to pay it over to Mr. Allen. If Mr. Hoyt were dishonest, might he not have shared the money before the receiver-general could get at it? The scheme doubles the chances of loss, by doubling the hands which are to keep the money.

But this scheme is to encourage the circulation of specie. I certainly shall not detain you on a matter with which you are more familiar than I am; but let me ask you a few questions. By one clause of the sub-treasury law, one fourth of all the duties bonded is to be paid in specie, and the residue according to the resolution of 1816. Now I want to know one thing: if one of you has a custom-house bond to pay, you go to the collector with a certified check, purporting to be payable *in specie*, for one fourth of the amount, and another check, in common form, for the other three fourths. Does not the collector receive these checks? That is the question I ask you. (Loud cries of "Yes! yes!" "He does! he does!") Well, then, is not all that part of the law which requires the payment of one fourth in specie a mere sham? If you go to him with a draft and demand specie, he will, no doubt, give it to you if you request it; but if not, he gives you good notes. Where, then, is all this marching and countermarching of specie, which was to gladden our eyes? Is it not all humbug? What does the collector do with the money when he gets it? Does he not deposit it in a bank of a very unsavory name? I do not certainly know, but I believe he deposits it in the Bank of the United States. He afterwards pays it over to the receiver-general, and gives him all the specie he wants; and yet, after all, there is no general use of specie in the matter.

They speak about a divorce between bank and state; and what does it amount to? I ask you, Is not the great amount of government funds at this moment in safe keeping in some bank? I believe it is. Then there is no separation. The government gives the money to individuals to keep, and they, like sensible men, put it into bank. Is this separation? If any change is made in the connection, it is to render it more close; and, like other illicit connections, the closer it is, the more secret it is kept.

It is called the "Independent Treasury," and some of its friends have called it "a second Declaration of Independence." Independence! how? of what? It is dependent on individuals, who immediately go to the bank; and is it to be tolerated that there should be this outcry about the use of specie, when here, in the heart of the commercial community, you see and know that there is no such thing?

But though at present this is all sham, yet that power to demand specie which the law contains, when its requirements shall cover the whole revenue of the government, and when that revenue shall be large, may, in its exercise, become a most dangerous instrument. When government shall have in the banks of this city from twelve to fifteen millions of dollars on deposit, as it has had, it will be in the power of the government to break down, at its pleasure, one, if not all, of these institutions. And when you go to the West, where the money is received for the public lands, every specie-paying bank in the country may, at the mere pleasure of the government, be compelled to shut up its doors.

But this independent treasury is to be independent of the banks! Well, if the sub-treasury law is to be called the second Declaration of Independence, then there is a third Declaration of Independence, and that is the treasury-note law. How marvellously free does that make us of banks! While two millions of these notes, bearing interest, are deposited there, — and there, — and there, — in all these banks around me! Deposited? How deposited? They are sold. And how sold? They are deposited in these banks, carrying interest, while the bank gives the government authority to draw for money when needed. Now, I say the bank may make, not a very unreasonable, but a very reasonable, amount by the interest in these notes, before it is called on to pay out any of its own money. One of these accounts between bank and government was examined by a friend of mine; I had not myself time to look at it. The bank received treasury-notes bearing interest; it passed these to the credit of government, at the nominal amount; the government was then to draw for money as it wanted it; and, on that single transaction, the bank realized between eighty and a hundred thousand dollars in interest. Now, this is what I call a third Declaration of Independence! You know, by the Secretary's report, that the government has already issued nearly the whole of the five millions authorized by Congress. Two millions lie in the banks, drawing interest, the banks paying government drafts as they come in. And this is setting up for independence of the banks!

Again, the fashion now is, since Mr. Calhoun has forced the administration to insert in the law the specie clause, for government to discredit the use of bank paper whenever it can. That is the general tone of the government communications. They avow such to be their object, and I believe them. But who can tell the consequence of discrediting bank paper, if our revenues should ever again become what they have been in times past? It is a power by which government can break the solvent banks, but can never make the insolvent return to their duty.

But then, it is said, all this cannot be any great matter, be-

7 *

cause Mr. Wright tells us, that, in ordinary times, five millions of dollars will perform all the operations of receipt and expenditure. Now, that proposition depends upon Mr. Wright's estimate of what the expenditure will be. Does he expect to reduce it to the standard of Mr. Adams's administration, once denounced as so extravagant? Does he expect to reduce the thirty-nine millions to thirteen millions? or will he go below that? He does not tell us. For my own part, I believe five or five and a half millions would be a moiety of the average amount of specie in all the banks in the city. You can judge for yourselves what must be the effect of withdrawing one half of all the specie in these banks, and of locking it up in the sub-treasury vaults.

But how does all this stand with Mr. Wright's main argument? He says that the great object to be effected by the sub-treasury law is to prevent fluctuations, by preventing the banks from discounting upon the public money. But if five millions of dollars only are needed for the ordinary treasury operations, can such a sum as this have produced all the fluctuations in the commercial community? Surely not. In his printed speech, he says that the chief practical difference produced by the law is, that the money is now kept by Mr. Allen, which used to be kept by the Bank of America. But is that all? What, then, becomes of the specie clause? I suppose he knows that was all a sham.

Gentlemen, I will not detain you longer on the practical operation of this sub-treasury scheme. So far as relates to the receipts and disbursements of the public treasure, you know better than I. A great part of these operations take place in your own city. But permit me now to go, for a moment, into the political objection to this sub-treasury scheme; I mean *its utter omission of all concern with the general currency of the country.* This objection is cardinal and decisive. It is this which has roused the country, and which is to decide the fate of the present administration. But the question is so general, it has so long been before the country, and so frequently discussed in all quarters, that I will not farther extend my remarks in regard to it. I believe that the mind of the people is now thoroughly awakened, and that the day rapidly approaches when their final judgment will be pronounced.

There is yet one topic on which I must detain you for a moment, and I will then relieve you. We have the good fortune, under the blessing of a benign Providence, to live in a country which we are proud of for many things, — for its independence, for its public liberty, for its free institutions, for its public spirit, for its enlightened patriotism. But we are proud also, — and they are among the things we should be the most proud of, — we are proud of its public justice, of its sound faith, of its substantially correct morals in the administration of the government, and the general conduct of the country, since she took her place among the nations of the world. But among the events which most threaten our character and standing, and which are so greatly at war with the moral principles that have hitherto distinguished us, are certain sentiments which have been broached among us, and, I am sorry to say, have more supporters than they ought, because they strike at the very foundation of the social system. I do not speak especially of those which have been promulgated by some persons in my own State, but of others which go yet deeper into our political condition. I refer to the doctrine, that one generation of men, acting under the Constitution, cannot bind another generation who are to be their successors; on which ground it is held, among other things, that State bonds are not obligatory. What! one generation cannot bind another? Where is the line of separation? It changes hourly. The American community to-day is not the same with the American community to-morrow. The community in which I began this day to address you was not the same as it is at this moment.

How abhorrent is such a doctrine to those great truths, which teach us that, though individuals flourish and decay, states are immortal, that political communities are ever young, ever green, ever flourishing, ever identical! The individuals who compose them may change, as the atoms of our bodies change, but the political community still exists in its aggregate capacity, as our bodies still exist in their natural capacity; with this only difference, that we know that our natural frames must soon dissolve, and return to their original dust; but for our country, she yet lives, she ever dwells in our hearts, and it will, even at the last solemn moment, go up as our final aspiration to Heaven, that she may be immortal.

WHIG CONVENTION AT RICHMOND.

WHIG CONVENTION AT RICHMOND.*

VIRGINIANS, — The wisdom of our fathers has established for us a Constitution of government which enables me to appear before you to-day, and to address you as *my fellow-citizens;* and half a century of experience has shown how favorable to our common interest, how conducive to our common renown and glory, is that Constitution by which we are thus united. I desire to pay due honor to those illustrious men who made us, the children of those who fell at Bunker Hill and Yorktown, members of the same political family, bound together by the same common destiny, and awaiting the same common prosperity, or common adversity, in all time to come. It is the extraordinary nature of the times, together with a long-cherished desire to visit Virginia, which has procured me the pleasure I enjoy of being in the midst of you all to-day. I have come more for the purpose of seeing and hearing you than of speaking to you myself. I have come to mingle myself among you, to listen to the words of your wise and patriotic men, that I may improve my own patriotic feeling by communication with the chivalrous spirits of this Ancient Dominion. But, inasmuch as there are, or may be, some questions of national policy, or of constitutional power, on which you and I differ, there are some amiable persons who are so very considerate of your reputation, and of my reputation, as to signify that they esteem it a great breach of propriety that you should invite me to come here, or that I should accept your invitation. Let us hope that these amiable persons will allay their fears.

If there be any question or questions on which you and I differ in opinion, those questions are not to be the topics of dis-

* A Speech delivered on the 5th of October, 1840, in the Capitol Square at Richmond, Virginia, before the Whig Convention.

cussion to-day. No! We are not quite soft enough for that. While in the presence of a common enemy, who is armed to the teeth against us both, and putting forth as many hands as Briareus to destroy what we think it most important to preserve, does he imagine that, at such a moment, we shall be carrying on our family controversies? that we are going to give our-selves those blows which are due to him? No! Regarding him as the enemy of our country, we mean to pursue him till we bring him to capitulation or to flight; and when we have done that, if there are any differences of opinion among us, we will try to settle them ourselves, without his advice or assist-ance; and we will settle them in a spirit of conciliation and mutual kindness. If we do differ in any of our views, we must settle that difference, not in a spirit of exasperation, but with moderation, with forbearance, in a temper of amity and brother-hood.

It is an era in my life to find myself on the soil of Virginia addressing such an assemblage as is now before me; I feel it to be such; I deeply feel the responsibility of the part which has this day been thrown upon me. But, although it is the first time I have addressed an assembly of my fellow-citizens upon the soil of Virginia, I hope I am not altogether unacquainted with the history, character, and sentiments of this venerable State. The topics which are now agitating the country, and which have brought us all here to-day, have no relation what-ever with those on which I differ from the opinions she has ever entertained. The grievances and the misgovernment which have roused the country pertain to that class of subjects which especially and peculiarly belong to Virginia, and have from the very beginning of our history. I know something of the com-munity amidst which I stand, its distinguished and ardent at-tachment to civil liberty, and its habits of political disquisition. I know that the landholders of Virginia are competent, from their education and their leisure, to discuss political questions in their elements, and to look at government in its tendencies, as well as in the measures it may at present pursue. There is a sleepless suspicion, a vigilant jealousy of power, especially of executive power, which for three quarters of a century has marked the character of the people of the Old Dominion; and if I have any right conception of the evils of the time, or of the true objection to the measures of the present administration, it is, that they are of such a kind as to expose them, in an especial manner, to that sleepless jealousy, that stern republican scrutiny, that acute and astute inspection, which distinguish the present as they have distinguished all preceding generations of men in this ancient Commonwealth. Allowing this to be so, let me present to you my own views of the present aspect of our public affairs.

In my opinion, a decisive majority of all the people of the United States has been, for several years past, opposed to the policy of the existing administration. I shall assume this in what I have further to say, because I believe it to be true ; and I believe that events are on the wing, and will soon take place, which will proclaim the truth of that position, and will show a majority of three fourths of the votes of the electoral colleges in favor of a CHANGE OF MEN. Taking this, for the present, as the true state of political feeling and opinion, I next call your attention to the very extraordinary excitement, agitation, and I had almost said commotion, which mark the present moment throughout every part of the land. Why are these vast assemblages everywhere congregated ? Why, for example, am I here, five hundred miles from my own place of residence, to address such an assembly of Virginians on political subjects ? And why does every day, in every State, witness something of a similar kind ? Has this ever been seen before ? Certainly not in our time, and once only in the time of our fathers. There are some present here who witnessed, and there are others who have learned from the lips of their parents, the state of feeling which existed in 1774 and 1775, before the resort was made to arms in order to effect the objects of the Revolution. I speak now of the time when Patrick Henry, standing, as we now do, in the open air, was addressing the Virginians of that day, while at the same moment James Otis and his associates were making the same rousing appeal to the people of Massachusetts. From that time to this there has been nothing in any degree resembling what we now behold. This general earnestness, this universal concern of all men in relation to public affairs, is now witnessed for the first time since the Revolution. Do not men abandon their fields in the midst of seed-time or of harvest, do they not leave their various occupations, as you have now done, to attend to matters which they deem more important ? And is it not so

through all classes of our citizens throughout the whole land?
Now, the important question I wish to put, and I put it as a
question fit for the mind of the statesmen of Virginia, — I propose it, with all respect, to the deep deliberation and reflection
of every patriotic man throughout the country, — is this: If it be
true that a majority of the people of the United States have, for
some years, been opposed in sentiment to the policy of the present administration, WHY IS IT NECESSARY that these extraordinary efforts should be put forth to turn that administration out
of power, and to put better men in their places? We inhabit
a free country; — every office of public trust is in our own
hands, at the disposal of the people's own suffrages; all public
concerns are controlled and managed by them, at their own
pleasure; and the reliance has always been on the ballot-box, as
an effectual means to keep the government at all times in conformity with the public will. How, then, has it happened, that,
with all this, such extraordinary efforts have been necessary to
put out a particular administration? Why has it not been done
by the silent power of the elective franchise? Why has not the
government been changed both in its policy and in the men
who administer it? I desire from the free, the thinking men of
Virginia, an answer to that question. When the elections are
everywhere showing that a large majority of the people are opposed in sentiment to the existing administration, I desire them
to tell me how that administration has held its place and pursued its own peculiar system of measures so long?

My answer to my own question is this: In my judgment, it
has come to be true, in the actual working of our system of government, that the executive power has increased its influence
and its patronage to such a degree as to counteract the will of a
majority of the people, and has continued to do so until that majority has not only become very large, but till it has united in its
objects and in its candidate, and, by these strenuous and extraordinary efforts, is enabled to turn the administration out of
power. I believe that the patronage of the executive in our government has increased, is increasing, and ought to be diminished.
I believe that it does enable the incumbents to resist the public
will, until the country is roused to a high and simultaneous
effort, and the imperative mandate of the public voice dismisses
the unfaithful servants from their places. The citadel of the
administration can only be carried by general storm.

Now, I ask, can it be supposed that this government can go on long in a course of successful operation, if no change can be produced without such an effort as that in which the people of this country are now engaged? I put it to the old-fashioned republicans of Virginia. I ask them, whether it can be supposed that this free republican government of ours can last for half a century longer, if its administration cannot be changed without such an excitement, I may say such a civil revolution, as is now in progress, and, I trust, is near its completion?

I present this case as the greatest and strongest of all proofs that executive power in this country has increased, and is become dangerous to liberty.

If this be so, then I ask, What are the causes which have given and have augmented this force of executive power? The disciples of the ancient school of Virginia long entertained the opinion, that there was great danger of encroachment by the general government on the just rights of the States; but they were also alarmed at the possibility of an undue augmentation of the executive power. It becomes us, at a crisis like the present, to recur to first principles, — to go back to our early history, and to see how the question actually stands.

You all well know that, in the formation of a constitution for the government of this country, the great difficulty its framers encountered was with regard to the executive power. It was easy to establish a House of Representatives, and a second branch of the government in the form of a Senate, for it was a very obvious principle, that the States should be represented in one House of Congress as the people were represented in the other. But the great and perplexing question was, how to limit and regulate the executive power in such a manner, that, while it should be sufficiently strong and effective for the purposes of government, it should not be able to endanger civil liberty. Our fathers had seen and felt the inconvenience, during the Revolutionary war, of a weak executive in government. The country had suffered much from that cause. There was no unity of purpose or efficiency of action in its executive power. As the country had just emerged from one war, and might be plunged into another, they were looking intently to such a constitution as should secure an efficient executive. Perhaps it remains to be seen whether, in this respect, they had not better have given

less power to this branch, and taken all the inconvenience arising from the want of it, rather than have hazarded the granting
of so much as might prove dangerous, not only to the other
departments of government, but to the safety and freedom of the
country at large.

In the first place, it is the executive which confers all the
favors of a government. It has the patronage in its hands,
and if we look carefully at the proceedings of the past and
present administrations, we shall see that in the course of
things, and to answer the purposes of men, this patronage has
greatly increased. We shall find that the expenditures for
office have been augmented. We shall find that this is true of
the civil and diplomatic departments; we shall find it is true of
all the departments; of the post-office, and especially of the
commercial department. Thus, to take an instance from one
of our great commercial cities, in the custom-house at New
York, the number of officers has, in twelve years, increased
threefold, and the whole expense, of course, in the same proportion.

Then there is the power of removal, a power which, in some
instances, has been exercised most remorselessly. By whatever
party it is wielded, unless it be called for by the actual exigencies of the public service, Virginia, more than any State of the
Union, has ever rejected, disowned, disavowed, the practice of removal for opinion's sake. I do honor to Virginia in this respect.
That power has been far less practised in Virginia than in certain States where the spoils doctrine is known to be more popular. But this power of removal, sanctioned as it is by time,
does exist, and I have seen it exercised, in every part of the
country where public opinion tolerated it, with a most unsparing hand.

I will now say, however, that which I admit to be very presumptuous, because it is said notwithstanding the illustrious authority of one of the greatest of your great men, — a man better
acquainted with the Constitution of the United States than any
other man; a man who saw it in its cradle, who held it in his
arms, as one may say, in its infancy, who presented and recommended it to the American people, and who saw it adopted
very much under the force of his own reasoning and the weight
of his own reputation, who lived long enough to see it prosper-

ous, to enjoy its highest honors, and who at last went down to the grave beneath ten thousand blessings, for which, morning and evening, he had thanked God; I mean James Madison. Yet even from this great and good man, whom I hold to be chief among the just interpreters of the Constitution, I am constrained, however presumptuous it may be considered, to differ in relation to one of his interpretations of that instrument. I refer to the opinion expressed by him, that the power of removal from office does exist in the Constitution as an independent power in the hands of the President, without the consent of the Senate. I wish he had taken a different view of it. I do not say that he was wrong; that in me would be too hazardous. I advert to this here, to show that I am not now for the first time preaching against the danger of an increase of executive power; for when the subject was in discussion before Congress, in 1835, I expressed there the same opinions which I have now uttered, and which have been only the more confirmed by recent experience. The power of removal places the hopes and fears, the living, the daily bread of men, at the disposal of the executive, and thereby produces a vast mass of executive influence and control. Then, again, from the very nature of things, the executive power acts constantly; it is always in being, always in the citadel and on the look-out; and it has, besides, entire unity of purpose. They who are in have but one object, which is to keep all others out; while those who are not in office, and who desire a change, have a variety of different objects, as they are to be found in different parts of the country. One complains of one thing, another of another; and, ordinarily, there is no strict unity of object, nor agreement on candidates, nor concert of action; and therefore it is that those wielding power within the fortress are able to keep the others out, though they may be more numerous. Hence we have seen an administration, though in a minority, yet, by the continued exercise of power, able to bring over a majority of the people's representatives to the support of such a measure as the sub-treasury, which, when it was first proposed, received but little favor in any part of the country.

Again; though it may appear comparatively inconsiderable, yet, when we are looking at the means by which the executive power has risen to its present threatening height, we must not overlook the power of, I will not say a pensioned, but of a patron-

ized press. Of all things in a popular government, a *government press* is the most to be dreaded. The press furnishes the
only usual means of public address; and if government, by supporting, comes to control it, then they take to themselves, at the
public expense, the great channel of all communication with the
people. Unless France be an exception, where the minister
regularly demands so many thousand francs for the management of the public press, I know of no government in the world
where the press is avowedly patronized to the same extent as it
is in this country. Have not you, men of Virginia, been morti-
fied to witness the importance which is attached, at Washington, to the election of a public printer? to observe the great
anxiety and solicitude which even your own friends have been
obliged to exercise to keep that appointment out of the hands
of executive power? One of the first things which, in my opinion ought to be done, is, when a new administration shall come
in, to separate the government press from the politics of the
country. I don't want the government printer to preach politics
to the people; beause I know beforehand what politics he will
preach; it will all be one *Io triumphe* from the beginning of
the first page to the end of the last paragraph. I am for cut-
ting off this power from the executive. Give the people fair
play. I say, *give the people fair play.* If they think the govern
ment is in error, or that better men may be found to administer
it, give them a chance to turn the present men out, and put better men in; but don't let them be compelled to give their money
to pay a man to persuade them not to change the government.

Well, there are still other modes by which executive power is
established and confirmed. The first thing it seeks to do is to
draw strict lines of party distinction, and then to appeal to the
party feelings of men. This is a topic which might lead me
very far into an inquiry as to the causes which have overturned
all popular governments. It is the nature of men to be credu-
lous and confiding toward their friends. If there exists in the
country a powerful party, and if the head of that party be the
head of the government, and, avowing himself the head of that
party, gives thanks for the public honors he has received, not to
the country, but to his party, then we can see the causes in operation, which, according to the well-known character and tendencies of man, lead us to give undue trust and confidence to

party favorites. Why, Gentlemen, kings and queens of old, and probably in modern times, have had their favorites, and they have placed unbounded trust in them. Well, there are sometimes among the people persons who are no wiser than kings and queens, who have favorites also, and give to those favorites the same blind trust and confidence. Hence it is very difficult, nay, sometimes impossible, to convince a party that the man at its head exercises an undue amount of power. They say, " He is our friend; the more power he wields, the better for us, because he will wield it for our benefit." There are two sorts of republicans in the world: one is a very good sort; the other, I think, quite indifferent. The latter care not what power persons in office possess, if they have the election of those persons. They are quite willing their favorites should exercise all power, and are perfectly content with the tendencies of government to an elective despotism, if *they* may choose the man at the head of it, and more especially if they have a chance of being chosen themselves. That is one sort of republicanism. But that is not our American liberty; that is not the republicanism of the United States, and especially of the State of Virginia. Virginians do not rush out into that extravagant confidence in men; they are for restraining power by law; they are for hedging in and strictly guarding all who exercise it. They look upon all who are in office as limited agents, and will not repose too much trust in any. That is American republicanism. What was it that Thomas Jefferson said with so much emphasis? " Have we found angels in the form of men to govern us? " However it might have been then, we of this day may answer, No! No! We have found them at least like others, "a little *lower* than the angels." In the same spirit he has said, an elective despotism is not the government we fought for. And that is true. Our fathers fought for a limited government, a government hedged all round with securities, or, as I heard an eminent son of Virginia say, a government fenced in with ten rails and a top-rider.

Gentlemen, a distinguished lover of liberty of our own time, in another hemisphere, said, with apparent paradox, that the quantity of liberty in any country is exactly equal to the quantity of restraint; because, if government is restrained from putting its hand upon you, to that extent you are free; and all regular liberty consists in putting restraints upon government and individuals, so that they shall not interfere with your freedom of action and purpose. You may easily simplify government; shallow thinkers talk of a simple government; Turkey is the simplest government in the world. But if you wish to secure entire personal liberty, you must multiply restraints upon the government, so that it cannot go farther than the public good requires. Then you may be free, and not otherwise.

Another great power by which executive influence augments itself, especially when the man who wields it stands at the head of a party, consists in the use of names. Mirabeau said that words are things; and so they are. But I believe that they are often fraudulent things, though always possessed of real power. The faculty of taking to ourselves a popular name, and giving an unpopular name to an adversary, is a matter of very great concern in politics. I put it to you, Gentlemen, whether, for the last month or two, the activity of this government has not consisted chiefly in the discharge of a shower of hard names. Have you, for a month past, heard any man defend the sub-treasury? Have you seen any man, during that time, burn his fingers by taking hold of Mr. Poinsett's militia project? Their whole resort has been to pour out upon us a tide of denunciation as aristocrats, aristocrats; taking to themselves, meanwhile, the well-deserved designation of true Democrats. How cheering, how delightful, that a man, independent of any regard to his own character or worth, may thus range himself under a banner the most acceptable of all others to his fellow-citizens! It is with false patriotism as with base money; it relies on the stamp. It does not wish to be weighed; it hates the scales; it is thrown into horrors at the crucible; it must all go by tale; it holds out the king's head, with his name and superscription, and, if challenged, replies, Do you not see the stamp on my forehead? I belong to the Democratic family; make me current. But we live in an age too enlightened to be gulled by this business of stamping; we have learned to inquire into the true nature and value of things. Democracy most surely is not a term of reproach, but of respect. Our government is a constitutional, democratic, republican government; and if they mean that only, there is none will dispute that they are good Democrats. But if they set up qualifications and distinctions, if there are *genera* and *species*, it may require twenty political Linnæuses to say to which class they belong.

There is another contrivance for the increase of executive power, which is utterly abhorrent to all true patriots, and against which, in an especial manner, General Washington has left us his farewell injunction; I mean, the constant recurrence to local differences, prejudices, and jealousies. That is the great bane and curse of this lovely country of ours. That country extends over a vast territory. There are few from among us in Massachusetts who enjoy the advantage of a personal intercourse with our friends in Virginia, and but few of you who visit us in Massachusetts. The farther South is still more remote. The difference which exists in habits and pursuits between us enables the enemy to sow tares, by exciting local prejudices on both sides. Sentiments are mutually ascribed to us which neither ever entertained. By this means a party press is enabled to destroy that generous spirit of brotherhood which should exist between us. All patriotic men ought carefully to guard themselves against the effects of arts like these.

And here I am brought to advert for one moment to what I constantly see in all the administration papers, from Baltimore south. It is one perpetual outcry, admonishing the people of the South that their own State governments, and the property they hold under them, are not secure, if they admit a Northern man to any considerable share in the administration of the general government. You all know that that is the universal cry. Now, I have spoken my sentiments in the neighborhood of Virginia, though not actually within the State, in June last, and again in the heart of Massachusetts in July, so that it is not now that I proclaim them for the first time. But further, ten years ago, when obliged to speak on this same subject, I uttered the same sentiment in regard to slavery, and to the absence of all power in Congress to interfere, in any manner whatever, with that subject. I shall ask some friend connected with the press to circulate in Virginia what I said on this subject in the Senate of the United States, in January, 1830.* I have nothing to add

---

* Mr. Webster had reference here to the remarks on the subject of slavery contained in his speech delivered in the Senate of the United States, in reply to Mr. Hayne, on the 21st of January, 1830, which will be found in a subsequent volume of this collection.

to or subtract from what I then said. I commend it to your attention, or, rather, I desire you to look at it. I hold that Congress is absolutely precluded from interfering in any manner, direct or indirect, with this, as with any other of the institutions of the States. [The cheering was here loud and long continued, and a voice from the crowd exclaimed, " We wish this could be heard from Maryland to Louisiana, and we desire that the sentiment just expressed may be repeated. Repeat! Repeat!"] Well, I repeat it; proclaim it on the wings of all the winds, tell it to all your friends, — [cries of " We will! We will!"] — tell it, I say, that, standing here in the Capitol of Virginia, beneath an October sun, in the midst of this assemblage, before the entire country, and upon all the responsibility which belongs to me, I say that there is no power, direct or indirect, in Congress or the general government, to interfere in the slightest degree with the institutions of the South.

And now, fellow-citizens, I ask you only to do me one favor. I ask you to carry that paper home; read it; read it to your neighbors; and when you hear the cry, " Shall Mr. Webster, the Abolitionist, be allowed to profane the soil of Virginia?" that you will tell them that, in connection with the doctrine in that speech, I hold that there are two governments over us, each possessing its own distinct authority, with which the other may not interfere. I may differ from you in some things, but I will here say that, as to the doctrines of State rights, as held by Mr. Madison in his last days, I do not know that we differ at all; yet I am one, and among the foremost, to hold that it is indispensable to the prosperity of these governments to preserve, and that he is no true friend to either who does not labor to preserve, a true distinction between both.

We may not all see the line which divides them alike; but all honest men know that there is a line, and they all fear to go either on the one or the other side of it. It is this balance between the general and the State governments which has preserved the country in unexampled prosperity for fifty years; and the destruction of this just balance will be the destruction of our government. What I believe to be the doctrine of State rights, I hold as firmly as any man. Do I not belong to a State? and, may I not say, to a State which has done something to give herself renown, and to her sons some little share of participated distinction? I say again, that the upholding of State rights, on the one hand, and of the just powers of Congress, on the other, is indispensable to the preservation of our free republican government.

And now, Gentlemen, permit me to address to you a few words in regard to those measures of the general government which have caused the existing excitement throughout the country. I will pass rapidly over them. I need not argue to you Democrats the question of the sub-treasury, and I suppose it is hardly necessary to speak to you of Mr. Poinsett's militia bill. Into which of your mountains has not its discussion penetrated? Up which of all your winding streams has not its echo floated? I am sure he must be very tired of it himself. Remember always that the great principle of the Constitution on that subject is, that the militia is the militia of the States, and not of the general government; and being thus the militia of the States, there is no part of the Constitution worded with greater care, and with a more scrupulous jealousy, than that which grants and limits the power of Congress over it. Does it say that Congress may make use of the militia as it pleases? that it may call them out for drill and discipline under its own pay? No such thing. The terms used are the most precise and particular: — " Congress may provide for calling out the militia to execute the laws, to suppress insurrection, and to repel invasion." These three cases are specified, and these are all. Call out the militia to drill them! to discipline them! March the militia of Virginia to Wheeling to be drilled! Why, such a thing never entered into the head of any man, — never, never. What is not very usual in the Constitution, after this specific enumeration of powers, it adds a negative in those golden words reserving to the States the appointment of officers and the *training* of the militia. That's it. Read this clause, and then read in Mr. Poinsett's project that the militia are to be trained by the *President!* Look on this picture, and on that. I do Virginia no more than justice when I say, that she first laid hold upon this monstrous project, and has continued to denounce it, and will never consent to it, by whatever weight of authority it may be urged on the country.

As to the sub-treasury, the subject is worn out. The topic is almost as empty of new ideas as the treasury itself is of money

I had, the other day, the honor to address an assemblage of the merchants of New York. I asked them, among other things, whether this eternal cry about a separation of bank and state was not all mockery and humbug; and thousands of merchants, intimately acquainted with the whole subject, cried, "Yes, yes; it is!" The fact unquestionably is, that the funds of the government are just as much in the custody of the banks at this moment as they ever were; yet at the same time I believe that, under the law, there does exist, whenever the revenues of the country shall be uncommonly large, a power to stop at pleasure all the solvent banks in the community. Such is the opinion uniformly held by the best-informed men in the commercial parts of the country.

There is another expedient to augment executive power, quite novel in its character. I refer to the power conferred upon the President to select from among the appropriations of Congress such as he may consider entitled to preference, if the treasury is unable to meet them all, and to give or withhold the public money accordingly. This is certainly a marvellously democratic doctrine. Do you not remember the emphasis with which Mr. Jefferson expressed himself on the subject of specific appropriations? The law, as it now stands, requires them to be specific. If Congress, for instance, appropriate so many dollars for the building of ships, no part of the money may be applied to the pay of sailors or marines. This is the common rule. But how has this subject been treated in regard to those objects over which this Presidential discretion extends? The appropriations are specific still; but then a specific power is given to the President to dispense with the restriction; and thus one specific is set against the other. Let this process be carried but one step farther, and, although there may be a variety of appropriations made by Congress, yet, inasmuch as we have entire trust and confidence in the executive discretion, that the President will make the proper selections from among them, therefore we may enact, or say it shall be enacted, that what little money there may at any time be found in the treasury, the President may expend very much according to his own pleasure.

There is one other topic I must not omit. I am now endeavoring to prove, that, of all men on the face of the earth, you of Virginia, the descendants and disciples of some of the greatest men of the Revolution, are most called to repudiate and to condemn the doctrines of this administration. I call upon you to apply to this administration all that body of political truth which you have learned from Henry, from Jefferson, from Madison, from Wythe, and that whole constellation of Revolutionary worthies, of whom you are justly proud, and under this light to examine and to say whether this exclusively Democratic administration are the favorers of civil liberty and of State rights, or the reverse. In furtherance of this design, I call your attention to the conduct of the President, of the executive departments, and of the Senate of the United States, in regard to the right and practice of the States to contract debts for their own purposes. Has it occurred to you what a deadly blow they have struck at the just authority and rights of the States? Let us follow this matter out a little. In the palmy times of the treasury, when it was not only full, but overflowing with the public money, the States, to a very considerable extent, engaged in works of internal improvement, and, in consequence of doing so, had occasion to borrow money. We all know that money can be had on much cheaper terms on the other continent than on this; hence the bonds of the States went abroad, and absorbed capital in Europe; and so long as their credit was unassailed and remained sound, this was accomplished, for the most part, at very reasonable rates. During this process, and while a number of the States had thus their State securities in the foreign market, the President of the United States, in his opening message to Congress at the commencement of the last session, comes out with a series of the most discouraging and most disparaging remarks on the credit of all the States. He tells Congress that the States will repent what they have done, and that they will find it difficult to pay the debts they have contracted; and this official language of the chief magistrate to the legislature goes out into the very market where these State bonds are held for sale. Then comes his Secretary, Mr. Woodbury, with a report in the same strain, giving it as his opinion, that the States have gone too far in this assumption of liabilities. But the thing does not stop here. Mr. Benton brings forward a resolution in the Senate declaring that the general government ought not to assume these debts of the States; that resolution is sent to a committee, and that committee make a report upon the subject as long as yonder bridge, (though, I believe, by no means as often gone over,) the whole object and tendency of which are to disparage the credit of the States; and then Mr. Grundy makes a speech upon it to the same effect. What had Mr. Benton or Mr. Grundy to do with the matter? Were they called on to guarantee the debts of Virginia or of Maryland? Yet the effect very naturally and inevitably was, to depress the value of State securities in the foreign market. I was in Europe last summer. Massachusetts had her bonds in that market; and what did I see? The most miserable, pitiful, execrable lucubrations taken from the administration press in New York, endeavoring to prove that the States had not sovereignty enough to contract debts. These wretched productions declared that the bonds issued by the States of this Union were all void; that they were no better than waste paper; and exhorted European capitalists not to touch one of them. These articles, coming, as they did, from this side the water, were all seized on with avidity, and put into circulation in the leading journals of Europe. At the same time, the administration press in this country, unrebuked by the government, put forth arguments going to show that Virginia has no authority to contract a debt in the name and on the credit of the Commonwealth; that Massachusetts is so completely shorn of every particle of sovereignty whatever, that she can issue no public security of any kind on which to borrow money! And this is the doctrine of State rights! Well, Gentlemen, I was called on to meet this question, and I told those who put to me the inquiry, that the States of the American Union were, in this respect, just as sovereign as any of their states in Europe. I held a correspondence on the subject, which was published at length; and for that, yes, for defending State rights before the face of all Europe, I have been denounced as one who wants the general government to assume the debts of the States, as one who has conspired to buy up British Whigs (as they call us) with foreign gold! All this, however, has not ruffled my temper. I have seen it all with composure.

But I confess there is one thing which has disturbed the serenity of my mind. It is what appears to be a studied attempt, on the part of this whole administration, including its head, to fix a spot upon the good name of the early founders of our Constitution. Read the letter of the President to some of his friends in Kentucky, to what he calls "the entire Democracy of Kentucky." (I should like much to know what constitutes the Democracy of a State.) These good friends of the President write to him that the entire Democracy of the State is with him, and he writes back how happy he is to hear that such is the fact. The State comes to the vote, and two thirds of the people of the State are found to be against him; yet still he clasps to his breast, with exultation, the "entire Democracy of Kentucky!" And so it will be a month hence. General Harrison will have been elected by a simultaneous rush of the free voters of the whole Union; yet Mr. Van Buren will still insist that he has in his favor "the entire Democracy" of the country. Be this as it may, he does, in that letter, ascribe to President Washington, in 1791, and to Mr. Madison, in 1816, corrupt motives for their public conduct. I may forgive this, but I shall not forget it. I ask you to read that letter, and one other written on a similar occasion; and then, if it comes in your way, I ask you to peruse an address put forth by the administration members of the New York Legislature. What do you think they say? You, countrymen of Jefferson and of Madison, of Henry, of Wythe, of the Lees, and a host of kindred spirits of the same order, — you, who inherit the soil and the principles of those men who shed their blood for our national independence, — what do you think they say of your fathers and of my fathers? Why, that, in all their efforts and sacrifices in that great struggle, they meant, not independence, not civil liberty, not the establishment of a republican government, but merely to transfer the throne from England to America, and to be themselves peers and nobles around it! Does it not disturb the blood of Virginians to hear language like this? I do say that this attempt to scorch the fair, unsullied reputation of our ancestors —— But no, no, they cannot scorch it; it will go through a hotter furnace than any their detraction can kindle, and even the smell of fire shall not be upon their garments. Yet it does raise one's indignation to see men, certainly not the greatest of all benefactors of their country, thus attempt to blight the fame of men both then and ever since universally admitted to have been among her greatest and her best of friends.

While speaking of the attacks of this administration on State rights, I should not do my duty if I omitted to notice the outrage recently perpetrated on the most sacred rights of the State and people of New Jersey. By the Constitution of the United States, New Jersey, like the other States, is entitled to have a certain quota of representatives in Congress; and she chooses them by general ticket or in districts, as she thinks fit. The right to have a specific number of representatives is a State right under the Constitution. Under the constitutional guaranty of this right, New Jersey sends up to the House of Representatives her proper number of men. Now, I say that, by universal principles, although Congress be the judge, in the last resort, of the election return and qualification of her own members, those who bring in their hand the prescribed evidence of their election, by the people of any State, are entitled to take their seats upon the floor of that House, and to hold them until disturbed by proof preferred on petition. That this is so must be apparent from the fact, that those members who voted them out of their seats possessed no better or other means of proving their own right to sit and to vote on that question, than that held by any one of those whom they excluded. Were there other States situated precisely in this respect as New Jersey, would it not be as fair for the New Jersey members to vote these representatives out of the Representative Hall as it was for them to vote hers out? I think it is Virginia law, it is at least plantation law, that is to say, the law of common sense, and that is very good law, that, until the house is organized, he who has the evidence of his return as a representative elected by the people of his district, is entitled to take his seat. But the representatives of New Jersey, with this evidence in their hand, were voted out of their seats; their competitors, while the evidence was still under examination, were voted in, and immediately gave their complacent votes for the sub-treasury bill.

Gentlemen, I cannot forget where I am. I cannot forget how often you have heard these subjects treated with far greater ability than I can bring to the discussion. I will not further dwell upon these topics. The time has come when the public mind is nearly made up, and is very shortly about to settle these questions, together with the prosperity of the country for many years to come. I am only desirous of keeping myself to the line of remark with which I commenced. I say, then, that the enemy has been driven to his last citadel. He takes to himself a popular name, while beneath its cover he fires all manner of abuse upon his adversaries. That seems to be his only remaining mode of warfare. If you ask him what are his pretensions to the honors and confidence of the country, his answer is, "I am a Democrat." But are you not in love with Mr. Poinsett's bill? The answer still is, "I am a Democrat, and support all the measures of this Democratic administration." But do you approve of the turning out of the members from New Jersey? "O, yes, because the words are written on our banner (words actually placed on one of the administration flags in a procession in the interior of New York), *'The Democracy scorns the broad seal of New Jersey.'*"

My friends, I only desire that the professions and principles of this administration may be examined. We are coming to those times when men can no longer be deceived by mere professions. Virginia has once been deceived by them; but that day is past; the times are coming, they are, I trust, just at hand, when that distinguished son of Virginia, that eminent and patriotic citizen who has been put in nomination for the chief executive office under this government, will be elected by the unbought, unconstrained suffrages of his countrymen. To that event I look forward with as much certainty as to the duration of his life.

My acquaintance with the feelings and sentiments of the North has been extensive; and I believe that, from Pennsylvania east, New Jersey, New York, and the whole of New England, with the solitary exception, probably, of New Hampshire, — I say, I have not a doubt that the whole of this part of the country is in favor of the election of William Henry Harrison to the Presidency. Of my native State of New Hampshire I shall always speak with respect. I believe that the very foundations of her granite hills begin to shake; indeed, my only fear for her is, that she will come into the great family of her sister States only when her aid is no longer needed, and therefore too late for her own reputation.

Fellow-citizens, we are on a great march to the triumphant victory of the principles of liberty over executive power. If we do not accomplish it now, the future, I own, appears to me full of darkness and of doubt. If the American people shall sanction the course and the principles of this administration, I, for one, though I have been thought hitherto of rather a sanguine temperament, shall begin not a little to despair of the republic. But I will not despair of it. The public mind is aroused; men

9*

are beginning to think for themselves; and when they do this, they are not far from a right decision. There is an attempt on the part of the administration, — who seem beginning, at length, to fear for the perpetuity of their power, — to excite a feeling of acrimony and bitterness among neighbors. Have you not seen this, particularly of late, in the administration papers? Be above it. Tell your neighbors that we are all embarked in one cause, and that we must sink or swim *together*. Invite them, not in a taunting, but in a generous and a temperate spirit, to come forth and argue the great questions of the day, and to see if they can give good and solid reasons why there should not be a change. Yes, a CHANGE. I said when I was in Baltimore, in May last, and I repeat it here, the cry, the universal cry, is for a change. However well many may think of the motives and designs of the existing administration, they see that it has not succeeded in securing the well-being of the country, and they are for a change. Let us revile nobody; let us repel nobody. They desire but light; let us give it to them. Let us discuss with moderation and coolness the great topics of public policy, and endeavor to bring all men of American heart and feeling into what I sincerely believe to be the true AMERICAN CAUSE. How shall I, — O, how shall I express to you my sense of the obligation which rests upon this generation to preserve from destruction our free and happy republican institutions? Who shall spread fatal dissensions among us? Are we not together under one common government, to obtain which the blood of your fathers and of mine was poured out together in the same hard-fought fields? Nay, does imagination itself, in its highest flight, suggest any thing in the form of political institutions for which you would exchange these dearly-bought constitutions of our own? For my part, having now arrived at that period of life when men begin to reflect upon the past, I love to draw around me in thought those pure and glorious spirits who achieved our Revolution, and established our forms of government. I cannot find a deeper or more fervent sentiment in my heart than that these precious institutions and liberties which we enjoy may be transmitted unimpaired to the latest posterity; that they may terminate only with the termination of all things earthly, when the world itself shall terminate, —

"When, wrapped in flames, the realms of ether glow,
And Heaven's last thunders shake the world below."

REMARKS TO THE LADIES OF RICHMOND.

REMARKS TO THE LADIES OF RICHMOND.*

REMARKS TO THE LADIES OF RICHMOND

THE visit of Mr. Webster to Richmond was short, and his public engagements so numerous, as to put it out of his power to return the calls of his friends, or to pay his respects to their families. It was accordingly proposed that the ladies who might desire to do so should assemble in the "Log Cabin," and that he should there pay his respects to them collectively. The meeting was large, and the building quite full. On being introduced to them, in a few appropriate remarks, by Mr. Lyons, Mr. Webster addressed them in the following speech : —

LADIES, — I am very sure I owe the pleasure I now enjoy to your kind disposition, which has given me the opportunity to present my thanks and my respects to you thus collectively, since the shortness of my stay in the city does not allow me the happiness of calling upon those, severally and individually, from members of whose families I have received kindness and notice. And, in the first place, I wish to express to you my deep and hearty thanks, as I have endeavored to do to your fathers, your husbands, and your brothers, for the unbounded hospitality I have received ever since I came among you. This is registered, I assure you, in a grateful heart, in characters of an enduring nature. The rough contests of the political world are not suited to the dignity and the delicacy of your sex; but you possess the intelligence to know how much of that happiness which you are entitled to hope for, both for yourselves and for your children, depends on the right administration of government, and a proper tone of public morals. That is a subject on which the moral perceptions of woman are both quicker and juster than

* Remarks made at a Public Reception by the Ladies of Richmond, Virginia, on the 5th of October, 1840.

those of the other sex. I do not speak of that administration
of government whose object is merely the protection of industry,
the preservation of civil liberty, and the securing to enterprise of
its due reward. I speak of government in a somewhat higher
point of view; I speak of it in regard to its influence on the
morals and sentiments of the community. We live in an age
distinguished for great benevolent exertion, in which the affluent
are consecrating the means they possess to the endowment of
colleges and academies, to the building of churches, to the support of religion and religious worship, to the encouragement of
schools, lyceums, and athenæums, and other means of general
popular instruction. This is all well; it is admirable; it augurs
well for the prospects of ensuing generations. But I have
sometimes thought, that, amidst all this activity and zeal of the
good and the benevolent, the influence of government on the
morals and on the religious feelings of the community is apt to
be overlooked or underrated. I speak, of course, of its indirect
influence, of the power of its example, and the general tone
which it inspires.

A popular government, in all these respects, is a most powerful institution; more powerful, as it has sometimes appeared to
me, than the influence of most other human institutions put together, either for good or for evil, according to its character. Its
example, its tone, whether of regard or disregard for moral obligation, is most important to human happiness; it is among those
things which most affect the political morals of mankind, and
their general morals also. I advert to this, because there has
been put forth, in modern times, the false maxim, that there is
one morality for politics, and another morality for other things;
that, in their political conduct to their opponents, men may say
and do that which they would never think of saying or doing in
the personal relations of private life. There has been openly
announced a sentiment, which I consider as the very essence
of false morality, which declares that " all is fair in politics." If
a man speaks falsely or calumniously of his neighbor, and is re-
proached for the offence, the ready excuse is this: — " It was in
relation to public and political matters; I cherished no personal
ill-will whatever against that individual, but quite the contrary;
I spoke of my adversary merely as a political man." In my
opinion, the day is coming when falsehood will stand for false-

hood, and calumny will be treated as a breach of the command-
ment, whether it be committed politically or in the concerns of
private life.

It is by the promulgation of sound morals in the community,
and more especially by the training and instruction of the young,
that woman performs her part towards the preservation of a free
government.   It is generally admitted that public liberty, and the
perpetuity of a free constitution, rest on the virtue and intelligence of the community which enjoys it.   How is that virtue to
be inspired, and how is that intelligence to be communicated?
Bonaparte once asked Madame de Staël in what manner he
could best promote the happiness of France.   Her reply is full
of political wisdom.   She said, " Instruct the mothers of the
French people."   Mothers are, indeed, the affectionate and effective teachers of the human race.   The mother begins her process of training with the infant in her arms.   It is she who directs, so to speak, its first mental and spiritual pulsations.   She
conducts it along the impressible years of childhood and youth,
and hopes to deliver it to the stern conflicts and tumultuous
scenes of life, armed by those good principles which her child
has received from maternal care and love.

If we draw within the circle of our contemplation the mothers of a civilized nation, what do we see ?   We behold so many
artificers working, not on frail and perishable matter, but on the
immortal mind, moulding and fashioning beings who are to
exist for ever.   We applaud the artist whose skill and genius
present the mimic man upon the canvas ; we admire and celebrate the sculptor who works out that same image in enduring
marble ; but how insignificant are these achievements, though
the highest and the fairest in all the departments of art, in comparison with the great vocation of human mothers !   They
work, not upon the canvas that shall perish, or the marble that
shall crumble into dust, but upon mind, upon spirit, which is to
last for ever, and which is to bear, for good or evil, throughout
its duration, the impress of a mother's plastic hand.

I have already expressed the opinion, which all allow to be
correct, that our security for the duration of the free institutions
which bless our country depends upon habits of virtue and the
prevalence of knowledge and of education.   The attainment of
knowledge does not comprise all which is contained in the

larger term of education. The feelings are to be disciplined; the passions are to be restrained; true and worthy motives are to be inspired; a profound religious feeling is to be instilled, and pure morality inculcated, under all circumstances. All this is comprised in education. Mothers who are faithful to this great duty will tell their children, that neither in political nor in any other concerns of life can man ever withdraw himself from the perpetual obligations of conscience and of duty; that in every act, whether public or private, he incurs a just responsibility; and that in no condition is he warranted in trifling with important rights and obligations. They will impress upon their children the truth, that the exercise of the elective franchise is a social duty, of as solemn a nature as man can be called to perform; that a man may not innocently trifle with his vote; that every free elector is a trustee, as well for others as himself; and that every man and every measure he supports has an important bearing on the interests of others, as well as on his own. It is in the inculcation of high and pure morals such as these, that, in a free republic, woman performs her sacred duty, and fulfils her destiny. The French, as you know, are remarkable for their fondness for sententious phrases, in which much meaning is condensed into a small space. I noticed lately, on the title-page of one of the books of popular instruction in France, this motto: — "Pour instruction on the heads of the people! you owe them that baptism." And, certainly, if there be any duty which may be described by a reference to that great institute of religion, — a duty approaching it in importance, perhaps next to it in obligation, — it is this.

I know you hardly expect me to address you on the popular political topics of the day. You read enough, you hear quite enough, on those subjects. You expect me only to meet you, and to tender my profound thanks for this marked proof of your regard, and will kindly receive the assurances with which I tender to you, on parting, my affectionate respects and best wishes.

RECEPTION AT BOSTON.

INTRODUCTORY NOTE.

On the accession of General Harrison to the Presidency of the United States, on the 4th of March, 1841, Mr. Webster was called to the office of Secretary of State, in which, after the President's untimely death, he continued under Mr. Tyler for about two years. The relations of the country with Great Britain were at that time in a very critical position, as is more particularly stated in the introduction to a subsequent volume of this collection containing Mr. Webster's diplomatic correspondence. The most important and difficult subject which engaged the attention of the government, while he filled the Department of State, was the negotiation of the treaty with Great Britain, which was signed at Washington on the 9th of August, 1842. The other members of General Harrison's Cabinet having resigned their places in the autumn of 1841, discontent was felt by some of their friends, that Mr. Webster should have consented to retain his. But as Mr. Tyler continued to place entire confidence in Mr. Webster's administration of the Department of State, the great importance of pursuing a steady line of policy in reference to foreign affairs, and especially the hope of averting a rupture with England by an honorable settlement of our difficulties with that country, induced Mr. Webster to remain at his post.

On occasion of a visit made by him to Boston, after the adjournment of Congress, in August, 1842, a number of his friends were desirous of manifesting their sense of the services which he had rendered to the country by pursuing this course, and the following correspondence took place.

To the Hon. Daniel Webster : —

Sir, — The undersigned, desirous of evincing their gratitude for your eminent and patriotic public services, during a long term of years, and especially for the part sustained by you in the late negotiations which have been so skilfully conducted and happily terminated in a treaty with Great Britain, invite you to meet them at a public dinner, at such time as shall be convenient to yourself.

HARRISON GRAY OTIS,	LEMUEL SHAW,
JEREMIAH MASON,	THOMAS B. WALES,
WILLIAM STURGIS,	GEORGE MOREY,
JOSIAH BRADLEE,	C. W. CARTWRIGHT,
CHARLES G. LORING,	E. BALDWIN,
CHARLES P. CURTIS,	HORACE SCUDDER,
WILLIAM APPLETON,	FRANCIS WELCH,
ABBOTT LAWRENCE,	JOHN L. DIMMOCK,
NATHAN APPLETON,	FRANCIS C. LOWELL,
PATRICK T. JACKSON,	CALEB CURTIS,
JOSEPH BALCH,	GEORGE HAYWARD,
JAMES K. MILLS,	AMOS LAWRENCE,
F. SKINNER,	GEORGE DARRACOTT,
J. T. STEVENSON,	SIDNEY BARTLETT,
HENRY CABOT,	SEWELL TAPPAN,
PETER C. BROOKS,	SAMUEL L. ABBOT,
ROBERT G. SHAW,	JOSEPH BALLISTER,
BENJAMIN RICH,	HENRY D. GRAY,
PHINEAS SPRAGUE,	GEORGE B. CARY,
HENRY OXNARD,	NATHAN HALE,
J. INGERSOLL BOWDITCH,	J. M. FORBES,
S. AUSTIN, JR.,	S. HOOPER,
J. T. BUCKINGHAM,	GEORGE HOWE,
THOMAS B. CURTIS,	WILLIAM H. GARDINER,
ABEL PHELPS,	J. H. WOLCOTT,
PETER HARVEY,	DANIEL C. BACON,
EBENEZER CHADWICK,	J. DAVIS, JR.,
ROBERT HOOPER, JR.,	W. C. AYLWIN,
SAMUEL QUINCY,	FRANKLIN DEXTER,
OZIAS GOODWIN,	ISAAC LIVERMORE,
JOS. RUSSELL,	THOMAS KINNICUTT,
JACOB BIGELOW,	EDMUND DWIGHT,
JONATHAN CHAPMAN,	JOHN P. ROBINSON,
G. R. RUSSELL,	HENRY WILSON,
H. WAINWRIGHT,	GEORGE T. CURTIS,
FRANCIS FISHER,	GEORGE T. BIGELOW,
JOHN S. BLAKE,	WILLIAM W. GREENOUGH,
FRANCIS C. GRAY,	THOMAS LAMB,
B. R. CURTIS,	JOSEPH GRINNELL.

Boston, *September* 8, 1842.

Boston, September 9, 1842.

Gentlemen, — I have received your letter of the 8th instant, inviting me to a public dinner, and am duly sensible of the value of this proof of your regard.

It will give me great pleasure to meet all my fellow-citizens, who may desire to see me ; and the mode of such meeting I should leave to them, with a preference, however, on my part, if equally agreeable to others, that the dinner should be dispensed with, and that the meeting should be had in such a manner as shall impose the least restrictions, and best suit the convenience of all who may be disposed to attend it.

I am, Gentlemen, with very sincere regard,

Your obliged fellow-citizen, and obedient servant,

DANIEL WEBSTER.

To Messrs. H. G. Otis, J. Mason, William Sturgis, Josiah Bradlee, Charles G. Loring, Charles P. Curtis, William Appleton, Abbott Lawrence, and others.

In pursuance of this correspondence, a public meeting was appointed to be held in Faneuil Hall, on the 30th of September. Some time before the hour appointed for the reception of Mr. Webster, the hall was filled. Very many of the most distinguished citizens came at an early hour, to make sure of admission, and the hall was soon crowded to its utmost capacity. Great numbers were obliged to turn away without being able to come within the doors.

Just before eleven o'clock, His Honor Jonathan Chapman, Mayor of the city, rose, and said that he had received a letter from a committee of those gentlemen who had extended the invitation to Mr. Webster, requesting him to preside. This he had consented to do, unless objection should be made. He would only add, that the committee would introduce Mr. Webster precisely at eleven o'clock.

Amid the enthusiastic applause that followed this information, Mr. Webster, with the committee of his friends, entered the hall. Mr. Chapman led him forward upon the platform, and, after the assembly had given nine hearty cheers, addressed its guest as follows.

" Mr. Webster : — I have the honor, Sir, to be the organ of this large assembly of your former constituents, and still fellow-citizens and friends, who have gathered to greet you with a cordial welcome, upon your visit to what we are proud to call, and trust you will always feel to be, your home. We sought to meet you at a social festival ; but it has taken the present far better form, at your own request. The pointed meaning, however, of the occasion is unchanged. Believing that, as a true republican, you will find the richest reward of your public services in the respect and gratitude of those whom you serve, we would assure you in the most emphatic manner, that, so far as your friends here are concerned, you have them from the heart. We would assure you, that though your duties, at your country's call, have separated you from us for a season, you are not forgotten ; but that wherever your destiny may place you, so long as you shall be nobly defending your country's Constitution, as in time past, and maintaining untarnished her honor, there will be living and beating here hearts in which you will ever be enshrined.

" A large portion, Sir, of your mature life has been spent in the public service, and of that portion, a great part as the immediate representative of this city and Commonwealth. We rejoice in this opportunity of testifying to you, that your long and eminent services in our behalf are still held in most grateful remembrance. We acknowledge our deep obligations to you, for your unwavering fidelity to our interests, for your able support of that cause of American industry, whose protection has so distinguished the recent session of Congress, and for the broad and comprehensive spirit in which your legislative duties were ever discharged. Bright, Sir, ever bright, will be the page of history which records the efforts of your commanding intellect in the councils of the nation. And New England, — glorious New England, your birthplace and your home, whose heart, you know, is warm, though her skies be cold, — New England, from every summit of her granite hills, will never cease to hail you as her worthy representative.

" We resigned you with regret, indeed, but still with ready acquies-

10 *

cence in the wise judgment of that good old man, who, himself placed in the Presidential chair amidst a people's acclamations, from amongst the bright lights of this broad land selected you to stand at his right hand. It pleased a wise but inscrutable Providence, too soon, alas! to mortal eyes, to remove him from his elevated seat on earth to, we trust, a higher one above. But nobly, Sir, have you sustained the momentous interests, which, in a most critical period of the country's history, he committed to your charge. No sound, indeed, of his glad voice shall ever again greet your ear. But we feel that his benignant spirit has been, and will still be, near to bless you, and approve the loud 'Well done!' with which every true patriot must salute you.

"It is to your eminent services, Sir, on this broader field which you have lately occupied, that we look this day with special pride and admiration. Sir, in simple but heartfelt language, we thank you for the honorable attitude in which, so far as your department has been concerned, you have placed your country before the world. Would to God that it stood as well in other respects! In the many emergencies in our foreign relations which the two past years have presented, you have been faithful throughout to the true interests and honor of the country, and nowhere in its archives can abler, manlier, wiser, or more dignified papers be found, than those which bear your signature.

"When the dark cloud lowered upon our neighboring frontier, when a great and fundamental law of nations had wellnigh yielded to popular passion, when a single step only intervened between us and a war that must have been disastrous, as it would have found us in the wrong, it was your wise and energetic interference that dispelled the storm, by seeking to make us just, even under galling provocation.

"When a gasconading upstart from a neighboring republic, so called, presumed to address to this government a communication worthy only of his own, but which no one of his coadjutors was bold enough to present in person, one firm and dignified look from our own Secretary of State, a single sweep of his powerful arm, relieved the country from any further specimens of Mexican diplomacy.

"And, crowning act of all, when, amidst the numerous and perplexing questions which had so long disturbed the harmony of two nations whom God meant should always be friends, England sent forth her ambassador of compromise and peace, you met him like a man. Subtle diplomacy and political legerdemain you threw to the winds; and taking only for your guides simple honesty, common sense, and a Christian spirit, behold! by their magic influence, there is not a cloud in the common heavens above us, but only the glad and cheering sunlight of friendship and peace.

"We have already, Sir, on this same spot, expressed our approbation of this treaty with England, while paying a merited tribute of respect to the distinguished representative of that country * who was associated with you in its adjustment. We repeat to you our satisfaction with the result, and with the magnanimous spirit by which it was accomplished. We may add now, as we might not then, that we know not the other

---

* Lord Ashburton.

individual within the limits of the country who could have so success-fully achieved this happy event.

"We are aware, Sir, that this treaty is not yet completed, but that an important act is yet necessary for its accomplishment. We antici-pate no such result, and yet it may be that still further work is ne-cessary for the crowning of our hopes. You have brought skill and labor, ay, and self-sacrifice too, to this great work, we know. And whatever may befall the country, in this or any other matter, we are sure that you will be ready to sacrifice every thing for her good, save honor. And on that point, amidst the perplexities of these perplexing times, we shall be at ease; for we know that he who has so nobly main-tained his country's honor may safely be intrusted with his own.

"And permit us, Sir, most warmly to greet you as our personal friend and fellow-citizen. Though the few and brief intervals of leisure which your public duties have permitted you, have allowed us far less inter-course with you in private life than we have wished, we have never ceased to feel that you were one of us. We rejoice in the kind Provi-dence which has been with you in the past, and may Heaven still smile upon your future years. Long may you live to be an ornament and support of your native republic. And when at last your sun goes down, as every orb, the brightest even, must set, may it be from a serene and tranquil sky. It was bright at its rising; it is brilliant at its meridian. May no clouds gather around its departing; but, life's labors done and honors won, may it, — in your own classical and beautiful words, — may it go down with 'slow-descending, long-lingering light.'

"And now, fellow-citizens, it would be the idlest ceremony in the world, to presume to introduce to you our distinguished guest. It was his privilege, upon the occasion of an important trial in the Supreme Court of this Commonwealth, a few years since, to introduce to that court, and to the bar, the late lamented William Wirt, his opposing counsel in the cause. He did it by a just and beautiful tribute to his eminent talents and worth. It was the no less just and beautiful reply of Mr. Wirt, when he rose in turn to address the court, that he had one reason to regret the very kind introduction which he had just received; for his friend, Mr. Webster, had thereby placed him under an obligation which it never would be in his power to return, — for he never could meet that gentleman at any bar in the United States where his name and his fame had not gone before him.

"And here, fellow-citizens, in Boston, — here in Faneuil Hall, last place of all, and amongst you, last people of all, is such a ceremony needed. I have only to say that Daniel Webster, the faithful representative, the manly and able statesman, your fellow-citizen and friend, is before you, and I leave his name to do the rest."

Mr. Webster then delivered the following speech.

RECEPTION AT BOSTON.

I KNOW not how it is, Mr. Mayor, but there is something in the echoes of these walls, or in this sea of upturned faces which I behold before me, or in the genius that always hovers over this place, fanning ardent and patriotic feeling by every motion of its wings, — I know not how it is, but there is something that excites me strangely, deeply, before I even begin to speak. It cannot be doubted that this salutation and greeting from my fellow-citizens of Boston is a tribute dear to my heart. Boston is indeed my home, my cherished home. It is now more than twenty-five years since I came to it with my family, to pursue, here in this enlightened metropolis, those objects of professional life for which my studies and education were designed to fit me. It is twenty years since I was invited by the citizens of Boston to take upon myself an office of public trust in their service.* It gives me infinite pleasure to see here to-day, among those who hold the seats yielded to such as are more advanced in life, not a few of the gentlemen who were earnestly instrumental in inducing me to enter upon a course of life wholly unexpected, and to devote myself to the service of the public.

Whenever the duties of public life have withdrawn me from this home, I have felt it, nevertheless, to be the attractive spot to which all local affection tended. And now that the progress of time must shortly bring about the period, if it should not be hastened by the progress of events, when the duties of public life shall yield to the influences of advancing years, I cherish no hope more precious, than to pass here in these associations and among these friends what may remain to me of life; and to

* The office of Representative in Congress.

leave in the midst of you, fellow-citizens, partaking of your fortunes, whether for good or for evil, those who bear my name, and inherit my blood.

The Mayor has alluded, very kindly, to the exertions which I have made since I have held a position in the Cabinet, and especially to the results of the negotiation in which I have been recently engaged. I hope, fellow-citizens, that something has been done which may prove permanently useful to the public. I have endeavored to do something, and I hope my endeavors have not been in vain. I have had a hard summer's work, it is true, but I am not wholly unused to hard work. I have had some anxious days, I have spent some sleepless nights; but if the results of my efforts shall be approved by the community, I am richly compensated. My other days will be the happier, and my other nights will be given to a sweeter repose.

It was an object of the highest national importance, no doubt, to disperse the clouds which threatened a storm between England and America. For several years past there has been a class of questions open between the two countries, which have not always threatened war, but which have prevented the people from being assured of permanent peace.

His Honor the Mayor has paid a just tribute to that lamented personage, by whom, in 1841, I was called to the place I now occupy; and although, Gentlemen, I know it is in very bad taste to speak much of one's self, yet here, among my friends and neighbors, I wish to say a word or two on subjects in which I am concerned. With the late President Harrison, I had contracted an acquaintance while we were both members of Congress, and I had an opportunity of renewing it afterwards in his own house, and elsewhere. I have made no exhibition or boast of the confidence which it was his pleasure to repose in me; but circumstances, hardly worthy of serious notice, have rendered it not improper for me to say on this occasion, that as soon as President Harrison was elected, without, of course, one word from me, he wrote to me inviting me to take a place in his Cabinet, leaving to me the choice of that place, and asking my advice as to the persons that should fill every other place in it. He expressed rather a wish that I should take the administration of the treasury, because, as he was pleased to say, I had devoted myself with success to the examination of the questions of currency and finance, and he felt that the wants of the country, — the necessities of the country, on the great subjects of currency and finance, — were moving causes that produced the revolution which had placed him in the presidential chair.

It so happened, Gentlemen, that my preference was for another place, — for that which I have now the honor to fill. I felt all its responsibilities; but I must say, that, with whatever attention I had considered the general questions of finance, I felt more competent and willing to undertake the duties of an office which did not involve the daily drudgery of the treasury.

I was not disappointed, Gentlemen, in the exigency which then existed in our foreign relations. I was not unaware of all the difficulties which hung over us; for although the whole of the danger was not at that moment developed, the cause of it was known, and it seemed as if an outbreak was inevitable. I allude now to that occurrence on the frontier of which the chairman has already spoken, which took place in the winter of 1841, the case of Alexander McLeod.

A year or two before, the Canadian government had seen fit to authorize a military incursion, for a particular purpose, within the territory of the United States. That purpose was to destroy a steamboat, charged with being employed for hostile purposes against its forces and the peaceable subjects of the crown. The act was avowed by the British government at home as a public act. Alexander McLeod, a person who individually could claim no regard or sympathy, happened to be one of the agents who, in a military character, performed the act of their sovereign. Coming into the United States some years after, he was arrested under a charge of homicide committed in this act, and was held to trial as for a private felony.

According to my apprehensions, a proceeding of this kind was directly adverse to the well-settled doctrines of the public law. It could not but be received with lively indignation, not only by the British government, but among the people of England. It would be so received among us. If a citizen of the United States should as a military man receive an order of his government and obey it, (and he must either obey it or be hanged,) and should afterwards, in the territory of another power, which by that act he had offended, be tried for a violation of its law, as for a crime, and threatened with individual punishment, there is not a man in the United States who would not cry out for redress and for vengeance. Any elevated government, in a case like this, where one of its citizens, in the performance of his duty, incurs such menaces and danger, assumes the responsibility; any elevated government says, " The act was mine, — I am the man"; " Adsum qui feci, in me convertite ferrum."

Now, Gentlemen, information of the action of the British government on this subject was transmitted to us at Washington within a few days after the installation of General Harrison. I did not think that it was proper to make public then, nor is it important to say now, all that we knew on the subject; but I will tell you, in general terms, that if all that was known at Washington then had been divulged throughout the country, the value of the shipping interest of this city, and of every other interest connected with the commerce of the country, would have been depressed one half in six hours. I thought that the concussion might be averted, by holding up to view the principles of public law by which this question ought to be settled, and by demanding an apology for whatever had been done against those principles of public law by the British government or its officers. I thought we ought to put ourselves right in the first place, and then we could insist that they should do right in the next place. When in England, in the year 1839, I had occasion to address a large and respectable assemblage; and allusion having been made to the relations of things between the two countries, I stated then, what I thought and now think, that in any controversy which should terminate in war between the United States and England, the only eminent advantage that *either* would possess would be found in the rectitude of its cause. With the right on our side, we are a match for England; and with the right on her side, she is a match for us, or for any body.

We live in an age, fellow-citizens, when there has been established among the nations a more elevated tribunal than ever before existed on earth; I mean the tribunal of the enlightened public opinion of the world. Governments cannot go to war now, either with or against the consent of their own subjects or people, without the reprobation of other states, unless for grounds and reasons justifying them in the general judgment of mankind. The judgment of civilization, of commerce, and of that heavenly light that beams over Christendom, restrains men, congresses, parliaments, princes, and people from gratifying the inordinate love of ambition through the bloody scenes of war. It has been wisely said, and it is true, that every settlement of national differences between Christian states by fair negotiation, without resort to arms, is a new illustration and a new proof of the benign influence of the Christian faith.

With regard to the terms of this treaty, and in relation to the other subjects connected with it, it is somewhat awkward for me to speak, because the documents connected with them have not been made public by authority. But I persuade myself, that, when the whole shall be calmly considered, it will be seen that there was throughout a fervent disposition to maintain the interest and honor of the country, united with a proper regard for the preservation of peace between us and the greatest commercial nation of the world.

Gentlemen, while I receive these commendations which you have bestowed, I have an agreeable duty to perform to others. In the first place, I have great pleasure in bearing testimony to the intelligent interest manifested by the President of the United States, under whose authority, of course, I constantly acted throughout the negotiation, and his sincere and anxious desire that it might result successfully. I take great pleasure in acknowledging here, as I will acknowledge everywhere, my obligations to him for the unbroken and steady confidence reposed in me through the whole progress of an affair not unimportant to the country, and infinitely important to my own reputation.

A negotiator disparaged, distrusted, treated with jealousy by his own government, would be indeed a very unequal match for a cool and sagacious representative of one of the proudest and most powerful monarchies of Europe, possessing in the fullest extent the confidence of his government, and authorized to bind it in concerns of the greatest importance. I shall never forget the frankness and generosity with which, after a full and free interchange of suggestions upon the subject, I was told by the President that on my shoulders rested the responsibility of the negotiation, and on my discretion and judgment should rest the lead of every measure. I desire also to speak here of the hearty coöperation rendered every day by the other gentlemen connected with the administration, from every one of whom I received important assistance. I speak with satisfaction, also, of the useful labors of all the Commissioners, although I need hardly say here, what has been already said officially, that the highest respect is due to the Commissioners from Maine and Massachusetts for their faithful adherence to the rights of their own States, mingled with a cordial coöperation in what was required by the general interests of the United States. And I hope I shall not be considered as trespassing on this occasion, if I speak of the happy selection made by England of a person to represent her government on this occasion,* — a thorough Englishman, understanding and appreciating the great objects and interests of his own government, of large and liberal views, and of such standing and weight of character at home, as to impress a feeling of approbation of his course upon both government and people. He was fully acquainted with the subject, and always, on all occasions, as far as his allegiance and duty permitted, felt and manifested good-will towards this country.

Aside from the question of the boundary, there were other important subjects to be considered, to which I know not whether this is a proper occasion to allude. When the results of the negotiation shall be fully before the public, it will be seen that these other questions have not been neglected, questions of great moment and importance to the country; and then I shall look with concern, but with faith and trust, for the judgment of that country upon them. It is but just to take notice of a very important act, intended to provide for such cases as McLeod's, for which the country is indebted to the Whig majorities in the two houses of Congress, acting upon the President's recommendation. Events showed the absolute necessity of removing into the national tribunals questions involving the peace and honor of the United States.

There yet remain, Gentlemen, several other subjects still unsettled with England. First, there is that concerning the trade between the United States and the possessions of England, on this continent and in the West Indies. It has been my duty to look into that subject, and to keep the run of it, as we say, from the arrangement of 1829 and 1830, until the present time. That

---

* Lord Ashburton.

arrangement was one unfavorable to the shipping interests of the United States, and especially so to the New England States. To adjust these relations is an important subject, either for diplomatic negotiation, or the consideration of Congress. One or both houses of Congress, indeed, have already called upon the proper department for a report upon the operations of that arrangement, and a committee of the House of Representatives has made a report, showing that some adjustment of these relations is of vital importance to the future prosperity of our navigating interests.

There is another question, somewhat more remote; that of the Northwest Boundary, where the possessions of the two countries touch each other upon the Pacific. There are evident public reasons why that question should be settled before the country becomes peopled.

There are also, Gentlemen, many open questions respecting our relations with other governments. Upon most of the other States of this continent, citizens of the United States have claims, with regard to which the delays already incurred have caused great injustice; and it becomes the government of the United States, by a calm and dignified course, and a deliberate and vigorous tone of administration of public affairs, to secure prompt justice to our citizens in these quarters.

I am here to-day as a guest. I was invited by a number of highly valued personal and political friends to partake with them of a public dinner, for the purpose of giving them an opportunity to pass the usual greeting of friends upon my return; of testifying their respect for my public services heretofore; and of exchanging congratulations upon the results of the late negotiation. It was at my instance that the proposed dinner took the form of this meeting, and instead of meeting them at the festive board, I agreed to meet them, and those who chose to meet me with them, here. Still, the general character of the meeting seems not to be changed. I am here as a guest; here to receive greetings and salutations for particular services, and not under any intimation or expectation that I should address the gentlemen who invited me or others here, upon subjects not suggested by themselves. It would not become me to use the occasion for any more general purpose. Because, although I have a design, at some time not far distant, to make known my sentiments upon political matters generally, and upon the political state of the country and that of its several parties, yet I know very well that I should be trespassing beyond the bounds of politeness and propriety, should I enter upon this whole wide field now.   I will not enter upon it, because the gentlemen who invited me entertain on many of these topics views different from my own, and they would very properly say, that they came here to meet Mr. Webster, to congratulate him upon the late negotiation, and to exchange sentiments upon matters about which they agreed with him; and that it was not in very correct taste for him to use the occasion to express opinions upon other subjects on which they differ.   It is on that account that I shall forbear discussing political subjects at large, and shall endeavor to confine my remarks to what may be considered as affecting myself, directly or indirectly.

The Mayor was kind enough to say, that having, in his judgment, performed the duties of my own department to the satisfaction of my country, it might be left to me to take care of my own honor and reputation.   I suppose that he meant to say, that in the present distracted state of the Whig party, and among the contrariety of opinions that prevail (if there be a contrariety of opinion) as to the course proper for *me* to pursue, the decision of that question might be left to myself.   I am exactly of his opinion.   I am quite of opinion that on a question touching my own honor and character, as I am to bear the consequences of the decision, I had a great deal better be trusted to make it.   No man feels more highly the advantage of the advice of friends than I do; but on a question so delicate and important as that, I like to choose myself the friends who are to give me advice; and upon this subject, Gentlemen, I shall leave you as enlightened as I found you.

I give no pledges, I make no intimations, one way or the other; and I will be as free, when this day closes, to act as duty calls, as I was when the dawn of this day —— (Here Mr. Webster was interrupted by tremendous applause.   When silence was restored he continued:)

There is a delicacy in the case, because there is always delicacy and regret when one feels obliged to differ from his friends; but there is no embarrassment.   There is no embarrassment, because, if I see the path of duty before me, I have that within me which will enable me to pursue it, and throw all embarrassment to the winds. A public man has no occasion to be embarrassed, if he is honest. Himself and his feelings should be to him as nobody and as nothing; the interest of his country must be to him as every thing; he must sink what is personal to himself, making exertions for his country; and it is his ability and readiness to do this which are to mark him as a great or as a little man in time to come.

There were many persons in September, 1841, who found great fault with my remaining in the President's Cabinet. You know, Gentlemen, that twenty years of honest, and not altogether undistinguished service in the Whig cause, did not save me from an outpouring of wrath, which seldom proceeds from Whig pens and Whig tongues against any body. I am, Gentlemen, a little hard to coax, but as to being driven, that is out of the question. I chose to trust my own judgment, and thinking I was at a post where I was in the service of the country, and could do it good, I staid there. And I leave it to you to-day to say, I leave it to my country to say, whether the country would have been better off if I had left also. I have no attachment to office. I have tasted of its sweets, but I have tasted of its bitterness. I am content with what I have achieved; I am more ready to rest satisfied with what is gained, than to run the risk of doubtful efforts for new acquisition.

I suppose I ought to pause here. (Cries of "Go on!") I ought, perhaps, to allude to nothing more, and I will not allude to any thing further than it may be supposed to concern myself, directly or by implication. Gentlemen, and Mr. Mayor, a most respectable convention of Whig delegates met in this place a few days since, and passed very important resolutions. There is no set of gentlemen in the Commonwealth, so far as I know them, who have more of my respect and regard. They are Whigs, but they are no better Whigs than I am. They have served the country in the Whig ranks; so have I, quite as long as most of them, though perhaps with less ability and success. Their resolutions on political subjects, as representing the Whigs of the State, are entitled to respect, so far as they were authorized to express opinion on those subjects, and no further. They were sent hither, as I supposed, to agree upon candidates for the offices of Governor and Lieutenant-Governor for the support of

11 *

the Whigs of Massachusetts; and if they had any authority to speak in the name of the Whigs of Massachusetts to any other purport or intent, I have not been informed of it. I feel very little disturbed by any of those proceedings, of whatever nature; but some of them appear to me to have been inconsiderate and hasty, and their point and bearing can hardly be mistaken. I notice among others, a declaration made, in behalf of all the Whigs of this Commonwealth, of "a full and final separation from the President of the United States." If those gentlemen saw fit to express their own sentiments to that extent, there was no objection. Whigs speak their sentiments everywhere; but whether they may assume a privilege to speak for others on a point on which those others have not given them authority, is another question. I am a Whig, I always have been a Whig, and I always will be one; and if there are any who would turn me out of the pale of that communion, let them see who will get out first. I am a Massachusetts Whig, a Faneuil Hall Whig, having breathed this air for five-and-twenty years, and meaning to breathe it, as long as my life is spared. I am ready to submit to all decisions of Whig conventions on subjects on which they are authorized to make decisions; I know that great party good and great public good can only be so obtained. But it is quite another question whether a set of gentlemen, however respectable they may be as individuals, shall have the power to bind me on matters which I have not agreed to submit to their decision at all.

"A full and final separation" is declared between the Whig party of Massachusetts and the President. That is the text: it requires a commentary. What does it mean? The President of the United States has three years of his term of office yet unexpired. Does this declaration mean, then, that during those three years all the measures of his administration are to be opposed by the great body of the Whig party of Massachusetts, whether they are right or wrong? There are great public interests which require his attention. If the President of the United States should attempt, by negotiation, or by earnest and serious application to Congress, to make some change in the present arrangements, such as should be of service to those interests of navigation which are concerned in the colonial trade, are the Whigs of Massachusetts to give him neither aid nor succor?

If the President of the United States shall direct the proper department to review the whole commercial policy of the United States, in respect of reciprocity in the indirect trade, to which so much of our tonnage is now sacrificed, if the amendment of this policy shall be undertaken by him, is there such a separation between him and the Whigs of Massachusetts as shall lead them and their representatives to oppose it? Do you know (there are gentlemen now here who do know) that a large proportion, I rather think more than one half, of the carrying trade between the empire of Brazil and the United States is enjoyed by tonnage from the North of Europe, in consequence of this ill-considered principle with regard to reciprocity. You might just as well admit them into the coasting trade. By this arrangement, we take the bread out of our children's mouths and give it to strangers. I appeal to you, Sir, (turning to Captain Benjamin Rich, who sat by him,) is not this true? (Mr. Rich at once replied, True!) Is every measure of this sort, for the relief of such abuses, to be rejected? Are we to suffer ourselves to remain inactive under every grievance of this kind until these three years shall expire, and through as many more as shall pass until Providence shall bless us with more power of doing good than we have now?

Again, there are now in this State persons employed under government, allowed to be pretty good Whigs, still holding their offices; collectors, district attorneys, postmasters, marshals. What is to become of them in this separation? Which side are they to fall? Are they to resign? or is this resolution to be held up to government as an invitation or a provocation to turn them out? Our distinguished fellow-citizen, who, with so much credit to himself and to his country, represents our government in England,* — is *he* expected to come home, on this separation, and yield his place to his predecessor,† or to somebody else? And in regard to the individual who addresses you, — what do his brother Whigs mean to do with him? Where do they mean to place me? Generally, when a divorce takes place, the parties divide their children. I am anxious to know where, in the case of this divorce, I shall fall. This declaration announces a full and final separation between the

* Mr. Edward Everett.   † Mr. Andrew Stevenson.

Whigs of Massachusetts and the President. If I choose to remain in the President's councils, do these gentlemen mean to say that I cease to be a Massachusetts Whig? I am quite ready to put that question to the people of Massachusetts.

I would not treat this matter too lightly, nor yet too seriously. I know very well that, when public bodies get together, resolutions can never be considered with any degree of deliberation. They are passed as they are presented. Who the honorable gentlemen were who drew this resolution I do not know. I suspect that they had not much meaning in it, and that they have not very clearly defined what little meaning they had. They were angry; they were resentful; they had drawn up a string of charges against the President, — a bill of indictment, as it were, — and, to close the whole, they introduced this declaration about " a full and final separation." I could not read this, of course, without perceiving that it had an intentional or unintentional bearing on my position; and therefore it was proper for me to allude to it here.

Gentlemen, there are some topics on which it has been my fortune to differ from my old friends. They may be right on these topics; very probably they are; but I am sure *I* am right in maintaining my opinions, such as they are, when I have formed them honestly and on deliberation. There seems to me to be a disposition to postpone all attempts to do good to the country to some future and uncertain day. Yet there is a Whig majority in each house of Congress, and I am of opinion that now is the time to accomplish what yet remains to be accomplished. Some gentlemen are for suffering the present Congress to expire; another Congress to be chosen, and to expire also; a third Congress to be chosen, and then, if there shall be a Whig majority in both branches, and a Whig President, they propose to take up highly important and pressing subjects. These are persons, Gentlemen, of more sanguine temperament than myself. " Confidence," says Lord Chatham, " is a plant of slow growth in an old bosom." He referred to confidence in men, but the remark is as true of confidence in predictions of future occurrences. Many Whigs see before us a prospect of more power, and a better chance to serve the country, than we now possess. Far along in the horizon, they discern mild skies and halcyon seas, while fogs and darkness and mists blind other sons of humanity from beholding all this bright vision. It was not so that we accomplished our last great victory, by simply brooding over a glorious Whig future. We succeeded in 1840, but not without an effort; and I know that nothing but union, cordial, sympathetic, fraternal union, can prevent the party that achieved that success from renewed prostration. It is not, — I would say it in the presence of the world, — it is not by premature and partial, by proscriptive and denunciatory proceedings, that this great Whig family can ever be kept together, or that Whig counsels can maintain their ascendency. This is perfectly plain and obvious. It was a party, from the first, made up of different opinions and principles, of gentlemen of every political complexion, uniting to make a change in the administration. They were men of strong State rights principles, men of strong federal principles, men of extreme tariff, and men of extreme anti-tariff notions. What could be expected of such a party, unless animated by a spirit of conciliation and harmony, of union and sympathy? Its true policy was, from the first, and must be, unless it meditates its own destruction, to heal, and not to widen, the breaches that existed in its ranks. It consented to become united in order to save the country from a continuation of a ruinous course of measures. And the lesson taught by the whole history of the revolution of 1840 is the momentous value of conciliation, friendship, sympathy, and union.

Gentlemen, if I understand the matter, there were four or five great objects in that revolution. And, in the first place, one great object was that of attempting to secure permanent peace between this country and England. For although, as I have said, we were not actually at war, we were subjected to perpetual agitations, which disturb the interests of the country almost as much as war. They break in upon men's pursuits, and render them incapable of calculating or judging of their chances of success in any proposed line or course of business. A settled peace was one of the objects of that revolution. I am glad if you think this is accomplished.

The next object of that revolution was an increase of revenue. It was notorious that, for the several last years, the expenditures for the administration of government had exceeded the receipts; in other words, government had been running in debt, and in the mean time the operation of the compromise act was still further and faster diminishing the revenue itself. A sound revenue was one of those objects; and that it has been accomplished, our thanks and praise are due to the Congress that has just adjourned.

A third object was protection, protection incidental to revenue, or consequent upon revenue. Now as to that, Gentlemen, much has been done, and I hope it will be found that enough has been done. And for this, too, all the Whigs who supported that measure in Congress are entitled to high praise: they receive mine, and I hope they do yours; it is right that they should. But let us be just. The French rhetoricians have a maxim, that there is nothing beautiful that is not true; I am afraid that some of our jubilant oratory would hardly stand the test of this canon of criticism. It is not true that a majority, composed of Whigs, could be found, in either house, in favor of the tariff bill. More than thirty Whigs, many of them gentlemen of lead and influence, voted against the law, from beginning to end, on all questions, direct and indirect; and it is not pleasant to consider what would have been the state of the country, the treasury, and the government itself, at this moment, if the law actually passed, for revenue and for protection, had depended on Whig votes alone. After all, it passed the House of Representatives by a single vote; and there is a good deal of *éclat* about that single vote. But did not every gentleman who voted for it take the responsibility and deserve the honor of that single vote? Several gentlemen in the opposition thus befriended the bill; thus did our neighbor from the Middlesex District of this State,* voting for the tariff out and out, as steadily as did my honored friend, the member from this city.† We hear nothing of his " coming to the rescue," and yet he had that *one vote*, and held the tariff in his hand as absolutely as if he had had a presidential veto! And how was it in the Senate? It passed by one vote again there, and could not have passed at all without the assistance of the two Senators from Pennsylvania, of Mr. Williams of Maine, and of Mr. Wright of New York. Let us then admit the truth (and a lawyer may do that when it helps his case), that it was necessary that a large portion of the other party should come to the assistance of the

---

* Mr. Parmenter.   † Mr. R. C. Winthrop.

Whigs to enable them to carry the tariff, and that, if this assistance had not been rendered, the tariff must have failed.

And this is a very important truth for New England. Her children, looking to their manufactures and industry for their livelihood, must rejoice to find the tariff, so necessary to these, no party question. Can they desire, can they wish, that such a great object as the protection of industry should become a party object, rising with party, and with the failure of the party that supported it going to the grave? This is a public, a national question. The tariff ought to be inwrought in the sentiments of all parties; and although I hope that the preëminence of Whig principles may be eternal, I wish to take bond and security, that we may make the protection of domestic industry more durable even than Whig supremacy.

Let us be true in another respect. This tariff has accomplished much, and is an honor to the men who passed it. But in regard to protection it has only restored the country to the state in which it was before the compromise act, and from which it fell under the operation of that act. It has repaired the consequences of that measure, and it has done *no more*. I may speak of the compromise act. My turn has come now. No measure ever passed Congress during my connection with that body that caused me so much grief and mortification. It was passed by a few friends joining the whole host of the enemy. I have heard much of the motives of that act. The personal motives of those that passed the act were, I doubt not, pure; and all public men are supposed to act from pure motives. But if by motives are meant the objects proposed by the act itself, and expressed in it, then I say, if those be the motives alluded to, they are worse than the act itself. The principle was bad, the measure was bad, the consequences were bad. Every circumstance, as well as every line of the act itself, shows that the design was to impose upon legislation a restraint that the Constitution had not imposed; to insert in the Constitution a new prohibitory clause, providing that, after the year 1842, no revenue should be collected except according to an absurd horizontal system, and none exceeding twenty per cent. It was then pressed through under the great emergency of the public necessities. But I may now recur to what I then said, namely, that its principle was false and dangerous, and that,

when its time came, it would rack and convulse our system. I
said we should not get rid of it without throes and spasms.
Has not this been as predicted? We have felt the spasms and
throes of this convulsion; but we have at last gone through
them, and begin to breathe again. It is something that that act
is at last got rid of; and the present tariff is deserving in this,
that it is specific and discriminating, that it holds to common
sense, and rejects and discards the principles of the compromise
act, I hope for ever.

Another great and principal object of the revolution of 1840
was a restoration of the currency. Our troubles did not begin
with want of money in the treasury, or under the sapping and
mining operation of the compromise act. They are of earlier
date. The trouble and distress of the country began with the
currency in 1833, and broke out with new severity in 1837.
Other causes of difficulty have since arisen, but the first great
shock was a shock on the currency; and from the effect of this
the country is not yet relieved. I hope the late act may yield
competent revenue, and am sure it will do much for protection.
But until you provide a better currency, so that you may have
a universal one, of equal and general value throughout the land,
I am hard to be persuaded that we shall see the day of our former prosperity. Currency, accredited currency, and easy and
cheap internal exchanges, — until these things be obtained, depend upon it, the country will find no adequate relief.

And now, fellow-citizens, I will say a word or two on the history of the transactions on this subject. At the special session
of Congress, the Secretary of the Treasury, Mr. Ewing, arranged
a plan for a national bank. That plan was founded upon the
idea of a large capital, furnished mainly by private subscriptions,
and it included branches for local discounts. I need not advert, Gentlemen, to the circumstances under which this scheme
was drawn up, and received, as it did, the approbation of the
President and Cabinet, as the best thing that could be done. I
need not remind you, that he whom we had all agreed should
hold the second place in the government had been called to the
head of it. I need not say that he held opinions wholly different from mine on the subjects which now came before us.
But those opinions were fixed, and therefore it was thought the
part of wisdom and prudence not to see how strong a case might

be made against the President, but to get along as well as we might. With such views, Mr. Ewing presented his plan to Congress. As most persons will remember, the clause allowing the bank to establish branches provided that those branches might be placed in any State which should give its consent. I have no idea that there is any necessity for such a restriction. I believe Congress has the power to establish the branches without, as well as with, the consent of the States. But that clause, at most, was theoretical. I never could find any body who could show any practical mischief resulting from it. Its opponents went upon the theory, which I do not exactly accord with, that an omission to exercise a power, in any case, amounts to a surrender of that power. At any rate, it was the best thing that could be done; and its rejection was the commencement of the disastrous dissensions between the President and Congress.

Gentlemen, it was exceedingly doubtful at the time when that plan was prepared whether the capital would be subscribed. But we did what we could about it. We asked the opinion of the leading merchants of the principal commercial cities. They were invited to Washington to confer with us. They expressed doubts whether the bank could be put into operation, but they expressed hopes also, and they pledged themselves to do the best they could to advance it. And as the commercial interests were in its favor, as the administration was new and fresh and popular, and the people were desirous to have something done, a great earnestness was felt that that bill should be tried.

It was sent to the Senate at the Senate's request, and by the Senate it was rejected. Another bill was reported in the Senate, without the provision requiring the consent of the States to branches, was discussed for six weeks or two months, and then could not pass even a Whig Senate. Here was the origin of distrust, disunion, and resentment.

I will not pursue the unhappy narrative of the latter part of the session of 1841. Men had begun to grow excited and angry and resentful. I expressed the opinion, at an early period, to all those to whom I was entitled to speak, that it would be a great deal better to forbear further action at present. That opinion, as expressed to the two Whig Senators from Massachusetts, is before the public. I wished Congress to give time for consultation

to take place, for harmony to be restored; because I looked for
no good, except from the united and harmonious action of all the
branches of the Whig government. I suppose that counsel was
not good, certainly it was not followed. I need not add the
comment.

This brings us, as far as concerns the questions of currency,
to the last session of Congress. Early in that session the Secretary of the Treasury sent in a plan of an exchequer. It met
with little favor in either House, and therefore it is necessary for
me, Gentlemen, lest the whole burden fall on others, to say that
it had my hearty, sincere, and entire approbation. Gentlemen,
I hope that I have not manifested through my public life a very
overweening confidence in my own judgment, or a very unreasonable unwillingness to accept the views of others. But
there are some subjects on which I feel entitled to pay some
respect to my own opinion. The subject of currency, Gentlemen, has been the study of my life. Thirty years ago, a little before my entrance into the House of Representatives, the
questions connected with a mixed currency, involving the proper
relation of paper to specie, and the proper means of restricting
an excessive issue of paper, came to be discussed by the most
acute and well-disciplined understandings in England in Parliament. At that time, during the suspension of specie payments
by the bank, when paper was fifteen per cent. below par, Mr.
Vansittart had presented his celebrated resolution, declaring that
a bank-note was still worth the value expressed on its face; that
the bank-note had not depreciated, but that the price of bullion
had risen. Lord Liverpool and Lord Castlereagh espoused this
view, as we know, and it was opposed by the close reasoning
of Huskisson, the powerful logic of Horner, and the practical
sagacity and common sense of Alexander Baring, now Lord
Ashburton. The study of those debates made me a bullionist.
They convinced me that paper could not circulate safely in any
country, any longer than it was immediately redeemable at the
place of its issue. Coming into Congress the very next year,
or the next but one after, and finding the finances of the country in a most deplorable condition, I then and ever after devoted
myself, in preference to all other public topics, to the consideration of the questions relating to them. I believe I have read
every thing of value that has been published since on those

questions, on either side of the Atlantic. I have studied by close observation the laws of paper currency, as they have exhibited themselves in this and in other countries, from 1811 down to the present time. I have expressed my opinions at various times in Congress, and some of the predictions which I have made have not been altogether falsified by subsequent events. I must therefore be permitted, Gentlemen, without yielding to any flippant newspaper paragraph, or to the hasty ebullitions of debate in a public assembly, to say, that I believe the plan for an exchequer, as presented to Congress at its last session, is the *best* measure, the *only* measure for the adoption of Congress and the trial of the people. I am ready to stake my reputation upon it, and that is all that I have to stake. I am ready to stake my reputation, that, if this Whig Congress will take that measure and give it a fair trial, within three years it will be admitted by the whole American people to be the most beneficial measure of any sort ever adopted in this country, the Constitution only excepted.

I mean that they should take it as it was when it came from the Cabinet, not as it looked when the committees of Congress had laid their hands upon it. For when the committees of Congress had struck out the proviso respecting exchange, it was not worth a rush; it was not worth the parchment it would be engrossed upon. The great desire of this country is a general currency, a facility of exchange; a currency which shall be the same for you and for the people of Alabama and Louisiana, and a system of exchange which shall equalize credit between them and you, with the rapidity and facility with which steam conveys men and merchandise. That is what the country wants, what you want; and you have not got it. You have not got it, you cannot get it, but by some adequate provision of government. Exchange, ready exchange, that will enable a man to turn his New Orleans means into money to-day, (as we have had in better times millions a year exchanged, at only three quarters of one per cent.,) is what is wanted. How are we to obtain this? A Bank of the United States founded on a private subscription is out of the question. That is an obsolete idea. The country and the condition of things have changed. Suppose that a bank were chartered with a capital of fifty millions, to be raised by private subscription. Would it not be out of all possibility to find the money? Who would subscribe? What would you get for shares? And as for the local discount, do you wish it? Do you, in State Street, wish that the nation should send millions of untaxed banking capital hither to increase your discounts? What then shall we do? People who are waiting for power to make a Bank of the United States may as well postpone all attempts to benefit the country to the incoming of the Jews.

What, then, shall we do? Let us turn to this plan of the exchequer, brought forward last year. It was assailed from all quarters. One gentleman did say, I believe, that by some possibility some good might come out of it, but in general it met with a different opposition from every different class. Some said it would be a perfectly lifeless machine, — that it was no system at all, — that it would do nothing, for good or evil; others thought that it had a great deal too much vitality, admitting that it would answer the purpose perfectly well for which it was designed, but fearing that it would increase the executive power: thus making it at once King Log and King Serpent. One party called it a ridiculous imbecility; the other, a dangerous giant, that might subvert the Constitution. These varied arguments, contradicting, if not refuting, one another, convinced me of one thing at least, — that the bill would not be adopted, nor even temperately and candidly considered. And it was not. In a manner quite unusual, it was discussed, assailed, denounced, before it was allowed to take the course of reference and examination.

The difficulties we meet in carrying out our system of constitutional government are indeed extraordinary. The Constitution was intended as an instrument of great political good; but we sometimes so dispute its meaning, that we cannot use it at all. One man will not have a bank, without the power of local discount, against the consent of the States; for that, he insists, would break the Constitution. Another will not have a bank with such a power, because he thinks that would break the Constitution. A third will not have an exchequer, with authority to deal in exchanges, because that would increase executive influence, and so might break the Constitution. And between them all, we are like the boatman who, in the midst of rocks and currents and whirlpools, will not pull one stroke for safety, lest he break his oar. Are we now looking for the time when we can charter a United States Bank with a large private subscription? When will that be? When confidence is restored. Are we, then, to do nothing to save the vessel from sinking, till the chances of the winds and waves have landed us on the shore? He is more sanguine than I am, who thinks that the time will soon come when the Whigs have more power to work effectually for the good of the country than they now have. The voice of patriotism calls upon them not to postpone, but to act at this moment, at the very next session; to make the best of their means, and to try. You say that the administration is responsible; why not, then, try the plan it has recommended. If it fails, let the President bear the responsibility. If you will not try this plan, why not propose something else?

Gentlemen, in speaking of events that have happened, I ought to say, and will, since I am making a full and free communication, that there is no one of my age, and I am no longer very young, who has written or spoken more against the abuse and indiscreet use of the veto power than I have. And there is no one whose opinions upon this subject are less changed. I presume it is universally known, that I have advised against the use of the veto power on every occasion when it has been used since I have been in the Cabinet. But I am, nevertheless, not willing to join those who seem more desirous to make out a case against the President, than of serving their country to the extent of their ability, vetoes notwithstanding. Indeed, at the close of the extra session, the received doctrine of many seemed to be, that they would undertake nothing until they could amend the Constitution so as to do away with this power. This was mere mockery. If we were now reforming the Constitution, we might wish for some, I do not say what, guards and restraints upon this power more than the Constitution at present contains; but no convention would recommend striking it out altogether. Have not the people of New York lately amended their constitution, so as to require, in certain legislative action, votes of two thirds? and is not this same restriction in daily use in the national House of Representatives itself, in the case of suspension of the rules? This constitutional power, therefore, is no greater a restraint than this body imposes on itself. But it is utterly hopeless to look for such an amend-

12*

ment; who expects to live to see its day? And to give up all practical efforts, and to go on with a general idea that the Constitution must be amended before any thing can be done, was, I will not say trifling, but treating the great necessities of the people as of quite too little importance. This Congress accomplished, in this regard, nothing for the people. The exchequer plan which was submitted to it will accomplish some of the objects of the people, and especially the Whig people. I am confident of it; I know it. When a mechanic makes a tool, an axe, a saw, or a plane, and knows that the temper is good and the parts are well proportioned, he knows that it will answer its purpose. And I know that this plan will answer its purpose.

There are other objects which ought not to be neglected, among which is one of such importance that I will not now pass it by; I mean, the mortifying state of the public credit of this country at this time. I cannot help thinking, that if the statesmen of a former age were among us, if Washington were here, if John Adams, and Hamilton, and Madison were here, they would be deeply concerned and soberly thoughtful about the present state of the public credit of the country. In the position I fill, it becomes my duty to read, generally with pleasure, but sometimes with pain, communications from our public agents abroad. It is distressing to hear them speak of *their* distress at what they see and hear of the scorn and contumely with which the American character and American credit are treated abroad. Why, at this very time, we have a loan in the market, which, at the present rate of money and credit, ought to command in Europe one hundred and twenty-five per cent. Can we sell a dollar of it? And how is it with the credit of our own Commonwealth? Does it not find itself affected in its credit by the general state of the credit of the country? Is there nobody ready to make a movement in this matter? Is there not a man in our councils large enough, comprehensive enough in his views, to undertake at least to *present* this case before the American people, and thus do something to restore the public character for morals and honesty?

There are in the country some men who are indiscreet enough to talk of *repudiation*,—to advise their fellow-citizens to *repudiate* public debt. Does repudiation pay a debt? Does it discharge the debtor? Can it so modify a debt that it shall not be always binding, in law as well as in morals? No, Gentlemen; repudiation does nothing but add a sort of disrepute to acknowledged inability. It is our duty, so far as is in our power, to rouse the public feeling on the subject; to maintain and assert the universal principles of law and justice, and the importance of preserving public faith and credit. People say that the intelligent capitalists of Europe ought to distinguish between the United States government and the State governments. So they ought; but, Gentlemen, what does all this amount to? Does not the general government comprise the same people who make up the State governments? May not these Europeans ask us how long it may be before the national councils will repudiate public obligations?

The doctrine of repudiation has inflicted upon us a stain which we ought to feel worse than a wound; and the time has come when every man ought to address himself soberly and seriously to the correction of this great existing evil. I do not undertake to say what the Constitution allows Congress to do in the premises. I will only say, that if that great fund of the public domain properly and in equity belongs, as is maintained, to the States themselves, there are some means, by regular and constitutional laws, to enable and induce the States to save their own credit and the credit of the country.

Gentlemen, I have detained you much too long. I have wished to say, that, in my judgment, there remain certain important objects to engage our public and private attention, in the national affairs of the country. These are, the settlement of the remaining questions between ourselves and England; the great questions relating to the reciprocity principle; those relating to colonial trade; the most absorbing questions of the currency, and those relating to the great subject of the restoration of the national character and the public faith; these are all objects to which I am willing to devote myself, both in public and in private life. I do not expect that much of public service remains to be done by me; but I am ready, for the promotion of these objects, to act with sober men of any party, and of all parties. I am ready to act with men who are free from that great danger that surrounds all men of all parties, — the danger that patriotism itself, warmed and heated in party contests, will run into partisanship. I believe that, among the sober men of this country, there is a growing desire for more moderation of party feeling, more predominance of purely public considerations, more honest and general union of well-meaning men of all sides to uphold the institutions of the country and carry them forward.

In the pursuit of these objects, in public life or in a private station, I am willing to perform the part assigned to me, and to give them, with hearty good-will and zealous effort, all that may remain to me of strength and life.

THE NORTHEASTERN BOUNDARY.

INTRODUCTORY NOTE.

PENDING the negotiation of the treaty of Washington, in the spring and summer of 1842, Mr. Webster was made acquainted with the existence at Paris of a copy of D'Anville's map of America on a small scale, on which the boundary between the British Provinces and the United States was indicated by a red line, in a manner favorable to the British claim. This map (which was soon extensively known as the *red-line map*) had been discovered by President Sparks in the foreign office at Paris. He also found a letter from Dr. Franklin to the Count de Vergennes, from which it appeared that the boundary had been delineated by Dr. Franklin upon some map, at the request of the Count, and for his information. There was no proof, however, that this letter referred to the map discovered by Mr. Sparks.

After the negotiation of the treaty, and the publication of the debates in the Senate on the question of its ratification, much importance was attached by the opposition press in England to this map, as proving incontestably the soundness of the British claims relative to boundary. It was also absurdly made a matter of reproach against Mr. Webster, that he had not, as soon as he became acquainted with the existence of this map, communicated it to Lord Ashburton.

So conclusive was this piece of evidence deemed in England in favor of the British claim, and so much importance was attached to it in the debates in Parliament, that it became necessary for Sir Robert Peel, by way of offset, to refer to another map not before publicly known to exist; namely, the copy of Mitchell's map which had been used by Mr. Oswald, the British commissioner for negotiating the provisional treaty, and by him sent home to his government. This map had been preserved in the library of George the Third, and with that library was sent to the British Museum. On this map the line as claimed by the United States is boldly and distinctly traced throughout its whole extent, and the words " Boundary as described by Mr. Oswald" written in four places with great plainness. It was asserted by Lord Brougham in the House of Peers, that these words are in the handwriting of George the Third.

The writer of this note was assured by Lord Aberdeen, that he had no knowledge of the existence of this map till after the conclusion of the treaty of Washington. He was also assured by Lord Ashburton, that he was equally ignorant of it till after his return from America. It is supposed to have been accidentally discovered in the British Museum, and, under Lord Melbourne's administration, to have been placed in the hands of Mr. Featherstonhaugh, with other documents and materials relative to the boundary, although no allusion to this map is made in his report. He was directed by Lord Aberdeen to hand over to Lord Ashburton all the documents and maps in his possession, but this, by far the most important of them all, was not among those transferred by him.

At about the same time, a copy of Mitchell's map was found among the papers of Mr. Jay, one of the American commissioners for negotiating the treaty of 1783. It contains a line drawn from the mouth to the source of the St. John's, which is described upon the map as " Mr. Oswald's line." It no doubt represents the boundary line as offered by Mr. Oswald on the 8th of October, 1782, but not agreed to by the British government.

On the discovery of Mr. Jay's map, a meeting of the New York Historical Society was held, at which a very learned memoir on the Northeastern Boundary was read by the venerable Mr. Gallatin, who had acted as one of the commissioners for preparing the American statement to be submitted to the King of the Netherlands as arbiter, and whose knowledge of the subject was not surpassed, if equalled, by that of any other person.

At the time this meeting was held, the knowledge of Oswald's map had not reached America. The simultaneous discovery of these two maps in England and the United States, the most important in their bearing on the controversy of all the maps produced in the discussion, — one of them in fact (Oswald's) decisive as to the point at issue, — a discovery not made till after the conclusion of the treaty of 1842, — is among the most singular incidents in the history of the protracted negotiations which resulted in that treaty. Taken together, and in connection with the official correspondence, they leave no doubt that Mr. Jay's map exhibits the proposed line of the 8th of October, 1782, and that Oswald's map exhibits the line of the treaty of 1783, and which is that always contended for by the United States.

Mr. Webster, happening to be in New York, was present by invitation at the meeting of the Historical Society above alluded to, and after the reading of Mr. Gallatin's memoir, having been called upon by its Vice-President, Mr. W. Beach Lawrence, made the following speech.

THE NORTHEASTERN BOUNDARY.*

Mr. President: — I have had very great gratification in listening to your dissertation on the topics connected with the newly found map of the late Mr. Jay. I came here to be instructed, and I have been instructed, by an exhibition of the results of your information, and consideration of that subject. I came, however, without the slightest expectation of being called on to say any thing upon that or any other topic connected with the treaty, in the negotiation of which it was my fortune to bear a part. I am free to say, Sir, that the map which hangs over your head does appear to be proved, beyond any other documents now producible, to have been before the commissioners in Paris in 1782.† That fact, and the lines and marks which the map bears, lead to inferences of some importance. If they be not such inferences as remove all doubts from these contested topics, they may yet have no inconsiderable tendency towards rebutting or controlling other inferences of an opposite character, drawn, or attempted to be drawn, from similar sources.

Before making any particular remarks upon the subject of the several maps, I will advert to two or three general ideas, which it is always necessary to carry along with us in any process of reasoning upon this subject. Let us remember, then, in the first place, that the treaty of 1783 granted nothing to the United States, — nothing. It granted no political rights. It granted not one inch of territory. The political rights of the United States

---

* Remarks made at a Meeting of the New York Historical Society, on the 15th of April, 1843.

† It must be particularly borne in mind, in reading this speech, that intelligence of the discovery of Oswald's map, and of the line marked upon it, had not yet reached America.

had been asserted by the Declaration of Independence in 1776, and stood, and stand, and always will stand, upon that Declaration. The territorial limits of the several States stood upon their respective ancient charters and grants from the British crown, going back to the times of the Stuarts. The treaty of peace of 1783 acknowledged, it did not grant, the independence of the United States. It acknowledged the independence of the United States as they then existed, with the territories that belonged to them, respectively, as colonies. That which has since become, or afterwards became, the subject of dispute, was territory claimed by Great Britain on the one hand, and by Massachusetts on the other. The question was the definition of the boundary between the English Provinces of Canada and Nova Scotia or New Brunswick, and Massachusetts. But as, by the acknowledgment of the independence of the United States, England had put herself in a condition to treat diplomatically with the whole Union, this matter of disputed boundary between England and the State of Massachusetts thenceforward became a question of boundary between the United States and England; because the treaty-making power necessarily devolved upon the whole Union, as well according to the Articles of Confederation, as, afterwards, according to the Constitution of the United States. Well, then, the question was, What is, or what was, the boundary between the State of Massachusetts and the British Province of Nova Scotia? Nova Scotia did not join in the war of independence, and did not separate from the mother country; Massachusetts did, and the question therefore arose, What was the boundary between them?

Now, in order to a general understanding of that, we must go a little back in the history of political occurrences on this continent. The war of 1756 brought on a general conflict in America between England on the one side, and France and Spain on the other. From that period till the peace of 1763, which terminated the war, Spain possessed Florida, and Canada belonged to the French. By the peace of Paris, in 1763, Canada on the north, and Florida on the south, were ceded by France and Spain, respectively, to Great Britain. Other conquests were made by British power in the West Indies; and the British ministry, in October of that year, by the celebrated proclamation of the 7th of that month, defined the boundaries of these respective Colonies thus obtained from France and Spain; and so far as the present subject is concerned, it may be enough to say, that the British government, in issuing the proclamation of 1763, defining, describing, and settling the boundaries of the newly acquired Province of Canada or Quebec, asserted as the boundary of Canada a line against which Massachusetts had contended with France during the preceding thirty or forty years. That is to say, the Colony of Massachusetts had insisted that her territory ran to the north bank of the St. Lawrence. She claimed not *to* the highlands, but *over* them *down to the river.* England had never discountenanced this claim of her colony as against France. England, then becoming owner of Canada by conquest and subsequent cession, described its boundaries as she desired to fix them, by the celebrated line of "highlands." According to the proclamation, the line from Lake Nepissing (at the northwest) was to cross the St. Lawrence and Lake Champlain in the 45th degree of north latitude, and thence to proceed along the highlands which divide the rivers that empty themselves into the St. Lawrence from those which fall into the sea.

Massachusetts complained of the proclamation of 1763 as taking into Canada what she had insisted on as matter of her own right. Mr. Borland, the Massachusetts agent, presented it strongly to the British ministry, as an invasion of the territorial rights of that Colony. It happened, however, that in the interior of Maine, near the Kennebec, there was a tract of country to which it was alleged the crown of England had rightful claim. There grew up, therefore, a tacit consent, soon after the peace of 1763, between the crown of England and Massachusetts, that, if the former would forbear to assert any right to this territory, included within the general limits of the Province of Maine, Massachusetts would not press the matter respecting the boundary between that Province and Canada. Well, under these circumstances, when the peace of 1783 was made, the question was to ascertain what was the boundary between Massachusetts and Nova Scotia. The country was a wilderness, and the line was not easily defined. Many historical documents, the proclamation of 1763, and many prior and subsequent proceedings of the governments, were resorted to. Now I suppose that the object of the commissioners of 1783 was to ascertain what was the existing line, and not to run any new line, as England, being possessor of Canada by conquest from France, claimed under the French, and, acccording to general principles, would be bound by what had been the claims of her grantor. Now it is certain, that whilst the French owned Canada, down to the very day of its cession to Great Britain by the peace of 1763, the French maps, so far as I know, with hardly an exception, if any, represent the divisional line between Massachusetts and Nova Scotia exactly according to the line contended for by us. The French maps which gave another representation were the production of a subsequent epoch. It was fair, therefore, to say to England, " You must claim under your grantors, and according to their claim."

The provisions of the treaty of 1783 undoubtedly meant to ascertain what the line was as it then existed, and so to describe it. In regard to the map now presented, supposing the fact to be as I take it to be, that it was before the commissioners, because it has Mr. Jay's memorandum upon it, and connecting it with the proposition of the British minister of the 8th of October, 1782, several things seem very fairly to be deducible; and an important one is, that the northwest angle of Nova Scotia and the sources of the River St. John are identical according to this map and according to Mr. Oswald's proposition. How comes it, then, the northwestern angle of Nova Scotia and the sources of the St. John being identical in the minds of men of that day, that that idea has not been followed up? And this leads to one of the questions about which it is impossible to say that any one can lay down beforehand any positive rule, or decide fairly, without a full knowledge of the facts of the particular case. The commissioners proceeded upon a conviction of the accuracy and correctness of the geographical delineation upon the paper on their table. Should it afterwards turn out, either that that delineation was in some small degree incorrect, or that it was materially incorrect, or that it was altogether incorrect, what is the rule for such a case, or how far are mutual and common mistakes of this kind to be corrected? On the face of Mitchell's map, (and a copy of that map was before the commissioners, as all admit,) the Madawaska is laid down as a north and south line, or a river running from the north to the south. Mr. Oswald accordingly says, " beginning at the northwest angle of Nova Scotia," and then tracing the boundary to the Mississippi, down that river to latitude thirty-one north, and so to the sea, and along the sea; and then says, the eastern boundary shall be the River St. John, from its source to its mouth. He goes, therefore, on the idea, evidently, that the source of the St. John is at the northwest angle of Nova Scotia; or else he leaves a *hiatus* in his description. The fact, as stated by you, Sir, is, that this delineation of the Madawaska was erroneous. It is not a north and south river. Errors in the calculation of the longitude had led to giving it a north and south direction on the map, whereas it should have had a northwest and southeast direction; and this error carries it, in order to conform to the fact, from forty to fifty miles farther to the west. Now, of the various questions which we may reasonably suppose to arise in a case of this sort, one would be, whether, in a case of mutual mistake of that kind, founded on a mutual misapprehension, this error was to be corrected, or whether the parties were to be bound by it, let the true course of that river be what it might. These questions are no longer of great importance to us, since the whole matter has been settled; but they may have their influence, and are worthy of consideration in an historical point of view.

The conflict of these maps is undoubtedly a pretty remarkable circumstance. The great mass of contemporaneous maps are favorable to the claims of the United States, and the remarks read by the President of the Society are most cogent to evince this. The treaty negotiated in Paris by Mr. Oswald, on the part of the British government, met with great opposition in Parliament. It was opposed on the very ground that it made a line of boundary "exceedingly inconvenient to Great Britain"; or, as a leading member of Parliament said, that it made the United States masters both of Nova Scotia and New Brunswick; and maps were published exhibiting this line exactly as claimed by the United States. These maps accompanied the Parliamentary papers and debates. Now, it is very extraordinary, it would be deemed almost incredible, that, if these maps, thus making out a case on which so much stress had been laid against the British ministry and their negotiation, had been erroneous, nobody in the Foreign Office, nor the minister, nor Mr. Oswald himself, should have one word to suggest against the accuracy of these maps. They defended the treaty and boun-

13 *

dary as presented on the maps, not going on the ground at all that those maps exhibited any erroneous presentation. Nevertheless, it is a matter of historical notoriety, that, from the time of the conclusion of that treaty till our day, it had been impossible to bring the two governments to any agreement on the matter. That on the words of the treaty, on the fair and necessary import of the words of the treaty, the case is, and has always been, with the United States, I very much doubt if any intelligent Englishman at this day would be found ready to deny. The argument has been, not that it is possible to show the line anywhere else, not that it is possible to bring the northwest angle of Nova Scotia this side of all the waters that run into the St. John, — I suppose no man of sense and common candor would undertake to maintain seriously such a proposition as that, — but the argument always has been that which was successfully pressed upon the king of Holland, that there is a difficulty in ascertaining the meaning of these words, when we look to localities, the highlands, the streams, and face of the country; and that difficulty led his Majesty, as difficulties of a similar character in other cases lead referees and arbitrators, into the notion of "splitting the difference," or compromising the claim, and drawing a line between that claimed by us, on the one hand, and that claimed by the British government, on the other. The English government, therefore, has always proceeded less upon the terms of the treaty themselves, than on those external considerations, and especially upon that of the great inconvenience of such a line of demarcation; and has founded upon that, as its natural result, another inference, the great improbability that England would have agreed to a line, unnecessarily, which separated her own provinces from one another, and made the communication between them dependent on the will and pleasure of a foreign power. The treaty of Washington, and the negotiations which preceded it, were entered into in a spirit of compromise and settlement.

When the present administration came into power, it determined, that, as an arbitration conducted with the greatest diligence, ability, and learning, on the part of the United States, had failed, and, as the matter was likely at all events to terminate in compromise at last, it might be quite as wise for the parties to attempt to compromise it themselves, on such considerations as they might see fit to adopt. Rather wiser this, indeed, you must surely admit, than to refer it to the consideration of a third power. It was upon that principle and in that spirit that the negotiations of 1842 were entered into. It was altogether in that amicable and rational spirit in which one neighbor says to another, according to the Scripture, " Let us agree with our adversary while we are in the way with him." Or as one might suppose two landed proprietors would have done, whose contiguous estates had projecting corners, and irregular lines, producing inconvenience in the management of plantations and farms. These things, in private life, are adjusted, not on the principle that one shall get all he can and grant nothing, or yield every thing and get nothing, but on the principle that the arrangement shall be for the mutual convenience and advantage of both parties, if the terms can be made fair, and equal, and honorable to both.

I believe, or at least I trust with great humility, that the judgment of the country will ultimately be, that the arrangement in this case was not an objectionable one. In the first place, I am willing to maintain everywhere, that the States of Massachusetts and Maine are better off this day than if Lord Ashburton had not signed the treaty, but had signed, in behalf of his government, a relinquishment of the claim of England to every square foot of the territory in dispute, and gone home. These States get more by the opening of the navigation of the rivers, and by the other benefits obtained through the treaty, than all the territory north of the St. John is worth, according to any estimate any one has yet been pleased to make of it. And as to the United States, if we can trust the highest military judgment in the country, if we can trust the general sense of intelligent persons acquainted with the subject, if we can trust our own common sense on looking to the map, an object of great importance has been attained for the United States and the State of New York, by the settlement of the question relative to the forty-fifth degree of north latitude, from Vermont to the St. Lawrence across the outlet of Lake Champlain. At the same time that these are gains or advantages, it does not follow, because this whole arrangement is highly advantageous to the States of Massachusetts and Maine, of great importance to the United States, and particularly useful to the States of New

York, Vermont, and New Hampshire, that therefore it must be disadvantageous or dishonorable to the other party to the treaty. By no means. It is a narrow and selfish, a crafty and mean spirit, which supposes that in things of this sort there can be nothing gained on one side without a corresponding loss on the other. Such arrangements may be, and always should be, for the mutual advantage of all parties. England has no reason to complain. She has obtained all she wanted, a reasonable boundary and a fair communication, a " convenient " communication and line of intercourse between her own provinces. Who is therefore to complain? Massachusetts and Maine, by the unanimous vote of all their agents, have adopted the treaty. It has been ratified by the English government. And though in party times, and in contests of men, some little dust may be thrown into the air, and some little excitement of the political elements may be produced occasionally, yet, so far as we know, no considerable discontent exists on the subject. How far the United States consider themselves benefited by it, let the votes of the two houses of Congress decide. A greater majority, I will undertake to say, was never given, in either house, in favor of any treaty, from the foundation of the government to the present time.

With respect, Sir, to the publication of Mr. Featherstonhaugh, and the tone of sundry articles in the London press, concerning the Paris map, I hope nobody supposes, so far as the government of the United States is concerned, that these things are exciting any sensation at Washington. Mr. Featherstonhaugh does not alarm us for our reputation. Assuming that there must either be a second arbitration or a settlement by compromise, finding that no arbitration which did not end in a compromise would be successful in settling the dispute, the government thought it its duty to invite the attention of the two States immediately concerned to the subject, — to ask them to take part in negotiations about to be entered into, with an assurance that no line of boundary should be agreed to without their consent, and without their consent, also, to all the conditions and stipulations of the treaty respecting the boundary. To this the two States agreed, with the limitation upon the consent of their agents, that, with regard to both States, it should be unanimous. In this state of things, undoubtedly it was the duty of the government of the United States to lay before these States thus admitted into the negotiations all the information in its power. Every office in Washington was ransacked, every book of authority consulted, the whole history of all the negotiations, from the treaty of Paris downward, was produced, and among the rest this discovery in Paris, to go for what it was worth. If these afforded any evidences to their minds to produce a conviction that it might be used to obscure their rights, to lead an arbitration into an erroneous, unjust compromise, that was all for their consideration. The map was submitted as evidence, together with all the other proofs and documents in the case, without the slightest reservation on the part of the government of the United States. I must confess that I did not think it a very urgent duty on my part to go to Lord Ashburton and tell him that I had found a bit of doubtful evidence in Paris, out of which he might perhaps make something to the prejudice of our claims, and from which he could set up higher claims for himself, or throw further uncertainty over the whole matter.

I will detain you, Sir, by no remarks on any other part of the subject. Indeed, I had no expectation of being called upon to speak on the subject, in regard to which my own situation is a delicate one. I shall be quite satisfied if the general judgment of the country shall be, in the first place, that nothing disreputable to the Union, nothing prejudicial to its interests in regard to the line of boundary, has been done in the treaty; and in the next place, and above all things, that a fair, honorable, manly disposition has been manifested by the government in settling the question, and putting an end to a controversy which has disturbed the relations of the country for fifty years, not always without some danger of breaking the public peace, often with the effect of disturbing commercial intercourse, spreading distrust between those having daily dealings with one another, and always tending to excite alarm, jealousy, and suspicion.

CONVENTION AT ANDOVER.

INTRODUCTORY NOTE.

The annual election in the autumn of 1843 was conducted with great spirit in Massachusetts. Large conventions came together in several of the counties of the Commonwealth. Among them, that which met at Andover on the 9th of November, composed of delegates from all the towns in Essex County, and attended by many persons from the neighboring parts of the State, was one of the largest and most animated. The presence of Mr. Webster had been requested by special invitation from a committee of the citizens of Andover, immediately charged with the arrangements for the day. He was accompanied by a large number of personal and political friends from Boston. The place of meeting was a sequestered dell of a circular form, partly surrounded and sheltered by the native forest, about a quarter of a mile from the village, where a platform had been erected in front of the amphitheatrical slope, which furnished accommodation to a very large audience.

The meeting was called to order by Hon. Stephen C. Phillips of Salem, on whose motion William Stevens, Esq., of Andover, was chosen to preside over the Convention. After a few appropriate remarks from the chair introducing the business of the day, Mr. Phillips addressed the Convention at considerable length and with great ability, and concluded by moving a series of resolutions, setting forth with much power the principles of the Whig party and the objects to be effected at the coming election. The concluding resolution was in the following terms : —

" *Resolved*, That while regarding ourselves as especially engaged in the defence of the Constitution, we welcome on this occasion the much-desired presence of the great Defender ; that we submit to his hands the responsible task of repelling all open or insidious attacks upon this palladium of our rights ; and that we shall rejoice once more to hear from his lips the counsels of wisdom and the exhortations of patriotism."

After the enthusiastic cheering had subsided with which this resolution had been received, Mr. Webster was introduced to the meeting and delivered the following speech.   The Rev. Professor Stuart, of the Theological Seminary at Andover, having taken an active part in all the arrangements of the day, the pamphlet edition of the Speech was dedicated to him by Mr. Webster in the following letter.*

" *Boston, November* **13, 1843.**

" My dear Sir, — At the suggestion of friends, I have looked over the printed reports of my remarks at Andover, for the purpose of publication, in a pamphlet, with some of the papers and extracts which I read, or to which I referred, put into an Appendix.

" I doubt, my dear Sir, whether, at this season of the year, and under the circumstances, I should have gone to Andover to address a large collection of people, if a disposition to comply with your own personal wishes, so kindly expressed, had not formed a large part of the inducement.

" Will you allow me now, as a manifestation of my esteem and regard, to present the pamphlet in this public manner to you ; and to avail myself of the opportunity for expressing the gratification which I feel in knowing, not only your intelligent and warm regard for the maintenance of the institutions of the country, but also, that amidst the duties of your chair, and the labor which you are known to bestow on the deeper studies belonging to your profession, you still find time to acquaint yourself extensively with its great and leading interests.

" Daniel Webster.

" To Rev. Professor Moses Stuart, Andover."

---

* The topics of this speech, and Mr. Webster's political course generally, were made the subject of two very able letters written by Professor Stuart and published about this time in a pamphlet form.

CONVENTION AT ANDOVER.*

IT is not without considerable reluctance, fellow-citizens, that I present myself before this meeting to-day. It had been my purpose to abstain, for the time to come, from all public addresses before such vast assemblages. The invitation, however, came from sources which I so much respect, and appeared to urge my attendance with so much earnestness, that it was not in my yielding nature to withhold my consent. And that consent I cannot regret, when I look around me and before me, and see such a collection from Andover, from all parts of this county, and from the adjacent counties.

Gentlemen, I concur most zealously in the hope of the election of George N. Briggs and John Reed to the offices of Governor and Lieutenant-Governor of the Commonwealth, and am ready to perform any duty towards the accomplishment of what we all desire. I do not propose, on this occasion, any extended discussion of State politics; but I may say, generally, that I wish to see Massachusetts restored to what she has been, and characteristically is. In the proceedings of last year, I have seen much that does not belong to Massachusetts; much that has no flavor, no relish, of the Old Bay State about it. Gentlemen, I entertain not a particle of doubt that the good sense and good feelings of the people, when once aroused, — and they are now aroused, — will accomplish all that patriotism can desire, to this end. The proof of this I see, not in a noisy and vaporing spirit among the people, but in the deep earnestness and sobriety with which sensible and patriotic men are preparing for the performance of their duty, as electors, at the present crisis.

* An Address delivered at a Convention of the Whigs of Essex County, Massachusetts, held at Andover, on the 9th of November, 1843.

Gentlemen, the Andover Committee have desired me to address this assembly on a number of vastly important topics. It is quite impossible that I should enter far into so broad a field; I shall confine myself, in the remarks I have to make, to some of the subjects suggested by them.

They desire that I should express my sentiments upon the respective duties of the national and State governments; upon the duties of the general government to farmers, merchants, and manufacturers; upon the importance, the necessity, of a sacred observance of public faith; upon the currency and its relations, and the utility and importance of a universal medium of payment.

In reference to the discussion of these topics, I am embarrassed by the fact, that I have little new to say of any of them. By the favor of the people, I have been a good deal in public life, and upon these subjects my opinions are well known. They are unchanged. And I avail myself of this occasion, not so much to announce any new doctrines held by me, as to refer to sentiments long entertained, and often expressed.

The general government, all agree, is vested with certain powers, and held to certain duties. It is its duty to defend the country from foreign invasion, to provide armies and equip navies; the treaty-making power is confided to it; the superintendence of the foreign relations, and the maintenance of the country's honor in foreign States, belong to it. This all acknowledge. But upon its domestic duties there has grown up a difference of opinion of great breadth, leading to diverse conclusions on the one side and the other.

Upon these duties it is my intention briefly to say something, and it is my wish that all remarks made upon the subject may be taken in that spirit of conciliation and candor from which they proceed. I wish to persuade others of their correctness. I know we have a common destiny; that the good of the whole country embraces the good of all its parts; and I desire that at all times, by free and candid discussion and consideration, the differences of opinion which men entertain on these topics may be reconciled, and that all may approach, and finally stand upon, the same ground.

A contest has agitated the country for years upon the true extent of the powers of Congress in two particulars; —

1. As to its authority over the currency;

2. As to its power to encourage domestic industry by discrimination in laying duties on articles of manufacture imported from abroad.

And first, as to the currency. All agree that Congress possesses the power to regulate commerce, for that provision is found in the Constitution in terms; and that it has the power to coin money, for those words are also found in the Constitution. But there is a wide difference of opinion as to what duties are or are not fairly inferable from these grants of power. In regard to this matter, which has so long divided the country, and which will continue to agitate it till it shall be effectually settled, I must begin by a reference to some general principles and leading facts.

Congress possesses the commercial power, that is, the power of regulating commerce, and the power of coining money; and it may issue its own bills of credit. No State can either coin money, regulate commerce, or emit its own bills of credit. But, right or wrong, banking corporations are established under State authority, and issue bills; and these bills form, in fact, the mass of the circulating medium of the country. And now, since the use of these bills has become almost, if not wholly, universal, the question arises, On what government devolves the power of regulating the paper currency? Now, Gentlemen, in my opinion, which I have entertained for many years, the general government is bound to take care of the currency of the country; I think that it has a duty beyond merely coining money and fixing its value; that the power to regulate commerce gives Congress authority over that great instrument and means of commerce, the actual circulating medium of the country; and that if paper is to take the place of coin, Congress is bound to see that it is safe paper, and such as is not likely to defraud and oppress the people, to become base in character, or run to excess. On these topics my opinions have been frequently expressed, and are well known.*

As I have observed already, Gentlemen, I have very little

---

* In the original pamphlet edition of this speech, large extracts were here made from speeches in the Senate of the 28th of September, 1837, and the 12th of March, 1838, which will be found in a subsequent volume of this collection; and from the speech in Faneuil Hall, of the 24th of July, 1838, in Volume I. p. 417.

that is new to say on these points. The ground I have ever taken, and to which I adhere to this day, is, that if Congress is bound to furnish a currency for the people, as well as for the government, then something beyond a sub-treasury, something more than a vault, or series of vaults, where the public money can be collected, and whence it can be distributed, is necessary; on the other hand, if Congress is not bound to do this, then it may resort to any scheme it may deem proper for the collection and disbursement of revenue; although, even for that purpose, it is quite idle and ridiculous, in my opinion, to talk about vaults, and safes, and bolts, and locks.

Now, Gentlemen, there are three propositions which I would gladly submit to every candid man in every part of the country; because it is my wish to establish the principles I espouse, in the minds of men, by convincing them that they are honest, just, and will tend to the benefit of community. These propositions are, —

1st. That paper, in the present state and condition of society, will, and must, constitute the greater part of the currency, — the mass of the circulation.

All the humbug about a specie currency, a hard-money system, is altogether unworthy of a man of sense. We know that we *must*, from some source or other, have paper for circulation, and for the greater part of the circulation. Is there a man here, is there a man anywhere, who will say without a blush, that he expects an exclusive specie currency? Can any sensible man so say, without feeling his cheek burn with shame? There is none such. Well, then, is there any one not satisfied, —

2d. That a part, at least, of this paper currency, should be in every part of the country of equal value, and that value equivalent to specie?

Is it not highly desirable that we should have a circulating medium of universal receivability, if I may use such a word? The inhabitants of Maine, Georgia, the valley of the Mississippi, — is it not to be wished that they all may have some paper which every body will take? All candid men must admit that it is. It is an object of high importance that the people of Illinois, Indiana, Alabama, should have something which they can remit, without loss, to pay the manufacturers of Essex for their goods; it is as great an object to the Essex manufacturers that they should. Well, if this be admitted, there is only one more proposition, and that is, —

3d. That no State institution, nothing but the authority of the United States, can furnish such a universal circulating medium.

Can any State institution furnish such a currency? Have we seen any instance of it whatever? We all know the contrary. We have, in Massachusetts, bills of State banks which are good and current throughout Massachusetts. They have the same in Virginia. But if any of you were to go to-morrow to Richmond, or Petersburg, you would not find your Massachusetts money current there, although, indeed, you might find brokers who would give you a premium on the bills, for the purpose of Northern remittances; still, your Massachusetts bills would not be generally received.

The citizens of each State know the condition of their own institutions; and they trust them as far as they ought. But they do not know, and ought not to be expected to know, the condition and credit of all the institutions of all the States. On the other hand, they do know the general laws and the general institutions of the general government, and the credit to which those institutions are entitled. We must then revert to the government which has the control of commerce and the control of the currency, whose "spread eagle" is good everywhere. And it is but a reasonable and just demand, to require such a government to give us a currency which shall be welcome everywhere, and trusted everywhere.

Now, where is this power? I answer, In the authority of Congress to regulate commerce, and the great agent of commerce, money. Congress has the power of commercial regulation by the Constitution; it has also the power to coin; and according to Mr. Madison's matured judgment, the power to coin implies the power to say what shall take the place of the coinage, if that coinage be displaced by paper. I will not go over the whole range of the constitutional argument. Suffice it to say, that those who made the Constitution did not doubt this power. General Washington did not doubt it, for he established an institution for this very purpose; or at least, it was established under his immediate authority and sanction. Mr. Madison did not doubt it, and I mention his name because his authority is much relied on, as not generally favoring liberal constructions of constitutional powers. If not convinced in his own private judgment, he said, as any reasonable man would say, that the Constitution had thus been long interpreted, that its meaning was fixed and must not be disturbed. That was right. We have had a bank for forty years; some say now it is unconstitutional. Will they say so forty years hence? Will they then think that what was thought right by our fathers and grandfathers, who formed the Constitution and established the government, was wholly wrong? I suspect not. We must take the meaning of the Constitution as it has been solemnly fixed, — fixed by practice, fixed by successive acts of Congress, fixed by solemn judicial decision, — or we never shall have any settled meaning at all. It is absurd to say, that no precedent, no practice, no judicial decision, no assent of successive legislators, nor all these together, can fix the meaning of an article in the fundamental law.

I am well aware, Gentlemen, that at the present moment, and in the commercial States, the evils of a disordered currency are partially remedied, and not so severely felt. But in some parts of the country they are as great as ever. In the South and West, there is no money which deserves the name. The people trade almost wholly by barter. What they do call money is entirely without a fixed or general value; and the great depreciation and fluctuation in the currency is the cause of much demoralization in the community, and a fruitful source of other evils. Of all bad systems this is the worst. And though we in this part of the country, just now, feel no particular harm from this source, yet the evil day will come.

There are certain laws of trade which will always operate, so long as man is man, and which cannot be violated with impunity; and just as surely as this is the case, just so sure shall we again feel the effects of a disordered currency. There is now, in the mercantile phrase, a better feeling in the community, at least in the Atlantic States. There is an appearance of returning prosperity and a revival of business; but there are a thousand banks in the country, ready to lend money to good customers, under the doctrine, to which I cannot wholly agree, that all safe business paper may be discounted without danger. A plenty of money will raise prices, prosperity will beget excess, and excess must result in revulsion. And these alternations will be our lot and our history so long as we have no general regulator of the currency.

Now, I will not say, I never have said, that a Bank of the United States is absolutely necessary; but I have said that it has been tried for forty years with success, and is therefore entitled to respectful consideration. Some eight years ago, in the Senate of the United States, I said that a national bank had done much good to the country, yet it was not worth my while to propose its reëstablishment while there was no general call of the people for such a measure. I remain of that opinion. I have said, more recently, that a national bank whose capital should be derived from private subscriptions, and with the power of private discounts, is out of the question. I think so still, though it may be I am mistaken. My reason is, that State institutions for these purposes have become so much multiplied, and that many States derive large portions of their revenue from taxes upon the capital of such banks. Nevertheless, I am quite willing to agree that a Bank of the United States, upon the old model, is perfectly constitutional; and if, in the opinion of a future Congress and in the judgment of the country, such an institution should be deemed expedient, it shall have my hearty support. But my opinion is, that the country much more needs some institution under national authority, with power to restrain in some just mode the amount of paper issues, than it needs a bank which may itself make large discounts to individuals.

I have thus spoken upon commerce and the currency. These lead directly to the tariff, or the policy of encouraging domestic industry by laying discriminating duties on foreign importations.

I wish to state my opinions on this topic with some degree of precision, because I believe there is a sort of ultraism prevailing with regard to it, characteristic of the age. People run into extremes, not only in politics, but in all other matters. They are either on the Ganges, or at the extremity of the West. There are men who would carry a tariff to prohibition. Again, there are those who assert it to be perfectly unconstitutional to lay duties with the least regard to favoring or encouraging the products of our own country. My opinion is, that the power of favoring or encouraging productions of our own, by just discriminations in imposing duties for revenue on imports, does belong to Congress, and ought to be exercised in all proper cases.

This, Gentlemen, is my opinion, and I should be perfectly willing to discuss the matter with any candid man in the Commonwealth.

There are two propositions to which I invite your attention; —

1st. Congress has the power to lay duties of impost. No State has this power. This is a most important consideration.

2d. Before the adoption of the Constitution, and while the States could lay impost duties, several of them laid such duties, with discriminations avowedly intended to foster their own products. They now can do no such thing. It must accordingly be done by Congress, or not at all.

Now the power of Congress is to regulate commerce. And in all English history, and all our own history, down to the Revolution, and to the time of the adoption of the Constitution, importation of some articles was encouraged, and of others discouraged or prohibited, by *regulations of trade.* The regulation of trade, therefore, was a term of well-known meaning, and did comprehend the duty or object of discriminating, with a view to favor home productions. We find this to have been so in England, from the time of her Tudors and Stuarts down; and in America, the opinion I have stated was held by Otis, Adams, and the other great and eminent men of the Revolution. But upon this point I need not dwell, for the whole doctrine has been placed upon immutable foundations by a son of your own county, a most distinguished member of the Senate of the United States (Hon. Rufus Choate), in his speech of March, 1842.

The amount of the whole matter is this. History instructs us, that, before the Constitution was formed, the States laid duties of imposts; but each only for itself, and therefore the duties were very different and unequal; and the States which laid duties for the protection of their own manufactures were immediately exposed to competition from others that had no manufactures, who would open their ports freely to the goods taxed by their neighbors. We see at once how vain it would be for one State to look only to her own interests, while all the others were looking only to theirs. Take a supposed instance, for example, in the case of Massachusetts and Rhode Island. Massachusetts had manufactures, Rhode Island had not. Massachusetts laid duties on imported goods, Rhode Island did not. The consequence would be, that the goods taxed by Massachusetts in her seaport towns would be brought free into Newport or Providence, and it would only be by a cordon of custom-houses throughout the whole extent of her border, that Massachusetts could prevent the introduction of those goods into her territories.

The case is suppositious, but I speak to Massachusetts men who understand the effect of such a system, whose fathers experienced it, and I tell them that this obvious effect produced in Massachusetts, as much as any thing, the disposition to come under a general government, and to ratify the Constitution. It was, in fact, the full belief of the people, that this power of laying discriminating duties was granted to Congress, as part of the revenue power, and that it would be exercised. They had a right to expect, and did expect, that it would be used beneficially for their interests.

The whole history of the country from 1783 to 1788 proves this. That history is as important as that of any period of our national existence. We see in it the then infant States struggling under a load of debt incurred in the sacred cause of the Revolution, struggling under the extinction of commerce and prostration of manufactures, and struggling all in vain. These things produced that strong disposition which prevailed from 1784 to 1788, to establish a uniform system of commercial regulations, and extend also all proper encouragement to manufactures.

Gentlemen, a native of Massachusetts, certainly inferior to none in sagacity, and whose name confers honor upon the whole country, Dr. Benjamin Franklin, in 1787, indicated his sentiments upon these points in a very remarkable manner. The convention to deliberate upon the formation of the Constitution was held in Philadelphia, in May, 1787. Dr. Franklin was, if I remember aright, the President, as the office was then called, of Pennsylvania, and was chosen also as a member of the convention. As the delegates were assembling, he invited them to a meeting at his house, on which occasion a paper on this subject was read, which was subsequently printed, and to extracts from which I would call your attention.* They will show you what were the sentiments of Dr. Franklin. They prove that far-sighted sagacity, which could discern what was then visible to so few eyes; and that wisdom, which pointed out a course so greatly beneficial.

Let me now revert to the opinions of Massachusetts in this respect; to this good old Bay State, whose citizens we are proud to be, and whose early espousal of the cause of a national government is so well known. I will observe, first, that at the time these opinions were sanctioned by Dr. Franklin, and, indeed, till a very recent period, the manufacturers of the country were shop-workmen; tailors, hatters, smiths, shoemakers, and others, who wrought in their own shops; but still the principle is the same as if they were banded into corporations. He who denies to Congress the power to protect manufactures, as now carried on, denies protection as much to every individual workman as to Andover or Lowell. Let all classes of artisans, in the cities and villages, think well of this.

Now, Gentlemen, it so happened, that, in the years of severe disaster between the peace and the formation of the Constitution, the merchants and mechanics of Boston had their attention called to the subject, and their proceedings, only a little earlier than the paper just referred to, sprang from the same sense of necessity. I will trouble you to listen to some of them, which I gather from the publications of that day.

At a numerous and respectable meeting of "the merchants, traders, and others, convened at Faneuil Hall," on Saturday, the 16th of April, 1785, the following, among other resolutions, were adopted : —

"Whereas no commercial treaty is at present established between these United States and Great Britain, and whereas certain British merchants, factors, and agents from England are now residing in this town, who have received large quantities of English goods, and are in expectation of receiving further supplies, imported in British bottoms, or otherwise, greatly to the hinderance of freight in all American vessels ; and as many more such persons are daily expected to arrive among us, which threatens an entire monopoly of all British importations in the hands of such

* See Appendix, No. I.

merchants, agents, or factors, which we apprehend will operate to the prejudice of the interest of this country ; therefore, to prevent as far as possible the evil tendency of such persons continuing among us (excepting those of them who shall be approved by the selectmen), and to discourage the sale of their merchandise, we, the merchants, traders, and others of the town of Boston, do agree, —

" First, That a committee be appointed to draft a petition to Congress, representing the embarrassments under which the trade now labors, and the still greater to which it is exposed ; and that the said committee be empowered and directed to write to the several seaports in this State, requesting them to join with the merchants in this town in similar applications to Congress, immediately to regulate the trade of the United States agreeably to the powers vested in them by the government of this Commonwealth ; and also to obtain instructions to their representatives at the next General Court, to call the attention of their delegates in Congress to the importance of bringing forward such regulations as shall place our commerce on a footing of equality.

" Voted, That the said committee be requested to write to the merchants in the several seaports of the other United States, earnestly recommending to them an immediate application to the legislatures of their respective States to vest such powers in Congress (if not already done) as shall be competent to the interesting purposes aforesaid, and also to petition Congress to make such regulations as shall have the desired effect.

" Voted, That we do pledge our honor that we will not directly or indirectly purchase any goods of, or have any commercial connections whatever with, such British merchants, factors, or agents as are now residing among us, or may hereafter arrive, either from England or any part of the British dominions (excepting such persons as shall be approved as aforesaid), and we will do all in our power to prevent all persons acting under us from having any commercial intercourse with them, until the salutary purposes of these resolutions shall have been accomplished."

So far the merchants. Now what said the mechanics, the artisans, the shop-workmen, to this ? At an adjourned meeting of persons belonging to those classes at the Green Dragon Tavern, on Monday, the 25th of April, 1785, the following resolutions, among others, were passed : —

" Voted, that a committee be appointed by this body to draft a petition to the next General Court, setting forth the difficulties the manufacturers of this town labor under by the importation of certain articles (to be enumerated in the petition), and praying a prohibition, or that such duties may be laid as will effectually protect the manufacture of the same.

" Voted, That we do bear our public testimony against sending away our circulating cash for foreign remittances, as this practice, we conceive, is calculated to impoverish the country, to distress individuals in the prosecution of their business and in the payment of their taxes.

" Voted, That a committee be appointed to write to the committee of merchants and traders of this town, inclosing them a copy of these votes, and desiring a mutual correspondence on the subject."

The committee appointed under the foregoing resolution addressed the following letter to "the Committee of Merchants, Traders, and others" : —

" *Boston, April* 26, 1785.

" GENTLEMEN, — We, being appointed by the tradesmen and manufacturers of this town to inform you what measures they have adopted at this important crisis of our affairs, beg leave to inclose a copy of their proceedings, which they hope will meet with your approbation.

" We shall, by all measures in our power, endeavor to cultivate that harmony so essentially necessary at this time, and recollect with pleasing satisfaction the union that has always subsisted between the merchants, tradesmen, and manufacturers of this town ; we should regret if any measures should be now adopted by either, to impair that affection which it has ever been our happiness to boast.

" But as the several branches of our occupations have of late been materially affected by European importations, we conceive ourselves in duty bound to prevent, if possible, those supplies either by foreigners or our own merchants.

" We have therefore voted a petition to be presented to the next General Court for this purpose, and as we doubt not the sincerity of your declaration ' to encourage the manufactures of this country,' we trust you will support with your whole influence any measures calculated to promote so desirable an object.

" We are, Gentlemen, with every sentiment of esteem,
        " Your obedient and humble servants,
                JOHN GRAY,
                BENJAMIN AUSTIN, JR.,
                SAMUEL G. JARVIS,
                JOHN SKINNER,
                SARSON BELCHER.

" To the Committee of Merchants, Traders, and others."

Well, how did the merchants receive this? I will show you. Here is a letter, signed in their behalf, by that great patriot, and prince of merchants, John Hancock. Here was a full coöperation between merchants and manufacturers, for the united support of their own interests.

"*Boston, May* 2, 1785.

"GENTLEMEN, — Your communications of the 26th ult. were interesting and agreeable. Our situation is truly critical. To the United States in Congress we look for effectual relief, and to them we have accordingly appealed.

"We rejoice to find our sentiments and views harmonizing with yours, and hope that our united exertions will be crowned with the desired success.

"We shall cheerfully use what influence we have in promoting and encouraging the manufactures of our country, and for obtaining at the next General Court such restrictions and excises as may have so happy a tendency.

"We derive great support from that unanimity which appears to actuate our respective proceedings, and while that subsists we can no more despair of the commerce, trade, and manufactures, than of the liberties of America.

"We are, Gentlemen, with much esteem,

"Your most humble servants,

"JOHN HANCOCK,

In the name and in behalf of the Committee
of Merchants, Tradesmen, and others.

"To JOHN GRAY, ESQ., Chairman of the Committee of Tradesmen, Manufacturers, &c."

But the mechanics did not limit their addresses to the merchants of Boston. They addressed a spirited and sensible letter to all the tradesmen and manufacturers of Massachusetts, in which the same topics are urged with force and earnestness.[*]

Now, what is all this? and what does it prove? Why, though at peace with England, our ships could not visit her ports, or, in fact, those of any European nation. We had no national flag; we were unknown upon the seas; consequently, British vessels enjoyed the monopoly of our trade. So great, indeed, was the depression among all classes, that some gentlemen, who had a little property left from the Revolu-

[*] See Appendix, No. II.

tion, made a contribution to build three or four ships, on the Mystic River, so as to give some employment to working ship-builders. But, having no national character, and no means of sustaining commerce, these ships rotted on the ways, or at the wharves. The merchants of Boston thought that voluntary agreements were the only means in their power, and the agreement quoted above was one result of their opinions.

Now, Gentlemen, you have seen what happened in this state of things. The merchants having thus resolved not to use goods imported in foreign bottoms, in order to protect their own interests, the manufacturing classes assembled, and, in view of protecting *their* interests, they resolved not to use imported goods at all. They appealed to the merchants, as you have seen, and the appeal was answered with expressions of sympathy and support. The artisans, with Paul Revere and John Gray at their head, next addressed themselves to the mechanics in various parts of the State, setting forth the fatal consequences to their interests, not only of importations in British vessels, but of importations of foreign goods, free of tax, in any vessels whatever. They petitioned Governor Bowdoin and the Legislature for relief, by the establishment of imposts. But, as I have before asked, what could a single State do?

This state of things continued till 1788, when the Massachusetts Convention to consider the Constitution was held in Boston. Some of the most eminent persons who have shed lustre on the State were members of that Convention, and many of them, as is well known, felt great doubts about adopting the Constitution. Among these were two individuals, none other than John Hancock and Samuel Adams, the proscribed patriots. But the energy, determination, perseverance, and earnestness of the mechanics and tradesmen of Boston influenced even these wise and great men, and tended to, and did, in an eminent degree, contribute to the ratification of the Constitution. Any man will see this, who will look into the public transactions of that day.

There was a particular set of resolutions, founded on this very idea of favoring home productions, full of energy and decision, passed by the mechanics of Boston. And where did the mechanics of Boston meet to pass them? Full of the influence of these feelings, they congregated at the head-quarters of the

Revolution. I see, waving among the banners before me, that of the old Green Dragon. It was there, in Union Street, that John Gray, Paul Revere, and others of their class, met for consultation. There, with earnestness and enthusiasm, they passed their resolutions. A committee carried them to the Boston delegation in the Convention. Mr. Samuel Adams asked Colonel Revere, how many mechanics were at the meeting; and Colonel Revere answered, " More than there are stars in heaven."

The resolutions had their effect. The Constitution was established, and a universal burst of joy from all classes, merchants, manufacturers, and mechanics, proclaimed the exultation of the people at the thrice happy event. The journals of the day tell us, that

" On the ratification being declared, a very large concourse of spectators testified their satisfaction by repeated huzzas, and the whole Convention, having been previously invited, partook with a number of respectable citizens of a decent repast prepared in the Senate Chamber where, in mutual congratulations and testimonials of satisfaction, all party ideas were done away, and such a spirit of joy, union, and urbanity diffused, as, if continued, must be attended with the most happy consequences through the Commonwealth. The toasts given were truly conciliatory, and were, we believe, drunk with sincerity by every one present. All appeared willing to bury the hatchet of animosity, and to smoke the calumet of union and love.

" After this repast, the Convention dissolved."

Thus far the proceedings of the Convention. Now for those of the people.

" The Committee of Tradesmen met, and, by public advertisement, requested the attendance of the mechanics and artisans of every description in town at Faneuil Hall, in order to form and proceed in grand procession therefrom, to testify their approbation of the ratification of the Federal Constitution by the Convention."

This " grand procession " took place; and the artisans, mechanics, and manufacturers of Boston, together with the merchants and all other classes, indulged in the hope, not more sanguine than the event warranted, that, under the operation of the new national Constitution, prosperity would return, business revive, cheerfulness and contentment overspread the land, and

15 *

the country go rapidly forward in its career of growth and success.

But, Gentlemen, this sentiment and feeling were not merely the sentiment and feeling of Massachusetts. We may look at the debates in all the State conventions, and the expositions of all the greatest men in the country, particularly in Massachusetts and Virginia, the great Northern and Southern stars, and we shall find it everywhere held up as the main reason for the adoption of the Constitution, that it would give the general government the power to regulate commerce and trade. This power was thus considered established by the framers of the Constitution, and has been steadily recognized by the government. It was distinctly and in terms recognized by the very first act laying duties of imposts; and notwithstanding doubts and denial of it in excited times, it yet pervades the whole history of our legislation. The power, therefore, being clear, and its application in times past certain, the remaining question respects its utility and expediency.

Here, again, let me say, that I wish no exercise of the power, without much consideration and moderation. The shipping interest, the mercantile interest, as well as the mechanic interest, are concerned; and both and all must be looked after and cared for. I wish, in fixing all laws on this subject, that nothing excessive may be introduced; that no traps shall be laid; that nothing unexpected shall spring up in the way of the mercantile, or any other interest; and that nothing shall be enacted which will be expedient for the whole country.

And here let me remark upon the extreme injustice of attacking the tariff on the ground that it favors the rich corporations of New England. We know that this opinion has no real foundation. We know that corporations are only partnerships, carried on in a more convenient manner than they could be by indenture; that they are no monopolies; and that it is because of their convenience only that they are employed.

Gentlemen, I believe that a tariff of moderate duties, carefully laid, is expedient for the whole country; —

1st. Because it augments the aggregate of national wealth, by stimulating labor.

Moderate imposts upon such articles as we can and do manufacture must inevitably furnish a stimulus to our labor, and it is now the general, nearly the universal opinion, that labor is the source of wealth. Capital is a stimulus to labor. Now to me it appears very plain, that the stimulus can be applied here with greater effect than at a distance, and that, consequently, the country will be benefited accordingly. On this point, I am aware of the authority of McCulloch and Mr. Senior, writers of the very highest repute, both of whom I have the honor to know, and whom I greatly esteem.

Mr. McCulloch is a gentleman who has contributed more than any man of our age to a correct knowledge of statistics and political economy. But, if I may venture to say so, I think some of his opinions a little too abstract, or at least not applicable here. Our condition, I think, is peculiar; we have no such broad distinction between capital and labor as prevails in England. There is, indeed, no subject which so much requires an essay to set forth all its prominence, importance, and peculiarity, as American labor; there is nothing like it on the globe; and there never was any thing like it.

Our labor reaches beyond mere subsistence. In Europe the case is different. We know that, with us, labor earns for itself and creates a capital; and, looking at our country, we see that for this reason her condition is, and will be, most fortunate and happy for a century to come.

Gentlemen, the labor of the United States is respectable. We are emphatically a country of labor; and labor with us is not reluctant drudgery. It is cheerful, contented, spirited, because it is respectable, and because it is certain of its reward. Labor everywhere mixes itself with capital. The fields around us, how many of them are tilled by their owners! The shops in our towns, how many are occupied by their proprietors, for the convenient pursuit of their callings! Hence, in the United States, we see labor and capital mixed together in a degree unequalled in the world. What is the value of a hundred acres of land at the foot of the Rocky Mountains or in the remote regions of Spanish South America? Nothing at all. There is no value to any land till man has mixed his labor with it. But the moment an American laborer drives his plough through these acres, or fells a tree upon them, that moment he creates a capital, which every step he takes, and every stroke he gives, constantly augments. He thus not only lives by labor, but every day's work, while it gives him subsistence, adds to his means, his property, his capital.   Where else in this world shall we find the same state of things to such a degree?

I have ventured to express a doubt whether all the opinions of McCulloch are applicable to us; but I acknowledge with pleasure, that on the subject of the importance of high wages he has expressed himself in the justest and soundest terms.   He has laid down maxims on this subject which lie at the foundation of national prosperity in its highest state.   This is what he says: —

" The best interests of society require that the rate of wages should be elevated as high as possible ; that a taste for the comforts, luxuries, and enjoyments of human life should be widely diffused, and, if possible, interwoven with the national habits and prejudices.   A low rate of wages, by rendering it impossible for increased exertions to obtain any considerable increase of comforts and enjoyment, effectually hinders any such exertion from ever being made, and is, of all others, the most powerful cause of that idleness and apathy that contents itself with what can barely continue animal existence.   The experience of all ages and nations proves that high wages are at once the keenest spur, the most powerful stimulus to unremitting and assiduous exertion, and the best means of attaching the people to the institutions under which they live."

On this subject, Gentlemen, I refer with approbation and pleasure to a very able speech in Congress, ten years ago, by Mr. Nathan Appleton, which I heartily commend to the perusal of every one who desires to see the principles of political economy applicable to our condition fairly set forth.

It is our good fortune, Gentlemen, to live in a country distinguished, as the whole world says, by a high rate of wages.   We are here this day, in the midst of a county agricultural, manufacturing, and commercial.   This very township and its institutions show the happy results of this condition of things.   It is a beautiful township ; few are more so.   In an agricultural point of view it is very fertile.   There are streams in it which afford facilities, improved to the fullest extent of their capacity, to turn mills and drive machinery.   And what rate of wages do we see existing here?   We find that female operatives, after paying their board, receive two dollars, or nine shillings sterling, per week.   Is there any thing like this in the manufacturing districts of England, France, Germany, or Prussia? Nothing. The male workmen, after paying their board, in like manner, clear twelve dollars a month. We cannot see this in any other country. There is also a degree of personal elevation of character, of respectability, of education, among our laboring classes, which is to be found nowhere else. To instance, again, in Andover; here is a township of about nine miles square, occupied by an intelligent, well-fed, well-clothed, well-housed population; there are ten or twelve neat and commodious places of worship; twenty of those gems of New England, free schools, where the sons of the rich and the poor meet on an equal footing, and receive the same useful instruction. Here, too, is a classical seminary, which has long been distinguished for its ripe and elegant scholars; and, of more recent establishment, a theological institution, the piety, talents, and learning of whose professors have made it most honorably known, not only in the United States, but in Europe.

Why should we wish to change this happy condition, by any speculation, or experiment, which will not be likely to improve, and may destroy it?

I confess that many persons in the Commonwealth, and perhaps in the crowd around me, entertain opinions directly the reverse of those which, in their operation and practical effect, have produced, as I think, these results and this state of things. I attribute them to misapprehensions, and am therefore desirous that our opponents, for I will not call them enemies or adversaries, may hear us with a spirit of candor, so that we may see if our opinions and actions cannot be made to coincide.

Gentlemen, I believe, —

2d. That the tariff favors every interest of the country. The sugar-planters of Louisiana, we know, it encourages. The cotton-growers of the South, I firmly believe, it helps, because I deem the maintenance of a steady market here of very essential benefit to them. I believe, moreover, that it is favorable to the agricultural interest; but upon this I need not enlarge, as I have recently, in another place, taken occasion to speak upon this point.

There is one essential difference between the United States and England, with respect to agriculture. There the produce of the soil does not feed the population; consumers, therefore, demand a free importation of foreign produce. With us it is exactly the reverse. Our agriculture is productive far beyond our consumption, and the great objects of our producers are an augmented demand at home, and as much increase as possible in the demand from abroad. We are sellers, the English are buyers, of agricultural produce, and this makes all the difference in the world in the reasoning upon the case.

Gentlemen, the manufacturing interest is not a local interest, and so much progress has elsewhere been made in certain manufactures, that I cannot but think a more just feeling, as to this point, must follow. There is hardly a State at the South, that has not, at this moment, cotton manufactories; and in New York there are now for sale considerable quantities of Southern goods. I have been furnished by a friend with statements on this subject of the most instructive character.*

I say, therefore, to all our brethren, that the manufacturing is not an exclusive, but a general interest, and is to be properly sustained, not by persuading the North to vote down the South, for fear the South should destroy our interests, but by patriotism, moderation, and mutual conciliation and regard.

A tariff does not necessarily increase prices. One year after the present tariff was established, many articles embraced in its provisions were considerably lower than they had before been.† And I ask any one if there is now any complaint of undue high prices in any article to which the present tariff extends.

The Andover Committee, Gentlemen, have mentioned the public lands. Upon this topic I have but very little now to say. Congress has affirmed the proposition, that, in the present condition of the country, the proceeds of the public lands belong rightfully to the States. If it be so, then I say that *this* is the time to make the appropriation of the lands, because now is the time when the States need all their means.

In my opinion, though I reproach nobody, for I myself voted for the bill, our legislation upon this subject has been inconsistent in this; that when the land-bill was passed, provision was made that the appropriation should be void in case of war, and

---

* See Appendix, No. III.   † See Appendix, No. IV.

at any rate limited to five years. I think this inconsistent, and a sort of contradiction; because, if the lands rightfully belong to the States, they belong to them as well in war as in peace, and for ever, as well as for a time limited. And if we do any thing in regard to the public lands, by way of ceding their income to the States, the good of the country requires that it should be done once for all. The good of the country requires that this question should be removed from the political arena, and disposed of permanently.

Connected somewhat with this topic is the present condition of the public credit. We live in a State, the credit of which is good, is unimpaired. But there are States in the Union whose credit is gone, and I believe that their people, and all the people, should make every effort to restore that credit, at whatever sacrifice of personal convenience or comfort. There is danger of remissness in this respect, danger of want of effort and want of resolution. But we should all remember that we all suffer. The country as a whole country, and every individual as a part of the country, suffer daily from the existing state of things respecting those State debts. We are all of the same American family. None of us can shake off that character, or, when abroad, disavow the relationship. Our States are much more than independent individuals or corporations; they are sovereign, but connected communities. Their faith is public faith; their failure is the failure of public faith. And each and every one of us suffers from it. Nothing in a State can be trustworthy, if the State itself be not.

I hold in my hand an address from the Congress of the Confederation to the people, in 1783, one of the darkest periods in our history. It shows you what principles, what honesty, what determination to preserve the public faith untarnished, pervaded the bosoms of the great men of those days. I commend it to your reflections.*

This declaration of Congress is in favor of paying the debts of the States, and of every one of the States. A similar crisis has arisen now, and our country is again put to the severest test of republican virtue. I may say that the question which now

* See Appendix, No. V.

rings throughout Europe is this : " Will the republican governments of America maintain their faith ? " If they will not, they
must be abandoned.   The society of the world cannot exist
without faith among nations, any more than society at home
can exist without faith and trust among individuals.

But I say this faith and credit will be redeemed.   At any sacrifice it must be.   The tarnish shall be wiped off from the non-
paying States, the credit of the country restored.   And now is
the time to apply the public lands to this end.   The doctrine of
repudiation is at present avowed by nobody.   Nobody will stand
up, and give the State to which he belongs open advice to adopt
that measure.   Times are growing better; there are omens of
returning prosperity ; and I am sure that true and good men, in
every State, will exert themselves for the entire reëstablishment
of character and credit.

Gentlemen, having detained you so long, I beg to say a little,
and it shall be very little, of a personal nature.

I am not a candidate for any office in the gift of the government, or in the gift of the people.   I have not been named for
any office at my own suggestion, or, indeed, recently, with my
own previous knowledge.   I am a private citizen ; and that condition will never be changed by any movement or effort made
for that purpose by myself, or at my suggestion.   In my opinion, nominations for the high offices of the country should
come, if they come at all, from the free and spontaneous exercise
of that respect and confidence which the people themselves may
feel.   All solicitations of such nominations, and all canvassing
for such high trusts, I regard as equally inconsistent with personal dignity, and derogatory to the character of the institutions
of the country.

As a private man, I hold my opinions on public subjects.
They are all such, in their great features and general character, as I have ever held.   It is as impossible that I should tread
back the path of my political opinions, as that I should retrace,
step by step, the progress of my natural life, until I should
find myself again a youth.   On the leading questions arising
under our constitutions and forms of government; on the importance of maintaining the separation of powers, which those
constitutions establish ; on the great principles of such a policy

as shall promote all interests, maintain general harmony in the country, and perpetuate the blessings of political and religious liberty, — my opinions, the result of no little study, and some experience, have become part of myself. They are identified with all my habits of thought and reflection; and though I may change my views of particular measures, or not deem the same measures equally proper at all times, yet I am sure it is quite impossible I should ever take such a view, either of the public interest or of my own duty, as should lead to a departure from any cardinal principles.

As a private man, I am ready to do all in my power to uphold principles which I have ever deemed important, and to support measures which the public interest, in my judgment, requires. And as measures cannot be accomplished without the agency of men, I am of course entirely willing to support the men of the highest character, most unexceptionable principles, and who may be most able to take an efficient and successful lead in such measures. And here, perhaps, I ought to pause. But the gentlemen who invited me to this meeting were pleased to express their approbation of my conduct in remaining in the Cabinet at Washington after the other members, originally appointed by General Harrison, had withdrawn. I should not have alluded to this subject, Gentlemen, on this occasion, but for the reference which the committee have made to it. I am aware that there are many persons in the country, having feelings not unfriendly toward me, personally, and entertaining all proper respect for my public character, who yet think I ought to have left the Cabinet with my colleagues. I do not complain of any fair exercise of opinion in this respect; and if, by such persons as I have referred to, explanation be desired of any thing in the past, or any thing in my present opinions, it will be readily and cheerfully given. On the other hand, those who deal only in coarse vituperation, and satisfy their sense of candor and justice simply by the repetition of the charge of dereliction of duty, and infidelity to Whig principles, are not entitled to the respect of an answer from me. The burning propensity to censure and reproach by which such persons seem to be actuated would probably be somewhat rebuked, if they knew by whose advice, and with whose approbation, I resolved on staying in the Cabinet.

Gentlemen, I could not but be sensible that great responsibility attached to the course which I adopted. It was a moment of great excitement. A most unfortunate difference had broken out between the President and the Whig members of Congress. Much exasperation had been produced, and the whole country was in a very inflamed state. No man of sense can suppose, that, without strong motives, I should wish to differ in conduct from those with whom I had long acted; and as for those persons whose charity leads them to seek for such motive in the hope of personal advantage, neither their candor nor their sagacity deserves any thing but contempt. I admit, Gentlemen, that if a very strong desire to be instrumental and useful in accomplishing a settlement of our difficulties with England, which had then risen to an alarming height, and appeared to be approaching a crisis, — if this be a personal motive, then I confess myself to have been influenced by a personal motive. The imputation of any other personal motive, the charge of seeking any selfish advantage, I repel with utter scorn.

To be sure it excites contempt, but hardly any thing so respectful as regret or indignation, when persons capable of no effort in any cause but that of making a noise, and with no other merit than that of interested partisanship, — men, indeed, yet reeking from their labors in the support of the most questionable measures of General Jackson's administration, and others still odorous with the perfumes of the sub-treasury, — distend their throats, and admonish the country to beware of Mr. Webster's infidelity to Whig principles.

Gentlemen, I thought I saw an opportunity of doing the state some service, and I ran the risk of the undertaking. I certainly do not regret it, and never shall regret it. And it is in no spirit of boasting or vainglory, it is from no undue feeling of self-respect, that I say now, that I am ready to leave it to the public judgment to decide whether my remaining in the Cabinet was best for the country, or, on the other hand, whether my leaving it would have been better for the country.

On this question I am in the judgment of this generation and the next generation; and am willing that my name and fame and character shall abide the result.

There was no difference between the President and myself on the great questions of our foreign relations. I neither foresaw then, nor experienced afterward, any embarrassment from such a cause as that. And it is but an act of justice, which I always perform with pleasure, to say, that in the English negotiation, and in other negotiations, I found the President influenced by just principles and proper sentiments, desirous of maintaining, at the same time, the honor and the peace of the country.

Gentlemen, exception has been taken to a note addressed by me to the editors of the National Intelligencer of the 13th of September, 1841, on the ground that that note implied a censure on my colleagues for leaving the President's Cabinet. But I intended no such reproach. I intended, certainly, only to speak for myself, and not to reproach others. This was the note.

"*Washington, September* 13, 1841.

" To Messrs. Gales & Seaton : —

" Gentlemen, — Lest any misapprehension should exist as to the reasons which have led me to differ from the course pursued by my late colleagues, I wish to say that I remain in my place, first, because I have seen no sufficient reasons for the dissolution of the late Cabinet by the voluntary act of its own members.

" I am perfectly persuaded of the absolute necessity of an institution, under the authority of Congress, to aid revenue and financial operations, and to give the country the blessings of a good currency and cheap exchanges.

" Notwithstanding what has passed, I have confidence that the President will coöperate with the legislature in overcoming all difficulties in the attainment of these objects ; and it is to the union of the Whig party, by which I mean the Whig President, the Whig Congress, and the Whig people, that I look for the realization of our wishes. I can look nowhere else.

" In the second place, if I had seen reasons to resign my office, I should not have done so without giving the President reasonable notice, and affording him time to select the head to whom he should confide the delicate and important affairs now pending in this department.

" I am, Gentlemen, respectfully,

" Your obedient servant,

" Daniel Webster."

If in this there was any ambiguity, or any expression not well chosen, or not well considered, candor, I think, might have interpreted it by another letter, written and published about the same time, addressed to a friend in New York, which I will read.

"*Washington, September* 11, 1841.

" MY DEAR SIR, — I thank you for your kind and friendly letter.

" You will have learned that Messrs. Ewing, Bell, Badger, and Crittenden have resigned their respective offices. Probably Mr. Granger may feel bound to follow the example. This occurrence can hardly cause you the same degree of regret which it has occasioned to me ; as they are not only friends, but persons with whom I have had, for some time, a daily official intercourse. I could not partake in this movement.

" It is supposed to be justified, I presume, by the differences which have arisen between the President and Congress, upon the means of establishing a proper fiscal agency, and restoring a sound state of the currency ; and collateral matters, growing out of these differences. I regret these differences as deeply as any man ; but I have not been able to see in what manner the resignation of the Cabinet was likely either to remove or mitigate the evils produced by them. On the contrary, my only reliance for a remedy for those evils has been, and is, on the union, conciliation, and perseverance of the whole Whig party, and I by no means despair of seeing yet accomplished, by these means, all that we desire. It may render us more patient under disappointment in regard to one measure, to recollect, as is justly stated by the President in his last message, how great a number of important measures have been already successfully carried through. I hardly know when such a mass of business has been despatched in a single session of Congress.

" The annual winter session is now near at hand ; the same Congress is again soon to assemble ; and feeling as deeply as I ever did the indispensable necessity of some suitable provision for the keeping of the public money, for aid to the operations of the treasury, and to the high public interests of currency and exchanges, I am not in haste to believe that the party which has now the predominance will not, in all these respects, yet fulfil the expectations of the country. If it shall not, then our condition is forlorn indeed. But for one, I will not give up the hope.

" My particular connection with the administration, however, is with another department. I think very humbly, none can think more humbly, of the value of the services which I am able to render to the public in that post. But as there is, so far as I know, on all subjects affecting our foreign relations, a concurrence in opinion between the President and myself ; and as there is nothing to disturb the harmony of our intercourse, I have not felt it consistent with the duty which I owe to the country, to run the risk, by any sudden or abrupt proceeding, of embarrassing the executive, in regard to subjects and questions now immediately pending, and which intimately affect the preservation of the peace of the country.

       "I am, dear Sir, with constant regard, yours,
                        "DANIEL WEBSTER.
"H. KETCHUM, ESQ., New York."

Gentlemen, it must have been obvious to all, that my remaining in the Cabinet of the President, notwithstanding the personal good-will between us, after the separation between him and the great body of the Whigs, could only be inconvenient and unpleasant to both. My retirement, therefore, was the necessary consequence of political occurrences, and I am not, I think, called on to say more.

I hope I have not extended these remarks beyond the purpose which I proposed; and I close them by repeating the declaration made by me in another place, last year, that I am a Whig, a Massachusetts Whig, a Faneuil Hall Whig, and none shall have the power, now or hereafter, to deprive me of the position in which that character places me.

16*

APPENDIX.

No. I. — Page 168.

Extracts from an Essay entitled "An Inquiry into the Principles on which a Commercial System for the United States of America should be founded." *

THERE are in every country certain important crises when exertion or neglect must produce consequences of the utmost moment. The period at which the inhabitants of these States have now arrived will be admitted by every attentive and serious mind to be clearly of this description.

Our money absorbed by a wanton consumption of imported luxuries, a fluctuating paper medium substituted in its stead, foreign commerce extremely circumscribed, and a federal government not only ineffective, but disjointed, tell us indeed too plainly, that further negligence may ruin us for ever. Impressed with this view of our affairs, the writer of the following pages has ventured to intrude upon the public. But as neither his time nor opportunities will permit him to treat of all the great objects which excite his apprehensions or engage his wishes, he means principally to confine himself to that part of them which has been most subjected to his observations and inquiries.

In a country blessed with a fertile soil, and a climate admitting steady labor, where the cheapness of land tempts the European from his home, and the manufacturer from his trade, we are led by a few moments of reflection to fix on agriculture as the great leading interest. From this we shall find most of our other advantages result, so far as they arise from the nature of our affairs, and where they are not produced by the coercion of laws, the fisheries are the principal exception. In order to make a true estimate of the magnitude of agriculture, we must remember that it is encouraged by few or no duties on the importation of rival

---

* The paper from which these extracts are given is published in the American Museum, Vol. I. p. 432, with the name of Tench Toxe, Esq., as its author. It is also incorporated into his work called "View of the United States of America," p. 4.

produce, that it furnishes outward cargoes not only for all our own ships, but those also which foreign nations send to our ports, or, in other words, that it pays for all our importations ; that it supplies a part of the clothing of our people and the food of them and their cattle ; that what is consumed at home, including the materials for manufacturing, is four or five times the value of what is exported ; that the number of people employed in agriculture is at least nine parts in ten of the inhabitants of America ; that therefore the planters and farmers do form the body of the militia, the bulwark of the nation ; that the value of property occupied by agriculture is manifold greater than that of the property employed in every other way ; that the settlement of our waste lands, and subdividing our improved farms, is every year increasing the preëminence of the agricultural interest ; that the resources we derive from it are at all times certain and indispensably necessary ; and lastly, that the rural life promotes health and morality, by its active nature, and by keeping our people from the luxuries and vices of the towns. In short, agriculture appears to be the spring of our commerce and the parent of our manufactures.

The commerce of America, including our exports, imports, shipping, manufactures, and fisheries, may be properly considered as forming one interest. So uninformed or mistaken have many of us been, that it has been stated as the great object, and I fear it is yet believed to be the most important interest, of New England. But, from the best calculations I have been able to make, I cannot raise the proportion of property or the number of men employed in manufactures, fisheries, navigation, and trade to one eighth the property and the people occupied by agriculture, even in that commercial quarter of the Union.

While I feel an absolute conviction that our true interests should restrain us from burdening or impeding agriculture in any way whatever, I am not only ready to admit, but must beg leave to urge, that sound policy requires our giving every encouragement to commerce and its connections, which may be found consistent with a due regard to agriculture.

The communication between the different ports of every nation is a business entirely in their power. The policy of most countries has been to secure this domestic navigation to their own people. The extensive coasts, the immense bays and numerous rivers of the United States, have already made this an important object, and it must increase with our population. As the places at which the cargoes of coasting vessels are delivered must be supplied with American produce from some part of the Union, and as the merchant can always have American bottoms to transport the goods of the producing State to the State consuming them, no interruption to the market of the planters and farmers can be apprehended from prohibiting transportation in foreign bottoms from port to port within the United States. A single exception may perhaps be proper, permitting foreign vessels to carry from port to port, for the purpose of finishing their sales, any goods that shall be part of the cargoes they brought into the Union from the last foreign place at which they loaded. The fleets of colliers on the British coasts evince the possible benefits of such a regulation.

The consumption of fish, oil, whalebone, and other articles obtained through the fisheries, in the towns and counties that are convenient to navigation, has become much greater than is generally supposed. I am informed that no less than five thousand barrels of mackerel, salmon, and pickled codfish are vended in the city of Philadelphia annually; add to them the dried fish, oil, spermaceti candles, whalebone, &c., and it will be found a little fleet of sloops and schooners are employed in the business. The demand for the use of the inhabitants of those parts of the Union to which these supplies can be carried is already considerable, and the increase of our towns and manufactures will render it more so every year. In the present state of our navigation we can be in no doubt of procuring these supplies by means of our own vessels. The country that interferes most with us at our own market is Nova Scotia, which also, I am informed, has had some emigrants from our fishing towns since the decline of their business. Such encouragement to this valuable branch of commerce as would secure the benefits of it to our own people, without injuring our other essential interests, is certainly worth attention. The convention will probably find, on consideration of this point, that a duty or prohibition of foreign articles, such as our own fisheries supply, will be safe and expedient.

These are the principal encouragements to foreign commerce which occur to me at present as proper to form a part of a permanent system for the United States. Regulations for temporary purposes, such as restrictions and prohibitions affecting particular nations, I do not mean to speak of here. I must, however, observe, that they should be adopted with great prudence and deliberation, as they may affect us very unfavorably, if they should be tried in vain. In taking measures to promote manufactures, we must be careful that the injuries to the general interests of commerce do not exceed the advantages resulting from them. The circumstances of the country, as they relate to this business, should be dispassionately and thoroughly examined. Though it is confessed that the United States have full employment for all their citizens in the extensive field of agriculture, yet as we have a valuable body of manufacturers already here, and as many more will probably emigrate from Europe, who will choose to continue at their trades, and as we have some citizens so poor as not to be able to effect a little settlement on our waste lands, there is a real necessity for some wholesome general regulations on this head.

By taking care not to force manufactures in those States where the people are fewer, tillage much more profitable, and provisions dearer, than in several others, we shall give agriculture its full scope in the former, and leave all the benefits of manufacturing (so far as they are within our reach) to the latter. South Carolina, for instance, must manufacture to an evident loss, while the advancement of that business in Massachusetts will give the means of subsistence to many, whose occupations have been rendered unprofitable by the consequences of the Revolution. A liberal policy on this subject should be adopted, and the produce of the Southern States should be exchanged for such manufactures as can be made by the Northern, free from impost.

Another inducement to some salutary regulations on this subject will be suggested by considering some of our means of conducting manufactures. Unless business of this kind is carried on, certain great *natural powers* of the country will remain inactive and useless. Our numerous mill-seats, for example, by which flour, oil, paper, snuff, gunpowder, iron-work, woollen cloths, boards and scantling, and some other articles, are prepared or perfected, would be given by Providence in vain. If properly improved, they will save us an immense expense for the wages, provisions, clothing, and lodging of workmen, without diverting the people from their farms. Fire, as well as water, affords, if I may so speak, a fund of assistance, that cannot lie unused without an evident neglect of our best interests. Breweries, which we cannot estimate too highly, distilleries, sugar-houses, potteries, casting and steel furnaces, and several other works, are carried on by this powerful element, and attended with the same savings that were particularized in speaking of water machines. It is probable, also, that a frequent use of steam-engines will add greatly to this class of factories. In some cases where fire and water are not employed, horses are made to serve the purpose as well, and on much lower terms than men. The cheapness and the easy increase of these serviceable animals insure us this aid to any extent that occasion may require, which, however, is not likely to be very great.

The encouragement to agriculture afforded by some manufactories is a reason of solid weight in favor of pushing them with industry and spirit. Malt liquors, if generally used, linseed oil, starch, (and, were they not a poison to our morals and constitutions, I might add corn spirits,) would require more grain to make them than has been exported in any year since the Revolution. I cannot omit to observe here, that beer strengthens the arm of the laborer without debauching him, while the noxious drink now used enervates and corrupts him. The workers in leather, too, of every kind, in flax and hemp, in iron, wood, stone, and clay, in furs, horn, and many other articles, employ either the spontaneous productions of the earth or the fruits of cultivation.

A further encouragement to manufactures will result from improvements and discoveries in agriculture. There are many raw materials, that could be produced in this country on a large scale, which have hitherto been very confined. Cotton, for many years before the Revolution, was not worth more than nine pence sterling in the West India Islands. The perfection of the factories in Europe has raised it to such a pitch, that, besides the prohibition against shipping it from the colonies to any foreign port, the price has risen fifty per cent. The consumers in Pennsylvania have paid near two shillings sterling for the importation of this year. This article must be worth the attention of the Southern planters.

If the facts and observations in the preceding part of this paper be admitted to be true and just, and if we take into consideration with them the acknowledged superiority of foreign commerce and the fisheries over our manufactories, we may come to the following conclusions : —

That the United States of America cannot make a proper use of the natural advantages of the country, nor promote her agriculture and other lesser interests, without manufactures ; that they cannot enjoy the attainable benefits of commerce and the fisheries, without some general restrictions and prohibitions affecting foreign nations ; that in forming these restrictions and prohibitions, as well as in establishing manufactories, there is occasion for great deliberation and wisdom, that nothing may be introduced which can interfere with the sale of our produce, or with the settlement and improvement of our waste lands.

It will not be amiss to draw a picture of our country, as it would really exist under the operation of a system of national laws formed upon these principles. While we indulge ourselves in the contemplation of a subject at once so interesting and dear, let us confine ourselves to substantial facts, and avoid those pleasing delusions into which the spirits and feelings of our countrymen have too long misled them.

In the foreground we should find the mass of our citizens the cultivators, (and what is happily for us, in most instances, the same thing,) the independent proprietors of the soil. Every wheel would appear in motion that could carry forward the interests of this great body of our people, and bring into action the inherent powers of the country. A portion of the produce of our lands would be consumed in the families or employed in the business of our manufacturers, a farther portion would be applied in the sustenance of our merchants and fishermen and their numerous assistants, and the remainder would be transported, by those that could carry it at the lowest freight (that is, with the smallest deduction from the aggregate profits of the business of the country), to the best foreign markets.

On one side, we should see our manufacturers encouraging the tillers of the earth by the consumption and employment of the fruits of their labors, and supplying them and the rest of their fellow-citizens with the instruments of their occupations, and the necessaries and conveniences of life, in every instance where it could be done without injuriously and unnecessarily increasing the distress of commerce, the labors of the husbandmen, and the difficulties of changing our native wilds into scenes of cultivation and plenty. Commerce, on the other hand, attentive to the general interests, would come forward with offers to range through foreign climates in search of those supplies which the manufacturers could not furnish but at too high a price, or which nature has not given us at home, in return for the surplus of those stores that had been drawn from the ocean or produced by the earth.

The commercial citizens of America have for some time felt the deepest distress; among the principal causes of their unhappy situation were the inconsiderate spirit of adventure to this country, which pervaded every kingdom in Europe, and the prodigious credits from thence given to our merchants. To these may be added the high spirits and the golden dreams that naturally followed such a war, closed with so much honor and success. Triumphant over a great enemy, courted by the most powerful nations in the world, it was not in human nature that America should immediately comprehend her new situation. Really possessed of the means of future greatness, she anticipated the most distant benefits of the Revolution, and considered them as already in her hands. She formed the highest expectations, many of which, however, serious experience has taught her to relinquish, and now that the thoughtless adventures and imprudent credits from foreign countries take place no more, and time has been given for cool reflection, she will see her true situation, and need not be discouraged.

The foundations of national wealth and consequence are so firmly laid in the United States, that no *foreign* power can undermine or destroy them. But the enjoyment of these substantial blessings is rendered precarious by domestic circumstances. Scarcely held together by a weak and half-formed federal constitution, the powers of our national government are unequal to the complete execution of any salutary purpose, foreign or domestic. The evils resulting from this unhappy state of things have again shocked our reviving credit, produced among our people alarming instances of disobedience to the laws, and, if not remedied, must destroy our property, liberties, and peace. Foreign powers, however disposed to favor us, can expect neither satisfaction nor benefit from treaties with Congress, while they are unable to enforce them. We can, therefore, hope to secure no privileges from them, if matters are thus conducted.

We must immediately remedy this defect, or suffer exceedingly.

Desultory commercial acts of the legislatures, formed on the impression of the moment, proceeding from no uniform or permanent principles, clashing with the laws of the other States, and opposing those made in the preceding year by the enacting State, can no longer be supported, if we are to continue one people. *A system which will promote the general interests with the smallest injury to particular ones, has become indispensably necessary.* Commerce is more affected by the distractions and evils arising from the uncertainty, opposition, and errors of our trade laws, than by the restrictions of any one power in Europe. A negative upon all commercial acts of the legislatures, if granted to Congress, would be perfectly safe, and must have an excellent effect. If thought expedient, it should be given as well with regard to those that exist, as to those that may be devised in future. Congress would thus be enabled to prevent every regulation that might oppose the general interests, and, by restraining the States from impolitic laws, would gradually bring our national commerce to order and perfection. Such of the ideas suggested in the preceding part of this paper as shall be honored with the public approbation, may be better digested, and, if they appear worthy of it, may form new articles of confederation, which would be the foundation of the commercial system.

I have ventured to hint at prohibitory powers, but shall leave that point, and the general power of regulating trade, to those who may undertake to consider the political objects of the convention, suggesting only the evident propriety of enabling Congress to prevent the importation of such foreign commodities as are made from our own raw materials. When any article of that kind can be supplied at home, upon as low terms as it can be imported, a manufacture of *our own produce*, so well established, ought not by any means to be sacrificed to the interests of foreign trade, or subjected to injury by the wild speculations of ignorant adventurers. In all cases, careful provision should be made for refunding the duties on exportation, which renders the impost a virtual excise without being liable to the objections against an actual one, and is a great encouragement to trade.

The restoration of public credit at home and abroad should be the first wish of our hearts, and requires every economy, every exertion we can make. The wise and virtuous axioms of our political constitutions, resulting from a lively and perfect sense of what is due from man to man, should prompt us to the discharge of debts of such peculiar obligation. We stand bound to no common creditors. The friendly foreigner, the widow and the orphan, the trustees of charity and religion, the patriotic citizen, the war-worn soldier, and a magnanimous ally, — these are the principal claimants upon the feeling and justice of America. Let her apply all her resources to this great duty and wipe away the darkest stain that has ever fallen upon her.

The general impost, the sale of the lands and every other unnecessary article of public property, restraining with a firm hand every needless expense of government and private life, steady and patient industry, with proper dispositions in the people, would relieve us of part of the burden, and enable Congress to commence their payments, and, with the aid of taxation, would put the sinking and funding of our debts within the power of all the States.

No. II.— Page 171.

To the Tradesmen and Manufacturers of the Commonwealth of Massachusetts : —

Gentlemen, — The large importations from Europe of the manufactures of this country call loudly on us to join in some united effort to remedy a measure so destructive. It is with regret we observe, that since the peace the importations into this State have consisted of many articles which are usually manufactured among ourselves, on which thousands of individuals depend for the maintenance of themselves and families, and many of our brethren who have been engaged in the war, and are now returned to their occupations, rely for subsistence and support; we therefore view the continuance of such a practice as tending to the ruin of those several manufacturers, and impoverishing great numbers of industrious members of society.

Nothing can be more desirable, at this important period, than a firm, united exertion to prevent the evils we apprehend, and, as we conceive, the interest of the whole is so infinitely connected with those branches already affected, we should wish to establish a union upon so broad a basis that it cannot fail of producing the most extensive and permanent advantages to the collective body of mechanics.

We conceive ourselves interested in one common cause, although the evils we complain of are not equally felt by all. Yet we trust our brethren will view the concern as general, and will be ready to join with us in all legal measures to obtain a regulation in the present system of commerce, which, if not speedily checked, must prove fatal to the whole.

If ever the attention of the manufacturers and mechanics of this Commenwealth was required, *this is the interesting moment.* If we let this opportunity pass without some endeavors on our part, we shall for ever have reason to repent of our remissness. Every day brings fresh proofs of the necessity of our exertions, and we cannot answer it to God, our

COUNTRY, our POSTERITY, or OURSELVES, if we are inactive at this decisive crisis.

The restrictions by the British government on all American vessels, and the shipping of goods from England to America in British bottoms, must eventually operate to the destruction of ship-building among ourselves, and render our vessels of little value in prosecuting voyages to any part of the British dominions, and entirely destroy our carrying trade, an object so essentially important to America.

We have reason to apprehend, from what has hitherto taken place, that not only our ship-building will be ruined, but that every article of rigging, sails, blocks, and also cordage ready fitted for the rigger, together with all the variety of ship-chandlery, will soon be imported by British merchants or factors, or brought in vessels freighted as English bottoms. The consequence must be the entire ruin of our ship-builders, blacksmiths, rope-makers, riggers, block-makers, sail-makers, with every other branch of business connected with the equipment of vessels.

We need not mention other branches of trade and manufacture more immediately affected by foreign importation, — they are too keenly felt to need repetition, — being sensible that every implement throughout the whole system of mechanism will ere long (without speedy assistance) be wrested from the hands of the industrious American.

These things are not surmises, they are *truths* which cannot be controverted; they therefore require our joining in a petition to the next General Court, praying that such duties may be laid on foreign importations of all articles usually manufactured here, as will prevent their being brought among us to the injury of such individuals as are now employed in those branches.

As the time is now approaching for the choice of persons to represent us the ensuing year, on whom we greatly rely for the success of our petition, it is hoped the tradesmen and manufacturers will exert their whole influence to make choice of those men who are avowedly friends to the manufactures of this country. Your own judgment will dictate to you such persons, whose connections, whose steadiness, and whose patriotism will bear the test of scrutiny.

We are, Gentlemen, with every sentiment of esteem, your friends and brethren in a common cause.

JOHN GRAY.

The following letter was addressed to Governor Bowdoin : —

May it please your Excellency, — We, the Committee of Tradesmen and Manufacturers of the town of Boston, do in their names congratulate your Excellency on your appointment to the chief seat of government.

It affords us the greatest satisfaction, that a gentleman is placed at the head of this Commonwealth who is so particularly acquainted with the interests of the country, and on whose integrity, wisdom, and decision we can confidently rely.

Your Excellency's disposition to encourage the manufactures of this country (the embarrassed state of which has not escaped your notice) gives us the most pleasing expectation of your patronage and support, and we anticipate the fond idea that measures will soon be adopted by this State fully adequate to the removal of the difficulties under which we at present labor.

The unanimity which so generally prevails throughout the several branches of the legislature, we conceive a happy presage of those national blessings so earnestly desired by every sincere friend to the independence of America.

May your administration be happy. May union and stability prevail in all our public counsels. And may your Excellency, by a faithful discharge of the important duties of your station, ever receive the warmest acknowledgments of the people over whom you preside.

To which his Excellency made the following reply : —

GENTLEMEN, — I am greatly indebted to the worthy body of tradesmen and manufacturers in the town of Boston for their congratulations, and in particular to you, Gentlemen, for the obliging manner in which you have communicated them.

You certainly are not mistaken in your idea of my disposition to encourage the manufactures of this country, and for that purpose I hope to see measures adopted fully adequate to the removal of the difficulties under which the several classes of my fellow-citizens do at present unhappily labor. To the forwarding and completing of such adequate measures, I shall be happy to contribute.

I thank you for your good wishes, and especially for the wish that my administration may be happy. Be assured, Gentlemen, it shall be my endeavor to make it so to every class of citizens throughout the Commonwealth, and particularly to the tradesmen and manufacturers of Boston, whose prosperity it will give me great pleasure to see, but much greater to promote.

JAMES BOWDOIN.

No. III. — P. 178.

Statement of Manufactures in Virginia.

COTTON. — Three cotton manufactories, which have **14,200** spindles, **263** looms, and employ **610** hands or operatives. They consume

$ 153,000 of raw material, and turn out $ 378,000 in value of cotton fabrics per annum, with a capital of $ 477,500.

IRON. — There are two rolling-mills, one nail factory, three extensive iron founderies, two saw and axe manufactories, and three extensive establishments for the manufacture of agricultural implements, in which is a greater or less amount of castings. The capital invested in these is about $ 500,000; they employ about 325 men, many of them with families, and consume about $ 200,000 worth of iron and $ 50,000 worth of coal, and turn out fabrics now to the value of about $ 700,000.

Besides the above, which embraces cotton and iron alone, there is an extensive paper-mill, a woollen manufactory, flouring-mills that manufacture about 100,000 barrels of flour per annum, upward of $ 1,000,000 of tobacco manufactured into chewing tobacco per annum, and in addition coach factories, manufactories of boots and shoes, guns and locks, one of pianos, brass founderies, &c., &c.

Just previous to the adoption of the present tariff, the manufacturing operations of Richmond, Petersburg, and other places throughout the State, were curtailed one half. They gradually recovered during the first six months after the passage of the tariff, and most rapidly during the last eight months; so that they are all doing a fair business now, while some of them, the cotton factories, are pushed to their utmost to supply the demand, which they are scarcely able to do.

Richmond memorialized Congress for the passage of that tariff, and so did Petersburg, I believe. The memorial sent from Richmond, which had the largest number of signatures ever put to a paper in the city, asserted these propositions : —

" That duties should be adequate to the purposes of revenue. That they should be discriminating also, not only with a view to favor domestic productions, but to benefit the consumer by enlarging the supply, and by adding domestic competition, which is always active, to foreign competition, which is sometimes inefficient, and never regular and constant."

It was also further asserted, that, " under the tariff policies of different civilized nations, the only mode of relieving or aiding agriculture was by diverting to other occupations a portion of the labor applied to it, and by increasing, at the same time, the domestic market for its products; and that therefore no branch of industry in the country has a clearer interest in the due encouragement and support of home manufactures than the agricultural."

The total capital invested in the more important manufactures of Richmond is about $ 5,000,000.

The town of Petersburg has eight cotton manufacturing establishments now in full operation. She has leased three flouring-mills, a paper-mill, a woollen factory, &c., with a fixed capital of near

$ 1,000,000 in cotton manufactories, $ 125,000 in flouring-mills, and $ 1,000,000 in tobacco manufactories.

Wheeling, with a population of over 10,000 inhabitants, has 136 establishments for the manufacture of domestic goods, raising annually 1,243,000 bushels of coal, and giving employment to more than 1,700 persons, yielding an annual product worth $ 2,000,000. Her chief manufactures are iron castings, bar iron, and glass. Near Wheeling, and in the vicinity of Richmond, 7,000,000 bushels of coal are raised annually. Near Richmond alone, the quantity raised exceeds 5,000,000 bushels.

The small town of Fredericksburg has several iron and woollen manufactories, which, with flouring and other mills, employ a capital of about $ 250,000.

Lynchburg. — This large and flourishing town, with near 7,000 inhabitants, is a place of large operations in the manufacture of tobacco, iron, flour, cotton, &c., amounting to several millions of dollars annually.

From other places where manufactories are in operation, I have no particular information.

General Estimate.

In Wheeling, Petersburg, Richmond, Lynchburg, Fredericksburg, and Kanawha County, there are more than $ 11,000,000 employed in the leading manufactures of these places. There are, besides, cotton manufactories, blast furnaces, and founderies, in many of the counties. Virginia has every element and every advantage for manufacturing. Cotton, iron, lead, hemp, and wool are diffused in each of her four grand divisions, and salt in the Southwest. Her water power is not excelled, and I doubt whether it is equalled, in any other State in the Union. The importance of her manufactures is far better appreciated among her citizens than formerly. I doubt whether so rapid, so general, and so great a change in favor of this object has taken place anywhere else in the United States as has occurred in this old Commonwealth during the last two years. She was the tobacco State a few years ago; now, the West, but for the peculiar excellence of her tobacco, would crowd her out of foreign markets, or put the price down so low that the cost of its productions, and the advantage of more profitable pursuits she enjoys by reason of her position, would induce her perhaps to abandon entirely, certainly in a great degree, its culture in a few years.

Last year there were received at the port of New Orleans, from the tobacco regions of the West, more than twice as many hogsheads of tobacco as the entire crop of Virginia, while a large portion of the Western crop was *via* Pennsylvania to Baltimore and elsewhere. This is

17 *

an important fact regarding the destinies of Virginia. She must become a manufacturing State.

The people generally are fast giving up their old notions on the tariff, or those notions which were once regarded as peculiarly Virginian. A majority may now be found in favor of the tariff views, as advocated by the people of Richmond in their memorial adverted to in the early part of this review.

Hurried as I am, I deem it of importance to give you this additional sketch, showing the probable amount of raw cotton manufactured or used by our factories in Virginia.

		Bales.	
In Petersburg, by the	Elluch Co.,	1,500	
"	" Matoaca Co.,	1,300	
"	" Mechanics' Co.,	1,200	
"	" Merchants' Co.,	1,200	
"	" Canal Co.,	1,000	
"	" Battersea,	600	
"	" Washington,	400	
"	" Eagle,	400	
			7,600
In Richmond,	" Manchester,	2,200	
"	" Richmond,	1,400	
"	" Spring Hill,	400	
			4,000
In Albemarle County,	Thadwell,	500	
"	" Union,	400	
			900
In Isle of Wight County,			600
In Fredericksburg,			600
In Lynchburg,			600
In the other smaller factories in the State,			1,000
			15,300

No. IV. — Page 178.

New York, 6th November, 1843.

My DEAR SIR, — In conformity with my promise on Saturday last, I now send you the annexed statement of prices of articles of American manufacture in this city, in the months of July, August, and September of 1842, and the corresponding months of 1843.

Prices of Nails in 1842.	*Prices of Nails in 1843.*
July, . . 4¼ to 4½ cents per lb.	July, . . 3¾ cents per lb.
August, . 4¼ to 4½ " "	August, . . 4 " "
September, . 4½ to 4¾ " "	September, . 4 " "
Prices of best Penn. Pig Iron, 1842.	*Prices of best Penn. Pig Iron, 1843.*
July, Aug., and Sept., $30 per ton.	July, Aug., and Sept., $25 per ton.
Penn. rolled Bar Iron, 1842.	*Penn. rolled Bar Iron, 1843.*
July, August, and to Sept. 10th, $70.	July, August, and September, $65.
From Sept. 10th to October 1st, $75.	

Since August, 1842, there have been but very few, if any, nails manufactured in this country of imported iron. Prior to January, 1842, the bulk of nails sold in this market were from Swedes' iron, when the wholesale price of that description of iron seldom reached so low a point as $80 per ton. Since August, 1842, the price has ranged from $70 to $75 per ton. Competition among American manufacturers (aided, probably, by low prices in Europe) has reduced the prices of bar iron and nails in this country. Prices of iron in Europe have been depressed in consequence of our tariff, and consequently it is the operation of the tariff alone which now enables the consumer to purchase these articles at their present reduced rates. I have long been satisfied that English iron, particularly, could be afforded to us even under the present tariff; the prices in England being regulated rather by what the articles would command here, than the cost of production there. If this be true, the reduction of duties designed by the compromise tariff was defeated, and the benefit accrued to the foreign producers.

Since writing the above, a friend has furnished me with the following facts relative to the prices of Scotch pig-iron in this city, and also in Scotland, in August, 1842, and August, 1843 : —

Say — In August, 1842, the price in this city was, . . $25.00 per ton.
   In August, 1843,   "   "   "   . $23.50 per ton.
Say — In August, 1842, the price of same iron in Scotland was £2 15s. per ton.
   In August, 1843, it would be, ... £2 per ton.

No. V. — Page 179.

Extract from an Address to the States, adopted by Congress on the 24th of April, 1783, on the Report of a Committee consisting of Messrs. Madison, Hamilton, and Ellsworth.

If other motives than those of justice be requisite on this occasion, no nation could ever feel stronger; for to whom are the debts to be paid ?

To an ally, in the first place, who, to the exertion of his arms in support of our cause, has added the succor of his treasure ; who, to his important loans, has added liberal donations; and whose loans themselves carry the impression of his magnanimity and friendship.

To individuals in a foreign country, in the next place, who were the first to give so precious a token of their confidence in our justice, and of their friendship for our cause, and who are members of a republic which was second in espousing our rank among nations.

Another class of creditors is *that illustrious and patriotic band of our fellow-citizens*, whose blood and whose bravery have defended the liberties of their country ; who have patiently borne, among other distresses, the privation of their stipends, while the distresses of their country disabled it from bestowing them; and who even now ask for no more than such a portion of their dues as will enable them to retire from the field of victory and glory into the bosom of peace and private citizenship, and for such effectual security for the residue of their claims as their country is now unquestionably able to provide.

The remaining class of creditors is composed partly of such of our fellow-citizens as originally lent to the public the use of their funds, or have since manifested most confidence in their country by receiving transfers from the lenders, and partly of those whose property has been either advanced or assumed for the public service.

To discriminate the merits of these several descriptions of creditors would be a task equally unnecessary and invidious. If the voice of humanity plead more loudly in favor of some than of others, the voice of policy, no less than of justice, pleads in favor of all. A wise nation will never permit those who relieve the wants of their country, or who rely most on its faith, its firmness, and its resources, when either of them is distrusted, to suffer by the event.

Let it be remembered, finally, that it has ever been the pride and boast of America, that the rights for which she contended were the rights of human nature. By the blessing of the Author of these rights on the means exerted for their defence, they have prevailed against all opposition, and form the basis of thirteen independent States. No instance has heretofore occurred, nor can any instance be expected hereafter to occur, in which the unadulterated forms of republican government can pretend to so fair an opportunity of justifying themselves by their fruits. In this view, the citizens of the United States are responsible for the greatest trust ever confided to a political society. If justice, good faith, honor, gratitude, and all other qualities which ennoble the character of a nation, and fulfil the ends of governments, be the fruits of our establishment, the cause of liberty will acquire a dignity and lustre which it has never yet enjoyed, and an example will be set which cannot but have the most favorable influence on the rights of mankind. If, on the other side, our government should be unfortunately blotted with the reverse of these cardinal and essential virtues, the great cause which we have engaged to vindicate will be dishonored and betrayed; the last and fairest experiment in favor of the rights of human nature will be turned against them, and their patrons and friends exposed to be insulted and silenced by the votaries of tyranny and usurpation.

THE LANDING AT PLYMOUTH.

THE LANDING AT PLYMOUTH.*

THE great Pilgrim festival was celebrated on the 22d of December, 1843, by the New England Society of New York, with uncommon spirit and success. A commemorative oration was delivered in the morning by Hon. Rufus Choate, in a style of eloquence rarely equalled. The public dinner of the Society, at the Astor House, at which M. H. Grinnell, Esq., presided, was attended by a very large company, composed of the members of the Society and their invited guests. Several appropriate toasts having been given and responded to by the distinguished individuals present, George Griswold, Esq., rose to offer one in honor of Mr. Webster. After a few remarks complimentary to that gentleman, in reference to his services in refuting the doctrine of nullification and in averting the danger of war by the treaty of Washington, Mr. Griswold gave the following toast : —

"DANIEL WEBSTER, — the gift of New England to his country, his whole country, and nothing but his country."

This was received with great applause, and on rising to respond to it, Mr. Webster was greeted with nine enthusiastic cheers, and the most hearty and prolonged approbation. When silence was restored, he spoke as follows : —

MR. PRESIDENT : — I have a grateful duty to perform in acknowledging the kindness of the sentiment thus expressed towards me. And yet I must say, Gentlemen, that I rise upon this occasion under a consciousness that I may probably disappoint highly raised, too highly raised expectations. In the scenes of this evening, and in the scene of this day, my part is an humble one. I can enter into no competition with the fresh-

---

* A Speech delivered on the 22d of December, 1843, at the Public Dinner of the New England Society of New York, in Commemoration of the Landing of the Pilgrims.

er geniuses of those more eloquent gentlemen, learned and reverend, who have addressed this Society. I may perform, however, the humbler, but sometimes useful, duty of contrast, by adding the dark ground of the picture, which shall serve to bring out the more brilliant colors.

I must receive, Gentlemen, the sentiment proposed by the worthy and distinguished citizen of New York before me, as intended to convey the idea that, as a citizen of New England, as a son, a child, a *creation* of New England, I may be yet supposed to entertain, in some degree, that enlarged view of my duty as a citizen of the United States and as a public man, which may, in some small measure, commend me to the regard of the whole country. While I am free to confess, Gentlemen, that there is no compliment of which I am more desirous to be thought worthy, I will add, that a compliment of that kind could have proceeded from no source more agreeable to my own feelings than from the gentleman who has proposed it, — an eminent merchant, the member of a body of eminent merchants, known throughout the world for their intelligence and enterprise. I the more especially feel this, Gentlemen, because, whether I view the present state of things or recur to the history of the past, I can in neither case be ignorant how much that profession, and its distinguished members, from an early day of our history, have contributed to make the country what it is, and the government what it is.

Gentlemen, the free nature of our institutions, and the popular form of those governments which have come down to us from the Rock of Plymouth, give scope to intelligence, to talent, enterprise, and public spirit, from all classes making up the great body of the community. And the country has received benefit in all its history and in all its exigencies, of the most eminent and striking character, from persons of the class to which my friend before me belongs. Who will ever forget that the first name signed to our ever-memorable and ever-glorious Declaration of Independence is the name of John Hancock, a merchant of Boston? Who will ever forget that, in the most disastrous days of the Revolution, when the treasury of the country was bankrupt, with unpaid navies and starving armies, it was a merchant, — Robert Morris of Philadelphia, — who, by a noble sacrifice of his own fortune, as well as by the exercise of his great financial abilities, sustained and supported the wise men of the country in council, and the brave men of the country in the field of battle? Nor are there wanting more recent instances. I have the pleasure to see near me, and near my friend who proposed this sentiment, the son of an eminent merchant of New England (Mr. Goodhue), an early member of the Senate of the United States, always consulted, always respected, in whatever belonged to the duty and the means of putting in operation the financial and commercial system of the country; and this mention of the father of my friend brings to my mind the memory of his great colleague, the early associate of Hamilton and of Ames, trusted and beloved by Washington, consulted on all occasions connected with the administration of the finances, the establishment of the treasury department, the imposition of the first rates of duty, and with every thing that belonged to the commercial system of the United States, — George Cabot, of Massachusetts.

I will take this occasion to say, Gentlemen, that there is no truth better developed and established in the history of the United States, from the formation of the Constitution to the present time, than this, — that the mercantile classes, the great commercial masses of the country, whose affairs connect them strongly with every State in the Union and with all the nations of the earth, whose business and profession give a sort of nationality to their character, — that no class of men among us, from the beginning, have shown a stronger and firmer devotion to whatsoever has been designed, or to whatever has tended, to preserve the union of these States and the stability of the free government under which we live. The Constitution of the United States, in regard to the various municipal regulations and local interests, has left the States individual, disconnected, isolated. It has left them their own codes of criminal law; it has left them their own system of municipal regulations. But there was one great interest, one great concern, which, from the very nature of the case, was no longer to be left under the regulations of the then thirteen, afterwards twenty, and now twenty-six States, but was committed, necessarily committed, to the care, the protection, and the regulation of one government; and this was that great unit, as it has been called, the commerce of the United States. There is no commerce of New York, no commerce of

Massachusetts, none of Georgia, none of Alabama or Louisiana. All and singular, in the aggregate and in all its parts, is the commerce of the United States, regulated at home by a uniform system of laws under the authority of the general government, and protected abroad under the flag of our government, the glorious *E Pluribus Unum*, and guarded, if need be, by the power of the general government all over the world. There is, therefore, Gentlemen, nothing more cementing, nothing that makes us more cohesive, nothing that more repels all tendencies to separation and dismemberment, than this great, this common, I may say this overwhelming interest of one commerce, one general system of trade and navigation, one everywhere and with every nation of the globe. There is no flag of any particular American State seen in the Pacific seas, or in the Baltic, or in the Indian Ocean. Who knows, or who hears, there of your proud State, or of my proud State? Who knows, or who hears, of any thing, at the extremest north or south, or at the antipodes, — in the remotest regions of the Eastern or Western Sea, — who ever hears, or knows, of any thing but an American ship, or of any American enterprise of a commercial character that does not bear the impression of the American Union with it?

It would be a presumption of which I cannot be guilty, Gentlemen, for me to imagine for a moment, that, among the gifts which New England has made to our common country, I am any thing more than one of the most inconsiderable. I readily bring to mind the great men, not only with whom I have met, but those of the generation before me, who now sleep with their fathers, distinguished in the Revolution, distinguished in the formation of the Constitution and in the early administration of the government, always and everywhere distinguished; and I shrink in just and conscious humiliation before their established character and established renown; and all that I venture to say, and all that I venture to hope may be thought true, in the sentiment proposed, is, that, so far as mind and purpose, so far as intention and will, are concerned, I may be found among those who are capable of embracing the whole country of which they are members in a proper, comprehensive, and patriotic regard. We all know that the objects which are nearest are the objects which are dearest; family affections, neighborhood affections, social relations, these in truth are nearest and dearest to us all:

but whosoever shall be able rightly to adjust the graduation of his affections, and to love his friends and his neighbors, and his country, as he ought to love them, merits the commendation pronounced by the philosophic poet upon him

" Qui didicit patriæ quid debeat, et quid amicis."

Gentlemen, it has been my fortune, in the little part which I have acted in public life, for good or for evil to the community, to be connected entirely with that government which, within the limits of constitutional power, exercises jurisdiction over all the States and all the people. My friend at the end of the table on my left has spoken pleasantly to us to-night of the reputed miracles of tutelar saints. In a sober sense, in a sense of deep conviction, I say that the emergence of this country from British domination, and its union under its present form of government beneath the general Constitution of the country, if not a miracle, is, I do not say the most, but one of the most fortunate, the most admirable, the most auspicious occurrences, which have ever fallen to the lot of man. Circumstances have wrought out for us a state of things which, in other times and other regions, philosophy has dreamed of, and theory has proposed, and speculation has suggested, but which man has never been able to accomplish. I mean the government of a great nation over a vastly extended portion of the surface of the earth, *by means of local institutions for local purposes, and general institutions for general purposes.* I know of nothing in the history of the world, notwithstanding the great league of Grecian states, notwithstanding the success of the Roman system, (and certainly there is no exception to the remark in modern history,) — I know of nothing so suitable on the whole for the great interests of a great people spread over a large portion of the globe, as the provision of local legislation for local and municipal purposes, with, not a confederacy, nor a loose binding together of separate parts, but a limited, positive general government for positive general purposes, over the whole. We may derive eminent proofs of this truth from the past and the present. What see we to-day in the agitations on the other side of the Atlantic? I speak of them, of course without expressing any opinion on questions of politics in a foreign country; but I speak of them as an occurrence which shows the great expediency, the utility, I may say

the necessity, of local legislation.   If, in a country on the other
side of the water (Ireland), there be some who desire a severance
of one part of the empire from another, under a proposition of
repeal, there are others who propose a continuance of the existing relation under a federative system: and what is this?   No
more, and no less, than an approximation to that system under
which we live, which for local, municipal purposes shall have a
local legislature, and for general purposes a general legislature.

This becomes the more important when we consider that the
United States stretch over so many degrees of latitude, — that
they embrace such a variety of climate, — that various conditions and relations of society naturally call for different laws and
regulations.   Let me ask whether the legislature of New York
could wisely pass laws for the government of Louisiana, or
whether the legislature of Louisiana could wisely pass laws
for Pennsylvania or New York?   Every body will say, " No."
And yet the interests of New York and Pennsylvania and Louisiana, in whatever concerns their relations between themselves
and their general relations with all the states of the world, are
found to be perfectly well provided for, and adjusted with perfect congruity, by committing these general interests to one common government, the result of popular general elections among
them all.

I confess, Gentlemen, that having been, as I have said, in my
humble career in public life, employed in that portion of the
public service which is connected with the general government,
I have contemplated, as the great object of every proceeding,
not only the particular benefit of the moment, or the exigency
of the occasion, but the preservation of this system; for I do
consider it so much the result of circumstances, and that so
much of it is due to fortunate concurrence, as well as to the
sagacity of the great men acting upon those occasions, — that it
is an experiment of such remarkable and renowned success, —
that he is a fool or a madman who would wish to try that experiment a second time.   I see to-day, and we all see, that the
descendants of the Puritans who landed upon the Rock of Plymouth ; the followers of Raleigh, who settled Virginia and
North Carolina ; he who lives where the truncheon of empire,
so to speak, was borne by Smith ; the inhabitants of Georgia ;
he who settled under the auspices of France at the mouth of

the Mississippi; the Swede on the Delaware, the Quaker of Pennsylvania, — all find, at this day, their common interest, their common protection, their common *glory*, under the united government, which leaves them all, nevertheless, in the administration of their own municipal and local affairs, to be Frenchmen, or Swedes, or Quakers, or whatever they choose. And when one considers that this system of government, I will not say has produced, because God and nature and circumstances have had an agency in it, — but when it is considered that this system has not prevented, but has rather encouraged, the growth of the people of this country from three millions, on the glorious 4th of July, 1776, to seventeen millions now, who is there that will say, upon this hemisphere, — nay, who is there that will stand up in any hemisphere, who is there in any part of the world, that will say that the great experiment of a united republic has *failed* in America? And yet I know, Gentlemen, I feel, that this united system is held together by strong tendencies to union, at the same time that it is kept from too much leaning toward consolidation by a strong tendency in the several States to support each its own power and consideration. In the physical world it is said, that

> "All nature's difference keeps all nature's peace,"

and there is in the political world this same harmonious difference, this regular play of the positive and negative powers (if I may so say), which, at least for one glorious half-century, has kept us as we have been kept, and made us what we are.

But, Gentlemen, I must not allow myself to pursue this topic. It is a sentiment so commonly repeated by me upon all public occasions, and upon all private occasions, and everywhere, that I forbear to dwell upon it now. It is the union of these States, it is the system of government under which we live, beneath the Constitution of the United States, happily framed, wisely adopted, successfully administered for fifty years, — it is mainly this, I say, that gives us power at home and credit abroad. And, for one, I never stop to consider the power or wealth or greatness of a State. I tell you, Mr. Chairman, I care nothing for your Empire State as such. Delaware and Rhode Island are as high in my regard as New York. In population, in power, in the government over us, you have a greater share. You would have

18 *

the same share if you were divided into forty States. It is not, therefore, as a State sovereignty, it is only because New York is a vast portion of the whole American people, that I regard this State, as I always shall regard her, as respectable and honorable. But among State sovereignties there is no preference; there is nothing high and nothing low; every State is independent and every State is equal. If we depart from this great principle, then are we no longer one people; but we are thrown back again upon the Confederation, and upon that state of things in which the inequality of the States produced all the evils which befell us in times past, and a thousand ill-adjusted and jarring interests.

Mr. President, I wish, then, without pursuing these thoughts, without especially attempting to produce any fervid impression by dwelling upon them, to take this occasion to answer my friend who has proposed the sentiment, and to respond to it by saying, that whoever would serve his country in this our day, with whatever degree of talent, great or small, it may have pleased the Almighty Power to give him, he cannot serve it, he will not serve it, unless he be able, at least, to extend his political designs, purposes, and objects, till they shall comprehend the whole country of which he is a servant.

Sir, I must say a word in connection with that event which we have assembled to commemorate. It has seemed fit to the dwellers in New York, New-Englanders by birth or descent, to form this society. They have formed it for the relief of the poor and distressed, and for the purpose of commemorating annually the great event of the settlement of the country from which they spring. It would be great presumption in me to go back to the scene of that settlement, or to attempt to exhibit it in any colors, after the exhibition made to-day; yet it is an event that in all time since, and in all time to come, and more in times to come than in times past, must stand out in great and striking characteristics to the admiration of the world. The sun's return to his winter solstice, in 1620, is the epoch from which he dates his first acquaintance with the small people, now one of the happiest, and destined to be one of the greatest, that his rays fall upon; and his annual visitation, from that day to this, to our frozen region, has enabled him to see that progress, *progress*, was the characteristic of that small people. He has seen them from a handful, that one of his beams coming through a key-hole might illuminate, spread over a hemisphere, which he cannot enlighten under the slightest eclipse. Nor, though this globe should revolve round him for tens of hundreds of thousands of years, will he see such another incipient colonization upon any part of this attendant upon his mighty orb. What else he may see in those other planets which revolve around him we cannot tell, at least until we have tried the fifty-foot telescope which Lord Rosse is preparing for that purpose.

There is not, Gentlemen, and we may as well admit it, in any history of the past, another epoch from which so many great events have taken a turn; events which, while important to us, are equally important to the country from whence we came. The settlement of Plymouth — concurring, I always wish to be understood, with that of Virginia — was the settlement of New England by colonies of Old England. Now, Gentlemen, take these two ideas and run out the thoughts suggested by both. What has been, and what is to be, Old England? What has been, what is, and what may be, in the providence of God, *New* England, with her neighbors and associates? I would not dwell, Gentlemen, with any particular emphasis upon the sentiment, which I nevertheless entertain, with respect to the great diversity in the races of men. I do not know how far in that respect I might not encroach on those mysteries of Providence which, while I adore, I may not comprehend; but it does seem to me to be very remarkable, that we may go back to the time when New England, or those who founded it, were *subtracted* from Old England; and both Old England and New England went on, nevertheless, in their mighty career of progress and power.

Let me begin with New England for a moment. What has resulted, embracing, as I say, the nearly contemporaneous settlement of Virginia, — what has resulted from the planting upon this continent of two or three slender colonies from the mother country? Gentlemen, the great epitaph commemorative of the character and the worth, the discoveries and glory, of Columbus, was, that he had *given a new world to the crowns of Castile and Aragon.* Gentlemen, this is a great mistake. It does not come up at all to the great merits of Columbus. He gave the territory of the southern hemisphere to the crowns of Castile and Aragon; but as a place for the plantation of colonies, as a place for the habitation of men, as a place to which laws and religion, and manners and science, were to be transferred, as a place in which the creatures of God should multiply and fill the earth, under friendly skies and with religious hearts, he gave it to the whole world, he gave it to universal man! From this seminal principle, and from a handful, a hundred saints, blessed of God and ever honored of men, landed on the shores of Plymouth and elsewhere along the coast, united, as I have said already more than once, in the process of time, with the settlement at Jamestown, has sprung this great people of which we are a portion.

I do not reckon myself among quite the oldest of the land, and yet it so happens that very recently I recurred to an exulting speech or oration of my own, in which I spoke of my country as consisting of nine millions of people. I could hardly persuade myself that within the short time which had elapsed since that epoch our population had doubled; and that at the present moment there does exist most unquestionably as great a probability of its continued progress, in the same ratio, as has ever existed in any previous time. I do not know whose imagination is fertile enough, I do not know whose conjectures, I may almost say, are *wild* enough to tell what may be the progress of wealth and population in the United States in half a century to come. All we know is, here is a people of from seventeen to twenty millions, intelligent, educated, freeholders, freemen, republicans, possessed of all the means of modern improvement, modern science, arts, literature, with the world before them! There is nothing to check them till they touch the shores of the Pacific, and then, they are so much accustomed to water, that *that's* a facility, and no obstruction!

So much, Gentlemen, for this branch of the English race; but what has happened, meanwhile, to England herself since the period of the departure of the Puritans from the coast of Lincolnshire, from the English Boston? Gentlemen, in speaking of the progress of English power, of English dominion and authority, from that period to the present, I shall be understood, of course, as neither entering into any defence or any accusation of the policy which has conducted her to her present state. As to the justice of her wars, the necessity of her conquests, the propriety of those acts by which she has taken possession of so great a portion of the globe, it is not the business of the present occasion to inquire. *Neque teneo, neque refello.* But I speak of them, or intend to speak of them, as facts of the most extraordinary character, unequalled in the history of any nation on the globe, and the consequences of which may and must reach through a thousand generations. The Puritans left England in the reign of James the First. England herself had then become somewhat settled and established in the Protestant faith, and in the quiet enjoyment of property, by the previous energetic, long, and prosperous reign of Elizabeth. Her successor was James the Sixth of Scotland, now become James the First of England; and here was a union of the crowns, but not of the kingdoms, — a very important distinction. Ireland was held by a military power, and one cannot but see that at that day, whatever may be true or untrue in more recent periods of her history, Ireland was held by England by the two great potencies, the power of the sword and the power of confiscation. In other respects, England was nothing like the England which we now behold. Her foreign possessions were quite inconsiderable. She had some hold on the West India Islands; she had Acadia, or Nova Scotia, which King James granted, by wholesale, for the endowment of the knights whom he created by hundreds. And what has been her progress? Did she then possess Gibraltar, the key to the Mediterranean? Did she possess a port in the Mediterranean? Was Malta hers? Were the Ionian Islands hers? Was the southern extremity of Africa, was the Cape of Good Hope, hers? Were the whole of her vast possessions in India hers? Was her great Australian empire hers? While that branch of her population which followed the western star, and under its guidance committed itself to the duty of settling, fertilizing, and peopling an unknown wilderness in the West, were pursuing their destinies, other causes, providential doubtless, were leading English power eastward and southward, in consequence and by means of her naval prowess, and the extent of her commerce, until in our day we have seen that within the Mediterranean, on the western coast and at the southern extremity of Africa, in Arabia, in hither India and farther India, she has a population *ten times* as great as that of the British Isles two centuries ago. And recently, as we have witnessed, — I will not say with how much truth and justice, policy or impolicy, I do not speak at all to the morality of the action, I only speak to the *fact*, — she has found admission into China, and has carried the Christian religion and the Protestant faith to the doors of three hundred millions of people.

It has been said that whosoever would see the Eastern world before it turns into a Western world must make his visit soon, because steamboats and omnibuses, commerce, and all the arts of Europe, are extending themselves from Egypt to Suez, from Suez to the Indian seas, and from the Indian seas all over the explored regions of the still farther East.

Now, Gentlemen, I do not know what practical views or what practical results may take place from this great expansion of the power of the two branches of Old England. It is not for me to say. I only can see, that on this continent *all* is to be *Anglo-American* from Plymouth Rock to the Pacific seas, from the north pole to California. That is certain; and in the Eastern world, I only see that you can hardly place a finger on a map of the world and be an *inch* from an English settlement.

Gentlemen, if there be any thing in the supremacy of races, the experiment now in progress will develop it. If there be any truth in the idea, that those who issued from the great Caucasian fountain, and spread over Europe, are to react on India and on Asia, and to act on the whole Western world, it may not be for us, nor our children, nor our grandchildren to see it, but it will be for our descendants of some generation to see the extent of that progress and dominion of the favored races.

For myself, I believe there is no limit fit to be assigned to it by the human mind, because I find at work everywhere, on both sides of the Atlantic, under various forms and degrees of restriction on the one hand, and under various degrees of motive and stimulus on the other hand, in these branches of a common race, the great principle *of the freedom of human thought, and the respectability of individual character*. I find everywhere an elevation of the character of man as man, an elevation of the individual as a component part of society. I find everywhere a rebuke of the idea, that the many are made for the few, or that government is any thing but an *agency* for mankind. And I care not beneath what zone, frozen, temperate, or torrid; I care not of what complexion, white or brown; I care not under what circumstances of climate or cultivation, if I can find a race of men on an inhabitable spot of earth whose general sentiment it is, and whose general feeling it is, that government is made for man — man, as a religious, moral, and social being — and not man for government, there I know that I shall find prosperity and happiness.

Gentlemen, I forbear from these remarks. I recur with pleasure to the sentiment which I expressed at the commencement of my observations. I repeat the gratification which I feel at having been referred to on this occasion by a distinguished member of the mercantile profession; and without detaining you further, I beg to offer as a sentiment, —

" *The mercantile interest of the United States*, always and everywhere friendly to a united and free government."

Mr. Webster sat down amid loud and repeated applause ; and immediately after, at the request of the President, rose and said : —

Gentlemen, I have the permission of the President to call your attention to the circumstance that a distinguished foreigner is at the table to-night, Mr. Aldham; a gentleman, I am happy to say, of my own hard-working profession, and a member of the English Parliament from the great city of Leeds. A traveller in the United States, in the most unostentatious manner, he has done us the honor, at the request of the Society, to be present to-night. I rise, Gentlemen, to propose his health. He is of that Old England of which I have been speaking; of that Old England with whom we had some fifty years ago rather a serious family quarrel, — terminated in a manner, I believe, not particularly disadvantageous to either of us. He will find in this, his first visit to our country, many things to remind him of his own home, and the pursuits in which he is engaged in that home. If he will go into our courts of law, he will find those who practise there referring to the same books of authority, acknowledging the same principles, discussing the same subjects, which he left under discussion in Westminster Hall. If he go into our public assemblies, he will find the same rules of procedure — possibly not always quite as regularly observed — as he left behind him in that house of Parliament of which he is a member. At any rate, he will find us a branch of that great family to which he himself belongs, and I doubt not that, in his sojourn among us, in the acquaintances he may form, the notions he may naturally imbibe, he will go home to his own country somewhat better satisfied with what he has seen and learned on this side of the Atlantic, and somewhat more convinced of the great importance to both countries of preserving the peace that at present subsists between them.   I propose to you, Gentlemen, the health of Mr. Aldham.

Mr. Aldham rose and said : — " Mr. President and Gentlemen of the New England Society, I little expected to be called on to take a part in the proceedings of this evening ; but I am very happy in being afforded an opportunity of expressing my grateful acknowledgments for the very cordial hospitality which you have extended to me, and the very agreeable intellectual treat with which I have been favored this evening.   It was with no little astonishment that I listened to the terms in which I was introduced to you by a gentleman whom I so much honor (Mr. Webster).   The kind and friendly terms in which he referred to me were, indeed, quite unmerited by their humble object, and nothing, indeed, could have been more inappropriate.   It is impossible for any stranger to witness such a scene as this without the greatest interest.   It is the celebration of an event which already stands recorded as one of the most interesting and momentous occurrences which ever took place in the annals of our race.   And an Englishman especially cannot but experience the deepest emotion as he regards such a scene.   Every thing which he sees, every emblem employed in this celebration, many of the topics introduced, remind him most impressively of that community of ancestry which exists between his own countrymen and that great race which peoples this continent, and which, in enterprise, ingenuity, and commercial activity, — in all the elements indeed of a great and prosperous nation, — is certainly not exceeded, perhaps not equalled, by any other nation on the face of the globe.   Gentlemen, I again thank you for the honor you have done me, and conclude by expressing the hope that the event may continue to be celebrated in the manner which its importance and interest merit."

Mr. Aldham sat down amid great applause.

MASS MEETING AT ALBANY.

MASS MEETING AT ALBANY.*

Among the numerous political meetings in the summer and autumn of 1844, none, perhaps, surpassed that which was held at Albany on the 27th of August. It was attended by an immense number of the inhabitants of that city and of the neighboring counties, and by many thousands of persons from a distance. By some estimates the numbers present exceeded fifty thousand. Among the distinguished persons present by invitation were Mr. Webster, Messrs. Dawson and Berrien of Georgia, Messrs. Granger, Hasbrouck, and Greely, of New York, and others of political eminence from several parts of the country. The meeting, of course, was held in the open air. Samuel Stevens, Esq., of Albany, presided, and, after a few appropriate remarks by him on the nature of the occasion, Mr. Webster was introduced to the meeting and delivered the following speech.

In the history of states and of governments, as in the lives of individuals, there are epochs at which it is wise to pause, to review the past, to consider attentively the present, and to contemplate probable futurity. We are, fellow-citizens, upon the eve of a general election, full of importance and of interest, involving questions which rise far above all considerations of the personal qualities of the candidates for office, questions of the greatest and the nearest bearing upon present and existing interests, and likely to affect the prosperity of the country for a long time to come.

In my judgment, therefore, it is highly proper, in such a state of things and on such an occasion, that we should bring the past into our immediate presence, and consider and examine it; that we should ponder assiduously existing interests and exist-

* A Speech delivered at a very large Meeting held at Albany, on the 27th of August, 1844, with Reference to the Presidential Election of that Year.

ing duties, and that we should exercise whatever of forecast and sagacity we possess, in endeavoring to discern what is, or what may be, yet before us.

On the 3d of March next, fifty-six years will have expired since we began our national character and existence under the present Constitution of the United States. In the lapse of that period, we have gone through fourteen Presidential elections, and have chosen eight-and-twenty successive Congresses of the United States. Of these fourteen Presidential elections, twelve have been effected by the popular vote, according to the provisions of the Constitution; and two have taken place, in pursuance of other constitutional provisions, by the House of Representatives in Congress, and in default of an election in the primary mode by the people of the Union. These several elections have all been legal and regular. Every successive incumbent of the Presidential office has been acknowledged, in succession, to be rightfully in possession of that office. All these elections have been conducted without violence or disorder, without the interference of an armed force, and by the regular, peaceable, constitutional exertion of the public will.

In my estimation, Gentlemen, this is a fact of the highest importance to us, and of great interest and importance to the whole civilized world; because it proves that a republican government is capable of existing over a great country, of various interests, connections, associations, and pursuits; that it has a possible permanence; that it may be continued and exercise its functions. For such a government has existed, has continued itself, has exercised its functions, as I have said, for more than half a century; and that half-century, be it always remembered, has been a marked period in history, — for during its progress fierce wars have afflicted the nations of Europe, and revolutions, without parallel for convulsion and violence, have shaken the dynasties of the elder world.

It is true, therefore, that on a great area there has existed, during this period, a republican and popular form of government. Its officers have been renewed during this period, by the choice of the people, and the succession of power has been as peaceable and regular as in any of the established monarchies or dynasties of the ancient world.

In the second place, our history proves, that not only is such a republican government capable of continuance, and, as we hope, of perpetuity, but it is capable also of exercising all the functions and all the powers necessary to an efficient government, and of performing all the duties requisite to the protection and defence of the country, and to the advancement of the prosperity of the people.

In the third place, our history shows, that the government established by this Constitution, though spread over a vast territory, when administered by wise and good men, and supported by a virtuous community, is in its tendency a salutary government; that its general tendency is to act for the good of the people; and that, therefore, as parental and guardian in its character, as exercising its functions for the common weal, it attaches to itself a sentiment of general support and approbation.

And finally, our history proves that such a system may exist, with all the necessary attributes of government, with all the powers of salutary administration; and exist, at the same time, with the perfect safety of popular liberty and of private rights; — because, in this respect, looking back over the half-century which has passed, we may somewhat proudly challenge the world, including the most advanced and enlightened nations of Europe, to show that there is anywhere on the face of the earth a government which provides greater security for private right, for life and property, and greater security for popular, public liberty, than have been maintained in these United States.

Now, as I have said, it appears to me, that, in reviewing the past, we may congratulate ourselves that we have set this great example, not only to our posterity, but to the whole civilized world, — an example which the world has desired to see, which all the lovers of civil liberty and all who are friendly to popular government have anxiously sought to behold.

You know, fellow-citizens, that it has been a current opinion with those who speculate upon the subject, that republican forms of government are adapted only to the affairs of small countries. A distinguished English philosopher, writing some sixty or seventy years ago, observed that the truth of this opinion was about to be brought to the test of experiment; and that this great experiment was to be made in America. If that distinguished writer had lived to the present time, if he had reviewed with us the occurrences and incidents of the last fifty years, if he

19*

could be here to-day and see with what order and quiet and intelligence great public questions are discussed by the great body of the people, he would have said, and he would have rejoiced to be able to say, that the great experiment had succeeded in America.

Now, Gentlemen, there are two propositions which it is my purpose to submit to you, and in support of which I shall offer such remarks as I may be able to make, and you may be able to hear, in the vast concourse assembled on this occasion.

The first is, that, if this government, under which we shall have lived fifty-six years on the third day of March next, has fully and fairly, to the satisfaction of all men, and to the admiration of the world, fulfilled the objects designed by it, then it is our interest, if we value our happiness or the happiness of those who are to come after us, *to support* that constitution and government.

And, in the second place, if the success of this Constitution, for the period I have mentioned, be fairly referable to the adoption and practice of any great system of measures, which we can comprehend, which we can understand, of which we have had experience, then I say, if we love the Constitution, and if we mean to defend and transmit it to our children, our plain duty is, as far as in us lies, to pursue the same system of public measures, and to *adhere* to all, and each, and every one, of those great principles.

The question then, is, Gentlemen, Has the Constitution of the United States fulfilled the objects for which it was established?

To the intelligible understanding of this question, and the rendering a satisfactory answer, we must first look back to the period of its adoption, and ascertain what were its objects. To what great end, for what significant and especial purpose, did our fathers adopt the Constitution of the general government?

Now, Gentlemen, however commonplace it may be, it is vastly important that we should never fail, on these occasions, to bear in mind the condition of the country while it yet consisted of individual States, united only by the loose bands of the old confederacy. The Revolutionary war, and its termination, by the peace of 1783, made the thirteen States independent States; but it left them with feeble powers, conferred for certain purposes, and to be exercised under certain conditions. They formed one government to no purpose, and with no object. They had no common revenue, no common commerce, no common nationality. A man could call himself a citizen of New York, a citizen of Massachusetts, a citizen of Georgia; but no man with any emphasis, and certainly not in any particular which makes us proud so to call ourselves, could call himself, anywhere on the face of the earth, an *American* citizen; because there was no unity, no identity, no specific idea, attached to that term, now so glorious throughout the habitable world.

The war left the States embarrassed, with a disordered trade, with every variety of custom-house regulation, and involved in debt. The country called for a general Congress. The debts of the Revolution pressed heavily upon it. All the States were indebted, all were overwhelmed with a depreciated paper money; there was no unity of action, no general concert, in short, no "perfect union" among the States. Especially did this variety exist in reference to the intercourse which each State had with its neighbors and with foreign states. It constituted not only variety, but contradiction. There was a state of things in this respect which Mr. Madison, with his clear perception and patriotic regard for the best interests of the American people, did not hesitate to call a "wonderful anarchy of trade."

It was under these circumstances that the formation of the Constitution of the United States entered into the conception and purposes of the wise men of those days. They entertained that conception; they sought to accomplish that purpose. This was no easy purpose to accomplish with thirteen independent States, each jealous of its liberties and its rights, and sufficiently prone to think highly of its local advantages and powers. Yet the wisdom and patriotism, and general devotion to the interests of the whole, felt everywhere, pervading all classes, in the end accomplished that object of almost supreme importance.

Let us now look a little more closely into this matter, and inquire something more definitely into the objects for which the Constitution was formed. It was, for certain purposes, to make us *one people*, though surely not for all purposes; and the extent to which it was desired and designed that the people of all the States should be one people, and the government over these people should be one government, is expressed in a document of the most authentic character, I mean the letter addressed to the Congress of the Confederation by the Convention which formed the Constitution.　That letter, written on behalf of the Convention, and having the great name of Washington subscribed to it, says : —

" The friends of our country have long seen and desired, that the power of making war, peace, and treaties, that of levying money and regulating commerce, and the correspondent executive and judicial authorities, should be fully and effectually vested in the general government of the Union."

We see here, then, that the object of this Constitution was to make the people of the United States one people, and to place them under one government, in regard to every thing respecting their relation to foreign states and the aspect in which the nations of the world were to regard them.　It was not an amalgamation of the whole people under one government; not an extinguishment of the State sovereignties.　That would have been an extinction, not a union, of existing States.　There was no pressing necessity, therefore, for making the local institutions of the several States approach each other in any closer affinity. As governments existed, each within its own territory, for all purposes of territorial supremacy and power, in a word, for all State purposes, it was no matter what variety the States should have in these respects, and it was left to their own discretion.　And it is the very beauty of our system, as I conceive, that the Federal and the State governments are kept thus distinct; that local legislation is left to the local authorities, and the general legislation is given to the general government.

This I take to be the true idea and definition of those purposes for which the general government, under the present Constitution, was organized and established.　Indeed, Gentlemen, a most authoritative, a perfectly authoritative, declaration of the objects of the people of the United States in forming a Constitution, is contained in that instrument itself, on its very face. There the words stand, an everlasting record of the intentions and purposes of those who framed it.　It says it is established "in order to form a more perfect union."　They, the people, framed the Constitution of the United States, for their " more perfect union," — to " establish justice, insure domestic tranquillity, provide for the common defence, and promote the general welfare," and, finally, " to secure the blessings of liberty " to them and their posterity. Here, at the head of all these objects, stands, in bold and prominent relief, the great, noble object, TO FORM A MORE PERFECT UNION *among the people of the United States*.

And I will take the liberty to refer to another passage in the letter to which I have just alluded, from the Federal Convention to Congress, in submitting to them the plan of the Constitution : —

" In all our deliberations on this subject, we kept steadily in our view that which appears to us the *greatest* interest of every true American, the consolidation of our UNION, in which is involved our prosperity, felicity, safety, perhaps our national existence."

You will please to observe, that this language is not applied to the powers of government; it does not say that they aim at consolidation *in* the general government, nor *of* all the powers of government; it does not at all usurp the local authorities of the States, nor interfere with any thing that belongs to the local legislation and administration. But the consolidation of which Washington and his associates spoke was a consolidation *of the Union*, for the just purposes of a Union, of a strong Union, — for those purposes for which the Union itself ought to exist.

I have said, and I beg leave to repeat, because it lies at the foundation of all just conceptions of the Constitution of the country, that the Union created by the Constitution was a union among the people in every thing which regards their diplomatic and foreign relations and concerns, and the intercourse between the world and themselves. The Union created by the old Confederation was imperfect; indeed, it hardly existed at all, certainly with no efficiency and productive of no good. This was the object, as stated by the members of the Convention themselves, in the document to which I have referred, and distinctly announced on the face of the Constitution itself.

In pursuance of these purposes, the Constitution proceeded to institute a general government, with such powers and authority as would accomplish the object intended. The Constitution assigned to the general government the power of war and peace, the power of making treaties, and that other important, and, as it has turned out, absolutely indispensable power, *the regulation of commerce.*

Government has attempted to perform all these duties. It

has exercised the power of regulating commerce. So has it sought to establish justice, another of its objects. It has done so especially in the great matter of paying off the debt of the Revolution. It has enacted laws to insure domestic tranquillity, and it has effected that object. It has provided for the common defence, by organizing armies, equipping navies, and such other preparations as the exigencies of our position have rendered necessary. In these and other ways it has endeavored to promote the public welfare; and it has not neglected any means for securing the blessings of liberty.

Such being the objects of the Constitution, you and I and our contemporaries throughout the country, who have a part to act, a vote to give, an opinion to express,— you and I, and all of us, after the experience of half a century, are bound to put it to ourselves and to our consciences, whether these objects have been accomplished by that instrument. Because if they have not, if the Constitution has shown itself, under the best administrations, inefficient and useless, it is time to revert to that great power inherent in the people, of reforming the government, and establishing a system more suited to their purposes and desires. But if the Constitution, on the whole, upon this conscientious examination, shall prove to have accomplished its ends, to have subserved the public prosperity, carried the nation forward in wealth, in business, in enterprise, and to have raised us to a pitch of glory and renown, of which you and I and all of us are proud, — then, I say, we are bound to it by every tie of gratitude, by every feeling of patriotism. We are bound to support it with all our hearts, for all our lives, and to transmit it unimpaired to our children.

Now, I say, in my humble but conscientious judgment, and I say it under a mixed sense of gratitude to God and of profound reverence for the wisdom of our ancestors, making all reasonable allowances for the frailties which beset all men and the misfortunes which sometimes betide all governments, — I say to you as my judgment, I say it to the country, and would to Heaven I could say it to the whole human race, and in tones which would echo to the last generation of men, that this Constitution *has* prosperously, greatly, and gloriously answered the ends of its establishment. And if there be any one among you, or if there be in the country a man, who doubts or denies this, he is a man for whose judgment I have no great respect, and with whose feelings I have no manner of sympathy.

Gentlemen, this government was established at one of the most fearful periods in the history of the human race in modern times, — just at the breaking out of that tremendous convulsion which so terribly shook Europe to her foundation, in all her interests and all her concerns, all her thrones and all her dynasties, — the French Revolution. We had just entered upon the first administration of the government under the great leader of the Revolution, who had been chosen to be our great leader in the times which succeeded, the times of peace. When the French Revolution broke out, we had just commenced our national being under the present Constitution. It proved the ark of our safety. It proved competent to preserve our neutrality. It proved competent, under his administration, to keep us clear from the overwhelming and submerging Maelstrom of European war and European conquest. In its progress it covered every sea with our flag. It replenished the treasury. It paid the debt of the Revolution. Above all, it gave us name and fame, it gave us character and standing. It made the flag *E Pluribus Unum* known wherever any thing could be water-borne. In the northern and southern, the eastern and western seas, wherever our navy went, the stars and stripes went with it, and they made known that the United States of America had become *one* in all that related to their intercourse with foreign nations. It gave a general significance, a new respect, to the power-importing name of America: and on that foundation we still rest.

Under this Constitution we have attained the rank of the second commercial nation in the world. We have risen from a population of three millions to one of twenty millions. Every interest, in my judgment, has been successfully maintained, sustained, cherished, and nourished by a wise and paternal government.

And now, Gentlemen, is there a man among you, or in the country, who, in a just and candid examination of this history, is not ready to stand by the Constitution? or are there those who prefer another form of government? I put it to you to-day, whether, in the history of the past, which we have briefly scanned, you see any thing which you wish reversed. Do you wish to revolutionize the history of the past? Do you wish to blot it out? Is there any thing in the history of your country thus far which makes you ashamed that you are Americans? I put it to the elderly men assembled here to-day, whose career of life is fast drawing to a close, — do they know any better government, any better political system, to which they would wish to intrust the lives and property of their children? I put it to you, men in middle life, engaged in the concerns and business of life, — do you wish for, can you conceive, have you a notion of, any system better calculated to secure industry, to maintain liberty, to protect property, and to enable you to provide for yourselves and for those who are near and dear to you? And you, young men, full of the aspirations of ingenuous youth, full, I know, of patriotic feeling, and eagerly desirous to enjoy, to honor, and to serve your country, — do you wish to render public service under any other banner?

Then, Gentlemen, then, fellow-Americans, then, friends, if it be true that the Constitution of the United States, under the various and successive administrations that have taken place since 1789, has fulfilled all the just hopes, and more than even the most sanguine hopes, of the country, is there a question that it is the part of gratitude to God, of respect to our ancestors, the part of regard for every interest that is dear to us and to ours, to cleave to it as to the ark of our political salvation? that, however it may be with others, however others may stray from the great object of national regard, for us and ours we will *adhere* to it, we will maintain, we will defend it, to our dying day?

If this be so, if the Constitution of the country has been, in fact, proved eminently useful, the next question is, Upon what system of general policy, according to what measures relating to the great interests of the country, has the Constitution, on the whole, been administered? How did it commence? What measures were deemed necessary, if I may so say, from its cradle?

Gentlemen, this leads us back to that interesting and important epoch, the commencement of Washington's administration, in the city of New York, under the present Constitution of the United States.

For myself, I always revisit those scenes with delight. I refresh myself by going back to this spring-time of the republic, to contemplate the characters of the men, and, above all, to admire the purity of their patriotism and the elevation of their principles. In idea I love to gather round me the circle of Washington and his great compatriots, not in the field of battle, but in a greater field, the field of political wisdom, the field of patriotism, the field where prudence, and discretion, and firmness are as necessary as in the greatest conflict in arms. I carry myself back to the halls of the Congress which sat in the spring of 1789. I can present to myself a sort of living image of that great assembly of wise men. In the centre you may see Washington himself, and his immediate advisers, — Mr. Jay, who had not yet ceased to be Secretary for Foreign Affairs under the authority of the old Confederation, Mr. Hamilton, and General Knox. In the House of Representatives were Ames, and Goodhue, and Benson, and Lawrence, and Boudinot, and Fitzsimmons, and Madison, and Huger. In the Senate were King, and Schuyler, and Strong, and Robert Morris, and Baldwin of Georgia, and Richard Henry Lee of Virginia, — he who had moved the resolution of Independence in 1776 then in the Senate, and he* who had proved himself the champion in debate of that resolution then presiding over the Senate. In one department or another were the warriors of many a well-fought field; and civilians and statesmen, who had been tried in the fiery ordeal of the Revolution, and come forth like burnished gold, surrounded the great chief of the government.

Gentlemen, I can realize the scene when General Washington assembled these houses of the legislature before him, and made to them his first speech, and paid to them the tribute due to their character, and laid before them and before the country those great principles of public and private virtue, on which he wished and desired to see the administration of the government established.

"It will be more consistent," he says, "with those circumstances, and far more congenial with the feelings which actuate me, to substitute, in place of a recommendation of particular measures, the tribute that is due to the talents, the rectitude, and the patriotism which adorn the characters selected to devise and adopt them. In these honorable qualifications I behold the surest pledges, that as, on one side, no local preju-

* John Adams, Vice-President of the United States.

dices or attachments, no separate views or party animosities, will mis-
direct the comprehensive and equal eye which ought to watch over this
great assemblage of communities and interests ; so, on another, that the
foundations of our national policy will be laid in the pure and immutable principles of private morality, and the preëminence of a free government be exemplified by all the attributes which can win the affections
of its citizens and command the respect of the world ; since the preservation of the sacred fire of liberty and the destiny of the republican
model of government are justly considered as *deeply*, perhaps as *finally*,
staked on the experiment intrusted to the hands of the American people."

And in this sentiment, Gentlemen, uttered by Washington, I
concur with all my heart. I believe that we have this great
pledge in our hands; and I believe that every lover of liberty in
the whole earth is looking steadily and earnestly to see if this
great model of a republican government may be held up to the
imitation of mankind.

This is the scene in which our government commenced.
These were the auspices under which it began; worthy, in
my judgment, of America, worthy of liberty, worthy of everlasting renown!

But now, Gentlemen, that we have turned back and contemplated this great first meeting of the chief magistrate and legislature under the Constitution, the inquiry is, What system of
administration did they adopt? What measures appeared to
them to be consonant with the objects of the Constitution, and
called for by the general voice of the people? And I wish to
put the question at once, without any preliminary remarks, and
I put it not only to the Whigs of this assembly, but, if there is
any gentleman present who has attachments to the other party,
or if there be any such in the country who may hear my words,
I put it to him, to his conscience, to his love of truth, to say
whether the great measures with which the administration of
that day proposed to carry on the government are such as our
opponents hold out for our adoption at this day? Did General
Washington and his Congress begin by denying entirely all power
to foster the labor and industry of the United States, as a power
forbidden by the Constitution? Did they deny that Congress
has any power over the currency? Did they deny that Congress
has power to adopt suitable means to collect and disburse its

revenue? Did they begin by denying to Congress the right to make, from the treasury, improvements which were absolutely necessary for the convenience and facility of commerce? Did they, in short, enter upon the administration with the notion that, after all that was done, after all the measures adopted to make a more united people, there still remained in the States a power of State interference, by which one State could set up its will against the wishes of all the other States, and so defeat the operations of the general government? An administration upon these principles, or any of these principles, would defeat the whole object of forming a more perfect union among the people; it would make the bands of the confederacy as loose as before the adoption of the Constitution; it would have untied, instead of tying closer, the knots of concord and union.

Now, in the early administration of the government some trusts and duties were conferred upon the general government, about which there could not be much dispute. It belonged to the general government to make war and peace, and to make treaties. There was no room for dispute as to these powers; they were liable to no great diversity of opinion. But then comes the other power, which has been, and is now, of the utmost importance, that *of regulating commerce*. What does that import? On this part of the Constitution there has sprung up in our day a great diversity of opinion. But it is certain that when the Constitution had been framed, and the first Congress assembled to pass laws under it, there was no diversity of opinion upon it, no contradictory sentiments. The power of regulating commerce granted to Congress was most assuredly understood to embrace all forms of regulation belonging to those terms under other governments,—all the meaning implied in the terms, in the same language, employed in all laws and in the intercourse of modern nations. And I consider it as capable of mathematical demonstration, as capable of demonstration as any proposition in Euclid, that the power of discriminating in custom-house duties, for the protection of American labor and industry, was understood, not by some, but by all, by high and low, everywhere, as included in the regulation of trade.

The term was well understood in our colonial history, and if we go back to the history of the Constitution, and of the Convention which adopted it, we shall find that everywhere, when masses of men were assembled, and the wants of the people were brought forth into prominence, the idea was held up, that domestic industry could not prosper, manufactures and the mechanic arts could not advance, the condition of the common country could not be carried up to any considerable elevation, unless there should be one government, to lay one rate of duty upon imports throughout the Union, from New Hampshire to Georgia; regard to be had, in laying this duty, to the protection of American labor and industry. I defy the man in any degree conversant with history, in any degree acquainted with the annals of this country from 1787 to the adoption of the Constitution in 1789, to say that this was not a leading, I may almost say, the leading motive, South as well as North, for the formation of the new government. Without that provision in the Constitution, it never could have been adopted.

I shall add one or two circumstances which occurred immediately on organizing the government, to show that this was the expectation, the belief, the conviction of what was the duty, and what would be the conduct, of the new government, which prevailed everywhere.

The House of Representatives formed a quorum for the first time under the Constitution, in the city of New York, and elected its speaker, on the 1st day of April, 1789. And now, Gentlemen, the House being thus organized, what do you imagine was the very first petition ever presented to it? I hold an account of that petition in my hand, copied from the Journal of the House; and here it is: —

"A petition of the tradesmen, manufacturers, and others, of Maryland, whose names are thereunto subscribed, was presented to the House, and read, stating certain matters, and praying an imposition of such duties on all foreign articles which can be made in America, as will give a just and decided preference to the labors of the petitioners, and that there may be granted to them, in common with the other manufacturers and mechanics of the United States, such relief as in the wisdom of Congress may appear proper."

There, Gentlemen, was the very first petition ever presented to the Congress of the United States, and it came from the monumental city, the capital of Maryland!

And now what do you suppose was the second petition?

Why, it was a like petition from certain mechanics of Charleston; — not Charlestown in Massachusetts, that Commonwealth now scoffed at and derided as narrow and selfish in her politics; not that Charlestown which was burned and laid in ashes by a foreign foe on the 17th of June, 1775, but which, under a fostering government, sprung up again like another phœnix, with renovated and increased beauty; not that Charlestown which skirts the base of Bunker Hill; — but Charleston, the refined and elegant city, the pride of the South, Charleston in South Carolina, always distinguished for intelligence, hospitality, and all the social virtues; Charleston, the mention of which always brings up by association the names of Pinckney, of Sumpter, of Huger, and of Lowndes. From the bosom of that Charleston came this second petition to Congress; and it was a petition of the *shipwrights* of that city, praying Congress to protect them against foreign competition. Here it is : —

" A petition of the shipwrights of the city of Charleston, in the State of South Carolina, was presented to the House and read, stating the distress they are in, from the decline of that branch of business and the present situation of the trade of the United States, and praying that the wisdom and policy of the national legislature may be directed to such measures, in a general regulation of trade and the establishment of a proper navigation act, as will tend to relieve the particular distresses of the petitioners, and, in common with them, those of their fellow-shipwrights throughout the United States."

Well, Gentlemen, and where did the next petition on this subject come from? What city, what people, what country, whose inhabitants, followed close upon these petitions and made similar applications to Congress? It was from the mechanics and manufacturers of that city which is now the great commercial emporium of the whole western continent, the city of New York. Let us see in what terms they address themselves to what they justly call " the *new* government," and what hopes inspired their bosoms, from the fact that a new government had been formed on which was bestowed the power of protecting mechanical labor. Here is the petition : —

" A petition of the mechanics and manufacturers of the city of New York, whose names are thereunto subscribed, was presented to the House and read, setting forth that, in the present deplorable state of commerce and manufactures, they look with confidence to the operations

20 *

of the new government for a restoration of both, and that relief which they have so long and anxiously desired; that they have subjoined a list of such articles as can be manufactured in the State of New York, and humbly pray the countenance and attention of the national legislature thereto."

And yet, Gentlemen, in that great and noble city, which has so far gone ahead of all its competitors, and presents itself to the world as the great city of the American continent, abounding in commerce and successful manufactures, rich in all things, the products of industry of all countries, there are persons in that very city, from which this earnest application of the manufacturers and mechanics was addressed to Congress, in the first days of its existence, who *deny all power* to Congress thus to relieve their fellow-citizens!

Lamentable, lamentable indeed, in my judgment, is that great departure (by what causes produced I will not say), that wide departure of public opinion from the plain, clear, and rational wishes of the people, in the formation of the government, as expressed in these memorials.

Now, I ask you again, how were these petitions for protection treated? Did Congress deny its power? Did it say that it could not possibly give them this protection, unless it should happen to be *in-ci-den-tal?* Did it say, We have only a *revenue* power in regard to this matter? that is, We have the clear and undoubted power to take so much money out of your pockets, and apply it to our own purposes; but God forbid that, in doing so, we should do you any good at the same time? Were these petitioners told that they must take care of themselves? that these were days of free trade, and every body must have a right to trade on equal terms with every body else? Far, far from it. In regard to the subject of these petitions, we all know that the very first Congress secured to the navigation of the United States that which has been, from that time to this, the great foundation, not only of preference, but of *monopoly*, the whole coasting trade of the Union; and the shipwrights of America enjoy that monopoly to the present day, and I hope they will enjoy it for ever. Look at the coasting trade of the United States, so vast in its extent. It is entirely confined to American shipping. But why thus confine it? Why not let in other ships, all other ships which wish to come in, — the Dane, the man of the Hanse Towns and of Hamburg,—with their cheap means of navigation? Why not let them, if they wish, become carriers between New Orleans and New York and Boston? Why not, if you support the system of free trade, why not carry it out? Be impartial. We say you have no more right to protect the carrying trade than any other mode of carrying on traffic among the people; and yet the coasting trade of the United States, employing half our tonnage, is a close monopoly to American shipwrights and sailors; and so may it ever remain!

When I say that, nobody complains of it, but every body says it is right and should be so. But when we come to the government and ask them to protect the hat-maker, or boot-maker, or worker in brass, and all the various mechanic arts of the country, or the man who makes cloth on a larger scale, then is raised the outcry of "Free trade!" and "Down with protection!" And sometimes, I am very sorry to say, this cry comes from the cities, from the exchanges, though not always, and recently, thank Heaven! not often. But sometimes it does come from those people who have long enjoyed, and justly enjoyed, this monopoly of the whole coasting trade of the country, and who have been enriched, honestly enriched, by it.

But how did Congress treat these applications from the cities of New York and Baltimore, to extend protection to the mechanic arts? It *granted* them! It yielded it. And, except a formal act for taking the oaths, the very first act passed by Congress was to secure the coasting trade and protect the mechanic arts, by discriminating duties, and thus carry out the clear, and, according to historical testimony, the most manifest object of the Constitution.

Now, Gentlemen, I know I weary you with these details. But if public discussion is worth any thing, if we mean to exercise the elective franchise intelligently, it seems to me we must go back and drink deep of these original fountains of legislation and administration. I will call your attention, then, to the history of the first act ever passed by Congress, except the one concerning oaths. The following is the preamble of that act: — "Whereas it is necessary for the support of government, for the discharge of the debts of the United States, and the encouragement and *protection of manufactures*, that duties be laid on

goods, wares, and merchandise imported." Ay, the very term
on the face of the act is that derided and now much abhorred
word, *Protection.* There it is on the parchment record of Congress, and on the paper record of our statute-books. It cannot
be erased, and it shall not be erased!

Now, Gentlemen, Congress, as I have mentioned, assembled,
and the House of Representatives formed a quorum on the first
day of April, 1789. It was just before the spring importations;
the treasury was empty, the debt unprovided for; there was
not money enough on hand to pay the expenses of members
of Congress. Mr. Madison, who took a great and admirable
lead in the public business of the day, introduced a measure
into Congress to lay the necessary imposts. In the emergency
of the moment he proposed, not a discriminating law, laying
specific duties for protection as well as for revenue, but a general law, laying a general average duty, so much per cent. on all
articles. He said the principle must be regarded. The general
rule was doubtless that of free trade, but we have the example
of protection, and it must be followed until all other countries
adopt free trade. He urged upon Congress the passage of a
law to raise a little money, without going into the imposition
of specific discriminating duties, article by article. He urged it
with his accustomed power, ability, and authority, and no man
in the house had equal authority.

But the House of Representatives steadily and sturdily, finally
and to the end, refused any such course of proceeding. They
said, " No! we will begin, on this subject of laying duties on
imports, as we intend to go on. Here, and to-day, we will take
up the list of goods, article by article, as requested in the New
York petition, and on some we will lay lighter, and on some
we will lay heavier duties; we will discriminate, and we will
make this discrimination with a view, while answering the
wants of the treasury, to protect the industry and answer the
expectations of our own people." To this principle they adhered, and voted down Mr. Madison's proposition. Mr. Madison
himself, who never denied the principle, came into the measure,
and put his great talents at work upon the bill, and it passed
the house, and stands now upon the statute-book, bearing upon
its face, as one of its objects, the protection of American industry, and adopting the true and lawful, and only true and just
discrimination, that of specific duties.

the general government, General Washington addressed a letter to the port wardens of the city of New York, telling them that, of course, the support of the light-houses, &c., would devolve upon Congress; but as Congress had then no money, and no provision had been made, he requested them not to extinguish the lights, to hold up their lanterns, and pledged himself that he would see them refunded out of the national treasury. And he did so. But now it is supposed to be a great heresy to call upon the national treasury for one cent to clear a harbor, to remove a sand-bar, or to facilitate the commerce of the country in any respect.

These local ideas mislead. Some years ago, while I had the honor of a seat in Congress, I voted for a large expenditure for a harbor at Mobile. A constituent of mine wrote to me to know how, as a Massachusetts man, I could make up my mind to vote so large a sum for a local improvement so far away as a harbor at Mobile, on the Gulf of Mexico. I told him I would not answer him on the general principle, but I would give him a very satisfactory matter-of-fact answer: two or three of *his neighbors* had suffered shipwreck on that very bar at Mobile, in their own vessels, from Massachusetts.

Gentlemen, I will occupy your attention no longer with the other novelties of these times. I hope that they are sufficiently exploded with the generality of American citizens, at least the idea that the laws of Congress can be set aside by individual States. If allowed to prevail, we are no longer *one* people, — only, at any rate, so long as all the States of the present Union choose to remain so. If one State goes off, we are two people; if nine go off, we are ten. It is sufficient to say, that if that idea is allowed to prevail, the Constitution becomes a mere rope of sand; it will grow feebler and feebler every day, and will become, ere long, the object of all men's derision and of all men's contempt.

And now, fellow-citizens, having stated to you what I conscientiously believe to be, and what is proved to be, the real system, the true policy, and the measures by which the government has been administered since most of us were born, I put it to you to-day, whether it is your pleasure to reverse all this course of administration, to entertain the doctrines now presented by our opponents, who deny the power of Congress over protection, over the currency, and over internal improvements, and, when they assert any thing, assert only the power of nullification.

I desire, however, to consider their principles with all candor and fairness. And our opponents tell us, in the first place, that they are not all nullifiers. I am glad of it. But who are the leaders? Who speak for them? Whose standard do they follow? Whose words do they echo? Whose sympathy and support do they seek? That's the question. A party speaks through its organs, its leaders. What folly it is to say, "That's not *my* opinion." Suppose it is not: your influence goes to maintain it, and it is idle to profess that the party goes farther than you wish to go, if all the time you contribute your power to sustain them. You must not give them the power, if you do not mean to have it exercised.

And so it is said, that all are not against protection. Who are not against it? Or if any are not against it, do they not follow the lead of those who are? Justice requires us to say, that there are those of that party in favor of protection in this and other Northern States. But those whom we feel obliged to oppose have chosen a leader; they have presented to us a candidate for our support. How is he on the subject of protection? In other words, what is Mr. Polk's opinion of the subject? Mr. Polk says he is in favor of a judicious tariff. But what sort of a tariff is a judicious tariff in his opinion? His brethren of Carolina say it is a *horizontal* tariff, one which makes no discriminations, but rejects all protection. That is the judgment of Mr. Polk's Carolinian friends on a judicious tariff; and I am strongly of the opinion that it is *his* judgment also.

Again, he says he is in favor of "*incidental* protection." What is incidental protection? Does it mean accidental, casual? I suppose, if a duty of ten per cent. was imposed upon all articles without any discrimination whatever, it would accidentally give some such incidental protection. If that is the meaning of incidental protection, I eschew the word altogether. No, no. The true principle is this. You lay a duty to raise a necessary amount of revenue; in laying it you discriminate, not accidentally, but studiously, cautiously, designedly, discreetly; and in raising a dollar of revenue, you consider upon what article you can collect that dollar so as best to advance the industry of the nation. That's the question, and that's all of it. If you look *only* to the revenue in laying the duty, and say you are in favor of the protection which *that* duty will incidentally allow, you may as well say you are in favor of a rain, or a fog, or a thunderstorm. You are in favor of an accident. It is something which you cannot control. It will take place against your volition, or without it; whether you are in favor of it or not. This, certainly, is not a statesmanlike view of the subject.

The great principle is this. One of you has to contribute five dollars a year to maintain the government; and you pay it in the form of duties on what you consume. Now, if you happen to be a consumer mainly, it is of very little consequence to you on what particular articles this duty is imposed. But it makes the greatest difference in the world to your neighbor, whether it is laid on such articles as he produces, or whether it is so laid as to keep him down and subservient to the labor of other countries. I say again, there must be an intended, designed, discreet discrimination, for real, efficient, substantial protection; and the man who is not for that, is for nothing but incidents, and accidents, and casualties.

We hear much of reciprocity, and I take the rule upon this subject to be well laid down by a distinguished gentleman from another section of the United States,* whom you will probably have the pleasure of hearing when I shall have relieved your patience, that reciprocity is a matter to be secured with foreign nations when it is evidently a true reciprocity. But I have yet to learn, from some new dictionary, that a system of reciprocity is a system with advantages only on one side. I am for reciprocity treaties. No, I will not say treaties, but arrangements; for the whole power over the subject lies with Congress, and not with the treaty-making power. But I am for a *real* reciprocity; not such as was provided by the treaty arrangement lately negotiated, and which the Senate, greatly to their honor, in my judgment, rejected.† I am not for giving away substantial rights, and, without ascribing blame to any party, I must say, not that we were overreached, but that the arrangement of this kind, commonly called Mr. McLane's arrangement of 1831, has turned out greatly to our disadvantage,

* Hon. Mr. Berrien, of Georgia.
† A Treaty with the Hanse Towns.

and that all our reciprocity treaties, as they are called, with the North of Europe, have been, and are, manifestly injurious to American navigation. It will, in my judgment, be one of the first duties of the new administration (if we get one), to revise the whole of that matter, to take care that we protect ourselves, and not to rely on the good-will of our national competitors.

Now, Gentlemen, having detained you so long on the history of the government, to show that protection has been one of its objects from the beginning, I will consider for a moment the reasons, the theory of the matter. Why is protection to domestic labor useful and necessary to the country? It comes to this. We have a variety of occupations, and allow me to say that this variety of employments is a matter of great importance to society, for it gives scope to every degree of ingenuity and talent. I admit freely, notwithstanding the multitude of avocations in life, that the culture of the soil is the great leading interest of the country. I admit this freely, and am willing, if you choose, that trade and manufactures should be regarded as subordinate, as auxiliary to it. I am willing to admit, that, if the theory and practice of protection can be shown distinctly and clearly to militate against the great agricultural interest of the country, it ought to be given up.

But consider the matter; take even this only, the fact that in this country wages are high. They are, and they ought to be, higher than in any other country in the world. And the reason is, that the laborers of this country *are* the country. The vast proportion of those who own the soil, especially in the Northern States, cultivate the soil. They stand on their own acres. The proprietors are the tillers, the laborers on the soil. But this is not all. The members of the country here are part and parcel of the government, and every man is one of the sovereign people, whose combined will constitutes the government. This is a state of things which exists nowhere else on the face of the earth. An approximation to it has been made in France, since the revolution of 1831, which secured the abolition of primogeniture and the restraint of devises.

But nowhere else in the world does there exist such a state of things as we see here, where the proprietors are the laborers, and, at the same time, help to frame the government. If, therefore, we wish to maintain the government, we must see that labor with us is not put in competition with the pauper, untaught, ignorant labor of Europe.   Our men who labor have families to maintain and to educate.   They have sons to fit for the discharge of most duties of life; they have an intelligent part to act for themselves and their connections.   And is labor like that to be reduced to a level with that of the forty millions of serfs of Russia, or the half-fed, half-clothed, ignorant, dependent laborers of other parts of Europe?   America must cease then to be America.   We should be transferred to I know not what sort of government, transferred to I know not what state of society, if the laborers in the United States were to do no more to maintain and educate their families, and to provide for old age, than they do in the Old World.   And may my eyes never look upon such a spectacle as that in this free country!

I believe, that, so far from injuring the great interest of the cultivation of the soil, the reasonable protection of manufactures is useful to that department of industry in all its branches. I believe, in the first place, that the protection of manufactures is useful to the planting States themselves, though I know most of those engaged in that pursuit are of a contrary opinion.   I believe the planter of South Carolina is better off than if there were no manufacturers of his staple in the United States. These take a considerable proportion of every crop of his cotton. They take it early, they fix a price, they are near customers, and to them he disposes of no small portion of his annual crop.

Again, I believe the establishment and successful prosecution of manufactures at the North materially diminishes the price of those articles which the Southern planter has to buy.   But a gentleman from the South, already alluded to, is present, to whom I will leave these matters, and speak of something nearer home, the great farming interests of the Middle and Western States.

Now I hold it to be as demonstrable as any moral proposition, that the agricultural interest of this State, and of the adjoining Western and Southern States, is materially, substantially, and beyond measure benefited by the existence of the manufactures of the North.   To elucidate this, allow me to inquire what is it that the farmer of the county of Albany, or Duchess, or Rensselaer, desires?   Next to the favor of Heaven, in showers and summer heat, and the blessing of health, he desires *a market of sale, at fair prices, for his produce*, and a market, near and reasonable, for what he has occasion to buy. If he has a market where he can *sell* reasonably, and *buy* reasonably, these two conditions fill up the measure of his exigencies.

Where shall he go for a market of sale? I wish to put the question to those who decry the Northern and Eastern manufacturers. Where shall a farmer in any great county of New York find a market for his produce? Why, say some, abroad, in England. But England will not take it. France will not take it.

I see it is insisted, in some of the leading presses in the interest of those opposed to us, that our tariff prevents the sending of our bread stuffs to England. There is nothing more absurd, nothing more entirely destitute of all truth and fact. I assert it as my opinion, that, if our tariff were abolished to-morrow, you would not sell one bushel more corn in England than you do now. Why does not England take it now? Not because she cannot pay for it; but the laws of England prevent the importation of grain or flour, except when the price rises so high in England as to exceed a certain rate (which it seldom does), and then it comes in under a low duty.

This happens sometimes, but not often. Flour, therefore, is sent abroad to wait these occasions, but only in small quantities. You have sent a good deal of wheat to Canada, where it is ground and becomes Canadian flour. This gives a vent for some, and so far it is well. Some beef and cheese and other provisions go from New York to England, and this is all well. The more the better. But depend upon it, that nothing of this kind is affected by the tariff. The reason England takes no more is because her laws (and of their alteration I see no prospect) do not admit it, except when there is a short crop in England, and then under a reduced duty.

Now what becomes of the surplus produce of the grain-growing States? Where does it go to? Who consumes it? The great demand is at home, *at home*, in the manufacturing districts of this State and of other States, and in the consumption of the persons engaged in navigation and commerce. The home demand is the great demand, which takes off the surplus agricultural produce.

I think it sheds light upon the subject, which must satisfy reasonable minds, to look at facts. The New England States, three of them at least, do not raise their own bread-stuffs. They are consumers largely of the flour and grain of this and other

States, as well as of other articles. I have taken some pains to ascertain the amount of the products of other States consumed by Massachusetts alone. I know, in the absence of official returns, it is not easy to speak positively and certainly; but I have given some attention to the subject, and a very intelligent, accurate, and careful member of Congress from Massachusetts (Mr. Hudson) has attended to it also. The result of these estimates I wish to lay before the people of this community, and of all the States, planting States as well as others, and to show them what amount of produce is consumed in Massachusetts.

In the first place, Massachusetts takes and pays for cotton to the value of $ 7,000,000 annually.

And now, if you go to Boston, and look at the great depot of the Western Railroad, you will find it filled with flour; and on every road, and on the hill-sides of New Hampshire, and wherever there is water to float or steam-power to convey it, in every village and town, and at every cross-road, you will find flour bearing every brand, from the State of New York and the West; and there is where it is consumed. Massachusetts takes and pays for flour annually to the value of $ 4,000,000.

She takes and pays for Indian corn and other grain to the value of $ 4,000,000 more, the produce of New York, of the Southern, and of the Northwestern States.

Of wool, — and let the farmers of Duchess understand *that*, and the farmers of Pennsylvania, and the farmers of Vermont, and the farmers everywhere; let them understand, when the price of their wool is raised, what raised it. Massachusetts herself receives $ 3,000,000 worth of wool; and let the farmers get that amount, if they can, out of an *incidental* and *judicious* tariff!

Of leather and hides, from the mountains of New York mainly, Massachusetts buys every year $ 700,000 worth. She buys and consumes beef, pork, and other provisions to the value of $ 3,000,000. Of butter and cheese, mostly from New York, she buys to the value of $ 1,000,000. She takes $ 500,000 worth of pig lead from Missouri and Illinois; $ 300,000 worth of rice from South Carolina, for consumption; and $ 1,000,000 worth of tar, pitch, &c., from what they call the " Glorious Old North State." * And not to overlook Pennsylvania, she pays her annually $ 800,000 for iron.

* North Carolina.

21 *

Here, then, are $ 40,000,000 worth of products, of the raw materials of other States, paid for and consumed by Massachusetts, to say nothing of the other States. Here is a sum equal to almost half of the whole export of raw material from the United States to all Europe! And now what do Mr. Polk and the followers of Mr. Polk propose? They say to agriculturists, " Your produce is low." How do they propose to increase the prices? They say, " Your consumption is too small." They propose to diminish it! You produce too much. They propose to *increase* it! They desire to stop the manufacturing operations of the Eastern States. They propose to convert all those engaged in these operations into farmers, to raise wheat and oats on our sterile hills, or to emigrate South and raise them in a far more fertile and prolific soil. At the same time, therefore, that they *diminish* the *demand*, they would *increase* the *supply*. And this is their way of remedying the evils under which agriculture suffers.

I know that agriculture is now apparently in a state of depression. The produce of farmers sells at prices which I wish were higher. But look at the state of things. No doubt the works of internal improvement, which have brought the produce of the West into the midst of you, have had some effect. No doubt in times past the depression of manufactures has had some effect. After all, we hope there is a tendency to a better state of things; that the progress of things is onward, and that agriculture will soon receive its just reward. Sure I am, as sure as I am of any principle, moral or political, that, if there is such a thing as benefiting the agriculture of the country, it is to be accomplished by urging forward manufactures and the mechanical arts. This will multiply the number of consumers, and thus raise the prices of what they consume.

Gentlemen, I see a little printed tract which has been circulated largely over the country, full of what I think are errors. I will not not call them misrepresentations. It is dedicated to Mr. Greely, who, I hope, will acknowledge the dedication, and answer it in his own way. It purports to state prices, which it appears to me are all imaginary. The tariff was passed in 1842, in the summer. The writer of this tract states that there has been a fall in the price of beef, from $ 8 in 1843 to $ 5 in 1844. What has the tariff to do with beef? I wish I had known where beef could have been sold in 1843 for $ 8; as I happened then to have a little of the article to dispose of. And so of the rest; the prices are all imaginary. If the price-currents ever set forth such prices as are here stated, they never met my eye.

In the next place, he says that the price of manufactured goods has risen. What does he mean by this? He says, Cocheco, and other prints with hard names, have risen in 1844. Every one must see the fallacy of all such reasoning as this. In 1841 and 1842 manufactures were greatly depressed; a great many establishments stopped. The business of the country was stagnant, for in order to have business active, people must be able to buy as well as to sell. It is generally known that no dividends were made by manufacturers during these years. When the tariff was passed, the goods then made were brought into market. But the question is not, if a man will be candid and just, whether the act of 1842 raised or lowered the prices of American goods. The question is, whether the general protection of American manufactures has not, on the whole, reduced the price of goods, so that a man can clothe himself cheaper than before. The inquiry should be, not as to the prices of a piece of cloth in 1842 and 1844, but as to the general effect of the tariff on the business of the country and the prosperity of the people.

Having thus, I fear at too great length, spoken of our past history and present condition, I will submit what I think is likely to be the future progress of the country. Under the favor of Providence, it is in our power, in a great measure, to prescribe this futurity, and to say what it shall be. If we choose to go in the path we have trod before, to adhere to the course of measures thus far in the main pursued, there is no reason to doubt that our prosperity will make progress, that we shall go on, step by step, until we attain any desirable degree of national greatness. If, on the contrary, we run counter to all that has hitherto been done, then, whatever others may expect, I look for nothing but disaster and distress.

Gentlemen, there is another question about to be decided, most interesting to us and the whole country, to which I shall only allude by saying, that this subject of the annexation of Texas is one of those which give the greatest intensity of interest to the impending election.

But the great question before the public is in regard to the general policy of the country, whether we shall follow in the tracks of our fathers, or reverse all their opinions and all their measures, and take a new course for ourselves. And I put it to you to-day, and I am willing to leave the decision to this great State and to you, how the people of New York mean to bear themselves, how this great State means to conduct herself, in the decision of this question. Whosoever looks upon the map, and sees her stretching over so great an extent of the Union, or looks at the census and sees her large population, or looks at the commercial returns, must contemplate New York as holding a great, I had almost said a fearful, responsibility for the future conduct of this government. I do not doubt that her intelligent people will acquit themselves on this occasion as they think their own interests and the interests of the Union require. If I were to doubt that, I should doubt the continuance of the prosperity of our country; I should doubt that the interests of the United States would go forward, but I should expect to see them steadily decline, till they finally sunk in ruin.

Gentlemen, I will detain you no longer. To as many of you as are inhabitants of Albany, I desire to give my thanks for the kindness of this invitation, and for your hospitality. Of late years my intercourse with the good city of Albany has not been frequent. Of the great and good men of the State whom I have had the good fortune to know, some are not now among the living. Mr. De Witt Clinton, a man never to be mentioned by any American without entire respect; the late General Van Rensselaer, whose many virtues and amiable qualities seemed to enable him to overcome the difficulty of a " camel's going through the eye of a needle"; Governor Tompkins, and Mr. Van Vechten, are gone to their final homes. Among those with whom, in early life or early manhood, I had the pleasure to form acquaintance here, two are still living, at an advanced age, having enlightened a whole profession, and reflected great honor by their public life on the State and country, Chancellor Kent and Chief Justice Spencer. They are not here to-day; but they are with us, I doubt not, in sympathy and feeling, full of the same patriotic purpose. I pray God they may long live to see and enjoy the prosperity and glory of our common country.

And now, Gentlemen, with my best good wishes for you all, allow me most respectfully to take my leave.

WHIG CONVENTION AT PHILADELPHIA.

INTRODUCTORY NOTE.

THE meeting at which the following speech was delivered was one of the largest and most enthusiastic ever held in the city of Philadelphia. Besides the inhabitants of the city, there was a great attendance from the eastern counties of the State. The United States Gazette of the 2d of October, 1844, gives an animated account of the celebration, of which the following is an abridgment: —

"Philadelphia has been the scene of many gallant displays, — heart-cheering and evincing the fulness of enthusiasm. Brilliant processions have swept through her streets; shouts have arisen from living masses congregated to evince their attachment to principles or to men; and multitudes have gathered to listen to the inspiring eloquence of some favorite orator. There have been great occasions and great displays in honor of them; but there never was one which, in grand and imposing effect, as an evidence of attachment to great principles, and to the great men who advocate them, can at all compare with that of yesterday.

"Never have we seen the population of Philadelphia so completely, either marshalled into a procession, or poured into the streets through which it passed. Business was completely at a stand, for it was felt by the mass of the population that the time had come when it was necessary for all to make a sacrifice of private interest to the public good.

"The previous evening gave promise in various ways of the stirring interest of the ensuing day. At the earliest dawn the work of preparation was visible. In many streets flags and streamers were stretched across from house to house. Market Street presented a forest of flags and pennons. Fourth Street, Front Street, and the shipping at the wharves, were adorned in the same way. The sky was without a cloud.

"The crowds soon increased to throngs. The houses in the streets through which the procession was to pass were filled, many of the windows being occupied by ladies. The masses in the streets were so compact, that it was at times difficult for the procession to make its way.

"From the beginning to the end of the route, there was a continuous mass of people; and when at last the procession poured into the fields, where the meeting was to be held, a most magnificent spectacle was presented. When the meeting was organized, it was estimated that at least fifty thousand persons were assembled on the ground.

"Hon. John Sergeant was chosen President of the Convention, and introduced the business of the day by an appropriate and eloquent address. The following speech was then delivered by Mr. Webster."

WHIG CONVENTION AT PHILADELPHIA.*

FELLOW-CITIZENS OF PENNSYLVANIA: — I am happy to be with you, in this assembling of ourselves together, to manifest the interest I feel in the great cause which has convened you, and my deep concern for the issue of the election now pending. But I come with no expectation of adding any thing of information or argument to the side which you and I espouse. The questions at issue have been discussed, by persons of abilities, all over the country. Most reading men have had opportunity to examine for themselves; and most thinking men, time to mature their judgments. Yet, Gentlemen, if this meeting shall have the effect of awakening what may remain of listlessness and indifference, and of inspiring new activity and new firmness of purpose, an important end will be accomplished, and much good done. Political friends are cheered, we are all cheered, by manifestations of common feeling and a common resolution. We take courage from one another; we obtain new impulses from sympathy. If this meeting shall arouse public attention, if unthinking men shall be made by it to think and to observe, if we shall find ourselves prompted by new zeal, and resolved on more vigorous efforts, then we have assembled for good, and may congratulate ourselves that a duty to our country has been performed.

Gentlemen, although there are two great parties in the country, with distinct and opposing candidates for high office, and avowing and maintaining, in general, different and opposing principles and opinions, yet in this great Commonwealth of Pennsylvania there is something quite peculiar in the pretensions

* Speech delivered at a great Whig Convention at Philadelphia, on the 1st of October, 1844.

and conduct of one of these parties, in regard to the principles which it claims for itself, or assigns to its candidates. I pray permission, Gentlemen, to invite your attention to this peculiarity. A singular stratagem seems to be attempted; the putting on of a new face, the speaking with a new voice, and the assumption of quite a new deportment and behavior. This is worthy of close observation and regard. Generally speaking, the two parties, throughout the whole country, are divided and opposed upon one great and leading question of the times, I mean the subject of Protection, as it is called.

The Whig party maintain the propriety of protecting, by custom-house regulations, various pursuits and employments among ourselves. Our opponents repudiate this policy, and embrace the doctrines of what is called free trade. This is the general party line. The distinction is not a local, but a party distinction. Thus, while the Whig States of New England are all in favor of a protective tariff, New Hampshire and Maine, which are not Whig States, are opposed to it. And south of the Potomac, it would be difficult, I suppose, to find any men, but avowed Whigs, who favor the tariff policy.

Tariff or no tariff, protection or no protection, thus becomes a great leading question. All Whigs are on one side, and, generally speaking, all who are not Whigs on the other. But then arises the *peculiarity* in the state of things in Pennsylvania. Pennsylvania is a strong tariff State. Among her citizens, the protective policy overrides the general division of political parties, and men who are not Whigs support that policy, firmly and ardently. This is clear. Every body knows it, and it needs no proof. Well, then, what has happened in consequence of this well-known state of opinion in Pennsylvania?

Does the party here act against the tariff? Does it speak the same language which it speaks in Carolina? O, no! nothing like it. In Carolina, and other States, the whole party exists, principally, for the purpose of putting down the tariff, and rooting it out to the last fibre. They call it the "black tariff"; they denounce it as cruel and oppressive; and they openly intimate the idea that a disruption of the bonds of our national union would be a less evil, than the establishment and continuance of protective principles. But lo! when they come into Pennsylvania, all is changed. Here they themselves are professed tariff

men. Mr. Polk, their candidate for the Presidency, is declared
to be a supporter of the tariff, a protectionist, a thorough Pennsylvanian on all these subjects.   This is, at least, a bold stroke
of policy.   I will not say how respectful it is to the intelligence
of Pennsylvania; I will only say it is a bold, a very bold, political movement.   In every State where the anti-tariff policy is
predominant, or in which the party holds anti-tariff opinions,
there Mr. Polk is pressed upon the confidence of the people as
an anti-tariff man, and because he is an anti-tariff man; an
anti-tariff man, as they commonly say, "up to the hub."   But
in Pennsylvania his claims to confidence and support are urged
with equal zeal on the opposite ground, that is to say, because
he is a tariff man, and a tariff man equally "up to the hub."
Here the whole party, their speakers, their writers, their press,
adopt fully, and support warmly, the tariff principles of the
Whigs, the tariff principles of Pennsylvania.   Here they sail
under the Whig flag, they would get into the Whig ship, seize
the Whig rudder, and throw the old crew overboard.   Or, if
they keep in their own craft, they still hoist false colors, give
their vessel a new name, and destroy the old log-book.

Gentlemen, I think if Mr. Polk were in a circle of friends,
composed partly of citizens of Carolina, and partly of those of
Pennsylvania, he would find himself in a curious dilemma.   It
would be a wonder, if he did not set these two sorts of friends
at once by the ears.   The Carolina gentlemen would shout,
"Polk for ever, and down with the tariff of 1842!"   The Pennsylvania gentlemen would say, "Polk *and* the tariff of 1842
for ever!"   And what would Mr. Polk say?   Why, uttering his
own well-known opinions, he would say to his Carolina friends,
"Gentlemen, you do me no more than justice.   I am opposed
to the tariff of 1842, and think it ought to be repealed.   In
the canvass against Governor Jones, in Tennessee, last year, I
made more than one hundred speeches against it.   I am for
bringing all duties down to the point they were at in June,
1842; that is to say, to one uniform rate of twenty per cent.
You know I have agreed with you throughout on this great
question of tariff for protection.   I have opposed it by my
speeches, by my pledges, by numerous and repeated declarations,
and by my votes.   All show what I have thought, and what I
think now.   I now repeat my opposition, and renew my pledges."

This would be manly, this would be fact, this would be all right; and Carolina huzzas, and Carolina clapping of hands, would not unnaturally, with characteristic earnestness, follow this plain and frank declaration. But how would the Pennsylvania gentlemen stand this? How could Mr. Polk appease them? I will not say that he would, with his own tongue, and from his own lips, speak a directly contrary language to them. I do not think him capable of such effrontery. But if he were to give utterance to the opinions which those put in his mouth who support him here in Pennsylvania, he would say, " My dear friends of Pennsylvania, you have heard what I have said to the Carolina gentlemen. Never mind. I don't know exactly what I am, but I rather think I am a better tariff man than Henry Clay! I am for *incidental* protection; and that is a great matter. It is rather strong, to be sure, after all I have said in Tennessee, to raise, in Pennsylvania, the cry of ' Polk *and* the tariff of 1842!' Nevertheless, let the cry go forth!"

Now, Gentlemen, what excellent party harmony would be produced, if Mr. Polk's two sets of friends could hear him utter these sentiments at the same time, and in the same room! And yet they are uttered every day in the same country, and in regard to the same election. The more loudly Carolina, and other States holding her sentiments, cry out, " Polk, and down with the tariff!" the more sturdily does the party press in Pennsylvania raise the opposite shout. Now, Gentlemen, there is an old play, named, I think, " *Who's the Dupe?*" An answer, and here it is an important one, is to be given to the question, " Who is the dupe?" and we shall see, in the end, on which party the laugh falls.

Gentlemen, incidental protection, which some persons, just now, would represent as transcendental protection, what is it? It is no protection at all, and does not deserve the name. It is a result which comes, if it comes at all, without design, without certainty, and without discrimination. It falls on tea and coffee, as well as on iron and broadcloth. Let us not be deluded by such a thin and flimsy pretext. It is an insult to our understandings. Gentlemen, I have come here for no purpose of oratory, nor eloquence, nor display. This is not the occasion for any thing of that kind. If I ever had any such ambition, it has long since passed away, and I hope now only to be useful to you, useful to the great cause in which we are all engaged; and this, and this only, has brought me here. I shall speak with that plainness and frankness with which a man ought to speak, directly and earnestly, feeling as a man ought to feel who has at heart the importance of what he says. This service in which we are engaged is no holiday service, no mere display, no passing pageant, but serious and solemn; serious, as far as any thing can be serious in the secular affairs of men. I come here, then, to use no ornaments of speech, no trope, no metaphor. Honestly and sincerely I come to speak to you out of the abundance of my heart, and I beg you to receive what I have to say in the spirit with which it is delivered.

No wonder that among you, Pennsylvanians, the party that is opposed to us represents itself friendly to the tariff. It is well known that Pennsylvania is favorable to the tariff, and that is no wonder. She is a State of great mineral interests, and is therefore as much interested in the tariff as any State in the Union, not to say more. She has, it is probable, more to lose than any other State by a change of policy on the part of the federal government, because she cannot so easily recover as other States might from the effect of any great change. In addition to her minerals, which are her richest treasures, she has her artisans, her workers in iron, her workers in metals, her spinners, her weavers, her laborers of every pursuit and occupation. Her treasures not only lie embosomed in the earth, but are spread out in every workshop in the country. There is not an operative, nor a working man, who is not interested in, and supported by, the protective laws of the government. Protection touches every man's bread. If ever, then, there was a subject worthy of the attention of a public man or of a statesman, it is this of protection. No wonder, I repeat, that every Pennsylvanian is engaged in the cause of protection; the wonder would be if he were not.

I have often said heretofore, and I repeat it now, that there is not on the globe a spot naturally richer in all the elements of greatness than Pennsylvania, except England, if, indeed, England be an exception. This is the view of the subject which, it appears to me, both public men and private individuals in Pennsylvania ought to consider. Pennsylvania is full of capacities, full of natural wealth. What policy is best calculated to exhibit those capacities, and to draw out that natural wealth? That is the great question; that forms the great topic; and now, fellow-citizens of Pennsylvania, what have you to say to it?

Pennsylvania is favored in climate, far more than the State to which I belong. She is favored, too, by position, her eastern line being closely connected with the sea, and her western with the great rivers of the West; while large and useful streams flow from her mountains, east and west, and north and south. She has a soil of remarkable fertility, especially suited to the production of wheat and other kinds of grain. But these are far from being all. She is rich, most rich, in treasures which lie beneath the surface. England possesses her East Indies and her West Indies; but it has been said, with truth, that, as sources of wealth, these are little in comparison with her " Black Indies." Coal and iron are among the chief productive causes of English opulence and English power. The acquisition of the whole empire of the Great Mogul is far less important, and all the mines of Mexico and Peru, if she should acquire them, would be less valuable, than these exhaustless treasures, lying in her own bosom.

Now, Gentlemen, how does Pennsylvania compare with England? In the first place, England and Wales embrace an extent of fifty-seven thousand square miles; Pennsylvania has an area of forty-three thousand. Here, as you perceive, is an approach to equality. Both abound in coal and iron ; and probably Pennsylvania has as great a variety of the former, both anthracite and bituminous, as England. The value of coal, in its application to that new agent in human affairs, the use of steam, it is impossible to calculate or estimate. Steam has so far altered the modes of motion, and the forms of human industry and human action, that it may be said to have changed the world. It almost seems that we are whirling round the sun on a new orb, or at least had got into a new creation of things. We fly over the earth's surface, with a rapidity greater than that of the wings of the wind; we penetrate beneath its surface, and with a new and mighty power bring its hidden treasures up to the light of the sun. New agencies are at work, in all departments of business, and the processes of labor are everywhere revolutionized.

In this change, and in the causes which have produced it,

Pennsylvania is singularly and eminently interested; more so, probably, than any other State in the Union. Steam develops her resources, and turns them all to good account; but the development is yet only partial. Probably the coal field of Pennsylvania may be something less in area than that of England and Wales; but this is of little importance, as the supply seems adequate for ages and centuries to come. But the actual annual product is small, compared with that of England. England produces annually thirty millions of tons of coal, worth, at the pit's mouth, sixty or seventy millions of dollars. What an amount of wealth is this, from a single source! Pennsylvania is supposed to produce a million and a half of tons of anthracite coal, and perhaps as much of the bituminous kind. This is all her present product, with a capacity to supply the continent. Now, Gentlemen, how does this product bear on the employment and occupation of her citizens? How does it affect the great interests of labor and industry? This is an important point. If the existence of mines be useful to capitalists alone, it is one thing; but if their existence, and the working of them, be beneficial to the industrious and working classes, then they become quite another thing. Let us see how this is. I am told that coal in the mines may be regarded as worth, generally, thirty cents a ton, that is to say, the right of digging it may be obtained at that price. When dug and made ready for delivery, it is worth two dollars, or two dollars and a quarter, a ton. Now, what does this prove? Why, it proves, certainly, that, of the whole value of a ton of coal, the raw material composes thirty cents, and the labor employed and paid for in producing it from a hundred and seventy to a hundred and ninety-five cents. This last sum, therefore, is earned, by the labor and industry of Pennsylvania, on every ton of coal, making, of course, proper allowance for capital employed in machinery. But then this machinery, again, is itself a product of labor. We may pursue this subject into its details, as far as we please; the pursuit will always end in the establishment of the great principle, that labor is the source of wealth, and another great principle, fairly deducible from it, and equally clear, that, to judge of the general prosperity and happiness of a people, we are to look, in the first place, to the amount of useful, healthy, and well-paid *labor* which that people performs. It is this new demand for labor, created by the working of the mines, that makes the subject so important to the whole people of Pennsylvania. Every new demand for well-paid labor is a new source of prosperity and happiness to the great mass of the community. But this is a vast topic, and I have not now time to go far into it. It so happened, that ten or twelve years ago I addressed an assembly of the citizens of Pennsylvania at Pittsburg. On that occasion I expressed my opinions at some length, on the subject of American labor. Those opinions I still hold, with increased confidence in their truth and justice, and to them I beg leave respectfully to refer you.*

Another great mineral product of Pennsylvania is iron; in this respect, too, your State resembles England. England produces, annually, one million and a half of tons of pig iron. Eight or ten years ago, she did not produce one third of this amount; and this vast increase shows the extent of the new demand for the article, and her increased activity in producing it. But the chief value of iron, as well as of coal, consists of labor, directly or indirectly employed in the production. In the first place, it may be remarked, that the manufacture of iron consumes a vast quantity of coal. It has been computed that the production of a million and a half tons of iron, in England, requires six million tons of coal. Here is a case in which one occupation acts most favorably on another. But in the next place, miners of iron, and all classes of laborers employed in bringing the crude ore through the several stages of progress till it assumes the shape of bar iron, are, of course, to be fed, and clothed, and supported. All this creates a demand for provisions and various agricultural products. It has been estimated, that, for every ton of iron brought to market, twenty dollars have been paid away for agricultural labor and productions.

Now, Gentlemen, if these things be so, if this view of the case be substantially correct, how plain is it, that it is for the interest of every working man in Pennsylvania, of every occupation, that coal and iron should be produced at home, instead of being imported from abroad? To be sure, if the mines were poor and scanty, and could only be wrought at a far greater expense than mines elsewhere; or if the material, when produced, were of an

* The speech here referred to was delivered at Pittsburg, July 9th, 1833. See Vol. I. p. 285.

inferior sort, then the case might be different. But, in fact, richer mines, or mines more easily wrought, do not exist on the face of the earth. Nothing is wanted but a policy which shall give to our own enterprise and our own labor a fair chance, and a just encouragement to begin with. Pennsylvania, indeed, is not the only iron-producing State. Much of that metal is found in New York, in Maryland, in Tennessee; and some in other States. The interest, therefore, is in a good degree general.

But it is said that twenty per cent. *ad valorem* is duty enough, and, if iron cannot be made at home under such a duty, we ought to send for it to England or to Sweden. Now, in all reason, and according to all experience, this must very much depend upon the state, the degree of advancement, in which the interest proposed to be protected is found. Useful undertakings often require encouragement and stimulus in the beginning, which may afterwards be dispensed with. The product of English iron exemplifies this. At present that interest needs no protection; but up to 1820 it enjoyed the protection of quite as high a rate of duty as now exists in the United States. Now, it may well defy competition for the market at home. And it is well to bear in mind, that the existing tariff of duties in England imposes no less a rate than £42 19s. 6d. on every hundred pounds in value of imported goods, making an average of the whole. Certainly there is not much of the spirit of free trade in this.

Now, I repeat, Gentlemen, that it is not wonderful that a State in the condition of Pennsylvania, and of the character of Pennsylvania, — a State industrious, full of resources, and every way capable of drawing them out, — should favor a policy favorable to their development. It would be wonderful if it were otherwise. It would be wonderful, indeed, if she should manifest a disposition to throw off the steam from her thousand engines, put out the fires, and close up her mines. The interest of all her people points the other way. And her aggregate interest, her interest as represented by her government, her own State policy, — does that not point in the same direction? The government of Pennsylvania has created a heavy debt, and it has embarrassed its finances, for the purpose of constructing canals and railroads, to furnish means and facilities of transportation, and to bring the great products of the State to market. She will not slumber over this debt. She knows it must be paid, and she intends to pay it. I never for a moment doubted this. Her faith is pledged, and she will redeem it. She requests, and she needs, no *assumption* of her debt by the government of the United States. She contracted it herself, and she can pay it herself, and she will pay it. But she has a right to demand something of the general government, and that something is *a permanent settled, steady, protective policy*, to be established by means of custom-house regulations. Pennsylvania cannot establish this policy for herself. She has parted with the power of laying duties at her own ports. All this is gone to the general government. And that government has solemnly bound itself to exercise the power, fairly, justly, and beneficially. What the State can do, it does, and will do. It makes roads and canals, and creates all the facilities in its power. What the people can do, they do, and will continue to do. They show enterprise, and bestow labor. They make the wilderness blossom, and crown their fields with golden harvests. They are ready to bore the earth and extract its treasures.

But there is one thing which is altogether essential, which neither the government of Pennsylvania nor the people of Pennsylvania can do. They are unable to protect themselves, by custom-house regulations, against the poorer and cheaper labor of Europe. This Congress must do for them, or it cannot be done at all. Pennsylvania has no longer the power. It is given up. All the world knows that the coal and iron of Pennsylvania, and the other great interests of Pennsylvania, cannot be protected and regulated but through the custom-house, and Pennsylvania has not control over one in the world. That power is parted with. Pennsylvania surrendered it to the federal government. The power of laying duties on imports, which was once a Pennsylvania power, belongs to Pennsylvania no more. But this truth is clear, that this high prerogative, thus parted with, should be exercised, and must be exercised, by the trustee who has it, for the benefit of Pennsylvania, to raise up, bring forth, and reward American labor. The federal government, I say, fails in its duty to Pennsylvania, and in its duty to every other State in this Union, if it lets the power lie latent, and refuses to use it. That is the pinch, the very exigence, that made this government of the United States.

For that, Massachusetts came into it; for that, Pennsylvania came into it. The power of protection was in both States. It existed on all sides. The compact was made to give it identity, universality, union, and that is all we want. Now, Gentlemen, the State may do what it pleases; we may do what we please; but unless the federal government exercises its legitimate power, unless it acts in our behalf, as we, if left alone, would act for ourselves, there is no security for any interest, no promise of perpetuity.

I have said Pennsylvania will pay her own debt. Every body expects it. I expect it. The whole world expects it. Pennsylvania will pay her own debt. I should despair of self-government, I should cease to be a defender of popular institutions, I should hold down my head as an American, if this popular and rich commonwealth should sneak away from the payment of her debt. Never, no, never, will it be done! Between this place and the Ohio River there may be a half-dozen who would repudiate. Black spots there are on the sun, but the dazzling effulgence of that bright orb hides them all. There may be a man in Pennsylvania whose principles and whose morals would lead him to cry out against or evade the payment of such a debt, but who could hear his voice amid the loud, long shouts of all honest men? I never had a doubt Pennsylvania would pay all she owes. I know what Pennsylvania always has been. I therefore know what she always will be. Her character for the past is her pledge for the future. I cannot be dissuaded out of my impression, while a man in Pennsylvania reads her history, or knows any thing of her character, from the time when William Penn first put his foot on her shore.

But the time is now come when the policy of a reasonable, permanent protection must be settled. (A voice in the crowd shouted, "Now or never!") I say, *Now or never!* It is a question that is most exciting to the whole country, and absolutely vital to the interests of the people of Pennsylvania; and it is "Now or never!"

And now it is very important that we should not be deceived in the men whom we choose for our rulers. Let us know all about them! If we do take Mr. Polk for our chief magistrate, let us take him for what he is, not for what he is not. I trust we have too much consciousness of truth for —— (Here a voice cried out, "We won't have him at all.") Well, I'm pretty much of that opinion myself. But let us take our ruler for what he really is, not for what he is not, and thereby show that we have been duped and deceived. Let us have too much consciousness of truth, too much self-respect, too much regard for the opinion of the world, to take Mr. Polk for that which he is not, and never was, and does not profess to be.

Let us, then, see what are the sentiments of Mr. Polk on the protective policy. Is he with us, or is he against us? What does he say himself on this subject? I know no reason why he should not be believed. I don't go back to the time of his boyhood. I don't go back to the days of his grandfather, Ezekiel Polk. I need not even go back to the period of his Congressional services, but I will take the Mr. Polk of last year, running for a popular office, not that of President of the United States, but that of Governor of Tennessee. You know that, in that part of the country, it is common for the candidates for popular offices to go forth, and state frankly to the people whose suffrages they solicit what their opinions are on all the great subjects, social and political, of the day. Now, what does Mr. Polk say of himself on this occasion?

" I am opposed to direct taxes, and to prohibitory and *protective duties;* and in favor of such moderate duties as will not cut off importations. In other words, I am in favor of reducing the duties to the rates of the Compromise Act, where the Whig Congress found them on the 29th of June, 1842."

These are his own words, his own opinions, from his own speech; and, as the lawyers say, I lay the venue, and I give the date, in order that there may be no misunderstanding. It is from his speech of the 3d of April, 1843, in reply to Milton Brown, at Jackson, and was published in the Nashville Union of the 5th of May, 1843.

Here he is plain, distinct, direct, and cannot be misunderstood. He is for bringing all duties to the same rate, and that rate is twenty per cent. *ad valorem,* and no more; for that was the rate at which the Whig Congress found all duties on the 29th of June, 1842.

He is therefore for repealing the act which altered that rate;

that is to say, he is for abolishing the present tariff. No language can make this plainer. And let me add, that any man in the United States who wishes to abolish the present tariff will vote for Mr. Polk. It remains to be seen whether those who are in favor of the present tariff, who are of opinion that it ought to be continued and upheld, can be brought, by misrepresentation and false pretences, to join its enemies and coöperate for its overthrow. That is the true and real question.

Again, Mr. Polk says he is "for such moderate duties as will not cut off importations." Very well; this is explicit; all can understand it.

Now if we do not wish to cut off the importations of coal and iron, and the various products of English manufactures, then we shall agree with Mr. Polk; but if we do wish to cut off these importations, then we shall disagree with him and disagree with his policy; for he would have only such moderate duties as will not cut off importations. But, as I have said, he is quite explicit, and I thank him for it. He would reduce the duties to the rates of the Compromise Act, as they existed in 1842, when they afforded no protection at all. But there is a tariff in existence at present, and some questions were put to him to this effect: Are you in favor of that tariff, or are you not? Will you support it, or will you try to repeal it? To these questions, put since he has been a candidate for the Presidency, he stands mute. There are humane considerations occasionally employed in courts of law, when persons are mute; but when a man can answer and does not answer, when he is perfectly able, but entirely unwilling, to make a reply, then we have a right to put our own construction on the case. But it was entirely unnecessary to put these questions to Mr. Polk; he had already stated that he wanted the duties reduced to the Compromise standard. The duties in June, 1842, had come down to twenty per cent. without discrimination; so, therefore, Mr. Polk was in favor of bringing down the duties to twenty per cent. on all imported articles.

In a written address to the people of Tennessee, dated May 29, 1843, Mr. Polk expresses his sentiments in a still more considerate manner. Here is the address: —

" To the People of Tennessee.

" *Winchester*, May 29, 1843.

" The object which I had in proposing to Governor Jones at Carrol-
ville, on the 12th of April last, that we should each write out and publish
our views and opinions on the subject of the tariff, was, that our respective positions might be distinctly known and understood by the people.
That my opinions were already fully and distinctly known I could not
doubt. I had steadily, during the period I was a Representative in Congress, been opposed to a protective policy, as my recorded votes and
published speeches prove. Since I retired from Congress I had held
the same opinions. In the present canvass for Governor, I had avowed
my opposition to the tariff of the late Whig Congress, as being highly
protective in its character, and not designed by its authors as a revenue
measure. I had avowed my opinion in my public speeches, that the
interests of the country, and especially of the producing classes, required its repeal, and the restoration of the principles of the Compromise Tariff Act of 1833."

Now come forth, any man in this assembly who pretends to
be a tariff man, and tell us what he has to say to this? Is Mr.
Polk a tariff man, or is he not? Honor is due to Mr. Polk's
sincerity. Indeed, he does not speak like a man who is making
a confession, but rather as a man who is claiming a merit. Before the people of Tennessee, he insisted upon it that he was
an original, consistent, thorough, whole-souled anti-tariff man.
He says he wishes his opinions to be distinctly known and understood by the people. I hope he means still that his opinions
shall be distinctly understood by the people; for he says, he had
been steadily opposed to a protective policy while in Congress,
and he had held the same opinions ever since. Now there cannot be any thing more explicit than this declaration, out of the
mouth of the man himself; and he will no more deny this than
he will deny his own name. And since he avers all this, insists
upon it, and repeats it over and over again, what friend of his
will stand up to deny it and give him the lie to his face?

But let us see again. How did those regard him who brought
him forward as their candidate for the Presidency of the United
States? Take the case of the South Carolina members, for
instance. A resolution was brought forward by Mr. Elmore, in
Charleston, by which the anti-tariff gentlemen of that part of

the world resolved to support him with all their hearts. This is the resolution : —

"Resolved, That by the election of James K. Polk, and the defeat of Henry Clay, a substantial victory will be gained by the Constitution, — the Presidential power and influence will be in the hands of a Southern man, *a friend of free trade*, and identified with us in our institutions, and an enemy of the protective policy and Abolitionism ! and we ought not, by any action of our State, to embarrass or lessen the chances of his election, in which much may be gained, or cause his defeat, by which so much must be lost, and by which we shall draw on ourselves the blame of our friends in other States, change their kind feelings into coldness, perhaps resentment and hostility, by unnecessarily weakening and embarrassing them, and thus increasing the numbers and spirit of our enemies, and adding to our difficulties in obtaining justice."

Now please remember, all ye citizens of Pennsylvania, — please remember, all ye who are tariff men, and who are yet disposed to follow the party, and to vote for Mr. Polk, — please remember, I say, one and all, that the fixed, unalterable anti-tariff men of the South support Mr. Polk, because they regard him as one of themselves.

We have recently, Gentlemen, seen a published letter from Mr. H. L. Pinkney, of Charleston, S. C., a gentleman of much personal respectability, and of high standing with his political friends. The letter was written to the committee of what was called the Macon Democratic Mass Meeting, and it was dated the 19th of August last.

In this letter Mr. Pinkney says, —

"It is the policy of the Whigs, and some of our Democrats, too, to represent Colonel Polk as a protectionist, in consequence of his recent letter to Mr. Kane of Philadelphia. But no charge was ever more unfounded. It is contradicted by the whole tenor of his political life. It is refuted by all his speeches and votes in relation to the tariff, for a long series of years.

"His doctrine of a tariff for revenue as the primary object, with incidental protection to manufactures, is the very doctrine of South Carolina. It is the doctrine of the Baltimore Convention, in which he concurs, and which has been generally assented to by the Democratic party of South Carolina. It is the doctrine of the celebrated exposition published by the Legislature of this State, and has always been recognized as the creed of the State Rights party."

I have one more proof to lay before you, and I then take leave of this part of the subject. It is the declaration of Mr. Holmes of Charleston, a man of lead and influence with his friends, and now member of Congress from that city.

After Mr. Polk had been nominated, at Baltimore, some of Mr. Holmes's political friends wrote to him, propounding certain questions relating to Mr. Polk, and calling with emphasis for answers. The first question was this: —

"Are you in favor of the election of Mr. Polk and Mr. Dallas, the Democratic candidates for the Presidency and Vice-Presidency of the United States; and are you, or not, of the opinion that the vote of South Carolina should be given, in good faith, for them?"

The second question was this: —

"Whatever may be your opinion of Mr. Polk's ability, in the event of his election, to effect a repeal of the tariff of 1842, and to break down the protective system, have you any doubt of the sincerity of his opposition to the entire system of protection, and that the influence of his high office will be in good faith exerted to subvert it?"

To these questions Mr. Holmes returned the following prompt, brief, and pithy answer: —

"Gentlemen, — I have just received your letter, in which two queries are distinctly put, and as distinctly will I reply.

"1st. I am in favor of the election of Mr. Polk and Mr. Dallas, and am decidedly of the opinion that South Carolina ought to vote for them.

"2d. I have no doubt of Mr. Polk's sincerity when he declared his opposition to the entire system of protection, and that, if elected, he will endeavor to subvert it."

Here is the opinion of Mr. Holmes, a distinguished member of Congress, of the anti-tariff party; and let me tell you, once more, that he speaks the opinions of the whole anti-tariff party of the South.

These evidences might be accumulated, but it would be useless. Those who really desire to know the truth, and are willing to embrace it, and act upon it, surely can need nothing more on this point.

Gentlemen, I remember that Mr. Polk has said that he is against the duty on wool. Very well; so are other anti-tariff men. Let this be known, fully and fairly, to your great county

of Washington (Penn.), as well as to other wool-growing districts; and if the people of that county still say they are in favor
of Mr. Polk, I must admit they have a right to be so. But, still,
let them take him as he is, and for what he is, and not for something which he is not.   There are some who say, that, even if
Mr. Polk be an anti-tariff man, and should be elected President
of the United States, yet he cannot repeal the tariff or overcome our policy. Strange doctrine! We choose him that he
may not triumph over us after choosing him! We elect him
that he may not destroy the policy he is opposed to! We
choose him to prevent his destroying that which we think ought
to be preserved! Strange argument for sensible men! If we
knew that he would not be able to carry out his policy, or to
exercise that power which the office would give him to abolish the tariff, would that be a reason why we should withhold
our opposition? Not at all! There is the evil of perpetual
agitation, of perpetual doubt, of perpetual uncertainty; there is
the evil of perpetual opposition to the duration of the protective
policy.   Will capital be employed to bring out the mineral
wealth of this great State, if it be doubtful whether those so
employing it will be protected in their enterprise or not? No!
Once more I say, most assuredly, No! What the country needs
is security and stability; a permanent, settled policy, that enterprising and industrious men may be enabled to give direction to
their capital and means, and labor with the assurance, with the
unshaken confidence, that there will be no violent fluctuation in
the state of the law.

  Gentlemen, the citizens of Massachusetts have no especial
interest of their own in favoring the coal and iron of Pennsylvania. We are large purchasers of the articles, and free trade,
or free admission, in regard to them, would be best for us. But
we have other interests, and we see other interests all over the
country, calling for a wise system of custom-house duties; and
we embrace that policy which we think essential to the good of
the whole. We desire no favoritism, no partial system. The
interests of the people of these two great States, the interests of
the people of all the States, are bound up in one bond. But I
say, that, if Mr. Polk be elected President of the United States,
with the general concurrence of the popular branch of the legislature, either the tariff will be repealed, or so much disturbed

23*

as to dishearten its friends, and make them turn from it with disgust. This is a thing of the deepest interest. It rests with you of Pennsylvania to decide this; for without the vote of Pennsylvania, I undertake to say, he cannot be elected President of the United States. It is for you to say. Give me your assurance that he will not get the vote of Pennsylvania, and I will give you my assurance that he will not be elected President of the United States. Any man may make the canvass, any man may go over the votes from Maine to Missouri, and he will, he must, be convinced that it is absolutely certain that Mr. Polk cannot be elected without the vote of the Keystone State! And it is equally certain, that without the vote of this State he remains at home, a private and respectable citizen of the State of Tennessee.

I wish every man in Pennsylvania to consider this, that on his vote, and the vote of his fellow-citizen, his neighbor, or his kinsman, depends the issue whether Mr. Polk be elected President or not. And I say that any man who attempts to convey the impression to another, any man of information, — whether it be done in the highways or by-ways, in parlor or kitchen, in cellar or garret, — any man, who shall be found telling another that Mr. Polk is in favor of the tariff, means to cheat an honest Pennsylvanian out of the fair use of the elective franchise! And if there be not spirit enough in Pennsylvania to repel so gross a misrepresentation, then Pennsylvania is not that Pennsylvania which I have so long respected and admired.

I am admonished, my friends, by the descent of the sun, that I must bring my remarks to a close. I was desirous of saying a few words to you about Texas. (Cries of " Go on!" " Go on!" " Tell us about Texas.") Well, I will only say, in relation to Texas, that you will find in the archives of your own State that which is far more important than all I can say upon the subject. But I do say that the annexation of Texas would tend to prolong the duration and increase the extent of African slavery on this continent. I have long held that opinion, and I would not now suppress it for any consideration on earth! And because it does increase the evils of slavery, because it will increase the number of slaves and prolong the duration of their bondage, — because it does all this, I oppose it without condition and without qualification, at this time and all times, now and for ever.

In 1780 the Legislature of Pennsylvania passed the act abolishing slavery in this State. It was introduced by a grateful acknowledgment to God for the achievement of American liberty, for that assistance by which the people had been enabled to break the chains of a foreign power, and by the enjoyment and assumption of a duty conformable to that, to do all that they could to break all other chains and set the world free.

That preamble was the work of your fathers; they sleep in honored graves; there is not, I believe, one man living now who was engaged in that most righteous act. There are words in that preamble fit to be read by all who inherit the blood, by all who bear the name, by all who cherish the memory, of an honored and virtuous ancestry. And I ask every one of you now present, ere eight-and-forty hours pass over your heads, to turn to that act, to read that preamble, and if you are Pennsylvanians the blood will stir and prompt you to your duty. There are arguments in that document far surpassing any thing that my poor ability could advance on the subject, and there I leave it.*

In answering an invitation to address the citizens of Pennsylvania, in another place, a short time ago, I observed that I had a desire to say a few words to the people of the State. I have now said them. I have said, and I repeat, that the result of the approaching election rests much in your hands. You may decide it favorably to the interests and honor of the country. Without your concurrence, Mr. Polk cannot be chosen. I wish to state this to you, and to leave it with you, in the strongest possible manner.

We are all, in Massachusetts, interested in the manner you give your votes at the coming Presidential election, and you are as much interested in the manner in which we give ours. But there is another election to be shortly decided in this State besides the Presidential election. It would ill become me to interfere in the elections by another State of its own State officers. I will not do so farther than to say, that the manner in which this first election of yours is conducted, and shall result, will have a great effect on the hopes and prospects of the Whigs in reference to that which is so soon to come after it.

---

* See preamble to the act of the Legislature of Pennsylvania for the gradual abolition of slavery, passed 1780, Pennsylvania Laws, Vol. I. p. 492.

I need not tell you that there is a great curiosity among the Whigs of other States, — *curiosity* is a term that is not strong enough for the feeling that exists, — there is a deep and strong *anxiety* prevailing all over the Union in relation to the way in which the Whigs shall conduct the next election in this State. Because it is perfectly plain to every one, that if the venerable man who was introduced to you this day,* — if that distinguished son of this great State, who was recently here on this platform, shall be elected Governor, there will be a brightening of the political skies, at the sight of which every true Whig in the Union will rejoice.

I have a few words to say to the people of this city, this fair and beautiful Philadelphia, this city of the Declaration of Independence, this city in which was matured and perfected the glorious Constitution of the United States, this noble city, which is connected with so much of the early history of our country and its subsequent prosperity! Can there be a doubt of the side which this city will take in the coming contest? I ask every young man to sit down and ask his conscience how he can give a vote for the subversion of all the best interests and the only correct policy of our beloved country! I ask every old man to remember the past, to reflect on the policy, the principles, and the men of other times, and to consider if all in that past does not prompt him to one course of action!

Fellow-citizens of Pennsylvania! There are subordinate questions, on which those may differ, without great injury, who agree in general principles. And there are questions of a temporary interest, in regard to which a wrong decision made now may be corrected hereafter. Such are not the questions now before us. The questions now before us touch, and touch vitally, great, and deep, and permanent interests of the country.

On these questions, brethren of the same principles must not differ. In saying this, while I look round about me, and see who compose this vast assembly, I have not, I hope, transcended the bounds of propriety. You understand me. I need not press the point more explicitly.

When great principles of government are at stake, when high and lasting interests are at hazard, I repeat, that, in such a crisis,

---

* General Markle, the Whig candidate for Governor.

friends must not allow themselves to divide upon questions respecting men, so as to defeat or endanger all their own dearest objects.

What we now do, we cannot undo.   We do it once, and we do it for our generation, perhaps for ever.   And so much of all our highest interests, our truest prosperity, and our best hopes depends on having this work well done, that I say once more, — I say it from the very bottom of my heart, — I say it with the most profound conviction of its importance, — brethren of the same principles must not be allowed to differ with regard to men.

CONVENTION AT VALLEY FORGE.

CONVENTION AT VALLEY FORGE.*

Two days after the foregoing speech was delivered at Philadelphia, Mr. Webster was invited to address a general convention of the Whigs of Chester and Montgomery Counties. The place appointed for the meeting was Valley Forge, a spot for ever famous in the annals of the Revolution, and still preserving the most interesting memorials of the dreadful winter of 1777 – 78. The information that Mr. Webster was expected to address the meeting had circulated widely throughout the neighboring townships, few of whose inhabitants had ever had an opportunity of hearing him. They accordingly assembled in great numbers, and of both sexes. The village was filled, at an early hour, by the multitude, which poured in from every quarter. Processions were formed, with banners, wreaths, and emblems appropriate to the Revolutionary associations of the place, and significant of the principles and feelings which belonged to the present occasion. A strong mounted escort was in attendance at the railway station ; and at nine o'clock, A. M., the train arrived from Philadelphia, with Mr. Webster and a large number of political friends from that city.

After a short time passed in a survey of the interesting localities of the spot, especially the house in which General Washington's quarters were established during the winter of 1777 – 78, the convention was organized by the appointment of Hon. Jonathan Roberts as President. After a forcible address from the chair, on the general objects of the meeting, Mr. Webster was introduced to the company, and delivered the following speech.

LADIES AND GENTLEMEN, — There is a mighty power in local association. All acknowledge it, and all feel it ! Those places naturally inspire us with emotion, which, in the course of human history, have been connected with great and interesting events ;

* Speech delivered at a great Convention of the Whigs of Chester and Montgomery Counties, in Pennsylvania, at Valley Forge, on the 3d of October, 1844.

and this power over all ingenuous minds never ceases, until frequent visits familiarize the mind to the scenes.

There are in this vast multitude many who, like myself, never before stood on the spot where the Whig army of the Revolution, under the immediate command of their immortal leader, went through the privations, the sufferings, and the distress, of the winter of 1777 and 1778. The mention of Washington, the standing on the ground of his encampment, the act of looking around on the scenes which he and his officers and soldiers then beheld, cannot but carry us back, also, to the Revolution, and to one of its most distressing and darkest periods.

In September, the battle of Brandywine had been fought; in October, that of Germantown; and before Christmas, a little before the severity of winter set in, General Washington repaired to this spot, and put his army into huts for the winter. He had selected the position with great care, for the safety of his army, and with equal judgment, also, for the protection of as large a portion of the country as possible, the British troops being then in possession of Philadelphia.

We see, then, the Whig chief of the Whig army of the Revolution, as it were, before us. We see him surrounded by his military friends, distinguished not less for their social virtues than for their bravery in the field. Anthony Wayne was here, that great and good man. He was a native of the County of Chester, where his bones still rest. Green was here, and Knox, and Hamilton; and at that anxious moment, in order to keep alive the connection between the civil authority and the army, (for be it remembered now and at all times, that Washington and his army always acted in submission to the civil authority), a committee of Congress was here, Dana of Massachusetts, Gouverneur Morris, and that worthy gentleman, the especial favorite of Washington, who was afterwards President of your Commonwealth, General Reed.*

And now, Gentlemen, I could not depict, I could not describe, I could not trust my own feelings in attempting to describe, the horrible sufferings of that Whig army. Destitute of clothing, destitute of provisions, destitute of every thing but their trust in

* A very interesting letter from the Committee to the President of Congress, on the state of the army, written by General Reed, will be found in the Life and Correspondence of Joseph Reed, by his Grandson, William B. Reed. Vol. I. p. 360 *et seq.*

God, and faith in their immortal leader, they went through that winter. The grounds now around us, particularly the grounds contiguous to the hospital, are rich in Revolutionary dust. Every excavation, as often as the season returns, brings to the surface the bones of Revolutionary officers and soldiers, who perished by disease, brought on by want of food, want of clothing, want of every thing but that boundless sympathy and commiseration for sufferings which he could not alleviate, that filled the bleeding heart of their illustrious leader. Long after peace returned, General Washington declared, at his own table, that it was no exaggeration, it was the literal truth, that the march of the army from Whitemarsh, to take up their quarters at this place, could be tracked by the blood on the snow from the unshod feet of the soldiers.

It is impossible to recall the associations of such a place without deep and solemn reflection. And when we, as Whigs, professing the principles of that great Whig leader and that Whig army, come here to advocate and avow those principles to one another, and professing to exercise the political rights transmitted to us by them, for the security of that liberty which they fought to establish, let us bring ourselves to feel in harmony with the scenes of the past. Let us endeavor to sober and solemnize our minds. For, if I have any apprehension of the condition of things under which we have met here, it is one that ought to produce that effect upon us. I feel, and all should feel, that there is a calamity impending over us. If we would avert that impending calamity, it is only to be done by a serious and manly course. And by the blood of our fathers, which cries to us from this hallowed ground, by the memory of their many virtues and brilliant achievements, by the sad story of their intense sufferings, by the blessings of that blood-bought inheritance of liberty which they suffered and died to obtain for us, we are called upon to perform the important duty that lies before us in the present crisis, to perform that duty fearlessly, to perform it promptly, and to perform it effectually.

It is under this feeling, my friends, that I come here to-day; and it is under this feeling that I intend to speak plainly and manfully, as man should speak to man, at a moment like this, on the important duties which are incumbent on us all.

We are on the eve of a general election, in which the people are to choose a President and Vice-President of the United States. It is the great action of the citizen in carrying on his own plan of self-government. But the circumstances connected with this election render it peculiarly interesting, and of more importance than any former Presidential election. There are two candidates in the field, Mr. Clay of Kentucky, and Mr. Polk of Tennessee. I shall speak of them both with the respect to which their character and position entitle them; and at the same time with that freedom and candor which ought to be observed in discussing the merits of public men, especially those who are candidates for the highest office in the gift of the people.

Mr. Clay has been before the country for a long period, nearly forty years. Over thirty years he has taken a leading and highly important part in the public affairs of this country. He is acknowledged to be a man of singular and almost universal talent. He has had great experience in the administration of our public affairs in various departments. He has served for many years with wonderful judgment and ability, in both houses of Congress, of one of which he performed the arduous and difficult duties of its presiding officer, with unexampled skill and success. He has rendered most important services to his country of a diplomatic character, as the representative of this government in Europe, at one of the most trying periods of our history, and ably assisted to conduct to a satisfactory conclusion a very delicate and important negotiation. He has performed the duties of the department of state with ability and fidelity. He is a man of frankness and honor, of unquestioned talent and ability, and of a noble and generous bearing.

Mr. Polk is a much younger man than Mr. Clay. He is a very respectable gentleman in private life; he has been in Congress; was once Speaker of the House of Representatives of the United States, and once Governor of the State of Tennessee.

Such are the candidates before the country for its choice; and it will not be invidious to say, that, in point of character and talent, and general standing before the country and the world, there is no sort of comparison between the two men.

It is for the people to choose between them; and if they prefer one who is secondary to one who is first rate, such preferences can only be ascribed to one of two causes. If they prefer

Mr. Polk to Mr. Clay, it will be either because party attachment is so strong, that they will vote for any man that may be nominated by their party, independent of any other consideration whatever; or it will be because his measures, principles, and opinions are such as they approve, whilst the measures, principles, and opinions of Mr. Clay are such as they do not approve.

I suppose that the existence of parties in a republican government cannot be avoided; and to a certain extent, perhaps, under such form of government, they may exercise a wholesome, restraining, and necessary influence upon the rulers. But I still think that, when party spirit carries men so far that they will not inquire into the men and measures that are placed before them for their sanction and support, but will only inquire to what party the men belong, or what party recommends the measures, that is a state of things which is dangerous to the stability of a free government.

It has been said that party is the madness of many for the gain of the few. This is true, because of all inventions dangerous to liberty, of all inventions calculated to subvert free institutions and popular forms of government, of all inventions calculated to apply a bandage to the eyes of man, an unscrupulous, heated, undistinguishing spirit of party is the most effectual. I will ask you all to talk to your neighbors who propose to vote for Mr. Polk, on this point; to reason with them, to ask them the question, and you will find, when you come to bring them to it, that they purpose doing so because Mr. Polk is of their party, and Mr. Clay is of the other party. You will find, when you come to ask them, that many who propose to vote for Mr. Polk desire, nevertheless, to see all his policy defeated. Of this there is no doubt. Many of the leading men among our opponents, and many of those connected with the public press, have openly expressed themselves dissatisfied with the nomination. They have issued their manifestoes to that effect, and they advise the people to do what they intend to do themselves, that is, support Mr. Polk for the Presidency, but take especial care to support also, as members of Congress, those men that will defeat his policy.

Now, I do not suppose that our free government could long be maintained by such a miserable, crooked policy as this. The plan of our opponents is to elect Mr. Polk to the office of chief

24 *

magistrate of this country, and at the same time to give him, intentionally, and by design, a Congress that shall defeat his policy; to elect him to an office wherein he is to be the guardian of the whole people, an office that has been filled by Washington, and an office that we had hoped always to see filled by men of Washington's principles, if not of his ability, — to select and elect a man to fill this office, and then to put him under guardianship in order to defeat his measures!

The case is a serious one. It addresses itself to the conscience of every man, to see that he does not support in any way, as candidate for the Presidency, a man whose whole course of policy and opinions he is utterly opposed to. And it comes to this: Is there such a sense of the great duty which they owe to their fellow-men, to their children, and to generations yet unborn, such a sense of the necessity of preserving unimpaired the benefits and efficiency of our free, our noble institutions, such a sense of the deep responsibility that rests on them at this important crisis, such a sense of patriotism and integrity, that men will prefer their country to their party in the coming contest, or not? (Cries of " There is!" " There is!")

I believe it. And, to take the other hypothesis, if those who vote for Mr. Polk do not do it under the stimulus of party feeling, then it must be that they vote for him because they are opposed to Mr. Clay's principles. They may be supposed to say, " It is true that Mr. Clay is the most distinguished man, it is true that he has rendered infinitely more important services to his country than Mr. Polk, it is true that the country regards him with far more favor than his opponent, still his measures and principles, as he has avowed them, incline us to elect an inferior man, because we like the principles of the latter better, and believe that they will be more beneficial to the country." Very well. If that case be made out, then you and I, and all Pennsylvania and Massachusetts, are bound to take Mr. Polk. Because, if we suppose and believe that his principles and his measures will conform to our principles and our interests, and the interests of the country, and that Mr. Clay's principles and measures will not conform to our principles and our interests, and the interests of the country, then we are bound to take the second best.

And this leads us directly to the inquiry, What are the measures, principles, and opinions of the one and of the other, as submitted to the consideration and judgment of the people? Now, Gentlemen, there would be a stop to all republican government, a dead halt made by those who desire to see the prosperity of free institutions, if we were to give up this first great principle, that electors are inquisitive enough to desire to know the opinions and sentiments of those whom they may choose to rule over them, that they have intelligence enough thoroughly to analyze those opinions and those sentiments, and discretion and candor enough to make the proper application of the knowledge thus acquired. If this great principle be given up, then the substratum of popular government falls to the ground. I believe there is intelligence enough to do this, and integrity enough to choose those whose principles are best calculated to effect the great objects which we all have in view.

There are two leading questions for our consideration in the very important contest before us. One is the protective system. This subject has been so ably and thoroughly discussed before you by men much more able to do justice to it than I am, that it is not necessary I should dwell upon it here. It is a favorite measure with you, with us at home, and with all our party. We deem it a most necessary system, one that cannot under any circumstances be dispensed with, as being necessary to the comfort, necessary to the happiness, the prosperity of all; and vitally touching the permanent, as well as the present, interests of the community.

This brings us at once to the inquiry, What are the opinions which these two candidates hold upon this protective policy? and it leads us first to ask what are Mr. Polk's sentiments thereon.

This is easily answered. It is notorious, that, when Mr. Polk was nominated, it was partly on account of his hostility to the tariff of 1842. I had supposed that there was not a man in the Union, of information or intelligence, not a man who could read a newspaper, who did not fully understand, who did not know, who was not morally certain, that Mr. Polk was put forth as a strong, uncompromising anti-tariff man, a warm friend and advocate of free trade; and that he was nominated on those very grounds to run against Mr. Clay. The thing was not disguised with us. All his adherents in Massachusetts, New Hampshire, and Maine avowed that he was a strong anti-tariff man, and declared that on that very ground they would vote for him. But in course of time his friends found that this doctrine was not popular in some parts of the Union, and they therefore resolved that he should go to them, not in his true, but in his assumed, garb; that he, who was the steady, regular, original enemy to protection, should be dressed and undressed, and undressed and dressed again, and finally exhibited in his new garments as a protectionist. I do not believe that Mr. Polk, after undergoing such a change, after donning his new, and for him unaccustomed garments, — I do not think that he would have that continuity of ideas which philosophers say constitutes "personal identity"; he would not know himself. Indeed, so far as I know any thing of Mr. Polk, I do not believe that he would submit to any such degradation. I do not believe that he would for a moment lend himself to the perpetration of such deception. I believe he would scorn it. If he were here to-day, and the question were to be put to him, to be sure he would look grave, and would not like to make any answer; but if he were forced to speak, under the penalty of forfeiting the good opinion of all men, he would say, directly and honestly, " I am opposed to protection; I came into public life opposed to it; all my votes, speeches, and public acts have been in direct hostility to it, my sentiments have undergone no change up to this hour in regard to it, and I expect to remain an uncompromising enemy to it, till the day I die."

This is strong language, but it is not stronger than Mr. Polk used in stating his views last year, in the general discussion and controversy with Mr. Jones, in Tennessee, when they were rival candidates for the office of Governor of that State. Tennessee had been a strong anti-tariff State; she had followed closely the lead of South Carolina on this subject. But the sentiments of the people had undergone a change; several of the most eminent men in the State thought that the tariff operated beneficially, even to Tennessee, and were satisfied that it benefited the whole country immensely, and with true patriotism abandoned all local prejudices, for the general welfare. Mr. Polk remained on the old anti-tariff ground. He proposed to Mr. Jones, that they should write letters to the people explaining their respective opinions, and fully discuss this great question in their approaching contest; and it is notorious that the contest was strictly tariff and anti-tariff, and that Mr. Polk came off second best.

That Mr. Polk ever has been, and still is, regarded as thoroughly opposed to all protection, is quite clear from the occurrences at the Baltimore Convention, where Mr. Polk was nominated and Mr. Van Buren defeated. Mr. Van Buren was not much of a tariff man, nor much of an anti-tariff man; he was not much of a proslavery man, nor much of an antislavery man, nor much of a decided man in any thing or on any question. He was not much for Texas, and he was not much against Texas. He was not against the tariff, nor pledged up to his chin for Texas. How did he fare? He had a majority of the votes in the convention, and was, therefore, put under the ban of the two-thirds rule. He could not get two thirds of the votes, and after a course of proceeding which it would not become me to characterize in appropriate terms here, he was defeated, and Mr. Polk was chosen, the thorough anti-tariff and pro-Texas man!

This is all true. It is not more true that the battles of Brandywine and Germantown were fought in 1777, and that Washington and his army were here in the winter of 1778, than that Mr. Polk was brought forward because he was anti-tariff. If it had not been for his opposition to the tariff and his advocacy of the annexation of Texas, we should never have heard any more of Mr. James K. Polk of Tennessee! And yet I have seen banners floating in the air, in this intelligent county of Chester, on which were inscribed, "POLK AND DALLAS, AND THE TARIFF OF 1842!"

Why, is there no shame in men? Mr. Polk openly avows that he is for reducing the duties on all imported goods to the level of the Compromise Act, as that law stood on the 29th of June, 1842. That is to say, to twenty per cent. on every thing. He says, "Down with the tariff!" And his friends here say, "Polk and the tariff for ever!" Is there no shame in men? Or do they suppose that they will be enabled to put such a veil of blindness over men's eyes, that, if the cry be right, that is, if it come from the right quarter, they will take the leap, lead where it may? If men could be misled by such means, if they could be deceived by such a miserable juggle as this, I should despair of the practicability of popular governments. If a man can thus stifle the voice of his conscience, if he can throw aside his integrity and patriotism, if he can forget the duty he owes to himself, his family, his country, and his God, for such a shallow device as this, how can he be worthy of being a citizen of this free and happy country?

It becomes our duty, then, to expose, in every way and everywhere, this infamous juggle. Let us put it down, and put it down at once and for ever. Let us declare it a fraud and a cheat. I declare it a fraud and a cheat; and if my voice could be heard throughout the whole of this country, I would say that, whoever he is, if he be a man of common information and common knowledge, and comes to an elector of this or any other State, and says that Mr. Polk is in favor of the tariff, he means to cheat and defraud that elector out of the proper exercise of the elective franchise! And after he has got him to vote for Mr. Polk, he will turn his back on him and say, "What intolerable gulls *the people* are!"

If this were not so serious a matter, it would be supremely ridiculous. But it is so serious a thing as to excite our deepest indignation, that men should try to get the honest votes of an honest community for the support of men and of measures which they know that honest community do not desire. We owe it, therefore, as a duty to our neighbors, to go among them; to explain this whole matter to them; to read Mr. Polk's declarations to them, and to undeceive them. We owe it to them as a sacred duty. We owe it to them inasmuch as we are all embarked in the same bottom. If they go down, we shall go down with them; we cannot prosper if they are ruined. For reason, and philosophy, and experience, and common sense, all teach that one portion of the community cannot flourish at the expense of another portion. Let us by every exertion possible, by the use of calm, sober reasoning and fair argument, bring our neighbors who are of opposite opinions to ours to see things in their proper light, and to induce them to give their support to those who are their friends and the friends of that policy which they desire themselves to see perpetuated.

I shall not go at great length into a discussion of the tariff. It is well understood in this part of the country. There would not be the slightest doubt in my mind of the result of the coming election in Pennsylvania, if the people could be made to understand what the issue really is. The tariff policy is founded on this. We have vast resources of natural wealth; by these, if properly protected, and, as a natural consequence, properly and fully developed, we have the means of providing other vast sources of wealth, which will contribute, not to the emolument of a few, as has been falsely asserted, but to the prosperity and lasting happiness of every class in the community. We are in a situation that does not require us all to be farmers, or all lawyers, or all mechanics. There must necessarily be another class, that of manufacturers and operatives. And a system which shall create a demand for labor, which shall amply remunerate that labor, which shall thereby create such a wholesome demand for agricultural products, as to properly compensate the tiller of the ground for his toil, — a system which would enable the farmers to raise up their families (those families which are the main pride and boast of the country) in comfort and happiness, and thus to benefit and preserve all that is dear to them in the world, — such a system ought to be pursued, and no other.

I am addressing here, I suppose, an assembly, a large majority of whom are engaged in agricultural pursuits. And I put it to the farmer to say how the tariff affects him. There are many false prophets going to and fro in the land, who declare that the tariff benefits only the manufacturer, and that it injures the farmer. This is all sheer misrepresentation.

Every farmer must see, that it is his interest to find a near purchaser for his produce, to find a ready purchaser, and a purchaser at a good price. Now, the tariff supposes, that, if there be domestic manufactures carried on successfully, there will inevitably be those engaged therein who will consume a large amount of agricultural products, because they do not raise any for themselves, — a new class of consumers of the farmer's commodities, an enlarged class of consumers. Now if that general rule be false, then our policy is false. But if that general rule be true, then our policy is true. If it be for the interest of the Chester farmer, that there should be many consumers, that the number should be largely increased of those who do not raise agricultural products, then our policy is true; and if it be not for the interest, but for the injury, of the Chester farmer, that the number of those who consume but do not raise agricultural products should be increased, then our policy is false.

To illustrate this, I will here give an estimate that has been made with very great care, by a most intelligent writer, a friend of mine, in whose judgment I have the highest confidence. This estimate shows the exact state of things in this country, in connection with the subjects before us. And, before I go into it, allow me to say that the great wealth, the great happiness, of the country consists in the interchange of domestic commodities.

In illustrating this point, let us take the article of bread-stuffs. What do you do with it? Who consumes it? What becomes of it? You send your flour to Philadelphia, New York, and Baltimore; but where does it go to from those places? There must be an ultimate consumer. There must be a last man into whose hands the barrel of flour must go before the hoops are knocked off. And where is he to be found? Why, the chief consumption of wheat flour in this country is in the East, where the great manufacturing interests are carried on; and in the districts where large and extensive mining operations are successfully making progress; and in those other districts inhabited by the workers in wool, and workers in cotton, and workers in iron and the various metals. These are the classes who are the great and profitable consumers of the farmer's produce, whilst they never compete with him in raising it.

The amount of cotton imported into New England is very large, but the amount of bread-stuffs imported is still larger. But here is the extract before referred to:—

"Bread-stuffs are a more valuable import into New England than cotton. Of flour (wheat) we do not raise, in Massachusetts, over 120,000 bushels of wheat, equal to 24,000 barrels of flour,—about enough for the Lowell operatives. The balance comes from States out of New England. I should say we consumed, at least, 600,000 barrels of imported wheat flour, and a large amount of maize, rye, and oats. Maine may raise one half its wheat, but imports a large quantity of maize, oats, and rye, and New Hampshire, Connecticut, and Rhode Island import still more. Of sugar, we do not take any great quantity of Louisiana. It goes more to the Middle, but chiefly to the Western States. Of tobacco, we are, in New England, large consumers; and our ships to Africa and the East find a market for large quantities, in small parcels. Of naval stores, we, of course, consume immensely; for in Massachusetts we have 550,000 tons of shipping, and in Maine about 350,000 more; and in New England, in the whole, about 1,050,000. We distil a large quantity of turpentine for exportation to all parts of the world.

" There is no population except that of London which has a greater consuming ability for the necessaries, comforts, and most of the luxuries of life, than the 800,000 people of Massachusetts ; consequently, there is no population so advantageous to trade with. The Middle, and Southern, and Western States have laid great stress on the Zollverein treaty, on account of reductions in duties, which would not augment the sales of tobacco, cotton, &c., to the extent of five hundred thousand dollars. Now, the commerce which those sections have with Massachusetts, — which Mr. McDuffie ranks as one of the *poor States*, because we have but few exports for foreign countries, — I say, the commerce which these sections, namely, the South, and West, and Middle States, have with Massachusetts, is of more value, and of greater magnitude, than all the products which those sections sell to the *whole population of Germany ;* and, I will add, to Russia, Sweden, and Denmark.

" What may be the amount of imports into Massachusetts from these sections, I cannot ascertain ; but of grain of all kinds, it cannot be less, at average prices of the past five years, than $ 7,000,000 ; of cotton, 180,000 bales at $ 35 per bale, average of five years, $ 6,300,000 ; making $ 13,300,000 for those two staples. On reference to the returns of 1842, the last published, I find the domestic exports to the countries referred to as follows : —

Hanse Towns, ...	$ 3,814,994
Russia, ...	316,026
Prussia, ...	149,141
Sweden, and Swedish West Indies, . . .	368,675
Denmark, and the Danish West Indies, . .	862,594
	$ 5,511,430
Add, to Trieste, ...	748,179
	$ 6,259,609

" Commercially speaking, if this portion of the European population, amounting to at least 120,000,000, were to suspend their intercourse with the United States, it would be less detrimental to the States out of New England, than a cessation of intercourse with the poor State, as she is termed by many Southern men, of Massachusetts, with her population of 800,000 (last census 737,000), and increasing, in spite of the great density of her population, at the rate of about 18 per cent. in ten years.

" As to the other five New England States, I suppose the aggregate of their transactions with States out of New England may not equal the amount of the transactions of Massachusetts. This difference results from the nature of our products, and the superior amount of our capital, which, *per capita*, is greater than exists in any other State, and four times as great as in a majority of the States. Of course, such estimates are in some measure conjectural, but they are partly based on facts which are before the country.

"There never was a traffic carried on in any country, more advantageous, from its magnitude and its character, than the interchange of products between New England and the other States. We are large consumers. We *pay cash* for all we buy, and in good money, while we sell on credit, and have lost by bad debts south of the Hudson, within twenty years, more wealth than some of the cotton States, who call us poor, are now possessed of."

Now, the question is, Does not this show the true policy of the country to be, to build up interests that shall contribute to the healthy employment and mutual happiness of each other, and thus benefit equally the whole community? And with this, knowing, as I do, that the whole sentiments of the people of Pennsylvania are in favor of the protective system, I leave the topic.

Now, there is another and a very important subject that I desire briefly to speak of. We are trying the great experiment of the success of popular government, — whether these seventeen millions of people will exercise so much intelligence, integrity, virtue, and patriotism, as shall secure to this great country for ever the blessings of a free, enlightened, liberal, and popular government. In the first place, we have laid at its base a Constitution, — I had almost said, and may say, a miraculous Constitution, when we take into view all the circumstances connected with its origin and maturity, — a Constitution unequalled in its scope and design, its construction and its effect, which secures the full enjoyment of all human rights alike to every one. We are bound by a solemn duty to see that, among the candidates for the high offices in the gift of a free people, we give our votes to such as venerate that Constitution, and to none other. The principles of our government are liberty and equality, established law and order, security for public liberty and private right, a general system of education liberally diffused, the free exercise of every religious creed and opinion, and brotherly love and harmony, this last being considered peculiarly the characteristic of a happy people under a free form of government. It is to preserve all these, to see that not one of these rights and privileges is soiled in passing through the hands appointed to administer them, that not one is weakened, none injured or destroyed, that we are called upon to exercise our judgment and our privileges at the ensuing election. All these call on us with a sense of deep responsibility, whenever it is our duty to give our suffrages to the candidates for the high offices of our respective States and common country.

Now the subject for your serious consideration at this time is the annexation of another large territory to the twenty-six States we already possess. I have seen the dismemberment of Texas from Mexico with much hope. She sprung into existence of a sudden, perhaps prematurely, but she seemed competent to sustain herself in her position; and you and I and all wished her well, for we wished to see the advancement of human liberty. Men who set up a government after the plan of our own, and sincerely take our Washington for their model, are always entitled to our regard. But, whatever may be our feelings and desires in relation to Texas, we must not take such a vast extent of territory into our Union without looking a little into the internal condition of things there, and to the institutions of that country! And it has always appeared to me that the slavery of the blacks, and the unavoidable increase both of the numbers of these slaves and of the duration of their slavery, formed an insuperable objection to its annexation. For I will do nothing, now or at any time, that shall tend to extend the slavery of the African race on this continent. Now, our opponents are in favor of immediate annexation, at all hazards! The Secretary of State says, in the correspondence transmitted with the treaty to the Senate of the United States, that the United States are ready to take all the responsibility of annexing it immediately; because, he says, the annexation of Texas is necessary to preserve the domestic institutions of the two countries, — that is, to preserve slavery in the United States, and to preserve slavery in Texas. To secure these objects, the United States will take all the responsibility.

Now slavery, in this country, stands where the Constitution left it. I have taken an oath to support the Constitution, and I mean to abide by it. I shall do nothing to carry the power of the general government within the just bounds of the States. I shall do nothing to interfere with the domestic institutions of the South; and the government of the United States have no right to interfere therewith. But that is a different thing, very, from not interfering to prevent the extension of slavery, by adding a large slave country to this. Why, where would this lead us to? Some day, England may become deeply involved in domestic difficulties, and the people of the North may want the annexation of Canada. We have territory enough, we are happy enough, each State moulds its own institutions to suit its own people, and is it not best to leave them alone?

Others will address you on other topics, and I must take my leave. I came among you only to tell you the deep interest I feel in your ensuing State election. The election of a President of the United States depends on the next gubernatorial election of Pennsylvania, or at least may be materially affected by it. As far as we can go for the maintenance of our Constitution and our rights, we of Massachusetts intend to do our duty, and we believe that you will do yours.

A feeling of delicacy will restrain me from attempting to advise you in aught that concerns your State election. A letter has been read from Governor Ritner, showing the important bearing of the election for Governor, in this State, upon the next November contest, and I concur in every word of that letter. I know there is nothing in the North which interests all so much, there is nothing to which a man so quickly and intently turns his thoughts, after the performance of his daily devotional duties, as to inquire into the prospects of your next ensuing election. For it will be ominous of the contest next November. It stands to reason, that, where eight hundred thousand votes are cast, any party decidedly beaten in October will require very great exertion to rouse itself a second time. And it is therefore from the election of next week that I shall deduce my conclusions whether Pennsylvania next November will stand side by side with Massachusetts, or not.

One word more, though I do not intend to canvass the merits of the respective candidates. I may be allowed to say that I had, a few days ago, the honor and pleasure of making the acquaintance of General Markle; and whether he be elected Governor of this Commonwealth or not, or whatever may betide him or me in after life, I am very glad to know him. He is a frank, open-hearted, intelligent, and noble citizen. And if I were a Pennsylvanian, as you are Pennsylvanians, there is no man in the Commonwealth to whom I would sooner give my vote, or with whom I would sooner intrust the destinies of my State. And I pray Heaven, that at the next election you will all do your duty.

The duties before us must be regarded as serious and sober; the times are serious and sober; the occasion is serious and sober. The result of the next election will give a tone to the government and to the whole country for many years to come. It will decide whether the government is to remain upon the track which it has pursued since the days of Washington, or whether we are to shoot athwart the sky, and go off into some unknown region of political darkness.

There is no man who possesses so much or so little power, no man so elevated or so humble, as to be excused from exerting all the power he possesses to bring about the desired result; because there is no man so high in station or prosperity, no man so secure in life, or the possession of this world's goods, no man so intrenched in every way, and so persuaded that he is proof against fortune or fate, as not to be in danger from the effects of that disastrous course of policy which will be pursued should our adversaries succeed at the election.

Nor is there a man so low, so much bound to daily toil, as not to have an interest in the principles which the Whigs avow, those principles which reward labor, those principles which will elevate him in society, which shall fill his mouth with bread, his home with happiness, his heart with gladness.

Ladies and Gentlemen, I thank you for the honor and kindness of your patient attention, and respectfully bid you farewell.

25 *

MR. JUSTICE STORY.

MR. JUSTICE STORY.*

AT a meeting of the Suffolk Bar, held in the Circuit Court Room, Boston, on the morning of the 12th of September, the day of the funeral of Mr. Justice Story, Chief Justice Shaw having taken the chair and announced the object of the meeting, Mr. Webster rose and spoke substantially as follows: —

YOUR solemn announcement, Mr. Chief Justice, has confirmed the sad intelligence which had already reached us, through the public channels of information, and deeply afflicted us all.

JOSEPH STORY, one of the Associate Justices of the Supreme Court of the United States, and for many years the presiding judge of this Circuit, died on Wednesday evening last, at his house in Cambridge, wanting only a few days for the completion of the sixty-sixth year of his age.

This most mournful and lamentable event has called together the whole Bar of Suffolk, and all connected with the courts of law or the profession. It has brought you, Mr. Chief Justice, and your associates of the Bench of the Supreme Court of Massachusetts, into the midst of us; and you have done us the

---

* The following letter of dedication to the mother of Judge Story accompanied these remarks in the original edition: —

"*Boston, September* 15, 1845.

"VENERABLE MADAM, — I pray you to allow me to present to you the brief remarks which I made before the Suffolk Bar, on the 12th instant, at a meeting occasioned by the sudden and afflicting death of your distinguished son. I trust, dear Madam, that as you enjoyed through his whole life constant proofs of his profound respect and ardent filial affection, so you may yet live long to enjoy the remembrance of his virtues and his exalted reputation.

"I am, with very great regard, your obedient servant,

"DANIEL WEBSTER.

"To MADAM STORY."

honor, out of respect to the occasion, to consent to preside over us, while we deliberate on what is due, as well to our own afflicted and smitten feelings, as to the exalted character and eminent distinction of the deceased judge. The occasion has drawn from his retirement, also, that venerable man, whom we all so much respect and honor, (Judge Davis,) who was, for thirty years, the associate of the deceased upon the same Bench. It has called hither another judicial personage, now in retirement, (Judge Putnam,) but long an ornament of that Bench of which you are now the head, and whose marked good fortune it is to have been the professional teacher of Mr. Justice Story, and the director of his early studies. He also is present to whom this blow comes near; I mean, the learned judge (Judge Sprague) from whose side it has struck away a friend and a highly venerated official associate. The members of the Law School at Cambridge, to which the deceased was so much attached, and who returned that attachment with all the ingenuousness and enthusiasm of educated and ardent youthful minds, are here also, to manifest their sense of their own severe deprivation, as well as their admiration of the bright and shining professional example which they have so loved to contemplate, — an example, let me say to them, and let me say to all, as a solace in the midst of their sorrows, which death hath not touched and which time cannot obscure.

Mr. Chief Justice, one sentiment pervades us all. It is that of the most profound and penetrating grief, mixed, nevertheless, with an assured conviction, that the great man whom we deplore is yet with us and in the midst of us. He hath not wholly died. He lives in the affections of friends and kindred, and in the high regard of the community. He lives in our remembrance of his social virtues, his warm and steady friendships, and the vivacity and richness of his conversation. He lives, and will live still more permanently, by his words of written wisdom, by the results of his vast researches and attainments, by his imperishable legal judgments, and by those juridical disquisitions which have stamped his name, all over the civilized world, with the character of a commanding authority. " Vivit, enim, vivetque semper; atque etiam latius in memoria hominum et sermone versabitur, postquam ab oculis recessit."

Mr. Chief Justice, there are consolations which arise to mitigate our loss, and shed the influence of resignation over unfeigned and heartfelt sorrow. We are all penetrated with gratitude to God that the deceased lived so long; that he did so much for himself, his friends, the country, and the world; that his lamp went out, at last, without unsteadiness or flickering. He continued to exercise every power of his mind without dimness or obscuration, and every affection of his heart with no abatement of energy or warmth, till death drew an impenetrable veil between us and him. Indeed, he seems to us now, as in truth he is, not extinguished or ceasing to be, but only withdrawn; as the clear sun goes down at its setting, not darkened but only no longer seen.

This calamity, Mr. Chief Justice, is not confined to the bar or the courts of this Commonwealth. It will be felt by every bar throughout the land, by every court, and indeed by every intelli gent and well-informed man in or out of the profession. It will be felt still more widely, for his reputation had a still wider range. In the High Court of Parliament, in every tribunal in Westminster Hall, in the judicatories of Paris and Berlin, of Scockholm and St. Petersburg, in the learned universities of Germany, Italy, and Spain, by every eminent jurist in the civilized world, it will be acknowledged that a great luminary has fallen from the firmament of public jurisprudence.

Sir, there is no purer pride of country than that in which we may indulge when we see America paying back the great debt of civilization, learning, and science to Europe. In this high return of light for light and mind for mind, in this august reckoning and accounting between the intellects of nations, Joseph Story was destined by Providence to act, and did act, an important part. Acknowledging, as we all acknowledge, our obligations to the original sources of English law, as well as of civil liberty, we have seen in our generation copious and salutary streams turning and running backward, replenishing their original fountains, and giving a fresher and a brighter green to the fields of English jurisprudence. By a sort of reversed hereditary transmission, the mother, without envy or humiliation, acknowledges that she has received a valuable and cherished inheritance from the daughter. The profession in England admits, with frankness and candor, and with no feeling but that of respect and admiration, that he whose voice we have so recently heard within these walls, but shall now hear no more, was, of all men who have yet appeared, most fitted by the comprehensiveness of his mind, and the vast extent and accuracy of his attainments, to compare the codes of nations, to trace their differences to difference of origin, climate, or religious or political institutions, and to exhibit, nevertheless, their concurrence in those great principles upon which the system of human civilization rests.

Justice, Sir, is the great interest of man on earth. It is the ligament which holds civilized beings and civilized nations together. Wherever her temple stands, and so long as it is duly honored, there is a foundation for social security, general happiness, and the improvement and progress of our race. And whoever labors on this edifice with usefulness and distinction, whoever clears its foundations, strengthens its pillars, adorns its entablatures, or contributes to raise its august dome still higher in the skies, connects himself, in name, and fame, and character, with that which is and must be as durable as the frame of human society.

All know, Mr. Chief Justice, the pure love of country which animated the deceased, and the zeal, as well as the talent, with which he explained and defended her institutions. His work on the Constitution of the United States is one of his most eminently successful labors. But all his writings, and all his judgments, all his opinions, and the whole influence of his character, public and private, leaned strongly and always to the support of sound principles, to the restraint of illegal power, and to the discouragement and rebuke of licentious and disorganizing sentiments. " Ad rempublicam firmandam, et ad stabiliendas vires, et sanandum populum, omnis ejus pergebat institutio."

But this is not the occasion, Sir, nor is it for me to consider and discuss at length the character and merits of Mr. Justice Story, as a writer or a judge. The performance of that duty, with which this Bar will no doubt charge itself, must be deferred to another opportunity, and will be committed to abler hands. But in the homage paid to his memory, one part may come with peculiar propriety and emphasis from ourselves. We have known him in private life. We have seen him descend from the bench, and mingle in our friendly circles. We have

known his manner of life, from his youth up. We can bear
witness to the strict uprightness and purity of his character, his
simplicity and unostentatious habits, the ease and affability of
his intercourse, his remarkable vivacity amidst severe labors,
the cheerful and animating tones of his conversation, and his
fast fidelity to friends. Some of us, also, can testify to his large
and liberal charities, not ostentatious or casual, but systematic
and silent, — dispensed almost without showing the hand, and
falling and distilling comfort and happiness, like the dews of
heaven. But we can testify, also, that in all his pursuits and
employments, in all his recreations, in all his commerce with
the world, and in his intercourse with the circle of his friends,
the predominance of his judicial character was manifest. He
never forgot the ermine which he wore. The judge, the judge,
the useful and distinguished judge, was the great picture which
he kept constantly before his eyes, and to a resemblance of
which all his efforts, all his thoughts, all his life, were devoted.
We may go the world over, without finding a man who shall
present a more striking realization of the beautiful conception
of D'Aguesseau: " C'est en vain que l'on cherche à distinguer
en lui la personne privée et la personne publique; un même
esprit les anime, un même objet les réunit; l'homme, le père
de famille, le citoyen, tout est en lui consacré à la gloire du
magistrat."

Mr. Chief Justice, one may live as a conqueror, a king, or a
magistrate; but he must die as a man. The bed of death
brings every human being to his pure individuality; to the intense contemplation of that deepest and most solemn of all
relations, the relation between the creature and his Creator.
Here it is that fame and renown cannot assist us; that all
external things must fail to aid us; that even friends, affection,
and human love and devotedness, cannot succor us. This relation, the true foundation of all duty, a relation perceived and
felt by conscience and confirmed by revelation, our illustrious
friend, now deceased, always acknowledged. He reverenced
the Scriptures of truth, honored the pure morality which they
teach, and clung to the hopes of future life which they impart.
He beheld enough in nature, in himself, and in all that can be
known of things seen, to feel assured that there is a Supreme

Power, without whose providence not a sparrow falleth to the
ground.   To this gracious being he trusted himself for time and
or eternity ; and the last words of his lips ever heard by mortal ears were a fervent supplication to his Maker to take him
to himself.

PUBLIC DINNER AT PHILADELPHIA.

INTRODUCTORY NOTE.*

In the spring of 1846, a large number of the merchants and other citizens of Philadelphia proposed to offer to Mr. Webster a distinguished mark of their approbation of his political course. For this purpose it was determined to invite him to a public dinner, and the proposal was eagerly embraced by the most respectable members of the community, of all parties, professions, and pursuits in life. On the 25th of April a meeting of the subscribers was called to make the preliminary arrangements for the dinner, and a large committee was appointed for that purpose.

In the performance of their duty the following letter was addressed by the committee to Mr. Webster : —

"*Philadelphia, April* 27, 1846.

"Dear Sir, — Your fellow-citizens of this city, desirous of expressing their friendly regard and admiration of your services to your country, tender to you a public dinner, to be given at a time the most convenient to yourself.

"Nearly all who offer this mark of esteem are men of business, removed from the party strifes of the country, though deeply interested and affected in all their relations by the action and agitation of party. With these your name has long been associated as one of those whose advice, whether heeded or not, whose abilities, whether successfully exerted or not, were always directed towards the advancement of their interests, and the promotion of their prosperity. They offer to you this token of respect, not only as an evidence of personal esteem, but as a mark of sincere and grateful feeling.

"But, in this expression of regard, they will not limit themselves to what may be considered as more peculiarly their own interests. As members of this great republic, they desire in this way to express their approbation and pride in those efforts that have multiplied and strengthened our ties with the family of nations; that have increased and made more stable, as well as intimate, our own national sympathies; and

---

* Abridged from the account contained in the Introduction to the original pamphlet edition of the following speech.

26 *

which, by extending your reputation, have given credit and fame to your country.

"None cherish with more interest these, the lasting memorials that you have given of your patriotism and devotion to the welfare of your fellow-citizens, than those who now tender this token of their esteem.

"We have the honor to be, with the highest respect,

"Your friends and fellow-citizens,

"ALFRED L. ELWYN,	HENRY WHITE,
CHARLES W. CHURCHMAN,	JACOB M. THOMAS,
DAVID S. BROWN,	GEORGE McCLELLAND,
JOHN S. RIDDLE,	ISAAC R. DAVIS,
FREDERICK FRALEY,	WILLIAM D. LEWIS,
JOHN ASHHURST,	JOHN RICE,
ALEXANDER H. FREEMAN,	WILLIAM E. WHELAN,
JOSEPH B. MYERS,	JOHN H. MARTIN,
SINGLETON A. MERCER,	JOHN McCANDLESS,
THOMAS CHAMBERS,	THOMAS SMITH,
SAMPSON TAMS,	WILLIAM STRUTHERS."
DANIEL HADDOCK, Jr.,	

To this letter Mr. Webster made the following reply in acceptance of the invitation : —

"*Washington, May* 1, 1846.

"GENTLEMEN, — I have the honor to acknowledge the receipt of your communication of the 27th of April, inviting me to a public dinner in Philadelphia.

"The character of this invitation, as well as the friendly manner in which it is expressed, give it a peculiar claim on my regard, and render it indeed, on my part, not easy to be declined.

"You describe those whom you represent, or who join you in this mark of respect, as 'men of business, removed from the party strifes of the country, though deeply affected and interested in all their relations by the action and agitation of party movements.'

"I deem it a high honor, Gentlemen, to be requested by such men to accept a mark of their esteem ; and when my public duties shall allow, I will gladly meet you and your friends on such day as may suit your convenience.

"We are in the midst of all the business of one of the most important sessions of Congress which have been held under the Constitution. During its continuance I shall hardly be able to leave the duties of my place, even for a few days ; but after its conclusion, if you will allow me, I will confer with you upon the time for carrying your very respectful purpose into effect.

"I am, Gentlemen, with entire regard,

"Your obedient servant,

"DANIEL WEBSTER.

"To MESSRS. A. L. ELWYN, C. W. CHURCHMAN, D. S. BROWN, and other Gentlemen of the Committee."

Mr. Webster's duties at Washington prevented this invitation from taking immediate effect, and other causes of delay occurring, the dinner was postponed till the 2d of December, when it took place in the great saloon of the Museum Building. Every arrangement was made to give the most imposing and agreeable effect to the festival. Preparation was made for the reception of a very large company, consisting of the subscribers to the dinner, and of guests particularly invited from the principal neighboring cities of the Union. The entertainment was of the most liberal description. The hall and the tables were richly and tastefully decorated. Wreaths, banners, arches, vases, and flowers, skilfully disposed, met the eye in every direction; and before the speaking commenced, the galleries were filled with ladies.

The Hon. Samuel Breck presided at the table, and, after one or two patriotic sentiments, addressed the company as follows : —

" Gentlemen, — I rise to propose a toast, expressive of the great esteem and honor in which we hold the illustrious guest whom we are assembled to welcome. It is cause for felicitation to have this opportunity to receive him, and to meet him at our festive board.

" In Philadelphia, we have long been accustomed to follow him, with earnest attention, in his high vocations in the legislative hall and in the Cabinet; and have always seen him there exercising his great talents for the true interests of our wide-spread republic. And we, in common with the American people, have felt the influence of his wisdom and patriotism. In seasons of danger, he has been to us a living comforter; and more than once has restored this nation to serenity, security, and prosperity.

" In a career of more than thirty years of political agitation, he, with courageous constancy, unwavering integrity, and eminent ability, has carried out, as far as his agency could prevail, the true principles of the American system of government.

" For his numerous public services we owe him much, and we open our grateful hearts to him in thanks; we say to him, with feelings of profound respect and warm affection, that we are rejoiced at his presence here, amid his Philadelphia friends, — his faithful Philadelphia friends and admirers.

" I offer you the health of

" DANIEL WEBSTER, — the faithful representative, the able negotiator, the fearless statesman, the eloquent Defender of the Constitution. His patriotic services demand our gratitude, his untarnished honor is the nation's property."

Mr. Breck, while making these remarks, was frequently interrupted by the cheers of the audience ; and when at the close he introduced their distinguished guest, the most enthusiastic acclamations burst forth from the whole company. A considerable time elapsed before the excited feelings of the occasion were sufficiently subdued, to allow the voice of the orator to be heard in reply. When silence was at length restored, Mr. Webster delivered the following speech.

It seems proper to state, that, owing to the length of this speech, and the eagerness of the public to possess it without delay, it appears to have been written off from the reporter's notes with haste, and to have received very little, if any, revision from the author. It is evident that portions of it are presented in a fragmentary form.

PUBLIC DINNER AT PHILADELPHIA.*

MR. CHAIRMAN, — It is my duty, in the first place, to express the uncommon emotions which I feel in rising to discuss important subjects in a presence like this. It has not been my fortune, heretofore, to enter upon such a duty as is now before me, while galleries like these have been filled by an assemblage of the worth and beauty of the sex. Gentlemen, I come among you to address you as men of business of the city of Philadelphia, men engaged in the honorable pursuits of private life, and having no other interest in the political events and occurrences of the day, than as the course and acts of government affect life and liberty, property and industry. You are merchants, you are therefore deeply concerned in the peace of the country, and in whatever respects its commercial prosperity. You are manufacturers, mechanics, artisans; you have an interest, therefore, in all those wise laws which protect capital and labor thus employed, all those laws which shed their benign influence over the industrial pursuits of human life. You are holders of city property, many of you are landholders in the country, many of you are occupiers and cultivators of your own land in the neighborhood of the city. Finally, I know you are all Americans, you are all members of this great and glorious republic, bound to its destiny, partaking of all the happiness which its government is calculated to afford, and interested in every thing that respects its present prospects and its future renown.

I am honored, Gentlemen, by an invitation to address such an

* A Speech delivered at a Great Public Dinner, given to Mr. Webster at Philadelphia, on the 2d of December, 1846, Hon. Samuel Breck in the Chair.

assemblage of my fellow-citizens. I will say that it is always agreeable to me to speak, and to think, upon great questions respecting our political institutions, their progress and their results, in this city of Philadelphia. With no habits of public life but such as have connected me with the Constitution of the United States, accustomed somewhat to study its history and its principles, and called upon now, for some years, to take a part in its administration, so far as the action of Congress is concerned, it is natural that I should look back to the origin of that independence from which the Constitution sprung, and to the Constitution itself, out of which the government now established over us arose. These reflections bring with them agreeable local associations. The independence of our country was declared in yonder hall, the Constitution was framed, also, within the same venerable walls; and when one to whom that Declaration of Independence and that Constitution are objects of the highest human regard enters that hall, it is natural that he should gather around him, in imagination, the great men, the illustrious sages, who filled it on those successive occasions. They are all gone to their graves. But they have left their works behind them, as imperishable memorials of their wisdom.

The city of Philadelphia is, in all respects, much connected with the history of our country. She is, in all respects, interested in what affects the weal or woe of the republic. Her position along the line of the coast is central and important, her population is large, the occupations of her people are various; she is the capital of the great State of Pennsylvania, not improperly called the "KEYSTONE" of the arch of this Union.

Gentlemen, some years ago, in addressing a public meeting in the neighborhood of this city, I said, what I believed and now believe, that, with the exception of England, perhaps there is no spot upon the globe so abounding in natural riches as the State of Pennsylvania. She enjoys a mild and delightful climate, a rich and exuberant soil, certainly one of the best in the world, with mineral wealth beyond calculation. I know no portion of the globe that can go beyond her in any just statement of natural advantages, and of productive power. Pennsylvania, too, Gentlemen, is concerned in every interest that belongs to the country. On her eastern boundary she touches the tide-waters of the Atlantic, on her western border she reaches to the great river which carries, westward and southward, her products raised beyond the Alleghanies to the Gulf of Mexico. Thus she is open to the Gulf on the south and west, and to the ocean on the east. Her position is central, her population is numerous. If she chooses to say that she will connect the navigable waters which flow into the Gulf with the navigable waters of the Atlantic, she can do it without trespassing on any stranger's territory. It is with her a family affair. She has made one line of communication, she can make another, and as many as she pleases, to wed the waters of the Ohio with those of the Atlantic.

Gentlemen, I cannot help thinking that what Pennsylvania is, and that greater which Pennsylvania is to be, is and will be mainly owing to the constitutional government under which we live. I would not regard the Constitution of the United States, nor any other work of man, with idolatrous admiration; but, this side of idolatry, I hold it in profound respect. I believe that no human working on such a subject, no human ability exerted for such an end, has ever produced so much happiness, or holds out now to so many millions of people the prospect, through such a succession of ages and ages, of so much happiness, as the Constitution of the United States. We who are here for one generation, for a single life, and yet, in our several stations and relations in society, intrusted, in some degree, with its protection and support, — what duty does it devolve, — what duty does it *not* devolve upon us!

Gentlemen, there were those in the country at the time the Constitution was adopted who did not approve it. Some feared it from an excessive jealousy of power; others, for various causes, disliked it. The great majority of the people of the United States, however, adopted it, and placed Washington at the head of the first administration of the government. This Constitution, fairly expounded and justly interpreted, is the bond of our Union. Those who opposed it were all bound, in honor and justice, to follow the example of Patrick Henry, who himself opposed it, but who, when it had been adopted, took it in the fulness of its spirit, and to the highest extent of its honest interpretation. It was not, then, fair for those who had opposed the adoption of the Constitution to come in under it afterwards, and attempt to fritter away its provisions because they disliked them. The people had adopted the instrument as it stood, and they were bound by it, in its fair and full construction and interpretation. For the same reason, Gentlemen, those called upon to exercise high functions under the Constitution, in our day, may think that they could have made a better one. It may be the misfortune of the age of our fathers, that they had not the intelligence of this age. These persons may think that they could have made it much better, — that this thing and that ought not to have been put in it, and therefore they will try to get them out of it. That is not fair. Every man that is called upon to administer the Constitution of the United States, or act under it in any respect, is bound, in honor, and faith, and duty, to take it in its ordinary acceptation, and to act upon it as it was understood by those who framed it, and received by the people when they adopted it; and as it has been practised upon since, through all administrations of the government.

It may have happened, I think it has happened, on more than one occasion, that the spirit of this instrument has been departed from; that serious violations of that spirit have taken place. What of that? Are we to abandon it on that account? Are we to abandon it? Why, I should as soon think of abandoning my own father when ruffians attacked him! No! we are to rally around it with all our power and all our force, determined to stand by it, or fall with it. What was the conduct of the great lovers of liberty in the early periods of English history? They wrested from a reluctant monarch, King John, a great charter. The crown afterwards violated that charter. What did they then do? They remonstrated, they resisted, they reasserted, they reënforced it; and that, Gentlemen, is what we are to do.

Gentlemen, I have never felt more interested, I may say never so much interested, in the course of my public life, as during some periods of the last session of Congress. I could not but feel that we were in the midst of most important events. It was my purpose, towards the close of the session, to consider with some care the acts of Congress, and the course of the administration during that session, and to express my opinions on them, in my place in the Senate. It so happened, however, that, in the fleeting hours of the last week of the session, no opportunity was offered; and I therefore announced a purpose of taking some occasion before the public of reviewing the acts of

Congress during the last session, and of making such comments upon them as, in my humble judgment, they deserved. The present may be a proper occasion for fulfilling that duty. But my purpose has been so long deferred, that it has been anticipated. Other commentators have arisen, more effective and authoritative than I, and they have expressed their opinions upon the conduct of the last session of Congress, with an emphasis which must have penetrated the dullest perception.

Gentlemen, the political events that have occurred in the country since the termination of the session have impressed me with very profound feelings. The results of the elections, especially in the central States on the Atlantic, while they have awakened new hopes and new prospects, have been, nevertheless, of a nature to excite emotions far too deep to be expressed in any evanescent glow of party feeling. It appears to me quite plain, that no such revolution of public opinion as we have now witnessed has happened in this country before, for nearly fifty years. I may confine my remarks, in this respect, to those two great States, Pennsylvania and New York. When has such a change of public sentiment been manifested before, in the State of Pennsylvania, since the great controversy of 1799 and 1800? At that period, a very strong political dispute was carried on in this city, as well as elsewhere throughout the State, of which controversy the election between Governor McKean and Mr. Ross was one part and one element. The former was elected, and certain highly important political results followed. Since that time, no such entire revolution of popular sentiment, in regard to questions connected with the general government, as that witnessed within the last year, has taken place in Pennsylvania. I may say the same, in substance, I believe, of New York. Since the time of the great controversy in that State about the same period, I know of no change of sentiment in New York of such magnitude, and which has taken every body so much by surprise. At the same time, it is quite manifest that these changes have not been produced by effort. The country has been calm, the public mind serene. There have been no mass meetings, no extraordinary efforts of the press, no great attempts of any kind to influence men's opinions. It seems to me that the most remarkable circumstance connected with the occurrence is the spontaneous, self-moved, conscientious conviction and feeling of the people, producing this great result.

Now, Gentlemen, the question is, What is this revolution? What is its character? For whom, and against whom, for what, and against what, has it taken place?

Gentlemen, I intend to perform the duty before me this evening, without denunciation, without vituperation; I intend to avoid, as far as possible, all reflections upon men, and all unjust reflections upon parties. But it does appear to me as clear as the light of noonday, that the revolution which has now taken place in the country, in public sentiment, is a revolution against the measures and the principles of this now existing administration. It is against the manner in which this war with Mexico has been brought on. (Loud cries of "You're right!" "You're right!" and great applause.) It is against the tariff of 1846. (Deafening applause.) It is against that absurdity of all absurdities, the sub-treasury bill. (Shouts of laughter.) It is against the duplicate vetoes. (Great applause.)

Gentlemen, the present administration is not regarded as the just representative or the regular successor of any administration. In its principles and in its measures, it certainly does not resemble the administration of General Jackson, or of Mr. Van Buren, and most certainly it resembles no other. Now we must be just, we must be just to those who, in time past, have differed from us. We must, in some measure, forget the things which are behind. I take this to be the truth, that this administration has adopted a system of its own, and measures of its own, and assumed a character of its own, distinct and separate from what was the character of all preceding administrations. I take it to be for that reason, that hundreds and thousands of our fellow-citizens in this State and in other States, who were supporters of General Jackson's administration and Mr. Van Buren's administration, repudiate this administration. I think, therefore, that this administration stands alone, I will not say in its glory, but certainly in its measures and its policy. I think it is certain, that the sober-minded and intelligent portion of the community who have heretofore sustained what has been called the Democratic party have found that this administration of Mr. Polk either adopts new measures, not before known to the party, or has carried the sentiments of the party hitherto received and expressed to such extremes, that it is impossible for honest and just men to follow it; and that therefore they have come out, laying aside the natural reluctance which men feel in acting against the party of their friends, — they have come out, nevertheless, and in order to manifest their disapprobation of the principles and measures of this administration, they have flocked to the polls by thousands, and given plumpers to Whig candidates. Now, are they right in this? Are they right in supposing that this administration has adopted new doctrines, or carried old doctrines to extremes? Gentlemen, it is perfectly evident to me that they are right; that on questions of vital interest to these central States, and to all the States, the principles and measures of the present administration are marked departures from the principles and measures of General Jackson.

I will, with your permission and patience, illustrate this sentiment by one or two instances, beginning with that of the protective policy of the country.

It seems to me almost too light a question to ask, whether in this respect Young Hickory is like Old Hickory. But it is a great question to be put to the people of the United States, and which has been put, and which they have answered, whether the principles of the present administration, in regard to the protective policy of the country, are or are not entire departures from the principles of Andrew Jackson. I say they are.

Gentlemen, I have not been an advocate of the policy of General Jackson. We all know that he was a man of decided and strong character. For one, I believe that in general his wishes were all for the happiness and glory of the country. He thought, perhaps, that, to establish that happiness and perfect that glory, it was incumbent on him to exert a little more power than I believed the Constitution gave him. But I never doubted that he meant well; and that, while he sought to establish his own glory and renown, he intended to connect them with the glory and renown of the whole country.

Gentlemen, after the passage of what is called, or has been called, the Compromise Act of 1833, no great agitation arose on the tariff subject until the expiration, or near the expiration, of the period prescribed by that act. Within that time, Mr. Van Buren's administration began, went through, and terminated. The circumstances of the country, therefore, and the business presented to the consideration of the President and Congress, did not call on Mr. Van Buren, during his Presidency, to express an opinion, in any particular or formal manner, respecting the protective policy.

But I will now compare the opinions and principles of the present President of the United States, as expressed by him officially, with the principles and opinions of General Jackson during his Presidency, as expressed by him officially. I begin, Gentlemen, by reading to you what Mr. Polk says upon this subject of protection, in his message at the commencement of the last session of Congress, being his first annual message. It will require some attention from you, Gentlemen. I hope you will not think me presuming too much upon your patience.

Hear, then, what Mr. Polk says in his message of last December, on the opening of Congress : —

" The object of imposing duties on imports should be to raise revenue to pay the necessary expenses of government. Congress may, undoubtedly, in the exercise of a sound discretion, discriminate in arranging the rates of duty on different articles ; but the discriminations should be within the revenue standard, and be made with a view to raise money for the support of government.

" If Congress levy a duty, for revenue, of one per cent. on a given article, it will produce a given amount of money to the treasury, and will, incidentally and necessarily, afford protection or advantage to the amount of one per cent. to the home manufacturer of a similar or like article over the importer. If the duty be raised to ten per cent., it will produce a greater amount of money, and afford greater protection. If it be raised to twenty, twenty-five, or thirty per cent., and if, as it is raised, the revenue derived from it is found to be increased, the protection and advantage will also be increased, but if it be raised to thirty-one per cent., and it is found that the revenue produced at that rate is less than at the rate of thirty, it ceases to be revenue duty. The precise point in the ascending scale of duties, at which it is ascertained from experience that the revenue is greatest, is the maximum rate of duty which can be laid for the *bonâ fide* purpose of collecting money for the support of the government."

Now, Gentlemen, there are those who find difficulty in understanding exactly what Mr. Polk means by the " revenue standard." Perhaps this is not entirely plain. But one thing is clear, whatever else he may or may not mean, he means to be against all protection. He means that the sole and exclusive object to be regarded by the legislator, in imposing duties on imports, is to obtain money for the revenue. That is to be the only thing aimed at. He says, truly, that if a duty be laid on an imported article, an incidental benefit may accrue to the producer of a like article at home. But then this is incidental; it is altogether adventitious, an accident, a collateral or consequential result. It is not a matter to be taken into the view of the law-makers. It is to form no part of their purpose in framing or passing the law. That purpose is to be confined altogether to the inquiry after that " maximum rate of duty which can be laid for the *bonâ fide* purpose of collecting money for the support of the government."

This is his doctrine, as plain as words can make it. It is to lay such duties as may be most beneficial to revenue, and nothing but revenue; and if, in raising a revenue duty, it shall happen that domestic manufactures are protected, why that's all very well. But the protection of domestic manufactures is not to be any object of concern, nor to furnish any motive, to those who make the law. I think I have not misrepresented Mr. Polk. I think his meaning is sufficiently plain, and is precisely as I state it. Indeed, I have given you his own words. He would not, himself, deny the meaning of his words, as I have stated it. He is for laying taxes for revenue, and for revenue alone, just as if there were no iron manufactures, or other manufactures, in the United States. This is the doctrine of Mr. Polk.

Now, was this General Jackson's doctrine? Was it ever his doctrine? Let us see. I read you an extract from General Jackson's first message. He says: —

" The general rule to be applied in graduating the duties upon articles of foreign growth or manufacture is that which will place our own in fair competition with those of other countries; and the inducements to advance even a step beyond this point are controlling, in regard to those articles which are of primary necessity in time of war."

What is this doctrine? Does it not say in so many words, that, in imposing duties upon articles of foreign manufactures, it is the business of the framers of the law to lay such duties, and to lay them in such a way, as shall give our own producers a fair competition against the foreign producer? And does not

27 *

General Jackson go further, and say, — and you, Pennsylvanians, from here to Pittsburg, and all you workers in iron and owners of iron mines, may consider it, — does he not go further, and say, that, in regard to articles of primary importance, in time of war, we are under controlling reasons for going a step farther, and putting down foreign competition? Now, I submit to you, Gentlemen, instead of putting down foreign competition, is not the tariff of 1846 calculated to put down our own competition?

But I will read to you, Gentlemen, an extract from General Jackson's second message, which, in my opinion, advances the true doctrine, the true American constitutional rule and principle, fully, clearly, admirably.

" The power to impose duties on imports originally belonged to the several States ; the right to adjust those duties, with the view to the encouragement of domestic branches of industry, is so completely identical with that power, that it is difficult to suppose the existence of the one without the other.

" The States have delegated their whole authority over imports to the general government, without limitation or restriction, saving the very inconsiderable reservation relating to their inspection laws. This authority having thus entirely passed from the States, the right to exercise it for the purpose of protection does not exist in them, and consequently, if it be not possessed by the general government, it must be extinct. Our political system would thus present the anomaly of a people stripped of the right to foster their own industry, and to counteract the most selfish and destructive policy which might be adopted by foreign nations.

" This, surely, cannot be the case ; this indispensable power thus surrendered by the States, must be within the scope of the authority on the subject expressly delegated to Congress.

" In this conclusion I am confirmed, as well by the opinions of Presidents Washington, Jefferson, Madison, and Monroe, who have each repeatedly recommended the exercise of this right under the Constitution, as by the uniform practice of Congress, the continued acquiescence of the States, and the general understanding of the people."

It appears to me, Gentlemen, that these extracts from General Jackson's messages read very differently from the extracts from President Polk's message at the opening of the last session of Congress, which I have quoted. I think that his notion of a revenue standard — if President Polk means any thing by it beyond this, that it is the sole business of this government to obtain as much money as it needs, and to obtain it in the best way it can, if he means to say that there is any other object belonging to the revenue standard which is not incidental, which may or may not happen — is all visionary, vague, ideal, and, when touched by the principles announced by General Jackson, explodes like gun-cotton. You perceive, Gentlemen, that in his message to Congress General Jackson addressed himself directly to the object. He says, in raising revenues, consider that your duty is so to arrange duties on imports as to give to the manufacturer of the country a fair competition, and, in certain articles, to suppress foreign competition. There is an object, a purpose, a motive, in protection and for protection, and it is not left to the cabalistic word "incidental."

I have said that I believe that the people of this country see the difference between the principles of General Jackson and the principles of this administration on the great subject of protection, and I have endeavored to present that difference plainly, and in the very words of each. I think they see the difference, also, upon other important subjects.

Take, for instance, the war with Mexico. I am accustomed, Gentlemen, to mix so far as I am able, and as my circumstances will allow, with men of all classes and conditions in life; men of various political opinions. Your own avocations and concerns in life will have led you to do the same; and I now ask you, if you ever found a sensible and reasonable man who said to you that he believed that, if General Jackson or Mr. Van Buren had been at the head of the government, we should have had this Mexican war. I have found none such. Why, we all know, Gentlemen, that the President, — I have not to settle questions of greater or less worth, or the peculiar claims between members of a party to which I do not belong, — but we all know the fact that Mr. Polk came into office against Mr. Van Buren; that he came in on the Texas interest and for a Texas purpose; and we all know that Texas and Texas purposes have brought on this war. Therefore I say, I know no man of intelligence and sound judgment who believes that, if the Baltimore Convention had nominated, and the people elected, Mr. Van Buren to the Presidency, we should now have on hand a Mexican war.

The purpose of these remarks has been to show you, Gentle-

men, what I consider to have been the causes of the great
change which has taken place in public opinion itself; and it is
vain for any body to say, that any local causes here, or local
causes there, have brought about this result.   That Anti-rentism
in New York and some other *ism* in Pennsylvania have produced such important consequences, it is folly to say; there is
nothing at all in it.   The test is this.   Do you say that questions of State policy or State elections only have influenced this
result?   If you say so, then look at the elections for members
of Congress.   Members of Congress have nothing to do with
these State questions; and the truth is, that elections of members of Congress in this State and in New York have been carried by larger majorities than any other elections.   These elections have been governed mainly by questions of national policy.   There were counties in New York in which there was no
Anti-rentism.   There were others in which Anti-rent influence
was as much on one side as the other.   But take the test even
in regard to them.   I find it stated, and I believe correctly, that
Mr. Fish, the Whig candidate for Lieutenant-Governor, a most
respectable and honorable man, but certainly not a supporter of
those who profess themselves in favor of Anti-rent doctrine, — I
find it stated that he obtained more votes for the office of Lieutenant-Governor than Mr. Wright received as the Democratic
candidate for Governor.   That flattering unction, therefore,
gentlemen cannot lay to themselves.   There is, in truth, no
getting over the result of the popular election, nor getting beyond it, nor getting around it, nor behind it, nor doing any thing
with it, but acknowledging it to be the expression of public
opinion against the measures of the present administration.

I proceed to make some remarks upon the occurrences of the
session, connected with the previous course of the administration, since Mr. Polk assumed the office of President.

The question respecting the territory of Oregon is a settled
question, and all are glad that it is so.   I am not about to disturb it, nor do I wish to revive discussions connected with it;
but in two or three particulars it is worth while to make some
remarks upon it.

By the treaty of Washington of 1842, all questions subsist-
ing between the United States and England were settled and
adjusted, with the exception of the Oregon controversy.   (Great

applause.) I must beg pardon for the allusion. I did not mean by any allusion of that sort to give occasion for any expression of public feeling in connection with my own services. As I said, the Oregon question remained; and it is worthy of remark, that its importance, and the intensity with which it was pressed upon the people of the United States, increased when every other subject of dispute was adjusted.

I do not mention it as a matter of reproach at all, for I hold every man, especially every man in public life, to have an undoubted right to the expression of his own opinion, and to discharge his own duty according to the dictates of his own conscience; but I hope it may not be out of place to say, that, upon his accession to the Presidential office, it pleased the President of the United States to intrust the duties of the State Department, which has charge of our foreign relations, and pending this Oregon controversy, to the hands of a distinguished gentleman,* who was one of the few who opposed — and he did oppose with great zeal and all his ability — the whole settlement of 1842.

The Baltimore Convention assembled in May, 1844. One of its prominent proceedings was the sentiment which it expressed respecting our title to Oregon. It passed a resolution in these memorable words: —

" *Resolved,* That our title to the whole of the territory of Oregon is clear and unquestionable; that no part of the same ought to be ceded to England, or any other power."

Mr. Polk, in his inaugural address, makes the same declaration in the very same words, with marks of quotation, as if in acknowledgment of the authority of the Convention. Mr. Buchanan, by direction of the President, repeats the declaration in his letter to Mr. Packenham, of the 30th of August, 1845; and the President, in his message to Congress, last December, having made some apology for entering into a negotiation on the basis of former offers of this government, informs them, that our title to the whole of Oregon had been asserted and maintained, as was believed, by irrefragable facts and arguments. Through all the debates in the two houses, on all occasions, down to the

* Mr. James Buchanan.

day of the treaty, our right to the whole territory was pronounced " clear and unquestionable."

In and out of Congress, the universal echo was, that " our title to the *whole* of Oregon was clear and unquestionable." The Baltimore resolutions, in sentiment and in words, ran through all documents, all speeches, and all newspapers. If you knew what the Baltimore Convention had said, you knew what all those who were attached to the party had said, would say, or might, could, would, or should have said.

I remember, Gentlemen, that when I was at school I felt exceedingly obliged to Homer's messengers for the exact literal fidelity with which they delivered their messages. The seven or eight lines of good Homeric Greek in which they had received the commands of Agamemnon or Achilles, they recited to whomsoever the message was to be carried; and as they repeated them verbatim, sometimes twice or thrice, it saved me the trouble of learning so much more Greek.

Any body who attended the Baltimore Convention, and heard this resolution, would, in like manner, be familiar with what was to come, and prepared to hear again of " our clear and unquestionable title."

Nevertheless, Gentlemen, the clearness of the title was a good deal questioned by a distinguished gentleman from Missouri (Mr. Benton), and the end was, I think, a just and satisfactory settlement of the question by division of the Territory; forty-nine carrying it against fifty-four forty.* Now, Gentlemen, the remarkable characteristic of the settlement of this Oregon question by treaty is this. In the general operation of government, treaties are negotiated by the President and ratified by the Senate; but here is the reverse, — here is a treaty negotiated by the Senate, and only agreed to by the President. In August, 1845, all effort of the administration to settle the Oregon question by negotiation had come to an end; and I am not aware that, from that day to the absolute signature of the treaty, the administration, or its agents at home, or its agents abroad, did the least thing upon earth to advance the negotiation towards settlement in any shape one single step; and if it had

* The claim of the United States, as asserted by President Polk, extended to 54° 40' of north latitude ; the 49th degree was adopted as the boundary in the final arrangement.

stood where they left it, it would have remained unsettled at this moment. But it was settled. The discussions in Congress, the discussions on the other side of the water, the general sense of the community, all protested against the iniquity of two of the greatest nations of modern times rushing into war and shedding Christian blood in such a controversy. All enforced the conviction, that it was a question to be settled by an equitable and fair consideration, and it was thus settled. And that being settled, there is only one other topic connected with this subject upon which I will detain you with any remarks. I would not do this, if I did not think the honor of the country somewhat concerned, and if I did not desire to express my own dissatisfaction with the course of the administration.

What I refer to is the repeated refusal, on the part of the administration, to submit this question to honorable, fair arbitration. After the United States government had withdrawn all its offers, and the case stood open, the British Minister at Washington, by order of his government, offered arbitration. On the 27th of December, 1845, Mr. Packenham wrote to Mr. Buchanan as follows, viz. : —

" An attentive consideration of the present state of affairs, with reference to the Oregon question, has determined the British government to instruct the undersigned, her Britannic Majesty's Envoy, &c., again to represent, in pressing terms, to the government of the United States, the expediency of referring the whole question of an equitable division of that territory to the arbitration of some friendly sovereign or state.

" Her Majesty's government deeply regret the failure of all their efforts to effect a friendly settlement of the conflicting claims, by direct negotiation between the two governments.

" They are still persuaded that great advantages would have resulted to both parties from such a mode of settlement, had it been practicable; but there are difficulties now in the way in that course of proceeding, which it might be tedious to remove, while the importance of an early settlement seems to become, at each moment, more urgent.

" Under these circumstances, her Majesty's government think that a resort to arbitration is the most prudent, and perhaps the only feasible step which could be taken, and the best calculated to allay the existing effervescence of popular feeling," &c.

To this Mr. Buchanan replied, on the 3d of January, 1846, that

" This proposition assumes the fact, that the title of Great Britain to a portion of the territory is valid, and thus takes for granted the very question in dispute. Under this proposition, the very terms of the submission would contain an express acknowledgment of the right of Great Britain to a portion of the territory, and would necessarily preclude the United States from claiming the whole, before the arbitration, and this too in the face of the President's assertion of the 30th of August, 1845, made in the most solemn manner, of the title of the United States to the whole territory. This alone would be deemed sufficient reason for declining the proposition."

To remove this difficulty, Mr. Packenham, on the 16th of January, 1846, addressed Mr. Buchanan, to inquire " whether, supposing the British government to entertain no objection to such a course, it would suit the views of the United States government to refer to arbitration, not (as has already been proposed), the question of an equitable partition of the territory, but the question of title in either of the two powers to the whole territory; subject, of course, to the condition, that, if neither should be found, in the opinion of the arbitrator, to possess a complete title to the whole territory, there should, in that case, be assigned to each that portion which would, in the opinion of the arbitrating power, be called for by a just appreciation of the respective claims of each."

Mr. Packenham proposed a reference to some friendly sovereign or state, or " to a mixed commission with an umpire appointed by common consent; or, to a board composed of the most distinguished civilians and jurists of the time, appointed in such a manner as shall bring all pending questions to the decision of the most enlightened, impartial, and independent minds."

This proposition, also, Mr. Buchanan, in a note of the 4th of February, declines; and for thus refusing it, he says one reason was alone conclusive on the mind of the President, and that was, " that he does not believe the territorial rights of this nation to be a proper subject of arbitration."

Now, Sir, how is this? What sort of new doctrine is here advanced? I take it, that every question of boundary is a question of territory, and that from the origin of our government, from General Washington's time, under all successive administrations, down to the present time, we have been in the habit of referring questions of boundary to arbitration. The matters in dispute with England, in General Washington's time, were referred to arbitration. Each government appointed two commissioners; these four were to agree upon a fifth, or if they could not agree, he was to be selected by lot, and the government remains bound by their doings from that day to this. This reference of disputed boundaries to some form of arbitration has received the sanction of Washington, Jefferson, Madison, Jackson, and Van Buren, and has always been sanctioned by the Senate and House of Representatives and people. Now comes President Polk and says that no question of territory ought to be referred to any arbitration whatever, however constituted. Well, what does this lead to? How are disputes between different governments to be settled? Consider the infirmity of human nature. Two governments, like two men, do not see their respective rights in the same light. Is there no way to adjust this dispute, but to draw the sword? Who does not see that this doctrine leads directly to the assertion of the right of the strongest? Why, let us suppose a question of boundary between Russia and Sweden. There is a dispute about a boundary, or about national territory, which is the same thing. The parties cannot agree. His Majesty, the Emperor of all the Russias, holds his right to the disputed territory to be clear and unquestionable. Sweden doubts it, she argues the question, she puts forth her own claim. But the Emperor is an inflexible fifty-four forty man, and still insists that his right is clear and unquestionable. Sweden then proposes arbitration, either to some friendly sovereign, or to a board of intelligent, independent, and distinguished private individuals. She offers to bring the matter, for decision, before the most enlightened minds of the times. But his Majesty is of opinion, that a question of territory is not to be made the subject of arbitration. And what then remains to the weaker power, but submission or hopeless war?

Do not all perceive, that sentiments like these lead only to establish the right of the strongest? that they withdraw public questions between nations from all the jurisdiction of justice, and all the authority of right, from the control of enlightened opinion and the general judgment of mankind, and leave them entirely to the decision of the longest sword? I do not think this correspondence has raised the character of the United States in the estimation of the civilized world. Its spirit does not partake of the general spirit of the age. It is at war with that spirit, as much as it is at war with all our own history, from 1789 to the present day. The sense of modern times, the law of humanity, the honor of civilized states, and the authority of religion, all require that controversies of this sort, which cannot be adjusted by the parties themselves, should be referred to the decision of some intelligent and impartial tribunal. And now that none can doubt our ability and power to defend and maintain our own rights, I wish that there should be as little doubt of our justice and moderation.

The remaining topic, and it is one of vast interest, connected with our foreign relations, is the present war with Mexico. As that is an existing war, and as what we all say, in or out of Congress, will of course be heard or read, if thought worthy of being read, in Mexico, as well as in the United States, I wish, for one, to speak with caution and care, as well as with candor, in every thing respecting it. Nevertheless, there are some opinions connected with the history of this case which I sincerely entertain, and which I must avow. Allow me, therefore, to go back and bring up in short the history of the whole case. Texas achieved her independence of Mexico unexpectedly, by bravery and good fortune, displayed and obtained in a single battle. Texas threw off the dominion of Mexico, and for many years maintained a government of her own. Her independence was acknowledged by the government of this country, and by the governments of Europe. Mexico, nevertheless, did not acknowledge the independence of Texas. She made no effort, however, to re-subjugate or re-annex the territory to herself. Affairs remained in this condition for many years.

Here I am reminded of a very strange state of diplomatic things which existed in Washington, not long ago, growing out of these successive revolutions which have taken place in the world during the last thirty or forty years. There was at Washington a representative of Texas, but Texas was not acknowledged by Mexico. There was a representative of Mexico, but Mexico was not recognized by Old Spain. There was a minister from Old Spain; but the present dynasty of Spain was not recognized by Russia; and there was a minister of Russia, who, in common with all the other ministers alluded to, was recognized by the government of the United States.

I am not about to go into a history of the annexation of Texas. I do not wish to revert to that matter. I have to say, however, that, according to my view of the case, the objections which were urged, and properly urged, against the annexation of Texas, had no great relation to any claim of Mexico. They were, first, that the annexation of Texas was not a fair exercise of constitutional power. I thought so, and others thought so, but a majority in the counsels of the country overruled the objection. Secondly, it was thought that we had already territory enough, and that there was some degree of danger in extending our territory further than it was already extended. But in the third place, and this was insurmountable in my judgment, it was an objection that the annexation of Texas was to bring under the control of our government, and make part of this Union, a country which was then free from slavery, but into which, when annexed, slavery and slave representation would be introduced. That objection was insurmountable in my mind, and would be so at all times, under all circumstances, and in all like cases. In the fourth place, it was evident, and so was urged in Congress again and again, that the annexation of Texas might lead to a war with Mexico. These are the four grounds upon which the annexation of Texas was opposed by those who did oppose it.

Now, Gentlemen, there is not a man in the country who thinks less respectfully than I do of the Mexican government. Unhappy, unfortunate, miserable Mexico has nothing, and for a long time has had nothing, that deserves to be called a government. When she broke off the yoke of Spain, and proclaimed herself disposed to follow the example of the United States, and uttered the name of Washington with respect; when she professed to cherish free principles, a representative government, trial by jury, and security of personal property; why, we all hailed her, and wished her well. But unfortunately the result has been, that she has had no true constitutional government; has had no government under the influence of representative principles. All her presidents from time to time have been men created through the *pronunciamentos* of the military. A fortunate general of to-day supersedes him who was fortunate yesterday and is unfortunate to-day. One military man seizes the government, and obtains what he can from the people, and uses it in maintaining an army. Another man to-morrow makes another seizure of public or private property, and supersedes his predecessor. Meantime the people are the victims :

> " Quicquid delirant reges, plectuntur Achivi."

It has been one of the most irregular and worst governments, in my judgment, that has ever existed upon the face of the earth.

But the annexation was completed. The western boundary was a matter about which disputes existed or must arise. There was, as between us and Mexico, as there had been between Texas and Mexico, no ascertained and acknowledged western boundary.

This was the state of things after the annexation of Texas, and when the President began military movements in that direction. Now, Gentlemen, that I may misrepresent nobody, and say nothing which has not been clearly proved by official evidence, I will proceed to state to you three propositions, which, in my opinion, are fairly sustained by the correspondence of the government in its various branches and departments, as officially communicated to Congress.

1st. That the President directed the occupation of a territory by force of arms, to which the United States had no ascertained title ; a territory which, if claimed by the United States, was also claimed by Mexico, and was at the time in her actual occupation and possession.

The Texan Convention was to assemble July 4th, 1845, to pass upon the annexation. Before this date, to wit, on the 28th of May, General Taylor was ordered to move towards Texas ; and on the 15th of June he was instructed by a letter from Mr. Bancroft to enter Texas, and concentrate his forces on its " western boundary," and to select and occupy a position " on or near the Rio Grande, to protect what, in the event of annexation, will be our western border."

That the United States had no ascertained title to the territory appears from Mr. Marcy's letter to General Taylor of July 30th, 1845. General Taylor is there informed, that what he is to " occupy, defend, and protect" is " the territory of Texas, to the extent that it has been occupied by the people of Texas."

It appears in the despatch last quoted, that this territory had been occupied by Mexico.

Mr. Marcy goes on to say, "The Rio Grande is *claimed* to be the boundary between the two countries, and *up to this* boundary you are to extend your protection, only *excepting any posts on the eastern side thereof* which are in the actual occupancy of Mexican forces, or Mexican *settlements* over which the republic of Texas did not exercise jurisdiction at the period of annexation, or shortly before that event."

This makes it perfectly clear, that the United States had neither an ascertained nor an apparent title to this territory; for it admits that Texas only made a *claim* to it, Mexico having an adverse claim, and having also actual possession.

2d. That as early as July, 1845, the President knew as well as others acquainted with the subject, that this territory was in the actual possession of Mexico; that it contained Mexican settlements, over which Texas had not exercised jurisdiction, up to the time of annexation.

On the 8th of July, the Secretary of War wrote to General Taylor, that "This department is informed that Mexico has some military *establishments* on the east side of the Rio Grande, which are and for some time have been in the actual occupancy of her troops." On the 30th of July, the Secretary wrote as already mentioned, directing General Taylor to except from his protection "any posts on the eastern side thereof [of the Rio Grande], which are in the actual occupancy of Mexican forces, or Mexican settlements over which the republic of Texas did not exercise jurisdiction at the period of annexation, or shortly before that event."

It manifestly appears to have been the intention of the President, from the 28th of May down to the consummation of his purpose, to take possession of this territory by force of arms, however unwilling Mexico might be to yield it, or whatever might turn out on examination to be her right to retain it. He intended to extinguish the Mexican title by force; otherwise his acts and instructions are inexplicable.

The government maintained from the first, that the Rio Grande was the western boundary of Texas, as appears from the letters to General Taylor of the 28th of May and 15th of June, 1845. On the 15th of June, General Taylor was instructed to take such a position "on or near the Rio Grande" as "will be best to repel invasion, and protect what, in the event of annexation, will be our western boundary." In accordance with these are also the instructions of July 30th, to which I have already referred.

On the 6th of August, the Secretary wrote to General Taylor, " Although a state of *war* with Mexico, or an invasion of Texas by her forces, may not take place, it is, nevertheless, deemed proper and necessary, that your force should be fully equal to meet with certainty of success any crisis which may arise in Texas, and which would require you by *force of arms to carry out the instructions of the government.*" He is then, in the same letter, authorized to procure volunteers from Texas. On the 23d of August, the Secretary instructed General Taylor thus: " Should Mexico assemble a large body of troops on the Rio Grande, and cross it with a considerable force, such a movement must be regarded as an invasion of the United States, and the commencement of hostilities." He is then instructed how to assemble a large force. On the 30th of August he was instructed, in case any Mexican force crossed the Rio Grande, " to drive *all* Mexican troops beyond it"; that any *attempt* by the Mexicans to cross the river with a considerable force, would be regarded as an invasion; and that on such an event, namely, " in case of war, either declared or made manifest by hostile acts," he was not to confine his action within the territory of Texas. On the 16th of October, the Secretary wrote, that " the information which we have here renders it probable that no serious attempts will, at present, be made by Mexico to invade Texas." But General Taylor is still instructed to hold the country between the Nueces and the Rio Grande. " Previous instructions will have put you in possession of the views of the government of the United States, not only as to the extent of its territorial claims, but of its determination to assert them."

He is directed to put his troops into winter quarters, accordingly, as near the Rio Grande as circumstances will permit. Up to this time and to the 11th of March, 1846, General Taylor was at Corpus Christi. The open and decided step was taken on the 13th of January. On that day the Secretary at War directed General Taylor to march to the Rio Grande, and to take up a position opposite Matamoras. He is instructed, in so doing, in case Mexico should declare war, or commit any open act of hostility, not to act merely on the defensive. Throughout the correspondence, it is plain that the intention was to extinguish the Mexican title to this territory by armed occupation; and the instructions are explicit, to treat every assertion of title or movement on the part of Mexico as an act of hostility, and to proceed accordingly and resist it.

To show how General Taylor understood the instructions of his government, it may be observed that on the 2d of March, thirty miles from Matamoras, at a stream called the Arroyo Colorado, he was met by a party of Mexicans, whose commanding officer informed him, that if he crossed the stream it would be deemed a declaration of war, and put into his hand a copy o General Mejias's proclamation to that effect. Notwithstanding this, General Taylor put his forces in order of battle, crossed the stream, and pushed on, the Mexicans retreating. He arrived on the Rio Grande, opposite Matamoras, on the 29th of March.

Let me now ask your attention to an extract of a letter from Mr. Buchanan to Mr. Slidell, of January 20th, 1846. In this letter Mr. Buchanan says: —

" In the mean time the President, in anticipation of the final refusal of the Mexican government to receive you, has ordered the army of Texas to advance and take position on the left bank of the Rio Grande ; and has directed that a strong fleet shall be immediately assembled in the Gulf of Mexico. He will thus be prepared to act with vigor and promptitude the moment that Congress shall give him the authority."

Now, if, by this advance of troops, possession would be taken on the extreme line claimed by us, what further vigorous action did the President expect Congress to authorize? Did he expect Congress to make a general declaration of war? Congress was then in session. Why not consult it? Why take a step not made necessary by any pressing danger, and which might naturally lead to war, without requiring the authority of Congress in advance? With Congress is the power of peace and war; to anticipate its decision, by the adoption of measures leading to war, is nothing less than an executive interference with legislative power. Nothing but the necessity of self-defence could justify the sending of troops into a territory claimed and occupied by a power with which at that time no war existed. And there

was, I think, no case of such necessity of self-defence.   Mr.
Slidell replied to Mr. Buchanan on the 17th of February, saying, " The advance of General Taylor's force to the left bank
of the Rio Grande, and the strengthening our squadron in the
Gulf, are wise measures, which may exercise a salutary influence
upon the course of this government."

The army was thus ordered to the extreme limits of our
claim; to our utmost boundary, as asserted by ourselves; and
here it was to be prepared to act further, and to act with promptitude and vigor.   Now, it is a very significant inquiry, Did the
President mean by this to bring on, or to run the risk of bringing on, a general war?   Did he expect to be authorized by Congress to prosecute a general war of invasion and acquisition?
I repeat the question, Why not take the opinion of Congress, it
then being in session, before any warlike movement was made?
Mr. Buchanan's letter is of the 20th of January.   The instructions to march to the Rio Grande had been given on the 13th.
Congress was in session all this time; and why should, and
why did, the executive take so important a step, not necessary
for self-defence and leading to immediate war, without the authority of Congress?   This is a grave question, and well deserves an answer.

Allow me to repeat, for it is matter of history, that before and
at the time when these troops were ordered to the left bank of
the Rio Grande, there was no danger of invasion by Mexico or
apprehension of hostilities by her.   This is perfectly evident
from General Taylor's letters to the government through the
preceding summer, and down to the time the orders were
given.

I now refer to these letters.

On the 15th of August, General Taylor writes : " In regard
to the force at other points on the Rio Grande, except the militia
of the country, I have no information; nor do I hear that the
reported concentration at Matamoras is for any purpose of invasion."   On the 20th of August, he says: " Caravans of traders arrive, occasionally, from the Rio Grande, but bring no
news of importance.   They represent that there are no regular
troops on that river, except at Matamoras, and do not seem to
be aware of any preparations for a demonstration on this bank
of the river."   On the 6th of September, he writes thus : " I

have the honor to report that a confidential agent, despatched some days since to Matamoras, has returned, and reports that no extraordinary preparations are going forward there; that the garrison does not seem to have been increased, and that our consul is of opinion there will be no declaration of war." On the 11th of October, he says: "Recent arrivals from the Rio Grande bring no news or information of a different aspect from that which I reported in my last. The views expressed in previous communications relative to the pacific disposition of the border people on both sides of the river are continually confirmed." This was the last despatch, I presume, received by the War Department before giving the order of January 13th, for the march of the army.

A month after the order of march had been given, all General Taylor's previous accounts were confirmed by him. On the 16th of February, he thus writes to the Adjutant-General at Washington: "Many reports will doubtless reach the Department, giving exaggerated accounts of Mexican preparations to resist our advance, if not indeed to attempt an invasion of Texas. Such reports have been circulated even at this place, and owe their origin to personal interests connected with the stay of the army here. I trust that they will receive no attention at the War Department. From the best information I am able to obtain, and which I deem as authentic as any, I do not believe that our advance to the banks of the Rio Grande will be resisted. The army, however, will go fully prepared for a state of hostilities, should they unfortunately be provoked by the Mexicans."

This official correspondence proves, I think, that there was no danger of invasion, or of hostilities of any kind, from Mexico, at the time of the march of the army. It must in fact be plain to every body, that the ordering the army to the Rio Grande was a step naturally, if not necessarily, tending to provoke hostilities, and to bring on war. I shall use no inflammatory or exciting language, but it seems to me that this whole proceeding is against the spirit of the Constitution, and the just limitations of the different departments of the government; an act pregnant with serious consequences, and of dangerous precedent to the public liberties.

No power but Congress can declare war; but what is the

value of this constitutional provision, if the President of his own authority may make such military movements as must bring on war? If the war power be in Congress, then every thing tending directly or naturally to bring on war should be referred to the discretion of Congress? Was this order of march given, in the idle hope of coercing Mexico to treat? If so, idle it was, as the event proved. But it was something worse than a mistake or a blunder; it was, as it seems to me, an extension of executive authority, of a very dangerous character. I see no necessity for it, and no apology for it; since Congress was in session at the same moment, at the other end of Pennsylvania Avenue, and might have been consulted.

It will be contended, probably, that the conduct of the President was all sanctioned by Congress, by the act of May 11th. That act has a preamble, of which much has been said. I have only to remark, that neither a preamble, nor any other declaration of a legislative body, can create a fact or alter a fact. I remember to have heard Chief Justice Marshall ask counsel, who was insisting upon the authority of an act of legislation, if he thought an act of legislation could create or destroy a fact, or change the truth of history. Would it alter the fact, said he, if a legislature should solemnly enact, that Mr. Hume never wrote the history of England? A legislature may alter the law, but no power can reverse a fact. I hardly suppose Congress, by the act of the 11th of May, meant more than to enable the President to defend the country, to the extent of the limit claimed by him. If those who concurred in that act meant thereby to encourage the President to invade Mexico, and to carry on with the whole force committed to his charge a war of acquisition, to establish provinces, to appoint governors, to call elections, to annex new worlds to the United States, — if that was their intention they have never said it, and I for one do not believe it was their intention. But I repeat, Gentlemen, that Mexico is highly unjustifiable in having refused to receive a minister from the United States. My remarks on this subject have been drawn forth by no sympathy with Mexico. I have no desire, Heaven knows, to show my country in the wrong. But these remarks originate purely in a desire to maintain the powers of government as they are established by the Constitution between the different departments, and a hope that, whether we have conquests or no conquests, war or no war, peace or no peace, we shall yet preserve, in its integrity and strength, the Constitution of the United States.

War, however, is upon us. Armies are in the field, navies are upon the sea. We believe that the government ought immediately, in any honorable and satisfactory manner, to bring that war to a conclusion, if possible. We believe that every reasonable effort should be made to put an end to this war. But while the war lasts, while soldiers are upon the land, and seamen on the sea, upholding the flag of the country, you feel, and I feel, and every American feels, that they must be succored and sustained. They bear the commission of their government. They are under its order and control. Their duty is obedience to superior command. They are engaged on a foreign service. They have done honor to the country to which they belong, and raised the character of its military prowess.

I am behind no man in ascribing praise and honor to General Taylor and all his forces; and I am behind no man, and perhaps forward of most men, in the respect and admiration which I feel for the good conduct of the volunteers who have entered the field. We know no period in our history, there is nothing in our annals, which shows superior gallantry on the part of raw recruits, taken suddenly from the pursuits of civil life and put into military service. Where can we look for such steadiness, coolness, bravery, and modesty as in these volunteers? The most distinguished incident in the history of our country relative to the good conduct of militia, of new raised levies from amongst the people, is perhaps that of the battle of Bunker Hill. The gentleman who sits by me, though not of years to bear arms, was of years to be present, and to look on and see others engaged in that conflict. He did all he could, he poured his fervent youthful wishes into the general cause. I might go further, and say that at Bunker Hill the newly raised levies and recruits sheltered themselves behind some temporary defences, but at Monterey the volunteers assailed a fortified city. At any rate, Gentlemen, whatever we may think of the origin of the contest which called them there, it is gratifying to see to what extent the military power of the Union may be depended on, whenever the exigencies of the country may require it. It is gratifying to know, that, without the expense or the danger of large standing armies, there is enough military spirit, enough intelligence, enough perseverance, and patience, and submission to discipline, amongst the young men of the country, to uphold our stars and stripes whenever the government may order them to be unfurled.

I will now leave all topics connected with the foreign relations of the country, and pass to a consideration of some of the subjects connected with measures bearing upon our internal and domestic interests. Of these there is one of great public importance; and another, connected with which hundreds and thousands of individuals have been made — shall I say it? — the victims of the exercise of the veto power. I speak of the Harbor Bill, and of the bill making indemnity for French depredations on our commerce before 1800.

There is, Gentlemen, a clear veto power in the Constitution of the United States. There is an express provision that the President of the United States may withhold his approbation, if he see fit, from a law of Congress; and unless, after reasons stated by him for so withholding his approbation, it shall be passed by two thirds of both houses, it fails of legal validity and becomes a dead letter. This, in common discourse, we call the veto power. Something like it existed in ancient Rome. But the framers of our Constitution borrowed it from England, and then qualified it. By the constitution of England, it theoretically exists in the monarch, and without qualification. The framers of our Constitution, in placing it in the hands of the President, qualified it, so that if, upon reconsideration of the same measure, two thirds of both houses concurred in it, the bill should become a law, the President's negative notwithstanding.

In England, the power of the crown to negative acts of Parliament has not been exercised since the reign of William the Third, nearly two hundred years; and the reason is generally stated to be, that since that period, such has been the course of the British government in its administration, that the influence of the crown, in one or both houses of Parliament, connected with the power which the king possesses of dissolving Parliament, has been sufficient, without recourse to the exercise of the obnoxious veto power, to prevent the passage of bills with which the crown was not satisfied. Modern commentators say that influence, in this respect, has taken the place of prerogative. The king uses his influence, but never actually negatives bills presented to him. As I have said, our Constitution places the power in the hands of the executive in a qualified manner. It is valid, unless two thirds of both houses concur in the measure. The result of this provision has been rather singular.

I will not impute to Congress at any time, or to its members under any administration, any liability to corrupt influence; certainly not. But I suppose all will admit that frequently, and especially in party times, party connections, perhaps some little hope of office, some desire to benefit friends out of Congress, may soften opposition to particular measures in particular men's minds, and may produce something which, if we would talk straight out, we might call " undue influence." It has happened, and, if we are curious in such researches to fix the chronology of occurrences, we might find instances not very remote, that persons, still members of Congress, but who had failed in their reëlection or were pretty sure of failing, have concurred in certain measures; and then, not being longer called on to serve their country in the halls of Congress, and particularly unwilling that the country should entirely lose their services, have condescended to take office under the executive. Therefore the result in the practical administration of our government seems to be this. Some degree of influence may be exerted sufficient to bring one third to concur with the sentiments of the administration; and then the President, by his veto, overwhelms the other two thirds; so that if the purpose be to defeat a measure passed by majorities of both houses of Congress, if Influence will come in and do one third of the work, Veto is ready to do the rest.

The first victim of the veto power, at the last session, was connected with what is called, though not very correctly, Internal Improvements. It was the Harbor Bill. I confess to a feeling of great interest in that bill. Seeing nothing in it, as I thought, but such things as General Jackson's administration had approved, and Mr. Van Buren's administration had approved over and over again, I had no more apprehension that the President of the United States would veto that bill, than that he would veto an ordinary appropriation bill for the support of the army or navy. I was as much surprised when it was announced that, probably, he would send us the veto, as if it had been stated to me that he would veto a bill necessary to carry on the government. But the veto came. Now, Gentlemen, that bill made an appropriation of one million three hundred thousand dollars, for certain harbor improvements, on the ocean, the Gulf, the lakes, and the great and important navigable rivers of the country; — a work of peace, of improvement, of national progress; something to carry us forward, in convenience and prosperity, and in the acquisition of wealth; something to make permanent fixtures in the land, that should do some good to us and our posterity for ever. That was its object. The appropriation was small. The particular objects were somewhat numerous. The amount was no burden at all upon the treasury; in connection with its objects, not worth considering. And yet here comes the veto!

Well, now, what is to be done? We cannot shut our eyes to what is around us. Here we are. This vast country, with the ocean on the east, and the Gulf on the south, and the great lakes on the north and the west, and these great rivers penetrating it through hundreds and thousands of miles, — what are we to do? Is it not, of all countries in the world, that for which nature has done mighty things, and yet calls most loudly for man to do his part? Providence has given us a country capable of improvement. It is not perfected; we are called to do something for ourselves; to wake up, in this day of improvement, and do the deeds that belong to improvement; to facilitate internal intercourse; to furnish harbors for the protection of life and property; to remove obstructions from the rivers; to do every thing, all and singular, which a large and liberal policy will suggest to an intelligent people, with abundance of means for the advancement of the national prosperity. We live in an age, Gentlemen, when we are not to shut our eyes to the great examples set us, all over the European continent. I do not speak of England, where private enterprise and wealth have gone so far ahead. But look to Russia, to Prussia, to Austria, to Saxony, to Sardinia; everywhere we see a spirit of improvement, active, stimulated, and persevering. We behold mountains penetrated by railroads, safe harbors constructed, every thing done by government for the people, which, in the nature of the case, the people cannot do for themselves.

Let us contemplate, for a moment, the Mississippi. This noble and extraordinary stream, with seven or eight millions of people on its banks, and on the waters falling into it, absolutely calls for the clearing out rivers and for the removal of *snags* and other obstacles to safe navigation. Who is to do this? Will any one of the States do it? Can all of the States do it? Is it the appropriate duty of any one State or any number of States? We know it is not. We know that, unless this government be placed in the hands of men who feel that it is their constitutional duty to make these improvements, they never will be made; and the waters of the Mississippi will roll over *snags*, and *snags*, and *snags*, for a century to come. These improvements must come from the government of the United States, or in the nature of things they cannot come at all; and I say that every steamboat that is lost by one of these *snags*, every life that is sacrificed, goes to make up a great account against this government. Why, what a world is there! What rivers and what cities on their banks! — Cincinnati, Louisville, St. Louis, Natchez, New Orleans, and others that spring up while we are talking of them, or, indeed, before we begin to speak of them; commercial marts, great places for the exchange of commodities along these rivers, which are, as it were, so many inland seas! And what! the general government no authority over them, — no power of improvement! Why, that will be thought the most incredible thing, hereafter, that ever was heard of. It will not be believed that it ever entered into the head of any administration, that these were not objects deserving the care and attention of the government. I think, therefore, that the Harbor Bill negatived by the President raises a vital question. This question was put in Congress, it has been put since, it was put at the polls. I put the question now, whether these internal improvements of the waters of the lakes and rivers shall be made or shall not be made; and those who say they shall not be made are right to adhere to Mr. Polk; and those who say they shall be made, and must be made, and that they will have them made, why, they have the work in their own hands, and, if they be a majority of the people, they will do it.

I do not know that we of the East and North have any especial interest in this; but I tell you what we of the East think that we have an especial interest in. I have thought so, at least, ever since I have been in Congress, and I believe all my associates from Massachusetts have also thought so. We think we have an interest, and an especial interest, in manifesting a spirit of liberality in regard to all expenses for improvements of those parts of the country watered by the Mississippi and the lakes. We think it belongs both to our interest and our reputation, to sustain improvements on the Western waters.

Now, Gentlemen, what was the Harbor Bill of the last session? What was that bill, which both houses passed, and the President vetoed? Here it is. And although this bill had three readings in Congress, and one more when it came back vetoed, I would ask for it a fifth reading now.*

Such, Gentlemen, is an enumeration of the appropriations of this bill, running along the shores of the sea and the lakes down the Gulf and the rivers; forty-nine objects in all. I notice but one important omission. I think there ought to have been a very liberal appropriation for the better navigation of Salt River! This is the bill which the President negatived, and I will shortly state to you his reasons, as I collect them from his messages, and make such remarks on those reasons as I may, whilst I go along.

The President assumes that these harbors are internal improvements, and because there is no power vested in Congress by the Constitution under that specific head, he denies the existence of such a power altogether. The course of the government has been just the other way. The people have not only acquiesced in these improvements, but clamored for them, and they are now very likely to clamor again.

The President assigns as a reason for the veto, that several of his predecessors had denied the constitutional power of Congress to make internal improvements. I know not where this denial is to be found. If he intends to say that some of his predecessors denied the general power of making all kinds of internal improvements, nobody contends that such a general power as that is in the Constitution. But then the question is, Does this bill imply any such power? These works are not internal improvements in that general sense; they are harbor improvements, connected with commerce, and the question is whether, as such, they are not provided for in the Constitution. Let us not be carried away by a vague notion that the Constitution of

* Mr. Hone of New York here read the bill, at the request of Mr. Webster. It will be found in the Appendix, No. I.

the United States gives no power to make internal improvements, and therefore does not authorize expenditures on a harbor. We are speaking of things not by any general name, not by classification or classes, but by phrases descriptive of the things themselves. We call a harbor a harbor. If the President of the United States says that is a matter of internal improvement, why then I say, that the name cannot alter the thing; the thing is a harbor. And does not every one of these harbors touch navigable waters? Is not every one of them on the shore of the sea, bay, gulf, or navigable river? and are not the navigable waters of the ocean, and Gulf, and bays and rivers, — are they not all for commercial purposes out of the jurisdiction of the States, and in the jurisdiction of the United States?

The President says that some of the objects provided for by the bill are local, and lie within the limits of a single State. Well, I dare say they do. It would be somewhat remarkable if a harbor were found lying in two or three States. It would be rather a large harbor that would embrace parts even of Connecticut and Rhode Island, two of the smallest of the States. The question is not whether the site be local, or whether the expenditure be local, but whether the purpose be general, a national purpose and object. As well might it be said that expenditure upon the Capitol was local, and not provided for, as to say that expenditure upon a harbor or breakwater, which is necessary for the general purposes of the commerce of the country, is a local expenditure made within a State, and therefore not constitutional. Wherever the money is so expended, it is expended within the jurisdiction of the United States, and for purposes conceded to it by the Constitution; that is to say, the regulation and protection of commerce.

The President draws a distinction between improvements for the benefit of foreign commerce and those for the benefit of internal trade, and states that the objects provided for by this bill are for the benefit of internal trade only. I wonder where he finds any authority to rest a distinction on that fact, even if it existed, which is hardly the case, I think, in any one instance.

The President says that many of the appropriations for these particular objects were made for the first time by this bill. Well, if appropriations had been made for them before, and they had been adequate, there would be no occasion for making new ones; but the question is, Are not these new objects the same in principle as those for which appropriations have been made very many times? I think they are; but I shall return to that point.

But let us now go to the origin of this power. Let us appeal from the opinions of the President of the United States to the written text of the Constitution; and let us see what that is. The power of the government of the United States in this respect is expressed in the Constitution in a very few words. It says, that "Congress shall have power to regulate commerce with foreign nations, and among the several States, and with the Indian tribes."

The whole force of the provision is concentrated in that word "regulate." Well, Mr. Polk himself admits that the word "regulate," as applied to facilities for foreign trade, does extend to the making of beacons, piers, and light-houses; but his message attempts to run a distinction between foreign trade and trade between the States. But the power over each is given in the same clause of the Constitution, in the very same words, and is of exactly equal length and breadth. If one is denied, both are denied; if one is conceded, both must be conceded. It is impossible to separate them by any argument or logical process worthy of a statesman's mind. It is wholly arbitrary, I say, and without the least foundation, to affirm that Congress may make provision for a harbor for the accommodation of foreign commerce, and not of domestic trade. Is the latter not as important as the former? Is not the breakwater at the mouth of the Delaware Bay as important for the trade of Philadelphia with New Orleans as with Liverpool? and so everywhere else? Is not our coasting trade one of the largest branches of our maritime interest, and can we yet do nothing for that?

It is strange that any man should entertain the idea that such a distinction can be drawn. I have before me a long list of acts of Congress, of a good deal of importance, as I think, tending to show that the President is mistaken when he speaks of the acquiescence and approbation of the people in opinions adverse to harbor improvements. The opinion, both of Congress and the people, seems quite the other way. Here is a list of provisions of this kind, made in Mr. Adams's time, in General Jackson's time, and in Mr. Van Buren's time, for exactly similar objects, and some of them for the same objects; and I should tax your patience with the reading of this list, if I had not another more convincing statement to make to you, which will close the consideration of this part of the subject.*

I have already placed before you the Harbor Bill, as it passed both houses, at the last session. Some of its enactments have been read to you by my friend near me, Mr. Hone; and now let me add, that I have caused the objects of expenditure and appropriation in that bill to be carefully examined, and former legislation in regard to these several objects to be investigated; and I will state to you the result. Here are forty-nine distinct objects of appropriation in this bill of last session which was vetoed by the President; and out of this list of forty-nine, thirty-three of them are the identical objects for which appropriations were made during the administration of General Jackson. There remain sixteen; and, upon careful examination, it will appear that these sixteen objects that have grown up since the time of General Jackson, and which Congress thought proper to provide for in this bill, are every one harbors connected with the external trade of the country, and therefore strictly within Mr. Polk's own rule.

Gentlemen, I leave this question. In the free discussion of which it has been the subject, in and out of Congress, the argument is exhausted. The question is, whether we are convinced, and whether we will stand up to our convictions. The question is, whether the Great West, so important a part of the country, bearing its share of all the common burdens, is to be struck out of all participation in the benefits which are bestowed upon other portions of the Union? I think not. The question is put already. I expect to hear an answer to it from the North, the Northwest, and the South. But I do not rely upon conventions at Memphis or St. Louis; I do not rely on resolutions. I rely on the disposition of the people to understand what their constitutional rights are, and to take care that those constitutional rights shall be fairly protected, by being intrusted to proper hands.

Before I quite leave this part of the subject, I must say a word upon an important report made to the Senate at the last session, by a committee to whom the resolutions passed by the Memphis Convention were referred. A distinguished Senator

---

* The list here referred to will be found in the Appendix, No. II.

from South Carolina (Mr. Calhoun) was chairman of the committee, and framed that elaborate report. So far as he admits any thing done by Congress to have been rightfully done, and admits any degree of authority in Congress to do what has not yet been done, I concur with him. The rest I reject; for I do not think the distinctions taken by that eminent man are sound. I regret that it is my misfortune to differ from him. The report proposes, I may state in brief, that where a river divides two States, or only two States are concerned, these two States must make the necessary improvements themselves. I do not agree with that; I do not suppose that it is a matter of any consequence whether the necessary improvements are connected with two States, or four, or only one. It is not a question of location, — it is a question of public importance. Look, for instance, at that portion of the North River which runs between two shores, both of which belong to New York. There, I suppose, the power of Congress over Governor Marcy's overslaugh farm, as it is called, is as perfect, as it is to make a similar improvement farther down, where the river divides the States of New York and New Jersey. The distinction attempted, as it strikes me, is a distinction without a difference.

Having thus alluded to the report of the committee of the Senate, and not having time to discuss its propositions at any considerable length, I will now, by way of conclusion, give to you my views on all this question of the power of making harbors. It is my opinion, —

That Congress has the power to make harbors on the rivers and on the lakes, to the full extent to which it has ever proposed to exercise such power:

That whether these proposed harbors be judged useful for foreign commerce, or only for commerce among the States themselves, the principle is the same, and the constitutional power is given in the same clause, and in the same words:

That Congress has power to clear out obstructions from all rivers suited to the purposes of commerce, foreign or domestic, and to improve their navigation and utility, by appropriations from the treasury of the United States:

That whether a river divide two States, or more than two, or run through two States, or more than two, or is wholly confined to one State, is immaterial, provided its importance to commerce, foreign or domestic, be admitted:

I think it wholly immaterial whether a proposed improvement in a river, for commercial purposes, be above or below an actually existing port of entry:

If, instead of clearing out the rocks, and in that manner improving the channel of a river, it is found better to make a canal around falls which are in it, I have no doubt whatever of the power of Congress to construct such a canal. I think, for instance, that Congress has the power to purchase the Louisville Canal around the Falls of the Ohio; and that it ought to exercise that power now, if the work can be purchased for a reasonable price; and that the canal should then be free to all who have occasion to use it, reserving such tolls only as are sufficient to keep the works in repair.

It seems to me that these propositions all flow from the nature of our government, and its equal power over trade with foreign nations and among the States; and from the fact resulting from these powers, that the commerce of the United States is a unit. I have no conception of any such thing as seems to be thought possible by the report of the committee of the Senate, that is, an external commerce existing between two States, carried on by laws and regulations of their own, whether such laws and regulations were adopted with or without the consent of Congress. I do not understand how there can be a Pennsylvania vessel, built, manned, and equipped under Pennsylvania laws, trading as such with New York or Maryland, or having any rights or privileges not conferred by acts of Congress; and consequently I consider it an unfounded idea, that, when only two States are interested in the navigation of a river, or its waters touch the shores of only two States, the improvement of such river is excluded from the power of Congress, and must be left to the care of the two States themselves, under an agreement, which they may, with the consent of Congress, enter into for that purpose. In my opinion, the provision of the Constitution which forbids a State from entering into any alliance, compact, or agreement with another State, without consent of Congress, can draw after it no such conclusion as that, with the consent of Congress, two States ought to be bound to improve the navigation of a river which separates their territories; and that, therefore, the power of Congress to make such improvements is taken away. A river flowing between two States, and two States only, may be highly important to the commerce of the whole Union.

It can hardly be necessary to discuss this point. It is sufficient to say, that the whole argument is founded on the notion that the Constitution prohibits *more* than two States from entering into agreements, even *with* the consent of Congress. This is manifestly untenable. The Constitution extends as fully to agreements between three, four, or five States, as between two only; and the consent of Congress makes an agreement between five as valid as between two. If, therefore, two States can improve rivers with the consent of Congress, so can five or more; and, if it be a sufficient reason for denying the power of Congress to improve a river in a particular case, that two States can themselves do it, having first obtained the assent of Congress, it is an equally valid reason in the case where five or ten States are concerned. They, too, may do the same thing, with the consent of Congress. The distinction, therefore, between what may be done by Congress where only two States are concerned with a river, and what may be done in cases where more than two are so concerned, entirely vanishes. I hold the whole doctrine of the report of the committee, on this point, to be unsound. I am also of opinion, that there is no difference between the power to construct a pier and the power to construct a harbor. A single pier, of itself, affords a degree of shelter and protection from winds and seas; two parallel piers make a harbor; and if one pier may be rightfully constructed, it is no extravagant stretch of the constitutional power to construct another. In fine, I am of opinion that Congress does, constitutionally, possess the power of establishing light-houses, buoys, beacons, piers, breakwaters, and harbors, on the ocean, the Gulf, the lakes, and the navigable rivers; that it does constitutionally possess the power of improving the great rivers of the country, by clearing out their channels, by deepening them, or removing obstructions, in order to render navigation upon them more safe for life and property; and that, for the same reason, Congress may construct canals around falls in rivers, in all necessary cases.

All this authority, in my opinion, flows from the power over commerce, foreign and domestic, conferred on Congress by the Constitution; and if auxiliary considerations or corroborative argument be required, they are found in two facts, viz.: — First, that improvements such as have been mentioned, whether on the ocean or the Gulf, on the lakes or the rivers, are improvements which, from their nature, are such as no single State, nor any number of States, can make, or ought to be called on to make. All idea of leaving such improvements to be undertaken by the States is, in my opinion, preposterous. In the second place, as all the revenue derived from commerce accrues to the general government, and none of it to the States, the charge of improving the means of commerce and commercial intercourse by such works as have been mentioned properly devolves on the treasury of that government, and on that treasury alone.

I had intended to discuss at length the President's veto of the bill for the indemnification of the sufferers under French spoliations before 1800. I must omit much of what I had intended to say on that subject, but I will state the history of it in as few words as possible, so that there may be no mistake or misapprehension.

In the progress of the French Revolution, French privateers, for whose conduct the government of France was responsible, made, and continued to make, spoliations on American commerce. The United States remonstrated, and sent embassy after embassy to France. The French government repeatedly promised indemnification, but coupled these promises with the demand, that the United States on their part should carry into effect, for the benefit of France, the guaranties of the treaty of alliance of 1778. After repeated attempts to come to an understanding on this point, France insisting on her claims against the United States, growing out of the treaty of alliance, and the American government pressing their claims for spoliations, the result was (without going into any unnecessary detail of the negotiation) an agreement between the two governments, that, if France would relinquish all claim on her part to the fulfilment of the treaty of 1778, the United States would relinquish all claims of our citizens on France, for spoliations up to the year 1800. That was the result of the arrangement between the two governments as contained in the convention of that year. The wars of Europe, however, continued. New depredations were made; and after the peace of Europe and the restoration of the Bourbons, and, indeed, after the accession of the present king of France (Louis Philippe), the United States, through the agency of Mr. Rives, in Paris, negotiated a treaty with France for the satisfaction of claims of American citizens. The terms were general.

They embraced all claims, and twenty-five millions of francs, or five millions of dollars, were appropriated by the government of France to pay these claims, and a commission was appointed by the government of the United States, to whom the distribution of this fund was intrusted. This commission sat at Washington. Persons brought in their claims. One man said, " My ship was captured in 1801; here are my papers; my loss was $ 50,000." Very well; he was paid. But here comes another, whose ship was captured in 1799, and he says, " I have a good claim; I had a ship properly documented, seized by French cruisers, condemned, and confiscated. Here is the register and bill of lading; my damages are $ 50,000." But the commissioners say, You are not to be admitted to partake in this fund, because the government of the United States, by the convention of 1800, for a consideration useful and of great value to itself, relinquished to France all claims up to that time. Well, then, these claimants have come to Congress for redress, insisting, that, as the government did in fact apply their claims to its own use, it ought to indemnify the claimants, and Congress, at the last session, passed an act for that purpose. Mr. Polk vetoed the bill. This is an unwarrantable interference of the veto power with cases of private right, for there is no constitutional question at issue.

What is the ground assigned by the President for so harsh a procedure? I have said before, and I repeat it, that his whole reasoning is trivial. It wants the dignity of an argument. He says, for instance, to the claimants, " You have been long before Congress; there is no more reason for paying you now than there was near half a century ago." In the first place, this is not true in fact; for until within less than twenty years it had not been decided that the claimants had no right to call further on France. But suppose it were so. Suppose that these claimants, in pursuance of a just debt, had called upon Congress from year to year, and been put off by one evasion or another, and had at last succeeded in convincing Congress that the debt ought to be paid. Is it any reason for negativing the bill, to say, that there is no more reason for paying them now than twenty years ago? But I am compelled for want of time to leave the topic, which I will do with a single remark. There are opponents of the administration who are actuated by political dissatisfaction; but by the veto of this bill, which deprives so many poor persons, widows, and orphans of their last hope, the President has touched the hearts of hundreds and thousands with something much stronger than mere political dislike.

Another great subject of public interest at the present time is the recent tariff, which I discussed when it was established, and about which I have nothing new to say. My object is, and has been, in every thing connected with the protective policy, the true policy of the United States, to see that the labor of the country, the industry of the country, is properly provided for. I am looking, not for a law such as will benefit capitalists, — they can take care of themselves, — but for a law that shall induce capitalists to invest their capital in such a manner as to occupy and employ American labor. I am for such laws as shall induce capitalists not to withhold their capital from actual operations, which give employment to thousands of hands. I look to capital, therefore, in no other view than as I wish it drawn out and used for the public good, and the employment of the labor of the country. Now on this subject I shall hand to the gentlemen of the press, a series of resolutions passed in Massachusetts, which I have not now time to read, but which entirely embody my own sentiments.*

I will only say, that I am for protection, ample, permanent, founded on just principles; and that, in my judgment, the principles of the act of 1842 are the true principles, — *specific* duties, and not *ad valorem* assessment; just discrimination, and, in that just discrimination, great care not to tax the raw material so high as to be a bounty to the foreign manufacturer and an oppression on our own. Discrimination and specific duties, and such duties as are full and adequate to the purposes of protection, — these are the principles of the act of 1842. Whenever there is presented to me any proposition, from any quarter, which contains adequate protection, founded on those indispensable principles, I shall take it. My object is to obtain, in the best way I can, and when I can, and as I can, full and adequate and thorough protection to the domestic industry of the country, upon just principles.

In the next place, I have to say that I will take no part in

* See Appendix, No. III.

any tinkering of the present law, while its vicious principles remain. As far as depends upon me, the administration shall not escape its just responsibility, by any pretended amendments of the recent law with a view to particular political interests. Allow me to say, frankly, ye iron men and ye coal men of Pennsylvania, that I know you are incapable of compromising in such a case; but if you were, and any inducements were held out to you to make your iron a little softer, and your coal burn a little clearer, while you left the hand-loom weaver —— (The vociferous cheering which here burst forth drowned the remainder of the sentence.)

I understand there are seven thousand hand-loom weavers in the city and county of Philadelphia; that their wages have hitherto averaged five dollars a week; that the *ad valorem* duty, as applied to cottons, affects them very injuriously, in its tendency to reduce wages and earnings; especially as the wages of a hand-loom weaver in Scotland hardly exceed one dollar and seventy-five cents or two dollars per week. What the precise result may be, remains to be seen. The carpet-weavers, it is said, may find some indemnity in the reduced price of wool. If this be so, it only shows that the loss is shifted from the weaver to the wool-grower. Washington County, Fayette County, and other counties in this State, will probably learn how this is. In the aggregate it has been estimated that the value of manufactures in the city and county of Philadelphia scarcely falls short of the value of those at Lowell; and their production, it is supposed, employs more hands here than are employed in Lowell.

Gentlemen, on the tariff I have spoken so often and so much, that I am sure no gentleman wishes me to utter the word again. There are some things, however, which cannot be too often repeated. Of all countries in the world, England, for centuries, was the most tenacious in adhering to her protective principles, both in matters of commerce and manufacture. She has of late years relaxed, having found that her position could afford somewhat of free trade. She has the skill acquired by long experience, she has vast machinery and vast capital, she has a dense population; a cheaply working, because a badly fed and badly clothed, population. She can run her career, therefore, in free trade. We cannot, unless willing to become badly fed and badly clothed also. Gentlemen, for the gymnastic exercises, men strip themselves naked, and for this strife and competition in free trade, our laborers, it seems, must strip themselves naked also.

It is, after all, an insidious system, in a country of diversified arts and attainments, of varied pursuits of labor, and different occupations of life. If all men in a country were merely agricultural producers, free trade would be very well. But where divers employments and pursuits have sprung up and exist together, it is necessary that they should succor and support one another, and defend all against dangerous foreign competition.

We may see, at this moment, what consequences result from the doctrines of free trade carried to extremes. Ireland is a signal example. The failure of a potato crop half starves a population of eight millions. The people have no employment which enables them to purchase food. Government itself is already absolutely obliged to furnish employment, often on works of little or no value, to keep the people from positive famine. And yet there are able men, — able I admit them to be, but theoretic men I think them to be; distinguished men, nevertheless, — who maintain that Ireland now is no worse off than if all the great landholders owning estates in Ireland, instead of living in England and spending there the rents of their Irish estates, lived in Ireland, and supported Irish labor on their farms, and about their establishments, and in the workshops.

This opinion is maintained by theoretical economists, notwithstanding the cry of Ireland for employment, employment! And has it not come even to that pass, that the government is obliged to employ hundreds and thousands of the people and pay them, and put them on works of very little utility, merely to give them bread? I wish that every Irishman in the State of Pennsylvania could be here to-night, so that I could ask him to remember the condition of the people of his own country, who are starving for the want of employment, and compare that condition with his own, here in Pennsylvania, where he has good employment and fair wages.

Gentlemen, this notion of free trade, which goes to cut off the employment of large portions and classes of the population, on the ground that it is best to buy where you can buy cheapest, is a folly, in a country like ours. The case of England is not analogous. What is the cry of free trade in England? Why, it is for cheap bread. In England the deficiency is in bread. Labor is limited in its reward. It can earn but so much, and we have Mr. Cobden's authority for saying that there is a disposition to reduce its earnings still lower. It has, accordingly, a vital interest in reducing the price of food. Therefore free trade in England is but another name for cheap bread. It is not so with us. What we desire for our laboring population is employment. We do not expect food to be cheaper in this country; our object is to make it dear; that is to say, our agricultural interests desire to raise the price of grain; and the laboring classes can stand this, if their employments are protected, and the price of labor kept up. Our hope, and let all rejoice in it, is, that the price of our agricultural productions may rise for the benefit of the farmer. Manufacturers and operators, so long as they get steady employment and good wages, can buy at any reasonable rate.

These views are confirmed by the practice of most of the civilized governments of the world. Who of all Europe imitates England? Nobody, as far as I know, except Holland and Turkey. Austria, Russia, Spain, and France adhere to what I call the common-sense doctrine of protecting their own labor. M. Dupin, in the French Chamber of Deputies, said, last year, that the instincts of France were in favor of the protection of French labor. Our American instincts from the first have been very much of the same character. Whence arose all those *non*-importation agreements, soon after the Revolutionary war, but from an instinct, or feeling that the interests of our own industrious population ought to be consulted and promoted? I happen to have a very important document here, which one of your fellow-citizens caused to be copied and printed in a very handsome manner. It is a *non*-importation agreement, entered into in this city as early as 1765. That was an American instinct! Here are names to be for ever remembered! I perceive amongst them Robert Morris, the financier of the Revolution, Charles Thompson, the Secretary of Congress, and other illustrious names, whose representatives are still amongst us.

There is one imputation that honest men ought to resist, which is, that the protective policy aids capitalists, and is meant to do so, exclusively. We hear every day of the great capitalists and rich corporations of New England. A word dissipates

all this. A corporation in New England is a form of partnership. Any body enters into it that chooses. Where individuals
invest their property to build a mill, they do it in the form of a
corporation, for the sake of convenience in transacting the business of the concern, their private responsibility still remaining in
a qualified sense. The talk about rich and exclusive corporations
is idle and delusive. There is not one of them into which men
of moderate means may not enter, and many such men do enter,
and are interested in them to a considerable extent.

Gentlemen, I have already alluded to the great importance of
the protective policy, in this State and in other States, to the
handicrafts. That was the original specific aim and design of the
policy. At the time of the adoption of the Constitution, large
manufacturing corporations were not known. No great works
existed, though sagacious and far-seeing men perceived that the
application of water-power must one day greatly advance the
manufacturing interests. At that day, the handicrafts, the mechanics, and artisans in the city were looked upon as those
whose labor it was desirable to protect. Will you pardon me,
Gentlemen, for recalling to the recollection of your older fellow-
citizens an interesting celebration which took place in this city,
on the 4th day of July, 1788. On that day the citizens of Philadelphia celebrated the Declaration of Independence made by
the thirteen United States of America on the 4th of July, 1776,
and the establishment of the Constitution or frame of government, then recently adopted by ten States. A procession was
formed. The military and companies of the various trades and
professions united in it. It was organized and commanded by
Generals Mifflin and Stewart, and some other well-known personages. The various companies displayed their flags and banners with appropriate devices and mottoes. Richard Bache,
Esq., on horseback, as a herald, attended by a trumpet, proclaimed a "New Era." The Hon. Peter Muhlenberg carried a
blue flag, with the words "17th of September, 1787,"* in silver letters. Chief Justice McKean, and his associates, in their robes of
office, were seated in a lofty car, shaped like an eagle, and drawn
by six white horses. The Chief Justice supported a tall staff, on
the top of which was the Cap of Liberty; under the cap the

---

* The day on which the plan of the Constitution was definitively adopted by
the Federal Convention, and subscribed by its members.

"New Constitution," framed and ornamented, and immediately under the Constitution the words "The People," in large gold letters. Next followed various corps and troops and associations, consuls, collectors, judges, and others. Then came the Agricultural Society, with its flag and motto, "Venerate the Plough." Then the Manufacturing Society, with their spinning and carding machines, looms, and other machinery and implements. Mr. Gallaudet carried the flag, the device on which was a Beehive, standing in the beams of the sun, bees issuing from the hive; the flag a blue silk; motto, "In its rays we shall feel new vigor." This was followed by a carriage holding men weaving and printing. A lady and her four daughters sat upon it, pencilling a piece of chintz, all dressed in cotton of their own manufacture, and over them all, on a lofty staff, was a flag with this motto, "May the Union Government protect the Manufactures of America." The federal ship "Union" followed next, and after her, boat-builders, sail-makers, merchants, and others interested in commerce. Then other trades, such as cabinet and chair-makers, with a flag and motto, "By Unity we support Society." Next bricklayers, with a flag on which there was a brickyard and kiln burning; hands at work; and in the distance a federal city building, with this motto, "It was hard in Egypt, but this prospect makes it easy." Then came the porters, bearing on their flag the motto, "May Industry ever be encouraged." After them various trades again, and then whip and cane-makers, with the motto, "Let us encourage our own Manufactures." After them still others, and amongst the last the brewers, with a flag with this motto, "Home-brewed is best."

I now ask you, Gentlemen, whether these sentiments and banners indicated that government was to lay duties only for revenue, and without respect to home industry? Do you believe the doctrines of Mr. Polk, or those of the citizens of Philadelphia in 1788? (Loud shouts of "Eighty-eight," and long-continued cheering.)

Gentlemen, I had intended to make some remarks upon the present state of the finances and the prospects of the public treasury. But I have not time to go into this subject at any length. I can but offer you a general statement.

For the year ending 30th June, 1846, the Secretary of the

Treasury will be enabled to present to Congress a more favorable state of the finances than he had previously estimated.

In his annual report at the commencement of the last session, he estimated the receipts of the year at	$ 26,820,000
And he stated that the actual balance in the treasury on the 1st of July, 1845 (the beginning of that year), was	7,658,000
Making the total means for the year, as estimated,	34,478,000
He estimated the expenditures for the same year at	29,627,000
Leaving an estimated balance in the treasury on the 1st of July, 1846, of	4,851,000
But it is believed that the actual receipts for the year in question were about	29,500,000
And the actual expenditures no more than about .	28,000,000
If this be correct, the actual receipts exceeded the Secretary's estimate by	2,700,000
And the actual expenditures fell short of his estimate	1,600,000
Instead, then, of this balance remaining on the 1st of July, 1846, as the Secretary estimated, . .	4,851,000
The actual balance in the treasury at that date must have been about	9,151,000
Being $ 4,300,000 more than the estimate. Accordingly, it appears from the monthly statement of the Treasurer that the balance in treasury, 29th June, 1846, was	9,310,000

But the Secretary will probably not be so fortunate in respect to his estimate for the present fiscal year, ending 30th June, 1847.

He estimates the revenue for this year at . .	$ 25,000,000
And the expenditures for the same period at .	25,500,000
The actual revenue for the first quarter of the same year, viz. from 30th June to 30th September, 1846, was	6,772,000
And the actual expenditure for the same quarter was	14,088,000
Leaving a deficiency for that quarter of . .	$ 7,306,000

If the first quarter be a fair sample of the whole year, both as to the revenue and expenditures, the deficiency at the end of the year will be	$ 29,224,000
To this deficiency the balance in the Treasury on the 1st of July, 1846, is applicable, viz. . .	9,310,000
And the remainder, unless other provision be made, goes to increase the public debt, . . .	19,914,000
The previously existing public debt was . .	17,075,000
The whole public debt, therefore, on the 1st of July, 1847, including stocks and treasury-notes, on this calculation, would be	36,989,000

These are, of course, but estimates, except so far as they are collected from the monthly and quarterly reports from the treasury. It may be that the receipts and expenditures for the first quarter of the present fiscal year will not turn out to be a true index to the remaining three quarters. We have yet to see, too, what will be the actual effect of the new tariff on the revenue. It is also to be borne in mind, that, in stating the above receipts and expenditures, no allowance whatever is made for expenses incurred, but not yet defrayed. The raising of more troops of course enhances the expense of the war, and on the whole it is probable that the deficiency at the end of the year may be $ 30,000,000. It is evident enough, that the country is rapidly incurring a considerable debt, which must necessarily go on increasing while the war lasts. I make the following calculation, from the best data in my possession.

Estimated amount of the public debt, if the war should continue till next spring, . . .	$ 100,000,000
Annual interest of this, ...	6,000,000
Sinking fund, ...	2,000,000
Ordinary expenses, ...	28,000,000
	36,000,000
Deduct income from public lands and all other sources, as estimated by Mr. Secretary Walker, for the year ending 30th June, 1847, . . .	2,500,000
Leaving to be provided for by duties on imports, .	33,500,000

Amount brought forward, ... $ 33,500,000
If the imports under the new tariff should be the
  same as they were for the year ending June 30th,
  1845, say $ 103,000,000, after deducting exports,
  it is estimated that the net revenue from imports
  will be   23,000,000

Leaving to be raised by duties on increased imports, $ 10,500,000

To produce this sum, there must be an increased importation
of $ 47,021,190, making a total of $ 150,021,190 (after deduct-
ing all reëxports of foreign goods), to be consumed in the country and paid for if we have the ability. The exports of our agricultural products, fisheries, &c., for the present year of short
crops of grain in Europe, will not exceed $ 135,000,000, leaving
$ 15,000,000 to be paid for in specie, which we cannot spare. Its
loss would immediately derange our currency, depress business,
and destroy credit. If the public debt should reach only to fifty
millions, then three millions of annual expenditure would be
saved, and the exports of specie, on the foregoing calculation,
be twelve millions instead of sixteen.

I think there will be a great deficiency, and I rather expect
that the President will recommend a tax upon tea and coffee.
All I have to say is this, that there was a majority found in
either branch of Congress sufficient to carry the present tariff
measure, a measure which has, in my judgment destroyed the
best system which this country ever possessed, — I mean the
tariff of 1842, whether for revenue, or protection, or public credit.
This there were majorities found to destroy. These same majorities exist. By that act, they struck off five millions from the annual income. They may, or may not, — I will not anticipate, —
receive an equal amount under their own new tariff. Let events
decide that. If they do not, if they want more money, if they
must have more money, they have the same majorities, for any
measures which they may see fit to adopt. If they will take
my advice, should they be in want of money, I would say to
them, Restore what you have destroyed. Give us back that system of credit, and, as soon as you can honorably, put an end to
this war. You may have increased your public debt; give us a
good system to live under, and pay under, and we can meet the
loss. But if you mean to overwhelm us with foreign importa-

tions, if you think you will receive, as you will not, forty or fifty millions of new importations, how do you expect to meet this demand? It is true, the times favor and support the hope of getting along for a little while under the present system. The high price of iron in England keeps up the price of that article here, whilst the famine in Ireland, and the general scarcity in other parts of Europe, augment the exportation of American produce. But, looking to the end, I entertain a confident opinion that the importations of the country will not reach such an amount as will make good the loss sustained by the destruction of the tariff of 1842; and if such importation should take place, and the people of the United States were foolish enough to purchase foreign commodities to that extent, what must be the consequences? Why, that our exports would not pay for our imports, and the country would be drained of specie. This seems to me inevitable; and derangement of the currency and pressure in commercial affairs must follow.

I now take my leave of the company and of the occasion, by returning thanks to the ladies who have honored me, and all of us, by attending this meeting. If they have not received pleasure, they have fulfilled, so far, the duty and destiny of the sex in conferring it. If the audience immediately before me have sometimes felt that their ears were weary, their eyes, nevertheless, have been always pleased.

They may well rejoice in the prosperity of happy homes and a happy country, and in the innumerable blessings which Providence has vouchsafed to pour upon us. Who is there — are there any? — who can look back with more pleasure and honest pride upon the history of the past? Who is there, in any part of the earth, that can contemplate the present circumstances which surround them with more satisfaction than one of this goodly land? And where are there fathers and mothers, who can look forward with higher or better hopes for the happiness of their children, and their children's children, than the fathers and mothers now before me?

Let us soften political duties and political differences by surrounding them with friendly associations and kind feelings; and while the fathers and the sons, through successive generations, shall, with manly strength, uphold the pillars of the state, may those pillars be ornamented by the grace and beauty of mothers and daughters!

APPENDIX.

No. I. — Page 340.

THE following is the bill alluded to by Mr. Webster as having been vetoed by Mr. Polk. The articles to which the letter J. is prefixed are such as had been partly provided for by appropriations under General Jackson's administration.

Be it enacted by the Senate and House of Representatives of the United States of America, in Congress assembled, That a sum of money be, and the same is hereby, appropriated, to be paid out of any unappropriated money in the treasury, sufficient for the following purposes, viz. : —

1836. J.	For the continuation of the breakwater structure at Burlington, on Lake Champlain, . . .	$ 15,000
1836. J.	For the continuation of the breakwater structure at Plattsburg, on Lake Champlain, ...	15,000
1836. J.	For the repairs and working of the steam dredge, on Lake Champlain, ...	9,000
	For the improvement of the Harbor at Port Ontario, on Lake Ontario, ...	40,000
1831. J.	For the improvement of the Harbor at Oswego, on Lake Ontario, ...	10,000
1830. J.	For the improvement of Big Sodus Bay, on Lake Ontario, ...	5,000
	For the improvement of Little Sodus Bay, on Lake Ontario, ...	5,000
1830. J.	For the improvement of the Harbor at the mouth of the Genesee River, on Lake Ontario, . .	10,000
1836. J.	For the improvement of the Oak Orchard Harbor, State of New York, ...	7,000
	For the construction of a dredge boat, for Lake Ontario and River St. Lawrence, . . .	20,000

1831. J.	For repairing and improving the Harbor at Buffalo, on Lake Erie, and the continuation of the sea-wall for the protection of the same, . . .	$ 50,000
1830. J.	For improving the Harbor at Dunkirk, on Lake Erie, ...	15,000
	For improving the Harbor at Erie, on Lake Erie,	40,000
1830. J.	For improving Grand River Harbor, on Lake Erie,	100,000
1832. J.	For improving Ashtabula Harbor, on Lake Erie,	10,000
1830. J.	For improving the Harbor at Cleveland, on Lake Erie, ...	20,000
1830. J.	For improving the Harbor at Huron, on Lake Erie,	5,000
	For improving the Harbor at Sandusky City, on Lake Erie, ...	11,000
1836. J.	For improving the River Raisin Harbor, on Lake Erie, ...	13,000
1836. J.	For constructing a dredge boat to be used on Lake Erie, ...	20,000
1836. J.	For the improvement of the St. Clair Flats, so called, so as to prevent their obstructing the passage of vessels from Buffalo to the ports on Lake Michigan, ...	40,000
1830. J.	For improving the Grand River Harbor, on Lake Michigan, so as to give protection to vessels sailing on said lake, ...	10,000
	For improving the Harbor at the mouth of Kalamazoo River, on Lake Michigan, so as to give protection to vessels sailing on said lake, . . .	10,000
1836. J.	For improving the Harbor at St. Joseph, on Lake Michigan, ...	10,000
1831. J.	For improving the Harbor at Michigan City, on Lake Michigan, ...	40,000
	For the improvement of Little Fort Harbor, on Lake Michigan, ...	12,000
	For improving the Harbor at Racine, on Lake Michigan, ...	15,000
	For improving the Harbor at Southport, on Lake Michigan, ...	10,000
1836. J.	For improving the Harbor at Milwaukie, on Lake Michigan, ...	20,000
1836. J.	For improving the Harbor at Chicago, on Lake Michigan, ...	12,000
	For constructing a dredge boat, to be used on Lake Michigan, ...	15,000

1836. J.	For improving the Harbor at St. Louis,	$ 75,000
1836. J.	For constructing a breakwater structure at Stamford Ledge, Maine,	20,000
1832. J.	For improving the Harbor of Boston,	40,000
1836. J.	For continuing the works at Bridgeport, Connecticut,	15,000
	For removing the obstruction at the Crook in the Harbor of Providence, Rhode Island,	5,000
1830. J.	For improving the Harbor at New Castle, Delaware,	15,000
1830. J.	For improving the Harbor at Port Penn, Delaware,	5,000
1830. J.	For completing the Delaware Breakwater,	75,000
	For removing obstructions in Newark Bay, New Jersey,	15,000
1836. J.	For improving the Harbor at Baltimore City,	20,000
	For the improvement of the Harbor at Havre de Grace, Maryland,	20,000
1832. J.	For the improvement of Savannah Harbor and the Naval Anchorage, near Fort Pulaski,	50,000
1832. J.	For the improvement of the Great Wood Hole Harbor, Massachusetts,	1,450
1836. J.	For the continuing the improvements of the navigation of the Hudson River, above and below Albany, in the State of New York,	75,000
1837. J.	For the improvement of the Ohio River, above the Falls at Louisville,	80,000
1830. J.	For the improvement of the Ohio River, below the Falls at Louisville, and of the Mississippi, Missouri, and Arkansas Rivers,	240,000
1831. J.	For removing the Raft of Red River, and for the improvement of said river,	80,000
	For repairs and preservation of harbor works heretofore constructed on the Atlantic coast,	20,000

No. II. — Page 343.

List of Objects of Internal Improvement for which Appropriations had been made under preceding Administrations.

By the Act of March 2d, 1829.

For extending the pier of Black Rock Harbor, at the outlet of Lake Erie, to a point opposite Bird's Island, . . . $ 30,000

For removing obstructions at the entrance of the Harbor of Big Sodus Bay, on Lake Ontario, ... $ 12,500

For the improvement of the navigation of the Genesee River, in the State of New York, ... 10,000

For improving the navigation of Conneaut Creek, in the State of Ohio, by removing the bar at the mouth of the same, ... 75,000

By the Act of 23d April, 1830.

For removing obstructions at the mouth of Huron River, Ohio, ... 1,880.36

For completing the removal of obstructions at the mouth of Grand River, Ohio, ... 5,563.18

For completing the improvements of Cleveland Harbor, Ohio, ... 1,786.56

For removing sand-bar at or near the mouth of Black River, Ohio, ... 8,559.77

For improving the navigation of Conneaut Creek, Ohio, . 6,135.65

For completing piers at the mouth of Dunkirk Harbor, New York, ... 1,342.75

For completing piers at Buffalo Harbor, New York, . 15,488.00

For extending the pier at Black Rock, New York, . . 3,198.00

For improving the navigation of Genesee River, New York, 13,335.00

For removing obstructions at the mouth of Big Sodus Bay, New York, ... 15,280.00

For improving the navigation of the Mississippi and Ohio Rivers, ... 50,000.00

By the Act of March 2d, 1831.

For removing obstructions at the mouth of Huron River, Ohio, ... 3,480.00

For removing sand-bar at or near the mouth of Black River, Ohio, ... 9,275.00

For completing the removal of obstructions at the mouth of Grand River, Ohio, ... 5,680.00

For removing obstructions at the mouth of Big Sodus Bay, New York, ... 17,450.00

For completing piers at Oswego, New York, . . 2,812.92

For securing the works of Oswego Harbor, New York, by a stone pier head and mole, ... 18,600.00

For completing the pier at the mouth of Buffalo Harbor, New York, ... 12,900.00

For securing and completing the works at the Harbor of
Dunkirk, New York, ... $ 6,400.00
For completing improvements of Cleveland Harbor, Ohio,   3,670.00
For completing the removal of obstructions at the mouth of
Ashtabula Creek, Ohio, ...   7,015.00
For improving the navigation of Conneaut River, Ohio,   6,370.00
For improving the navigation of Genesee River, New York, 16,670.00

By the Act of June 28th, 1834.

For carrying on the improvements of Ocracoke Inlet, North
Carolina, ...   15,000.00
For improving the navigation of Ohio, Missouri, and Missis-
sippi Rivers, ...   50,000.00
For improving the Harbor of Chicago, Illinois,   .   .   32,801.00
For the piers at La Plaisance Bay, Michigan,   .   .   .   4,895.00
For continuing and securing the works at Oswego Harbor,
New York, ...   30,000.00
For completing the works at Genesee River, New York, on
the present plan, ...   20,000.00
For continuing the improvements of Black Rock Harbor,
New York, ...   12,000.00
For completing the works at Buffalo, New York, .   .   20,000.00
For completing and securing the works at Cleveland Har-
bor, Ohio, ...   13,315.00
For repairing and securing the works at Grand River, Ohio, 10,000.00
For securing the works at Black River, Ohio,   .   .   .   5,000.00
For extending and securing the works at Huron River, Ohio,   6,700.00
For continuing the improvements at Ashtabula Creek, Ohio,   5,000.00

And for defraying the expense of surveys pursuant to the Act
of the 30th of April, 1824, including arrearages for 1833,   29,000
Of which sum $ 5,000 shall be appropriated and applied
to geological and mineralogical surveys and researches.

By the Act of March 3d, 1835.

For improving the Harbor at Chicago, in addition to the bal-
ance of former appropriations, ...   32,800.00
For securing the works at Black River,   .   .   .   4,400.00
For continuing the improvement at Ashtabula Creek, in ad-
dition to the balance of former appropriations,   .   .   7,591.00
For completing the works at Genesee River, .   .   .   2,390.00
For improving the navigation of the Ohio River below the
Falls, and the Missouri and Mississippi Rivers,   .   .   50,000.00

For the improvement of the navigation of the Ohio River between Pittsburg and the Falls of the Ohio, to be expended under the direction of the War Department, and under the care of a Superintendent for that part of Ohio, ... $ 50,000.00

For completing the removal of the obstructions to the navigation of Red River, in addition to the appropriation of $ 50,000 made at the last session of Congress, the sum of   50,000.00

For improving the navigation of the Arkansas River, and for constructing a boat with an iron hull,   .   .   .   40,000.00

By the Act of July 7th, 1838.

For continuing the improvements of the Harbor of Chicago, Illinois, ...   30,000.00

For continuing the construction of a Harbor at Michigan City, Indiana, ...   60,733.59

For continuing the construction of a pier or breakwater at the mouth of the River St. Joseph, Michigan, .   .   .   51,113.00

For the continuation of the works at the Harbor near the mouth of the River Raisin, Michigan, ...   15,000.00

For continuing the improvement of the Harbor at Whitehall, New York, ...   15,000.00

For continuing the improvement of the channel at the mouth of the Genesee River, New York, ...   25,000.00

For continuing the removal of obstructions at Black River, Ohio, ...   5,000.00

For continuing the removal of obstructions at the mouth of the Huron River, in Ohio, ...   5,000.00

For continuing the improvement of the navigation at the mouth of Vermilion River, Ohio, ...   3,626.57

For continuing the improvement of Cleveland Harbor, Ohio,   51,856.00

For continuing the removal of obstructions at Cunningham Creek, Ohio, ...   5,000.00

For continuing the removal of obstructions at Ashtabula Creek, Ohio, ...   8,000.00

For continuing the improvement of Dunkirk Harbor, New York, ...   10,000.00

For continuing the improvement of the Harbor of Portland, Lake Erie, New York, ...   35,466.00

For continuing the improvements of the Harbor at Cataraugus Creek, Lake Erie, New York, ...   32,410.00

For continuing the improvement of the Harbor of Salmon River, Lake Ontario, New York, ...   30,000.00

For continuing the construction of a breakwater at Platts-
burg, New York, ... $ 27,500.00
For continuing the improvement of the Harbor at the mouth
of Oak Orchard Creek, New York, ...   5,000.00
For continuing the improvement at Big Sodus Bay, New
York, ...   10,000.00
For continuing the pier and mole at Oswego Harbor, New
York, ...   46,067.00
For continuing the construction of a breakwater at Burling-
ton, Vermont, ...   50,000.00
For continuing the improvement of the Cumberland River
in Kentucky and Tennessee, below Nashville,   .   .   20,000.00
For continuing the improvement of the Ohio River between
the Falls and Pittsburg, ...   50,000.00
For continuing the improvement of the Ohio and Mississippi
Rivers from Louisville to New Orleans,   .   .   .   70,000.00
For continuing the improvement of the Mississippi River
above the mouth of the Ohio and the Missouri River,   .   20,000
For continuing the removal of obstructions in Grand River,
Ohio, ...   10,000.00
For continuing the works at Buffalo, ...   20,500.00
For erecting a mound or sea-wall along the peninsula
which separates Lake Erie from Buffalo Creek, to pre-
vent the influx of the lake over said peninsula,   .   .   48,000.00
For the improvement of the Arkansas River,   .   .   40,000.00

And be it further enacted, That the several sums appropriated by the
first section of this act, which exceed twelve thousand dollars each, one
half thereof, if the public service require it, shall be paid out during the
year 1838, to be applied to the objects above specified, and the other
half, in like manner, in the year 1839.

No. III. — Page 349.

THE following are the resolutions referred to by Mr. Webster : —

" *Resolved,* That the passage of the Tariff Bill of 1846, adopting new
and vicious principles in our revenue system, is a portentous experiment, threatening disturbance and injury to the great interests of the
country.

" *Resolved*, That from the first establishment of the federal government, two principles have been embodied in our revenue laws; the first, that, as far as practicable, all duties should be specific, as most simple in collection, and most secure against fraud; the other, a discrimination in the rates of duty, with a view to foster and protect the industry of the country, and to invite capital into the establishment of manufactures.

" *Resolved*, That under this system the whole country has prospered in a degree which has no parallel in the history of nations. While the Western wilderness has been giving place to cultivation and civilization, the older States have been transplanting and establishing the arts and manufactures of Europe, thus converting the whole country into a scene of active industry, in which diversified labor, mutually exchanging its products on terms of equality, realizes a remuneration and reward wholly unknown in the overpeopled countries of the Old World.

" *Resolved*, That we deprecate the changes introduced by the tariff of 1846, for the following reasons:

" We deprecate the change from specific to *ad valorem* duties, as affording increased facilities for fraud, as setting aside the light of all experience, and the opinions of all commercial men. We deprecate it as a revenue measure, inasmuch as it reduces the revenue upwards of five millions of dollars on the average importation of the last three years, while our war expenditures require a great increase of revenue, and are actually met by an increase of debt in the issue of treasury-notes. We deprecate the principles of attempting to provide for this deficiency by an increased importation of products, to come in competition with our own, displacing and paralyzing to an equal extent our own industry, and eventually producing a great reduction in the wages of labor.

" We further deprecate the principle of increasing the importation of foreign manufactures, always tending to excess, and causing the exportation of specie in return, the fruitful source of derangement in our currency, and of embarrassment in all branches of trade and industry. We deprecate the sudden change, as wantonly sporting with the interests of capital invested under the implied pledge of government for its continued protection. But we deprecate it far more as wantonly sacrificing the interests of labor, by opening upon it the foreign competition of the under-fed and overworked labor of Europe, the avowed purpose of the new policy. We deprecate it as the result of executive dictation and stringent party discipline, adopted under the coercion of a minority, without examination and without discussion, against the sober judgment of a majority of both houses of Congress.

" *Resolved*, That the allegation that the protective system favors capital more than labor, is equally contradictory to every sound principle of political economy, to al experience, and to common sense. Whilst capital is considered necessary to set labor in motion, it is an admitted principle that there is a uniform tendency, in capital employed in different pursuits, to an equalization of profits through a free competition. Whilst other propositions are disputed, this is never contested. It is confirmed by all our experience. Every branch of manufacture which has been successful has been subjected to occasional checks and embarrassments through over-action. The prosperity which followed the establishment of the tariff of 1842 has led to new construction and new expenditure in all branches of industry beyond any former precedent. In fact, we are told by the friends of the administration, as if in double mockery of their own reasoning and our apprehensions, that the *manufacturer has more to fear from home competition and over-production than from any foreign competition which can reach him under the present tariff.* It is, in fact, obvious to the most simple understanding, that the investment of capital in works which can only be made productive by the employment of many hands, is putting capital in the power of labor, rather than in a position to control it.

" *Resolved*, That the assertion, so often repeated, that the tariff of 1842 has operated as an unequal tax upon the laboring classes, in the manufactures consumed by them, is wholly destitute of truth. Our application of manufacturing industry has always been made, in the first instance, to those productions requiring little labor in proportion to the raw material. In these the success has been greatest, and it is notorious that, in the manufacture of cotton, wool, leather, hats, &c., the common articles used by the laboring classes are produced at prices which may defy all foreign competition. Even the cotton minimum, the object of so much undeserved obloquy, is well known to be all but nominal in respect to the lower branches of the manufacture, and that its only actual effect is to levy a high duty on its higher branches, on what may well be termed luxuries.

" *Resolved*, That while the loss of capital by this change of system is sudden and determinate, the effect upon labor will be a continuous wasting disease, with no remedy but the retracing our steps.

" *Resolved*, That the high reward of labor, in all its branches, is the peculiar advantage of our country, is intimately connected with the general diffusion of education and intelligence, and is the best security for the permanence of our free institutions. The protective system acts as the proper guardian of this boon.

" *Resolved*, That while we welcome and approve the repeal of the British corn laws as a concession and benefit to the depressed labor of England, by increasing its means of subsistence, the government is acting a very different part towards our own labor in opening its products to a free competition with those of the underpaid laborers of Europe.

" *Resolved,* That the principles of free trade advocated by the modern economists of Europe are founded on a state of society essentially different from our own. It contemplates labor in excess, content with a bare subsistence, and with no hope of improving its condition. It regards only the profits of capital. With us, labor is active in accumulation for itself, going hand in hand with capital, and requiring especially the shield of the protective system against foreign interference.

" *Therefore resolved,* That it is the duty of the Whig party, and of all friends of their country, to urge upon Congress the duty of revising and modifying the existing tariff of 1846, so that it may furnish revenue sufficient for the wants of the government, and of reëstablishing the principle of specific duties in all practicable cases, and of discrimination in the rates of duty with a view to foster and protect the industry of the country in all its branches.

" *Resolved,* That, whilst Massachusetts is deeply interested in the protection of her capital, and her labor devoted to manufacturing and the mechanic arts, it is a great mistake, propagated for party purposes, and received by a too easy credulity, that protection is a local or party policy. We esteem it a policy equally favorable to every part of the country, and to all the States of the Union."

SOUTHERN TOUR.

INTRODUCTORY NOTE.

In the month of May, 1847, Mr. Webster made a visit to the Southern Atlantic States. He was everywhere, on his route, received with great respect and cordiality; and was hospitably entertained at Richmond, Charleston, Columbia, Augusta, and Savannah. His intention was to go as far as New Orleans, and to return to the North by way of the Mississippi. Unfortunately he was taken ill at Augusta, in Georgia, and was thus prevented from continuing his journey beyond that place.

Short speeches were made by Mr. Webster at the several public receptions attended by him. They were rendered peculiarly interesting by the unusual nature of such an occurrence as the visit of a highly distinguished New England statesman to the South, and the enthusiasm with which he was everywhere welcomed. No full notes, however, of his addresses appear to have been taken on any of these occasions, and in most cases a very brief summary is all that remains.

Of his speech at a public dinner at Richmond, on the 29th of April, no report whatever, it is believed, has been preserved. In addition to his remarks on this occasion, in acknowledgment of a toast complimentary to himself, Mr. Webster rose, when the memory of Chief Justice Marshall was proposed, and pronounced *impromptu* a brief eulogy upon the great jurist, which appears to have been of the most brilliant character. "We have never," says the editor of a Richmond journal, "had the pleasure of listening to a more finished specimen of Ciceronian eloquence. A gentleman, whose taste and acquirements entitle his opinions to the utmost respect, remarked to us, that not Burke nor Sheridan could have been more felicitious, in giving utterance to thoughts that breathe and words that burn." Unfortunately, no report of these remarks was given to the public.

On receiving intelligence of his intended visit to Charleston, a number of the most respectable citizens of that place were appointed a committee to wait upon Mr. Webster on his arrival, and tender him a public welcome to the city. It took place on the 7th of May. On the following day a brilliant entertainment was given to him by the New

England Society. On the 10th he partook of a public entertainment by invitation of the Charleston Bar. On the 12th he was received with great distinction by the faculty and students of the College of South Carolina, at Columbia. On the 17th he arrived at Augusta, in Georgia, where a public reception of the most flattering kind awaited him. Here, however, he became so much indisposed, as to be compelled to withdraw himself from the projected hospitalities of the citizens, as well as to forego the prosecution of his tour. On the 24th of May he was sufficiently recovered to proceed to Savannah, in which place, on the 26th, a public reception took place in Monument Square, at the base of the monument to Greene and Pulaski. On this occasion a very interesting address was made to Mr. Webster on behalf of the citizens of Savannah, by Mr. Justice Wayne, of the Supreme Court of the United States. From Savannah Mr. Webster returned to Charleston, and immediately took passage in a steamer for the North.

In connection with the speeches made by Mr. Webster, as far as they have been preserved, it has been thought that some of those made by other gentlemen, on the occasions just named, would be found interesting by the readers of these volumes, particularly in the present state of public affairs in reference to the relations between the South and the North. They have accordingly been given, as far as was practicable, with those of Mr. Webster.

ARRIVAL AT CHARLESTON.*

THE Hon. Daniel Webster arrived in this city yesterday morning, and took lodgings at the Charleston Hotel. At 12 o'clock, M., he was waited on by the Committee of Reception, consisting of the following gentlemen, viz. Messrs. F. H. Elmore, D. E. Huger, James L. Petigru, William Aiken, H. A. Desaussure, Henry Gourdin, J. B. Campbell, Francis K. Huger, B. F. Hunt, J. B. Legare, R. Yeadon, John S. Ashe, I. W. Hayne, Dr. John B. Irving, and Alexander Black.

The Committee conducted Mr. Webster to the spacious piazza or balcony of the hotel, which was thronged with ladies and citizens, gathered (as was also a large crowd of citizens in the street fronting the hotel) to give the distinguished guest a hearty welcome to the hospitalities of Charleston. Mr. Webster was there addressed as follows, by the Hon. Franklin H. Elmore, Chairman of the Committee of Reception : —

" SIR, — As representatives of our fellow-citizens of Charleston, we wait upon you to tender their welcome and good wishes. Having heard that it was your intention to pass through their city, in a tour through the Southern States, undertaken to obtain, by personal observation, a better knowledge of their people, pursuits, and interests, the citizens of Charleston, laying aside all differences of political opinion, in a common desire to further your wishes and to render your visit agreeable, assembled, and unanimously delegated to us the pleasing duty of expressing to you the great satisfaction they experience in thus meeting you in their homes. Although they well know there are essential differences of opinion between a great majority of them and yourself and the great Commonwealth of which you are the trusted and distinguished representative in the councils of the nation, yet, on this occasion, they remember

* Abridged from the Charleston Courier of the 8th of May, 1847.

with far more pleasure, that, whilst at the head of the State Department, you watched with fidelity over other sections of the Union ; that the South was not neglected, but her interests and her rights found in you an able and impartial vindicator ; that you made, amongst other public services, great and successful efforts to preserve our relations in peace and harmony with the most free and powerful nation of the Old World ; and that, while you served the general cause of humanity and civilization in so doing, you at the same time sustained the honor and promoted the best interests of our common country. They remember, too, that Massachusetts also is one of the Old Thirteen, that she was the leader in the struggles of the Revolution, and that, amid its common trials and dangers, she, with our own State, won our common heritage of freedom and a common stock of glory. They feel, also, that, in these grateful reminiscences, we should be bound up in a common love for each other, and in an unalterable determination to honor, maintain, and respect the rights, welfare, and feelings of each. They hope to see these tendencies cherished and these ties strengthened. Events, like this now transpiring with us, conduce happily to such results. The influence of public men is a powerful agency, and it is very much to be regretted, that, of American statesmen, whose enlarged and liberal minds make their opinions authority, and best qualify them to understand their character and to do them justice in their own, so few travel into other sections, and make themselves personally acquainted with and known to their distant countrymen. In such intercourse, and in the interchange of courtesies and opinions, prejudices disappear, misjudgments are corrected, and a just appreciation of each other created, leading to cordiality in feeling, harmony in public measures, and eminently conducing to their common prosperity and welfare.

" Entertaining these views, our constituents heard of the intention and objects of your visit to the South with unmixed satisfaction.

" They are happy in the opportunity of expressing these sentiments to you, Sir, especially. They welcome you with the frankness and cordiality due to your high station, to your representative character, and to your eminent abilities. And they will not, on this occasion, withhold the expression of hopes which they warmly cherish, that Massachusetts will see, in all she does, that, while South Carolina may not forbear the maintenance of her own rights with decision, she still entertains for your State all the kindness and affection due to a sister, illustrious for her great virtues, her great men, and her great achievements. For yourself, and as her representative, again, Sir, we bid you a cordial welcome to South Carolina and to Charleston."

To this address Mr. Webster returned the following reply.

GENTLEMEN,— It would be an act of as great violence to my own feelings, as of injustice and ingratitude to the hospitality of the citizens of Charleston, if I should fail to express my cordial thanks for the welcome you give me in their behalf, and to reciprocate, to you and to them, my sincere respect and good wishes.

You are quite right, Gentlemen, in supposing that my purpose, in undertaking the tour which has brought me into the midst of you, is to see the country, and the people of the country, and to obtain a better and fuller knowledge of both. Hitherto, I have not been a visitor so far south; and I was unwilling, quite unwilling, to be longer a stranger, personally, in the Southern States. The citizens of Charleston do me an honor, which I most deeply feel, when they say, through you, that they have satisfaction in meeting me at their own homes, and wish to render my visit agreeable. When one is made welcome to the homes of Charleston, I am quite aware that the warmth of hospitality can go no further.

Undoubtedly, Gentlemen, differences of opinion on many subjects exist between your fellow-citizens and myself, and between South Carolina and Massachusetts. But how poor must be that spirit, a spirit which I am sure prevails neither here nor in Massachusetts, which out of these differences would extract cause of social alienation or personal disrespect! What would be the value of our political institutions, if men might not differ on public questions, without sacrificing mutual esteem or destroying the sense of common brotherhood? We have diverse political sentiments, but we have but one country. We may differ as to the best manner of serving and honoring that country, but we agree that she is to be served by all to the utmost of their power, and honored by all with filial reverence and patriotic devotion. If we do not always think alike, we all feel alike. We feel that much of the individual happiness, as well as the national renown, which belongs to us now, or may belong to us hereafter, does and will attach to us as the undivided, and I hope always the indivisible, members of the great American republic.

I am happy, Gentlemen, if you think that, while discharging the duties of Secretary of State, I paid just regard to the protection of Southern interests. In my judgment, those interests, important in themselves, were connected with grave questions of public law, questions touching the immunity of flags, and the independence and equality of nations upon the ocean. To the magnitude of these questions I could not be insensible. It is true that they commanded my utmost attention; and if the result has been greater freedom from annoyance, more security for maritime rights, and a general advance in the maintenance of peace and the friendly intercourse of nations, I am bound to ascribe this result rather to the concurrence of fortunate circumstances, and to the encouragement and support of others, than to any ability displayed in my efforts.

I concur with you cordially, Gentlemen, in the sentiment, that mutual intercourse strengthens mutual regard; and that the more citizens of different parts of the country see of one another, the more will asperities be softened, and differences reconciled. I may undertake to say, for Massachusetts, that she is ready, at all times, to meet and to return the respect and the hospitality of South Carolina; and that she remembers ancient ties of union and fraternity; that she acknowledges a common interest, and a common fate, in a common country; that there is nowhere a juster or a higher appreciation of the men, or the deeds, of this her sister State; and nowhere the prevalence of more earnest wishes for whatever may advance her prosperity and distinction.

Gentlemen, I come among you, with my family, as travellers, but not feeling that we are entirely strangers. I wish to attract no ostentatious notice, but desire only to be regarded as a fellow-countryman and a fellow-citizen, and to see the country and the people without formality or constraint.

Thanking you, and the citizens of Charleston, again, for the cordial welcome extended to me, it remains that I offer you, Gentlemen, personally, the assurance of my high regard; and to this concourse of your fellow-citizens, which now surrounds us, and whose assembling together, on this occasion, I regard as so respectful, and so imperatively demanding my grateful acknowledgments, I must tender my sincere respects.

Citizens of Charleston! I am happy to regard you as countrymen. We are born to the same inheritance, won by the same patriotism and the same valor. New England blood has moistened the soil where we now stand, shed as readily as at Lexington, or Concord, or Bunker Hill. May it prove a durable cement of the union of our respective States! And may many generations, now far off, find themselves, when they arrive, as we now find ourselves, a free, respectable, united, and prosperous community! I pray you, Gentlemen, accept my sincere good wishes for you all.

32 *

DINNER OF THE NEW ENGLAND SOCIETY.*

ON the 8th of May a public dinner was given to Mr. Webster, in St. Andrew's Hall, by the New England Society. In the lamented absence, caused by indisposition, of the venerable President, Doddridge Crocker, Esq., the chair was occupied by A. S. Willington, Esq., Vice-President. The entertainment was attended by a large company, consisting of members of the Society, and of the most distinguished citizens of Charleston and the vicinity, present by invitation. After a toast from the chair in honor of Massachusetts and South Carolina, Hon. B. F. Hunt, one of the Vice-Presidents of the day, spoke as follows : —

" MR. PRESIDENT, — As our Society dispenses with the usual formalities of a set occasion, and is determined to receive our guest as an old family friend and connection, whom we have found journeying through the land of our adoption, I shall take leave to invite your attention to a few observations, after which I shall propose a toast.

" Our experience authorizes us to assure him, that he will return to his own New England farm more attached than ever to that Constitution which, we trust, is destined, through all time to come, to bind together all parts of our country in one great and glorious republic ; each State governing its own internal affairs, which practical experience enables it to do wisely, while the federal government is left free to manage our national concerns.

" We hail with pleasure the interchange of unofficial and social intercourse by the statesmen of the different quarters of the country. It cannot fail to wear away that distrust which is prone to render strangers distant and suspicious, and I may add selfish, in their conduct of affairs.

" We believe that the more Americans see and know of each other at

* Abridged from the Charleston Courier of the 10th of May, 1847.

home, the more easily will they be convinced that, although their internal arrangements may differ, all can join in a cordial and hearty union as one great people. A mutual respect, reciprocal benefit, and social intercourse will every day diminish those causes of difference that sometimes mar the harmony of our counsels. Each State will thus respect and regard the institutions and social arrangements of every other, and all combine to elevate and extend the honor and interests of the only republic which in art and in arms maintains a proud equality among the nations of the earth.

" No States have more reason to entertain the most cordial relations than South Carolina and Massachusetts. When the port of Boston was shut, and the stubborn spirit of her people rebuked and controlled by armed foreigners, South Carolina, distant as she was from the scene of wrong, and not necessarily included in its immediate effect, disdained to profit by the sufferings of a sister colony, but promptly made common cause with the Bay State, and resolved to cheer her spirits and share her fortunes.

" The scenes of Lexington and Bunker Hill soon roused her kindred spirit into action ; — the military stores and forts were seized ; — South Carolina became a rebel colony, and a British fleet entered Charleston harbor. If the sons of the Pilgrims fired the first morning gun of freedom's glorious day, Fort Moultrie thundered forth a gallant response, and rendered immortal the ever green Palmetto. The oppressor was taught that the good Old Thirteen, when right and liberty were at stake, were animated with one spirit, and true to their kindred blood.

" The sons of the wanderers of the Mayflower united with the descendants of the Huguenot in a firm phalanx, and stood shoulder to shoulder during the dark and stormy days of the Revolution. Is it not fitting, then, that their posterity should hand down to unborn ages, unimpaired, that fraternal kindness which was born of a common conflict and a common triumph?

" Fortune resolved to leave out no element essential to a perpetual and friendly union of the North and the South. The generous and high-souled chivalry, that led South Carolina without hesitation to peril her own existence in a combined opposition to the oppression by which the legislation of the mother country was seeking to humble and crush for ever the unyielding spirit of New England, was never to be forgotten. When overwhelming military power had laid prostrate the fortunes of the South and held her gallant spirits bound in inaction, — in this dark hour of her fate, the military spirit of a New England mechanic conceived the project of rescuing the South at every hazard, and gave pledge to Washington to do so or perish in the effort.

" Perilous as was the attempt, the commander-in-chief resolved to indulge the aspirations of his favorite general; and after a march, which might be tracked by the bloody footsteps of his barefoot and almost naked followers, the troops of Greene were united with the followers of Sumpter and Marion. Every gallant warrior of the South started at the beat of the drum and the blast of the clarion from the North. Conflict followed conflict, until, one by one, every post of the enemy, from Ninety-six to Charleston, fell before their united valor. The tide of war was rolled back, until at Yorktown the sword of the proud Cornwall is was delivered to another son of New England, and Lincoln was accorded a noble retribution for his gallant but unsuccessful defence of Charleston during its protracted siege.

" Every battle-field of our State contains beneath its sod the bones of New England men, who fell in the defence of the South. Is it not right that the land, won by the united energies and sprinkled with the common blood of both, should remain for ever one heritage, where the descendants of those who made it freedom's sacred soil may recognize, in its whole length and breadth, ' their own, their native land,' the land their fathers held by the glorious title of the sword?

" It is in this feeling that we hold every son of the South entitled to a home and a welcome among the green hills and pure streams of New England.

" The North and the South are but apartments in the house of our fathers, and long, long may their inmates live in harmony together in the ennobling relations of children of the common conquerors of a common country.

" You, Sir, for the first time, look upon that sunny side of the national domain where *we* have planted our habitations and garnered up our hearts. Here are our homes and our altars, here is the field of our labors, here are the laws and institutions which protect us; here, too, are to many the birthplace of their children and their own destined graves; here our first allegiance is due, which we feel is in all things consistent with fidelity to the great republic of which our State is an integral portion. Neither have we forgotten the happy days of early life, those well-loved scenes of ' our childhood's home.' Fidelity to the land of our adoption finds no guaranty in a renegade desertion of that of our birth; but we turn, with feelings of cherished veneration, to where our fathers, in sorrow and privation, laid the deep foundations of a new empire, based on the eternal principles of civil and religious liberty, and sustained by general education and public and private virtue. We hallow their memories and tread with reverence on their graves. Our filial piety is not abated by distance, and we hail the coming among us of a worthy son of New England as a messenger from our father-land.

" We recognize in you one who has exhibited the influence of her in-stitutions in a resplendent light. The son of a New England farmer, the pupil of the free schools and college of your native State, your own energies have placed you on an elevation at the bar, in the Senate, and in the cabinet, where the civilized world can behold an orator, a jurist, and a statesman, who bears no adventitious title, and yet is known and rec-ognized by nature's own stamp of greatness.

" As a diplomatist, you have secured peace without any sacrifice of national honor, and may wear your civic crown as proudly as the vic-torious soldier does his plume. We shall record your visit in our ar-chives as a part of our annals, and the recollection of it will always be among the most acceptable reminiscences in the history of our Society.

" Mr. President and Gentlemen, I offer as a toast, —

" Our guest : He has a heart large enough to comprehend his whole country, — a head wise enough to discern her best interests ; we cheer him on his way to view her in all her various aspects, well assured that, the more he sees of her, the better he will like her."

This address and sentiment having been received with loud and re-peated cheers and applause, Mr. Webster rose and made the following reply.*

GENTLEMEN, — I am bound to say a few words in acknowledg-ment of the numerous kind things which have been said by the gentleman who has just addressed you, and the kind manner in which they have been received by the company. In answer to the testimonials of respect and the high compliments so eloquently paid me by my New England friend, I must be permitted to say, that it is a high source of gratification to me to find my-self in the city of Charleston, the long-renowned and hospitable city of the South, among those whom I regard as fellow-country-men, and who look upon me in the same light. The marks of respect and affection thus tendered have penetrated my heart with the most grateful emotions. Colonel Hunt has been pleased, with much propriety and eloquence, to refer to that great instrument of government, the Constitution, and to speak of it in terms habitual to, and expressive of the sentiment of, all Amer-ican bosoms. Whatever difference of opinion may exist with

---

* The reporter, from whose notes this speech is here given, makes an earnest apology for the entire inadequacy of his sketch.

regard to some of its purposes, all agree that it is the basis of our liberty, the cement of our Union, and the source of our national prosperity and renown. True, the cardinal principle of that instrument and the interpretation of some of its provisions have, at times, led to agitating discussions and dangerous excitements, but every thing is now calm and repose, and

> " All the clouds that lowered upon our house
> In the deep bosom of the ocean buried."

I take great pleasure, Sir, in marking the wise choice that the sons of New England around me have made, in coming to this State. I trust they were not very badly off at home, but they appear to be exceedingly comfortable here. Since "the loud torrent and the whirlwind's roar" did not "bind them to their native mountains more," they have not only acted wisely in coming hither, but, if they must make a change, I really think they could not have made a better.

Where on this continent is there a higher freedom of social enjoyment, or a more ready extension of the relations of private friendship and the courtesies of refined society, than in this city and State? Nor can I forbear a tribute to the intelligence, enterprise, and hospitality of the citizens of Charleston, where the exiled and the oppressed of the earth, and the victims of religious persecution, the Huguenot as well as the Puritan, have ever found a sanctuary and a home ; whither, as the name of this hall instructs us,* the enterprising North-British merchant resorts in the prosecution of business, and for convivial enjoyment; and where that other people, the hapless sons of Ireland, in our day the subjects of so much suffering, and to whose relief the whole of our land, both North and South, are now hastening with one heart and one purse, have also gathered as the home of the oppressed.

My friend has been pleased, in speaking of my public services, to refer to my influence over recent negotiations, connected with the preservation of the peace of the earth. Our true national policy is a policy of peace. I have not felt, for many years, that it is at all necessary for us to make farther displays of prowess in arms in order to secure us an enduring national renown. There is no danger that we shall be underrated in the scale of nations,

---

* St. Andrew's Hall.

by any defect in this particular. With these views, I have in my public course directed my best efforts to promote the peace of the world, deeming that policy best for the honor and prosperity of our land, and in closest conformity to the benign precepts of Christianity and the humane spirit of modern civilization.

In reference to this policy, I can bear testimony to the able and honorable bearing of the distinguished sons of South Carolina in the councils of the nation. On all the great questions of peace and war, and other questions of national interest, that have been discussed in the halls of legislation, they have been arrayed on the side of the country, and a large debt of gratitude is their due.

It is natural on an occasion like this to reflect on the advantages to be derived from free intercourse between the inhabitants of the various sections of the Union, and on the importance of personal communication, to enable us to see and know more of one another, convinced as I am, that, the more we see and know of each other, the higher will be our mutual appreciation, the greater will be our deference for each other's judgments and opinions, and that, by cultivating reciprocal feelings of kindness and courtesy, the stronger will be our ties of fraternal peace and concord, the stronger the great bond of union which holds us together as *United States*. These considerations are especially applicable in this era of developments so favorable to transportation and conveyance, in which distance is so much less measured than formerly by space than time.

Nobody, Sir, will expect a set speech from me at this social board. I have had enough of such speeches elsewhere. I feel that it would be entirely out of keeping with the unceremonious character of the occasion to inflict on the company a formal address. Enough has been already said by me; and it only remains for me to tender my most earnest and cordial good wishes for the happiness and prosperity of the citizens of Charleston and the people of South Carolina.

Mr. Webster concluded with the following toast: —

The people of South Carolina: Distinguished for their hospitality and high social virtues, — as much so, as for the great names which, at all times, they have given to the public service of the country.

The great cheering and applause with which Mr. Webster's address had been received having subsided, he rose and remarked that he was happy to see, among the guests and sons of South Carolina around this festive board, a distinguished gentleman (General James Hamilton) with whom he had the honor to serve many years since, (he did not mean to insinuate that the gentleman was an old man any more than to put himself in that category,) in the national councils, and to whose gallantry, vigor, and courtesy in debate, he took pleasure in bearing ample testimony. He proposed, therefore, " The health of General Hamilton."

This toast was acknowledged by General Hamilton in the following speech.

" MR. PRESIDENT AND GENTLEMEN OF THE NEW ENGLAND SOCIETY,— Although I have retired from public life during the last three or four years, and hence am in no small degree out of the practice of public speaking, I nevertheless feel, under the inspiring invocation of our distinguished guest, that I am not absolutely bereft of the faculty of speech, although overwhelmed with the value of the compliment he has paid me, and the large addition you have made to it by the enthusiasm with which it has been received.

" I deem myself peculiarly fortunate, that, in a brief and accidental visit I have paid to this city, I should be present to unite with you in those just, and to yourselves eminently honorable tributes, which you have paid to the distinguished genius and estimable private worth of the Senator from Massachusetts.

" It is true that I served some four or five years on the floor of the House of Representatives in the Congress of the United States with this gentleman, during the discussion of many interesting, and I may say some heart-burning questions.

" I have often witnessed, and sometimes *felt*, his extraordinary vigor in debate. But if I have been made sensible of this, I have likewise recognized the gentlemanly courtesy, amiable temper, and generous spirit of contest which he uniformly carried into every discussion, surpassed, if it was possible, alone by those fine social qualities around the festive board, in the atmosphere of which, the torch of party spirit, if it was not at once extinguished, at least was lost in the blaze of his genius, or in the broad glare of the convivial sympathies which flowed from his kind and benevolent heart.

" I am happy to greet him, Sir, in the home of my fathers. It is right and fitting that he should come among us ; that the favored son of old Massachusetts Bay should at last see how old South Carolina stands, and what sort of people we are, after a lapse of more than eighty years since those two then heroic Colonies were united in common league to achieve the independence of our common country.

"This remark, Sir, recalls to my recollection a cherished tradition in my own family. A fact which you will find confirmed in the biographical history of our country, in a highly interesting life of Josiah Quincy, Jr., written by his son, the late distinguished President of Harvard University.

"When John Hancock and Samuel and John Adams determined to resist the oppressions of the mother-country, they sent Josiah Quincy, Jr. (than whom a more gallant and accomplished spirit our Revolution did not produce) to South Carolina, to obtain the support of this Cavalier and Huguenot Colony, the very pet of the British crown, to stand by them in the coming struggle. The first person on whom Mr. Quincy called was my grandfather, Thomas Lynch, Sen., who, with a princely fortune, had staked every thing from the jump in the glorious contest, and who, as early as the first Congress after the passage of the Stamp Act, wrote and reported, as a delegate from South Carolina, one of the addresses of the Colonies to the Imperial Parliament. Mr. Quincy, coming by land from Boston, drove up to my grandfather's residence on South Santee, then and now called Peach-Tree. After communicating his mission, which met with the warm concurrence of my distinguished relative, they both instantly started for Charleston, and in the house of Miles Brewton (the late residence of the late Colonel William Alston, in King Street), then an opulent and patriotic merchant, whose wealth greatly depended on peace with England, met John Rutledge, Christopher Gadsden, Miles Brewton, and the other patriots of South Carolina, and *there* was concocted the grand scheme of colonial resistance, which was afterwards uttered in the war-shout at Bunker Hill, and reëchoed in the thunders from our own Palmetto fort on the 28th of June following.*

"I glory that my noble old ancestor thus received the young Boston emissary and rebel. I would rather have sprung, as I have sprung, from his loins, than that the blood of all the Howards should flow in my veins.

---

* There is some inaccuracy in these details, which were evidently stated from general recollection. Mr. Quincy's visit to South Carolina took place several years after the patriots of Massachusetts "had determined to resist the oppressions of the mother country." He arrived in Charleston on the 28th of February, 1773. The voyage (for he went by sea) was undertaken purely from motives of health, it being decided that "his only hope of life depended upon an immediate change to a more southern climate." It is quite true, however, that during his visit to South Carolina he lost no opportunity of conferring with the patriots of Charleston and the vicinity, and of giving and receiving encouragement in reference to the approaching crisis. See Memoir of Josiah Quincy, Jr., by his son, Josiah (President) Quincy, p. 72.

"I ask, then, our distinguished guest, whether Massachusetts and South Carolina ought not ever to be indissolubly united? Fast friends, then, in the hour of utmost need, may they never be irreconcilable adversaries in the hour of the utmost exasperation.

"May we not hope, my friends, that our distinguished guest will recognize, in his journey through the South, some things to esteem and regard, and fresh cement, in his own cordial sympathies with the warm greetings which everywhere await him, to bind his cherished union of the States more closely to his heart?

"I know that none of us can go to New England, that garden of modern civilization, without instruction and delight. If we can learn much from the victorious industry of her sons in building up the finest social structure in the world, we must be captivated by the generous and gushing hospitality of her noble capital, where literature and the arts form the classic architrave which adorns the granite pillars of the religion and morals of that singularly interesting people.

"I have, Sir, some right to speak thus of New England. It was there that I acquired the rudiments of almost all I know in this world. On the banks of the beautiful Charles River, as it winds its silvery current through the county of Norfolk, I passed the hours of my childhood, under the parental instruction of a kind and gifted old clergyman, who has long since gone to his bright and easily adjusted account.

"All these scenes of my childhood, even at this moment, when approaching age has not chilled its fires, come gushing to my heart to receive a renewed vitality from its tenderness and warmth. There is not 'a bosky bourne or alley green' for miles around the humble parsonage of my revered preceptor, that I do not remember with fond affection. Yes, I now feel that these images of the past have come as it were again with throbbing tenderness to tell me that, next to my own native land, I perhaps love old Massachusetts best; for next to her who gives us life, we ought to love those who nurture. At least I think so. Perhaps the coming of our friend from this land has created this illusion. But if these are illusions, I find these emotions, these natural instincts of the human heart, are stronger than the strifes of party spirit, even in the hour of their utmost inflammation. If these, indeed, are delusions, they ought to be encouraged, for it is only by getting clear in this way of the dust and turmoil of this world, that we really 'seem to recover a part of the forgotten value of existence.'

"I have, however, Mr. President, sufficiently trespassed on the kind and flattering attention of this assembly. It is time that I should conclude.

"I know not that I can conclude more appropriately than by an allusion to a great event in the public history of our guest. When the

Greeks decreed to Achilles the greatest of his ovations, I am sure he would have greeted with cordial salutations a just tribute of respect to the memory of Hector. I know when I bring the name of Hayne to the recollection of our friend, his heart stands ready, unbidden, to unite in our tribute of sorrow, admiration, and esteem, to the shade of that gifted spirit.

"In the celebrated debate on Foot's Resolutions, (which was but a foreshadowing of coming events of far deeper interest,) the greatest and by far the ablest discussion of the principles of the Constitution of the United States which ever took place, occurred, as you well know, in the Senate of the United States, in the session of 1830.

"Our deeply lamented Hayne, our comparatively youthful champion, was pitted against the gentleman now honoring and honored by this festival. It is not for me, with all my strong sympathies, personal and political, to say in this 'War of Giants' who had the better part, either in his great argument, or in the mode or manner of enforcing it. A proper feeling of courtesy to our distinguished guest induces me to be silent on their relative merits, and on the relative value of the great truths involved in the discussion.

"But I can well say this, that I have often heard my deceased friend, in the hours of our unreserved confidence, bear testimony to the preëminent powers that his opponent brought to bear in that debate, the brilliancy of which he was not the last to recognize and acknowledge. Nor was he backward in likewise acknowledging his belief in the sincerity with which opinions thus entertained were thus so ably enforced.

"May I not thus likewise, my friends, say to such as knew our gifted and deceased countryman, that, if he had been spared to us and stood where I now stand, he would have been the first among us with an outstretched hand and willing heart to receive his great antagonist on his arrival on our shores?

"The accents of my voice almost reach the spot where he rests in his mourned and untimely grave. But, dear and never to be forgotten friend, thou canst not hear these accents which hail you with the tender and recollected association of a long-cherished friendship. Methinks I almost hear the music of thy once unrivalled voice in all the compass of its melody and power. Yes, I seem to gaze once more with unspeakable delight on that countenance which beamed in life with the blended rays of genius, virtue, and spotless honor, cheering and greeting our guest on his kindly advent among us. But, alas! thou art as silent, my friend, as thy thrice honored-grave.

"Let us, however, my friends, as a consecrated office of friendship and affection, approach his urn in a spirit of just pride, as well as with a feeling of unfeigned sorrow, and offer this libation to his shade.

"The memory of Robert Y. Hayne: A champion worthy to have contended with Daniel Webster, and to have borne on high the glorious banner of our State."

This toast was drank standing and in silence. On the company being again seated, Mr. Webster rose and said, —

The gentleman who has just taken his seat has anticipated me in the tribute he has paid to the memory of his friend, in what I intended to say in the course of the evening. I cordially concur, from the bottom of my heart, in every sentiment he has so eloquently and feelingly uttered. If it was my fortune to be opposed to that gentleman in debate, on an important national question, it only gave me a better opportunity of recognizing his very eminent ability, which was not even surpassed by his gentlemanly accomplishments. I am happy in this assembly to have an opportunity of bearing testimony to his elevated patriotism, his high honor, and incorruptible integrity. No one out of the circle of his immediate relatives and friends more sincerely sympathized in the great public loss that his death occasioned. With this appreciation, we can then well afford to offer another tribute to his distinguished worth. I will give you

The memory of Robert Y. Hayne: A gentleman of courteous and polished manners, of irreproachable life, a lawyer of distinction and eminence, a statesman of ability and talent, and a highly favored son of his native State.

DINNER OF THE CHARLESTON BAR.*

THE Bar Dinner in honor of Daniel Webster, the great master of law and leader of the profession in the Union, took place, at St. Andrew's Hall, on Monday, the 10th instant. Henry A. Desaussure, Esq., the senior practising lawyer, the courteous chief patriarch of the profession in Charleston, presided, assisted by Messrs. James L. Petigru, B. F. Hunt, H. Bailey, and Richard Yeadon, as Vice-Presidents. A number of retired members of the Bar participated in the festive scene, attracted by the desire to do honor to one who conferred such honor on the profession. After a sentiment from the chair in honor of the legal profession, James L. Petigru, Esq., one of the Vice-Presidents, rose and made a few remarks on the law as the noblest of human sciences, and on the tribute due to those who profoundly studied and illustrated its principles. He concluded with the following appropriate sentiment : —

"The accomplished orator, who, as well in private causes as in public affairs, has not only set an example to his contemporaries, but earned a name among the illustrious masters of a former age."

This sentiment was received with the greatest enthusiasm, and was responded to by Mr. Webster as follows : —

GENTLEMEN, — I feel highly honored by this tribute of respect and regard from my professional brethren of the Charleston Bar. I take pleasure in expressing my sincere and grateful satisfaction in thus meeting them at the friendly and social board. Such are the emotions of my bosom, I can scarcely trust myself with a response, or be expected to make a set speech in reply. Let me say, Gentlemen, that I love our common profession, and love

* Abridged from the Charleston Courier of the 12th of May, 1847.

33 *

all who honor it.   I regard it as the great ornament, and one of
the chief defences and securities, of free institutions.   It is indispensable to and conservative of public liberty.   I honor it from
the bottom of my heart.   If I am any thing, it is the law — that
noble profession, that sublime science which we all pursue —
that has made me what I am.   It has been my ambition, coeval
with my early manhood, nay, with my youth, to be thought
worthy to be ranged under the banner of that profession.   The
law has been my chief stimulus, my controlling and abiding
hope, nay, I might almost say, my presiding genius and guardian angel.

We have met this evening, Sir, my brothers and myself,
brethren in the law, under the influence of common feelings.
We are students of the same profession, followers and disciples
of the same great leaders and teachers whom history has chroni-
cled for our contemplation and example; such as the sages of the
Roman jurisprudence; such as D'Aguesseau and Domat, Coke
and Holt and Mansfield, and other great names in Europe; such
as the masters of the profession in our own country, — great
lights and luminaries in every branch of legal science and in
the principles of legislation.   I feel it no common good fortune
to belong to a profession so useful, so honorable, and so distinguished.   Although it may not always, although it does not
often, in this country, lead to wealth, it does what is infinitely
better and more important, — it enables us to do good in our
day and generation.   I repeat, it is not calculated to yield its
members the greatest fortunes.   It seldom, in this respect, fulfils
the sanguine expectations of beginners in the toilsome path.
After twenty-five years' observation, I can give it as the condensed history of most, if not all, good lawyers, that they lived
well and died poor.   In other countries, and in England especially, it is different.   Great fortunes are there accumulated in
every branch of the legal profession.   Many noble and wealthy
families in England have been built up on the acquisitions of
the law.   Such is not the course of things with us, nor, with our
habits and inclinations, is it to be expected.

The only regret to be felt at the slenderness of professional
emolument arises out of the difficulty of impressing on the general mind sufficiently strong inducements, to make adequate and
honorable provision for those who are selected from the legal

profession to go on the bench. In my opinion, there is no character on earth more elevated and pure than that of a learned
and upright judge. There is no cause to which I would more
cheerfully and more largely contribute the earnings of my life,
than the adequate support of the learned and upright judge.
But although such a character exerts an important agency in
the public service and influence for the public good, — an influence, like the dews of heaven, falling without observance, —
it is not always sure, among a people of great activity, like ours,
to attract the proper regard or proper reward. The inadequacy
of legal emolument is not the only reason which prevents the
profession in this country from accumulating wealth. Their
standing in society compels them to live somewhat expensively,
and, I may add, their inclinations too. Lawyers always think
themselves bound to be hospitable. Friends come to town, and
they must be entertained. These positions do not rest on dis-
putable authority, but are favored by every authority from Lord
Coke down.

But though not the road to wealth, our calling is not the less
honorable. Out of the profession of the law, magistrates are
chosen to dispense private and public justice. This is a great
proof of respectability of standing in a government like ours.
Merit, and not political favor, determines with us who shall occupy the seat of justice. He would profane our institutions
who should be bold and daring enough to put one on the bench
unqualified in mind and morals for the high position.

I have observed that the administration of justice is the great
end of human society. All the complex machinery of government has for its object that a magistrate should sit, in purity
and intelligence, to administer justice between individuals and
the country. The judiciary, selected from our profession, makes
every one feel safe in life, liberty, and property. Where is
there a higher function or dignity than that of a chancellor to
dispense equity between litigants and to the widow and orphan?
Learned and virtuous judges are the great masters, and lawyers
the apprentices of justice. No morality, save that of the Saviour of mankind, is more ennobling than that of a court of
equity, as illustrated in the judgments of men like D'Aguesseau and Hardwicke and Eldon, of Marshall and Desaussure
and Kent and Story. No moral lesson, except those of holy
writ, surpasses the teachings of these great lights of the law on

the subject of fiduciary relations, and in matters of trust and confidence. An eminent lawyer cannot be a dishonest man. Tell me a man is dishonest, and I will answer he is no lawyer. He cannot be, because he is careless and reckless of justice; the law is not in his heart, — is not the standard and rule of his conduct.

A great equity lawyer has truly said, that, ever since the Revolution of 1688, law has been the basis of public liberty. I hold it to be undoubted that the state of society depends more on elementary law, and the principles and rules that control the transmission, distribution, and free alienation of property, than on positive institutions. Written constitutions sanctify and confirm great principles, but the latter are prior in existence to the former. The Habeas Corpus Act, the Bill of Rights, the trial by jury, are surer bulwarks of right and liberty than written constitutions. The establishment of our free institutions is the gradual work of time and experience, not the immediate result of any written instrument. English history and our colonial history are full of those experiments in representative government which heralded and led to our more perfect system. When our Revolution made us independent, we had not to frame government for ourselves, to hew it out of the original block of marble; our history and experience presented it ready made and well proportioned to our hands. Our neighbor, the unfortunate, miserably governed Mexico, when she emerged from her revolution, had in her history nothing of representative government, habeas corpus, or trial by jury; no progressive experiments tending to a glorious consummation; nothing but a government calling itself free, with the least possible freedom in the world. She has collected, since her independence, $ 300,000,000 of revenue, and has unfortunately expended it all in putting up one revolution and putting down another, and in maintaining an army of forty thousand men in time of peace to keep the peace.

Liberty and law are in this respect intimately connected. Civil liberty consists in the establishment of those great and inherent principles of government and human regulation, which have prevailed in England from the time of Somers and Holt. I pray Heaven that we may never relinquish the independence of the judiciary. A timeserving judge is a spectacle to inspire abhorrence. The independent judge draws around him the respect and confidence of society. Law, equity, and justice require that *this* should be done and *that* should *not* be done, and judicial decisions should command entire acquiescence from full confidence in the purity, integrity, and learning of the judge. The profession of the law is the support of public liberty. True, there was once an Empson and a Dudley, blots and stains on the profession. There was *once* a Jeffreys, but never *twice*. Such a monster of judicial savageness and ferocity has never again appeared on the face of the earth. In England ever since her Revolution, eminent members of the bar have been eminent lovers and eminent supporters of public liberty; Somers, Holt, and Camden, and numerous others, eminent lawyers, are bright names on the honorable roll.

Liberty is the creature of law, essentially different from that authorized licentiousness that trespasses on right. It is a legal and a refined idea, the offspring of high civilization, which the savage never understood and never can understand. Liberty exists in proportion to wholesome restraint; the more restraint on others to keep off from us, the more liberty we have. It is an error to suppose that liberty consists in a paucity of laws. If one wants few laws, let him go to Turkey. The Turk enjoys that blessing. The working of our complex system, full of checks and restraints on legislative, executive, and judicial power, is favorable to liberty and justice. Those checks and restraints are so many safeguards set around individual rights and interests. That man is free who is protected from injury.

Again, the law is an instrument and means of instruction to the mass of the people. Merchants, planters, farmers, and every other class of the community, acting as litigants, jurors, witnesses, or spectators, find it a useful school. The trial by jury is the popular teacher of our system; the ægis of protection to individual rights, the shield and defence against the encroachments of power. "Why call a jury?" say some. "Let a judge, a learned, virtuous, impartial judge, decide." But no, let the judge give the charge to the jury on the law, but let the people in the jury-box adjudge the facts of the case. The people, it is true, as a mass, are not capable of understanding recondite subjects and abstruse reasoning. But, before juries, and especially unlearned ones, lawyers should have the good sense not to use terms which their hearers cannot understand. To be followed in a logical train of argument, they should speak plainly and intelligibly, so that, if you "lose a single word, a single link, you break the connection," according to a remark of Bishop Heber. When a jury is impanelled, the case should be plainly stated, without Latin, in our own vernacular English, and in this way the minds of commonly sensible men may be conducted to high results of argument.

There can be no better tribunal than the people brought together in the jury-box, under the solemn sanction of an oath, and acting under the instructions of enlightened judges. In what a vast majority of cases do they decide right! I am attached to this mode of trial, and will never consent to give it up. *Ad quæstionem facti respondeant juratores.* In cases of doubt, the special verdict, or case stated, is an admirable expedient. The judge's mind clearly made up on a case clearly stated, becomes authority for all other like cases. There is no system of jurisprudence but the common law that enjoys this advantage. The learned Court of Session in Scotland adjudges disputed questions of law and fact. It is composed of sixteen judges, and they often differ on both law and fact, and it has happened to Sir Walter Scott, as the clerk of court, finally to put the question, " Are you on the whole in favor of the pursuer or the defender?" The same objection applies to the Roman or civil law, — that system of law in every branch of which one of your distinguished citizens (the lamented Hugh S. Legaré), whose premature demise I most deeply and sincerely mourn, has been so eminent. To us it is only a great fountain of excellent general principles. There *the case* is not to be found; and general rules do not afford the precise analogy to the case in point.

Brethren, we are apprentices of the law, the honorable profession of the law; let us make our master a grateful return. For my own part, although largely connected with other pursuits, yet will I not forget the debt I owe to the profession of the law. It found me a youth among the granite hills of my native New England, fit for nothing but to try my fortune on any cast. It was my good fortune to be directed to the law, and the result is, I have earned an honorable competence, reared a family, and shall at least leave my children the possession of a good education, and the inheritance of a good name.

In conclusion, Gentlemen, I offer you the following toast: —

The Law: It has honored us, may we honor it.

RECEPTION AT COLUMBIA.*

Hon. Daniel Webster's Visit to Columbia. — This distinguished gentleman (accompanied by his family) visited our town last week, and remained from Wednesday evening to yesterday morning. He was received with such honors and hospitalities, public and private, as it is suitable to tender to one who fills so eminent a position in our Union. On arriving, he repaired to the mansion of his friend, the Hon. W. C. Preston, President of the South Carolina College (whose more especial guest he was), and in the course of the evening was greeted by several hundred ladies and gentlemen, who had been invited to meet him. The College buildings and grounds were brilliantly illuminated by the students, whose welcome Mr. Webster acknowledged in a brief address. On Thursday, with the ladies of his party, he was elegantly entertained at Millwood, the seat of Colonel Hampton, whose stately mansion and wide domain are among the most magnificent to be seen in the South. In the evening he attended a *soirée* at the residence of Dr. Lieber, the distinguished Professor of History in our College. Friday morning was employed in riding over and examining the extensive plantations of B. F. Taylor, Esq. and Colonel Hampton, until two o'clock, when Mr. Webster repaired to Clark's Hotel, to receive such of our citizens as might be disposed to make acquaintance with him. Here he was addressed, in behalf of the town authorities, by W. F. De Saussure, Esq., to whom he replied in suitable terms.

The students of the College having held a meeting, and appointed a committee to tender to Mr. Webster their respects and congratulations, at four o'clock he repaired to the chapel, where Mr. Farrow, of the Senior Class, made to him the following exceedingly well composed address: —

" Honorable Sir, — Allow me, in the name of my fellow-students of the South Carolina College, to present you the assurance of their sincere pleasure at being honored with your presence on this occasion.

* Abridged from the Columbia South Carolinian of the 17th of May, 1847.

Conscious we are that our humble tribute can add but little either to your pleasure or your fame. But taught from infancy to respect worth, we could not be silent when we see in our midst one in whom are blended the finished scholar, the able statesman, the pure patriot; one 'whose fame can no more be hemmed in by stateliness,' than the consecrated histories of Boston, Bunker Hill, and Lexington. However warm may be our gratitude to those who sustain our country's honor on the battle-field, we are not forgetful of those whose names are interwoven in the history of the councils of state and the debates of senates. And whilst we weave a willing wreath around the victor's brow, we equally offer the homage of our hearts and our understandings to men illustrious as you are, Sir, in civil life. Be assured, Sir, on our part, of a most hearty welcome amongst us."

To which Mr. Webster replied : —

YOUNG GENTLEMEN OF THE SOUTH CAROLINA COLLEGE, — I thank you for the manner in which you have been pleased to receive me, and for the respect which you have manifested. You are of the generation which is to come after us, and your judgments are to form part of the opinion of posterity, in respect to those who are now active in the scenes of life. It will be happy for me, if the mature sentiments of your manhood shall correspond with those thus expressed in your youth.

My young friends, I may well congratulate you on your present condition, and your prospects. You are members of a flourishing institution. You enjoy the teachings of a learned faculty, with a name at its head beloved in private life, highly distinguished in public life, and which confers grace as well as usefulness on these academic groves. Private and family affections cluster round you all; a thousand hopes are cherished for you; all good auspices hover over you. Every one of you may take to himself, in this respect, the language of the poet,

" Non sine Dis animosus infans."

Let me, then, say to each of you, " Carpe diem." Art is long and science is profound, and literature, in our day, is variou and extensive. But you have youth, and health, and the means of culture and improvement, and can accomplish great objects. With you it is the bright and breezy morn of life. A long day, I trust, is before you. Let me advise you to be early in prosecuting the great work, which in that day is to be done. Like the morning of the natural day, let the morning of life begin with devotion to the Great Giver of all good; and let every succeeding hour of that life be filled with acts of duty, and friendship, and private and public beneficence. The evening of such life will be full of hopes for a better; and all will be cheered and consoled by

> " that which should accompany old age,
> As honor, love, obedience, troops of friends."

Young Gentlemen, all my good wishes attend you! May you here sow, with liberal broadcast, the seeds of a future harvest of honor to yourselves, gratification to your friends, and usefulness to your country!

RECEPTION AT SAVANNAH.*

AGREEABLY to previous arrangements, at eleven o'clock on the morning of Wednesday, the 26th ultimo, the committee of thirteen waited upon Mr. Webster at his lodgings, and escorted him to the platform erected against the Greene and Pulaski monument, in Monument Square. A very large audience of both sexes was in attendance. We have seldom seen a brighter or more interesting spectacle in this city.

Mr. Webster having taken his place upon the stage, and quiet prevailing among the audience, he was addressed by Mr. Justice Wayne as follows : —

"SIR, — The people of Savannah, mindful of the services which you have rendered to our common country, welcome you to our city. We mean it to be a hearty welcome.

"Unaided by those accidents of fortune which give to some men temporary notoriety, you have achieved for yourself, and mostly in the service of your country, lasting reputation as a jurist, orator, and statesman. But, more than this, and that which we think you value most, you have also, in working your way to such distinction, won as much of the confidence and friendly regards of your contemporaries as in our day any public man can hope to enjoy. Proofs of it have been given to you everywhere. They were awaiting your arrival, if sickness had not shortened your journey, wherever you might have gone. Those kindly influences are worth a thousand other triumphs. It is in such a spirit we now address you, and, if the hundreds in our view could hear my voice, theirs would respond with the same feeling.

"All that you have done, Sir, and the manner in which it has been done, will be told in our history. More than thirty years of public service have identified you with the leading political incidents of that time. Memorable things have happened. The prominent actors in them will be judged, not alone by the parts they may have taken, but by the con-

* From the Savannah Republican of the 3d of June, 1847.

sequences and results of measures. Time removes contemporary mis-construction. Posterity will give its judgment free from the misguiding interests and prejudices of a past generation. History is God's provi-dence in human affairs, and it is a part of it to triumph over error, and to assign to the actors in great events their proper places.

" Yours, Sir, we believe, will be with those master-spirits who framed the Constitution of our Union. It has already made us a great nation and a numerous people. With it, we shall become all that a nation can be ; without it, nothing that a people should be. The effort of your life has been to maintain that Constitution in all that you believe to be its legitimate powers. Others, and some of them our ablest men, differ from you. But whenever those differences have been discussed, you have never failed to gain the respect of those who did not agree with you ; because your own opinions have always been openly avowed, and maintained with signal ability and conceded patriotic intention. All, too, admit that no man has been truer than yourself to the compromises of the Constitution. In the House of Representatives, in the Senate-chamber, in the courts, in your official despatches, and upon popular occasions, at home and elsewhere, when you have spoken, and when it was proper to say so, you have said that these compromises were to be kept as they were meant by the States which ratified it. We do not doubt that you will continue to think and to act so, with all that fervor of feeling with which you once exclaimed, in reference to the union of the States, ' Liberty and Union, now and for ever, one and inseparable.'

" From one of your constitutional suggestions every man in the land has been more or less benefited. We allude to it with the greater pleas-ure because it was in a controversy begun by a Georgian in behalf of the constitutional rights of the citizen. When the late Mr. Thomas Gibbons determined to hazard a large part of his fortune in testing the constitution-ality of the laws of New York, limiting the navigation of the waters in that State to steamers belonging to a company, his own interest was not so much concerned as the right of every citizen to use a coasting license upon the waters of the United States, in whatever way their vessels were propelled. It was a sound view of the law, but not broad enough for the occasion. It is not unlikely that the case would have been decided upon it, even if you had not insisted that it should be put upon the broader constitutional ground of commerce and navigation. The court felt the application and force of your reasoning, and it made a decision releasing every creek and river, lake, bay, and harbor, in our country, from the interference of monopolies, which had already provoked un-friendly legislation between some of the States, and which would have been as little favorable to the interest of Fulton as they were unworthy of his genius.

" Nor must we permit this occasion to pass without noticing your administration of the State Department. We of the South as a very
large portion of your fellow-citizens did everywhere, recognize in what
was then done practical ability remarkably suited to the time of action,
with a comprehensive support of every American interest and right,
domestic and foreign.

" One word more, Sir. The place from which we give you our welcome has been consecrated by us to the memory of Greene and Pulaski.
It is a fit place for a people's welcome to be given to one who has
deserved well of the republic. It reminds us of those Revolutionary
events which excite in all Americans a common sympathy. It should
be cultivated by all of us. It has hitherto resisted the contentions of
interest and the passion of party. And if, at any time hereafter, some
dark cloud shall threaten our harmony, it will be made harmless by
holding up to the people the remembrance of their fathers, united in the
cause of American freedom. Upon our part, we shall never forget that
Georgia gave an early response to the earlier remonstrance of Massachusetts against those acts of Parliament of which she was the immediate victim, but which were levelled against the liberties of all the Colonies. When the language of Suffolk, bolder than any which had been
used before,* proclaimed, for the first time, that the Colonies were only
a part of the realm of England by *compact*, which would be dissolved,
if the acts of which Massachusetts complained were not repealed, it
was repeated here with pledges to our sister Colonies to join them in any
and every measure of resistance. The patriots of Georgia were not
slow in showing that they were in earnest. Their sons, and grandsons,
and great-grandsons, bearing the honors of their paternity gracefully
and unobtrusively, but with all the sympathies of their fathers, are here
to-day to unite with the rest of us to give you our welcome. Accept it,
Sir, and should you, upon your return home, be called upon to tell any
thing of your visit to the South, tell those to whom you may speak that
you have been among a people who, in the real respect which they feel
and have shown to yourself, intended also to manifest their attachment
to their Northern and Eastern brethren, and to show that their prevailing
political feeling is devotion to our Union.

" May God animate all the people of all States with the same sentiment, and impress upon their hearts that it is a duty which we owe to
him, to our fathers, and our posterity, to maintain, defend, and preserve
the Union, and to transmit it entire to future generations ! "

* See resolutions of " the County of Suffolk in the Province of Massachusetts Bay," of the 6th of September, 1774, laid before the Continental Congress
on the 17th of that month.

To this speech Mr. Webster made the following reply.

SIR, — I beg you to believe me duly sensible of the respect paid me by the citizens of Savannah. They have appointed a committee to welcome me, composed of distinguished citizens, and placed at its head a gentleman well known to myself personally and to the public, as filling with equal honor to himself and the country the high station of an Associate Justice of the Supreme Court of the United States.

The topics alluded to in the address just delivered are of great and permanent importance. At their head stands that of the Union of the States, and the Constitution. To such parts of the address as are complimentary to myself, I can of course, beyond the expression of my thanks, make no reply. What most becomes me, certainly, in this respect, is a grateful and respectful silence.

Allow me to say, that no more than justice is done me, in ascribing to me a steady adhesion to the Union of the States, upon the principles and according to the provisions of the Constitution.

I have made this present tour, which has proved so delightful to me while enjoying it, and which will leave so many pleasant reminiscences to dwell upon after my return, for the purpose of visiting those younger sisters of the family of the Old Thirteen whom I had not before known. I heartily rejoice that I have done so, for the reception which has welcomed me has proved that we of the North and the South are still brethren in feeling, and members of the same great political family, bound together by the articles of agreement in our glorious Constitution. He must be a presumptuous man indeed, who would venture to think that he could suggest any new features of improvement, or in any way improve our present form of united government. By its provisions and compromises I stand, as I have ever stood, and woe to the meddling politicians who would assail them in the hope of getting surer and safer guaranties for State rights and State institutions. In itself it is already complete and perfect; any change could only result in marring the harmony of its separate parts. The Constitution was the result of concessions and compromises. It gave to the general government certain specific rights and duties, and it left to the States the free

34 *

exercise of their own appropriate rights, and the unrestricted enjoyment of their own laws and the control of their own social institutions. It has stood the test of experience, and proved itself capable, under a wise administration, of carrying forward the prosperity of the country. Our duty is to be content with the Constitution *as it is*, to resist all changes from whatever quarter, to preserve its original spirit and original purpose, and to commend it, as it is, to the care of those who are to come after us.

In reply to Judge Wayne's handsome allusion to the argument made by me before the Supreme Court, in the suit instituted by Thomas Gibbons, to try the exclusive right of the heirs of Fulton to the exclusive navigation by steam of all the waters within the State of New York, I would observe, that it has been my fortune in the courts of law, as well as in the halls of Congress, to take frequent parts in the discussion of constitutional questions of this character. The case referred to by Judge Wayne is one of them. It is true, that, in the case of Gibbons *v.* Ogden, I declined to argue the cause on any other ground than that of the great commercial question presented by it, — the then novel question of the constitutional authority of Congress *exclusively* to regulate commerce in all its forms, on all the navigable waters of the United States, their bays, rivers, and harbors, without any monopoly, restraint, or interference created by State legislation.

That question I regarded as all-important. Other grounds might have been sufficient for the disposal of this particular cause, but they were of no public or permanent importance. If that great point had then been waived or evaded, it is not easy now to see what inferences unfavorable to the just authority of Congress might have been drawn.

But my agency in this and similar questions before the Supreme Court has been but subordinate; the decision has rested with the court itself. No higher judicial tribunal exists than the Supreme Court of the United States, distinguished alike for the wisdom of its decisions and the eminent qualities of the judges who compose it, both in their private and public capacities. It is the expounder of fundamental principles of government; it is the appointed umpire on questions of the profoundest interest and most enduring consequences between conflicting sovereignties. The American people, if they are wise, will ever cherish it as their most valuable possession, since its duration will be coexistent with that of the Constitution, of which it is the sole interpreter. The decisions of this tribunal have in general commanded public respect and inspired public confidence. Great talents and great learning have adorned its bench. Some of its judgments on questions of great magnitude have manifested unsurpassed ability. Let us hope that its future may resemble its past, and that the same learning and dignity, the same integrity and firmness, which have characterized its decisions in times past, may also distinguish them in times to come.

I beg, Sir, leave also to acknowledge the kindness with which you have noticed the manner in which I have discharged the duties of the Department of State. I held that office but for a short period; during that period, however, the question of the Northeastern Boundary was definitively settled, and an opportunity was afforded for considering and discussing other objects of great interest, which had remained unsettled, and which had become attended with no small difficulty. That opportunity was embraced. I am happy to think that good has been done, and to learn from you that the conduct of that negotiation received the approbation of the citizens of Savannah. There was as much, perhaps, in the favorable circumstances of the occasion, as in any ability manifested in the conduct of the negotiation.

You have alluded, Sir, to the spot where we stand, and the monument which rises before us. It reminds us, indeed, of the days of the Revolution, when State called upon State for aid in the cause of independence. What citizen of Massachusetts can forget the noble response of Georgia to her call? Georgia was then far distant; the wonder-working agency of the telegraph, that annihilates space, was then undreamed of, and long and weary miles of wilderness intervened between the oldest and the youngest of the original Thirteen. But the call was heard and answered. The blood of New England, in her turn, was freely poured out upon Southern soil, and her sons stood shoulder to shoulder with those of Georgia in the common cause. Sons and grandsons of those patriots, whom I now address! Georgians! shall we not cherish the recollection of those common sufferings and common dangers; and make them the incentives towards establishing a more perfect harmony between their descendants? Those whom the dangers and perils of war could not sever, peace should not separate.

Others may value this union of confederated States as a convenience, or an arrangement or a compromise of interests; but I desire to see an attachment to the Union existing among the people, not as a deduction of political economy, nor as a result of philosophical reasoning, but cherished as a heartfelt *sentiment*. I wish to see that attachment extended from one extremity of this confederacy to the other, not by telegraphic communications alone, but through the medium of American sympathies acting upon the American heart. Massachusetts, it is true, cannot vie with Georgia in fertility of soil, abundance of resources, or the boundless facilities of internal improvement, which will render her, at no distant day, one of the mightiest of our confederated States. Seven States like Massachusetts might be carved out of Georgia, and yet abundant room be left for the formation of another State. The natural products of Massachusetts (as a Southern statesman once said) are granite and ice. Many of these stately buildings that tower above me are, I doubt not, indebted to Massachusetts for the granite upon which they are reared. Your lines of railroads, even now stretching almost to the foot of your mountain ranges, beds of entire granite, will soon deprive her of that privilege; but our hyperborean winters will long give us the monopoly of the other article of export, and if we are not destined to be your "hewers of wood and drawers of water," we shall at least be your "*hewers of ice and coolers of water.*"

Never before was I so forcibly impressed with the mighty influence of that great modern discovery, steam-power, as an engine of improvement, as when, during my journey hither, I witnessed the passage of the long train of cars through the dense and gloomy pine forests of your interior, self-moved by an inner power which gave no visible signs of its existence and left no trace behind it, cleaving those solitudes as a bird cuts the air, but urged by a power that could know no weariness and whose energies never flagged. It was a most impressive lesson of the might of man in removing natural impediments from his path of progressive improvement.

Knowing, as I do, the rapid march of improvement in your State, that you have already upwards of seven hundred miles of railroad completed, and much more projected, I cannot but reflect upon the great destinies open to the people of Georgia if they will but improve the opportunities within their power.

This mighty agent, steam, is the handmaid of improvements almost beyond contemplation. Each day develops new blessings to be derived from it. It lessens labor, it economizes time, it gives the poor man leisure and ability to travel, it joins together the most remote regions, and brings their inhabitants face to face, establishing a harmony of interest and feeling between them. It limits all distinctions. The poor and the rich, the prince and the peasant, enjoy now equal facilities of travel, and can procure the same comforts and luxuries from distant points, and, when they travel, they sit side by side in the same rail-car. The individual is sinking, and the mass rising up in the majesty of a common manhood. For a long time after the discovery and use of this potent agent, it was thought only applicable to navigation, and this prejudice retarded the march of improvements, which it might have expedited. For a long series of years a communication between the waters of the Atlantic and the Gulf of Mexico, through the peninsula of Florida, has been thought desirable; but this prejudice prevented it, as a canal was considered necessary for that purpose. But railroads are now taking the place of canals, and the completion of a southwestern railroad from Savannah to Pensacola is only needed to make those two cities respectively the most prosperous in the South, uniting as it would the best seaport on the Southern Atlantic coast, with almost the only good harbor on the Mexican Gulf.

Five-and-twenty years ago, from my place in Congress, I pressed this matter, but the times were not ripe for it then. Now it may be and ought to be carried out, and I pledge to this assembly all the aid and influence that I possess in carrying it into execution, as of infinite value to Georgia and the entire Union.

With a graceful and impressive farewell to the audience who had honored him with their presence and approbation, Mr. Webster, amidst tumultuous applause, concluded his eloquent address, of which our meagre sketch is but the faint reflection.

OPENING OF THE NORTHERN RAILROAD.

OPENING OF THE NORTHERN RAILROAD
TO GRAFTON, N. H.

At the opening of the Northern Railroad from Franklin to Grafton in New Hampshire, on the 28th of August, 1847, a large number of persons from all the adjacent towns were assembled at Grafton to witness the ceremonies of the occasion. Mr. Webster happened to be then at his farm in Salisbury, in the immediate neighborhood; and this fact being known to the company, he was spontaneously called upon, in the most enthusiastic manner, to address them. Mr. Webster readily complied with the unexpected summons, and made the following remarks.

I am very happy, fellow-citizens, to be here on this occasion, to meet here the Directors of the Northern Railroad, the directors of various other railroads connected with it below, and such a number of my fellow-citizens, inhabitants of this part of the State. Perhaps my pleasure and my surprise at the success of this great enterprise so far are the greater, in consequence of my early acquaintance with this region and all its localities.

But, Gentlemen, I see the rain is beginning to descend fast, and I pray you to take shelter under some of these roofs. (Cries of "Go on! go on! Never mind us!")

In my youth and early manhood I have traversed these mountains along all the roads or passes which lead through or over them. We are on Smith's River, which, while in college, I had occasion to swim. Even that could not always be done; and I have occasionally made a circuit of many rough and tedious miles to get over it. At that day, steam, as a motive power, acting on water and land, was thought of by nobody; nor were there good, practicable roads in this part of the State. At that day, one must have traversed this wilderness on horseback or on foot. So late as when I left college, there was no road from river to river for a carriage fit for the conveyance of persons. I well recollect the commencement of the system of turnpike roads. The granting of the charter of the fourth turnpike, which led from Lebanon to Boscawen, was regarded as a wonderful era. The champion in the legislature of this great enterprise was Benjamin J. Gilbert, then a lawyer at Hanover, always a most amiable and excellent man, and now enjoying a healthful old age in the city of Boston. I think he is eighty-four years old. He is well known to the elder inhabitants of this county, and I am glad of this opportunity to allude to him as a highly valued friend of long standing.

I remember to have attended the first meeting of the proprietors of this turnpike at Andover. It was difficult to persuade men that it was possible to have a passable carriage road over these mountains. I was too young and too poor to be a subscriber, but I held the proxies of several absent subscribers, and what I lacked in knowledge and experience I made up in zeal. As far as I now remember, my first speech after I left college was in favor of what was then regarded as a great and almost impracticable internal improvement, to wit, the making of a smooth, though hilly, road from Connecticut River, opposite the mouth of the White River, to the Merrimack River at the mouth of the Contoocook. Perhaps the most valuable result of making these and other turnpike roads was the diffusion of knowledge upon road-making among the people; for in a few years afterward, great numbers of the people went to church, to electoral and other meetings, in chaises and wagons, over very tolerable roads. The next step after turnpikes was canals. Governor Sullivan, Dr. Dexter, Colonel Baldwin, and other eminent citizens of Massachusetts, had planned the Middlesex Canal, connecting the Merrimack River at Pawtucket Falls, near where Lowell now is, with Boston. And a canal was built around those falls also, to complete a water conveyance to Newburyport. Great expense was incurred afterward in locking the various falls higher up the river, until at length the river was made navigable for boats as high up as Concord. This was thought to be a great and most useful achievement, and so indeed it was. But a vastly greater was now approaching, the era of steam. That is the invention which distinguishes this age. The application of steam to the moving of heavy bodies, on the water and on the land, towers above all other inventions of this or the preceding age, as the Cardigan Mountain now before us lifts itself above the little hillocks at its base.

Fellow-citizens, can we without wonder consider where we are, and what has brought us here? Several of this company left Boston and Salem this morning. They passed the Kearsarge on the left, the Ragged Mountain on the right, have threaded all the valleys and gorges, and here they now are at two o'clock at the foot of the Cardigan Hills. They probably went to the market this morning, ordered their dinners, went home to a leisurely breakfast, and set out on their journey hither. Here they now are, enjoying the collation of our hospitable friend, Mr. Cass, at the hour when their families are dining at home. By the way, if they had thought fit, (and it would have been a happy thought,) they might have brought us a few fish taken out of the sea at sunrise this morning, and we might here enjoy as good a fish dinner as our friends are now enjoying at Phillips's Beach or Nahant. This would have been rather striking; — a chowder at the foot of the Cardigan Hills would have been a thing to be talked about.

Fellow-citizens, this railroad may be said to bring the sea to your doors. You cannot, indeed, snuff its salt water, but you will taste its best products, as fresh as those who live on its shores. I cannot conceive of any policy more useful to the great mass of the community than the policy which established these public improvements. Let me say, fellow-citizens, that in the history of human inventions there is hardly one so well calculated as that of railroads to equalize the condition of men. The richest must travel in the cars, for there they travel fastest; the poorest can travel in the cars, while they could not travel otherwise, because this mode of conveyance costs but little time or money. Probably there are in the multitude before me those who have friends at such distances that they could hardly have visited them, had not railroads come to their assistance to save them time and to save them expense. Men are thus brought together as neighbors and acquaintances, who live two hundred miles apart.

We sometimes hear idle prejudices expressed against railroads because they are close corporations; but so from the necessity of the case they necessarily must be, because the track of a railway cannot be a road upon which every man may drive his own carriage. Sometimes, it is true, these railroads interrupt or annoy individuals in the enjoyment of their property; for these cases the most ample compensation ought to be made. I have myself had a little taste of this inconvenience. When the directors of the road resolved to lay it out upon the river (as I must say they were very wise in doing), they showed themselves a little too loving to me, coming so near my farm-house, that the thunder of their engines and the screams of their steam-whistles, to say nothing of other inconveniences, not a little disturbed the peace and the repose of its occupants. There is, beside, an awkward and ugly embankment thrown up across my meadows. It injures the looks of the fields. But I have observed, fellow-citizens, that railroad directors and railroad projectors are no enthusiastic lovers of landscape beauty; a handsome field or lawn, beautiful copses, and all the gorgeousness of forest scenery, pass for little in their eyes. Their business is to cut and to slash, to level or deface a finely rounded field, and fill up beautifully winding valleys. They are quite utilitarian in their creed and in their practice. Their business is to make a good road. They look upon a well-constructed embankment as an agreeable work of art; they behold with delight a long, deep cut through hard pan and rock, such as we have just passed; and if they can find a fair reason to run a tunnel under a deep mountain, they are half in raptures. To be serious, Gentlemen, I must say I admire the skill, the enterprise, and that rather bold defiance of expense, which have enabled the directors of this road to bring it with an easy ascent more than five hundred feet above the level of the Merrimac River. We shall soon see it cross yonder mountainous ridge, commonly called "the Height of Land," and thence pitch down into the fair valley of the Connecticut.

Fellow-citizens, you who live along the line of the road must already begin to feel its beneficial effects. Your country is rather a rough one. There are, indeed, good lands about the base of the Kearsarge, on Beach Hill, Babcock's Hill, and other places adjacent to the road. There are other portions not so fertile. We may infer this from the names they bear. We have come through "Little Gains," "Hard Scrabble," and "Dungeswamp," which latter, I understand, is an Indian word to signify the poorest land in creation. But, fellow-citizens, health and industry, good morals and good government, have made your homes among these mountains prosperous and happy. This great improvement comes to your farther assistance. It will give you new facilities, connect you more readily with other portions of the State, and most assuredly, according to all experience, create new objects for the application of your enterprise and your labor. You do not yet begin to feel the benefits which it will confer on you. I rejoice most heartily that my native State has adopted a policy which has led to these results. I trust that policy may be steadily pursued, till internal improvement in some really and intrinsically useful form shall reach every glen and every mountain-side of the State.

And now, my friends, having thus shortly complied with the wish expressed by you that I should address you in a few words, I take a respectful leave of you, tendering to you all at parting my best wishes for your health and prosperity.

35 *

OPENING OF THE NORTHERN RAILROAD
TO LEBANON, N. H.

On Wednesday, the 17th of November, 1847, the Northern Railroad was farther opened to Lebanon, in New Hampshire. This event was celebrated by a large number of persons who came from Boston for that purpose, and by a great concourse from the neighboring region. The train made a halt at South Franklin for the purpose of taking in Mr. Webster, then on a visit to his farm in that place. A collation had been prepared for the company at Lebanon. At this entertainment, a toast in honor of Mr. Webster was proposed by Charles T. Russell, Esq., of Boston, Chairman of the Committee of Arrangements, to which Mr. Webster responded as follows.

I WISH, Sir, that the gentleman who has done me the honor to propose the toast just given had called upon some other person than myself to address the meeting, and had left me in the position of a listener merely. But I could not properly refrain from expressing my sincere thanks for the manner in which my name has been announced by the president, and received by the assembly. Thus called upon to speak, I cannot disregard the summons. Undoubtedly the present is a moment of great interest, and I now have to perform the pleasing duty of congratulating the directors and stockholders of this road upon the successful completion of their enterprise; and also the citizens residing in this part of the country upon the result which has been witnessed to-day, the entire accomplishment of this most important work. It is an undertaking not only important in itself, but also very important when regarded as a link in the great chain of railroads which is to connect the West with the sea-coast.

For myself, in considering the progress of railroad structures throughout the country, I have been, doubtless many other individuals have been, generally contented with admiring the enterprise manifested, the ingenuity displayed, the industry shown in carrying them forward to completion. But here, on this occasion, there is to me a matter of peculiar interest. Perhaps, and very possibly, this is because the road whose completion is now to be hailed runs not only through New Hampshire, my native State, but also through that part of New Hampshire in which I have a considerable personal interest. This is but natural, for the road passes through my own farm, my own New Hampshire home.

This Northern Railroad is destined to be connected with two other roads of vast importance, each having Montreal for its end. The one will traverse Vermont, passing Montpelier, and proceeding along the valley of the Winooski to Lake Champlain, while the other will extend itself up the valley of the Passumpsic. Each, for the present, has its terminus at Montreal; so that the traveller from the Atlantic coast, arriving at Lebanon, might have a choice to make between the routes. This choice, perhaps, may occasionally be perplexing. The passenger from the coast to the St. Lawrence may not know on which line travel is best, or which is most convenient for his purposes. It may not improbably so happen, that the traveller will compromise the matter, deciding to go on by the one route, and return by the other. So far as I am concerned, both lines have my best wishes for their entire success.

My friend, the presiding officer, has spoken of Burlington and Montreal as the termini of this road. But in point of fact, this is a mere link, a part of a line of land navigation, by steam, from Boston to Ogdensburg, and thence, by land and water, to the Great West. I do not exactly remember whether it was Mr. Gouverneur Morris or Mr. Clinton who said, with regard to the Erie Canal, that the object and aim of that undertaking were to "tap Lake Erie, and draw down its waters to New York harbor." One or the other of these two great men it was, and the design has been carried out. It may not, perhaps, be proper for me to say, that the design of this road, with its extensions, is to tap the St. Lawrence, but it can be asserted, and with truth, that it was to relieve that noble river of a large portion of its great, rich, overwhelming burdens; and deliver its freight, or at least a great part of its freight, at the Atlantic shore, by a more safe, speedy, and cheap conveyance than any before available. That, I imagine, must be clear to all.

Again, no one can fail to perceive how greatly instrumental this road, with its extension, will prove in bringing Ogdensburg near to Boston, — as near, indeed, as Buffalo now is to Albany. This connection between Ogdensburg and the capital of New England would open at once a new thoroughfare for the products of the West, an outlet hitherto untried, through which the commodities of Lake Superior and the other upper lakes may seek and reach the Atlantic by the way of Massachusetts Bay and its chief port. I will not undertake to compare the little city of Boston with the great city of New York, preëminent as New York is, among the cities of America, for her extended commerce and her facilities for its increase. The great city of our neighboring State towers above all rivals in respect to every advantage of commercial position. Let her enjoy all the benefit she can, let her claim all the credit she can from this circumstance. Neither envy nor malice, on my part, shall contribute to rob her of one of her well deserved laurels. But without any very great arrogance, or any very undue exhibition of local pride, we may say that Boston, with her adjacent towns, throughout all the neighboring shore from Hingham to Marblehead, — which extent of country, in effect, is but one seaport, certainly one so far as commercial and manufacturing industry is concerned, — is entitled to command some degree of respect from the whole confederation of our States. Standing, indeed, upon the summit of Bunker Hill, one can look around upon a territory, and a population, equal to that of New York and her immediate suburbs. In fact, from Boston to Newburyport it is all one city; and by the development of her own enterprise, Boston, with her environs, has made herself a rival not lightly to be contemned by any city of the country. I will for one not undertake to estimate the increased extent of her commerce when all the links in her chain of railroad communication shall be completed.

There is another consideration which will commend itself to those who would contemplate the immediate future. It is this, that there will soon be an entire railroad line from New York, through New Haven, Hartford, and Springfield, not only to Boston, but up the valleys of the Connecticut and Passumpsic, to Montreal. It is the impression of many, that land in New England is poor; and doubtless such is the fact with regard to a great portion of it. But throughout the whole United States I do not know of a richer or more beautiful valley, as a whole, than that of the Connecticut River. Parts of it are worth two hundred and fifty dollars an acre for the purpose of cultivation, and there is no land in the West worth half so much. I cannot say so much for the land of the Merrimack valley for cultivation, but that portion of the country is rich in water-power, rich in manufacturing industry, and rich in human energy and enterprise. These are its elements of wealth; and these elements will soon be developed, in a great measure by the means of railroad communication, to a surprising extent. The whole region of country along this line of road, a distance say of about one hundred and twenty miles, will, before our children have ceased to be active among the sons of men, be one of the richest portions of the whole world. Such, I really believe, is the destiny of the Merrimack valley. Rich, not in the fertility of the soil on its banks, but in its almost illimitable water-power, the energy and industry of its people, and the application of these elements to the improvement and extension of productive machinery. It may soon be said of this beautiful river, with even more truth than applied to the poet's glorious lines upon the Thames,—

> " Though with those streams it no resemblance hold,
>   Whose foam is amber and whose gravel gold,
>   Its greater, but less guilty, wealth to explore,
>   Search not its bottom, but survey its shore."

And now what is the particular cause of all the prosperity and wealth which I foresee in this valley? What is it that has chiselled down these Grafton rocks, and made this road which brings my own house so near to the home of my most distant New Hampshire hearer? It is popular industry; it is free labor. Probably there never was an undertaking which was more the result of popular feeling than this. I am told that there are fifteen hundred stockholders in the enterprise, the capital being two millions and a half. That single fact would serve to show the generally diffused interest felt by the people in its success. It is but three or four years since, when, having occasion to visit my farm at Franklin, I observed a line of shingles stretching across my fields. Asking my farmer what was the meaning of all this, I was answered, " It is the line of our railroad." Our railroad! That is the way the people talked about it. I laughed at the idea at first; and, in conversation with a neighbor, inquired what in the world they wanted of a railroad there. " Why," was the reply, " the people want a ride behind the iron horse, and that ride they will have." This day they have had it. The result has proved, not that my friend was too sanguine, but that I was too incredulous.

It is the spirit and influence of free labor, it is the indomitable industry of a free people, that has done all this. There is manifested in its accomplishment that without which the most fertile field by nature must remain for ever barren. Human sagacity, skill, and industry, the zealous determination to improve and profit by labor, have done it all. That determination has nowhere been more conspicuously displayed than here. New Hampshire, it is true, is no classic ground. She has no Virgil and no Eclogues. She has a stern climate and a stern soil. But her climate is fitted to invigorate men, and her soil is covered with the evidences of the comforts of individual and social life. As the traveller pursues his way along her roads, he sees all this. He sees those monuments of civilization and refinement, churches; he sees those marks of human progress, schoolhouses, with children clustering around their doors as thick as bees. And they are bees, except in one respect. The distinction is, that whereas the insect day after day returns to its home laden with the spoils of the field, the human creature is admitted to the hive but once. His mind is furnished with the stores of learning, he is allowed to drink his fill at the fountains of knowledge, his energies are trained in the paths of industry, and he is then sent out into the world, to acquire his own subsistence and help to promote the welfare of his kind.

It is an extraordinary era in which we live. It is altogether new. The world has seen nothing like it before. I will not pretend, no one can pretend, to discern the end; but every body knows that the age is remarkable for scientific research into the heavens, the earth, and what is beneath the earth; and perhaps more remarkable still for the application of this scientific research to the pursuits of life. The ancients saw nothing like it.

The moderns have seen nothing like it till the present generation. Shakspeare's fairy said he would

> " Put a girdle round about the earth
> In forty minutes."

Professor Morse has done more than that; his girdle requires far less time for its traverse. In fact, if one were to send a despatch from Boston by the telegraph at twelve o'clock, it would reach St. Louis at a quarter before twelve. This is what may be called doing a thing in less than no time. We see the ocean navigated and the solid land traversed by steam power, and intelligence communicated by electricity. Truly this is almost a miraculous era. What is before us no one can say, what is upon us no one can hardly realize. The progress of the age has almost outstripped human belief; the future is known only to Omniscience.

In conclusion, permit me to say that all these benefits and advantages conferred upon us by Providence should only strengthen our resolves to turn them to the best account, not merely in material progress, but in the moral improvement of our minds and hearts. Whatsoever else we may see of the wonders of science and art, our eyes should not be closed to that great truth, that, after all, "the fear of the Lord is the beginning of wisdom."

SPEECH AT MARSHFIELD.

INTRODUCTORY NOTE.

The following correspondence explains the occasion of the meeting at Marshfield, at which the following speech was delivered.

> "*Marshfield, Mass., Aug. 2, 1848.*

"HON. DANIEL WEBSTER : —

"Dear Sir, — The undersigned, Whigs and fellow-citizens of yours, are desirous of seeing and conferring with you on the subject of our national policy, and of hearing your opinions freely expressed thereon. We look anxiously on the present aspect of public affairs, and on the position in which the Whig party, and especially Northern Whigs, are now placed. We should be grieved indeed to see General Cass — so decided an opponent of all those measures which we think essential to the honor and interests of the country and the prosperity of all classes — elected to the chief magistracy. On the other hand, it is not to be concealed, that there is much discontent with the nomination made by the late Philadelphia Convention, of a Southern man, a military man, fresh from bloody fields, and known only by his sword, as a Whig candidate for the Presidency.

"So far as is in our humble ability, we desire to preserve the Union and the Whig party, and to perpetuate Whig principles ; but we wish to see also that these principles may be preserved, and this Union perpetuated, in a manner consistent with the rights of the Free States, and the prevention of the farther extension of the slave power ; and we dread the effects of the precedent, which we think eminently dangerous, and as not exhibiting us in a favorable light to the nations of the earth, of elevating a mere military man to the Presidency.

"We think a crisis is upon us ; and we would gladly know how we may best discharge our duties as true Americans, honest men, and good Whigs. To you, who have been so long in public life, and are able from your great experience and unrivalled ability to give us information and advice, and upon whom, as neighbors and friends, we think we have some claims, we naturally look, and we should be exceedingly gratified if, in any way, public or private, you would express your opinion upon interesting public questions now pending, with that boldness and distinctness with which you are accustomed to declare your sentiments. If you can concur with our wishes, please signify to us in what manner it would be most agreeable to you that they should be carried into effect.

"With very great regard, your obedient servants,

"DANIEL PHILLIPS,
GEORGE LEONARD,
GEO. H. WETHERBEE,
and many others."

To this invitation Mr. Webster returned the following reply : —

"*Marshfield, Aug.* 3, 1848.

"GENTLEMEN, — I have received your letter. The critical state of things at Washington obliges me to think it my duty to repair thither immediately and take my seat in the Senate, notwithstanding the state of my health and the heat of the weather render it disagreeable for me to leave home.

"I cannot, therefore, comply with your wishes at present; but on my return, if such should continue to be your desire, I will meet you and the other Whigs of Marshfield, in an unceremonious manner, that we may confer upon the topics to which your letter relates.

"I am, Gentlemen, with esteem and friendship,

"Your obliged fellow-citizen,

"DANIEL WEBSTER.

"To Messrs. DANIEL PHILLIPS, GEORGE LEONARD,
GEO. H. WETHERBEE, and others."

Soon after Mr. Webster's return from Washington, it was arranged that the meeting should take place at the "Winslow House," the ancient seat of the Winslow family, now forming a part of Mr. Webster's farm at Marshfield, on Friday, the first day of September.

SPEECH AT MARSHFIELD.*

ALTHOUGH it is not my purpose, during the present recess of Congress, frequently to address public assemblies on political subjects, I have felt it my duty to comply with your request, as neighbors and townsmen, and to meet you to-day; and I am not unwilling to avail myself of this occasion to signify to the people of the United States my opinions upon the present state of our public affairs. I shall perform that duty, certainly with great frankness, I hope with candor. It is not my intention to-day to endeavor to carry any point, to act as any man's advocate, to put up or put down any body. I wish, and I propose, to address you in the language and in the spirit of conference and consultation. In the present extraordinary crisis of our public concerns, I desire to hold no man's conscience but my own. My own opinions I shall communicate, freely and fearlessly, with equal disregard to consequences, whether they respect myself or respect others.

We are on the eve of a highly important Presidential election. In two or three months the people of this country will be called upon to elect an executive chief magistrate of the United States; and all see, and all feel, that great interests of the country are to be affected, for good or evil, by the results of that election. Of the interesting subjects over which the person who shall be elected must necessarily exercise more or less control, there are especially three, vitally connected, in my judgment, with the honor and happiness of the country. In the first place, the honor and happiness of the country imperatively require that there shall be a chief magistrate elected who shall not plunge

* Delivered at a Meeting of the Citizens of Marshfield, Massachusetts, on the 1st of September, 1848.

36 *

us into further wars of ambition and conquest. In the second place, in my judgment, the interests of the country and the feeling of a vast majority of the people require that a President of these United States should be elected, who will neither use official influence to promote, nor feel any desire in his heart to promote, the further extension of slavery in this community, or its further influence in the public councils. In the third place, if I have any just estimate, if an experience not now a short one in public affairs has enabled me to know any thing of what the public interest demands, the state of the country requires an essential reform in the system of revenue and finance, such as shall restore the prosperity, by prompting the industry and fostering the labor of the country, in its various branches. There are other things important, but I will not allude to them. These three I hold to be essential.

There are three candidates presented to the choice of the American people. General Taylor is the Whig candidate, standing upon the nomination of the Whig Convention; General Cass is the candidate of the opposing and now dominant party in the country; and a third candidate is presented in the person of Mr. Van Buren, by a convention of citizens assembled at Buffalo, whose object, or whose main object, as it appears to me, is contained in one of those considerations which I have mentioned; and that is, the prevention of the further increase of slavery; — an object in which you and I, Gentlemen, so far as that goes, entirely concur with them, I am sure.

Most of us who are here to-day are Whigs, National Whigs, Massachusetts Whigs, Old Colony Whigs, and Marshfield Whigs, and if the Whig nomination made at Philadelphia were entirely satisfactory to the people of Massachusetts and to us, our path of duty would be plain. But the nomination of a candidate for the Presidency made by the Whig Convention at Philadelphia is not satisfactory to the Whigs of Massachusetts. That is certain, and it would be idle to attempt to conceal the fact. It is more just and more patriotic, it is more manly and practical, to take facts as they are, and things as they are, and to deduce our own conviction of duty from what exists before us. However respectable and distinguished in the line of his own profession, or however estimable as a private citizen, General Taylor is a military man, and a military man merely. He has had no training in civil affairs. He has performed no functions of a civil nature under the Constitution of his country. He has been known, and is known, only by his brilliant achievements at the head of an army. Now the Whigs of Massachusetts, and I among them, are of opinion that it was not wise, nor discreet, to go to the army for the selection of a candidate for the Presidency of the United States. It is the first instance in their history in which any man of mere military character has been proposed for that high office. General Washington was a great military character; but by far a greater civil character. He had been employed in the councils of his country from the earliest dawn of the Revolution. He had been in the Continental Congress, and he had established a great character for civil wisdom and judgment. After the war, as you know, he was elected a member of that convention which formed the Constitution of the United States; and it is one of the most honorable tributes ever paid to him, that by that assembly of good and wise men he was selected to preside over their deliberations. And he put his name first and foremost to the Constitution under which we live. President Harrison was bred a soldier, and at different periods of his life rendered important military services. But President Harrison, nevertheless, was for a much greater period of his life employed in civil than in military service. For twenty years he was either governor of a Territory, member of one or the other house of Congress, or minister abroad; and discharged all these duties to the satisfaction of his country. This case, therefore, stands by itself; without a precedent or justification from any thing in our previous history. It is for this reason, as I imagine, that the Whigs of Massachusetts feel dissatisfied with this nomination. There may be other reasons, there are others; they are, perhaps, of less importance, and more easily to be answered. But this is a well-founded objection; and in my opinion it ought to have prevailed, and to have prevented this nomination. I know enough of history to see the dangerous tendency of such resorts to military popularity.

But, if I may borrow a mercantile expression, I may now venture to say, that there is another side to this account. The impartiality with which I propose to discharge my duty to-day requires that it should be stated. And in the first place, it is to be considered, that General Taylor has been nominated by a Whig convention, held in conformity with the usages of the Whig party, and, so far as I know, fairly nominated. It is to be considered, also, that he is the only Whig before the people, as a candidate for the Presidency; and no citizen of the country, with any effect, can vote for any other Whig, let his preferences be what they might or may.

In the next place, it is proper to consider the personal character of General Taylor, and his political opinions, relations, and connections, so far as they are known. In advancing to a few observations on this part of the case, I wish every body to understand that I have no personal acquaintance whatever with General Taylor. I never saw him but once, and that but for a few moments in the Senate. The sources of information are open to you, as well as to me, from which I derive what I know of his character and opinions. But I have endeavored to obtain access to those sources. I have endeavored to inform and instruct myself by communication with those who have known him in his profession as a soldier, in his associations as a man, in his conversations and opinions on political subjects; and I will tell you frankly what I think of him, according to the best lights which I have been able to obtain.

I need not say, that he is a skilful, brave, and gallant soldier. That is admitted by all. With me, all that goes but very little way to make out the proper qualifications for President of the United States. But what is more important, I believe that he is an entirely honest and upright man. I believe that he is modest, clear-headed, of independent and manly character, possessing a mind trained by proper discipline and self-control. I believe that he is estimable and amiable in all the relations of private life. I believe that he possesses a reputation for equity and fair judgment, which gives him an influence over those under his command, beyond what is conferred by the authority of station. I believe that he is a man possessing the confidence and attachment of all who have been near him and know him. And I believe, that, if elected President, he will do his best to relieve the country from present evils, and guard it against future dangers. So much for what I think of the personal character of General Taylor.

I will say, too, that, so far as I have observed, his conduct since he has been a candidate for the office of President has been irreproachable. I hear no intrigue imputed to him, no contumelious treatment of rivals. I do not find him making promises or holding out hopes to any men or any party. I do not find him putting forth any pretensions of his own, and therefore I think of him very much as he seems to think of himself, that he is an honest man, of an independent mind and of upright intentions. And as for the subject of his qualifications for the Presidency, he has himself nothing to say about it.

And now, friends and fellow-townsmen, with respect to his political opinions and relations, I can say at once, that I believe him to be a Whig; I believe him to hold to the main doctrines of the Whig party. To think otherwise would be to impute to him a degree of tergiversation and fraudulent deception, of which I suppose him to be entirely incapable.

Gentlemen, it is worth our while to consider in what manner General Taylor has become a candidate for the Presidency of the United States. It would be a great mistake to suppose that he was made such merely by the nomination of the Philadelphia Convention. He had been nominated for the Presidency in a great many States, by various conventions and meetings of the people, a year before the convention at Philadelphia assembled. The whole history of the world shows, whether in the most civilized or the most barbarous ages, that the affections and admiration of mankind are at all times easily carried away towards successful military achievements. The story of all republics and of all free governments shows this. We know in the case now before us, that so soon as brilliant success had attended General Taylor's operations on the Rio Grande, at Palo Alto, and Monterey, spontaneous nominations of him sprang up.

And here let me say, that, generally, these were Whig nominations. Not universally, but generally, these nominations, made at various times before the meeting of the Philadelphia Convention, were Whig nominations. General Taylor was esteemed, from the moment that his military achievements brought him into public notice, as a Whig general. You all remember, that when we were discussing his merits in Congress, upon the question of giving thanks to the army under his command, and to himself, among other objections, the friends and supporters of Mr. Polk's administration denounced him as being, and because he was, a Whig general. My friends near me, whom I am happy to see here, belonging to the House of Representatives, will remember that a leading man of the party of the administration declared in his place in Congress, that the policy of the administration, connected with the Mexican war, would never prosper, till the President recalled those Whig generals, Scott and Taylor. The policy was a Democratic policy. The argument was, that the men to carry out this policy should be Democratic men. The officers to fight the battles should be Democratic officers, and on that ground, the ordinary vote of thanks was refused to General Taylor, on the part of the friends of the administration.

Let me remark, in the next place, that there was no particular purpose connected with the advancement of slavery entertained, generally, by those who nominated him. As I have said, they were Whig nominations, more in the Middle and Northern than in the Southern States, and by persons who never entertained the slightest desire, by his nomination, or by any other means, to extend the area of slavery of the human race, or the influence of the slaveholding States in the councils of the nation. The Quaker city of Philadelphia nominated General Taylor, the Whigs all over the Union nominated him, with no such view. A great convention was assembled in New York, of highly influential and respectable gentlemen, very many of them well known to me, and they nominated General Taylor with no such view. General Taylor's nomination was hailed, not very extensively, but by some enthusiastic and not very far-seeing people in the Commonwealth of Massachusetts. There were, even among us, in our own State, Whigs quite early enough, certainly, in manifesting their confidence in this nomination; a little too early, it may be, in uttering notes of exultation for the anticipated triumph. It would have been better if they had waited.

Now the truth is, Gentlemen, — and no man can avoid seeing it, unless, as sometimes happens, the object is too near our eyes to be distinctly discerned, — the truth is, that in these nominations, and also in the nomination at Philadelphia, in these conventions, and also in the convention at Philadelphia, General Taylor was nominated exactly for this reason; — that, believing him to be a

Whig, they thought he could be chosen more easily than any other Whig. This is the whole of it. That sagacious, wise, far-seeing doctrine of availability lies at the bottom of the whole matter. So far, then, from imputing any motive to these conventions over the country, or to the convention in Philadelphia, as operating on a majority of the members, to promote slavery by the nomination of General Taylor, I do not believe a word of it, — not one word. I see that one part of what is called the Platform of the Buffalo Convention says that the candidates before the public were nominated under the dictation of the slave power. I do not believe a word of it.

In the first place, a very great majority of the convention at Philadelphia was composed of members from the Free States. By a very great majority they might have nominated any body they chose. But the Free States did not choose to nominate a Free State man, or a Northern man. Even our neighbors, the States of New England, with the exception of New Hampshire and a part of Maine, neither proposed nor concurred in the nomination of any Northern man. Vermont would hear of nothing but the nomination of a Southern and slaveholding candidate. Connecticut was of the same mind, and so was Rhode Island. The North made no demand, nor presented any request for a Northern candidate, nor attempted any union among themselves for the purpose of promoting the nomination of such a candidate. They were content to take their choice among the candidates of the South. It is preposterous, therefore, to pretend that a candidate from the Slave States has been forced upon the North by Southern dictation.

In the next place, it is true that there were persons from New England who were extremely zealous and active in procuring the nomination of General Taylor, but they were men who would cut off their right hands before they would do any thing to promote slavery in the United States. I do not admire their policy, indeed I have very little respect for it, understand that; but I acquit them of bad motives. I know the leading men in that convention. I think I understand the motives that governed them. Their reasoning was this: " General Taylor is a Whig; not eminent in civil life, not known in civil life, but still a man of sound Whig principles. Circumstances have given him a reputation and *éclat* in the country. If he shall be the Whig candidate, he will be chosen; and with him there will come into the two houses of Congress an augmentation of Whig strength. The Whig majority in the House of Representatives will be increased. The Democratic majority in the Senate will be diminished. That was the view, and such was the motive, however wise or however unwise, that governed a very large majority of those who composed the Convention at Philadelphia. In my opinion, this was a wholly unwise policy; it was short-sighted and temporizing on questions of great principles. But I acquit those who adopted it of any such motives as have been ascribed to them, and especially of what has been ascribed to them in a part of this Buffalo Platform.

Such, Gentlemen, are the circumstances connected with the nomination of General Taylor. I only repeat, that those who had the greatest agency originally in bringing him before the people were Whig conventions and Whig meetings in the several States, Free States, and that a great majority of that convention which nominated him in Philadelphia was from the Free States, and might have rejected him if they had chosen, and selected any body else on whom they could have united.

This is the case, Gentlemen, as far as I can discern it, and exercising upon it as impartial a judgment as I can form,— this is the case presented to the Whigs, so far as respects the personal fitness and personal character of General Taylor, and the circumstances which have caused his nomination. If we were weighing the propriety of nominating such a person to the Presidency, it would be one thing; if we are considering the expediency, or I may say the necessity (which to some minds may seem to be the case), of well-meaning and patriotic Whigs supporting him after he is nominated, that is quite another thing.

This leads us to the consideration of what the Whigs of Massachusetts are to do, or such of them as do not see fit to support General Taylor. Of course they must vote for General Cass, or they must vote for Mr. Van Buren, or they must omit to vote at all. I agree that there are cases in which, if we do not know in what direction to move, we ought to stand still till we do. I admit that there are cases in which, if one does not know what to do, he had better not do he knows not what. But on a question so important to ourselves and the country, on a question of a popular election under constitutional forms, in which it is impossible that every man's private judgment can prevail, or every man's private choice succeed, it becomes a question of conscientious duty and patriotism, what it is best to do upon the whole.

Under the practical administration of the Constitution of the United States, there cannot be a great range of personal choice in regard to the candidate for the Presidency. In order that their votes may be effective, men must give them for some one of those who are prominently before the public. This is the necessary result of our forms of government and of the provisions of the Constitution. The people are therefore brought sometimes to the necessity of choosing between candidates, neither of whom would be their original, personal choice.

Now, what is the contingency? What is the alternative presented to the Whigs of Massachusetts? In my judgment, fellow-citizens, it is simply this; the question is between General Taylor and General Cass. And that is the only question. I am no more skilled to foresee political occurrences than others. I judge only for myself. But, in my opinion, there is not the least probability of any other result than the choice of General Taylor or General Cass. I know that the enthusiasm of a new-formed party, that the popularity of a new-formed name, without communicating any new-formed idea, may lead men to think that the sky is to fall, and that larks are suddenly to be taken. I entertain no such expectations. I speak without disrespect of the Free Soil party. I have read their platform, and though I think there are some unsound places in it, I can stand on it pretty well. But I see nothing in it both new and valuable. " What is valuable is not new, and what is new is not valuable." If the term Free Soil party, or Free Soil men, designate those who are fixed, and unalterably fixed, in favor of the restriction of slavery, are so to-day and were so yesterday, and have been so for some time, then I hold myself to be as good a Free Soil man as any of the Buffalo Convention. I pray to know who is to put beneath my feet a freer soil than that upon which I have stood ever since I have been in public life? I pray to know who is to make my lips freer than they always have been, or to inspire into my breast a more resolute and fixed determination to resist the advances and encroachments of the slave power, than has inhabited it since I for the first time

opened my mouth in the councils of the country? The gentlemen at Buffalo have placed at the head of their party Mr.
Van Buren, a gentleman for whom I have all the respect that
I ought to entertain for one with whom I have been associated, in some degree, in public life for many years, and who
has held the highest offices in the country. But really, speaking for myself, if I were to express confidence in Mr. Van Buren and his politics on any question, and most especially this
very question of slavery, I think the scene would border upon
the ludicrous, if not upon the contemptible. I never proposed
any thing in my life of a general and public nature, that Mr.
Van Buren did not oppose. Nor has it happened to me to
support any important measure proposed by him. If he and I
now were to find ourselves together under the Free Soil flag, I
am sure that, with his accustomed good nature, he would laugh.
If nobody were present, we should both laugh at the strange
occurrences and stranger jumbles of political life that should
have brought us to sit down cosily and snugly, side by side, on
the same platform. That the leader of the Free Spoil party
should so suddenly have become the leader of the Free Soil
party would be a joke to shake his sides and mine.

Gentlemen, my first acquaintance in public life with Mr. Van
Buren was when he was pressing with great power the election
of Mr. Crawford to the Presidency, against Mr. Adams. Mr.
Crawford was not elected, and Mr. Adams was. Mr. Van Buren was in the Senate nearly the whole of that administration;
and during the remainder of it he was Governor of the State of
New York. It is notorious that he was the soul and centre,
throughout the whole of Mr. Adams's term, of the opposition
made to him. He did more to prevent Mr. Adams's reëlection
in 1828, and to obtain General Jackson's election, than any
other man, — yes, than any *ten* other men in the country.

General Jackson was chosen, and Mr. Van Buren was appointed his Secretary of State. It so happened that in July, 1829, Mr.
McLane went to England to arrange the controverted, difficult,
and disputed point on the subject of the colonial trade. Mr.
Adams had held a high tone on that subject. He had demanded, on the ground of reciprocity and right, the introduction of
our products into all parts of the British territory, freely, in our
own vessels, since Great Britain was allowed to bring her prod-

uce into the United States upon the same terms. Mr. Adams placed this demand upon the ground of reciprocity and justice. Great Britain would not yield. Mr. Van Buren, in his instructions to Mr. McLane, told him to yield that question of right, and to solicit the free admission of American produce into the British colonies, on the ground of privilege and favor; intimating that there had been a change of parties, and that this favor ought not to be refused to General Jackson's administration because it had been demanded on the ground of right by Mr. Adams's. This is the sum and substance of the instruction.

Well, Gentlemen, it was one of the most painful duties of my life, on account of this, to refuse my assent to Mr. Van Buren's nomination. It was novel in our history, when an administration changes, for the new administration to seek to obtain privileges from a foreign power on the assertion that they have abandoned the ground of their predecessors. I suppose that such a course is held to be altogether undignified by all public men. When I went into the Department of State under General Harrison, I found in the conduct of my predecessor many things that I could have wished had been otherwise. Did I retract a jot or tittle of what Mr. Forsyth had said? I took the case as he had left it, and conducted it upon the principles which he left. I should have considered that I disgraced myself if I had said, " Pray, my Lord Ashburton, we are more rational persons than our predecessors, we are more considerate than they, and intend to adopt an entirely opposite policy. Consider, my dear Lord, how much more friendly, reasonable, and amiable we are than our predecessors."

But now, on this very subject of the extension of the slave power, I would by no means do the least injustice to Mr. Van Buren. If he has come up to some of the opinions expressed in the platform of the Buffalo Convention, I am very glad of it. I do not mean to say that there may not be very good reasons for those of his own party who cannot conscientiously vote for General Cass to vote for him, because I think him much the least dangerous of the two. But, in truth, looking at Mr. Van Buren's conduct as President of the United States, I am amazed to find that he should be placed at the head of a party professing to be, beyond all other parties, friends of liberty and enemies of African slavery in the Southern States. Why, the very first thing that Mr. Van Buren did after he was President was to declare, that, if Congress interfered with slavery in the District of Columbia, he would apply the veto to their bills. Mr. Van Buren, in his inaugural address, quotes the following expression from his letter accepting his nomination: "I must go into the Presidential chair the inflexible and uncompromising opponent of every attempt on the part of Congress to abolish slavery in the District of Columbia against the wishes of the slaveholding States; and also with a determination equally decided to resist the slightest interference with it in the States where it exists." He then proceeds: "I submitted also to my fellow-citizens, with fulness and frankness, the reasons which led me to this determination. The result authorizes me to believe that they have been approved and are confided in by a majority of the people of the United States, including those whom they most immediately affect. It now only remains to add, that no bill conflicting with these views can ever receive my constitutional sanction."

In the next place, we know that Mr. Van Buren's casting vote was given for a law of very doubtful propriety, — a law to allow postmasters to open the mails and see if there was any incendiary matter in them, and if so, to destroy it. I do not say that there was no constitutional power to pass such a law. Perhaps the people of the South thought it was necessary to protect themselves from incitements to insurrection. So far as any thing endangers the lives and property of the South, so far I agree that there may be such legislation in Congress as shall prevent such results.

But, Gentlemen, no man has exercised a more controlling influence on the conduct of his friends in this country than Mr. Van Buren. I take it that the most important event in our time tending to the extension of slavery and its everlasting establishment on this continent, was the annexation of Texas, in 1844. Where was Mr. Van Buren then? Let me ask, Three or four years ago, where was he THEN? Every friend of Mr. Van Buren, so far as I know, supported the measure. The two Senators from New York supported it, and the members of the House of Representatives from New York supported it, and nobody resisted it but Whigs. And I say in the face of the world,

I say in the face of those connected with, or likely to be benefited by, the Buffalo Convention, I say to all of them, that there
has been no party of men in this country which has firmly and
sternly resisted the progress of the slave power but the Whigs.

Why, look to this very question of the annexation of Texas.
We talk of the dictation of the slave power! At least they do,
I do not. I do not allow that any body dictates to me. They
talk of the triumph of the South over the North! There is not
a word of truth or reason in the whole of it. I am bound to say
on my conscience, that, of all the evils inflicted upon us by these
acquisitions of slave territory, the North has borne its full part in
the infliction. Northern votes, in full proportion, have been giv-
en in both houses for the acquisition of new territory, in which
slavery existed. We talk of the North. There has for a long
time been no North. I think the North Star is at last discovered;
I think there will be a North; but up to the recent session of
Congress there has been no North, no geographical section of
the country, in which there has been found a strong, conscientious, and *united* opposition to slavery. No such North has
existed.

Pope says, you know,

" Ask where 's the North? At York, 't is on the Tweed;
    In Scotland, at the Orcades ; and there,
    At Greenland, Zembla, or the Lord knows where."

Now, if there has heretofore been such a *North* as I have described, a North strong in opinion and united in action against
slavery, — if such a *North* has existed anywhere, it has existed
" the Lord knows where," I do not. Why, on this very question
of the admission of Texas, it may be said with truth, that the
North let in Texas. The Whigs, North and South, resisted
Texas. Ten Senators from slaveholding States, of the Whig
party, resisted Texas. Two, only, as I remember, voted for it.
But the Southern Whig votes against Texas were overpowered
by the Democratic votes from the free States, and from New
England among the rest. Yes, if there had not been votes from
New England in favor of Texas, Texas would have been out
of the Union to this day. Yes, if men from New England had
been true, Texas would have been nothing but Texas still.
There were four votes in the Senate from New England, in favor of the admission of Texas, Mr. Van Buren's friends, Dem-

ocratic members : one from Maine ; two from New Hampshire ; one from Connecticut. Two of these gentlemen were confidential friends of Mr. Van Buren, and had both been members of his cabinet. They voted for Texas ; and they let in Texas, against Southern Whigs and Northern Whigs. That is the truth of it, my friends. Mr. Van Buren, by the wave of his hand, could have kept out Texas. A word, a letter, though it had been even shorter than General Cass's letter to the Chicago Convention, would have been enough, and would have done the work. But he was silent.

When Northern members of Congress voted, in 1820, for the Missouri Compromise, against the known will of their constituents, they were called " Dough Faces." I am afraid, fellow-citizens, that the generation of " dough faces " will be as perpetual as the generation of men.

In 1844, as we all know, Mr. Van Buren was a candidate for the Presidency, on the part of the Democratic party, but lost the nomination at Baltimore. We now learn, from a letter from General Jackson to Mr. Butler, that Mr. Van Buren's claims were superseded, because, after all, the South thought that the accomplishment of the annexation of Texas might be more safely intrusted to Southern hands. We all know that the Northern portion of the Democratic party were friendly to Mr. Van Buren. Our neighbors from New Hampshire, and Maine, and elsewhere, were Van Buren men. But the moment it was ascertained that Mr. Polk was the favorite of the South, and the favorite of the South upon the ground I have mentioned, as a man more certain to bring about the annexation of Texas than Mr. Van Buren, these friends of Mr. Van Buren in the North all " caved in," not a man of them stood. Mr. Van Buren himself wrote a letter very complimentary to Mr. Polk and Mr. Dallas, and found no fault with the nomination.

Now, Gentlemen, if they were " dough faces " who voted for the Missouri Compromise, what epithet should describe these men, here in our New England, who were so ready, not only to change or abandon him whom they most cordially wished to support, but did so in order to make more sure the annexation of Texas. They nominated Mr. Polk at the request of gentlemen from the South, and voted for him, through thick and thin, till the work was accomplished, and Mr. Polk elected. For my part, I think that "dough faces" is an epithet not sufficiently reproachful. Such persons are dough faces, with dough heads, and dough hearts, and dough souls; they are *all* dough; the coarsest potter may mould them to vessels of honor or dishonor, — most readily to vessels of *dis*honor.

But what do we now see? Repentance has gone far. There are among these very people, these very gentlemen, persons who espouse, with great zeal, the interests of the Free Soil party. I hope their repentance is as sincere as it appears to be. I hope it is honest conviction, and not merely a new chance for power, under a new name and a new party. But, with all their pretensions, and with all their patriotism, I see dough still sticking on the cheeks of some of them. And therefore I have no confidence in them, not a particle. I do not mean to say, that the great mass of the people, especially those who went to the Buffalo Convention from this State, have not the highest and purest motives. I think they act unwisely, but I acquit them of dishonest intentions. But with respect to others, and those who have been part and parcel in the measures which have brought new slave territory into this Union, I distrust them all. If they repent, let them, before we trust them, do works worthy of repentance.

I have said, Gentlemen, that in my opinion, if it were desirable to place Mr. Van Buren at the head of government, there is no chance for him. Others are as good judges as I am. But I am not able to say that I see any State in the Union in which there is a reasonable probability that he will get the vote. There may be. Others are more versed in such statistics than I am. But I see none, and therefore I think that we are reduced to a choice between General Cass and General Taylor. You may remember, that in the discussions of 1844, when Mr. Birney was drawing off votes from the Whig candidate, I said that every vote for Mr. Birney was half a vote for Mr. Polk. Is it not true that the vote of the Liberty party taken from Mr. Clay's vote in the State of New York made Mr. Polk President? That is as clear as any historical fact. And in my judgment, it will be so now. I consider every Whig vote given to Mr. Van Buren, as directly aiding the election of Mr. Cass. Mark, I say, *Whig* vote. There may be States in which Mr. Van Buren may draw from the other side largely. But I speak of Whig votes, in this State and in any State. And I am of opinion, that any such vote given to Mr. Van Buren inures to the benefit of General Cass.

Now as to General Cass, Gentlemen. We need not go to the Baltimore platform to instruct ourselves as to what his politics are, or how he will conduct the government. General Cass will go into the government, if at all, chosen by the same party that elected Mr. Polk; and he will "follow in the footsteps of his illustrious predecessor." I hold him, I confess, in the present state of the country, to be the most dangerous man on whom the powers of the executive chief magistracy could well be conferred. He would consider himself, not as conservative, not as protective to present institutions, but as belonging to the party of Progress. He believes in the doctrine of American destiny; and that that destiny is, to go through wars, and invasions, and maintain vast armies, to establish a great, powerful, domineering government over all this continent. We know that, if Mr. Cass could have prevented it, the treaty with England in 1842 would not have been made. We know that, if Mr. Cass could have prevented it, the settlement of the Oregon question would not have been accomplished in 1846. We know that General Cass could have prevented the Mexican war; and we know that he was first and foremost in pressing that war. We know that he is a man of talent, of ability, of some celebrity as a statesman, in every way superior to his predecessor, if he should be the successor of Mr. Polk. But I think him a man of rash politics, pushed on by a rash party, and committed to a course of policy, as I believe, not in consistency with the happiness and security of the country. Therefore it is for you, and for me, and for all of us, Whigs, to consider whether, in this state of the case, we can or cannot, we will or will not, give our votes for the Whig nomination. I leave that to every man's conscience. I have endeavored to state the case as it presents itself to me.

Gentlemen, before General Taylor's nomination, I stated always, when the subject was mentioned by my friends, that I did not and could not recommend the nomination of a military man to the people of the United States for the office of President. It was against my conviction of what was due to the best interests of the country, and to the character of the republic. I stated always, at the same time, that if General Taylor should be nominated by the Whig convention, fairly, I should not oppose his election. I stand now upon the same declaration. General Taylor has been nominated fairly, as far as I know, and I cannot, therefore, and shall not, oppose his election. At the same time, there is no man who is more firmly of opinion that such a nomination was not fit to be made. But the declaration that I would not oppose General Taylor, if nominated by the Whig party, was of course subject, in the nature of things, to some exceptions. If I believed him to be a man who would plunge the country into further wars for any purpose of ambition or conquest, I would oppose him, let him be nominated by whom he might. If I believed that he was a man who would exert his official influence for the further extension of the slave power, I would oppose him, let him be nominated by whom he might. But I do not believe either. I believe that he has been, from the first, opposed to the policy of the Mexican war, as improper, impolitic, and inexpedient. I believe, from the best information I can obtain, — and you will take this as my own opinion, Gentlemen, — I believe, from the best information I can obtain, that he has no disposition to go to war, or to form new States in order to increase the limits of slavery.

Gentlemen, so much for what may be considered as belonging to the Presidency as a national question. But the case by no means stops here. We are citizens of Massachusetts. We are Whigs of Massachusetts. We have supported the present government of the State for years, with success; and I have thought that most Whigs were satisfied with the administration of the State government in the hands of those who have had it. But now it is proposed, I presume, on the basis of the Buffalo platform, to carry this into the State elections, as well as into the national elections. There is to be a nomination of a candidate for Governor, against Mr. Briggs, or whoever may be nominated by the Whigs; and there is to be a nomination of a candidate for Lieutenant-Governor, against Mr. Reed, or whoever may be nominated by the Whigs; and there are to be nominations against the present members of Congress. Now, what is the utility or the necessity of this? We have ten members in the Congress of the United States. I know not ten men of any party who are more zealous, and firm, and inflexible in their opposition against slavery in any form.

And what will be the result of opposing their reëlection?

Suppose that a considerable number of Whigs secede from the Whig party, and support a candidate of this new party, what will be the result? Do we not know what has been the case in this State? Do we not know that this district has been unrepresented from month to month, and from year to year, because there has been an opposition to as good an antislavery man as breathes the air of this district? On this occasion, and even in his own presence, I may allude to our Representative, Mr. Hale. Do we want a man to give a better vote in Congress than Mr. Hale gives? Why, I undertake to say that there is not one of the Liberty party, nor will there be one of this new party, who will have the least objection to Mr. Hale, except that he was not nominated by themselves. Ten to one, if the Whigs had not nominated him, they would have nominated him themselves; doubtless they would, if he had come into their organization, and called himself a third party man.

Now, Gentlemen, I remember it to have occurred, that, on very important questions in Congress, the vote was lost for want of two or three members which Massachusetts might have sent, but which, in consequence of the division of parties, she did not send. And now I foresee that, if in this district any considerable number of Whigs think it their duty to join in the support of Mr. Van Buren, and in the support of gentlemen whom that party may nominate for Congress, the same thing will take place, and we shall be without a representative, in all probability, in the first session of the next Congress, when the battle is to be fought on this very slavery question. The same is likely to happen in other districts. I am sure that honest, intelligent and patriotic Whigs will lay this consideration to their consciences, and judge of it as they think they ought to do.

Gentlemen, I will detain you but a moment longer. You know that I gave my vote in Congress against the treaty of peace with Mexico, because it contained these cessions of territory, and brought under the authority of the United States, with a pledge of future admission into the Union, the great, vast, and almost unknown countries of New Mexico and California.

In the session before the last, one of the Southern Whig Senators, Mr. Berrien of Georgia, had moved a resolution, to the effect that the war ought not to be continued for the purposes of conquest and acquisition. The resolution declared that the war with Mexico ought not to be prosecuted by this government with any view to the dismemberment of that republic, or to the acquisition, by conquest, of any portion of her territory. That proposition he introduced into the Senate, in the form of a resolution; and I believe that every Whig Senator but one voted for it. But the Senators belonging to the Locofoco or Democratic party voted against it. The Senators from New York voted against it. General Cass, from the free State of Michigan, Mr. Fairfield, from Maine, Mr. Niles, from Connecticut, and others, voted against it, and the vote was lost. That is, these gentlemen, — some of them very prominent friends of Mr. Van Buren, and ready to take the field for him, — these very gentlemen voted not to exclude territory that might be obtained by conquest. They were willing to bring in the territory, and then have a squabble and controversy whether it should be slave or free territory. I was of opinion that the true and safe policy was, to shut out the whole question by getting no territory, and thereby keep off all controversy. The territory will do us no good, if free; it will be an encumbrance, if free. To a great extent, it will produce a preponderance in favor of the South in the Senate, even if it be free. Let us keep it out, therefore. But no. We will make the acquisition, bring in the territory, and manage it afterwards. That was the policy.

Gentlemen, in an important crisis in English history, in the reign of Charles the Second, when the country was threatened by the accession to the throne of a prince, then called the Duke of York, who was a bigot to the Roman Catholic religion, a proposition was made to exclude him from the crown. Some said that was a very rash measure, brought forward by very rash men; that they had better admit him, and then put limitations upon him, chain him down, restrict him. When the debate was going on, a member is reported to have risen and expressed his sentiments by rather a grotesque comparison, but one of considerable force: —

> "I hear a lion, in the lobby, roar!
> Say, Mr. Speaker, shall we shut the door,
> And keep him out; or shall we let him in,
> And see if we can get him out again?"

I was for shutting the door and keeping the lion out. Other more confident spirits, who are of the character of Van Amburgh, were for letting him in, and disturbing all the interests of the country. When this Mexican treaty came before the Senate, it had certain clauses ceding New Mexico and California to the United States. A Southern gentleman, Mr. Badger, of North Carolina, moved to strike out those clauses. Now you understand, that if a motion to strike out a clause of a treaty be supported by one third, it will be struck out; that is, two thirds of the Senate must vote for each clause, in order to have it retained. The vote on this question of striking out stood 38 to 14, not quite one third being against the cession, and so the clause was retained. And why were there not one third? Just because there were four New England Senators voting for these new territories. That is the reason.

I hope I am as ardent an advocate for peace as any man living; but I would not be carried away by the desire for peace to commit an act which I believed highly injurious, likely to have consequences of a permanent character, and indeed to endanger the existence of the government. Besides, I believed that we could have struck out the cessions of territory, and had peace just as soon. And I would be willing to go before the people and leave it to them to say, whether they would carry on the war any longer for acquisition of territory. If they would, then they were the artificers of their own fortunes. I was not afraid of the people on that subject. But if this course had continued the war somewhat longer, I would have preferred that result, rather than that those territories lying on our southern border should come in hereafter as new States. I should speak, perhaps, with more confidence, if some Whigs of the North had not voted for the treaty. My own opinion was then clear and decisive. For myself I thought the case a perfectly plain one, and no man has yet stated a reason to convince me to the contrary.

I voted to strike out the articles of cession. They would have been struck out if four of the New England Senators had not voted against the motion. I then voted against the ratification of the treaty, and that treaty would have failed if three New England Senators had not voted for it, and Whig Senators too. I should do the same thing again, and with much more resolution I would have run a still greater risk, I would have endured a still greater shock, I would have risked any thing, rather than have been a participator in any measure which should have a tendency to annex Southern territory to the States of the Union. I hope it will be remembered, in all future time, that on this question of the accession of these new territories of almost boundless extent, I voted against them, and against the treaty which contained them, notwithstanding all inducements to the contrary, and all the cries, which I thought hasty and injudicious, of " Peace! Peace on any terms!" I will add, that those who voted against the treaty were gentlemen from so many parts of the country, that its rejection would have been an act rather of national than of local resistance. There were votes against it from both parties, and from all parties, the South and the West, the North and the East. What we wanted was a few more New England votes.

Gentlemen, after I had the honor of receiving the invitation to meet my fellow-citizens, I found it necessary, in the discharge of my duty, though with great inconvenience to my health, to be present at the closing scenes of the session. You know what there transpired. You know the important decision that was made in both houses of Congress, in regard to Oregon. The immediate question respected Oregon, or rather the bill respected Oregon, but the question more particularly concerned these new territories. The effect of the bill as passed in the Senate was to establish these new territories as slaveholding States. The House disagreed. The Senate receded from their ground, and the bill passed, establishing Oregon as a free Territory, and making no provision for the newly acquired territories on the South. My vote, and the reasons I gave for it, are known to the good people of Massachusetts, and I have not heard that they have expressed any particular disapprobation of them.

But this question is to be resumed at the first session of the next Congress. There is no probability that it will be settled at the next session of this Congress. But at least at the first session of the next Congress this question will be resumed. It will enter at this very period into all the elections of the South.

And now I venture to say, Gentlemen, two things; the first well known to you, that General Cass is in favor of what is called the Compromise Line; and is of opinion that the Wilmot Proviso, or the Ordinance of 1787, which excludes slavery from territories, ought not to be applied to territories lying south of 36° 30'. He announced this before he was nominated, and if he had not announced it, he would have been 36° 30' farther off from being nominated. In the next place, he will do all he can to establish that compromise line; and lastly, which is a matter of opinion, in my conscientious belief, he will establish it.

Give him the power and the patronage of the government, let him exercise it over certain portions of the country whose representatives voted on this occasion to put off that question for future consideration; let him have the power of this government with his attachments, with his inducements, and we shall see the result. I verily believe, that unless there is a renewed strength, an augmented strength of Whig votes in Congress, he will accomplish his purpose. He will surely have the Senate, and with the patronage of the government, with every interest which he can bring to bear, coöperating with every interest which the South can bring to bear, he will establish the compromise line. We cry safety before we are out of the woods, if we feel that the danger respecting the territories is over.

Gentlemen, I came here to confer with you as friends and countrymen, to speak my own mind and hear yours; but if we all should speak, and occupy as much time as I have, we should make a late meeting. I shall detain you no longer. I have been long in public life, longer, far longer than I shall remain there. I have had some participation for more than thirty years in the councils of the nation. I profess to feel a strong attachment to the liberty of the United States, to the Constitution and free institutions of this country, to the honor, and I may say the glory, of my native land. I feel every injury inflicted upon it, almost as a personal injury. I blush for every fault which I think I see committed in its public councils, as if they were faults or mistakes of my own. I know that, at this moment, there is no object upon earth so much attracting the gaze of the intelligent and civilized nations of the earth as this great republic. All men look at us, all men examine our course, all good men are anxious for a favorable result to this great experiment of republican liberty. We are on a hill and cannot be hid. We cannot withdraw ourselves either from the commendation or the reproaches of the civilized world. They see us as that star of empire which half a century ago was represented as making its way westward. I wish they may see it as a mild, placid, though brilliant orb, moving athwart the whole heavens to the enlightening and cheering of mankind; and not as a meteor of fire and blood, terrifying the nations.

SPEECH IN FANEUIL HALL

PREVIOUS TO

THE ELECTION IN 1848.

Once again, friends and fellow-citizens, once again, and quite unexpectedly, I find myself in Faneuil Hall. And I feel all the recollections of the past pathering upon me. I hear a thousand voices, silent elsewhere, but always speaking here, admonishing me, and admonishing you, who do me the honor to be here, to perform the whole duty which we owe to our country. I come here to-day, in obedience to an authority which I must always respect, the wishes of the people of Boston, and the Whigs of the Commonwealth, to express to them my opinions upon the present state of the internal affairs of the country, the concerns of business and the occupations of men, and their prospects for the future; and I proceed, without further preface, to the performance of that duty.

THE ELECTION IN 1815.

An election of President and Vice-President of the United States is now pending, and a choice of members to a Congress is already in progress. It is in vain to disguise the fact, that the result of these elections must produce a decided effect, for good or for evil, upon the interests of men and their prospects at the present moment, and upon the prospects which lie beyond the present. There are, in fact, Gentlemen, but two candidates for the Presidency, General Taylor, the Whig candidate, and General Cass, the Democratic candidate. As to the support of another gentleman, which some of our friends, I am sorry to say, have embraced and still pursue, I regard it as a military movement of the plainest and least imposing character. And if the subject were not solemn, and the occasion solemn, I should say it was a very much of a diversion, also, in the ordinary acceptation of that term.

* A Speech delivered in Faneuil Hall, on the 24th of October, at a general meeting of the Whigs of Boston and the vicinity, previous to the Presidential Election.

SPEECH IN FANEUIL HALL.*

ONCE again, friends and fellow-citizens, once again, and quite unexpectedly, I find myself in Faneuil Hall. And I feel all the recollections of the past gathering upon me. I hear a thousand voices, silent elsewhere, but always speaking here, admonishing me, and admonishing you, who do me the honor to be here, to perform the whole duty which we owe to our country. I come here to-day, in obedience to an authority which I must always respect, the wishes of the people of Suffolk and the Whigs of the Commonwealth, to express to them my opinions upon the present state of the internal affairs of the country, the concerns of business and the occupations of men, and their prospects for the future; and I proceed, without preface, to the performance of that duty.

An election of President and Vice-President of the United States is now pending, and a choice of members for the new Congress is already in progress. It is in vain to disguise, that the result of these elections must produce a decided effect, for good or for evil, upon the interests of men and their pursuits, at the present moment, and upon the prospects which lie beyond the present. There are, in fact, Gentlemen, but two candidates for the Presidency, General Taylor, the Whig candidate, and General Cass, the Democratic candidate. As to the support of another gentleman, which some of our friends, I am sorry to say, have embraced and still pursue, I regard it, in a military sense of the phrase, as a mere diversion; and if the subject were not solemn, and the occasion solemn, I should say it was very much of a diversion, also, in the ordinary acceptation of that term.

* A Speech delivered in Faneuil Hall, on the 24th of October, at a general meeting of the Whigs of Boston and the vicinity, previous to the Presidential Election.

38 *

There are, fellow-citizens, two candidates, and no more; and the election of one or the other, accompanied with a correspondent election in point of political character of members of Congress, will produce one or the other, respectively, of two results; and those results regard the present state of the business of the country, as it is affected by two acts of recent legislation. If General Taylor be elected President, and if there be, to sustain his measures, a Whig Congress, there are two existing laws of the country which will be essentially modified, or altogether repealed. I mean those commonly called the sub-treasury law and the tariff of 1846. If, on the other hand, General Cass be chosen, and a Congress elected, at the same time, to sustain his views of the public interests, both of these existing laws will be continued in force.

Gentlemen, I saw this morning a speech delivered lately in Washington by the present Secretary of State, Mr. Buchanan, a gentleman who is among the first, if not the very first, of his party, in point of character and standing in the country. Differing from most of the sentiments in this speech, I still do its author the credit and justice to say, that it is a manly speech. He says, having first paid a just, and no more than a just, tribute of respect to the military character, good sense and strong understanding, and the upright and pure motives of General Taylor, he says of him, nevertheless, that he is a Whig, and that being himself a Whig, if elected President by the Whigs, and surrounded, as he will be, by a Whig Cabinet, he must, from the necessity of his position, carry into effect Whig principles and Whig measures; and that he would be faithless to his friends and his party if he did not do that. I agree to all this, Gentlemen, and I believe that he would be prompted to Whig principles and Whig measures, not more by the necessities of his position, than from what I believe to be his deep conviction of the policy, propriety, justice, and soundness of those principles.

Well, Gentlemen, as Mr. Buchanan has stated one side of the case fairly, allow me to state the other. And I may say, upon the other hand, if General Cass be elected President, and a corresponding Congress be at the same time elected, he will carry out the Democratic platform of Baltimore, he will exert the influence of his office in favor of the sub-treasury and the tariff of

1846. He will follow the bright example of him whom he so much commends, Mr. Polk, and whatever, in the same career of legislation, Mr. Polk has left undone, General Cass will be on hand to do. So that it brings us exactly, as practical men, as men who are not carried away by theories, as men who do not attach all degree and all manner of importance to one single idea, as men who regard the various interests of the country, now and hereafter, to this position, to give our suffrages and our support heartily and cordially to General Taylor, or to consent to the election of General Cass.

Ought these measures, to which I have thus referred, to be further prolonged or continued, or ought they now to be repudiated, — to be set aside, and to give place to other and wiser measures of government? That is the question pending. And to begin with what is called the sub-treasury system. Ought that to be continued? Is it useful? Do the business men of the community find a benefit in it? Do the laboring classes find it to protect their interests? In short, does government find it convenient for its own purposes?

But before we consider what the results of the pending election may be, it may be well to understand what is the present state of the country, in regard to the business and occupations of men.

On that point, Gentlemen, I might, with great propriety, ask for information from you. And what I have to say upon it, I say with deference to your knowledge and experience. What, then, is the present state of things? I suppose I may answer, that there is a very unusual scarcity of money, or high price of money, in the community at the present moment; that it has lasted a very unusual length of time; that it has now continued for more than twelve months, without any apparent abatement. I suppose I may say, that there is a great depression of industry and stagnation of business, and discouragement to the occupations of men. I suppose I may say, with truth, that there is a diminished demand for manufacturing labor, and a great and increasing diminution in its reward. Is this a true, though brief, presentation of the actual state of things?

There are before me hundreds of men who, with some capital, like all other men of business, have occasion also, at times, for loans and discounts. Do they find, and do they admit, and do they feel, that money is scarce and dear? Do they find, in the daily operations of affairs in their own sphere of active life, that they are embarrassed on account of this dearness of money? All that I suppose every body can answer for himself. I suppose it is too notorious to be doubted for a moment; and having put this question to the active, industrious classes of society, engaged in trade and manufactures, and expecting to receive, if they were to speak, but one answer from them all, I would, in the next place, put the question to the rich men of the country, to the capitalists, to the men who have money to lend. I would ask them whether good notes are not now to be had at what they consider a *satisfactory* rate of discount; and I should expect to receive from them a very cheerful and satisfied answer.

In my judgment, Gentlemen, for a whole year back, the rich have been growing richer and richer; the active and industrious classes have been more and more embarrassed; and the poor have been growing poorer and poorer, every day throughout the whole year. And in my judgment, further, so long as this sub-treasury lasts, so long as the present rate of duties and customs lasts, that is to say, so long as the tariff of 1846 continues, this state of accumulation by the rich, of distress of the industrious classes, and of the aggravated poverty of the poor, will go on from degree to degree, to an end which I shall not attempt to calculate.

In the first place, Gentlemen, as to this constitutional sub-treasury, I look upon it as one of the strangest fantasies, as one of the greatest deceptions, and as one of the least plausible political delusions, ever produced by party power and party management. Is there a civilized and commercial country in the world that knows any such thing as locking up in chests and boxes, under bolts and bars, the public treasury? Is there any civilized people upon the earth, that separates the interest of the government, in respect to currency and money, from the interests of the people? Is there any such thing known in England, or France, or wherever a spirit of commerce has pervaded the people? If there is, I am ignorant of it.

And now, historically, let me ask, How did it arise, and what is its origin? It is all very plain, and soon told. General Jackson had a controversy with the Bank of the United States, in which the public moneys were deposited. He withdrew those public moneys from the Bank of the United States in the year 1833. How, then, should the public moneys be kept? He did not see fit to leave them as they were before there were banks, in the hands of collectors, to be drawn as wanted, but he adopted an "experiment," as he called it at the time, and placed them in deposit banks. That experiment failed in 1836 and 1837; and with a great explosion, these State deposit banks blew up.

By this time, Mr. Van Buren had come into office, and summoned an extra session of Congress, which assembled in September, 1837; and Mr. Van Buren and his counsellors produced on that day, as an original idea, — and it was altogether original, — as of their own invention, — and it was of their own invention, for in that respect they stole no man's thunder, — they produced this project of what they called a constitutional treasury, or sub-treasury, which was to lock up in the chests of the government every dollar which the government received, until it should be called for again by the government, thus abstracting it from the business of society, and obstructing all commercial proceedings as far as so much capital is concerned.

That system prevailed. The country tried it. It lasted during Mr. Van Buren's administration; and you and I, and all other Whigs in the country, exerted ourselves to expose the bad character, the uselessness, the inconvenience, and the mischievous operation of this sub-treasury; and upon that, the Whigs of the country turned Mr. Van Buren out of office. Yes, Gentlemen, there was no question which had more to do with the overthrow of Mr. Van Buren's administration and the election of General Harrison, in November, 1840, than this very question of the sub-treasury. Do we not all know that?

And now, by the way, if it be by the way and not too far out of the way, what are we Whigs requested to do by many members of the community, and, I am sorry to say, by some of our own party? We are requested to take back Mr. Van Buren, sub-treasury and all. We are requested to pass judgment against ourselves for our decision in 1840. And I see men in this Commonwealth, individuals, — but, thank Heaven, they are not a great number, — who, at the period of that discussion, in Congress and out of Congress, with a voice as distinct as mine, and talents far greater, opposed, decried, and condemned the sub-treasury system, as the greatest evil any government could inflict upon a commercial people, such as ours; I see them now taking Mr. Van Buren, sub-treasury and all, and locking him up in their embrace as fast as they can.

Gentlemen, I see with regret, that some of those who have been with us, — been with us here, been with us in the presence of these portraits of great men which hang around us, — denouncing, as we denounced, the policy of the government of Mr. Van Buren's time, upholding, as we endeavored to uphold, the necessity of a proper medium of currency for the people as well as the government, and the necessity of a fair tariff that should protect the industry of the laboring classes, — I see with pain and grief, that some gentlemen of that class now say that these are all "bygone" questions, and "obsolete," and not fit to be revived. In my judgment, that is a position unworthy of these gentlemen. We say, on the contrary, that here the substantial issues are the same. It is this sub-treasury which we would oppose, this tariff of 1846, which we felt as a millstone tied around our necks, as it has proved itself little else; these are still the things to be got rid of.

And those gentlemen who choose to say that these questions are sunk, overwhelmed, and forgotten in the presence of the "one idea," — such gentlemen mistake the sentiments of the people of Massachusetts. Why, let us again hear the friend of Mr. Polk (Mr. Buchanan) in his recent speech at Washington, a gentleman, certainly, who has as much right to speak for his party as any other man in the country. He puts the questions to be just such as they were in 1840, or rather in 1844. He says that the issue is between the party that will uphold this noble sub-treasury, and this glorious tariff of 1846, and those who would sacrilegiously destroy both the one and the other.

But here our brethren who take leave of us say that there is no difficulty about a tariff, — that every body agrees that we must have a tariff. But what sort of a tariff? They might as well say every body agrees that we must have a form of government; but what sort of government? Every body believes it will be some sort of weather to-morrow, but what sort of weather? Fair or foul? No, Gentlemen, these questions are inherent in our different views of policy. One side of them belongs to the Whigs, because they are Whigs, and the other side to our opponents, because they are opponents to Whigs; and so long as there shall be Whigs, and opponents to Whigs, upon questions which have lasted from the days of Washington, let me say, so long will this tariff question be important and distinctive. I say again, Mr. Buchanan is manly and fair. He does not go about now, as he or his friends did in 1844, to tell the people of Pennsylvania that they shall have a good tariff and specific duties. He does not say that their candidate is more of a tariff man than the Whig candidate. If he did not say this in 1844, his political friends said it. He says now the sub-treasury is a noble institution; and he speaks of the present existing tariff as a system that has answered all the purposes and sustained the business of the country. I am glad to say that there is no more equivocation; that the question is put fairly to us in Massachusetts, fairly to Pennsylvania, fairly to the Union, respecting the sub-treasury and the manner of disposing of the moneys of the government, and between the tariff of 1846 and something like the tariff of 1842, that is to say, a protective tariff.

Now, Gentlemen, I may be permitted to say, before going on to other things, that this sub-treasury, the invention of Mr. Van Buren, is still his favorite. As far as I remember, it has received no rebuke at the Buffalo Convention; and I believe, with all respect, that that Buffalo platform was constructed of such slight materials, that, while it would not bear a very heavy tread, it would sustain the fox-like footsteps of Mr. Van Buren. The creed was drawn up and made such as he could sign. And now, what is in point of fact the operation of this sub-treasury system? I am quite aware that I speak here in presence of merchants, manufacturers, and men of business, who understand it a great deal better than I do; but I shall state its actual operation, as far as I can inform myself of it. I am not now about to argue either against the sub-treasury or against the tariff of 1846. These measures have been the law of the land now for two years, and all men of business have had a taste of their effects. All I propose to-night is to bring them to the trial, to inquire into their actual operations, and see whether they have fulfilled the promises of their friends, either by doing good or averting evil.

And instead of going into general principles and statements, I have thought it would be more satisfactory to you, and more convenient to myself, to present to you the operation of this sub-treasury system in the great city of New York; because we know that New York is the great centre of the money market, as well as the great emporium of foreign commerce. I have been at some pains to investigate the matter, and I will state the results as I have learned them. The truth is this: when money is plenty, the sub-treasury is only a ludicrous, bungling, and annoying thing, forcing men of business to move about bags and kegs of specie, when the business would be just as well done by the passing of bank-notes. When money is plenty, it is only expensive, bungling, useless, annoying, and ridiculous; but the moment that, by the exportation of specie, or whatever other cause, money becomes scarce, and the exigencies of the business community begin to press, then it is not merely a harmless and ludicrous engine; it becomes then a means of torture and distress, because its inevitable effect, when money is scarce, is to make it scarcer, and when it is difficult to be had, to increase that difficulty.

I find that on the 25th day of August last, the commercial banks in the city of New York had in their vaults $5,800,000 in coin. That was the basis upon which they made their issues for the accommodation of the mercantile world. The sub-treasury had at that time in its vaults, in the same city, fourteen hundred thousand dollars. In the course of events, within one month that relation was greatly changed; for on the 29th of September the banks had but forty-six hundred thousand dollars, while the sub-treasury had increased its amount to twenty-four hundred thousand. Thus, in a few days more than a month, the banks parted with twelve hundred thousand dollars of specie, and the sub-treasury obtained the additional sum of one million. This change in the relation between the amounts of money in these respective depositories at once created a great scarcity of money; for every body knows that the specie or coin in the banks is the only safe basis for their circulation; and as, in this case, the banks in one month lost twelve hundred thousand dollars of coin, they must, of course, draw in their circulation, not merely to replace the twelve hundred thousand dollars, but to replace all that portion of their circulation represented by that amount. All practical mercantile men understand this. If

a bank loses a certain quantity of specie, it must curtail its discounts, not to the same extent, but to three or four times that
extent. I know that the proportion may be stated as three
to one, but it is more likely to exceed that proportion than to
fall short of it. Then this withdrawal of so large a sum as
twelve hundred thousand dollars would naturally lead to a curtailment by the banks. That is one turn of the sub-treasury
screw, and how many more such turns will it take to put the patient in perfect torture? The depression of business in the city
of New York, resulting from this curtailment, led, I suppose, to
the order of the Secretary of the Treasury, by which, by a certain
kind of habeas corpus writ, he should free from the sub-treasury
a certain sum, eight hundred thousand dollars, and, in its place,
put in confinement a quantity of treasury-notes. I have not examined the question, and will not therefore say that the proceedings are illegal. But it seems that the Secretary of the Treasury found that the government were not masters of the machinery, or else it was not a machine that any master could work.

This very operation, then, led to the necessary contraction of
three and a half or four millions of dollars in the commercial
business of the city of New York. Now this demand of the
sub-treasury could be made in a day, and when made in one
day or one week, it must be answered in one day or one week.
But then no banks could make the curtailment in one day or one
week or one month, to such an extent, without greatly distressing
the community. What is the consequence? The consequence
is, inevitably, to inspire mistrust and apprehension among those
who manage these institutions; to restrain them from what they
would otherwise do, for fear that events should show that they
have acted imprudently, if not even incurred great danger of ruin.
The merchants and dealers of the country, the superintend-
ents of banks, here and elsewhere, keep an accurate account of
the imports and exports of specie, the imports and exports of
goods, of the balance of trade, and can prepare for a change, because a shock of that sort does not come like lightning, — they
have some premonition of it. But who can calculate beforehand what will be the demands of the government, or what, in
a particular day or week, will be the amount of imports on
which the duties must be paid in coin? Who can foresee how
many vessels will arrive in a day or a week, and, out of this

money now in the vaults of the bank, what quantity may be demanded in an hour? Therefore there is a constant apprehension and fear. The consequence of this is a fluctuation from day to day in the money market, not from good to bad, but from bad to worse; then, perhaps, down again from worse to not quite so bad, but oftener up still further, to a degree of scarcity which is quite unexampled in the history of this country.

Gentlemen, upon this subject let me show you how I, with my partial means of information and my limited intercourse with men of business here in the capital of New England, — with some degree of acquaintance with men of business in the commercial emporium of the country, New York, — how far I differ from the great authority to which I have just alluded, Mr. Buchanan. In his speech four or five days ago, he said, " Where, since the Almighty first placed man upon the earth, has there been any nation to compare with ours in rapid and substantial improvement? " I say nowhere; I answer that question readily. " It has now become the wonder as well as the model of the world"; and I hope it will continue to be so. " Our prosperity has known no ebb in its sweeping course, except from the expansions and contractions of our paper currency, and the individual ruin which this has occasioned. For these temporary revulsions, we are indebted to Whig policy. And even for them, to a great extent, Democracy has found a preventive in the much-abused independent treasury." The independent treasury, then, is a preventive against expansions and fluctuations in the currency, against the course of things that makes money easy to-day and hard to-morrow. " Whilst this restrains wild speculation and over-trading on the part of banks and individuals, it has at the same time afforded the best and surest protection to domestic manufactures, a great and growing interest which must be ever dear to the country." Now, if the commercial interest and manufacturing interest see these things as Mr. Buchanan sees them, then nobody has a right to complain. If they see that the sub-treasury prevents fluctuations, instead of producing them; if they see that this sub-treasury has protected the interests of manufactures; if they see that, under the operation of this sub-treasury and the tariff of 1846, the iron mills are all flourishing, the woollen mills all going on, everywhere, in great prosperity, — if they see all that, then Mr. Buchanan is entirely right.

These remarks of Mr. Buchanan contain two propositions. One is, that the sub-treasury has in fact prevented fluctuations. Now, for one, I should say that, within my recollection, there has never been so great a fluctuation in the money market as we have witnessed for the last two years. Many of you have memories long enough to go back and review, in your own minds, the transactions of the past fifteen years. Did you ever know such great fluctuations in the value of money as you have witnessed in the last two years, with the exception that its fluctuations have generally been between prices always high?

The next proposition is, that protection to manufactures is afforded by the sub-treasury. So Mr. Buchanan says; but I can hardly think it is quite respectful to the intelligence and understanding of this community to hold or announce such a doctrine. I should think he supposed us ready to swallow camels of any size. The sub-treasury foster manufactures! The tariff of 1846 foster manufactures! Then why do they not prosper? Thus fostered and protected, how many of them have, within the last six months, sunk away and come to nothing? Among our most important manufactures here at the North, essential to the prosperity of the country and employing large capital, do we not see them sinking away every day? What, then, is the result of that fostering care, and the operation of these fostering laws?

Gentlemen, there is another consideration connected with this sub-treasury. Three fourths of all the importations from Europe are on foreign account; our importing merchants know nothing about them. If you go to State Street in Boston, or Wall Street in New York, and ask what importations are coming, they tell you they do not know. It is asserted, and I believe it is true beyond question, that three fourths of our importations from Europe are sent to this country on foreign account, consigned to commission merchants. They are sold, and their proceeds are remitted, and our merchants know no more of their probable coming or their amount than any body else. Therefore there is no knowledge among us, and can be no knowledge among us, of what will be the state of the money market; for when they arrive, the duties must be paid immediately, thus placing it in the power of foreign consignors of goods coming to this country to depress the money market at pleasure.

They may transfer from the banks into the sub-treasury, there to be locked up, an amount of money responsive to any importations they may choose to make.

I have spoken of the sub-treasury at New York. I have not inquired particularly into the state of the banks, and the operation upon them and their circulation of the sub-treasury, in this city. I suppose it probable that there may be four or five hundred thousand dollars now locked up in the sub-treasury in Boston, say half a million. Well, now if that were retained as the basis of bank circulation, under the ordinary terms and conditions which make such a circulation safe, it would enable the banks to make an issue of a million and a half of money, besides what is now in circulation. As it is, it answers no useful purpose in the community, but rather inspires terror and distrust, and, for all the uses of commerce, it would be just as well that it did not exist at all.

I have said that I supposed that money has not been known to be dearer for a long time. I suppose that, if we take the quantity loaned by the banks at the rate of interest to which they are limited, and if we then take the rates known to have been paid by private borrowers to private lenders last year, the rate of interest for the last twelve months, on the whole, can hardly be considered under ten per cent. Now, we have to carry on the business of the country, I mean the men of business have to do so, with money at this rate, while in England it certainly is not worth quite half so much. Therefore a man of business in the United States, at this moment, who has some capital, and at the same time, like most men, has occasion sometimes for bank facilities and to borrow money, pays twice as much as a man of the same circumstances pays for the like facilities in England. Every man can see the result of this.

I leave the sub-treasury, and turn to the tariff of 1846. Certainly I shall not argue now against that tariff; I shall not now discuss its apparent defects and its inconsistency with established principles. On another occasion and in another place, I went through all that, with very little success. It is the law of the land; it has been in operation for two years. But let me say, that it is a measure new to the history of the commercial world in modern times. It is a tariff of duties altogether *ad valorem*, with no specifications, with no just discrimination in favor of domestic industry and products.   If any body can find a tariff like that, let it be produced.   When under discussion in the Senate, we said all we could against it, and we said some pretty provoking things, but there was not a word uttered in its support.   Its friends maintained a most judicious silence.   One of them arose, and by an almost unnatural force of speech cried out, " The tariff will vindicate itself," and sat down.

Now we appeal to you, whether this tariff has vindicated itself; whether it has answered its ends; whether it is of the character ascribed to it.   I say, on the contrary, that it is purely a party measure.   I do not know but in the House of Representatives, here and there, a man straggling from his party voted for it or against it, but in the body of which I have the honor to be a member, it was strictly a party vote.   I know that Mr. Jarnegan voted for it, but his constituents in Tennessee instructed him so to vote; his masters were Democrats; he obeyed his masters, and his was therefore a Democratic vote.   Well, the Senate was equally divided, and how was it disposed of?   By the casting vote of the Vice-President of the United States, a citizen of the State of Pennsylvania!*

And now let me ask, after an experience of two years, who is helped by this tariff of 1846, — what portions of the country? Pray, is South Carolina helped by it?   It is in fact a measure dictated by South Carolina; it is a measure in which the South took the initiative, and led off, and the North, as has been too much its wont, followed.   There are men of the North who see the sun in the South, and they think they see all other light there.   Now, is South Carolina any richer for this tariff?   She is a great cotton-growing State.   Now that the tariff is passed now that we have free trade, said these friends of the new tariff, we shall see Carolina looming up like one of the Southern constellations.   She will become rich; she is enfranchised and set at liberty; hereafter she will take a great lead, and her cotton will enrich the people.

Pray, what has been the result?   When these glowing sentences were on the lips of her eloquent men, her cotton was from ten to eleven cents a pound.   Those words had hardly cooled, when, under this protection by free trade, and under this admi-

* Mr. Dallas.

39 *

rable tariff of 1846, which put down all other abominable tariffs, her cotton is down to five and a half and six cents a pound.

And Pennsylvania! Why, Gentlemen, it happened to me to be in Pennsylvania in the fall of 1844, before the election took place. I addressed multitudes of people in Philadelphia, at Valley Forge, and Pottsville, in the midst of the iron and coal of that region, and in other places; and what did I see there, all along the road, as I went from Philadelphia to the mines of Pottsville? I saw flags, holding out the motto, " Polk, Dallas, and the Tariff of '42," and I heard it again and again said, that Mr. Polk was a greater friend to the productive industry of Pennsylvania than the Whig candidate!* I may venture to say that all expectation founded upon this assurance has failed now, in a manner not a little mortifying. I regarded it then, and I regard it now, as false evidence, — the use of false signals and false tokens. The representations made then to the people of Pennsylvania, if it had been a case of jurisprudence and municipal trial, would, I think, have enabled a prosecuting officer to frame an indictment for false tokens and false pretences. It is right and fit there should be a new trial, now that the false evidence is made known; and I think the people of Pennsylvania are ready for a new trial. It is proper to try the case over again, when the fraud is discovered.

Now, Gentlemen, passing for a moment from this, I have already said, that if it be the pleasure of the country to elect a Whig President and a Whig Congress, this existing law will either be essentially modified or altogether repealed; and it is just as true, that, if there be no election of a Whig President, it will be continued. So, after all, Gentlemen, the support which we give to men should rest on our opinion as to what will be their measures. Public men are agents. One class of public men will do certain things, and support or pass one class of public measures, and another class of public men will do other things, and support or pass another class of public measures; and as we like or dislike the measures, so must we judge of the men.

While I say that General Cass will undoubtedly uphold the bill to which he gave an efficient support in 1846, and to which

* Mr. Clay.

he stands pledged, by his adherence to the Baltimore platform
of June last, I am bound to state, at the same time, that another gentleman, whose name has been mentioned in connection with the Presidency, is in exactly the same situation. I
have said that, if Mr. Van Buren is elected President of the
United States, he will not repudiate his own sub-treasury. I
say now, that, if elected President of the United States, unless
he repudiates himself, he will adhere to the tariff of 1846. I
have, Gentlemen, some short documents touching this point
which I will read. The first is the resolution adopted at Buffalo,
respecting revenue, protection, and customs.

" 5. *Resolved*, That the obligations of honor and patriotism require
the earliest practicable payment of the national debt; and we are therefore in favor of such a tariff of duties as will raise revenue adequate to
defray the necessary expenses of the federal government, and to pay
annual instalments of our debt and the interest thereon."

That is the philosophy and the extent of the protection and
encouragement to domestic industry set forth by the Buffalo
Platform. Now, Gentlemen, we see that the penman who drew
up that elaborate riddle was very much afraid of treading on
Mr. Van Buren's toes; because here is another document, a
line longer. It is a letter from Mr. Van Buren, written by him
soon after the passage of the tariff of 1842, the Whig tariff, and
is as follows: —

"*Albany*, Feb. 28, 1843.

" My DEAR SIR, — I thank you kindly for your friendly letter. I have
at no time nor anywhere hesitated to express my decided disapprobation of the tariff act of the last session, as well in respect to the *principle* on which it is founded, as to its details. In good time you will
have my views in respect to that and other subjects before the public.
In the mean time believe me to be, very sincerely, your friend and
obedient servant,

" MARTIN VAN BUREN."

Those " other views " have not come, unless they were con-
tained in this paper.*
Nevertheless, Gentlemen, our controversy is not with Mr. Van
Buren. We stand where we have for years. Our controversy

* The Buffalo resolution.

is with that political party who have been, and who are, our political opponents; who are numerous and powerful; men of great strength, long foresight, and calculation; who have contrived, I had almost said, to govern us; at least, they have contrived to exercise, for a long time, a great power and influence over the country. They are they with whom we have to deal hereafter. Let us see what is their opinion, what they mean to do on the great question of American industry. They said at the Baltimore Convention, which nominated Mr. Cass, —

" *Resolved*, That the fruits of the great political triumph of 1844, which elected James K. Polk and George M. Dallas President and Vice-President of the United States, have fulfilled the hopes of the democracy of the Union, in defeating the declared purposes of their opponents to create a national bank; in preventing the corrupt and unconstitutional distribution of the land proceeds, from the common treasury of the Union, for local purposes; in protecting the currency and the labor of the country from ruinous fluctuations, and guarding the money of the people for the use of the people, by the establishment of the constitutional treasury; in the noble impulse given to the cause of free trade, by the repeal of the tariff of 1842, and the creation of the more equal, honest, and productive tariff of 1846; and that, in our opinion, it would be a fatal error to weaken the bands of political organization by which these great reforms have been achieved, and risk them in the hands of their known adversaries, with whatever delusive appeals they may solicit our surrender of that vigilance, which is the only safeguard of liberty."

So Mr. Buchanan, in the extracts from his speech which I have read, has but recited by rote the doctrine of the party that this sub-treasury is the panacea which is to remove all the evils which press upon the productive industry of the country. The manufactures of the country are to find their most efficient support in the influence of the sub-treasury, and the sub-treasury has kept and will keep, according to them, the money concerns of the country free from all evil. Though always opposed by the Northern members of that party, whether of New England or other States, the Whigs succeeded in 1842, and as Whigs made what we thought a good tariff. We do also remember that the Southern Whigs helped in that which the Northern people of the other party did not. We had the intrepid Senator of Maine, Mr. Evans; but where were other votes from that State? Whom had we from New Hampshire, though she has been benefited by the uses to which her vast water power has been applied, against the policy of her government, and against all her opinions upon the subject? Yet Southern Whigs helped us. And I am sorry to say that Northern Whigs and Massachusetts Whigs, who stood by us in 1842, in Congress and out of Congress, and before 1842 and since 1842, to uphold this cause of domestic industry, to resist the sub-treasury and all its influences, — I am sorry to find them now leaving us, quitting us, saying good bye to us, and going where I think they will have the satisfaction of hearing as much applause of the tariff of 1846 as they will wish. These Whigs of ours, of whom I always speak with respect, because for some of them I have the deepest regard, and I speak more in sorrow than in anger when I allude to them, they say they do not mean to sustain the present tariff; but what sort of an argument is this? Is not every man held by the rules of law and common sense, and the understanding of all men, as meaning to do that which is the necessary tendency of his conduct? If his acts lead to a certain result known to him, and visible before his eyes, and he does those acts, is he free to say, I did not mean to do it, — it was not my purpose?

Now, Gentlemen, let us see how this policy of the administration, the united operation of the sub-treasury and the tariff of 1846, has operated to maintain the prosperity of the manufacturers. Here I can only instance a few things; and, so far as I am concerned, and this meeting is concerned, they must take them as specimens of the whole. I begin with wool and woollens, a great Northern interest. The production of wool and the manufacture of wool is a vast interest in the Northern and Middle States. It extends through Virginia, Ohio, the Western States, Pennsylvania, and certain parts of New York and New England; but the manufacture of it is established principally in the New England States. Now, I take a few instances of this. Here is a woollen establishment in our neighborhood, at Lowell, called the Middlesex Mills. Within a very short time, such has been the depression of that interest, and such the overwhelming effect of manufactures from abroad, that eight hundred hands have been discharged; and others, if not all, will be discharged soon. Wages are reduced twenty per cent., and the price of wool is reduced at least one third.

There are counties in Pennsylvania who will think of this upon the 7th of November. Washington, Greene, and other counties in the western part of Pennsylvania, may well take it into consideration, that this tariff and sub-treasury have protected them by depressing the price of their main commodity at least one third. It may not be amiss for our neighbors of Maine and Vermont, as well as New Hampshire, to notice that also. A respectable gentleman, well known to you, this afternoon placed in my hands a statement, according to which forty woollen mills, known to him, have within the last four months all stopped working from the pressure of the money market and the influx of foreign manufactures, and they have discharged nearly *three thousand hands*, and greatly reduced the wages of the remainder.

There is a singular fact connected with the woollen manufacture in the United States, I believe not generally known. A great portion of the imported article is from France and the Continent. I believe that it is not generally known that France pays a bounty upon the exportation of woollen manufactures, to the amount of fourteen per cent. It was formerly nine per cent. Belgium paid formerly a lower duty; but Belgian manufacturers now send their goods through France, and thus all these great importations of woollens come to the United States under a bounty equal to half the tax imposed upon them by our government, so that our tariff upon woollens is rendered null to one half its full extent, by bounties paid upon exported woollens abroad. Five sixths, and some say nine tenths, of all these fabrics come to the United States.

With respect to cotton I have nothing to say, excepting that I do not understand, and have not heard, that any establishments of that sort are supposed to be working at a profit. One or two other articles I mention as belonging to us at the North, and one of these is hemp, and the manufacture of hemp. I remember, when this tariff was under consideration in the Senate, a member addressed the Senate particularly on that subject. The tariff taxes the raw material higher than it taxes its manufacture. It seems to direct its artillery particularly against American labor, for the result of foreign labor comes cheap, while the material for American labor is dear.

I have spoken of labor as one of the great elements of our so-

ciety, the great substantial interest on which we all stand, — not
feudal service, not predial toil, not the irksome drudgery by one
race of mankind, subjected on account of color, to the control of
another race of mankind; but labor, intelligent, manly, independent, thinking and acting for itself, earning its own wages,
accumulating those wages into capital, becoming a part of society and of our social system, educating childhood, maintaining
worship, claiming the right of the elective franchise, and help-
ing to uphold the great fabric of the State. That is American
labor, and I confess that all my sympathies are with it, and my
voice, until I am dumb, will be for it.

There is another subject to which my attention has been a
little turned, not exactly professional, and yet not altogether remote from the circle of my habits; I mean the fisheries. To the
extent of the interest, I understand that the cod and mackerel
fisheries of New England are as great sufferers under this tariff
as any other pursuit; because it has reduced the duties upon
both, and because there are certain advantages belonging to the
British colonies, who live nearer the ground; and the result is,
as it was not formerly, that both codfish and mackerel are imported to a great extent. Fifty thousand barrels of mackerel
last year were imported into this State, and one hundred thousand more into the United States, amounting to no small aggregate. Although there is, in the tariff now existing, a right of
reëxportation, which seems to be plausible, inasmuch as it
may be supposed that this commodity is destined to other ports
as well as our own, there is still a great disadvantage to the
people of the United States; because, when there was no reëxportation or debenture, they commanded the whole of our own market; and to command the whole of our own market is a greater
advantage to them, than to have the right of reëxportation to other markets. My brethren, if they will allow me to call them so,
the fraternity of the line, if there are any here from Cape Ann,
Duxbury, or Plymouth, will understand it a great deal better
than I can explain it.

So much, Gentlemen, for a few of the instances that I
have ventured to select of the effects of this applauded tariff
of 1846 upon the fortunes of Massachusetts and the Northern
States.

And now go a little farther south, to the interests which it affects in the Middle States, and especially in the State of Pennsylvania. The great products of Pennsylvania are iron and coal. I propose to say a few words only upon the first, upon her iron. If there be any duty in political regulation, if there be any duty in society, which regards the great interests of the country, surely it must be that which protects the great masses of men in their daily employ. I know what duties belong to government in the first stages of civilization; they are confined, generally, to the repelling foreign invasions and maintaining internal peace. But as civilization proceeds, the objects of government become more various, — to regulate commerce and a hundred internal interests, and to foster manufactures to a reasonable extent; and this goes on just as far as civilization extends. Now I suppose in Pennsylvania there is no one of the manufacturing interests which involves the daily bread of the people beyond the iron interest. We have heard something of the sound of the hammer on those anvils within the last fortnight. When I was in Pennsylvania in the fall of 1844, I found every body attached to that great interest and to its support. The question was, Will Mr. Polk support it? Will Mr. Dallas support it? Every body said, Yes. Who doubts Mr. Dallas, from the State of Pennsylvania? Who doubts Mr. Polk, with the letter before him, which he wrote, stating it to be the duty of every government? Cannot we believe him? Will he impose upon us Pennsylvanians? Will he deceive us of the great Democratic State of Pennsylvania, which casts twenty-six electoral votes? Dare he, or his friends, come before us with misrepresentations? They yielded their confidence, and gave their great vote to Mr. Polk and Mr. Dallas. It made Mr. Polk President, and Mr. Dallas Vice-President; and when this question came up, Mr. Dallas himself in the chair, a native of Pennsylvania, made Vice-President by the votes of Pennsylvanians, when the vote on the tariff was equally divided upon the question of prostrating the tariff of 1842, he gave his casting vote in the affirmative, and settled the question. The tariff of 1842 was abolished, and this tariff of 1846 established in its stead by his casting vote.

Mr. Buchanan, in the speech to which I have already more than once alluded, tells his good friends in Pennsylvania, that it may, perhaps, be in their power to turn this pending election;

and he calls upon the Democracy of the State to do so. I am willing to take him upon that issue. Let Pennsylvania give her casting vote; but let her give it herself, by her own strong hand, and not by others. If at the polls, after the free discussion and experience of the past, Pennsylvania votes with her vast multitudes of intelligent people, and gives the CASTING vote for General Cass and General Butler, then so be it. Let her take the consequence. Thank Heaven, nobody but herself holds that casting vote at the present day. I hope she will give it; I hope she will consider it; and I hope she will give it, when she does give it, decisively and emphatically. Therefore I would say, if I could be heard by her, from the Delaware to the Ohio, from New Jersey to Maryland, — I would say to her, that now the people of the United States look to see how Pennsylvania WILL HERSELF GIVE HER OWN CASTING VOTE.

I will give a few facts in relation to the great interests of Pennsylvania. I understand that, after the law of 1842 was passed, sixteen or seventeen rolling-mills were erected to make railroad iron, a business then unknown in this country. Two thirds of them have stopped, and stopped for what? Forty-five hundred workmen have been discharged. Miners' wages have been known to be high, and the discharge of people from these mills for making railroad iron has thrown out of employment men earning together $1,800,000 a year Labor, therefore, to that amount, in these railroad iron mills, has been thrown out of employ. The imports of iron, since the new tariff, are enormous. All know that. It is said that orders have been sent out amounting to three millions. We shall see the difference by a short comparison of the imports of 1848 and of 1846: —

	1848.	1846.
Bar iron, ...	13,690 tons.	6,600 tons.
Pig iron, ...	24,000 "	7,716 "
Sheets, hoops, rods, and nails, .	75,500 "	20,428 "

And here the increase is in articles of the highest manufacture, that is, articles in which the greatest quantity of labor is incorporated; for there seems to be in this policy a bloodhound scent to follow labor, and to run it down, and to seize and strangle it wherever it may be found. Sheet iron, and those species of iron requiring the most labor, all come in cheapest under this system. As to some of these mills, and especially one at Danville in the State of Pennsylvania, which cost the proprietors seven hundred thousand dollars, which they paid in to the last cent, it is wholly stopped.

I will only add, that, if we mean to keep up American labor under these operations, we must hold to protecting our industry from the competition of foreign labor. Labor abroad is cheap, because the people live poor. English iron costs $ 8.02 per ton for wages; while American iron, the result of American labor, costs $ 15.82, because American labor means to live well, means to earn enough to educate its children, and to perform the duties of a citizen. Therefore I insist that it shall have wages, and high wages. We know that some others of these iron works are about to stop. The evil is not confined to this branch of industry. The wages of handicraft in Philadelphia are also cut down one third; I mean the hand-loom weavers, and fifteen hundred hands have been thrown out of employment in this branch of industry alone.

In connection with the tariff, in its operation upon these necessary articles, which I suppose it is the duty of our government to protect, I wish to advert to a fact or matter, I believe, not very much known. You know, Gentlemen, that the present tariff act was passed on the 30th of July, 1846. There seems to have been an apprehension that a state of things might arise under which there would be gross undervaluation, because all duties were *ad valorem*, and there was no specific duty laid upon any thing. The Secretary of the Treasury seems to have partaken of this apprehension. It would appear, that, under the influence of that fear, some few days afterwards, in the course of the same session, a bill was before Congress making the usual appropriations for civil and diplomatic services; and in that bill, at the suggestion of the Secretary of the Treasury, was inserted a section, not germain to the matter of the bill, but in close connection with this very tariff bill before us. It provides, —

" Sec. 2. And be it further enacted, That, in addition to the assistant appraisers authorized by law at the port of New York, there may be appointed, in the mode now prescribed by law, one additional assistant appraiser at said port, at a salary, as heretofore established, of fifteen hundred dollars per annum, to be paid out of any money in the Treasury not otherwise appropriated : Provided, said salary shall not commence, or appointment take effect, prior to the 30th of November next; and in appraising all goods, at any port of the United States, heretofore subjected to specific duties, but upon which *ad valorem* duties are imposed by the act of the 30th of July last, entitled ' An Act reducing the duty on imports and for other purposes,' reference shall be had to values and invoices of similar goods imported during the last fiscal year, under such general and uniform regulations for the prevention of fraud or undervaluation as shall be prescribed by the Secretary of the Treasury."

That is to say, that if the Secretary of the Treasury chose, he might, upon any such goods as had heretofore paid a specific duty, impose a value that should be ascertained, not by the appraisers, but by the invoices that accompanied the like article in the last fiscal year. Now, if the Secretary of the Treasury had seen fit to carry this section into operation, he might have kept the duties upon iron nearly as high as they now are. In point of fact I learn, that in November of last year the Secretary of the Treasury did send instructions to the appraisers of this port to look at their invoices, but never gave any direction whatever making it imperative upon them to adopt the value stated in the invoices of the preceding year. And from inquiry at the custom-house, through an intelligent source, I learn that to be the result. In 1845, the usual invoice price of iron was £ 10 sterling; now I believe it is about £ 5 6s. Then it was in the power, and it is now in the power, of the Secretary of the Treasury, if he sees fit, to say that all iron shall be taken according to the invoice of 1845, and pay *ad valorem* duty accordingly, instead of being taken according to the invoice of 1848. I learn that the difference will be just this. Taking the value of iron according to the invoices of 1845, and assessing the *ad valorem* duty which the present tariff provides, the duty would amount to $ 15 per ton, while by the recent invoices it would amount to but $ 9 per ton. So that at all times it has been in the power of the Secretary of the Treasury to keep the duty on iron from falling below $ 15 per ton. I say nothing as to the manner in which he should have discharged his duties. The probability is, that he has found the revenue from the custom-house sufficient to answer his purposes, and has not therefore seen fit to enhance this duty.

I have just adverted to certain interests affected by the present tariff, and a few more words remain for me to say respecting the more general question. And I say, if these hinderances to individual pursuits, individual occupations, and individual labor had not arisen or were not imposed by this tariff, yet the tariff, such as it is, is and must be destructive to the great interests of the whole people, whether manufacturers or not. I say that, because I see that we cannot stand for any length of time this overwhelming importation of foreign commodities, without an utter derangement of the currency of the country. That I take to be the great and general question after all, which embraces all interests, affects all men, and extends everywhere throughout the whole United States. Now let us look at some calculations upon this subject. The duties on imports for the year now current, that is, beginning with the 1st of July last, and ending with the 1st of July next, have been estimated at the treasury as likely to amount to $ 32,000,000. This is not an improbable estimate, because, for the year ending on the 1st of July last, they amounted to thirty-one millions and some odd thousand dollars. Now if this be so, taking the rates of duties as they now stand, to yield a revenue of $ 32,000,000, the present tariff requires an import of $ 155,000,000. We must import, therefore, to the amount of $ 155,000,000, if we expect to get thirty-two millions of revenue, according to the established rates. Now let me show you how this is; and I will give you a statement made up partly of these importations, and partly of the importations and exportations together.

"The import of specie during the year ending 30th June, 1847, was $ 24,121,289.

"Under the tariff of 1842 the imports (exclusive of specie and reëxportation) were for the year ending 30th June,

		Net revenue.
1844 . . . . $ 96,390,548	yielding	$ 26,183,570
1845 . . . 105,599,541	"	29,528,112
1846 110,048,859	"	26,712,667
Average of 3 years, 104,013,000	"	26,631,750
or 25.57 per cent.		

"Under tariff of 1846,

1847 116,258,310	"	23,747,864

less than 20½ per cent., a loss of five millions of revenue.

"It is thus quite obvious, that under the tariff of 1842 we should have derived more revenue from a less importation, and left the balance to remain with us in the form of specie.

"The revenue of the year ending 30th June, 1848, is reported to have been $31,700,000, which, at the same rate, requires an import of one hundred and fifty-three millions. The rate of import has apparently continued about the same.

"The export of specie commenced in October, 1847, and has continued without intermission for upwards of a year, and cannot amount to less than fifteen or sixteen millions.

"Our domestic exports, year ending Jan. 1846,   . $101,718,000
"   "   1847, the year of famine,   150,000,000
being an excess in bread-stuffs and other provisions of forty-one millions over 1846."

Such is the statement. The general opinion is, that the exportation of grain cannot continue at this rate. It has already fallen off. This importation must stop somewhere, for how are we to pay for it? We export cotton, and this year our crop is very great, but the price is very low. We have an export of provisions, but far less than a year or two ago, and this export must fall off. We send the stocks of the United States abroad to all who will buy, but that cannot last; and yet the specie is constantly going out of the country. Ten millions have been sent abroad, I understand, since January last. How are we to get over this? And of what is left under the effect of this importation, the sub-treasury locks up what would sustain a circulation of fifteen or twenty millions. I must suppose this state of the tariff and the sub-treasury always going on, and always found together, like Castor and Pollux, under a Democratic administration. And who is benefited by it? It is all from the unwillingness of party men to acknowledge themselves in error. I appeal to you. You are all acquainted with the state of commerce and business. Do you know twenty men, active in business, sensible men, who do not wish the sub-treasury anywhere but where it is? Do you know twenty mechanics and manufacturers, men of sense and industry, who do not wish the tariff of 1846 had never been born? What is it that keeps it in being but prejudice, party pride, and obstinacy? Gentlemen, I have no right to speak here to members of a party to which I do not belong, but yet I would venture to beseech them to consider whether there may not be some considerations,—whether our own daily business, the maintenance of our wives and families, the securing of a competence for a comfortable old age,—whether these considerations may not be of more importance than that we should learn by rote, and recite by rote, every dogma of the party to which we are attached?

I have spoken of the sub-treasury as I understand it, of its present and its future operations, and I have spoken of this tariff. If it shall remain unmodified and unremoved, it is one consolation to know that it is not because we have favored it. All the pursuits of society are certain to be affected by it; and looking to the present state of the country, it is not a matter of slight interest to inquire whether the hands into which we are now about, on the one side or the other, to commit the destinies of the nation,—whether they are men who believe that our true greatness and true glory consist in a conservative policy, in maintaining ourselves where we are, and in upholding ourselves in the view of the world, as a steady, just, enlightened, manly, and not encroaching republic; or whether we commit them to the hands of those who consider that our "manifest destiny" is war, aggression, turmoil, acquisition, annexation, and carrying our system, willing or unwilling, to the fullest extent of our power, to every land, by the bayonet and the sword.

Gentlemen, I think that the policy of the candidate proposed by our opponents, and of those who support him most vigorously, is of a dangerous character. I think that, in looking back to the past, we see that he and they are men who have opposed the adjustment of the Oregon question, and the settlement of the Northeastern Boundary. And one thing further strikes me, that, while there are of this school of politicians men whose views were heard in either house of Congress, and through the columns of all the newspapers, big with taunts, threats, and defiance to England, they are the men that, in all our own legislation upon tariffs and currency, act exactly the part that a British minister would most desire they should.

I know that confidence is to be placed by man in man. I feel the conviction that I must repose trust in somebody's hands to stand at the head of the nation, to uphold our essential interests, and to preserve the honor and peace of the country. I have made up my mind, and I give that trust to the Whig nomination, to GENERAL TAYLOR. I think he is bound up and wound up in his own principles and in his own declaration. I think with Mr. Buchanan, that he is a Whig, and I think he will be elected by the Whigs. I think he will surround himself, as Mr. Buchanan says, with a Whig Cabinet, and I believe he will honestly and faithfully adopt and pursue Whig principles and Whig measures.

Now I know that, on a certain other topic, great fears are inspired elsewhere, as well as in this State, in order to effect the election. I know that in a most respectable society in New Jersey and Pennsylvania, and containing numbers in other States, measures have been taken to influence them to give their votes either for the Free Soil party or for General Cass. I mean the Society of Friends. In thirty years of public life, I have formed a pretty general acquaintance in those States which I have mentioned; and I have the pleasure to know a great many men of this Society, the Society of Friends. I have always entertained a great respect for their public conduct as well as their private character. I have acquaintance with some, friendship for some, great personal regard for some, and to them I may venture to speak; and I would say to them, in the first place, that whatever else may be asserted before them, every vote given for Mr. Van Buren is a vote for General Cass; and the friends of General Cass, I think, will find that out. Why, Gentlemen, I was in New York last week, and while there, one gentleman of the Cass party said to a Whig, " We shall elect General Cass ; there is no doubt of that." " But how ? " " Why, the Liberty party, four years ago, helped us to elect Mr. Polk against the Whig candidate, and the Free Soil party will do just the same thing now." And therefore I say to those to whom I would now speak, whom I know to be urged in every variety of form to vote with that party, that every vote they give in that direction goes for General Cass. The question is, Do they prefer General Cass to General Taylor, as a man of peace, ay, as an anti-slavery man? I say to them, as I say to you,—and they do not suppose me, I trust, to be a pro-slavery man,— I say to them and to you, upon my honor and conscience, that I believe, under the present circumstances of the country, we are far more secure against the further progress of slavery and the slave power under the administration of General Taylor, than we are under the administration of General Cass. I will say that here. Let it be recorded, and let the result bring to the test the justness of the prophecy.

Gentlemen, it may be long before I shall again see you in this place in which we are assembled. I do not regret to have been invited hither; I am glad of an opportunity to unbosom myself upon the present condition of the country. I have done it. And I can only express the fervent hope in Divine Providence that while we — while our children, in ages to come — can continue to assemble in this hallowed place, to deliberate upon great political and national subjects, it may always be with that intelligence and uprightness, that pure patriotic spirit, and that high and determined resolve, which I believe at this moment animates the great body of the Whigs of Massachusetts.

JEREMIAH MASON.

JEREMIAH MASON.

THE death of the Hon. Jeremiah Mason, one of the most eminent members of the legal profession in the United States, took place at Boston, on the 14th of October, 1849. At a meeting of the Bar of the County of Suffolk, Mass., held on the 17th instant, appropriate resolutions in honor of the deceased, accompanied with a few eloquent observations, were introduced by Mr. Choate, and unanimously adopted. It was voted by the meeting, that Mr. Webster should be requested to present these resolutions to the Supreme Judicial Court at its next term in Boston. In compliance with this request, at the opening of the next term of the court, on the 14th of November, 1848, prayer having been offered, Mr. Webster rose and spoke as follows : —

MAY it please your Honors, — JEREMIAH MASON, one of the counsellors of this court, departed this life on the 14th of October, at his residence in this city. The death of one of its members, so highly respected, so much admired and venerated, could not fail to produce a striking impression upon the members of this bar; and a meeting was immediately called, at which a member of this court, just on the eve of leaving the practice of his profession for a seat on the bench,* presided; and resolutions expressive of the sense entertained by the bar of the high character of the deceased, and of sincere condolence with those whom his loss touched more nearly, were moved by one of his distinguished brethren, and adopted with entire unanimity. My brethren have appointed me to the honorable duty of presenting these resolutions to this court; and it is in discharge of that duty that I rise to address you, and pray that the resolutions which I hold in my hand may be read by the clerk.

* Mr. Justice Richard Fletcher.

The clerk of the court then read the resolutions, as follows : —

" *Resolved*, That the members of this bar have heard with profound emotion of the decease of the Honorable Jeremiah Mason, one of the most eminent and distinguished of the great men who have ever adorned this profession ; and, as well in discharge of a public duty, as in obedience to the dictates of our private feelings, we think it proper to mark this occasion by some attempt to record our estimate of his preëminent abilities and high character.

" *Resolved*, That the public character and services of Mr. Mason demand prominent commemoration ; that, throughout his long life, whether as a private person or in public place, he maintained a wide and various intercourse with public men, and cherished a constant and deep interest in public affairs, and by his vast practical wisdom and sagacity, the fruit of extraordinary intellectual endowments, matured thought, and profound observation, and by the soundness of his opinions and the comprehensiveness and elevated tone of his politics, he exerted at all times a great and most salutary influence upon the sentiments and policy of the community and the country ; and that, as a Senator in the Congress of the United States during a period of many years, and in a crisis of affairs which demanded the wisdom of the wisest and the civil virtues of the best, he was distinguished among the most eminent men of his country for ability in debate, for attention to all the duties of his great trust, for moderation, for prudence, for fidelity to the obligations of that party connection to which he was attached, for fidelity still more conspicuous and still more admirable to the higher obligations of a thoughtful and enlarged patriotism.

" *Resolved*, That it was the privilege of Mr. Mason to come to the bar, when the jurisprudence of New England was yet in its infancy ; that he brought to its cultivation great general ability, and a practical sagacity, logical power, and patient research, — constituting altogether a legal genius, rarely if ever surpassed ; that it was greatly through his influence that the growing wants of a prosperous State were met and satisfied by a system of common law at once flexible and certain, deduced by the highest human wisdom from the actual wants of the community, logically correct, and practically useful ; that in the fact that the State of New Hampshire now possesses such a system of law, whose gladsome light has shone on other States, are seen both the product and the monument of his labors, less conspicuous, but not less real, than if embodied in codes and institutes bearing his name ; yet that, bred as he was to the common law, his great powers, opened and liberalized by its study and practice, enabled him to grasp readily, and wield with entire ease, those systems of equity, applicable to the transactions of the land or the sea, which, in recent times, have so much meliorated and improved the administration of justice in our country.

" *Resolved*, That as respects his practice as a counsellor and advocate at this bar, we would record our sense of his integrity, prudence, fidelity, depth of learning, knowledge of men and affairs, and great powers of persuading kindred minds ; and we know well, that, when *he* died, there was extinguished one of the few great lights of the old common law.

" *Resolved*, That Mr. Webster be requested to present these resolutions to the Supreme Judicial Court, at its next term, in Boston ; and the District Attorney of the United States be requested to present them to the Circuit Court of the United States now in session.

" *Resolved*, That the Secretary communicate to the family of Mr. Mason a copy of these resolutions, together with the respectful sympathy of the bar."

The proprieties of this occasion (continued Mr. Webster) compel me, with whatever reluctance, to refrain from the indulgence of the personal feelings which arise in my heart, upon the death of one with whom I have cultivated a sincere, affectionate, and unbroken friendship, from the day when I commenced my own professional career, to the closing hour of his life. I will not say, of the advantages which I have derived from his intercourse and conversation, all that Mr. Fox said of Edmund Burke; but I am bound to say, that of my own professional discipline and attainments, whatever they may be, I owe much to that close attention to the discharge of my duties which I was compelled to pay, for nine successive years, from day to day, by Mr. Mason's efforts and arguments at the same bar. *Fas est ab hoste doceri;* and I must have been unintelligent, indeed, not to have learned something from the constant displays of that power which I had so much occasion to see and to feel.

It is the more appropriate duty of the present moment to give some short notice of his life, character, and the qualities of his mind and heart, so that he may be presented as an example to those who are entering upon or pursuing the same career. Four or five years ago, Mr. Mason drew up a biography of himself, from the earliest period of his recollection to the time of his removal to Portsmouth, in 1797; which is interesting, not only for the information it gives of the mode in which the habits of his life were formed, but also for the manner of its composition.

He was born on the 27th day of April, 1768, at Lebanon in Connecticut. His remotest ancestor in this country was Captain John Mason (an officer who had served with distinction in the Netherlands, under Sir Thomas Fairfax), who came from England in 1630, and settled at Dorchester in the Colony of Massachusetts. His great-grandfather lived at Haddam. His grandfather, born in 1705, lived at Norwich, and died in the year 1779. Mr. Mason remembered him, and recollected his character, as that of a respectable and deeply religious man. His ancestor on the maternal side was James Fitch, a learned divine, who came from England and settled in Saybrook, but removed to Lebanon, where he died. A Latin epitaph, in the ancient burying-ground of that town, records his merits. One of his descendants held a large tract of land in the parish of Goshen, in the town of Lebanon, by grant from the Indians; one half of which, near a century afterwards, was bequeathed to his daughter, Elizabeth Fitch, the mother of Mr. Mason. To this property Mr. Mason's father removed soon after his marriage, and there he died, in 1813. The title of this land was obtained from Uncas, an Indian sachem in that neighborhood, by the great-grandfather of Mr. Mason's mother, and has never been alienated from the family. It is now owned by Mr. Mason's nephew, Jeremiah Mason, the son of his eldest brother James. The family has been distinguished for longevity; the average ages of Mr. Mason's six immediate ancestors having exceeded eighty-three years each. Mr. Mason was the sixth of nine children, all of whom are now dead.

Mr. Mason's father was a man of intelligence and activity, of considerable opulence, and highly esteemed by the community. At the commencement of the Revolutionary war, being a zealous Whig, he raised and commanded a company of minute men, as they were called, and marched to the siege of Boston. Here he rendered important service, being stationed at Dorchester Heights, and engaged in fortifying that position. In the autumn of that year, he was promoted to a colonelcy, and joined the army with his regiment, in the neighborhood of New York. At the end of the campaign, he returned home out of health, but retained the command of his regiment, which he rallied and brought out with celerity and spirit when General Arnold assaulted and burned New London. He became attached to military life, and regretted that he had not at an early day entered the Continental service. Colonel Mason was a good man, affectionate to his family, kind and obliging to his neighbors, and faithful in the observance of all moral and religious duties.

Mr. Mason's mother was distinguished for a good understanding, much discretion, the purity of her heart and affections, and the exemplary kindness and benevolence of her life. It was her great anxiety to give all her children the best education, within the means of the family, which the state of the country would allow; and she was particularly desirous that Jeremiah should be sent to college. " In my recollection of my mother," says Mr. Mason, " she was the personification of love, kindness, and benevolence."

Destined for an education and for professional life, Mr. Mason was sent to Yale College, at sixteen years of age; his preparatory studies having been pursued under " Master Tisdale," who had then been forty years at the head of a school in Lebanon, which had become distinguished, and among the scholars of which were the Wheelocks, afterwards presidents of Dartmouth College. He was graduated in 1784, and performed a part in the Commencement exercises, which greatly raised the expectation of his friends, and gratified and animated his love for distinction. " In the course of a long and active life," says he, " I recollect no occasion when I have experienced such elevation of feeling." This was the effect of that spirit of emulation which incited the whole course of his life of usefulness. There is now prevalent among us a morbid and sickly notion, that emulation, even as honorable rivalry, is a debasing passion, and not to be encouraged. It supposes that the mind should be left without such excitement, in a dreamy and undisturbed state, flowing or not flowing, according to its own impulse, without such aids as are furnished by the rivalry of one with another. For one, I do not believe in this. I hold to the doctrine of the old school, as to this part of education. Quinctilian says: " Sunt quidam, nisi institeris, remissi; quidam imperio indignantur; quosdam continet metus, quosdam debilitat: alios continuatio extundit, in aliis plus impetus facit. Mihi ille detur puer, quem laus excitet, quem gloria juvet, qui victus fleat; hic erit alendus ambitu, hunc mordebit objurgatio, hunc honor excitabit; in hoc desidiam nunquam verebor." I think this is sound sense and just feeling.

Mr. Mason was destined for the law, and commenced the study of that profession with Mr. Baldwin, a gentleman who has lived to perform important public and private duties, has served his country in Congress, and on the bench of the Supreme Court of Connecticut, and still lives to hear the account of the peaceful death of his distinguished pupil. After a year, he went to Vermont, in whose recently established tribunals he expected to find a new sphere for the gratification of ambition, and the employment of talents. He studied in the office of Stephen Rowe Bradley, afterwards a Senator in Congress; and was admitted to the bar, in Vermont and New Hampshire, in the year 1791.

He began his career in Westmoreland, a few miles below Walpole, at the age of twenty-three; but in 1794, three years afterwards, removed to Walpole, as being a larger village, where there was more society and more business. There was at that time on the Connecticut River a rather unusual number of gentlemen, distinguished for polite accomplishments and correct tastes in literature, and among them some well known to the public as respectable writers and authors. Among these were Mr. Benjamin West, Mr. Dennie, Mr. Royall Tyler, Mr. Jacobs, Mr. Samuel Hunt, Mr. J. W. Blake, Mr. Colman (who established, and for a long time edited, the "New York Evening Post"), and Mr. Olcott. In the association with these gentlemen and those like them, Mr. Mason found an agreeable position, and cultivated tastes and habits of the highest character.

About this period, he made a journey to Virginia, on some business connected with land titles, where he had much intercourse with Major-General Henry Lee; and, on his return, he saw President Washington, at Philadelphia, and was greatly struck by the urbanity and dignity of his manner. He heard Fisher Ames make his celebrated speech upon the British treaty. All that the world has said with regard to the extraordinary effect produced by that speech, and its wonderful excellence, is fully confirmed by the opinion of Mr. Mason. He speaks of it as one of the highest exhibitions of popular oratory that he had ever witnessed; popular, not in any low sense, but popular as being addressed to a popular body, and high in all the qualities of sound reasoning and enlightened eloquence.

Mr. Mason was inclined to exercise his abilities in a larger sphere. He had at this time made the acquaintance of Aaron Burr and Alexander Hamilton. The former advised Mr. Mason to remove himself to New York. His own preference was for Boston; but he thought, that, filled as it then was by distinguished professional ability, it was too crowded to allow him a place. That was a mistake. On the contrary, the bar of this city, with the utmost liberality and generosity of feeling and sentiment, have always been ready to receive, with open arms, every honorable acquisition to the dignity and usefulness of the profession, from other States. Mr. Mason, however, removed to Portsmouth in the autumn of 1797; and, as was to be expected, his practice soon became extensive. He was appointed Attorney-General in 1802. About that time, the late learned and lamented Chief Justice Smith retired from his professional duties, to take his place as a judge; and Mr. Mason became the acknowledged head of his profession. He resigned the office of Attorney-General, three or four years afterwards, to the great regret of the court, the bar, and the country. As a prosecuting officer, he was courteous, inflexible, and just; careful that the guilty should not escape, and that the honest should be protected. He was impartial, almost judicial, in the administration of his great office. He had no morbid eagerness for conviction; and never permitted, as sometimes occurs, an unworthy wrangling between the official power prosecuting, and the zeal of the other party defending. His official course produced exactly the ends it was designed to do. The honest felt safe; but there was a trembling and fear in the evil disposed, that the transgressed law would be vindicated.

Very much confined to his profession, he never sought office or political elevation. Yet he held decided opinions upon all political questions, and cultivated acquaintance with all the leading subjects of the day; and no man was more keenly alive than he to whatever occurred, at home or abroad, involving the great interests of the civilized world.

His political principles, opinions, judgments, were framed upon those of the men of the times of Washington. From these, to the last, he never swerved. The copy was well executed. His conversation on subjects of state was as instructive and interesting as upon professional topics. He had the same reach of

41 *

thought, and exhibited the same comprehensive mind, and sagacity quick and far seeing, with regard to political things and men, as he did in professional affairs. His influence was, therefore, hardly the less from the fact that he was not actively engaged in political life. There was an additional weight given to his judgment, arising from his being a disinterested beholder only. The looker-on can sometimes form a more independent and impartial opinion of the course and results of the contest, than those who are actually engaged in it.

But at length, in June, 1813, he was persuaded to accept the post of a Senator of the United States, and took his seat that month. He was in Congress during the sessions of 1813 and 1814. Those were very exciting times, party spirit ran very high, and each party put forward its most prominent and gifted men. Both houses were filled by the greatest intellects of the country. Mr. Mason found himself by the side of Rufus King, Giles, Goldsborough, Gore, Barbour, Daggett, Hunter, and other distinguished public men. Among men of whatever party, and however much some of them differed from him in opinion or political principle, there was not one of them all but felt pleasure if he spoke, and respected his uncommon ability and probity, and his fair and upright demeanor in his place and station. He took at once his appropriate position. Of his associates and admirers in the other house, there are some eminent persons now living who were occasional listeners to his speeches and much struck with his ability; together with Pickering, Benson, Pitkin, Stockton, Lowndes, Gaston, and Hopkinson, now all deceased, who used to flock to hear him, and always derived deep gratification and instruction from his talents, character, and power.

He resigned his seat in the Senate in 1817. His published speeches are not numerous. The reports of that day were far less complete than now, and comparatively few debates were preserved and revised. It was a remarkable truth, that he always thought far too lightly of himself and all his productions. I know that he was with difficulty persuaded to prepare his speeches in Congress for publication; and in this memorial of himself which I have before me he says, with every appearance and feeling of sincerity, that he " has never acted any important part in life, but has felt a deep interest in the conduct of others."

His two main speeches were, first, one of great vigor, in the Senate, in February, 1814, on the Embargo, just before that policy was abandoned. The other was later, in December, 1815, shortly before the peace, on Mr. Giles's Conscription Bill, in which he discussed the subject of the enlistment of minors; and the clause authorizing such enlistment was struck out upon his motion.

He was afterwards for several years a member of the New Hampshire Legislature, and assisted in revising the code of that State. He paid much attention to the subject of the judicature, and performed his services fully to the satisfaction of the State; and the result of his labors was warmly commended. In 1824 he was again a candidate for the Senate of the United States. The election was to be made by the concurrent vote of the two branches of the Legislature. In the popular branch he was chosen by a strong vote. The Senate, however, non-concurred; by which means the election was lost, — a loss to the country, not to him, — by force of circumstances and agencies not now or ever fit to be recalled or remembered.

He continued to reside for many years in Portsmouth. His residence in that ancient town was a happy one. He was happy in his family and in the society of the town, surrounded by agreeable neighbors, respected by the bar and the court, and standing at the head of his profession. He had a great love of conversation. He took pleasure in hearing others talk, and gave an additional charm by the freshness, agreeableness, and originality of his own observations. His warm hospitality left him never alone, and his usefulness was felt as much within the walls of the homes, as of the tribunals, of Portsmouth. There are yet many in that town who love him and his; many who witnessed as children, and recollect, the enthusiasm with which he was greeted by their fathers and mothers; and all in New Hampshire old enough to remember him will feel what we feel here on this occasion.

Led at last partly by the desire of exerting his abilities in a larger sphere of usefulness, and partly by the fact of the residence here of beloved domestic connections, he came to this city, and entered upon the performance of his professional duties in 1832. Of the manner in which he discharged those duties, this court is the most competent judge. You, Mr. Chief Justice, and the venerable associate who usually occupies a place at your right,* have been witnesses of the whole. You know the fidelity with which he observed his duty to the court, as well as his duty to his clients. In learning, assiduity, respect for the bench, uprightness, and integrity, he stood as an example to the bar. You know the general probity and talent with which he performed, for so many years, the duty of a counsellor of this court.

I should hardly trust myself to make any analysis of Mr. Mason's mind. I may be a partial judge. But I may speak of what I myself admire and venerate. The characteristics of Mr. Mason's mind, as I think, were real greatness, strength, and sagacity. He was great through strong sense and sound judgment, great by comprehensive views of things, great by high and elevated purposes. Perhaps sometimes he was too cautious and refined, and his distinctions became too minute; but his discrimination arose from a force of intellect, and quick-seeing, far-reaching sagacity, everywhere discerning his object and pursuing it steadily. Whether it was popular or professional, he grasped a point and held it with a strong hand. He was sarcastic sometimes, but not frequently; not frothy or petulant, but cool and vitriolic. Unfortunate for him on whom his sarcasm fell!

His conversation was as remarkable as his efforts at the bar. It was original, fresh, and suggestive; never dull or indifferent. He never talked when he had nothing to say. He was particularly agreeable, edifying, and instructive to all about him; and this was the charm of the social intercourse in which he was connected.

As a professional man, Mr. Mason's great ability lay in the department of the common law. In this part of jurisprudence, he was profoundly learned. He had drunk copiously from its deepest springs; and he had studied with diligence and success the departures from the English common law which had taken place in this country, either necessarily, from difference of condition, or positively, by force of our own statutes. In his addresses, both to courts and juries, he affected to despise all eloquence, and certainly disdained all ornament; but his efforts, whether addressed to one tribunal or the other, were marked by

---

* Mr. Justice Wilde.

a degree of clearness, directness, and force not easy to be equalled. There were no courts of equity, as a separate and distinct jurisdiction, in New Hampshire, during his residence in that State. Yet the equity treatises and equity reports were all in his library, not "wisely ranged for show," but for constant and daily consultation; because he saw that the common law itself was growing every day more and more liberal; that equity principles were constantly forcing themselves into its administration and within its rules; that the subjects of litigation in the courts were constantly becoming, more and more, such as escaped from the technicalities and the trammels of the common law, and offered themselves for discussion and decision on the broader principles of general jurisprudence. Mr. Mason, like other accomplished lawyers, and more than most, admired the searching scrutiny and the high morality of a court of equity; and felt the instruction and edification resulting from the perusal of the judgments of Lord Hardwicke, Lord Eldon, and Sir William Grant, as well as of those of great names in our own country, not now among the living.

Among his early associates in New Hampshire, there were many distinguished men. Of those now dead were Mr. West, Mr. Gordon, Edward St. Loe Livermore, Peleg Sprague, William K. Atkinson, George Sullivan, Thomas W. Thompson, and Amos Kent; the last of these having been always a particular personal friend. All of these gentlemen in their day held high and respectable stations, and were eminent as lawyers of probity and character.

Another contemporary and friend of Mr. Mason was Mr. Timothy Bigelow, a lawyer of reputation, a man of probity and honor, attractive by his conversation, and highly agreeable in his social intercourse. Mr. Bigelow, we all know, was of this State, in which he filled high offices with great credit; but, as a counsellor and advocate, he was constant in his attendance on the New Hampshire courts. Having known Mr. Bigelow from my early youth, I have pleasure in recalling the mutual regard and friendship which I know to have subsisted between him and the subject of these remarks. I ought not to omit Mr. Wilson and Mr. Betton, in mentioning Mr. Mason's contemporaries at the bar. They were near his own age, and both well known as lawyers and public men.

Mr. Mason, while yet in New Hampshire, found himself engaged in causes in which that illustrious man, Samuel Dexter, also appeared. The late Mr. Justice Story was still more frequently at the bar of that State; and, at a period somewhat earlier, your great and distinguished predecessor, Chief Justice Parsons, occasionally presented himself before the courts at Portsmouth or Exeter, and he is known to have entertained a very high regard, personal and professional, as well for Mr. Mason as for the late Chief Justice Smith.

Among those still living, with whom Mr. Mason was on terms of intimacy, and with whom he associated at the bar, were Messrs. Plumer, Arthur Livermore, Samuel Bell, and Charles H. Atherton. If these respected men could be here to-day, every one of them would unite with us in our tribute of love and veneration to his memory.

But, Sir, political eminence and professional fame fade away and die with all things earthly. Nothing of character is really permanent but virtue and personal worth. These remain. Whatever of excellence is wrought into the soul itself belongs to both worlds. Real goodness does not attach itself merely to this life; it points to another world. Political or professional reputation cannot last for ever; but a conscience void of offence before God and man is an inheritance for eternity. *Religion*, therefore, is a necessary and indispensable element in any great human character. There is no living without it. Religion is the tie that connects man with his Creator, and holds him to his throne. If that tie be all sundered, all broken, he floats away, a worthless atom in the universe; its proper attractions all gone, its destiny thwarted, and its whole future nothing but darkness, desolation, and death. A man with no sense of religious duty is he whom the Scriptures describe, in such terse but terrific language, as living "without God in the world." Such a man is out of his proper being, out of the circle of all his duties, out of the circle of all his happiness, and away, far, far away, from the purposes of his creation.

A mind like Mr. Mason's, active, thoughtful, penetrating, sedate, could not but meditate deeply on the condition of man below, and feel its responsibilities. He could not look on this mighty system,

"This universal frame, thus wondrous fair,"

without feeling that it was created and upheld by an Intelligence, to which all other intelligences must be responsible. I am bound to say, that in the course of my life I never met with an individual, in any profession or condition of life, who always spoke, and always thought, with such awful reverence of the power and presence of God. No irreverence, no lightness, even no too familiar allusion to God and his attributes, ever escaped his lips. The very notion of a Supreme Being was, with him, made up of awe and solemnity. It filled the whole of his great mind with the strongest emotions. A man like him, with all his proper sentiments and sensibilities alive in him, must, in this state of existence, have something to believe and something to hope for; or else, as life is advancing to its close and parting, all is heart-sinking and oppression. Depend upon it, whatever may be the mind of an old man, old age is only really happy, when, on feeling the enjoyments of this world pass away, it begins to lay a stronger hold on those of another.

Mr. Mason's religious sentiments and feelings were the crowning glories of his character. One, with the strongest motives to love and venerate him, and the best means of knowledge, says : —

" So far as my memory extends, he always showed a deep conviction of the divine authority of the Holy Scriptures, of the institutions of Christianity, and of the importance of personal religion. Soon after his residence in Boston, he entered the communion of the Church, and has continued since regularly to receive the Lord's Supper. From that time, he also habitually maintained domestic worship, morning and evening. The death of two of his sons produced a deep impression upon his mind, and directed it in an increased degree to religious subjects.

" Though he was always reserved in the expression of religious feeling, still it has been very apparent, for several years, that his thoughts dwelt much upon his practical religious duties, and especially upon preparation for another world. Within three or four years, he frequently led the conversation to such subjects; and during the year past, immediate preparation for his departure has been obviously the constant subject of his attention. His expressions in regard to it were deeply humble; and, indeed, the very humble manner in which he always spoke of himself was most marked.

" I have observed, of late years, an increasing tenderness in his feelings and manner, and a desire to impress his family with the conviction that he would not remain long with them. His allusions of this kind have been repeated, even when apparently in his usual health; and they indicated the current of his thoughts.

" He retained his consciousness till within a few hours of his death, and made distinct replies to every question put to him. He was fully aware that his end was near; and in answer to the question, ' Can you now rest with firm faith upon the merits of your Divine Redeemer?' he said, ' I trust I do : upon what else can I rest?'

" At another time, in reply to a similar question, he said, ' *Of course*, I have no other ground of hope.' We did not often speak to him during those last three days, but had no doubt that he was entirely conscious of his state, knew that his family were all near, and that his mind was free from anxiety. He could not speak with ease, and we were unwilling to cause him the pain of exertion. His whole life, marked by uniform greatness, wisdom, and integrity; his deep humility, his profound reverence for the Divine Majesty, his habitual preparation for death, his humble trust in his Saviour, left nothing to be desired for the consolation of his family under this great loss. He was gradually prepared for his departure. His last years were passed in calm retirement; and he died as he wished to die, with his faculties unimpaired, without great pain, with his family around his bed, the precious promises of the Gospel before his mind, without lingering disease, and yet not suddenly called away."

Such, Mr. Chief Justice, was the life, and such the death, of JEREMIAH MASON. For one, I could pour out my heart like water, at the recollection of his virtues and his friendship, and in the feeling of his loss. I would embalm his memory in my best affections. His personal regard, so long continued to me, I esteem one of the greatest blessings of my life; and I hope that it may be known hereafter, that, without intermission or coolness through many years, and until he descended to his grave, Mr. Mason and myself were friends.

Mr. Mason died in old age; not by a violent stroke from the hand of death, not by a sudden rupture of the ties of nature, but by a gradual wearing out of his constitution. He enjoyed through life, indeed, remarkable health. He took competent exercise, loved the open air, and, avoiding all extreme theories or practice, controlled his conduct and habits of life by the rules of prudence and moderation. His death was therefore not unlike that described by the angel, admonishing Adam :—

"I yield it just, said Adam, and submit.
But is there yet no other way, besides
These painful passages, how we may come
To death, and mix with our connatural dust?

There is, said Michael, if thou well observe
The rule of ' Not too much,' by temperance taught,
In what thou eat'st and drink'st; seeking from thence
Due nourishment, not gluttonous delight;
Till many years over thy head return,
So mayst thou live; till, like ripe fruit, thou drop
Into thy mother's lap; or be with ease
Gathered, not harshly plucked; for death mature.
This is old age."

FESTIVAL

OF THE

SONS OF NEW HAMPSHIRE.

FESTIVAL OF THE SONS OF NEW HAMPSHIRE.

In the autumn of 1849 some of the natives of New Hampshire established in Massachusetts, and especially in Boston and the vicinity,
proposed to hold a festival in honour of the state of their birth. The
proposal was cordially approved, and a great many persons
took part in the festival. The subscribers assembled at three o'clock,
P.M. of the 7th of November, in the State House at Boston, when a
procession was formed which moved through the principal streets to the
large hall of the Fremont Railway Company. Mr. Webster presided
as president of the day. Mr. Levi Woodbury of the Supreme Court
of the United States, Hon. John P. Hale of the Senate of the United
States, Chief Justice Parker of the Law School of Cambridge, General
H. A. S. Dearborn, Mayor of Roxbury, Hon. Marshall P. Wilder, President of the Senate of Massachusetts, and other gentlemen of distinction, natives of New Hampshire, were present and addressed the company. Mr. Webster spoke twice in the course of the evening, the
first time as follows:—

Residents of Boston and its vicinity, natives born of New
Hampshire! we meet here to-day in honor of our native state,
to commemorate, and record, our grateful affection, for, or to
acknowledge the obligation which we all feel for birth-place and
nurture in our early days. Coming into this meeting along, we
have not brought away with us all our affection, or all our
attachments.

We have invited to meet us many distinguished citizens of
New Hampshire. They have answered our invitation and have
come in numbers. It may be considered properly the duty of
the place I occupy to bid them, one and all, welcome. Welcome, ye of New Hampshire, to-night, from every part and quarter
of our native State. If you come from the present valleys of

FESTIVAL OF THE SONS OF NEW HAMPSHIRE.

In the autumn of 1849 some of the natives of New Hampshire established in Massachusetts, and especially in Boston and the vicinity, proposed to hold a festival in honor of the State of their birth. The proposal was cordially welcomed, and about fifteen hundred persons took part in the festival. The subscribers assembled at three o'clock, P. M., of the 7th of November, in the State-House at Boston, when a procession was formed, which moved through the principal streets to the large hall of the Fitchburg Railway Company. Mr. Webster officiated as president of the day. Mr. Justice Woodbury of the Supreme Court of the United States, Hon. John P. Hale of the Senate of the United States, Chief Justice Parker of the Law School at Cambridge, General H. A. S. Dearborn, Mayor of Roxbury, Hon. Marshall P. Wilder, President of the Senate of Massachusetts, and other gentlemen of distinction, natives of New Hampshire, were present and addressed the company. Mr. Webster spoke twice in the course of the evening, the first time as follows: —

Residents of Boston and its vicinity, native born of New Hampshire! we meet here to-day in honor of our native State, to commemorate and record our grateful affection for her; to acknowledge the obligation which we all feel for her care and nurture in our early days. Coming into this, another State, we have not brought away with us all our affections, or all our attachments.

We have invited to meet us many distinguished citizens of New Hampshire. They have answered our invitation, and have come in numbers. It may be considered properly the duty of the place I occupy to bid them, one and all, welcome. Welcome, ye of New Hampshire origin, from every part and quarter of our native State! If you come from the pleasant valleys of

42*

the Connecticut and Merrimack, welcome! Are you from the sea-shore and the lakes of Strafford? welcome! Come ye from the Monadnock and the sides of the Crystal Hills? welcome! *welcome!* WELCOME!

It was not in my power, Gentlemen, to meet you in the hall of the State-House before dinner. But I meet you here, and in the name of those who have prepared this celebration, I greet our guests, and in my own name, I greet all. I think they say the Chinese have a heathenish custom, when they meet, of shaking their own hands to their friends. That is not our custom. Let us be more classical; —

> " Cur dextræ jungere dextram
> Non datur."

Let us follow the English and the Saxon custom, and shake hands with our friends. I give my hands to the friends next me. Let us embrace, *more majorum*, and have a good hearty shaking of hands.

Gentlemen, all the world admits that identity of local origin is a tie of connection and sympathy, especially if it be strengthened by early association, by the meeting with one another in the school-house, and in the society of early life. In the morning of life, the heart opens all its sympathies to those around it, and receives impressions which are deep and lasting. We have migrated from one State to another. Our migration has not, indeed, been far. Nor have we come among strangers; nor have we had a new tongue to learn, new principles to imbibe, new courses of life to pursue; but, nevertheless, we have changed our allegiance; we have changed our citizenship; we have changed our social relations. New Hampshire men once in all these respects, we have ceased to be New Hampshire men now in every thing, but grateful remembrance and affection for the past.

To-day we meet, to resume, for the time, the feelings which belong to us, as citizens of New Hampshire; to put on the New Hampshire character, and see how well it may fit us here, in the metropolis of the State to which we have come. Gentlemen, our lot is propitious; singularly, remarkably propitious. We are the native sons of one State, we are the adopted children of another, and we are proud of both. We desire not to forget whence we came, and Heaven forbid that we should forget where we are. We have met, I say, to commemorate our native State. We value it according to its merits, which we believe high and honorable. We value it for what Nature has conferred upon it, and for what its hardy sons have done for themselves. We have not forgotten that its scenery is beautiful; that its skies are all-healthful; that its mountains and lakes are surpassingly grand and sublime. If there be any thing on this continent, the work of Nature, in hills, and lakes, and seas, and woods, and forests, strongly attracting the admiration of all those who love natural scenery, it is to be found in our mountain State of New Hampshire.

It happened to me lately to visit the northern parts of the State. It was autumn. The trees of the forests, by the discoloration of the leaves, presented one of the most beautiful spectacles that the human eye can rest upon. But the low and deep murmur of those forests, the fogs and mists, rising and spreading, and clasping the breasts of the mountains, whose heads were still high and bright in the skies, — all these indicated that a wintry storm was on the wing; that the spirit of the mountains was stirred, and that ere long the voice of tempests would speak. But even this was exciting; exciting to those of us who had been witnesses before of such stern forebodings, and exciting in itself, as an exhibition of the grandeur of natural scenery. For my part, I felt the truth of that sentiment, applied elsewhere and on another occasion, that

"the loud torrent and the whirlwind's roar
But bound me to my native mountains more."

Ours is not one of the richest of the States. It does not compare with Massachusetts in its facilities of mercantile or commercial occupation and enterprise. Its soil is sterile and stubborn, but the resolution to subdue it is stubborn also. Unrelenting rocks have yielded, and do yield, to unrelenting labor; and there are productiveness, and health, and plenty, and comfort, over all her hills and among all her valleys. Manly strength, the nerved arm of freemen, each one tilling his own land, and standing on his own soil, enjoying what he earns, and ready to defend it, — these have made all comfortable and happy.

Nor need we be ashamed of her literary, her religious, or her social institutions.   I have seen, and others of my age have seen, the church and the school-house rise and stand in the very centre of the forest, and seen them resorted to in the midst of winter snows.   And where these things lie at the foundation and commencement of society, where the worship of God, the observance of morals, and the culture of the human mind, are springs of action with those who take hold of the original forest, to subdue it by strong arms and strong muscles, there, depend upon it, the people never fail.

Everywhere, *everywhere*, on her hills and rivers, are there school-houses.   The school-house ; who shall speak of that throughout New England as it ought to be spoken of ?   Who shall speak, in proper language, of the wisdom, and foresight, and benevolence, and sagacity of our forefathers, in establishing a general system of public instruction as a great public police for the benefit of the whole, as a business in which all are interested? The world had previously seen nothing like it, although some parts of the world, have since copied from it.   But where, when you talk of fostering governments, of guardian governments, of governments which render to subjects that protection which the allegiance of subjects demands, — where is it, I ask, that, as here with us, it has come to be a great and fundamental proposition, existing before constitutions, that it is the duty, the bounden duty, of governments composed by the representation of all, to lay the foundation of the happiness and respectability of society in universal education?   If you can tell me such a country out of New England, I would be glad to hear of it.   I know of none.   I have read of none.

Gentlemen, the inhabitants of our New Hampshire mountains were, it must be confessed, from the first, rather inclined to the indulgence of a military spirit.   I believe that this is common to mountainous regions in most parts of the world.   Scotland and Switzerland show the example of hardy, strong men in mountainous regions, attached to war and to the chase ; and it is not unfortunate in our New Hampshire history, that this sentiment, to a considerable degree, prevailed.   The position of the country and the state of the people called for its exercise. We know that New Hampshire was settled, in all its frontier towns, under circumstances of the most dangerous and difficult nature and character.   It was a border State.   It bordered on the Indians and on the French; names and nations always coupled together in the language of our fathers as common enemies to them. This exposed the frontier men, of New Hampshire especially, to perpetual war; to perpetual danger at least of war, and its frequent occurrence. People forget; they forget how lately it is, that the interior, the border country of New Hampshire, was settled and reclaimed, and made safe from Indian depredation. All the world reads that New England is the oldest part of the United States, or one of the oldest. It has been looked upon as the longest settled. But, in regard to the frontiers of our native State, the settlement has been recent. Even up to the time of the birth of some of us now living, there was some degree of danger from Indian depredations and Indian wars; liability to Indian assaults, murders, and burnings.

Whole generations, at least one entire generation, tilled the land and raised their bread with their arms in their hands, or in the fields with them at their labor. We do not now appreciate the difficulty of those frontier settlements, because subsequent prosperity and security have obliterated the recollection.

The pioneers of more fortunate countries in our day, what are their dangers compared with those of our fathers? They go to a mild climate. They go to a fertile land; and they have behind them a powerful government, capable of defending them against the foe, of protecting their interests, and of redressing the wrongs they may suffer. It was not so with our fathers in New Hampshire. There, on the border were the Indians, and behind the Indians were the hostile French. It was in this situation of border danger and border warfare, and border strife and border suffering, that our ancestors laid the foundation of the State from which we come.

In the language of Fisher Ames, " It is not in Indian wars that heroes are celebrated; but it is there they are formed. No enemy on earth is more formidable, in the skill of his ambushes, in the suddenness of his attack, or in the ferocity of his revenge." Not only was this foe to be encountered, but also a civilized state at enmity with us behind the Indians, supplying them with means, and always ready to purchase the victims that they could bring for sale to Canada. This was the condition of things in which the frontiers were settled. Let it be added, that half the year was winter, and that on the surface of the snow, incrusted by frosts, bands of savages, coming from a distance of two hundred miles, suddenly appeared, and set fire, at midnight, to the villages of the settlers.

It was in this discipline, it was in these Indian wars, it was especially in the war of 1756, against the French, in which almost every man in New Hampshire, capable of bearing arms, took part, — it was here that the military spirit of the country, the bravery, the gallantry of these mountain inhabitants, were all called forth. They were a people given to the chase and to the hunt in time of peace; fitted for endurance and danger; and when war came, they were ready to meet it. It was in the midst of these vicissitudes that they were formed to hardihood and enterprise, and trained to military skill and fearlessness.

As one example out of many, I might refer to General John Stark, well known for his military achievements in all the wars of his time; a hunter in peace, a soldier in war; and as a soldier, always among the foremost and the bravest. And since he is brought to my remembrance, let me dwell upon the recollection for a moment.

General Stark was my neighbor, the neighbor and friend of my father. One in a highly important, the other in a less distinguished situation, they had seen military service together, and had met the enemy in the same field. It was in the decline of Stark's life, comparatively speaking, that the Revolutionary war broke out. He entered into it, however, with all the manliness and all the fervor of his youthful character. Yet, in his advanced age, like other old men, he turned back fondly to earlier scenes; and when he spoke of the "war," he always meant the old French and Indian war. His remembrances were of Canada; of the exploits at Crown Point, and Ticonderoga, and Lake George. He seemed to think of the Revolution as only a family quarrel, in which, nevertheless, he took a warm and decided part; but he preferred to talk of the "war" in which he was taken by the Indians, as he was more than once, I think, and carried to Canada. The last time I saw him, he was seated around a social fire with his neighbors. As I entered, he greeted me, as he always did, with affection; and I believe he complimented me on my complexion, which he said was like my father's; and his was such, he said, that no one could tell whether he was covered with powder or not. The conversation turned, like other conversations among country neighbors, upon this man's condition and that man's condition; the property of one, and the property of another, and how much each was worth.   At last, rousing himself from an apparent slumber, he said, " Well, I never knew but once what I was worth.   In the war, the Indians took me, and carried me to Canada, and sold me to the French for forty pounds; and, as they say a thing is worth what it will fetch, I suppose I was worth forty pounds."

These are the scenes, ye native born, this is the history, ye sons of New Hampshire, of the times and the events that brought forth the gallant spirits of our native State into the midst of a still more important and more serious conflict, which began here in 1775.   New Hampshire was then full of soldiers; indeed, I may say that the whole of New England was full of soldiers, when the Revolutionary war broke out.   New Hampshire, especially, had hardly any body in it that had not been accustomed to bear arms in the previous war.   As proof of the soldierlike character of our New England yeomanry, I may mention a fact wich should not be forgotten; that, of all the soldiers, regular and militia, which served in the war of independence, Massachusetts and New Hampshire, Connecticut and Rhode Island,— these four little States, which, as you look upon a map of the United States, you can cover with your hand, — these States furnished more than one half of all the men that achieved our independence.   It appears from official and statistical records, that during the war, in the regular service and in the militia service, from three hundred and seventeen to three hundred and twenty thousand men were employed in our armies.   Of these, New England alone furnished more than half.

I may refer to a period further back.   I may revert to the time that Louisburg was taken from the French, in 1745.   How many men do you think the Colonies of New England maintained?   I believe, Gentlemen, they maintained, for one or two years at least, upon provincial pay, more men against the French, than were enlisted at any one time in our late war with England.   It was this which induced Lord Chatham to say, in his place in the House of Lords, " I remember, my Lords, when New England raised four regiments on her own bottom, and took Louisburg from the veteran troops of France."

Then came the war of the Revolution; it broke out here in the State of Massachusetts. Where was New Hampshire then? Was she alienated from the cause, or from her sister State? No. Neither then, nor at any time in the succeeding contest, was her soil subject to the tread of a hostile foot. Whether they thought it not worth entering, or whether they did not choose to encounter the dwellers in her mountains, I do not care to decide. The truth is, no enemy trod on the soil of New Hampshire. But when the strife began, when the beacon-fires were lighted here, when the march from Boston to Lexington and Concord had spread the flames of liberty, who answered to the call? Did New Hampshire need to be summoned to Bunker Hill? She came at the first blaze of the beacon-fires. None were earlier, none more ready, none more valiant.

I think it is Madame de Staël who says, that "from the mountains of the North there comes nothing but fire and the sword." And on this occasion there did indeed come from our native mountains both fire and the sword; not the fire of devastation and desolation, not the sword of ruthless plunder and massacre, but the fire of LIBERTY and the sword of PATRIOTISM. And how ardently the one burned, and how vigorously the other was wielded till the return of peace enabled the country to sheathe it and be at rest, let the whole history of that country tell.

Gentlemen, from Bunker Hill to Yorktown, there was not a battle in which New Hampshire blood was not shed. I may go further yet; and I may say that there is, probably, of the many hundreds now in this very hall, a representative of some New Hampshire officer or soldier who fell in every field, and left his bones where he fought his battle. The blood, *the blood* of New Hampshire men, falling everywhere, and in every year of the war, in defence of the liberty of the country, is here to-night. I hope it is worthy of its descent, and that it will transmit itself undefiled to ages, and ages yet to come.

Those who returned to New Hampshire from that seven years' contest have their graves on the mountain-sides and along the valleys of their native land; and those graves are ever objects of public regard and private affection.

> " How sleep the brave, who sink to rest,
>   By all their country's wishes blest !
>
>   And Freedom shall awhile repair,
>   And dwell, a weeping hermit, there."

They are ever pointed out to the passing traveller as the last resting-place of the patriotic and the brave; and they continue to be watered with the tears of a grateful posterity. But, alas! all did not return. McCleary, the earliest, or one of the earliest, of the New Hampshire victims of the Revolutionary struggle fell in Charlestown. His blood is mixed with the earth upon which yonder monument stands, raising its head to the skies, and challenging the respect and admiration of the world, for the spot where a military achievement was performed, which, in its results, in the long career of its consequences, in the great course of events which followed it, and their effects upon human happiness and human liberty, has no parallel in the history of mankind.

Adams and Coleman fell at Saratoga, and the soil of New York contains their ashes. Colonel Scammel, a scholar, a gentleman of high attainment and accomplishment, a soldier of undaunted valor, went through the whole career of the war, and lost his life at its close, when making a reconnoissance, as adjutant-general, before the redoubts at Yorktown. There he fell. He lies buried in the graveyard at Williamsburg. An affectionate friend and comrade, General Henry Dearborn, took pains to search out the spot where his remains were buried. He could find no more, than that they lay somewhere in that consecrated burial-ground. A braver or a better man did not belong to the army. I never read his history without being much affected. He left no descendants. He was never married. His career was short and brilliant, like that of the star that shoots across the horizon, and goes out to be seen no more. His friends came home from the army full of attachment and love for his name and fame. General John Brooks, formerly Governor of this State, beloved by every body and distinguished for every virtue, named a son for him, Alexander Scammel Brooks. This son was brought up to the army, like his predecessor and namesake, and lost his life in the Florida war. General Dearborn, another friend, also named a son for him, General Henry Alexander Scammel Dearborn, whom we have the pleasure of seeing here to-night.   Colonel Wadsworth also gave his name to a son who entered the navy, and is now Commodore Alexander Scammel Wadsworth.

The three namesakes, all about the same age, and early acquaintances and friends, lived until the Florida war broke up the trio, and reduced the number to General Dearborn and Commodore Wadsworth.* I wish, as a spontaneous tribute of the present generation, that somewhere within the sacred grounds of the churchyard at Williamsburg, at the expense of us, sons of New Hampshire, a monument should be raised to the memory of that distinguished soldier.

Gentlemen, I have no right to occupy much of your time. My voice is a little too familiar to you all.   There are others to whom you will listen with more gratification.   I will only refer, in a very few words, to the civil history of this, our native State, in the past and important era of our history ; and in doing that, I will mention only the great men who signed the Declaration of Independence, and those who put their names to the Constitution of the United States.   The Declaration of Independence, on the part of New Hampshire, was signed, in the first place, by Josiah Bartlett.   He was an unostentatious man, but able, sensible, and patriotic.   He left numerous descendants, and there are here those who belong to his family and kindred.   General William Whipple was another who signed the Declaration.   He left no descendants ; nothing but his character, his name, and his fame.   Dr. Matthew Thornton was a third.   And his descendants are in New Hampshire, in Boston, and elsewhere in the country ; some of them now in this hall.   Dr. Thornton was one of the most ardent sons of liberty, but was, as it happened, not at Philadelphia on the 4th of July, 1776, when the vote was passed.   He hurried immediately to Philadelphia.   You know that the official resolutions of Independence were only to be signed by the President.   But a Declaration, for individual signatures, was drawn up.   The first of the members who signed, after the President, was Josiah Bartlett, of New Hampshire ; the next was William Whipple of New Hampshire.   Matthew Thornton did not sign immediately, because he was not there. Others went on to sign ; and the Massachusetts delegation, you

---

* Commodore Wadsworth is since deceased.

remember, signed next to the two members from New Hampshire. Thornton hastened back to his post to sign with the rest, and the nearest place to his colleagues he could find was at the bottom of the right-hand column; and there it stands, " Matthew Thornton."

Well, Gentlemen, we now come to the Constitution of the United States. John Langdon and Nicholas Gilman represented New Hampshire in the Convention of 1789. Mr. Langdon has left descendants behind him, honorable and worthy. An excellent woman, a daughter, still lives, esteemed and regarded by all who know her.* Nicholas Gilman, of a family always an honor to his native State, and some of whom I dare say are here to-night, left no children.

At this period, without disturbing individual opinions or party feelings, I may speak of some of the early members of Congress. When the Constitution first went into operation, the members from New Hampshire assisted in forming the original organic laws, were confided in by the first President of the United States and did all that they could do to put the machine in operation. At the head of this list was Samuel Livermore, the father of several gentlemen of respectability in public life, in the State and in the national councils. Jeremiah Smith and William Gordon, also, both men of talent and industry, and warm friends of the first President, sat in Congress with high reputation.

This, Gentlemen, was the history, the early history, of our State, as one of the Union, so far as we may summarily comment upon it here to-night.

In regard to the military character of her Revolutionary heroes, and her early statesmen, and in regard to every thing which was done, or ought to have been done, or was expected to be done, to bring New Hampshire honorably and respectably into the great circle of our Union, Gentlemen, I leave all this for abler tongues, fresher recollections, and more persuasive accents. I sit down myself, filled with profound veneration for the character of my native State, and acknowledging to her my own personal debt for her culture and nurture, and determined, so far as in me lies, to transmit the sense of that obligation to those who shall come after me.

* Mrs. Langdon-Elwyn, now of Philadelphia.

After many other gentlemen had addressed the company, Mr. Webster again rose, and spoke as follows: —

THE regular toasts have now been gone through. I have occupied this chair as long as it seems to be convenient, and, with a few parting words, I propose to resign it to another.

Gentlemen, departing from the character of particular States, leaving for the present the agreeable thoughts that have entertained us, of our own homes and our own origin, it appears to me, before we part, that it is not improper that we should call to our attention the marked character of the age in which we live, and the great part that, in the dispensations of Divine Providence, we are called upon to act in it.

To act our part well, as American citizens, as members of this great republic, we must understand that part, and the duties which it devolves upon us. We cannot expect to blunder into propriety, or into greatness of action. We must learn the character of the age in which we live, we must learn our own place as a great and leading nation in that age, we must learn to appreciate justly our own position and character, as belonging to a government of a particular form, and we must act, in every case, and upon all subjects, as becomes our relations.

Now, Gentlemen, I venture to say, here and everywhere, in the face of the world, that there is not on earth any country, at the present moment, so interesting as the United States. I do not say, no country so strong, so rich, so beautiful, so high or commanding; but I say, no country so *interesting*, no country that sets such an example before the world of self-government, no country around which so many hopes and so many fears cluster, no country in regard to which the world with so much earnestness inquires, " What will she come to?"

I need not say that we are at the head of this continent. Who denies that? Who doubts it? Here are more than twenty millions of people, free, commercial, and enterprising, beyond example. They are spread over an immense territory, and that territory has been lately increased by a vast and an extraordinary addition. The country stretches from sea to sea, across the whole breadth of North America, and from the tropics to the great lakes and rivers of the North.

Forty or fifty years ago, an American poet said to his countrymen, —

> " No pent-up Utica contracts our powers,
> For the whole boundless continent is ours."

This was poetic; but the poetry has been advancing, and is still advancing, more and more, to sober truth and reality.

But this is not all, nor is it the most important point. We are brought by steam, and the improvements attendant upon its discovery, into the immediate neighborhood of the great powers of Europe, living under different forms of government; forms in which the aristocratic, or the despotic, or the monarchical element prevails. The United States, the second commercial country in the world, whose intercourse affects every other country, have entered the circle, and are become the immediate neighbors of them all. And what is expected to be the consequence of this proximity, this contiguity, this bringing the republican practice into the immediate presence of despotism, monarchy, and aristocracy? This is the philosophical view which attracts the attention of the observant part of mankind most strongly, and strikes us with the greatest power. What is to be the result?

Gentlemen, between us and the governments of Europe there is no political connection. They have their systems, and we have ours; but then their interests and ours approach, and sometimes coincide. Commercial interests are mingling together all over the civilized world. The information of mankind is becoming common to all nations, and the general tone of sentiment common, in learned circles, and among the masses of intelligent men. In matters of science, taste, commerce, in questions of right and justice, and matters of judicial administration, we think very much alike. But in regard to the origin of government, the form of government, and, in some cases, the end and objects of government, we differ. And yet it is certain that, of all human institutions, government is the chief, and by far the most important; and as the press, at least to a very great extent, in modern times, is free, government, its origin, its forms, its duties, its ends and objects, and its practical administration, are everywhere a constant subject of discussion. Now that steam has created such a daily intercourse, and brought countries so much nearer together, men of one nation seem to talk to those of another, on political subjects, as on other subjects, almost like inhabitants of the same city, or the same county.

This is a condition of things novel and interesting, and worthy of our reflection. In national relations, we sustain a rank, we hold a certain place, and we have high duties to perform. Of course it is our duty to abstain from all interference in the political affairs of other countries. But then there is one thing which we are bound to do. We are bound to show to the whole world, in the midst of which we are placed, that a regular, steady, conservative government, founded on broad, popular, representative systems, is a practicable thing. We are bound to show, that there may be such a government, not merely for a small, but for a great country, in which life and property shall be secure, religion and the worship of the Deity observed, good morals cultivated, commerce and the arts encouraged, and the general prosperity of all classes maintained and advanced.

It strikes me, and I repeat the sentiment only to show the strength of my own conviction, that our great destiny on earth is to exhibit the practicability of good, safe, secure, popular governments; to prove, and I hope we do prove, that there may be security for property, and for personal rights, that there may be provision for the maintenance of religion and morals, for an extensive diffusion of knowledge, and for carrying all branches of education and culture to their highest pitch, by means of institutions founded on republican principles. The prophecies and the poets are with us. Every body knows Bishop Berkeley's lines, written a hundred years ago: —

> " There shall be sung another golden age,
>   The rise of empire and of arts ;
> The good and great inspiring epic rage,
>   The wisest heads and noblest hearts."

> " Westward the course of empire takes its way ;
>   The four first acts already past,
> A fifth shall close the drama with the day :
>   Time's noblest offspring is the last."

And at a more recent period, but still when there was nothing to be seen in this vast North American continent but a few colonial settlements, another English poet suggests to his country, that she shall see a great nation, her own offspring, springing up, with wealth, and power, and glory, in the New World: —

> " In other lands, another Britain see ;
>   And what thou art, America shall be."

But, in regard to this country, there is no poetry like the poetry of events; and all the prophecies lag behind their fulfilment.

That is the doctrine which you, and I, of America, are bound to teach. Does any body doubt that, on this broad, popular platform, there exists now, in these United States, a safe government? Tell me where there is one safer. Or tell me of any on the face of the Old World on which public faith is more confidently reposed. I say the government of the United States is one of the safest. I do not know how long it may be before it will become one of the oldest governments in the world.

We are in an age of progress. That progress is towards self-government by the enlightened portion of the community, everywhere. And the great question is, how this impulse can be carried on, without running to excess; how popular government can be established, without falling into licentiousness. That is the great question, and we have seen how difficult it is, by those not taught in the school of experience, to establish such a system.

It is a common sentiment uttered by those who would revolutionize Europe, that, to be free, men have only to *will* it. That is a fallacy. There must be prudence and a balancing of departments, and there must be persons who will teach the science of free, popular governments; and there are but few, except in this country, who can teach that science. We have arrived at this ability by an experience of two hundred years. And how has it come? Why, we are an offshoot of the British constitution. In that constitution there is a popular element, that is, a representation of the people. This element is there mixed up with the monarchical and the aristocratic elements. But our ancestors brought with them no aristocracy, and no monarchical rule, except a general submission and allegiance to the crown of England. Their immediate government was altogether a popular representation; and the country has been thoroughly trained, and schooled, in the practice of such a government.

To abide by the voice of the representatives fairly chosen, by the edicts of those who make the legislative enactments, has been and is our only system. From the first settlement of the colony at Plymouth, through all our subsequent history, we have adhered to this principle. We threw off the power of the king, and we never admitted the power of the Parliament. That was the doctrine of Adams and Jefferson. That was the reason why the Parliament was not alluded to in the Declaration of Independence. The Colonies acknowledged the power of the crown, but never having acknowledged the authority of the Parliament, they disdained to give any reason for throwing it off.

When the Revolution severed us from the mother country, we had nothing to do but to go on with our elections, supplying the governors no longer appointed by the crown by our own election, thus making the whole government popular, and to proceed as at first. It was in this way that the Colonies of Connecticut and Rhode Island were enabled, down to a very late period, to continue their ancient constitutions.

If you look anywhere, beside at France, on the continent of Europe, can you find any thing that bears the aspect of a representative government? There is nothing. It is very difficult to establish a free conservative government for the equal advancement of all the interests of society. What has Germany done, learned Germany, fuller of ancient lore than all the world beside? What has Italy done, what have they done who dwell on the spot where Cicero and Cato lived? They have not the power of self-government which a common town-meeting with us possesses.

Yes, I say that those persons who have gone from our town-meetings to dig gold in California, are more fit to make a republican government than any body of men in Germany or Italy, because they have learned this one great lesson, that there is no security without law, and that, under the circumstances in which they are placed, where there is no military authority to overawe them, there is no sovereign will but the will of the majority; that therefore, if they remain, they must submit to that will.

It is the prevalence of this general sentiment of obedience to law, — that they must have representatives, and that, if they be fairly chosen, their edicts must stand for law, — it is the general diffusion of this opinion that enables our people everywhere to govern themselves. Where they have our habits, you will find that they will establish government upon the foundation of a free, popular constitution, and nothing else.

Now I think, Gentlemen, that while we prescribe no forms, while we dictate to nobody, our mission is to show that a constitutional, representative, conservative government, founded on the freest possible principles, can do, *can do*, for the advancement of general morals and the general prosperity, as much as any other government can do.   This is our business, this our mission among the nations; and it is a nobler destiny, even, than that which Virgil assigns to imperial Rome.

> " Excudent alii spirantia mollius aera,
>   Credo equidem; vivos ducent de marmore vultus;
>   Orabunt causas melius; cœlique meatus
>   Describent radio, et surgentia sidera dicent,
>   *Tu regere imperio populos, Romane, memento;*
>   *Hae tibi erunt artes, pacisque imponere morem,*
>   *Parcere subjectis, et debellare superbos.*"

Gentlemen, two things are to be maintained and insisted on. One, that men in an enlightened age are capable of self-government; that the enjoyment of equal rights is a practicable thing; and that freedom is not a dangerous thing for a body politic. And the other is, that freedom from restraint is not FREEDOM; that licentiousness, the discharge from moral duties, and that general scramble which leads the idle and the extravagant to hope for a time when they may put their hands into their neighbors' pockets, call it what you please, is tyranny.   It is no matter whether the Sultan of Turkey robs his subject of his property, or whether, under the notion of equal rights, the property earned by one shall be taken from him by a majority.   I would not choose the latter.   On the contrary, give me Turkey, for I would prefer one despot to ten thousand.   Who would labor if there were not a security that what he earns will be his own, for his own enjoyment, for the education of his children, for the support of his age, and the gratification of all his reasonable desires?

Gentlemen, the events of the past year are many, and some of them most interesting.   They seem to result from an indefinite purpose of those who wish to meliorate the condition of things in Europe.   They have had no distinct ideas.   There may be incidental benefits arising from the scenes of turmoil and of blood; but no general and settled change for the better. These wars may somewhat assuage the imperial sway of despots. They may serve to convince those who hold despotic power, that they may shake their own thrones if they do not yield something to popular demands. In that sense some good may come of these events.

Then, Gentlemen, there is another aspect. We have all had our sympathies much enlisted in the Hungarian effort for liberty. We have all wept at its failure. We thought we saw a more rational hope of establishing free government in Hungary than in any other part of Europe, where the question has been in agitation within the last twelve months. But despotic power from abroad intervened to suppress that hope.

And, Gentlemen, what will come of it I do not know. For my part, at this moment, I feel more indignant at recent events connected with Hungary than at all those which passed in her struggle for liberty. I see that the Emperor of Russia demands of Turkey that the noble Kossuth and his companions shall be given up, to be dealt with at his pleasure. And I see that this demand is made in derision of the established law of nations. Gentlemen, there is something on earth greater than arbitrary or despotic power. The lightning has its power, and the whirlwind has its power, and the earthquake has its power; but there is something among men more capable of shaking despotic thrones than lightning, whirlwind, or earthquake, and that is, the excited and aroused indignation of the whole civilized world. Gentlemen, the Emperor of Russia holds himself to be bound by the law of nations, from the fact that he negotiates with civilized nations, and that he forms alliances and treaties with them. He professes, in fact, to live in a civilized age, and to govern an enlightened nation. I say that if, under these circumstances, he shall perpetrate so great a violation of national law as to seize these Hungarians and to execute them, he will stand as a criminal and malefactor in the view of the public law of the world. The whole world will be the tribunal to try him, and he must appear before it, and hold up his hand, and plead, and abide its judgment.

The Emperor of Russia is the supreme lawgiver in his own country, and, for aught I know, the executor of that law, also. But, thanks be to God, he is not the supreme lawgiver or executor of national law, and every offence against that is an offence against the rights of the civilized world. If he breaks that law in the case of Turkey, or any other case, the whole world has a right to call him out, and to demand his punishment.

Our rights as a nation, like those of other nations, are held under the sanction of national law; a law which becomes more important from day to day; a law which none, who profess to agree to it, are at liberty to violate. Nor let him imagine, nor let any one imagine, that mere force can subdue the general sentiment of mankind. It is much more likely to diffuse that sentiment, and to destroy the power which he most desires to establish and secure.

Gentlemen, the bones of poor John Wickliffe were dug out of his grave, seventy years after his death, and burnt for his heresy; and his ashes were thrown upon a river in Warwickshire. Some prophet of that day said: —

> " The Avon to the Severn runs,
>   The Severn to the sea,
> And Wickliffe's dust shall spread abroad,
>   Wide as the waters be."

Gentlemen, if the blood of Kossuth is taken by an absolute, unqualified, unjustifiable violation of national law, what will it appease, what will it pacify? It will mingle with the earth, it will mix with the waters of the ocean, the whole civilized world will snuff it in the air, and it will return with awful retribution on the heads of those violators of national law and universal justice. I cannot say when, or in what form; but depend upon it, that if such an act take place, then thrones, and principalities, and powers, must look out for the consequences.

And now, Gentlemen, let us do our part; let us understand the position in which we stand, as the great republic of the world, at the most interesting era of its history. Let us consider the mission and the destiny which Providence seems to have designed for us, and let us so take care of our own conduct, that, with irreproachable hearts, and with hands void of offence, we may stand up whenever and wherever called upon, and, with a voice not to be disregarded, say, This shall not be done, at least not without our protest.

PILGRIM FESTIVAL AT NEW YORK IN 1850.

PILGRIM FESTIVAL AT NEW YORK IN 1850.

AFTER the customary toasts on this occasion had been given, the President of the day, Mr. Grinnell, asked attention to a toast which, as he said, was not on the list, but which he thought every one would vote ought to be placed there forthwith. He gave, " THE CONSTITUTION AND THE UNION, AND THEIR CHIEF DEFENDER." This sentiment was received with great applause ; and when Mr. Webster rose to respond to it, he was greeted with the most prolonged and tumultuous cheers. When the applause had subsided, he spoke as follows : —

MR. PRESIDENT, AND GENTLEMEN OF THE NEW ENGLAND SOCIETY OF NEW YORK : — Ye sons of New England ! Ye brethren of the kindred tie ! I have come hither to-night, not without some inconvenience, that I might behold a congregation whose faces bear lineaments of a New England origin, and whose hearts beat with full New England pulsations. I willingly make the sacrifice. I am here to attend this meeting of the Pilgrim Society of New York, the great offshoot of the Pilgrim Society of Massachusetts. And, gentlemen, I shall begin what I have to say, which is but little, by tendering to you my thanks for the invitation extended to me, and by wishing you, one and all, every kind of happiness and prosperity.

Gentlemen, this has been a stormy, cold, boisterous, and inclement day. The winds have been harsh, the skies have been severe ; and if we had been exposed to their rigor ; if we had no shelter against this howling and freezing tempest ; if we were wan and worn out ; if half of us were sick and tired, and ready to descend into the grave ; if we were on the bleak coast of Plymouth, houseless, homeless, with nothing over our heads but the heavens, and that God who sits above the heavens ; if we had distressed wives on our arms, and hungry and shivering children clinging to our skirts, we should see something, and feel something, of that scene, which, in the providence of God, was enacted at Plymouth on the 22d of December, 1620.

Thanks to Almighty God, who, from that distressed early condition of our fathers, has raised us to a height of prosperity and of happiness which they neither enjoyed, nor could have anticipated! We have learned much of them; they could have foreseen little of us. Would to God, my friends, that, when we carry our affections and our recollections back to that period, we could arm ourselves with something of the stern virtues which supported them, in that hour of peril, and exposure, and suffering! Would to God that we possessed that unconquerable resolution, stronger than bars of brass or iron, which strengthened their hearts; that patience, "sovereign o'er transmuted ill," and, above all, that faith, that religious faith, which, with eyes fast fixed upon heaven, tramples all things earthly beneath her triumphant feet!

Gentlemen, the scenes of this world change. What our ancestors saw and felt, we shall not see nor feel. What they achieved, it is denied to us even to attempt. The severer duties of life, requiring the exercise of the stern and unbending virtues, were theirs. They were called upon for the exhibition of those austere qualities, which, before they came to the Western wilderness, had made them what they were. Things have changed. In the progress of society, the fashions and the habits of life, with all its conditions, have changed. Their rigid sentiments, and their tenets, apparently harsh and exclusive, we are not called on, in every respect, to imitate or commend; or rather to imitate, for we should commend them always, when we consider the state of society in which they had been adopted, and in which they seemed necessary. Our fathers had that religious sentiment, that trust in Providence, that determination to do right, and to seek, through every degree of toil and suffering, the honor of God, and the preservation of their liberties, which we shall do well to cherish, to imitate, and to equal, to the utmost of our ability. It may be true, and it is true, that in the progress of society the milder virtues have come to belong more especially to our day and our condition. The Pilgrims had been great sufferers from intolerance; it was not unnatural that their own faith and practice, as a consequence, should become somewhat intolerant. This is the common infirmity of human nature. Man retaliates on man. It is to be hoped, however, that the greater spread of the benignant principles of religion, of the divine charity of Christianity, has, to some extent, improved the sentiments which prevailed in the world at that time. No doubt the " first-comers," as they were called, were attached to their own forms of public worship, and to their own particular and strongly cherished religious opinions. No doubt they esteemed those sentiments, and the observances which they practised, to be absolutely binding on all, by the authority of the word of God. It is true, I think, in the general advancement of human intelligence, that we find, what they do not seem to have found, that a greater toleration of religious opinion, a more friendly feeling towards all who profess reverence for God and obedience to his commands, is not inconsistent with the great and fundamental principles of religion; I might rather say, is itself one of those fundamental principles. So we see in our day, I think, without any departure from the essential principles of our fathers, a more enlarged and comprehensive Christian philanthropy. It seems to be the American destiny, the mission which has been intrusted to us here on this shore of the Atlantic, the great conception and the great duty to which we are born, to show that all sects, and all denominations, professing reverence for the authority of the Author of our being, and belief in his revelations, may be safely tolerated without prejudice either to our religion or to our liberties.

We are Protestants, generally speaking; but you all know that there presides at the head of the supreme judicature of the United States a Roman Catholic; and no man, I suppose, through the whole United States, imagines that the judicature of the country is less safe, that the administration of public justice is less respectable or less secure, because the Chief Justice of the United States has been, and is, a firm adherent of that religion. And so it is in every department of society amongst us. In both houses of Congress, in all public offices, and all public affairs, we proceed on the idea that a man's religious belief is a matter above human law; that it is a question to be settled between him and his Maker, because he is responsible to none but his Maker for adopting or rejecting revealed truth. And here is the great distinction which is sometimes overlooked, and which I am afraid is now too often overlooked, in this land, the glorious inheritance of the sons of the Pilgrims. Men, for their religious sentiments, are accountable to God, and to God only. Religion is both a communication and a tie between man and his Maker; and to his own master every man standeth or falleth. But when men come together in society, establish social relations, and form governments for the protection of the rights of all, then it is indispensable that this right of private judgment should in some measure be relinquished and made subservient to the judgment of the whole. Religion may exist while every man is left responsible only to God. Society, civil rule, the civil state, cannot exist, while every man is responsible to nobody and to nothing but to his own opinion. And our New England ancestors understood all this quite well. Gentlemen, there is the "Constitution" which was adopted on board the Mayflower in November, 1620, while that bark of immortal memory was riding at anchor in the harbor of Cape Cod. What is it? Its authors honored God; they professed to obey all his commandments, and to live ever and in all things in his obedience. But they say, nevertheless, that for the establishment of a civil polity, and for the greater security and preservation of their civil rights and liberties, they agree that the laws and ordinances, acts and constitutions, (and I am glad they put in the word "*constitutions*,") — they say that these laws and ordinances, acts and *constitutions*, which may be established by those whom they shall appoint to enact them, they, in all due submission and obedience, will support.

This constitution is not long. I will read it. It invokes a *religious* sanction and the authority of God on their *civil* obligations; for it was no doctrine of theirs that civil obedience is a mere matter of expediency. Here it is : —

"In the name of God, Amen: We, whose names are underwritten, the loyal subjects of our dread sovereign lord, King James, by the grace of God, of Great Britain, France, and Ireland, king, defender of the Faith, &c., having undertaken, for the glory of God, and advancement of the Christian faith, and honor of our king and country, a voyage to plant the first colony in the northern parts of Virginia, do by these presents solemnly and mutually, in the presence of God and one of another, covenant and combine ourselves together into a civil body politic, for our better ordering and preservation, and furtherance of the ends aforesaid, and by virtue hereof to enact, constitute, and frame such just and equal laws and ordinances, acts, constitutions, and offices, from time to time, as shall be thought most meet and convenient for the general good of the colony ; unto which we promise all due submission and obedience."

The right of private judgment in matters between the Creator and the individual, and submission and obedience to the will of the whole, in all that respects civil polity, and the administration of such affairs as concerned the colony about to be established, they regarded as entirely consistent; and the common sense of mankind, lettered and unlettered, everywhere establishes and confirms this sentiment.   Indeed, all must see that it is the very ligament, the very tie, which connects man to man, in the social system; and these sentiments are embodied in that constitution.   Discourse on this topic might be enlarged, but I pass from it.

Gentlemen, we are now two hundred and thirty years from that great event.   There is the Mayflower.*   There is an imitation on a small scale, but a correct one, of the Mayflower.   Sons of New England! there was in ancient times a ship that carried Jason to the acquisition of the Golden Fleece.   There was a flag-ship at the battle of Actium which made Augustus Cæsar master of the world.   In modern times, there have been flagships which have carried Hawke, and Howe, and Nelson of the other continent, and Hull, and Decatur, and Stewart of this, to triumph.   What are they all, in the chance of remembrance among men, to that little bark, the Mayflower, which reached these shores on the 22d day of December, 1620?   Yes, brethren of New England, yes! that Mayflower was a flower destined to be of perpetual bloom!   Its verdure will stand the sultry blasts of summer, and the chilling winds of autumn.   It will defy winter; it will defy all climate, and all time, and will continue to spread its petals to the world, and to exhale an ever-living odor and fragrance, to the last syllable of recorded time.

Gentlemen, brethren of New England! whom I have come some hundreds of miles to meet this night, let me present to you one of the most distinguished of those personages who came hither on the deck of the Mayflower.   Let me fancy that I now

* Pointing to a small figure of a ship, in confectionery, representing the Mayflower, that stood before him.

see Elder William Brewster entering the door at the farther end of this hall; a tall and erect figure, of plain dress, of no elegance of manner beyond a respectful bow, mild and cheerful, but of no merriment that reaches beyond a smile. Let me suppose that his image stood now before us, or that it was looking in upon this assembly.

"Are ye," he would say, with a voice of exultation, and yet softened with melancholy, "are ye our children? Does this scene of refinement, of elegance, of riches, of luxury, does all this come from our labors? Is this magnificent city, the like of which we never saw nor heard of on either continent, is this but an offshoot from Plymouth rock?

> ' Quis jam locus . . . .
> Quæ regio in terris nostri non plena laboris? '

Is this one part of the great reward for which my brethren and myself endured lives of toil and of hardship? We had faith and hope. God granted us the spirit to look forward, and we did look forward. But this scene we never anticipated. Our hopes were on another life. Of earthly gratifications we tasted little; for human honors we had little expectation. Our bones lie on the hill in Plymouth church-yard, obscure, unmarked, *secreted*, to preserve our graves from the knowledge of savage foes. No stone tells where we lie. And yet, let me say to you who are our descendants, who possess this glorious country and all it contains, who enjoy this hour of prosperity and the thousand blessings showered upon it by the God of your fathers, we envy you not, we reproach you not. Be rich, be prosperous, be enlightened. Live in pleasure, if such be your allotment on earth; but live, also, always to God and to duty. Spread yourselves and your children over the continent, accomplish the whole of your great destiny, and if it be that through the whole you carry Puritan hearts with you, if you still cherish an undying love of civil and religious liberty, and mean to enjoy them yourselves, and are willing to shed your heart's blood to transmit them to your posterity, then will you be worthy descendants of Carver and Allerton and Bradford, and the rest of those who landed from stormy seas on the rock of Plymouth."

Gentlemen, that little vessel, on the 22d of December, 1620, made her safe landing on the shore of Plymouth. She had been tossed on a tempestuous ocean; she approached the New England coast under circumstances of great distress and trouble; yet, amidst all the disasters of her voyage, she accomplished her end, and she bore a hundred precious pilgrims to the shore of the New World.

Gentlemen, let her be considered this night as an emblem of New England, the New England which now is. New England is a ship, staunch, strong, well built, and particularly well manned. She may be occasionally thrown into the trough of the sea by the violence of winds and waves, and may *wallow* there for a time; but, depend upon it, she will right herself. She will ere long *come round to the wind, and obey her helm.*

We have hardly begun, my brethren, to realize the vast importance to human society, and to the history and happiness of the world, of the voyage of that little vessel which brought hither the love of civil and religious liberty, and the reverence of the Bible, for the instruction of the future generations of men. We have hardly begun to realize the consequences of that voyage. Heretofore the extension of our race, following our New England ancestry, has crept along the shore. But now it has extended itself. It has crossed the continent. It has not only transcended the Alleghanies, but has capped the Rocky Mountains. It is now upon the shores of the Pacific; and on this day, or, if not on this day, then this day twelve-month, descendants of New England will there celebrate the landing ——

(A Voice. "To-day; they celebrate it to-day.")

God bless them! Here's to the health and success of the California Society of Pilgrims assembled on the shores of the Pacific. And it shall yet go hard if the three hundred millions of people of China, provided they are intelligent enough to understand any thing, shall not one day hear and know something of the rock of Plymouth too.

But, gentlemen, I am trespassing too long on your time. I am taking too much of what belongs to others. My voice is neither a new voice nor is it the voice of a young man. It has been heard before in this place; and the most that I have thought or felt concerning New England history and New England principles has been before, in the course of my life, said here or elsewhere.

Your sentiment, Mr. President, which called me up before this meeting, is of a larger and more comprehensive nature. It speaks of the Constitution under which we live; of the Union which has bound us together for sixty years, and made us the fellow-citizens of those who settled at Yorktown and the mouth of the Mississippi and their descendants, and now, at last, of those who have come from all corners of the earth and assembled in California. I confess I have had my doubts whether the republican system under which we live could be so vastly extended without danger of dissolution. Thus far, I willingly admit, my apprehensions have not been realized. The distance is immense; the intervening country is vast. But the principle on which our government is established, the representative system, seems to be indefinitely expansive; and wherever it does extend, it seems to create a strong attachment to the Union and the Constitution that protect it. I believe California and New México have had new life inspired into all their people. They feel themselves partakers of a new being, a new creation, a new existence. They are not the men they thought themselves to be, now that they find they are members of this great government, and hailed as citizens of the United States of America. I hope, in the providence of God, as this system of States and representative governments shall extend, that it will be strengthened. In some respects, the tendency is to strengthen it. Local agitations will disturb it less. If there has been on the Atlantic coast, somewhere south of the Potomac, and I will not define further where it is, — if there has been dissatisfaction, that dissatisfaction has not been felt in California; it has not been felt that side of the Rocky Mountains. It is a *localism*, and I am one of those who believe that our system of government is not to be destroyed by *localisms*, North or South. No; we have our private opinions, State prejudices, local ideas; but over all, submerging all, *drowning* all, is that great sentiment, that always, and nevertheless, *we are all Americans*. It is as Americans that we are known, the whole world over. Who asks what State you are from, in Europe, or in Africa, or in Asia? Is he an American? Does he belong to the United States? Does that flag protect him? Does he rest under the eagle and the stars and stripes? If he does, all else is subordinate and of but little concern.

Now it is our duty, while we live on the earth, to cherish this sentiment; to make it prevail over the whole country, even if that country should spread over the whole continent. It is our duty to carry English principles, I mean, Sir, [turning to Sir Henry Bulwer,] Anglo-Saxon *American* principles, over the whole continent; the great principles of Magna Charta, of the English Revolution, and especially of the American Revolution, and of the English language. Our children will hear Shakspeare and Milton recited on the shores of the Pacific. Nay, before that, American ideas, which are essentially and originally English ideas, will penetrate the Mexican, the Spanish mind; and Mexicans and Spaniards will thank God that they have been brought to know something of civil liberty, of the trial by jury, and of security for personal rights.

As for the rest, let us take courage. The day-spring from on high has visited us; the country has been called back to conscience and to duty. *There is no longer imminent danger of dissolution in these United States.* We shall live, and not die. We shall live as united Americans; and those who have supposed they could sever us, that they could rend one American heart from another, and that speculation and hypothesis, that secession and metaphysics, could tear us asunder, will find themselves wofully mistaken.

Let the mind of the sober American people remain sober. Let it not inflame itself. Let it do justice to all. And the truest course, and the surest course, to disappoint those who meditate disunion, is just to leave them to themselves, and see what they can make of it. No, Gentlemen; the time for meditated secession is past. Americans, North and South, will be hereafter more and more united. There is a sternness and severity in the public mind lately aroused. I believe that, North and South, there has been, in the last year, a renovation of public sentiment, an animated revival of the spirit of union, and, more than all, of attachment to the Constitution, regarding it as indispensably necessary; and if we would preserve our nationality, it is indispensable that this spirit of devotion should be still more largely increased. And who doubts it? If we give up that Constitution, what are we? You are a Manhattan man; I am a Boston man. Another is a Connecticut, and another a Rhode Island man. Is it not a great deal better, standing hand to hand, and clasping hands, that we should remain as we have been for sixty years, citizens of the same country, members of the same government, united all, united now, and united for ever? *That we shall be, Gentlemen.* There have been difficulties, contentions, controversies, angry controversies; but I tell you that, in my judgment, —

> " those opposed eyes,
> Which, like the meteors of a troubled heaven,
> All of one nature, of one substance bred,
> Did lately meet in th' intestine shock,
> Shall now, in mutual, well-beseeming ranks
> MARCH ALL ONE WAY."

VISIT TO BUFFALO IN 1851.

INTRODUCTORY NOTE.

In the month of May of the present year (1851), the New York and Erie Railroad was completed, and its entire length thrown open to the public, from Pyrmont on the North River to Dunkirk on Lake Erie, a distance of nearly five hundred miles. Great preparations were made to celebrate this important event, along the line of the railroad, and at its termination on Lake Erie. The President of the United States (a citizen of the western part of the State of New York) and the members of his Cabinet were invited to be present. Their reception, both at the city of New York and along the line of the railroad, was cordial and enthusiastic. At Dunkirk, Mr. Webster was detained by the illness of his son, and was on that account compelled to separate himself from the rest of the party.

On his arrival at Buffalo, the citizens of that place, without distinction of party, invited him to a public dinner. They also requested him to address the public in the Park. Similar invitations were tendered to him at Rochester, Syracuse, Albany, and other places through which he passed on his return to New York. From the numerous speeches delivered by him on these occasions, those at Buffalo and Albany have been selected as containing the fullest exposition of Mr. Webster's views on the important subjects which have engaged the public mind during the current year.

It may be mentioned as a circumstance strongly indicating the earnest wish on the part of the people to hear Mr. Webster, that, though the day appointed for the public address was extremely unfavorable, the citizens of Buffalo earnestly requested that the proposed meeting should not be given up. Although it rained steadily for the whole time that Mr. Webster was speaking, the audience, of which a considerable part were ladies, showed no disposition to disperse, but listened to the orator throughout with a fixed attention, interrupted only by continual bursts of applause.

PUBLIC DINNER AT BUFFALO.*

Mr. Mayor, and Fellow-Citizens of the City of Buffalo, I know that, in regard to the present condition of the country, you think as I think, that there is but one all-absorbing question, and that is the preservation of this Union. If I have strength, I propose to say something to you and your fellow-citizens on that subject to-morrow. In this social interview and intercourse, Gentlemen, I would not aspire to such a lofty, all-important theme. I desire, rather, on this occasion, to address you as citizens of Buffalo, many of whom I have had the pleasure of seeing in former times; many of whom belong to the generation which has grown up since I was first here; but with all of whom I feel a sympathy for the great prosperity which has distinguished their city, and the fair prospect which Providence holds out before them. Gentlemen, I have had the pleasure of being in the good city of Buffalo three times before this visit. I came here in 1825, with my family, accompanied by Mr. Justice Story and his family. We came mainly to see that all attractive neighbor of yours, the Falls of Niagara. I remember it was said, at that time, there were twenty-five hundred people in Buffalo. Even that was startling, because it was fresh in my recollection when it was only a waste, and when, as a member of Congress, I was called upon to ascertain the value of certain houses which were destroyed in the war of 1812. I came here afterwards, Gentlemen, in 1833. Your city then had been enlarged, manufactures were coming into existence, prosperity had begun. I had the pleasure of address-

---

* A Speech delivered at a Public Dinner at Buffalo, on the 21st of May, 1851

ing you or your fathers, or both, in the park, and I remember I was told, among other things, that I might say, with safety, that there were fifteen or eighteen steamboats on Lake Erie.

I remember another thing, Gentlemen, with great satisfaction, and I hope some parties to that transaction are here. The mechanics of Buffalo did me the great honor of tendering to me a present of an article of furniture, made from a great, glorious black-walnut tree, which grew to the south of us. They signified their desire to make a table out of that walnut-tree, and send it to me. The table was made, and I accepted it, of course, with great pleasure. When I left here in July, the tree was standing; and in about five weeks there was an elegant table, of beautiful workmanship, sent to my house, which was then in Boston. When I went to Marshfield it followed me to the sea-side, and there it stands now, in the best room in my house, and there it will stand as long as I live, and I hope as long as the house shall stand. I take this occasion to reiterate my thanks for that beautiful present. I am proud to possess it; I am proud to show it; I am proud in all the recollections that it suggests.

I was again in Buffalo some fourteen years ago, on my return from the West. That, I think, was in July also. I left the sea-coast in May. It was soon after the termination of General Jackson's administration, and the commencement of Mr. Van Buren's. I travelled by the way of the Pennsylvania Railroad and canals, and so on to the Ohio; and I was on the Ohio River, I think, at Wheeling, on the 25th of May, when we heard of the failure of all the banks, the breaking up of all the credit of the country, and Mr. Van Buren's proclamation for an extra session of Congress. That rather hastened our progress. I went by the way of Kentucky, Missouri, and Illinois, and had the pleasure of seeing my fellow-citizens of Buffalo on my return. Now, Gentlemen, it is a great pleasure for me to say, that between that time and the present the population of your city has augmented at least one half; and here is Buffalo, a city of fifty thousand inhabitants.

It is, undoubtedly, one of the wonders of the age and of this country. I enjoy it, Gentlemen, with a degree of pleasure inferior only to your own, because we are of the same country, because we participate in the same destiny, and because we are bound to the same fate for good or evil. All that is my interest is your interest, and I feel it to be so; and there is not in this region, or beyond the Lakes, a city planned, a tree felled, a field of wheat planted, or any other mark of prosperity, in which I, for one, do not take an interest. But then, Gentlemen, one thing strikes me. You are all a young race here. Here is my friend near me.* We were young men together. It seems to me but a short time ago, and here we are. Now, whom do I see around me here? Why, the rising generation have taken possession of Buffalo. Ye fathers, be frightened! Ye grandfathers, be alarmed! The youth of Buffalo have taken possession of the city. But then, you unmarried women of Buffalo, and you, young wives of Buffalo, be neither frightened nor alarmed; for those who have taken possession will be your protectors. And I believe that this is true throughout the whole county of Erie. The strong arms of young men till the soil. The vigorous resolution which takes hold of any improvement, and sustains every public project, takes counsel, no doubt, from age and experience; but young men in this country push forward every thing; complete every thing.

Gentlemen, I need not say that this great neighborhood of yours, and this great State of yours, are full of things most striking to the eye and to the imagination. The spectacle which your State presents, the waters of New York, the natural phenomena of New York, are exciting to a very high degree. There is this noble river, the Niagara; the noble lake from which it issues; there are the Falls of Niagara, the wonder of the world, and the numerous lakes and rivers of a secondary class. Why, how many things are there in this great State of New York that attract the wonder and draw the attention of Europe! I had the pleasure, some years ago, of being a few weeks in Europe, and every one asked me how long it took to go to Niagara Falls. New York, in all its relations, in its falls, its rivers, and secondary waters, is attractive to all the world. But then there is New York, in the State of New York. Gentlemen, the commercial character so far pervades the minds of commercial men all over the world, that there are many men, who are very respectable and intelligent, who do not seem to know there is any thing in the United States but New York.

* Hon. Albert H. Tracy.

When I was in England, it was asked of me if I did not come from New York. I told them my wife came from New York. That is something. Well, Gentlemen, I had the honor, one day, to be invited to a state dinner, by the Lord Mayor of London. He was a portly and a dignified gentleman. He had a big wig on his head, all powdered and ribboned down behind, and I had the honor to sit between him and the Lady Mayoress; and there were three hundred guests, with all the luxuries and gorgeousness of the Lord Mayor's dinner. Soon after the cloth was removed, his Lordship thought proper to take notice of his American guest. He seemed not to know exactly who I was. He knew I was a Senator; but he seemed to have but little idea of any place in the United States but New York. He arose: "Gentlemen," said he, "I give you the health of Mr. Webster, a member of the upper Senate of New York." Well, it was a great honor to be a member of any Senate of New York, but if there was an upper Senate, to be a member of that would be a great honor indeed.

Gentlemen, New York, the State of New York, — let me indulge in a moment's reflection on that great theme! It has so happened, in the dispensation of things, that New York stretches from east to west entirely across the country. Your fellow-citizens, to-day, are eating clams at Montauk Point, seven hundred miles from this spot, and you are regaling on lake trout. You stretch along and divide the whole country. New York extends from the frontier of Canada to the sea, and divides the Southern States from the Eastern. Here she is with two heads; one down at New York, and the other at Buffalo, like a double-headed snake. Well, what are you to do with her? Fixed, firm, and immovable, there she is. It has pleased Heaven, in assigning her a position in the configuration of the earth's surface, to cause her to divide the whole South from the East, and she does so, physically and geographically. As she stretches here, in the whole length and breadth, she divides the Southern from the Eastern States. But that is her inferior destiny, her lower characteristic; for, if I do not mistake all auguries, her higher destiny is likewise to unite all the States in one political union.

Gentlemen, nothing so fills my imagination, or comes up so nearly to my idea of what constitutes a great, enterprising, and energetic state, as those things which have been accomplished by

New York in reference to commerce and internal improvements. I honor you for it. When I consider that your canal runs from the Lakes to tide-water; when I consider, also, that you have had for some years a railroad from the Lakes to tide-water; and when I examine, as I have just examined, that stupendous work, hung up, as it were, in the air, on the southern range of mountains from New York to Lake Erie; when I consider the energy, the power, the indomitable resolution, which effected all this, I bow with reverence to the genius and people of New York, whatever political party may lead, or however wrongly I may deem any of them to act in other respects. It takes care of itself, it is true to itself, it is true to New York; and being true to itself, it goes far, in my opinion, in establishing the interest of the whole country. For one, I wish it so to proceed. I know that there are questions of a local and State character with which I have nothing to do. I know there is a proposition to make this canal of yours greater and broader, to give to New York and its commerce, if I may say so, the power to send forth what it has with greater facility. I know not how that may comport with State politics or State arrangements, but I shall be happy to see the day when there shall be no obstruction or hinderance to any article of trade or commerce going out right, straight and strong, with breadth enough and margin enough and room enough to carry all to its market. May I say, Gentlemen, that a broad, deep, and ample canal realizes, and more than realizes, what the poet has said of the River Thames : —

> " O, could I flow like thee, and make thy stream
> My great example, as it is my theme !
> Though deep, yet clear, though gentle, yet not dull,
> Strong without rage, without o'erflowing, full."

But, Gentlemen, there are other things about this State of yours. You are here at the foot of Lake Erie. You look out on the far expanse of the West. Who have come here? Of whom are you composed? You are already a people of fifty thousand, a larger population than that of any New England city except Boston; and yet you are but of yesterday. Who are your inhabitants? A great many of them are my countrymen from the East, and I see them with pleasure. But these are not all; there are also Irish and Germans. I suppose, on the whole and in the main, they are safe citizens; at any rate, they appear well disposed, and they constitute a large portion of your population. That leads us to consider generally what is the particular position of our country, and of your city, as one of the great outlets to the West, in regard to this foreign immigration. The emigration to this country is enormous; it comes from Ireland, Germany, Switzerland, and almost every other part of Continental Europe. I remember it used to be a simile, when any thing of a sudden or energetic nature took place, to say that it "broke out like an Irish rebellion, forty thousand strong, when nobody expected it." Forty thousand strong does not begin to compare with the emigration to the United States. Emigration comes here with a perfect rush from every part of Ireland; from Limerick and the Shannon, from Dublin and from Cork, from the Northern ports, from Londonderry and Belfast. Into this country they come, and will continue to come; it is in the order of things, and there is no possibility of preventing it. Gentlemen, it is about three centuries and a half since Columbus discovered America, and he came here by authority of the Spanish government. He gathered up some gold, and went back with a great name. It is a much shorter time since the Irish discovered America, and they come in much greater numbers; but they don't come here with the idea of carrying back money, or fame, or a name; they mean to abide here. They come to remain among us, and to be of us, and to take their chances among us. Let them come.

There are also Germans. Your city, I am told, has a very large number of thrifty, industrious German people. Let them also come. If his Majesty of Austria, and the Austrian ministry, will allow them to come, let them come. All we desire, whoever come, is, that they will Americanize themselves; that, forgetting the things that are behind, they will look forward; and if they look as far as Iowa and Minnesota, they will not look a rod too far. I know that many from Europe come here who have been brought up to different pursuits, to different modes of life, and to different systems of agriculture from ours; but I believe it is generally true, that, when they are removed from the temptations of the Atlantic cities, and when they get into regions where trees are to be felled and land cleared, they prove themselves worthy and respectable citizens.

And here, perhaps, Gentlemen, you will excuse me, if, without too long a speech, I say a little relative to our American system on this subject of foreign immigration. In the Declaration of Independence, declared on the 4th of July, 1776, a solemn and formal complaint is made against the British king, that he sought to prevent emigration from Europe to the Colonies, by refusing his assent to reasonable laws of naturalization, in consequence of which, it was stated, the country did not fill up and the public lands were not purchased. It is worthy the attention of any gentleman who wishes to acquaint himself with the early history of the country in this respect, to look back to the naturalization laws passed in the time of Washington. Every one can see what was the prevailing idea at that period. The idea of encouraging emigration from Europe was universal, and the only desire was, that those who wished to become naturalized should become acquainted with our system of government before they voted; that they should have an interest in the country; that they might not be led away by every designing demagogue. At that day, nobody foresaw such growth and such enlargement in the commerce of the country as we now see; and, therefore, in the early periods of Washington's administration, they were looking to see how they should pay the debt of the Revolution. Whatever we may think of it now, their great resource to pay their debt was, as they thought, the public domain. They had obtained from the separate States, before the Constitution was formed, a grant of the Northwest Territory, which was known to be capable of furnishing great products by agricultural labor. The Congress of that day looked to this. They had no idea how sudden would be the great increase of our commerce, or how plentiful would be the revenue from that source; and therefore their great care was to see how far they could encourage foreign immigration (which, it was expected, would bring capital into the country), consistently with such a conformity to our American system and our American institutions as would render immigration safe, and not dangerous, to the common weal.

Gentlemen, we are not arbiters of our own fate. Human foresight falters and fails. Who could foresee or conjecture at that day what our eyes now see and behold? We see this for good or for evil. Nor could we stay this immigration if we would. We see there is a rush of people from Europe to America that exceeds, in a single month, and at the single port of New York, the population of many single cities on the Atlantic coast. This is the case, and it is to be met and to be considered. It would be foolish to attempt to obstruct it, if obstruction were possible. The thing cannot be done. You may remember, Gentlemen, (though I ought not to suppose that you remember much about it,) that, in the correspondence with Lord Ashburton, who came out here to negotiate the treaty of 1842, we examined the subject of the impressment of American citizens. Up to that day, England had insisted on the right to visit every American ship in time of war, and, if she found any Englishmen, Irishmen, or Welshmen on board of her, to press them into her service, on the ground that they could not transfer their allegiance. I need not say that this subject had often been a matter of negotiation. It was at one time suggested by the British minister, that the right should be exercised only within certain latitudes. At another time, it was suggested that this right should not be extended to the deprivation of any American vessel of her crew. Gentlemen, I don't know that I ought to say it, but with your permission I will say, that on that occasion the ground was taken that every man on board of an American vessel, either mercantile or naval, was protected by the flag of America. No matter if his speech did betray him, no matter what brogue was on his tongue, if the stars and stripes were over him, he was for that purpose, while on board an American vessel, an American citizen. Well, Gentlemen, from that day to this, we have heard of no pretensions on the part of the British government that it could send an officer on board of any American ship and take from her any human being whatever, and, I venture to add, we never shall.

Lord Ashburton, with whom I negotiated and corresponded on that occasion, was a judicious and wise man. He had been a good deal in this country. He was married in this country. He knew something of it; and he saw various relations between this country and England in a far more philanthropical point of view than most others. He stated in a letter, which forms part of the correspondence: "I must admit that, when a British subject, Irish, English, or Welsh, becomes an American, and claims no longer the protection of his own country, his own country has no right to call him a subject, and to put him in a position to make war on his adopted country; and it appears to me," he added, " that we may count it among the dispensations of Providence, that these new facilities of transporting men from country to country, by the power of steam, and quickly, are designed by a high wisdom." He said, " We have more people than land, and you have more land than people. Take as many from us as you please, or as please to come. That seems to be the order of things; and it is not to be stopped." I told him that was my opinion too. Gentlemen, this immigration is not to be stopped; we must keep things as they are; we must inculcate upon all who come here the necessity of becoming Americans; we must teach them; we must endeavor to instil American sentiments into their bosoms.

Gentlemen, if it were not so late, I would say a few words more about the public lands of this country, and the best disposition to be made of them. What shall we do with them? They spread over a vast extent of territory, rich in its natural fertility; but can any one tell me what is the value of land unconnected with cultivation and social life? A thousand acres would not, in such a case, be worth a dollar. What is land worth in the remote interior? Land is a theatre for the application and exhibition of human labor; and when human labor goes upon it, and is exerted, then it creates its value. Without this, it is not worth a rush, from " Dan to Beersheba." I do not wish to say, that on every acre of land there must be a settlement; but there must be human labor somewhere near it; there must be something besides the mathematical division apportioning it into sections, half-sections, and quarter-sections, before land is of any value whatever.

But, Gentlemen, we have had a series of wonderful events in our commercial relations. The commerce of the country is filling the coffers of the country. It has supplied, and now supplies, every want of the government. What, then, shall we do with the public lands? During the last Congress, acts were passed, distributing large quantities of them, varying from one hundred and sixty acres, or more, down to forty acres, to those who had rendered military service to the country. This was all very well; nobody goes further than I do, in desiring to make happy those who have borne arms in their country's cause, as well as their widows and orphans; but this does not appear to me to answer the exigencies of the case. What is to be done? What is to become of those who come to this country and have nothing to buy land with? That is the question, Gentlemen. The last measure proposed by me while in the last Congress was the short and simple proposition, that every man of twenty-one years of age, who would go on any uncultivated land in the country, and take up one hundred and sixty acres and cultivate it for five years, should thereby make it his own, to the extinction of the public right; and if his widow and children did the same, they should have it. One of the great evils of this military bounty business is, that, when warrants are issued, manage it as you will, they fall into the hands of speculators, and do not accrue to those whom it was designed to benefit. Let me relate an anecdote on this subject. I brought forward this matter in the Senate of the United States, and soon afterwards I received a letter from Europe stating that it was wrong and unjust, because it would interfere with the rights of those who had purchased warrants to settle on the public lands, as a matter of speculation. I wrote back that it was just the thing I wished. I was glad it was so, and I had desired it should be so. My proposition was, that these lands should not be alienated; that they should be free of claims for debt; that they should not be transferable; and if a man left his land before five years, that he should lose it. My object was, simply, as far as the object could be accomplished by such an arrangement, to benefit those in the Northern States who were landless, and the thousands in the Southern States who were willing to toil if they had any thing of their own to toil upon. It was also to benefit the immigrant, by giving him a home; to let him feel that he had a homestead; that he trod upon his own soil; that he was a citizen, a freeholder. On his own good behaviour he must rely to make up all else to which he would aspire. I may have been wrong in my opinions, but they are my opinions still; and if ever an opportunity is given me, I shall endeavor to carry them out.

Well, Gentlemen, I revert once more to your great State. I see all her works, all her gigantic improvements, the respectability of her government. I hear of her greatness over the whole world. Your merchants have a character everywhere, which realizes my youthful idea of the character of a British merchant.

A friend of mine, in the days of the French Republic, had so much confidence in the men who stood at the head of affairs, that he invested largely in *assignats*. But after a while he found them to be worthless. His creditors would not touch them; and there they were, dead upon his hands. One day, after using some very extravagant language, he concluded by saying, "that if he were travelling in the deserts of Arabia, and his camel should kick up a British bill of exchange out of the sands, it would be worth ten per cent. premium, while these French government assignats were not worth a farthing." So your commercial character stands. Your vessels traverse every sea, and fill all the rivers. You invite Commerce to you from every region, and she comes. You call her from the vasty deep, and she responds to your call.

But, Gentlemen, I will conclude by offering a sentiment, for I am sure you are anxious to hear from others, from whom I have too long detained you. Permit me to give

The State of New York: not the envy, but the admiration, of her sister States.

RECEPTION AT BUFFALO.*

FELLOW-CITIZENS OF THE CITY OF BUFFALO, — I am very glad to see you; I meet you with pleasure. It is not the first time that I have been in Buffalo, and I have always come to it with gratification. It is at a great distance from my own home. I am thankful that circumstances have enabled me to be here again, and I regret that untoward events deprived me of the pleasure of being with you when your distinguished fellow-citizen, the President of the United States, visited you, and received from you, as he deserved, not only a respectful, but a cordial and enthusiastic welcome. The President of the United States has been a resident among you for more than half his life. He has represented you in the State and national councils. You know him and all his relations, both public and private, and it would be bad taste in me to say any thing of him, except that I wish to say, with emphasis, that, since my connection with him in the administration of the government of the United States, I have fully concurred with him in all his great and leading measures. This might be inferred from the fact that I have been one of his ordinary advisers. But I do not wish to let it rest on that presumption; I wish to declare that the principles of the President, as set forth in his annual message, his letters, and all documents and opinions which have proceeded from him, or been issued by his authority, in regard to the great question of the times, — all these principles are my principles; and if he is wrong in them, I am, and always shall be.

Gentlemen, it has been suggested to me that it would be agreeable to the citizens of Buffalo, and their neighbors in the

* A Speech delivered before a large Assembly of the Citizens of Buffalo and the County of Erie, at a Public Reception on the 22d of May, 1851.

county of Erie, that I should state to you my opinions, whatever may be their value, on the present condition of the country, its prospects, its hopes, and its dangers; and, fellow-citizens, I intend to do that, this day, and this hour, as far as my strength will permit.

Gentlemen, believe me, I know where I am. I know to whom I am speaking. I know for whom I am speaking. I know that I am here in this singularly prosperous and powerful section of the United States, Western New York, and I know the character of the men who inhabit Western New York. I know they are sons of liberty, one and all; that they sucked in liberty with their mothers' milk; inherited it with their blood; that it is the subject of their daily contemplation and watchful thought. They are men of unusual equality of condition, for a million and a half of people. There are thousands of men around us, and here before us, who till their own soil with their own hands; and others who earn their own livelihood by their own labor in the workshops and other places of industry; and they are independent, in principle and in condition, having neither slaves nor masters, and not intending to have either. These are the men who constitute, to a great extent, the people of Western New York. But the school-house, I know, is among them. Education is among them. They read, and write, and think. Here, too, are women, educated, refined, and intelligent; and here are men who know the history of their country, and the laws of their country, and the institutions of their country; and men, lovers of liberty always, and yet lovers of liberty under the Constitution of the country, and who mean to maintain that Constitution with all their strength. I hope these observations will satisfy you that I know where I am, under what responsibility I speak, and before whom I appear; and I have no desire that any word I shall say this day shall be withholden from you, or your children, or your neighbors, or the whole world; for I speak before you and before my country, and, if it be not too solemn to say so, before the great Author of all things.

Gentlemen, there is but one question in this country now; or, if there be others, they are but secondary, or so subordinate that they are all absorbed in that great and leading question; and that is neither more nor less than this: Can we preserve the union of the States, not by coercion, not by military power, not

46*

by angry controversies; but can we of this generation, you and I, your friends and my friends, — can we so preserve the union of these States, by such administration of the powers of the Constitution as shall give content and satisfaction to all who live under it, and draw us together, not by military power, but by the silken cords of mutual, fraternal, patriotic affection? That is the question, and no other. Gentlemen, I believe in party distinctions. I am a party man. There are questions belonging to party in which I take an interest, and there are opinions entertained by other parties which I repudiate; but what of all that? If a house be divided against itself, it will fall, and crush every body in it. We must see that we maintain the government which is over us. We must see that we uphold the Constitution, and we must do so without regard to party.

Now how did this question arise? The question is for ever misstated. I dare say, if you know much of me, or of my course of public conduct, for the last fourteen months, you have heard of my attending Union meetings, and of my fervent admonitions at Union meetings. Well, what was the object of those meetings? What was their purpose? The object and purpose have been designedly or thoughtlessly misrepresented. I had an invitation, some time since, to attend a Union meeting in the county of Westchester; I could not go, but wrote a letter. Well, some wise man of the East said he did not think it was very necessary to hold Union meetings in Westchester. He did not think there were many disunionists about Tarrytown! And so in many parts of the country, there is a total misapprehension of the purpose and object of these Union meetings. Every one knows, that there is not a county, or a city, or a hamlet in the State of New York, that is ready to go out of the Union, but only some small bodies of fanatics. There is no man so insane in the State, not fit for a lunatic asylum, as to wish it. But that is not the point. We all know that every man and every neighborhood, and all corporations, in the State of New York, except those I have mentioned, are attached to the Union, and have no idea of withdrawing from it. But that is not, I repeat, the point. The question, fellow-citizens, (and I put it to you now as the real question,) the question is, Whether you and the rest of the people of the great State of New York, and of all the States, will so adhere to the Constitution, will so enact and maintain laws to preserve that instrument, that you will not only remain in the Union yourselves, but permit your brethren to remain in it, and help to perpetuate it? That is the question. Will you concur in measures necessary to maintain the Union, or will you oppose such measures? That is the whole point of the case.

There are thirty or forty members of Congress from New York; you have your proportion in the United States Senate. We have many members of Congress from New England. Will they maintain the laws that are passed for the administration of the Constitution, and respect the rights of the South, so that the Union may be held together; and not only so that we may not go out of it ourselves, which we are not inclined to do, but so that, by maintaining the rights of others, they may also remain in the Union? Now, Gentlemen, permit me to say, that I speak of no concessions. If the South wish any concession from me, they will not get it; not a hair's breadth of it. If they come to my house for it, they will not find it, and the door will be shut; I concede nothing. But I say that I will maintain for them, as I will maintain for you, to the utmost of my power, and in the face of all danger, their rights under the Constitution, and your rights under the Constitution. And I shall never be found to falter in one or the other. It is obvious to every one, and we all know it, that the origin of the great disturbance which agitates the country is the existence of slavery in some of the States; but we must meet the subject; we must consider it; we must deal with it earnestly, honestly, and justly. From the mouth of the St. Johns to the confines of Florida, there existed, in 1775, thirteen colonies of English origin, planted at different times, and coming from different parts of England, bringing with them various habits, and establishing, each for itself, institutions entirely different from the institutions which they left, and in many cases from each other. But they were all of English origin. The English language was theirs, Shakspeare and Milton were theirs, the common law of England was theirs, and the Christian religion was theirs; and these things held them together by the force of a common character. The aggressions of the parent state compelled them to assert their independence. They declared independence, and that immortal act, pronounced on the 4th of July, 1776, made them independent.

That was an act of union by the United States in Congress assembled. But this act of itself did nothing to establish over them a general government. They had a Congress. They had Articles of Confederation to prosecute the war. But thus far they were still, essentially, separate and independent each of the other. They had entered into a simple confederacy, and nothing more. No State was bound by what it did not itself agree to, or what was done according to the provisions of the confederation. That was the state of things, gentlemen, at that time. The war went on; victory crowned the American arms; our independence was acknowledged. The States were then united together under a confederacy of very limited powers. It could levy no taxes. It could not enforce its own decrees. It was a confederacy, instead of a united government. Experience showed that this was insufficient and inefficient. Accordingly, beginning as far back almost as the close of the war, measures were taken for the formation of a united government, a government in the strict sense of the term, a government that could pass laws binding on the individual citizens of all the States, and which could enforce those laws by its executive powers, having them interpreted by a judicial power belonging to the government itself, and yet a government strictly limited in its nature. Well, Gentlemen, this led to the formation of the Constitution of the United States, and that instrument was framed on the idea of a limited government. It proposed to leave, and did leave, the different domestic institutions of the several States to themselves. It did not propose consolidation. It did not propose that the laws of Virginia should be the laws of New York, or that the laws of New York should be the laws of Massachusetts. It proposed only that, for certain purposes and to a certain extent, there should be a united government, and that that government should have the power of executing its own laws. All the rest was left to the several States.

We now come, Gentlemen, to the very point of the case. At that time slavery existed in the Southern States, entailed upon them in the time of the supremacy of British laws over us. There it was. It was obnoxious to the Middle and Eastern States, and honestly and seriously disliked, as the records of the country will show, by the Southern States themselves. Now, how was it to be dealt with? Were the Northern and Middle

States to exclude from the government those States of the South which had produced a Washington, a Laurens, and other distinguished patriots, who had so truly served, and so greatly honored, the whole country? Were they to be excluded from the new government because they tolerated the institution of slavery? Your fathers and my fathers did not think so. They did not see that it would be of the least advantage to the slaves of the Southern States, to cut off the South from all connection with the North. Their views of humanity led to no such result; and of course, when the Constitution was framed and established, and adopted by you, here in New York, and by New England, it contained an express provision of security to the persons who lived in the Southern States, in regard to fugitives who owed them service; that is to say, it was stipulated that the fugitive from service or labor should be restored to his master or owner if he escaped into a free State. Well, that had been the history of the country from its first settlement. It was a matter of common practice to return fugitives before the Constitution was formed. Fugitive slaves from Virginia to Massachusetts were restored by the people of Massachusetts. At that day there was a great system of apprenticeship at the North, and many apprentices at the North, taking advantage of circumstances, and of vessels sailing to the South, thereby escaped; and they were restored on proper claim and proof. That led to a clear, express, and well-defined provision in the Constitution of the country on the subject. Now I am aware that all these things are well known; that they have been stated a thousand times; but in these days of perpetual discontent and misrepresentation, to state things a thousand times is not enough; for there are persons whose consciences, it would seem, lead them to consider it their duty to deny, misrepresent, falsify, and cover up truths.

Now these are words of the Constitution, fellow-citizens, which I have taken the pains to transcribe therefrom, so that he who runs may read: —

" No PERSON HELD TO SERVICE OR LABOR IN ONE STATE, UNDER THE LAWS THEREOF, ESCAPING INTO ANOTHER, SHALL, IN CONSEQUENCE OF ANY LAW OR REGULATION THEREIN, BE DISCHARGED FROM SUCH SERVICE OR LABOR, BUT SHALL BE DELIVERED UP ON CLAIM OF THE PARTY TO WHOM SUCH SERVICE OR LABOR MAY BE DUE."

Is there any mistake about that? Is there any forty-shilling attorney here to make a question of it? No. I will not disgrace my profession by supposing such a thing. There is not, in or out of an attorney's office in the county of Erie, or elsewhere, one who could raise a doubt, or a particle of a doubt, about the meaning of this provision of the Constitution. He may act as witnesses do, sometimes, on the stand. He may wriggle, and twist, and say he cannot tell, or cannot remember. I have seen many such efforts in my time, on the part of witnesses, to falsify and deny the truth. But there is no man who can read these words of the Constitution of the United States, and say they are not clear and imperative. " No person," the Constitution says, " held to service or labor in one State, under the laws thereof, escaping into another, shall, in consequence of any law or regulation therein, be discharged from such service or labor, but shall be delivered up on claim of the party to whom such service or labor may be due." Why, you may be told by forty conventions in Massachusetts, in Ohio, in New York, or elsewhere, that, if a colored man comes here, he comes as a freeman; that is a *non sequitur*. It is not so. If he comes as a fugitive from labor, the Constitution says he is not a freeman, and that he shall be delivered up to those who are entitled to his service.

Gentlemen, that is the Constitution of the United States. Do we, or do we not, mean to conform to it, and to execute that part of the Constitution as well as the rest of it? I believe there are before me here members of Congress. I suppose there may be here members of the State legislature, or executive officers under the State government. I suppose there may be judicial magistrates of New York, executive officers, assessors, supervisors, justices of the peace, and constables before me. Allow me to say, Gentlemen, that there is not, that there cannot be, any one of these officers in this assemblage, or elsewhere, who has not, according to the form of the usual obligation, bound himself by a solemn oath to support the Constitution. They have taken their oaths on the Holy Evangelists of Almighty God, or by uplifted hand, as the case may be, or by a solemn affirmation, as is the practice in some cases; but among all of them, there is not a man who holds, nor is there any man who can hold, any office in the gift of the United

States, or of this State, or of any other State, who does not bind himself, by the solemn obligation of an oath, to support the Constitution of the United States. Well, is he to tamper with that? Is he to palter? Gentlemen, our political duties are as much matters of conscience as any other duties; our sacred domestic ties, our most endearing social relations, are no more the subjects for conscientious consideration and conscientious discharge, than the duties we enter upon under the Constitution of the United States. The bonds of political brotherhood, which hold us together from Maine to Georgia, rest upon the same principles of obligation as those of domestic and social life.

Now, Gentlemen, that is the plain story of the Constitution of the United States, on the question of slavery. I contend, and have always contended, that, after the adoption of the Constitution, any measure of the government calculated to bring more slave territory into the United States was beyond the power of the Constitution, and against its provisions. That is my opinion, and it always has been my opinion. It was inconsistent with the Constitution of the United States, or thought to be so, in Mr. Jefferson's time, to attach Louisiana to the United States. A treaty with France was made for that purpose. Mr. Jefferson's opinion at that moment was, that an alteration of the Constitution was necessary to enable it to be done. In consequence of considerations to which I need not now refer, that opinion was abandoned, and Louisiana was admitted by law, without any provision in, or alteration of, the Constitution. At that time I was too young to hold any office, or take any share in the political affairs of the country. Louisiana was admitted as a slave State, and became entitled to her representation in Congress on the principle of a mixed basis. Florida was afterwards admitted. Then, too, I was out of Congress. I had formerly been a member, but had ceased to be so. I had nothing to do with the Florida treaty, or the admission of Florida. My opinion remains unchanged, that it was not within the original scope or design of the Constitution to admit new States out of foreign territory; and, for one, whatever may be said at the Syracuse convention, or at any other assemblage of insane persons, I never would consent, and never have consented, that there should be one foot of slave territory beyond what the old thirteen States had at the time of the formation of the Union. Never, never! The man cannot show his face to me, and say he can prove that I ever departed from that doctrine. He would sneak away, and slink away, or hire a mercenary press to cry out, What an apostate from liberty Daniel Webster has become! But he knows himself to be a hypocrite and a falsifier.

But, Gentlemen, I was in public life when the proposition to annex Texas to the United States was brought forward. You know that the revolution in Texas, which separated that country from Mexico, occurred in the year 1835 or 1836. I saw then, and I do not know that it required any particular foresight, that it would be the very next thing to bring Texas, which was designed to be a slave-holding State, into this Union. I did not wait. I sought an occasion to proclaim my utter aversion to any such measure, and I determined to resist it with all my strength to the last. On this subject, Gentlemen, you will bear with me, if I now repeat, in the presence of this assembly, what I have before spoken elsewhere. I was in this city in the year 1837, and, some time before I left New York on that excursion from which I returned to this place, my friends in New York were kind enough to offer me a public dinner as a testimony of their regard. I went out of my way, in a speech delivered in Niblo's Garden, on that occasion, for the purpose of showing that I anticipated the attempt to annex Texas as a slave territory, and said it should be opposed by me to the last extremity. Well, there was the press all around me, — the Whig press and the Democratic press. Some spoke in terms commendatory enough of my speech, but all agreed that I took pains to step out of my way to denounce in advance the annexation of Texas as slave territory to the United States. I said on that occasion : —

" Gentlemen, we all see that, by whomsoever possessed, Texas is likely to be a slave-holding country ; and I frankly avow my entire unwillingness to do any thing that shall extend the slavery of the African race on this continent, or add other slave-holding States to the Union. When I say that I regard slavery in itself as a great moral, social, and political evil, I only use language which has been adopted by distinguished men, themselves citizens of slave-holding States. I shall do nothing, therefore, to favor or encourage its further extension. We have slavery already amongst us. The Constitution found it in the Union ; it recognized it, and gave it solemn guaranties. To the full extent of these guaranties we are all bound, in honor, in justice, and by the Constitution. All the stipulations contained in the Constitution in favor of the slave-holding States which are already in the Union ought to be fulfilled, and, so far as depends on me, shall be fulfilled, in the fulness of their spirit and to the exactness of their letter. Slavery, as it exists in the States, is beyond the reach of Congress. It is a concern of the States themselves; they have never submitted it to Congress, and Congress has no rightful power over it. I shall concur, therefore, in no act, no measure, no menace, no indication of purpose, which shall interfere or threaten to interfere with the exclusive authority of the several States over the subject of slavery as it exists within their respective limits. All this appears to me to be matter of plain and imperative duty. But when we come to speak of admitting new States, the subject assumes an entirely different aspect. Our rights and our duties are then both different. The free States, and all the States, are then at liberty to accept or to reject. When it is proposed to bring new members into this political partnership, the old members have a right to say on what terms such new partners are to come in, and what they are to bring along with them. In my opinion, the people of the United States will not consent to bring into the Union a new, vastly extensive, and slave-holding country, large enough for half a dozen or a dozen States. In my opinion, they ought not to consent to it."

Gentlemen, I was mistaken; Congress did consent to the bringing in of Texas. They did consent, and I was a false prophet. Your own State consented, and the majority of the representatives of New York consented. I went into Congress before the final consummation of the deed, and there I fought, holding up both my hands, and urging, with a voice stronger than it now is, my remonstrances against the whole of it. But you would have it so, and you did have it so. Nay, Gentlemen, I will tell the truth, whether it shames the Devil or not. Persons who have aspired high as lovers of liberty, as eminent lovers of the Wilmot Proviso, as eminent Free Soil men, and who have mounted over our heads, and trodden us down as if we were mere slaves, insisting that they are the only true lovers of liberty, they are the men, the very men, that brought Texas into this Union. This is the truth, the whole truth, and nothing but the truth, and I declare it before you, this day. Look to the journals. Without the consent of New York, Texas would not have come into the Union, either under the original resolutions or afterwards. But New York voted for the measure. The two Senators from New York voted for it, and decided the question; and you may thank them for the glory, the renown, and the happiness of having five or six slave States added to the Union. Do not blame me for it. Let them answer who did the deed, and who are now proclaiming themselves the champions of liberty, crying up their Free Soil creed, and using it for selfish and deceptive purposes. They were the persons who aided in bringing in Texas. It was all fairly told to you, both beforehand and afterwards. You heard Moses and the prophets, but if one had risen from the dead, such was your devotion to that policy, at that time, you would not have listened to him for a moment. I do not, of course, speak of the persons now here before me, but of the general political tone in New York, and especially of those who are now Free Soil apostles. Well, all that I do not complain of; but I will not now, or hereafter, before the country, or the world, consent to be numbered among those who introduced new slave power into the Union. I did all in my power to prevent it.

Then, again, Gentlemen, the Mexican war broke out. Vast territory was acquired, and the peace was made; and, much as I disliked the war, I disliked the peace more, because it brought in these territories. I wished for peace indeed, but I desired to strike out the grant of territory on the one side, and the payment of the $12,000,000 on the other. That territory was unknown to me; I could not tell what its character might be. The plan came from the South. I knew that certain Southern gentlemen wished the acquisition of California, New Mexico, and Utah, as a means of extending slave power and slave population. Foreseeing a sectional controversy, and, as I conceived, seeing how much it would distract the Union, I voted against the treaty with Mexico. I voted against the acquisition. I wanted none of her territory, neither California, New Mexico, nor Utah. They were rather ultra-American, as I thought. They were far from us, and I saw that they might lead to a political conflict, and I voted against them all, against the treaty and against the peace, rather than have the territories. Seeing that it would be an occasion of dispute, that by the controversy the whole Union would be agitated, Messrs. Berrien, Badger, and other respectable and distinguished men of the South, voted against the acquisition, and the treaty which secured it; and if the men of the North had voted the same way, we should have been spared all the difficulties that have grown out of it. We should have had peace without the territories.

Now there is no sort of doubt, Gentlemen, that there were some persons in the South who supposed that California, if it came into the Union at all, would come in as a slave State. You know the extraordinary events which immediately occurred, and the impulse given to emigration by the discovery of gold. You know that crowds of Northern people immediately rushed to California, and that an African slave could no more live there among them, than he could live on the top of Mount Hecla. Of necessity it became a free State, and that, no doubt, was a source of much disappointment to the South. And then there were New Mexico and Utah; what was to be done with them? Why, Gentlemen, from the best investigation I had given to the subject, and the reflection I had devoted to it, I was of the opinion that the mountains of New Mexico and Utah could no more sustain American slavery than the snows of Canada. I saw it was impossible. I thought so then; it is quite evident now. Therefore, when it was proposed in Congress to apply the Wilmot Proviso to New Mexico and Utah, it appeared to me just as absurd as to apply it here in Western New York. I saw that the snow-capped hills, the eternal mountains, and the climate of those countries would never support slavery. No man could carry a slave there with any expectation of profit. It could not be done; and as the South regarded the Proviso as merely a source of irritation, and as designed by some to irritate, I thought it unwise to apply it to New Mexico or Utah. I voted accordingly, and who doubts now the correctness of that vote? The law admitting those territories passed without any proviso. Is there a slave, or will there ever be one, in either of those territories? Why, there is not a man in the United States so stupid as not to see, at this moment, that such a thing was wholly unnecessary, and that it was only calculated to irritate and to offend. I am not one who is disposed to create irritation, or give offence among brethren, or to break up fraternal friendship, without cause. The question was accordingly left legally open, whether slavery should or should not go to New Mexico or Utah. There is no slavery there, it is utterly impracticable that it should be introduced into such a region, and utterly ridiculous to suppose that it could exist there. No one, who does not mean to deceive, will now pretend it can exist there.

Well, Gentlemen, we have a race of agitators all over the country; some connected with the press, some, I am sorry to say, belonging to the learned professions. They agitate; their livelihood consists in agitating; their freehold, their copyhold, their capital, their all in all, depend on the excitement of the public mind. The events now briefly alluded to were going on at the commencement of the year 1850. There were two great questions before the public. There was the question of the Texan boundary, and of a government for Utah and New Mexico, which I consider as one question; and there was the question of making a provision for the restoration of fugitive slaves. On these subjects, I have something to say. Texas, as you know, established her independence of Mexico by her revolution and the battle of San Jacinto, which made her a sovereign power. I have already stated to you what I then anticipated from the movement, namely, that she would ask to come into the Union as a slave State. We admitted her in 1845, and we admitted her as a slave State. We admitted her also with an undefined boundary; remember that. She claimed by conquest the whole of that territory commonly called New Mexico, east of the Rio Grande. She claimed also those limits which her constitution had declared and marked out as the proper limits of Texas. This was her claim, and when she was admitted into the United States, the United States did not define her territory. They admitted her as she was. We took her as she defined her own limits, and with the power of making four additional slave States. I say "we," but I do not mean that I was one; I mean the United States admitted her.

What, then, was the state of things in 1850? There was Texas claiming all, or a great part, of that which the United States had acquired from Mexico as New Mexico. She claimed that it belonged to her by conquest and by her admission into the United States, and she was ready to maintain her claim by force of arms. Nor was this all. A man must be ignorant of the history of the country who does not know, that, at the commencement of 1850, there was great agitation throughout the whole South. Who does not know that six or seven of the largest States of the South had already taken measures looking toward secession; were preparing for disunion in some way? They concurred apparently, at least some of them, with Texas, while Texas was prepared or preparing to enforce her rights by force of arms. Troops were enlisted by her, and many thousand persons in the South disaffected towards the Union, or desirous of breaking it up, were ready to make common cause with Texas; to join her ranks, and see what they could make in a war to establish the right of Texas to New Mexico. The public mind was disturbed. A considerable part of the South was disaffected towards the Union, and in a condition to adopt any course that should be violent and destructive.

What then was to be done, as far as Texas was concerned? Allow me to say, Gentlemen, there are two sorts of foresight. There is a military foresight, which sees what will be the result of an appeal to arms; and there is also a statesmanlike foresight, which looks not to the result of battles and carnage, but to the results of political disturbances, the violence of faction carried into military operations, and the horrors attendant on civil war. I never had a doubt, that, if the administration of General Taylor had gone to war, and had sent troops into New Mexico, the Texan forces would have been subdued in a week. The power on one side was far superior to all the power on the other. But what then? What if Texan troops, assisted by thousands of volunteers from the disaffected States, had gone to New Mexico, and had been defeated and turned back? Would that have settled the boundary question? Now, Gentlemen, I wish I had ten thousand voices. I wish I could draw around me the whole people of the United States, and I wish I could make them all hear what I now declare on my conscience as my solemn belief, before the Power who sits on high, and who will judge you and me hereafter, that, if this Texan controversy had not been settled by Congress in the manner it was, by the so-called adjustment measures, civil war would have ensued; blood, American blood, would have been shed; and who can tell what would have been the consequences? Gentlemen, in an honorable war, if a foreign foe invade us, if our rights are threatened, if it be necessary to defend them by arms, I am not afraid of blood. And if I am too old myself, I hope there are those connected with me by ties of relationship who are young, and willing to defend their country to the last drop of their blood. But I cannot express the horror I feel at the shedding of blood in a controversy between one of these States and the government of the United States, because I see in it a total and entire disruption of all those ties that make us a great and happy people. Gentlemen, this was the great question, the leading question, at the commencement of the year 1850.

Then there was the other matter, and that was the Fugitive Slave Law. Let me say a word about that. Under the provisions of the Constitution, during Washington's administration, in the year 1793, there was passed, by general consent, a law for the restoration of fugitive slaves. Hardly any one opposed it at that period; it was thought to be necessary, in order to carry the Constitution into effect; the great men of New England and New York all concurred in it. It passed, and answered all the purposes expected from it, till about the year 1841 or 1842, when the States interfered to make enactments in opposition to it. The act of Congress said that State magistrates might execute the duties of the law. Some of the States passed enactments imposing a penalty on any State officers who exercised authority under the law, or assisted in its execution; others denied the use of their jails to carry the law into effect; and, in general, at the commencement of the year 1850, it had become absolutely indispensable that Congress should pass some law for the execution of this provision of the Constitution, or else give up that provision entirely. That was the question. I was in Congress when it was brought forward. I was for a proper law. I had, indeed, proposed a different law; I was of opinion that a summary trial by a jury might be had, which would satisfy the people of the North, and produce no harm to those who claimed the service of fugitives; but I left the Senate, and went to another station, before any law was passed. The law of 1850 passed. Now I undertake, as a lawyer, and on my professional character, to say to you, and to all, that the law of 1850 is decidedly more favorable to the fugitive than General Washington's law of 1793; and I will tell you why. In the first place, the present law places the power in much higher hands; in the hands of independent judges of the Supreme and Circuit Courts, and District Courts, and of commissioners who are appointed to office for their legal learning. Every fugitive is brought before a tribunal of high character, of eminent ability, of respectable station. In the second place, when a claimant comes from Virginia to New York, to say that one A or one B has run away, or is a fugitive from service or labor, he brings with him a record of the court of the county from which he comes, and that record must be sworn to before a magistrate, and certified by the county clerk, and bear an official seal. The affidavit must state that A or B had departed under such and such circumstances, and had gone to another State; and that record under seal is, by the Constitution of the United States, entitled to full credit in every State. Well, the claimant or his agent comes here, and he presents to you the seal of the court in Virginia, affixed to a record of his declaration, that A or B had escaped from service. He must then prove that the fugitive is here. He brings a witness; he is asked if this is the man, and he proves it; or, in nine cases out of ten, the fact would be admitted by the fugitive himself.

Such is the present law; and, much opposed and maligned as it is, it is more favorable to the fugitive slave than the law enacted during Washington's administration, in 1793, which was sanctioned by the North as well as by the South. The present violent opposition has sprung up in modern times. From whom does this clamor come? Why, look at the proceedings of the antislavery conventions; look at their resolutions. Do you find among those persons who oppose this Fugitive Slave Law any admission whatever, that any law ought to be passed to carry into effect the solemn stipulations of the Constitution? Tell me any such case; tell me if any resolution was adopted by the convention at Syracuse favorable to the carrying out of the Constitution. Not one! The fact is, Gentlemen, they oppose the constitutional provision; they oppose the whole! Not a man of them admits that there ought to be any law on the subject. They deny, altogether, that the provisions of the Constitution ought to be carried into effect. Look at the proceedings of the antislavery conventions in Ohio, Massachusetts, and at Syracuse, in the State of New York. What do they say? "That, so help them God, no colored man shall be sent from the State of New York back to his master in Virginia!" Do not they say that? And, to the fulfilment of that they "pledge their lives, their fortunes, and their sacred honor." Their sacred honor! They pledge their sacred honor to violate the Constitution; they pledge their sacred honor to commit treason against the laws of their country!

I have already stated, Gentlemen, what your observation of these things must have taught you. I will only recur to the subject for a moment, for the purpose of persuading you, as public men and private men, as good men and patriotic men, that you ought, to the extent of your ability and influence, to see to it that such laws are established and maintained as shall keep you, and the South, and the West, and all the country, together, on the terms of the Constitution. I say, that what is demanded of us is to fulfil our constitutional duties, and to do for the South what the South has a right to demand.

Gentlemen, I have been some time before the public. My character is known, my life is before the country. I profess to love liberty as much as any man living; but I profess to love American liberty, that liberty which is secured to the country by the government under which we live; and I have no great opinion of that other and higher liberty which disregards the restraints of law and of the Constitution. I hold the Constitution of the United States to be the bulwark, the only bulwark, of our liberties and of our national character. I do not mean that you should become slaves under the Constitution. That is not American liberty. That is not the liberty of the Union for which our fathers fought, that liberty which has given us a right to be known and respected all over the world. I mean only to say, that I am for constitutional liberty. It is enough for me to be as free as the Constitution of the country makes me.

Now, Gentlemen, let me say, that, as much as I respect the character of the people of Western New York, as much as I wish to retain their good opinion, if I should ever hereafter be placed in any situation in public life, let me tell you now that you must not expect from me the slightest variation, even of a hair's breadth, from the Constitution of the United States. I am a Northern man. I was born at the North, educated at the North, have lived all my days at the North. I know five hundred Northern men to one Southern man. My sympathies, all my sympathies, my love of liberty for all mankind, of every color, are the same as yours. My affections and hopes in that respect are exactly like yours. I wish to see all men free, all men happy. I have few personal associations out of the Northern States. My people are your people. And yet I am told sometimes that I am not a friend of liberty, because I am not a Free Soil man. What am I? What was I ever? What shall I be hereafter, if I could sacrifice, for any consideration, that love of American liberty which has glowed in my breast since my infancy, and which, I hope, will never leave me till I expire?

Gentlemen, I regret that slavery exists in the Southern States; but it is clear and certain that Congress has no power over it. It may be, however, that, in the dispensations of Providence, some remedy for this evil may occur, or may be hoped for hereafter. But, in the mean time, I hold to the Constitution of the United States, and you need never expect from me, under any circumstances, that I shall falter from it; that I shall be otherwise than frank and decisive. I would not part with my character as a man of firmness and decision, and honor and principle, for all that the world possesses. You will find me true to the North, because all my sympathies are with the North. My affections, my children, my hopes, my every thing, are with the North. But when I stand up before my country, as one appointed to administer the Constitution of the country, by the blessing of God I will be just.

Gentlemen, I expect to be libelled and abused. Yes, libelled and abused. But it does not disturb me. I have not lost a night's rest for a great many years from any such cause. I have some talent for sleeping. And why should I not expect to be libelled? Is not the Constitution of the United States libelled and abused? Do not some people call it a covenant with hell? Is not Washington libelled and abused? Is he not called a bloodhound on the track of the African negro? Are not our fathers libelled and abused by their own children? And ungrateful children they are. How, then, shall I escape? I do not expect to escape; but, knowing these things, I impute no bad motive to any men of character and fair standing. The great settlement measures of the last Congress are laws. Many respectable men, representatives from your own State and from other States, did not concur in them. I do not impute any bad motive to them. I am ready to believe they are Americans all.

They may not have thought these laws necessary; or they may have thought that they would be enacted without their concurrence. Let all that pass away. If they are now men who will stand by what is done, and stand up for their country, and say that, as these laws were passed by a majority of the whole country, we must stand by them and live by them, I will respect them all as friends.

Now, Gentlemen, allow me to ask of you, What do you think would have been the condition of the country, at this time, if these laws had not been passed by the last Congress? if the question of the Texas boundary had not been settled? if New Mexico and Utah had been left as desert-places, and no government had been provided for them? And if the other great object to which State laws had opposed so many obstacles, the restoration of fugitives, had not been provided for, I ask, what would have been the state of this country now? You men of Erie County, you men of New York, I conjure you to go home to-night and meditate on this subject. What would have been the state of this country, now, at this moment, if these laws had not been passed? I have given my opinion that we should have had a civil war. I refer it to you, therefore, for your consideration; meditate on it; do not be carried away by any abstract notions or metaphysical ideas; think practically on the great question, What would have been the condition of the United States at this moment, if we had not settled these agitating questions? I repeat, in my opinion, there would have been a civil war.

Gentlemen, will you allow me, for a moment, to advert to myself? I have been a long time in public life; of course, not many years remain to me. At the commencement of 1850, I looked anxiously at the condition of the country, and I thought the inevitable consequence of leaving the existing controversies unadjusted would be civil war. I saw danger in leaving Utah and New Mexico without any government, a prey to the power of Texas. I saw the condition of things arising from the interference of some of the States in defeating the operation of the Constitution in respect to the restoration of fugitive slaves. I saw these things, and I made up my mind to encounter whatever might betide me in the attempt to avert the impending catastrophe. And allow me to add something which is not entirely unworthy of notice. A member of the House of Representatives told me that he had prepared a list of one hundred and forty speeches which had been made in Congress on the slavery question. "That is a very large number, my friend," I said; "but how is that?" "Why," said he, "a Northern man gets up and speaks with considerable power and fluency until the Speaker's hammer knocks him down. Then gets up a Southern man, and he speaks with more warmth. He is nearer the sun, and he comes out with the greater fervor against the North. He speaks his hour, and is in turn knocked down. And so it has gone on, until I have got one hundred and forty speeches on my list." "Well," said I, "where are they, and what are they?" "If the speaker," said he, "was a Northern man, he held forth against slavery; and if he was from the South, he abused the North; and all these speeches were sent by the members to their own localities, where they served only to aggravate the local irritation already existing. No man reads both sides. The other side of the argument is not heard; and the speeches sent from Washington in such prodigious numbers, instead of tending to conciliation, do but increase, in both sections of the Union, an excitement already of the most dangerous character."

Gentlemen, in this state of things, I saw that something must be done. It was impossible to look with indifference on a danger of so formidable a character. I am a Massachusetts man, and I bore in mind what Massachusetts has ever been to the Constitution and the Union. I felt the importance of the duty which devolved upon one to whom she had so long confided the trust of representing her in either house of Congress. As I honored her, and respected her, I felt that I was serving her in my endeavors to promote the welfare of the whole country.

And now suppose, Gentlemen, that, on the occasion in question, I had taken a different course. If I may allude so particularly to an individual so insignificant as myself, suppose that, on the 7th of March, 1850, instead of making a speech that would, so far as my power went, reconcile the country, I had joined in the general clamor of the Antislavery party. Suppose I had said, "I will have nothing to do with any accommodation; we will admit no compromise; we will let Texas invade New Mexico; we will leave New Mexico and

Utah to take care of themselves; we will plant ourselves on the Wilmot Proviso, let the consequences be what they may." Now, Gentlemen, I do not mean to say that great consequences would have followed from such a course on my part; but suppose I had taken such a course. How could I be blamed for it? Was I not a Northern man? Did I not know Massachusetts feelings and prejudices? But what of that? I am an American. I was made a whole man, and I did not mean to make myself half a one. I felt that I had a duty to perform to my country, to my own reputation; for I flattered myself that a service of forty years had given me some character, on which I had a right to repose for my justification in the performance of a duty attended with some degree of local unpopularity. I thought it my duty to pursue this course, and I did not care what was to be the consequence. I felt it was my duty, in a very alarming crisis, to come out; to go for my country, and my whole country; and to exert any power I had to keep that country together. I cared for nothing, I was afraid of nothing, but I meant to do my duty. Duty performed makes a man happy; duty neglected makes a man unhappy. I therefore, in the face of all discouragements and all dangers, was ready to go forth and do what I thought my country, your country, demanded of me. And, Gentlemen, allow me to say here to-day, that if the fate of John Rogers had stared me in the face, if I had seen the stake, if I had heard the faggots already crackling, by the blessing of Almighty God I would have gone on and discharged the duty which I thought my country called upon me to perform. I would have become a martyr to save that country.

And now, Gentlemen, farewell. Live and be happy. Live like patriots, live like Americans. Live in the enjoyment of the inestimable blessings which your fathers prepared for you; and if any thing that I may do hereafter should be inconsistent, in the slightest degree, with the opinions and principles which I have this day submitted to you, then discard me for ever from your recollection.

SPEECH TO THE YOUNG MEN OF ALBANY.

INTRODUCTORY NOTE.

On his journey from Buffalo to New York, Mr. Webster received, before reaching Albany, the following letter of invitation : —

" Sir, — The subscribers, having learned that you will probably pass through our city early in the ensuing week, respectfully request an opportunity for our citizens generally, irrespective of party, and especially the young men of Albany, to testify their admiration of your character and talents as an American statesman, and their high appreciation of your public services in the councils of the nation.

" They therefore respectfully invite you to partake with them of a dinner at Congress Hall, on the day of your arrival, or such other day as may suit your convenience.

" They beg leave to add, that, if your health will permit you to address our citizens at the Capitol, it would afford them great gratification to hear your views upon public affairs and the general condition of the country.

" *Albany, May 24, 1851.*"

This letter was signed by a large number of the most respectable citizens of Albany, without distinction of party.

The invitation having been accepted by Mr. Webster, arrangements were made for a public reception on the day of his arrival. A platform was erected near the Capitol, to which, at two o'clock, P. M., on the 28th of May, he was conducted by Messrs. Price and Porter, of the committee of the young men of Albany. Mr. Webster was introduced to the immense assembly by Hon. John C. Spencer, and, after the acclamation with which he was received had subsided, delivered the following speech.

The revised edition of the speech, in a pamphlet form, was introduced by the following

DEDICATION.

TO

THE YOUNG MEN OF ALBANY,

THIS SPEECH,

DELIVERED AT THEIR REQUEST,

IS MOST RESPECTFULLY DEDICATED.

"Cogitetis omnem dignitatem vestram cum Republica conjunctam esse debere. UNA NAVIS EST JAM BONORUM OMNIUM; quam quidem nos damus operam, ut rectam teneamus. Utinam prospero cursu. Sed quicunque venti erunt ars nostra certe non aberit."

SPEECH TO THE YOUNG MEN OF ALBANY.*

FELLOW-CITIZENS, — I owe the honor of this occasion, and I esteem it an uncommon and extraordinary honor, to the young men of this city of Albany, and it is my first duty to express to these young men my grateful thanks for the respect they have manifested towards me. Nevertheless, young men of Albany, I do not mistake you, or your object, or your purpose. I am proud to take to myself whatever may properly belong to me, as a token of personal and political regard on your part. But I know, young men of Albany, it is not I, but the cause; it is not I, but your own generous attachments to your country; it is not I, but the Constitution of the Union, which has bound together your ancestors and mine, and all of us, for more than half a century, — it is this that has brought you here to-day, to testify your regard toward one who, to the best of his humble ability, has sustained that cause before the country. Go on, young men of Albany! Go on, young men of the United States! Early manhood is the chief prop and support, the great reliance and hope, for the preservation of public liberty and the institutions of the land. Early manhood is ingenuous, generous, just. It looks forward to a long life of honor or dishonor, and it means that it shall, by the blessing of God, be a life of honor, of usefulness, and success, in all the professions and pursuits of life, and that it shall close, when close it must, with some claim to the gratitude of the country. Go on, then; uphold the institutions under which you were born. You are manly and bold. You fear nothing but to do wrong; dread nothing but to be found recreant to your country.

* Delivered on the 28th of May, 1851, at the Invitation of the Young Men of Albany, in the Public Square of the Capitol in that City.

48*

Gentlemen, I certainly had no expectation of appearing before such an assemblage as this to-day. It is not probable that, for a long time to come, I may again address any large meeting of my fellow-citizens. If I should not, and if this should be the last, or among the last, of all the occasions on which I am to appear before any great number of the people of the country, I shall not regret that that appearance was here. I find myself in the political capital of the greatest, most commercial, most powerful State of the Union. I find myself here by the invitation of persons of the highest respectability, without distinction of party. I consider the occasion as somewhat august. I know that among those who now listen to me there are some of the wisest, the best, the most patriotic, and the most experienced public and private men in the State of New York. Here are governors and ex-governors, here are judges and ex-judges, of high character and high station; and here are persons from all the walks of professional and private life, distinguished for talent, and virtue, and eminence. Fellow-citizens, before such an assemblage, and on such an invitation, I feel bound to guard every opinion and every expression; to speak with precision such sentiments as I advance, and to be careful in all that I say, that I may not be misapprehended or misrepresented.

I am requested, fellow-citizens, by those who invited me, to express my sentiments on the state of public affairs in this country, and the interesting questions which are before us. This proves, Gentlemen, that in their opinion there are questions sometimes arising which range above all party, and all the influences and considerations and interests of party. It proves more; it proves that, in their judgment, this is a time in which public affairs rise in importance above the range of party, and draw to them an interest paramount to all party considerations. If this be not so, I am here without object, and you are listening to me for no purpose whatever.

Then, Gentlemen, what is the condition of public affairs which makes it necessary and proper for men to meet, and confer together on the state of the country? What are the questions which are transcending, subduing, and overwhelming party, inciting honest, well-meaning persons to lay party aside, and to meet and confer for the general weal? I shall, of course, not enter at large into many of these questions, nor into any lengthened discussion of the state of public affairs, but shall endeavor in general to state what that condition is, what those questions are, and to pronounce a conscientious judgment of my own upon the whole.

The last Congress, fellow-citizens, passed laws called adjustment measures, or settlement measures; laws intended to put an end to certain internal and domestic controversies existing in the country, and some of which had existed for a long time. These laws were passed by the constitutional majorities of both houses of Congress. They received the constitutional approbation of the President. They are the laws of the land. To some or all of them, indeed to all of them, at the time of their passage, there existed warm and violent opposition. None of them passed without heated discussion. Government was established in each of the Territories of New Mexico and Utah, but not without opposition. The boundary of Texas was settled by compromise with that State, but not without determined and earnest resistance. These laws all passed, however, and, as they have now become, from the nature of the case, irrepealable, it is not necessary that I should detain you by discussing their merits or demerits. Nevertheless, Gentlemen, I desire, on this and all public occasions, in the clearest and most emphatic manner, to declare, that I hold some of these laws, and especially that which provided for the adjustment of the controversy with Texas, to have been essential to the preservation of the public peace.

I will not now argue that point, nor lay before you at length the circumstances which existed at that time; the peculiar situation of things in so many of the Southern States; the fact that many of those States had adopted measures for the separation of the Union; or the fact that Texas was preparing to assert her claims to territory which New Mexico thought was hers by right, and that hundreds and thousands of men, tired of the ordinary pursuits of private life, were ready to rise and unite in any enterprise that might offer itself to them, even at the risk of a direct conflict with the authority of this government. I say, therefore, without going into the argument with any detail, that in March of 1850, when I found it my duty to address Congress on these important topics, it was my conscientious belief, and it still remains unshaken, that if the controversy with

Texas could not be amicably adjusted, there must, in all probability, be civil war and bloodshed; and in the contemplation
of such a prospect, although we took it for granted that no
opposition could arise to the authority of the United States that
would not be suppressed, it appeared of little consequence on
which standard victory should perch. But what of that? I was
not anxious about military consequences; I looked to the civil
and political state of things, and their results, and I inquired
what would be the condition of the country, if, in this state of
agitation, if, in this vastly extended, though not generally pervading feeling at the South, war should break out and bloodshed should ensue in that quarter of the Union? That was
enough for me to inquire into and consider; and if the chances
had been but one in a thousand that civil war would be the result, I should still have felt that that one thousandth chance
should be guarded against by any reasonable sacrifice, because,
Gentlemen, sanguine as I am of the future prosperity of the
country, strongly as I believe now, after what has passed, and
especially after the enactment of those measures to which I
have referred, that it is likely to hold together, I yet believe
firmly that this Union, once broken, is utterly incapable, according to all human experience, of being reconstructed in its original character, of being re-cemented by any chemistry, or art, or
effort, or skill of man.

Now, then, Gentlemen, let us pass from those measures which
are now accomplished and settled. California is in the Union,
and cannot be got out; the Texas boundary is settled, and cannot be disturbed; Utah and New Mexico are Territories, under
provision of law, according to accustomed usage in former cases;
and these things may be regarded as finally adjusted. But then
there was another subject, equally agitating and equally irritating, which, in its nature, must always be subject to reconsideration or proposed amendment, and that is, the Fugitive Slave
Law of 1850, passed at the same session of Congress.

Allow me to advert, very shortly, to what I consider the
ground of that law. You know, and I know, that it was very
much opposed in the Northern States; sometimes with argument not unfair, often by mere ebullition of party, and often by
those whirlwinds of fanaticism that raise a dust and blind the
eyes, but produce no other effect. Now, Gentlemen, this ques-

tion of the propriety of the Fugitive Slave Law, or the enactment of some such law, is a question that must be met.   Its enemies will not let it sleep or slumber.   They will "give neither sleep to their eyes nor slumber to their eyelids" so long as they can agitate it before the people.   It is with them a topic, a desirable topic, and all who have much experience in political affairs know, that, for party men and in party times, there is hardly any thing so desirable as a topic.   Now, Gentlemen, I am ready to meet this question.   I am ready to meet it, and ready to say that it was right, proper, expedient, and just that a suitable law should be passed for the restoration of fugitive slaves, found in free States, to their owners in slave States.   I am ready to say that, because I only repeat the words of the Constitution itself, and I am not afraid of being considered a plagiarist, nor a feeble imitator of other men's language and sentiments, when I repeat and announce to every part of the Union, to you, here, and at all times, the language of the Constitution of my country.

Gentlemen, at the period of the Revolution, slavery existed in the Southern States, and had existed there for more than a hundred years.   We of the North were not guilty of its introduction.   That generation of men, even in the South, were not guilty of it.   It had been introduced according to the policy of the mother country, before the United States were independent; indeed, before there were any authorities in the Colonies competent to resist it.   Why, Gentlemen, men's opinions have so changed on this subject, and properly, the world has come to hold sentiments so much more just, that we can hardly believe, what is certainly true, that at the peace of Aix-la-Chapelle, in 1748, the English government insisted on the fulfilment, to its full extent, of a condition in the treaty of the Asiento, signed at Utrecht, in 1713, by which the Spanish government had granted the unqualified and exclusive privilege to the British government of importing slaves into the Spanish colonies in America!   That was not then repugnant to public sentiment; happily, such a contract would be execrated now.

I allude to this only to show that the introduction of slavery into the Southern States is not to be visited upon the generation that achieved the independence of this country.   On the contrary, all the eminent men of that day regretted its existence. And you, my young friends of Albany, if you will take the pains to go back to the debates of the period, from the meeting of the first Congress, in 1774, I mean the Congress of the Confederation, to the adoption of the present Constitution, and the enactment of the first laws under it, — you, or any body who will make that necessary research, will find that Southern men and Southern States, as represented in Congress, lamented the existence of slavery in far more earnest and emphatic terms than the Northern; for, though it did exist in the Northern States, it was a feeble taper, just going out, soon to end, and nothing was feared from it, while leading men of the South, and especially of Virginia, felt and acknowledged that it was a moral and political evil; that it weakened the arm of the freeman, and kept back the progress and success of free labor; and they said with truth, and all history verifies the observation, "that if the shores of the Chesapeake had been made as free to free labor as the shores of the North River, New York might have been great, but Virginia would have been great also." That was the sentiment.

Now under this state of things, Gentlemen, when the Constitution was framed, its framers, and the people who adopted it, came to a clear, express, unquestionable stipulation and compact. There had been an ancient practice, a practice a century old, for aught I know, according to which fugitives from service, whether apprentices at the North or slaves at the South, should be restored. Massachusetts had restored fugitive slaves to Virginia long before the adoption of the Constitution, and it is well known that in other States, in which slavery did or did not exist, they were restored also, on proper application. And it was held that any man could pursue his slave and take him wherever he could find him. Under this state of things, it was expressly stipulated, in the plainest language, and there it stands, —sophistry cannot gloss it, it cannot be erased from the page of the Constitution; there it stands, — that persons held to service or labor in one State, under the laws thereof, escaping into another, shall not, in consequence of any law or regulation therein, be discharged from such service or labor, but shall be delivered up upon claim of the party to whom such service or labor shall be due. This was adopted without dissent; it was nowhere objected to, North or South, but considered as a matter of absolute right and justice to the Southern States, and concurred in everywhere, by every State that adopted the Constitution; and we look in vain for any opposition to it, from Massachusetts to Georgia.

This, then, being the case, this being the provision of the Constitution, it was found necessary, in General Washington's time, to pass a law to carry that provision of the Constitution into effect. Such a law was prepared and passed. It was prepared by a gentleman from a Northern State. It is said to have been drawn up by Mr. Cabot, of Massachusetts. It was supported by him, and by Mr. Goodhue, and by Mr. Sedgwick, of Massachusetts, and generally by all the free States. It passed without a division in the Senate, and with but seven votes against it in the House. It went into operation, and for a time it satisfied the just rights and expectations of every body. That law provided that its enactments should be carried into effect mainly by State magistrates, justices of the peace, judges of State courts, sheriffs, and other organs of State authority. So things went on, without loud complaints from any quarter, until some fifteen years ago, when some of the States, the free States, thought it proper to pass laws prohibiting their own magistrates and officers from executing this law of Congress, under heavy penalties, and refusing to the United States authorities the use of their prisons for the detention of persons arrested as fugitive slaves. That is to say, these States passed acts defeating the law of Congress, as far as it was in their power to defeat it. Those of them to which I refer, not all, but several, nullified the law of 1793 entirely. They said, in effect, "We will not execute it. No runaway slave shall be restored." Thus the law became a dead letter, an entire dead letter. But here was the constitutional compact, nevertheless, still binding; here was the stipulation, as solemn as words could form it, and which every member of Congress, every officer of the general government, every officer of the State governments, from governors down to constables, is sworn to support. Well, under this state of things, in 1850, I was of opinion that common justice and good faith called upon us to make a law, fair, reasonable, equitable, and just, that should be calculated to carry this constitutional provision into effect, and give the Southern States what they were entitled to, and what it was intended originally they should receive, that is, the fair, right, and reasonable means to recover their fugitives from service from the States into which they had fled. I was of opinion that it was the bounden duty of Congress to pass such a law. The South insisted they had a right to it, and I thought they properly so insisted. It was no concession, no yielding of any thing, no giving up of any thing. When called on to fulfil a compact, the question is, Will you fulfil it? And, for one, I was ready. I said, "I will fulfil it by any fair and reasonable act of legislation."

Now, the law of 1850 had two objects, both of which were accomplished. First, it was to make the law more favorable for the fugitive than the law of 1793. It did so, because it called for a record, under seal, from a court in the State from which the fugitive came, proving the fact that he was a fugitive, so that nothing should be left, when pursued into a free State, but to produce the proof of his identity. Besides this, it secured a higher tribunal, and it placed the power in more responsible hands. The judges of the Supreme and District Courts of the United States, and learned persons appointed by them as commissioners, were to see to the execution of the law. It was, accordingly, a law more favorable, in all respects, to the fugitive, than the law passed under General Washington's administration in 1793. The second object was to carry the constitutional provision into effect by the authority of law, seeing that the States had prevented the execution of the former law.

Now, let me say that this law has been discussed, considered, and adjudged in a great many of the tribunals of the country. It has been the subject of discussion before judges of the Supreme Court of the United States; the subject of discussion before courts the most respectable in the States. Everywhere, on all occasions, and by all judges, it has been held to be, and pronounced to be, a constitutional law. So say Judges Grier, McLean, Nelson, Woodbury, and all the rest of the judges, as far as I know, on the bench of the Supreme Court of the United States. This is the opinion of Massachusetts herself, expressed by as good a court as ever sat in Massachusetts, its present Supreme Court, given unanimously, and without hesitation. And so says every body eminent for learning, and knowledge of constitutional law, and good judgment, without opposition, without intermixture of dissent, or difference of judicial opinion anywhere. And I hope I may be allowed on this occasion, Gentlemen, partly on account of a high personal regard, and partly for the excellence and ability of the production, to refer you all to a recent very short opinion of Mr. Prentiss, the district judge of Vermont. True, the case before him did not turn so much on the question of the constitutionality of this law, as upon the unconstitutionality, the illegality, and utter inadmissibility of the notion of private men and political bodies setting up their own whims, or their own opinions, above it, on the idea of the higher law that exists somewhere between us and the third heaven, I never knew exactly where.

All judicial opinions are in favor of this law. You cannot find a man in the profession in New York, whose income reaches thirty pounds a year, who will stake his professional reputation on an opinion against it. If he does, his reputation is not worth the thirty pounds. And yet this law is opposed, violently opposed, not by bringing this question into court; these lovers of human liberty, these friends of the slave, the fugitive slave, do not put their hands in their pockets, and draw funds to conduct lawsuits, and try the question; they are not much in that habit. That is not the way they show their devotion to liberty of any kind. But they meet and pass resolutions; they resolve that the law is oppressive, unjust, and should not be executed at any rate, or under any circumstances. It has been said in the States of New York, Massachusetts, and Ohio, over and over again, that the law shall not be executed. That was the language of conventions in Worcester, Massachusetts, in Syracuse, New York, and elsewhere. And for this they pledged their lives, their fortunes, and their sacred honor! Now, Gentlemen, these proceedings, I say it upon my professional reputation, are distinctly treasonable. Resolutions passed in Ohio, certain resolutions in New York, and in conventions held in Boston, are distinctly treasonable. And the act of taking away Shadrach from the public authorities in Boston, and sending him off, was an act of clear treason. I speak this in the hearing of men who are lawyers; I speak it out to the country; I say it everywhere, on my professional reputation. It was treason, and nothing less; that is to say, if men get together, and combine, and resolve that they will oppose a law of the government, not in any one case, but in all cases; if they resolve to resist the law, whoever may be attempted to be made the subject of it, and carry that purpose into effect, by resisting the application of the law in any one case, either by force of arms or force of numbers, that, Sir, is treason. You know it well [addressing Mr. Spencer]. The resolution, itself, unacted on, is not treason; it only manifests a treasonable purpose. When this purpose is proclaimed, and it is proclaimed that it will be carried out in all cases, and is carried into effect, by force of arms or of numbers, in any one case, that constitutes a case of levying war against the Union; and if it were necessary, I might cite in illustration the case of John Fries, convicted in 1799 for being concerned in an insurrection in Pennsylvania.

Now, various are the arguments, and various the efforts, to denounce this law; to oppose its execution; to hold it up as a subject of agitation and popular excitement. They are as diverse as the varied ingenuity of man, and the aspect of such questions when they come before the public. It is a common thing to say that the law is odious; and that therefore it cannot be executed, and will not be executed. That has always been said by those who do not mean it shall be executed; not by any body else. They assume the fact that it cannot executed, to make that true which they wish shall turn out to be true. They wish that it shall not be executed, and therefore announce to all mankind that it cannot be executed. When public men, and the conductors of newspapers of influence and authority, thus deal with the subject, they deal unfairly with it. Those who have types at command have a perfect right to express their opinions; but I doubt their right to express opinions as facts. I doubt whether they have a right to say, not as a matter of opinion, but of fact, that this particular law is so odious, here and elsewhere, that it cannot be executed. That only proves that they are of opinion that it ought not, that they hope it may not, be executed. They do not say, " Let us see if any wrong is inflicted on any body by it, before we wage war upon it; let us hope to find in its operation no wrong or injury to any body. Let us give it a fair experiment." Do any of them hold that language? Not one. " The wish is father to the thought." They wish that it may not be executed, and therefore they say it cannot and will not be executed. That is one of the modes of presenting the case to the people; and, in my opinion, it is not quite a fair mode of doing it.

There are other forms and modes of conducting the opposition to the law. I may omit to notice the blustering of Abolition societies at Boston and elsewhere, as unworthy of regard; but there are other forms more insidious, and equally efficacious. There are men who say, when you talk of amending that law, that they hope it will not be touched. You talk of attempting it, and they dissuade you. They say, " Let it remain as obnoxious as it can be, and so much the sooner it will disgust, and be detested by, the whole community." I am grieved to say that such sentiments have been avowed by those in Massachusetts who ought to be ashamed, utterly ashamed, to express such opinions. For what do they mean? They mean to make the law obnoxious; so obnoxious that it shall not be executed. But still they suggest no other law; they oppose all amendment; oppose doing any thing that shall make it less distasteful. What do they mean? They mean, and they know it, that there shall exist no law whatever, if they can prevent it, for carrying into effect this provision of the Constitution of the country, let the consequences be what they may. They wish to strike out this constitutional provision; to annul it. They oppose it in every possible form short of personal resistance, or incurring personal danger; and to do this they say the worse the law is the better. They say we have now a topic, and for mercy's sake don't amend the horrible law of 1850.

Then, again, they say, " We are for an eternal agitation and discussion of this question; the people cannot be bound by it. Every member of Congress has the right to move the repeal of this, as well as any other law." Who does not know this, Gentlemen? A member must act according to his own discretion. No doubt he has a right to-morrow, if Congress were in session, to move a repeal of the Fugitive Slave Law; but this takes with it another consideration. He has just as much right to move to tear down the Capitol, until one stone shall not be left on another; just as much right to move to disband the army, and to throw the ordnance and arms into the sea. He has just as much right to move that all the ships of war of the United States shall be collected and burned; an illumination like that which lit up the walls of ancient Troy. He may move to do any of these things. The question is, Is he prudent, wise, a real friend of the country, or adverse to it? That is all. And a greater question lies behind, Will the people support him in it Is it the result of the good sense of the Northern people, that the question shall have neither rest nor quiet, but shall be constantly kept up as a topic of agitation? I cannot decide this question for the people, but leave them to decide it for themselves.

And now, Gentlemen, this is a serious question, whether the Constitution can be maintained in part, and not as a whole; whether those interested in the preservation of one part of it, finding their interests in that particular abandoned, are not likely enough, according to all experience of human feeling and human conduct, to discard that portion which was introduced, not for their benefit, but for the benefit of others. That is the question. For one, I confess I do not see any reasonable prospect of maintaining the Constitution of the United States unless we maintain it as a whole, impartially, honorably, patriotically. Gentlemen, I am detaining you too long; but allow me a few words on another subject by way of illustration.

The Constitution of the United States consists in a series of mutual agreements or compromises, one thing being yielded by the South, another by the North; the general mind having been brought together, and the whole agreed to, as I have said, as a series of compromises constituting one whole. Well, Gentlemen, who does not see that? Had the North no particular interest to be regarded and protected? Had the North no peculiar interest of its own? Was nothing yielded by the South to the North? Gentlemen, you are proud citizens of a great commercial State. You know that New York ships float over the whole globe, and bring abundance of riches to your own shores. You know that this is the result of the commercial policy of the United States, and of the commercial power vested in Congress by the Constitution. And how was this commerce established? by what constitutional provisions, and for whose benefit? The South was never a commercial country. The plantation States were never commercial. Their interest always was, as they thought, what they think it to be now, free trade, the unrestricted admission of foreigners in competition in all branches of business with our own people. But what did they do? They agreed to form a government that should regulate commerce according to the wants and wishes of the Northern States, and when the Constitution went into operation, a commercial system was actually established, on which has risen up the whole glory of New York and New England. How was this effected? What did Congress do under a Northern lead with Southern acquiescence? What did it do? It protected the commerce of New York and the Eastern States, by preference, by discriminating tonnage duties; and that higher duty on foreign ships has never been surrendered to this day except in consideration of a just equivalent; so, in that respect, without grudging or complaint on the part of the South, but generously and fairly, not by way of concession, but in the true spirit of the Constitution, the commerce of New York and the New England States was protected by the provision of the Constitution to which I have referred. But that is not all.

Friends! fellow-citizens! men of New York! does this country not now extend from Maine to Mexico, and beyond? Have we not a State beyond Cape Horn, belonging nevertheless to us as part of our commercial system? And what does New York enjoy? What do Massachusetts and Maine enjoy? They enjoy an exclusive right of carrying on the coasting trade from State to State, on the Atlantic, and around Cape Horn to the Pacific. And that is a highly important branch of business, and a source of wealth and emolument, of comfort and good living. Every man must know this, who is not blinded by passion or fanaticism. It is this right to the coasting trade, to the exclusion of foreigners, thus granted to the Northern States, which they have ever held, and of which, up to this time, there has been no attempt to deprive them; it is this which has employed so much tonnage and so many men, and given support to so many thousands of our fellow-citizens. Now what would you say, in this day of the prevalence of notions of free trade, — what would you say, if the South and the Southwest were to join together to repeal this law? And they have the votes to do it to-morrow. What would you say if they should join hands and resolve that these men of New York and New England, who put this slight on their interest, shall enjoy this exclusive privilege no longer? that they will throw it all open, and invite the Dane, the Swede, the Hamburgher, and all the commercial nations of Europe who can carry cheaper, to come in and carry goods from New York coastwise on the Atlantic, and to California, on the Pacific? What would you say to that?

Now, Gentlemen, these ideas may have been often suggested before, but if there is any thing new in them I hope it may be regarded. But what was said in Syracuse and in Boston? It was this: " You set up profit against conscience; you set up the means of living: we go for conscience." That is a flight of fanaticism, and all I have to answer is, that if what we propose is right, fair, just, and stands well with a conscience not enlightened with those high flights of fancy, it is none the worse for being profitable; and that it does not make a thing bad which is good in itself, that you and I can live on it, and our children be supported and educated by it. If the compact of the Constitution is fair, and was fairly entered into, it is none the worse, one should think, for its having been found useful. Gentlemen, I believe it was in Cromwell's time, — for I am not very fresh in the recollection of my early reading; I have had more to do with other things than some of you younger men that love to look into the instructive history of that age, — but I think it was in Cromwell's time that there sprung up a race of saints who called themselves " Fifth Monarchy men"; and a happy, self-pleased, glorious people they were, for they had practised so many virtues, they were so enlightened, so perfect, that they got to be, in the language of that day, "above ordinances." That is the higher law of this day exactly. Our higher law is but the old doctrine of the Fifth Monarchy men of Cromwell's time revived. They were above ordinances, walked about prim and spruce, self-satisfied, thankful to God that they were not as other men, but had attained so far to salvation as to be " above all necessity of restraint and control, civil or religious." Cromwell himself says of these persons, if I remember rightly, " that *notions* will hurt none but those that have them; but when they tell us, not that law is to regulate us, but that law is to be abrogated and subverted, and perhaps the Judaical law brought in, instead of our own laws settled among us," this is something more than a notion, " this is worthy of every magistrate's consideration."

Gentlemen, we live under a Constitution. It has made us what we are. What has carried the American flag all over the world? What has constituted that " unit of commerce," that wherever the stars and stripes are seen, they signify that it belongs to America and united America? What is it now that represents us so respectably all over Europe? in London at this moment, and all over the world? What is it but the result of those commercial regulations which united us all together, and made our commerce the same commerce; which made all the States, New York, Massachusetts, and South Carolina, in the aspect of our foreign relations one and the same country, without division, distinction, or separation? Now, Gentlemen, to effect this was the original design of the Constitution. We in our day must see to it; and it will be equally incumbent on you, my young friends of Albany, to see that, while you live, this spirit is made to pervade the whole administration of the government. The Constitution of the United States, to keep us united, to keep a fraternal feeling flowing in our hearts, must be administered in the spirit in which it was framed.

And, Gentlemen, if I wished to convey to you an idea of what that spirit is, I would exhibit it to you in its living, speaking, animated form; I would refer now and always to the administration of the first President, George Washington. If I were now to describe a patriot President, I would draw his master-strokes and copy his design; I would present his picture before me as a constant study; I would display his policy, alike liberal and just, narrowed down to no sectional interests, bound to no personal objects, held to no locality, but broad and generous and open, as expansive as the air which is wafted by the winds of heaven from one part of the country to another.

I would draw a picture of his foreign policy, just, steady, stately, but withal proud, and lofty, and glorious. No man apprehended, in his day, that the broad escutcheon of the Union could receive injury or damage, or even contumely or disrespect, with impunity. His own character gave character to the foreign relations of the country. He upheld every interest of the United States in even the proudest nations of Europe; and while resolutely just, he was as resolutely determined that no plume in the honor of the country should ever be defaced or moved from its proper position by any power on earth. Washington was cautious and prudent; no self-seeker; giving information to Congress, as directed by the Constitution, on all questions, when necessary, with fairness and frankness, claiming nothing for himself, exercising his own rights, and preserving the dignity of his station, but taking especial care to execute the laws as a paramount duty, and in such manner as to give satisfaction to all just and reasonable men. It was always remarked of his administration, that he filled the courts of justice with the most spotless integrity, the highest talent, and the purest virtue; and hence it became a common saying, running through all classes of society, that our great security is in the learning and integrity of the judicial tribunals. This high character they justly possessed, and continue to possess in an eminent degree from the impress which Washington stamped on these tribunals at their first organization.

Gentlemen, a patriot President is the guardian, the protector, the friend, of every citizen of the United States. He should be, and he is, no man's persecutor, no man's enemy, but the supporter and the protector of all and every citizen, so far as such support and protection depend on his faithful execution of the laws. But there is especially one great idea which Washington presents, and which governed him, and which should govern every man high in office who means to resemble Washington; and that is, the duty of preserving the government itself; of suffering, so far as depends on him, no one branch to interfere with another; no power to be assumed by any department which does not belong to it, and none to be abandoned which does belong to it, but to preserve it and carry it on unharmed for the benefit of the present and future generations.

Gentlemen, a wise and prudent shipmaster makes it his first duty to preserve the vessel which carries him, and his passengers, and all that is committed to his charge; to keep her afloat, to conduct her to her destined port with entire security of property and life. That is his first object, and that should be, and is, the object of every chief magistrate of the United States, who has a proper appreciation of his duty. His first and highest duty is to preserve the Constitution which bears him, which sustains the government, without which every thing goes to the bottom; to preserve that, and keep it, with the utmost of his ability and foresight, off the rocks and shoals, and away from the quicksands. To accomplish this great end, he exercises the caution of the experienced navigator. He suffers nothing to betray his watchfulness, or to draw him aside from the great interest committed to his care; but is always awake, always solicitous, always anxious, for the safety of the ship which is to carry him through the stormy seas.

" Though pleased to see the dolphins play,
He minds his compass and his way;
And oft he throws the wary lead,
To see what dangers may be hid:
At helm he makes his reason sit;
His crew of passions all submit.
Thus, thus he steers his bark, and sails,
On upright keel, to meet the gales! "

Now, Gentlemen, a patriot President, acting from the impulses of this high and honorable purpose, may reach what Washington reached. He may contribute to raise high the public prosperity, to help to fill up the measure of his country's glory and renown. He may be able to find a rich reward in the thankfulness of the people,

" And read his history in a nation's eyes."

In the evening of the 28th of May, Mr. Webster was entertained at dinner by a large company of the most distinguished citizens of Albany. Hon. John C. Spencer presided at the table, and, after the cloth was removed, addressed the company as follows: —

" I am about to offer a sentiment, my friends, which you expect from the chair. The presence of the distinguished guest whom we have met to honor imposes restraints which may not be overleaped. Within those limits, and without offending the generous spirit which has on this occasion discarded all political and partisan feeling, I may recall to our recollection a few incidents in his public life, which have won for him the proud title of ' Defender of the Constitution.'

" When, in 1832 – 33, South Carolina raised her parricidal arm against our common mother, and the administration of the government was in the hands of that man of determined purpose and iron will, Andrew Jackson, whose greatest glory was his inflexible resolution to sustain the Union or perish with it, — in that dark and gloomy day, where was our guest found ? Did he think of paltry politics, of how much his party might gain by leaving their antagonists to fight the battle of the Union between themselves, and thus become a prey to their watchful opponents ? No, Gentlemen, you know what he did. He rallied his mighty energies, and tendered them openly and heartily to a political chieftain whose administration he had constantly opposed. He breasted himself to the storm. Where blows were thickest and heaviest, there was he;

and when he encountered the great champion of the South, Colonel Hayne, in that immortal intellectual struggle, the parallel of which no country has witnessed, the hopes, the breathless anxiety of a nation, hung upon his efforts. And, O, what a shout of joy and gratulation ascended to heaven at the matchless victory which he achieved! Had he then been called to his fathers, the measure of his fame would have been full to overflowing, and he would have left a monument in the grateful recollection of his countrymen such as no statesman of modern times had reared. But he was reserved by a kind Providence for greater efforts. For more than twenty years, in the Senate-chamber, in the courts of justice, and in the executive councils, he has stood sentinel over the Constitution. It seems to have been the master passion of his life to love, to venerate, to defend, to fight for the Constitution, at all times and in all places. He did so because the Union existed and can exist only in the Constitution; and the peace and happiness of the country can exist only in the Union. In fighting for the Constitution, he fought therefore for the country, for the whole country.

"I may not speak in detail of the many acts of his public life which have developed this absorbing love of country. But there are a few of the precious gems in the circlet which adorns his brow, that are so marked and prominent that they cannot be overlooked.

"When he first assumed the duties of the Department of State, war was lowering on our horizon like a black cloud, ready to launch its thunderbolts around us. The alarming state of our foreign relations at that time is shown by the extraordinary fact, that the appropriation bills passed by Congress, at the close of Mr. Van Buren's administration, contained an unusual provision, authorizing the President to transfer them to military purposes. In a few months after our guest took the matter in hand, the celebrated treaty with Lord Ashburton was concluded, by which the irritating question of boundary was settled, every difficulty then known or anticipated was adjusted, and among others, the detestable claim to search our vessels for British seaman was renounced.

"In connection with this treaty, I take this occasion, the first that has presented itself, to state some facts which are not generally known. The then administration had no strength in Congress; it could command no support for any of its measures. This was an obstacle sufficiently formidable in itself. But Mr. Webster had also to deal with a feeble and wayward President, an unfriendly Senate, a hostile House of Representatives, and an accomplished British diplomatist. I speak of what I personally know, when I say, that never was a negotiation environed with greater or more perplexing difficulties. He had at least three parties to negotiate with instead of one, to say nothing of Massachusetts and Maine, who had to be consulted in relation to a boundary that affected their territory.* You know the result ; glorious as it was to our country, how glorious was it also to the pilot that guided the ship through such difficulties !

" You have not forgotten how the generous sympathies of our guest were awakened in behalf of the noble Hungarians, in their immortal resistance against the forces of barbarism. And sure I am there is not a heart here that has not treasured up the contents of that world-renowned letter to Chevalier Hülsemann, in answer to the intimations of threats by Austria to treat our diplomatic agent as a spy. What American was not proud of being the countryman of the author of that letter ?

" I confess I cannot now think of that letter without recollecting the sensations a particular part of it produced upon my risible faculties. I mean the comparison between the territories and national importance of the house of Hapsburg and those of he United States of America.

" But I must stop the enumeration of the great deeds in the glory of which we all participate, and by the results of which the whole civilized world has been benefited. I must stop, or the setting sun would leave me still at the task, and the rising sun would find it unfinished.

" The same soul-absorbing devotion to the country and to the Constitution, as its anchor of safety, has been exhibited so recently and so remarkably, that no one can have forgotten it. In the view which I present of the matter, it is quite immaterial whether we regard our guest as having been right or wrong. He deemed the course he took to be the only one permitted to him by his sense of duty. On the one side were the strong feelings with which, as a Northern man, he had always sympathized ; there also were the friends of his youth and of his age ; the troops of ardent and devoted admirers ; all whose love was equal to their reverence ; all the associations and affections of life were clustered there ; while on the other side a feeling of enmity, engendered by former contests and the defeat of all their schemes ; nothing to allure or invite, but every thing to repel except one, and that was the Constitu-

* For the purpose of explanation it may be well to say, that, the Northeastern Boundary having been a matter of controversy for fifty years, and the award of the King of the Netherlands having failed to take effect, Mr. Webster proposed that a line should be established by agreement, upon the principle of fair equivalents, to be assented to by Massachusetts and Maine. Massachusetts accordingly appointed three commissioners, and Maine four, selected from both political parties, to proceed to Washington, and take part in the negotiations. The consent of all the commissioners was made the condition of binding their respective States. It will thus be seen, that the difficulty of making a treaty, when so many and such diverse interests were to be harmonized, was immeasurably increased.

tion of the country. That, as he conscientiously believed, required him to interpose and prevent a breach of faith, as well as of the organic law, and avert a civil war that he believed to be impending. He hesitated not a moment, but at once marched up to the deadly breach, and was ready to sacrifice upon his country's altar more than life, every thing that could render life worth retaining.

" My friends, whatever other view may be taken of that step, every one knows that it conformed to the whole plan of his public life to know no North, no South, where the Constitution is in question; and there is not a heart in this assembly that will not respond to my voice when I pronounce it heroism; heroism of the most sublime order. It can be compared only to that of the great Reformer, who, when advised not to proceed to the Diet that was convoked to condemn him, declared that, if fifty thousand legions of devils stood in the way, go he would !

" How poor and insignificant are all our efforts to express our appreciation of such a character and of such services ! They have sunk deep in our hearts; they will sink deeper still in the hearts of the unborn millions who are to people this vast continent; and when he and we sleep with our fathers, his name will reverberate from the Atlantic to the Pacific, as the defender of the Constitution and of his country.

" Gentlemen, I give you a sentiment which I think will be drunk in bumpers and standing. [The whole assembly rose at once with acclamation.]

" The Constitution of the United States and Daniel Webster: inseparable now, and inseparable in the records of time and eternity."

Mr. Webster rose to respond, when the whole company started from their seats, and greeted him with three times three cheers. Mr. Webster spoke as follows: —

I know, Gentlemen, very well, how much of the undeserved compliment, or I may say eulogy, which you have heard from my honorable friend at the head of the table, is due to a personal and political friendship which has now continued for many years. Of course, I cannot but most profoundly thank him for the manner in which he has expressed himself. Gentlemen, what shall I say? What shall I say to this outpouring of kindness? I am overwhelmed. I have no words. I cannot acknowledge the truth of what has been said, yet I hardly could find it in my heart to deny it. It is overstated. It is overstated. But that I love the Constitution of the country; that I have a passion for it, the only political passion that ever entered into my breast; that I cherish it day and night; that I live on its healthful, saving influences, and that I trust never, never, never to cease to heed it till I go to the grave of my fathers, is as true [turning to Mr. Spencer] as that you sit here. I do not suppose I am born to any considerable destiny, but my destiny, whatever it may be, attaches me to the Constitution of the country. I desire not to outlive it. I desire to render it some service. And, on the modest stone that shall mark my grave, whether within my native New Hampshire or my adopted Massachusetts, I wish no other epitaph than this: While he lived, he did what he could to support the Constitution of his country. I confess to you that as to mere questions of politics, of expediency, I have taken my share in them, as they have gone along, in the course of my public life, which is now fast running through. But I have felt no anxiety, no excitement; nothing has made me lie awake at night, when it is said honest men sleep, except what has concerned the preservation of the Union.

The Constitution of the United States! What is there on the whole earth; what is there that so fills the imaginations of men under heaven; what is there that the civilized, liberalized, liberty-loving people of the world can look at, and do look at, so much as that great and glorious instrument held up to their contemplation, blazing over this western hemisphere, and darting its rays throughout the world, the Constitution of the United States of America! In Massachusetts, in New York, in Washington, its ample folds are athwart the whole heavens. Are they not seen in all America, on all the continent of Europe, gazed at and honored in Russia, in Turkey, in the Indian seas, in all the countries of the Oriental world? What is it that makes you and me here, to-day, so proud as we are of the name of America? What is it? It is almost a miracle; the achievement of half a century, by wise men under propitious circumstances, acting from patriotic motives; a miracle achieved on earth and in view of all nations; the establishment of a government, taking hold on a great continent; covering ample space for fifty other governments; having twenty-five milli ns of people, intelligent, prosperous, brave, able to defend themselves against united mankind, and to bid defiance to the whole of them; a noble monument of republican honor and power, and of republican success, that throws a shade, and sometimes a deep and black shade, over the monarchies, and aristocracies, and despotisms of Europe. Who is there, who is there from the poles to the Mediterranean, despot, aristocrat, autocrat, who is there that now dares to speak reproachfully or in tones of derogation of the government of the United States of America? There is not one. And if we may judge, my friends, of the success of our system of government from the regard it attracts from all nations, we may flatter ourselves that in our primitive republicanism, in our representative system, in our departure from the whole feudal code and all the prerogatives of aristocratic and autocratic power, from all the show and pageantry of courts, we shall hold ourselves up like the face of the sun, not marred by inscription, but bright in glory, and glittering in the sight of all men. And so we will stand, so shine; and when the time comes when I shall be gathered to my fathers, and you to yours, that eternal, unfading sun of American liberty and republicanism, as steady in its course as the sun in the heavens, shall still pour forth its beams for the enlightenment of mankind.

Gentlemen, I again thank you for the manner in which you have been pleased to receive the complimentary sentiment proposed by my friend. I thank you, thank him. Gentlemen, I am happy to be here, in this ancient city. Of course, I like to see my Yankee brethren here, and a great many of them, of the ancient stock. But I have no objection to see the recent importations, so to describe them, come from where they may; because I am of opinion, and have expressed it again and again, that we have got to that stage in our affairs, that the world has reached that point in the system of change and innovation, that we have nothing to do but say to the inhabitants of the ancient world, — the Irish, the Welch, the German, — Gentlemen, come! and the fact is, "the cry is still, They come!" There are people enough imported into New York, twice a year, to make a city as large as old Salem or Naumkeag in Massachusetts. Every ship brings them to our shores, and off they start for Wisconsin. Well, they come, and whether they come from Dublin, Cork, or Kerry they are very happy to stay wher they are. If they come from the North of Ireland, if they have a little of the canny Scot in them, they still find themselves at home. Every steamboat brings them, and every packet; and when you think they are all here, "the cry is still, They come!" Well, we must meet this as well as we can.   Very many of them are excellent persons, and become excellent citizens of the United States.   I am a New England man.   I am of the Anglo-Saxon race; but it is my good fortune to be connected in life with a lady who has a portion of the old Knickerbocker blood.   I am happy to know that among this company there are many persons of Dutch descent.   I honor them all, and I accord to them credit for honesty, for sobriety of character, and for the great aid they have lent to the growth and prosperity of this and neighboring States.

Gentlemen, numerous and various as are the elements of our national life, they are harmonized into one great whole, — the Constitution and the Union.   With my dying breath, if I have my senses, my last prayer shall be, Heaven save my country and the Constitution!   I hear the cry of disunion, secession.   The secession of individual States, to my mind, is the most absurd of all ideas.   I should like to know how South Carolina is to get out of this Union.   Where is she to go?   The commercial people of Charleston say, with truth and propriety, if South Carolina secedes from the Union, we secede from South Carolina.   The thing is absurd.   A separate secession is an absurdity.   It could not take place.   It must lead to war.   I do, indeed, admit the possibility that a great mass of the Southern States, if they should come so far north as to include Virginia, might make a Southern confederation.   But it would put Virginia up to all she knows to accomplish it.   More than half of Virginia lies on the west slope of the Alleghanies, and is connected with the valley of the Mississippi, its people and interests, more than with those who live on tide-water.   Do they think that the great western slope of the Alleghanies is to be included in a secession movement?   Nevertheless, it is a most serious consideration.   All know what would be the result of any dismemberment of this Union, large or small.   The philosophic poet tells us, that in the frame of things, above us, beneath us, and around us, there are connections, mutual dependences and relations, which link them together in one great chain of existences, beginning from the throne on high, and running down to the lowest order of beings.   There seems to be some analogy between this great system of the universe and our association here as separate States; independent, yet connected; revolving in separate spheres, and yet mutually bound one with another. What the poet says of the great chain that holds all together in the moral, intellectual, and physical world, is applicable to the bond which unites the States: —

> " Whatever link you strike,
> Tenth, or ten thousandth, breaks the chain alike."

Now, Gentlemen, it is not for me to do much more, nor attempt much more, on this theatre of action. I look on to see what others shall do, and especially to see what the rising generation shall do. I look on to see what the young men of the country are determined to do. I see them intelligent, regardless of personal objects, holding on upon what their ancestors gave them, holding on with their whole strength to the institutions of the country. I know that, when I shall slumber in the dust, the institutions of the country will be free and safe; I know that the young men of the country can preserve the country. In the language of the old Greek orator, " The young are the spring-time of the people." I wish to leave my exhortation to the young men all over the country; to say to them, On you, young men of the republic, the hopes, the independence, the Union, the honor of the country, entirely depend. May God bless you! In taking leave of you, whilst I shall never forget the pleasure this occasion has given me, I give you, as a sentiment: —

" The young men of Albany, the young men of this generation and of the succeeding generations: may they live for ever, but may the Constitution and the Union outlive them all."

THE ADDITION TO THE CAPITOL.

50 *

THE ADDITION TO THE CAPITOL.*

FELLOW-CITIZENS, — I greet you well; I give you joy, on the return of this anniversary; and I felicitate you, also, on the more particular purpose of which this ever-memorable day has been chosen to witness the fulfilment. Hail! all hail! I see before and around me a mass of faces, glowing with cheerfulness and patriotic pride. I see thousands of eyes turned towards other eyes, all sparkling with gratification and delight. This is the New World! This is America! This is Washington! and this the Capitol of the United States! And where else, among the nations, can the seat of government be surrounded, on any day of any year, by those who have more reason to rejoice in the blessings which they possess? Nowhere, fellow-citizens! assuredly, nowhere! Let us, then, meet this rising sun with joy and thanksgiving!

This is that day of the year which announced to mankind the great fact of American Independence. This fresh and brilliant morning blesses our vision with another beholding of the birthday of our nation; and we see that nation, of recent origin, now among the most considerable and powerful, and spreading over the continent from sea to sea.

Among the first colonists from Europe to this part of America, there were some, doubtless, who contemplated the distant consequences of their undertaking, and who saw a great futurity.

* An Address delivered at the Laying of the Corner-stone of the Addition to the Capitol, on the 4th of July, 1851.

The following motto stands upon the title-page of the original pamphlet edition : —

     " Stet Capitolium
Fulgens;
     late nomen in ultimas
  Extendat oras."

But, in general, their hopes were limited to the enjoyment of a safe asylum from tyranny, religious and civil, and to respectable subsistence, by industry and toil. A thick veil hid our times from their view. But the progress of America, however slow, could not but at length awaken genius, and attract the attention of mankind.

In the early part of the second century of our history, Bishop Berkeley, who, it will be remembered, had resided for some time in Newport, in Rhode Island, wrote his well-known " Verses on the Prospect of planting ARTS and LEARNING in AMERICA." The last stanza of this little poem seems to have been produced by a high poetical inspiration : —

> " Westward the course of empire takes its way ;
> The four first acts already past,
> A fifth shall close the drama with the day :
> Time's noblest offspring is the last."

This extraordinary prophecy may be considered only as the result of long foresight and uncommon sagacity ; of a foresight and sagacity stimulated, nevertheless, by excited feeling and high enthusiasm. So clear a vision of what America would become was not founded on square miles, or on existing numbers, or on any common laws of statistics. It was an intuitive glance into futurity ; it was a grand conception, strong, ardent, glowing, embracing all time since the creation of the world, and all regions of which that world is composed, and judging of the future by just analogy with the past. And the inimitable imagery and beauty with which the thought is expressed, joined to the conception itself, render it one of the most striking passages in our language.

On the day of the declaration of independence our illustrious fathers performed the first scene in the last great act of this drama ; one in real importance infinitely exceeding that for which the great English poet invokes

> " A muse of fire,
> A kingdom for a stage, princes to act,
> And monarchs to behold the swelling scene ! "

The Muse inspiring our fathers was the Genius of Liberty, all on fire with a sense of oppression, and a resolution to throw it off ; the whole world was the stage, and higher characters than princes trod it ; and, instead of monarchs, countries and nations and the age beheld the swelling scene. How well the characters were cast, and how well each acted his part, and what emotions the whole performance excited, let history, now and hereafter, tell.

At a subsequent period, but before the declaration of independence, the Bishop of St. Asaph published a discourse, in which the following remarkable passages are found: —

"It is difficult for man to look into the destiny of future ages; the designs of Providence are vast and complicated, and our own powers are too narrow to admit of much satisfaction to our curiosity. But when we see many great and powerful causes constantly at work, we cannot doubt of their producing proportionable effects.

"The colonies in North America have not only taken root and acquired strength, *but seem hastening with an accelerated progress to such a powerful state as may introduce a new and important change in human affairs.*

"Descended from ancestors of the most improved and enlightened part of the Old World, they receive, as it were by inheritance, all the improvements and discoveries of their mother country. And it happens fortunately for them to commence their flourishing state at a time when the human understanding has attained to the free use of its powers, and has learned to act with vigor and certainty. They may avail themselves, not only of the experience and industry, but even of the errors and mistakes, of former days. Let it be considered for how many ages a great part of the world appears not to have thought at all; how many more they have been busied in forming systems and conjectures, while reason has been lost in a labyrinth of words, and they never seem to have suspected on what frivolous matters their minds were employed.

"And let it be well understood what rapid improvements, what important discoveries, have been made, in a few years, by a few countries, with our own at their head, which have at last discovered the right method of using their faculties.

"May we not reasonably expect that a number of provinces possessed of these advantages and quickened by mutual emulation, with only the common progress of the human mind, should very considerably enlarge the boundaries of science?

"The vast continent itself, over which they are gradually spreading, may be considered as a treasure yet untouched of natural productions that shall hereafter afford ample matter for commerce and contemplation. And if we reflect what a stock of knowledge may be accumulated by the constant progress of industry and observation, fed with fresh supplies from the stores of nature, assisted sometimes by those happy strokes of chance which mock all the powers of invention, and sometimes by those superior characters which arise occasionally to instruct and enlighten the world, it is difficult even to imagine to what height of improvement their discoveries may extend.

" *And perhaps they may make as considerable advances in the arts of civil government and the conduct of life.* We have reason to be proud, and even jealous, of our excellent constitution ; but those equitable principles on which it was formed, an equal representation (the best discovery of political wisdom), and a just and commodious distribution of power which with us were the price of civil wars, and the rewards of the virtues and sufferings of our ancestors, descend to them as a natural inheritance, without toil or pain.

" *But must they rest here, as in the utmost effort of human genius ? Can chance and time, the wisdom and the experience of public men, suggest no new remedy against the evils* which vices and ambition are perpetually apt to cause ? May they not hope, without presumption, to preserve a greater zeal for piety and public devotion than we have done ? For sure it can hardly happen to them, as it has to us, that when religion is best understood and rendered most pure and reasonable, then should be the precise time when many cease to believe and practise it, and all in general become most indifferent to it.

" May they not possibly be more successful than their mother country has been in preserving that reverence and authority which are due to the laws ? to those who make, and to those who execute them ? *May not a method be invented of procuring some tolerable share of the comforts of life to those inferior useful ranks of men to whose industry we are indebted for the whole ? Time and discipline may discover some means to correct the extreme inequalities of condition between the rich and the poor, so dangerous to the innocence and happiness of both.* They may fortunately be led by habit and choice to despise that luxury which is considered with us the true enjoyment of wealth. They may have little relish for that ceaseless hurry of amusements which is pursued in this country without pleasure, exercise, or employment. And perhaps, after trying some of our follies and caprices, and rejecting the rest, they may be led by reason and experiment to that old simplicity which was first pointed out by nature, and has produced those models which we still admire in arts, eloquence, and manners. *The diversity of new scenes and situations, which so many growing states must necessarily pass through, may introduce changes in the fluctuating opinions and manners of men which we can form no conception of;* and not only the gracious disposition of Providence, but the visible preparation of causes, seems to indicate strong tendencies towards a general improvement."

Fellow-citizens, this "gracious disposition of Providence," and this "visible preparation of causes," at length brought on the hour for decisive action. On the 4th of July, 1776, the Representatives of the United States of America, in Congress assembled, declared that these United Colonies are, and of right ought to be, FREE AND INDEPENDENT STATES.

This declaration, made by most patriotic and resolute men, trusting in the justice of their cause and the protection of Heaven, and yet made not without deep solicitude and anxiety, has now stood for seventy-five years, and still stands. It was sealed in blood. It has met dangers, and overcome them; it has had enemies, and conquered them; it has had detractors, and abashed them all; it has had doubting friends, but it has cleared all doubts away; and now, to-day, raising its august form higher than the clouds, twenty millions of people contemplate it with hallowed love, and the world beholds it, and the consequences which have followed from it, with profound admiration.

This anniversary animates and gladdens and unites all American hearts. On other days of the year we may be party men, indulging in controversies, more or less important to the public good; we may have likes and dislikes, and we may maintain our political differences, often with warm, and sometimes with angry feelings. But to-day we are Americans all; and all nothing but Americans. As the great luminary over our heads, dissipating mists and fogs, now cheers the whole hemisphere, so do the associations connected with this day disperse all cloudy and sullen weather in the minds and hearts of true Americans. Every man's heart swells within him; every man's port and bearing become somewhat more proud and lofty, as he remembers that seventy-five years have rolled away, and that the great inheritance of liberty is still his; his, undiminished and unimpaired; his in all its original glory; his to enjoy, his to protect, and his to transmit to future generations.

Fellow-citizens, this inheritance which we enjoy to-day is not only an inheritance of liberty, but of our own peculiar American liberty. Liberty has existed in other times, in other countries, and in other forms. There has been a Grecian liberty, bold and powerful, full of spirit, eloquence, and fire; a liberty which produced multitudes of great men, and has transmitted one immortal name, the name of Demosthenes, to posterity. But still it was a liberty of disconnected states, sometimes united, indeed, by temporary leagues and confederacies, but often involved in wars between themselves. The sword of Sparta turned its sharpest edge against Athens, enslaved her, and devastated Greece; and, in her turn, Sparta was compelled to bend before the power of Thebes. And let it ever be remembered, especially let the truth sink deep into all American minds, that it was the WANT OF UNION among her several states which finally gave the mastery of all Greece to Philip of Macedon.

And there has also been a Roman liberty, a proud, ambitious, domineering spirit, professing free and popular principles in Rome itself, but, even in the best days of the republic, ready to carry slavery and chains into her provinces, and through every country over which her eagles could be borne. What was the liberty of Spain, or Gaul, or Germany, or Britain, in the days of Rome? Did true constitutional liberty then exist? As the Roman empire declined, her provinces, not instructed in the principles of free popular government, one after another declined also, and when Rome herself fell, in the end, all fell together.

I have said, Gentlemen, that our inheritance is an inheritance of American liberty. That liberty is characteristic, peculiar, and altogether our own. Nothing like it existed in former times, nor was known in the most enlightened states of antiquity; while with us its principles have become interwoven into the minds of individual men, connected with our daily opinions, and our daily habits, until it is, if I may so say, an element of social as well as of political life; and the consequence is, that to whatever region an American citizen carries himself, he takes with him, fully developed in his own understanding and experience, our American principles and opinions, and becomes ready at once, in coöperation with others, to apply them to the formation of new governments. Of this a most wonderful instance may be seen in the history of the State of California.

On a former occasion I ventured to remark, that " it is very difficult to establish a free conservative government for the equal advancement of all the interests of society. What has Germany done, learned Germany, more full of ancient lore than all the world beside? What has Italy done? What have they done who dwell on the spot where Cicero lived? They have not the power of self-government which a common town-meeting, with us, possesses. . . . . . Yes, I say that those persons who have gone from our town-meetings to dig gold in California are more fit to make a republican government than any body of men in Germany or Italy; because they have learned this one great lesson, that there is no security without law, and that, under the circumstances in which they are placed, where there is no military authority to cut their throats, there is no sovereign will but the will of the majority; that, therefore, if they remain, they must submit to that will." And this I believe to be strictly true.

Now, fellow-citizens, if your patience will hold out, I will venture, before proceeding to the more appropriate and particular duties of the day, to state, in a few words, what I take these American political principles in substance to be. They consist, as I think, in the first place, in the establishment of popular governments, on the basis of representation; for it is plain that a pure democracy, like that which existed in some of the states of Greece, in which every individual had a direct vote in the enactment of all laws, cannot possibly exist in a country of wide extent. This representation is to be made as equal as circumstances will allow. Now, this principle of popular representation, prevailing either in all the branches of government, or in some of them, has existed in these States almost from the days of the settlements at Jamestown and Plymouth; borrowed, no doubt, from the example of the popular branch of the British legislature. The representation of the people in the British House of Commons was, however, originally very unequal, and is yet not equal. Indeed, it may be doubted whether the appearance of knights and burgesses, assembling on the summons of the crown, was not intended at first as an assistance and support to the royal prerogative, in matters of revenue and taxation, rather than as a mode of ascertaining popular opinion. Nevertheless, representation had a popular origin, and savored more and more of the character of that origin, as it acquired, by slow degrees, greater and greater strength, in the actual government of the country. The constitution of the House of Commons was certainly a form of representation, however unequal; numbers were counted, and majorities prevailed; and when our ancestors, acting upon this example, introduced more equality of representation, the idea assumed a more rational and distinct shape.   At any rate, this manner of exercising popular power was familiar to our fathers when they settled on this continent. They adopted it, and generation has risen up after generation, all acknowledging it, and all learning its practice and its forms.

The next fundamental principle in our system is, that the will of the majority, fairly expressed through the means of representation, shall have the force of law; and it is quite evident that, in a country without thrones or aristocracies or privileged castes or classes, there can be no other foundation for law to stand upon.

And, as the necessary result of this, the third element is, that the law is the supreme rule for the government of all.   The great sentiment of Alcæus, so beautifully presented to us by Sir William Jones, is absolutely indispensable to the construction and maintenance of our political systems : —

> " What constitutes a state ?
>   Not high-raised battlement or labored mound,
>   Thick wall or moated gate ;
>   Not cities proud, with spires and turrets crowned ;
>   Not bays and broad-armed ports,
>   Where, laughing at the storm, rich navies ride ;
>   Not starred and spangled courts,
>   Where low-browed baseness wafts perfume to pride.
>   No : MEN, high-minded MEN,
>   With powers as far above dull brutes endued,
>   In forest, brake, or den,
>   As beasts excel cold rocks and brambles rude :
>   Men who their duties know,
>   But know their rights, and, knowing, dare maintain ;
>   Prevent the long-aimed blow,
>   And crush the tyrant while they rend the chain :
>   These constitute a state ;
>   And SOVEREIGN LAW, that state's collected will,
>   O'er thrones and globes elate
>   Sits empress, crowning good, repressing ill."

And, finally, another most important part of the great fabric of American liberty is, that there shall be written constitutions, founded on the immediate authority of the people themselves, and regulating and restraining all the powers conferred upon government, whether legislative, executive, or judicial.

This, fellow-citizens, I suppose to be a just summary of our American principles, and I have on this occasion sought to express them in the plainest and in the fewest words. The summary may not be entirely exact, but I hope it may be sufficiently so to make manifest to the rising generation among ourselves, and to those elsewhere who may choose to inquire into the nature of our political institutions, the general theory upon which they are founded.

And I now proceed to add, that the strong and deep-settled conviction of all intelligent persons amongst us is, that, in order to support a useful and wise government upon these popular principles, the general education of the people, and the wide diffusion of pure morality and true religion, are indispensable. Individual virtue is a part of public virtue. It is difficult to conceive how there can remain morality in the government when it shall cease to exist among the people; or how the aggregate of the political institutions, all the organs of which consist only of men, should be wise, and beneficent, and competent to inspire confidence, if the opposite qualities belong to the individuals who constitute those organs, and make up that aggregate.

And now, fellow-citizens, I take leave of this part of the duty which I proposed to perform; and, once more felicitating you and myself that our eyes have seen the light of this blessed morning, and that our ears have heard the shouts with which joyous thousands welcome its return, and joining with you in the hope that every revolving year may renew these rejoicings to the end of time, I proceed to address you, shortly, upon the particular occasion of our assembling here to-day.

Fellow-citizens, by the act of Congress of the 30th of September, 1850, provision was made for the extension of the Capitol, according to such plan as might be approved by the President of the United States, and for the necessary sums to be expended, under his direction, by such architect as he might appoint. This measure was imperatively demanded, for the use of the legislative and judiciary departments, the public libraries, the occasional accommodation of the chief executive magistrate, and for other objects. No act of Congress incurring a large expenditure has received more general approbation from the people. The President has proceeded to execute this law. He has approved a plan; he has appointed an architect; and all things are now ready for the commencement of the work.

The anniversary of national independence appeared to afford an auspicious occasion for laying the foundation-stone of the additional building. That ceremony has now been performed by the President himself, in the presence and view of this multitude. He has thought that the day and the occasion made a united and imperative call for some short address to the people here assembled; and it is at his request that I have appeared before you to perform that part of the duty which was deemed incumbent on us.

Beneath the stone is deposited, among other things, a list of which will be published, the following brief account of the proceedings of this day, in my handwriting: —

"On the morning of the first day of the seventy-sixth year of the Independence of the United States of America, in the city of Washington, being the 4th day of July, 1851, this stone, designed as the corner-stone of the extension of the Capitol, according to a plan approved by the President, in pursuance of an act of Congress, was laid by

MILLARD FILLMORE,

PRESIDENT OF THE UNITED STATES,

assisted by the Grand Master of the Masonic Lodges, in the presence of many members of Congress, of officers of the Executive and Judiciary Departments, National, State, and District, of officers of the army and navy, the corporate authorities of this and neighboring cities, many associations, civil and military and masonic, members of the Smithsonian Institution and National Institute, professors of colleges and teachers of schools of the District, with their students and pupils, and a vast concourse of people from places near and remote, including a few surviving gentlemen who witnessed the laying of the corner-stone of the Capitol by President Washington, on the 18th day of September, A. D. 1793.

"If, therefore, it shall be hereafter the will of God that this structure shall fall from its base, that its foundation be upturned, and this deposit brought to the eyes of men, be it then known, that on this day the Union of the United States of America stands firm, that their Constitution still exists unimpaired, and with all its original usefulness and glory; growing every day stronger and stronger in the affections of the great body of the American people, and attracting more and more the admiration of the world. And all here assembled, whether belonging to public life or to private life, with hearts devoutly thankful to Almighty God for the preservation of the liberty and happiness of the country, unite in sincere and fervent prayers that this deposit, and the walls and arches, the domes and towers, the columns and entablatures, now to be erected over it, may endure for ever!

"GOD SAVE THE UNITED STATES OF AMERICA!

"DANIEL WEBSTER,
Secretary of State of the United States."

Fellow-citizens, fifty-eight years ago Washington stood on this spot to execute a duty like that which has now been performed. He then laid the corner-stone of the original Capitol. He was at the head of the government, at that time weak in resources, burdened with debt, just struggling into political existence and respectability, and agitated by the heaving waves which were overturning European thrones. But even then, in many important respects, the government was strong. It was strong in Washington's own great character; it was strong in the wisdom and patriotism of other eminent public men, his political associates and fellow-laborers; and it was strong in the affections of the people.

Since that time astonishing changes have been wrought in the condition and prospects of the American people; and a degree of progress witnessed with which the world can furnish no parallel. As we review the course of that progress, wonder and amazement arrest our attention at every step. The present occasion, although allowing of no lengthened remarks, may yet, perhaps, admit of a short comparative statement of important subjects of national interest as they existed at that day, and as they now exist. I have adopted for this purpose the tabular form of statement, as being the most brief and significant.

COMPARATIVE TABLE.

	Year 1793.	Year 1851.
Number of States, ...	15	31
Representatives and Senators in Congress,	135	295
Population of the United States, . .	3,929,328	23,267,498
Population of Boston, ...	18,038	136,871
Population of Baltimore, ...	13,503	169,054
Population of Philadelphia, . . .	42,520	409,045
Population of New York (city), . .	33,121	515,507
Population of Washington, ...	. . .	40,075
Population of Richmond, ...	4,000	27,582

51 *

	Year 1793.	Year 1851.
Population of Charleston, . . .	16,359	42,983
Amount of receipts into the Treasury,	$5,720,624	$52,312,980
Amount of expenditures, . . .	$7,529,575	$48,005,879
Amount of imports, ...	$31,000,000	$215,725,995
Amount of exports, ...	$26,109,000	$217,517,130
Amount of tonnage (tons), . .	520,764	3,772,440
Area of the United States in square miles,	805,461	3,314,365
Rank and file of the army, . .	5,120	10,000
Militia (enrolled), ...		2,006,456
Navy of the United States (vessels), .	(None.)	76
Navy armament (ordnance), ...		2,012
Treaties and conventions with foreign powers,	9	90
Light-houses and light-boats, . . .	12	372
Expenditures for ditto, . . .	$12,061	$529,265
Area of the Capitol, ...	½ acre	4⅓ acres.
Number of miles of railroad in operation,	. . . .	10,287
Cost of ditto, ...	. . . .	$306,607,954
Number of miles in course of construction,	. . . .	10,092
Lines of electric telegraph, in miles, .	. . . .	15,000
Number of post-offices, . . .	209	21,551
Number of miles of post route, . .	5,642	196,290
Amount of revenue from post-offices, .	$104,747	$6,727,867
Amount of expenditures of Post-Office Department, ...	$72,040	$6,024,567
Number of miles of mail transportation, .	. . . .	52,465,724
Number of colleges, ...	19	121
Public libraries, ...	35	694
Volumes in ditto, ...	75,000	2,201,632
School libraries, ...		10,000
Volumes in ditto, ...		2,000,000
Emigrants from Europe to the United States,	10,000	299,610
Coinage at the Mint, ...	$9,664	$52,019,465

In respect to the growth of Western trade and commerce, I extract a few sentences from a very valuable address before the Historical Society of Ohio, by William D. Gallagher, Esq., 1850 : —

" A few facts will exhibit as well as a volume the wonderful growth of Western trade and commerce. Previous to the year 1800, some eight or ten keel-boats, of twenty or twenty-five tons each, performed all the carrying trade between Cincinnati and Pittsburg. In 1802 the first government vessel appeared on Lake Erie. In 1811 the first steamboat (the Orleans) was launched at Pittsburg. In 1826 the waters of Michigan were first ploughed by the keel of a steamboat, a pleasure trip to Green Bay being planned and executed in the summer of this year. In 1832 a steamboat first appeared at Chicago. At the present time the entire number of steamboats running on the Mississippi and Ohio and their tributaries is more probably over than under six hundred, the aggregate tonnage of which is not short of one hundred and forty thousand; a larger number of steamboats than England can claim, and a greater steam commercial marine than that employed by Great Britain and her dependencies."

And now, fellow-citizens, having stated to you this infallible proof of the growth and prosperity of the nation, I ask you, and I would ask every man, whether the government which has been over us has proved itself an affliction or a curse to the country, or any part of it?

Ye men of the South, of all the original Southern States, what say you to all this? Are you, or any of you, ashamed of this great work of your fathers? Your fathers were not they who stoned the prophets and killed them. They were among the prophets; they were of the prophets; they were themselves the prophets.

Ye men of Virginia, what do you say to all this? Ye men of the Potomac, dwelling along the shores of that river on which WASHINGTON lived and died, and where his remains now rest, ye, so many of whom may see the domes of the Capitol from your own homes, what say ye?

Ye men of James River and the Bay, places consecrated by the early settlement of your Commonwealth, what do you say? Do you desire, from the soil of your State, or as you travel to the North, to see these halls vacated, their beauty and ornaments destroyed, and their national usefulness gone for ever?

Ye men beyond the Blue Ridge, many thousands of whom are nearer to this Capitol than to the seat of government of your own State, what do you think of breaking this great association into fragments of States and of people? I know that some of you, and I believe that you all, would be almost as much shocked at the announcement of such a catastrophe, as if you were to be informed that the Blue Ridge itself would soon totter from its base. And ye men of Western Virginia, who occupy the great slope from the top of the Alleghanies to Ohio and Kentucky, what benefit do you propose to yourselves by disunion? If you "secede," what do you "secede" from, and what do you "accede" to? Do you look for the current of the Ohio to change, and to bring you and your commerce to the tide-waters of Eastern rivers? What man in his senses can suppose that you would remain part and parcel of Virginia a month after Virginia should have ceased to be part and parcel of the United States?

The secession of Virginia! The secession of Virginia, whether alone or in company, is most improbable, the greatest of all improbabilities. Virginia, to her everlasting honor, acted a great part in framing and establishing the present Constitution. She has had her reward and her distinction. Seven of her noble sons have each filled the Presidency, and enjoyed the highest honors of the country. Dolorous complaints come up to us from the South, that Virginia will not head the march of secession, and lead the other Southern States out of the Union. This, if it should happen, would be something of a marvel, certainly, considering how much pains Virginia took to lead these same States into the Union, and considering, too, that she has partaken as largely of its benefits and its government as any other State.

And ye men of the other Southern States, members of the Old Thirteen; yes, members of the Old Thirteen; that always touches my regard and my sympathies; North Carolina, Georgia, South Carolina! What page in your history, or in the history of any one of you, is brighter than those which have been recorded since the Union was formed? Or through what period has your prosperity been greater, or your peace and happiness better secured? What names even has South Carolina, now so much dissatisfied, what names has she of which her intelligent sons are more proud than those which have been connected with the government of the United States? In Revolutionary times, and in the earliest days of this Constitution, there was no State more honored, or more deserving of honor. Where is she now? And what a fall is there, my countrymen! But I leave her to her own reflections, commending to her, with all my heart, the due consideration of her own example in times now gone by.

Fellow-citizens, there are some diseases of the mind as well as of the body, diseases of communities as well as diseases of individuals, that must be left to their own cure; at least it is wise to leave them so until the last critical moment shall arrive.

I hope it is not irreverent, and certainly it is not intended as reproach, when I say, that I know no stronger expression in our language than that which describes the restoration of the wayward son; " he came to himself." He had broken away from all the ties of love, family, and friendship. He had forsaken every thing which he had once regarded in his father's house. He had forsworn his natural sympathies, affections, and habits, and taken his journey into a far country. He had gone away from himself and out of himself. But misfortunes overtook him, and famine threatened him with starvation and death. No entreaties from home followed him to beckon him back; no admonition from others warned him of his fate. But the hour of reflection had come, and nature and conscience wrought within him, until at length " *he came to himself.*"

And now, ye men of the new States of the South! You are not of the original thirteen. The battle had been fought and won, the Revolution achieved, and the Constitution established, before your States had any existence as States. You came to a prepared banquet, and had seats assigned you at table just as honorable as those which were filled by older guests. You have been and are singularly prosperous; and if any one should deny this, you would at once contradict his assertion. You have bought vast quantities of choice and excellent land at the lowest price; and if the public domain has not been lavished upon you, you yourself will admit that it has been appropriated to your own uses by a very liberal hand. And yet in some of these States, not in all, persons are found in favor of a dissolution of the Union, or of secession from it. Such opinions are expressed even where the general prosperity of the community has been the most rapidly advanced. In the flourishing and interesting State of Mississippi, for example, there is a large party which insists that her grievances are intolerable, that the whole body politic is in a state of suffering; and all along, and through her whole extent on the Mississippi, a loud cry rings that her only remedy is " Secession," " Secession." Now, Gentlemen, what infliction does the State of Mississippi suffer under?

What oppression prostrates her strength or destroys her happiness? Before we can judge of the proper remedy, we must know something of the disease; and, for my part, I confess that the real evil existing in the case appears to me to be a certain inquietude or uneasiness growing out of a high degree of prosperity and consciousness of wealth and power, which sometimes lead men to be ready for changes, and to push on unreasonably to still higher elevation. If this be the truth of the matter, her political doctors are about right. If the complaint spring from over-wrought prosperity, for that disease I have no doubt that secession would prove a sovereign remedy.

But I return to the leading topic on which I was engaged. In the department of invention there have been wonderful applications of science to arts within the last sixty years. The spacious hall of the Patent Office is at once the repository and proof of American inventive art and genius. Their results are seen in the numerous improvements by which human labor is abridged.

Without going into details, it may be sufficient to say, that many of the applications of steam to locomotion and manufactures, of electricity and magnetism to the production of mechanical motion, the electrical telegraph, the registration of astronomical phenomena, the art of multiplying engravings, the introduction and improvement among us of all the important inventions of the Old World, are striking indications of the progress of this country in the useful arts. The network of railroads and telegraphic lines by which this vast country is reticulated have not only developed its resources, but united emphatically, in metallic bands, all parts of the Union. The hydraulic works of New York, Philadelphia, and Boston surpass in extent and importance those of ancient Rome.

But we have not confined our attention to the immediate application of science to the useful arts. We have entered the field of original research, and have enlarged the bounds of scientific knowledge.

Sixty years ago, besides the brilliant discoveries of Franklin in electricity, scarcely any thing had been done among us in the way of original discovery. Our men of science were content with repeating the experiments and diffusing a knowledge of the discoveries of the learned of the Old World, without attempting to add a single new fact or principle to the existing stock. Within the last twenty-five or thirty years a remarkable improvement has taken place in this respect. Our natural history has been explored in all its branches; our geology has been investigated with results of the highest interest to practical and theoretical science. Discoveries have been made in pure chemistry and electricity, which have received the approbation of the world. The advance which has been made in meteorology in this country, within the last twenty years, is equal to that made during the same period in all the world besides.

In 1793 there was not in the United States an instrument with which a good observation of the heavenly bodies could be made. There are now instruments at Washington, Cambridge, and Cincinnati equal to those at the best European observatories, and the original discoveries in astronomy within the last five years, in this country, are among the most brilliant of the age. I can hardly refrain from saying, in this connection, that the "Celestial Mechanics" of La Place has been translated and commented upon by Bowditch.

Our knowledge of the geography and topography of the American continent has been rapidly extended by the labor and science of the officers of the United States army, and discoveries of much interest in distant seas have resulted from the enterprise of the navy.

In 1807, a survey of the coast of the United States was commenced, which at that time it was supposed no American was competent to direct. The work has, however, grown within the last few years, under a native superintendent, in importance and extent, beyond any enterprise of the kind ever before attempted.

These facts conclusively prove that a great advance has been made among us, not only in the application of science to the wants of ordinary life, but in science itself, in its highest branches, in its adaptation to satisfy the cravings of the immortal mind.

In respect to literature, with the exception of some books of elementary education, and some theological treatises, of which scarcely any but those of Jonathan Edwards have any permanent value, and some works on local history and politics, like

Hutchinson's Massachusetts, Jefferson's Notes on Virginia, the Federalist, Belknap's New Hampshire, and Morse's Geography, and a few others, America had not produced a single work of any repute in literature. We were almost wholly dependent on imported books. Even our Bibles and Testaments were, for the most part, printed abroad. The book trade is now one of the greatest branches of business, and many works of standard value, and of high reputation in Europe as well as at home, have been produced by American authors in every department of literary composition.

While the country has been expanding in dimensions, in numbers, and in wealth, the government has applied a wise forecast in the adoption of measures necessary, when the world shall no longer be at peace, to maintain the national honor, whether by appropriate displays of vigor abroad, or by well-adapted means of defence at home. A navy, which has so often illustrated our history by heroic achievements, though in peaceful times restrained in its operations to narrow limits, possesses, in its admirable elements, the means of great and sudden expansion, and is justly looked upon by the nation as the right arm of its power. An army, still smaller, but not less perfect in its detail, has on many a field exhibited the military aptitudes and prowess of the race, and demonstrated the wisdom which has presided over its organization and government.

While the gradual and slow enlargement of these respective military arms has been regulated by a jealous watchfulness over the public treasure, there has, nevertheless, been freely given all that was needed to perfect their quality; and each affords the nucleus of any enlargement that the public exigencies may demand, from the millions of brave hearts and strong arms upon the land and water.

The navy is the active and aggressive element of national defence; and, let loose from our own sea-coast, must display its power in the seas and channels of the enemy. To do this, it need not be large; and it can never be large enough to defend by its presence at home all our ports and harbors. But, in the absence of the navy, what can the regular army or the volunteer militia do against the enemy's line-of-battle ships and steamers, falling without notice upon our coast? What will guard our cities from tribute, our merchant-vessels and our navy-yards from conflagration? Here, again, we see a wise forecast in the system of defensive measures, which, especially since the close of the war with Great Britain, has been steadily followed by our government.

While the perils from which our great establishments had just escaped were yet fresh in remembrance, a system of fortifications was begun, which now, though not quite complete, fences in our important points with impassable strength. More than four thousand cannon may at any moment, within strong and permanent works, arranged with all the advantages and appliances that the art affords, be turned to the protection of the sea-coast, and be served by the men whose hearths they shelter. Happy for us that it is so, since these are means of security that time alone can supply; and since the improvements of maritime warfare, by making distant expeditions easy and speedy, have made them more probable, and at the same time more difficult to anticipate and provide against. The cost of fortifying all the important points of our coast, as well upon the whole Atlantic as the Gulf of Mexico, will not exceed the amount expended on the fortifications of Paris.

In this connection one most important facility in the defence of the country is not to be overlooked; it is the extreme rapidity with which the soldiers of the army, and any number of the militia corps, may be brought to any point where a hostile attack shall at any time be made or threatened.

And this extension of territory embraced within the United States, increase of its population, commerce, and manufactures, development of its resources by canals and railroads, and rapidity of intercommunication by means of steam and electricity, have all been accomplished without overthrow of, or danger to, the public liberties, by any assumption of military power; and, indeed, without any permanent increase of the army, except for the purpose of frontier defence, and of affording a slight guard to the public property; or of the navy, any further than to assure the navigator that, in whatsoever sea he shall sail his ship, he is protected by the stars and stripes of his country. This, too, has been done without the shedding of a drop of blood for treason or rebellion; while systems of popular representation have regularly been supported in the State governments and in the general government; while laws, national and State, of such

a character have been passed, and have been so wisely administered, that I may stand up here to-day, and declare, as I now
do declare, in the face of all the intelligent of the age, that, for
the period which has elapsed from the day that Washington
laid the foundation of this Capitol to the present time, there has
been no country upon earth in which life, liberty, and property
have been more amply and steadily secured, or more freely enjoyed, than in these United States of America. Who is there
that will deny this? Who is there prepared with a greater or a
better example? Who is there that can stand upon the foundation of facts, acknowledged or proved, and assert that these our
republican institutions have not answered the true ends of government beyond all precedent in human history?

There is yet another view. There are still higher considerations. Man is an intellectual being, destined to immortality.
There is a spirit in him, and the breath of the Almighty hath
given him understanding. Then only is he tending toward his
own destiny, while he seeks for knowledge and virtue, for the
will of his Maker, and for just conceptions of his own duty. Of
all important questions, therefore, let this, the most important
of all, be first asked and first answered: In what country of the
habitable globe, of great extent and large population, are the
means of knowledge the most generally diffused and enjoyed
among the people? This question admits of one, and only
one, answer. It is here; it is here in these United States; it is
among the descendants of those who settled at Jamestown; of
those who were pilgrims on the shore of Plymouth; and of those
other races of men, who, in subsequent times, have become
joined in this great American family. Let one fact, incapable
of doubt or dispute, satisfy every mind on this point. The population of the United States is twenty-three millions. Now,
take the map of the continent of Europe and spread it out before you. Take your scale and your dividers, and lay off in one
area, in any shape you please, a triangle, square, circle, parallel-
ogram, or trapezoid, and of an extent that shall contain one hundred and fifty millions of people, and there will be found within
the United States more persons who do habitually read and write
than can be embraced within the lines of your demarcation.

But there is something even more than this. Man is not
only an intellectual, but he is also a religious being, and his re-

ligious feelings and habits require cultivation. Let the religious element in man's nature be neglected, let him be influenced by no higher motives than low self-interest, and subjected to no stronger restraint than the limits of civil authority, and he becomes the creature of selfish passion or blind fanaticism.

The spectacle of a nation powerful and enlightened, but without Christian faith, has been presented, almost within our own day, as a warning beacon for the nations.

On the other hand, the cultivation of the religious sentiment represses licentiousness, incites to general benevolence and the practical acknowledgment of the brotherhood of man, inspires respect for law and order, and gives strength to the whole social fabric, at the same time that it conducts the human soul upward to the Author of its being.

Now, I think it may be stated with truth, that in no country, in proportion to its population, are there so many benevolent establishments connected with religious instruction, Bible, Missionary, and Tract Societies, supported by public and private contributions, as in our own. There are also institutions for the education of the blind, of idiots, of the deaf and dumb; for the reception of orphan and destitute children, and the insane; for moral reform, designed for children and females respectively; and institutions for the reformation of criminals; not to speak of those numerous establishments, in almost every county and town in the United States, for the reception of the aged, infirm, and destitute poor, many of whom have fled to our shores to escape the poverty and wretchedness of their condition at home.

In the United States there is no church establishment or ecclesiastical authority founded by government. Public worship is maintained either by voluntary associations and contributions, or by trusts and donations of a charitable origin.

Now, I think it safe to say, that a greater portion of the people of the United States attend public worship, decently clad, well behaved, and well seated, than of any other country of the civilized world. Edifices of religion are seen everywhere. Their aggregate cost would amount to an immense sum of money. They are, in general, kept in good repair, and consecrated to the purposes of public worship. In these edifices the people regularly assemble on the Sabbath day, which, by all classes, is sacredly set apart for rest from secular employment and for religious meditation and worship, to listen to the reading of the Holy Scriptures, and discourses from pious ministers of the several denominations.

This attention to the wants of the intellect and of the soul, as manifested by the voluntary support of schools and colleges, of churches and benevolent institutions, is one of the most remarkable characteristics of the American people, not less strikingly exhibited in the new than in the older settlements of the country. On the spot where the first trees of the forest were felled, near the log cabins of the pioneers, are to be seen rising together the church and the school-house. So has it been from the beginning, and God grant that it may thus continue!

> " On other shores, above their mouldering towns,
>   In sullen pomp, the tall cathedral frowns ;
>   Simple and frail, our lowly temples throw
>   Their slender shadows on the paths below ;
>   Scarce steal the winds, that sweep the woodland tracks,
>   The larch's perfume from the settler's axe,
>   Ere, like a vision of the morning air,
>   His slight-framed steeple marks the house of prayer.
>   Yet Faith's pure hymn, beneath its shelter rude,
>   Breathes out as sweetly to the tangled wood,
>   As where the rays through blazing oriels pour
>   On marble shaft and tessellated floor."

Who does not admit that this unparalleled growth in prosperity and renown is the result, under Providence, of the union of these States under a general Constitution, which guaranties to each State a republican form of government, and to every man the enjoyment of life, liberty, and the pursuit of happiness, free from civil tyranny or ecclesiastical domination?

And, to bring home this idea to the present occasion, who does not feel that, when President Washington laid his hand on the foundation of the first Capitol, he performed a great work of perpetuation of the Union and the Constitution? Who does not feel that this seat of the general government, healthful in its situation, central in its position, near the mountains whence gush springs of wonderful virtue, teeming with Nature's richest products, and yet not far from the bays and the great estuaries of the sea, easily accessible and generally agreeable in climate and association, does give strength to the union of these States? that this city, bearing an immortal name, with its broad streets and avenues, its public squares and magnificent edifices of the general government, erected for the purpose of carrying on within them the important business of the several departments, for the reception of wonderful and curious inventions, for the preservation of the records of American learning and genius, of extensive collections of the products of nature and art, brought hither for study and comparison from all parts of the world; adorned with numerous churches, and sprinkled over, I am happy to say, with many public schools, where all the children of the city, without distinction, have the means of obtaining a good education; and with academies and colleges, professional schools and public libraries, should continue to receive, as it has heretofore received, the fostering care of Congress, and should be regarded as the permanent seat of the national government? Here, too, a citizen of the great republic of letters,* a republic which knows not the metes and bounds of political geography, has prophetically indicated his conviction that America is to exercise a wide and powerful influence in the intellectual world, by founding in this city, as a commanding position in the field of science and literature, and placing under the guardianship of the government, an institution " for the increase and diffusion of knowledge among men."

With each succeeding year new interest is added to the spot; it becomes connected with all the historical associations of our country, with her statesmen and her orators, and, alas! its cemetery is annually enriched by the ashes of her chosen sons.

Before us is the broad and beautiful river, separating two of the original thirteen States, which a late President, a man of determined purpose and inflexible will, but patriotic heart, desired to span with arches of ever-enduring granite, symbolical of the firmly cemented union of the North and the South. That President was General Jackson.

On its banks repose the ashes of the Father of his Country, and at our side, by a singular felicity of position, overlooking the city which he designed, and which bears his name, rises to his memory the marble column, sublime in its simple grandeur, and fitly intended to reach a loftier height than any similar structure on the surface of the whole earth.

* Hugh Smithson, whose munificent bequest has been applied to the foundation of " The Smithsonian Institution."

52 *

Let the votive offerings of his grateful countrymen be freely contributed to carry this monument higher and still higher. May I say, as on another occasion, " Let it rise; let it rise till it meet the sun in his coming; let the earliest light of the morning gild it, and parting day linger and play on its summit!"

Fellow-citizens, what contemplations are awakened in our minds as we assemble here to reënact a scene like that performed by Washington! Methinks I see his venerable form now before me, as presented in the glorious statue by Houdon, now in the Capitol of Virginia. He is dignified and grave; but concern and anxiety seem to soften the lineaments of his countenance. The government over which he presides is yet in the crisis of experiment. Not free from troubles at home, he sees the world in commotion and in arms all around him. He sees that imposing foreign powers are half disposed to try the strength of the recently established American government. We perceive that mighty thoughts, mingled with fears as well as with hopes, are struggling within him. He heads a short procession over these then naked fields; he crosses yonder stream on a fallen tree; he ascends to the top of this eminence, whose original oaks of the forest stand as thick around him as if the spot had been devoted to Druidical worship, and here he performs the appointed duty of the day.

And now, fellow-citizens, if this vision were a reality; if Washington actually were now amongst us, and if he could draw around him the shades of the great public men of his own day, patriots and warriors, orators and statesmen, and were to address us in their presence, would he not say to us: " Ye men of this generation, I rejoice and thank God for being able to see that our labors and toils and sacrifices were not in vain. You are prosperous, you are happy, you are grateful; the fire of liberty burns brightly and steadily in your hearts, while DUTY and the LAW restrain it from bursting forth in wild and destructive conflagration. Cherish liberty, as you love it; cherish its securities, as you wish to preserve it. Maintain the Constitution which we labored so painfully to establish, and which has been to you such a source of inestimable blessings. Preserve the union of the States, cemented as it was by our prayers, our tears, and our blood. Be true to God, to your country, and to your duty. So shall the whole Eastern world follow the morning sun to contemplate you as a nation; so shall all generations honor you, as they honor us; and so shall that Almighty Power which so graciously protected us, and which now protects you, shower its everlasting blessings upon you and your posterity."

Great Father of your Country! we heed your words; we feel their force as if you now uttered them with lips of flesh and blood. Your example teaches us, your affectionate addresses teach us, your public life teaches us, your sense of the value of the blessings of the Union. Those blessings our fathers have tasted, and we have tasted, and still taste. Nor do we intend that those who come after us shall be denied the same high fruition. Our honor as well as our happiness is concerned. We cannot, we dare not, we will not, betray our sacred trust. We will not filch from posterity the treasure placed in our hands to be transmitted to other generations. The bow that gilds the clouds in the heavens, the pillars that uphold the firmament, may disappear and fall away in the hour appointed by the will of God; but until that day comes, or so long as our lives may last, no ruthless hand shall undermine that bright arch of Union and Liberty which spans the continent from Washington to California.

Fellow-citizens, we must sometimes be tolerant to folly, and patient at the sight of the extreme waywardness of men; but I confess that, when I reflect on the renown of our past history, on our present prosperity and greatness, and on what the future hath yet to unfold, and when I see that there are men who can find in all this nothing good, nothing valuable, nothing truly glorious, I feel that all their reason has fled away from them, and left the entire control over their judgment and their actions to insanity and fanaticism; and more than all, fellow-citizens, if the purposes of fanatics and disunionists should be accomplished, the patriotic and intelligent of our generation would seek to hide themselves from the scorn of the world, and go about to find dishonorable graves.

Fellow-citizens, take *courage*; be of *good cheer*. We shall come to no such ignoble end. We shall live, and not die. During the period allotted to our several lives, we shall continue to rejoice in the return of this anniversary. The ill-omened sounds of fanaticism will be hushed; the ghastly spectres of *Secession* and *Disunion* will disappear, and the enemies of united constitutional liberty, if their hatred cannot be appeased, may prepare to have their eyeballs seared as they behold the steady flight of the American eagle, on his burnished wings, for years and years to come.

President Fillmore, it is your singularly good fortune to perform an act such as that which the earliest of your predecessors performed fifty-eight years ago. You stand where he stood; you lay your hand on the corner-stone of a building designed greatly to extend that whose corner-stone he laid. Changed, changed is every thing around. The same sun, indeed, shone upon his head which now shines upon yours. The same broad river rolled at his feet, and bathes his last resting-place, that now rolls at yours. But the site of this city was then mainly an open field. Streets and avenues have since been laid out and completed, squares and public grounds inclosed and ornamented, until the city which bears his name, although comparatively inconsiderable in numbers and wealth, has become quite fit to be the seat of government of a great and united people.

Sir, may the consequences of the duty which you perform so auspiciously to-day, equal those which flowed from his act. Nor this only; may the principles of your administration, and the wisdom of your political conduct, be such, as that the world of the present day, and all history hereafter, may be at no loss to perceive what example you have made your study.

Fellow-citizens, I now bring this address to a close, by expressing to you, in the words of the great Roman orator, the deepest wish of my heart, and which I know dwells deeply in the hearts of all who hear me: "Duo modo hæc opto; unum, UT MORIENS POPULUM ROMANUM LIBERUM RELINQUAM; hoc mihi majus a diis immortalibus dari nihil potest: alterum, ut ita cuique eveniat, ut de republicâ quisque mereatur."

And now, fellow-citizens, with hearts void of hatred, envy, and malice towards our own countrymen, or any of them, or towards the subjects or citizens of other governments, or towards any member of the great family of man; but exulting, nevertheless, in our own peace, security, and happiness, in the grateful remembrance of the past, and the glorious hopes of the future, let us return to our homes, and with all humility and devotion offer our thanks to the Father of all our mercies, political, social, and religious.

NOTE.

The following letter, received after the delivery of the foregoing Address, from a gentleman who witnessed the laying of the corner-stone of the Capitol by President Washington, will be read with interest : —

"Boston, July 8, 1851.

"My Honored Sir, — I cannot well refrain from thus thanking you for your address at the metropolis, on the 4th instant, which I have read from the newspapers. It has carried me back to that scene so happily adverted to by you, of which I was a witness, on the 18th of September, 1793, when in boyhood.

"The cavalcade on the morning of that day was formed at Suter's tavern, in Georgetown, three miles from the spot where Washington, in person, officiated at the ceremony of laying the corner-stone of the Capitol; that day, I remember, was clear sunshine, and very hot for the season. After the ceremony was over, a large company returned to Suter's, to partake of a dinner prepared for the occasion, and where a most joyous entertainment was realized. Living just opposite the dining-place, I had an opportunity to observe some of the most prominent of the company; namely, the City Commissioners; Ellicott, the surveyor; Major Benjamin Stoddert, afterwards Secretary of the Navy; Colonel Uriah Forrest, a Revolutionary officer, who had lost a leg in the battle of Brandywine; General Lingan, the then collector of the port of Georgetown, and who several years after was massacred by the mob in Baltimore, at a memorable and hateful period of party strife; Robert Peters, the father of Thomas Peters, who married one of Mrs. Washington's granddaughters; Colonel William Deakins, one of the best esteemed gentlemen in the State of Maryland; with many others I could name. They all, with Washington, sat down at the full board on that joyous occasion. I heard one of the company, after dinner, remark, that 'Washington himself was most happy.' To take a retrospect of fifty-eight years, and have that scene, with its present connections, so well expressed as your words have done it, is to me intensely interesting, and I shall, therefore, make no apology for thus intruding upon your time.

" We all see, that all which the most sanguine of dreams, or the inspired *prophecy of the poet*, could suggest, has been realized. I have only to regret, Sir, that I was not there to join the few remaining survivors who were also present at the former celebration.

" I am, respectfully and truly, your obedient and humble servant,

" HENRY LUNT.

"HON. DANIEL WEBSTER, *Washington, D. C.*"

END OF VOLUME SECOND.